GROWING EXOTIC FORESTS

Two of the most widespread genera used as exotics are Eucalyptus *and* Pinus, *as illustrated. These two genera are becoming well known genetically, silviculturally and with respect to their wood properties. The pine (top) is* Pinus caribaea var. hondurensis, *genetically improved and growing excellently in Queensland, Australia. The* Eucalyptus grandis *shown (below) is from South Africa (Photo, Courtesy R. J. Poynton, S. A. Forestry Research Institute).*

GROWING EXOTIC FORESTS

BRUCE J. ZOBEL
Zobel Forestry Associates, Inc.
Cary, North Carolina

GERRIT VAN WYK
South African Forest Research Institute
Pretoria, Republic of South Africa

PER STAHL
Swedish Forest Service
Falun, Sweden

A WILEY-INTERSCIENCE PUBLICATION
JOHN WILEY & SONS
New York Chichester Brisbane Toronto Singapore

Library of Congress Cataloging in Publication Data:

Zobel, Bruce, 1920–
  Growing exotic forests.

  "A Wiley-Interscience publication."
  Bibliography: p.
  Includes index.
    1. Exotic forestry. 2. Exotic forests. I. Van Wyk,
  Gerrit. II. Stahl, Pers. III. Title.
  SD387.E85Z63 1988   634.9   87-6087
  ISBN 0-471-80915-2

Printed in the United States of America

10 9 8 7 6 5 4 3 2 1

*This book is dedicated
to Dr. Lamberto Golfari.*

Dr. Lamberto Golfari is a leader in the area of exotic forestry. Born in Italy in 1914, Dr. Golfari worked primarily in Argentina and Brazil but has made study and advisory trips to many countries. Dr. Golfari's methodology and approach, partially based on the earlier European work, has been a model, followed by many researchers throughout the world, especially in South America. His work on the identification of ecological regions related to the choice of exotic forest trees has been admired and emulated by many persons. The authors of this book wish, by this dedication, to recognize the contributions of this outstanding forester.

PREFACE

The need for a large and reliable supply of inexpensive forest products of good quality is rapidly escalating. One of the most important ways to increase the supply of forest products is to expand the use of exotic species, that is, to grow trees in areas to which they are not indigenous or in areas not now forested. Exotics are currently being used on a very large scale in both the temperate and tropical regions and expansion in this area of forestry is very rapid. It is the purpose of this book to cover some of the most important aspects of growing exotic forest trees; a complete coverage of exotic forestry is impossible in one book.

Exotic forestry has special and sometimes unusual advantages and problems. It is the objective of this book to deal with these as they relate to the establishment, growth, and utilization of exotic forests. Special emphasis will be placed upon the methods necessary to assure a choice of the trees most useful for exotic plantations. Most chapters will deal with general principles that apply to all exotics. To aid in understanding which methods are best, results of past experiences in the growing of exotics in both the temperate and tropical regions will be covered in separate chapters.

If trees to be used for exotic forestry are carelessly chosen, the effects can be biologically disastrous because of poorly adapted trees or too great a restriction of the genetic base and economically disastrous because of poor yields or the production of low-quality products. Chapters have been included in the book on gene conservation, the politics of exotics, and the utilization of wood from exotics to emphasize the items necessary for the success of a well-balanced, long-term program dealing with exotic forest trees.

The book has been written so that it will be of value in the following ways:

1.   As a textbook for courses in exotic forestry. Much has been written about exotics, but this book is the first comprehensive summary of various aspects of general concepts related to the subject. A text covering exotic forestry is badly needed because many schools and universities are starting courses in this area. The need for good coverage of exotics is especially great in the developing countries, where the proper management of exotics determines the success or failure of large industrial and small private land and governmental forestry operations.

2.   As a reference for persons involved in the silviculture of exotics. Exotic forestry has become so widespread and important that all persons interested in forestry must have an understanding of what constitutes exotic forestry, what it can contribute, and what its limitations are. Suitable references covering the needed general concepts about exotic forestry have not previously been available in a single publication.

3.   As a guide and reference for those persons who are now, or soon will be, involved in growing exotic trees. Many foresters have no training or experience in this kind of forestry yet find themselves working with exotics. This book supplies information about growing and using exotics to which such persons can refer. Without proper information and guidance, very serious mistakes have been and will continue to be made; the book contains information which is necessary to help prevent mistakes in exotic forestry.

4.   As a source of information to help persons, corporations, and governments decide whether to become involved in exotic forestry and, if so, how to proceed and how difficult the operation will be. There is no greater area of misinformation and ignorance in forestry than in the field of exotic forestry, and many organizations become operationally deeply involved to the "point of no return" because of a lack of knowledge about exotic forest trees and how to handle them.

The book is written in a simple, easy-to-understand manner. Since much of it deals with general concepts, undoubtedly some exceptions to the general concepts developed have been overlooked for certain specific conditions or for different species. Most of the book deals with the use of conventional forest products such as pulp, paper, lumber, plywood, and particleboard. But there are sections dealing with "nonconventional" uses of forests such as for firewood, for industrial energy, and for social forestry.

Although many references and literature citations about exotics are included in the book, there are so many publications related to this area of forestry that only a small portion of those available to the authors could be cited. Despite this, the book will serve to organize and summarize some of the presently available information on exotic forestry. In addition, personal observations and concepts of the authors, based upon many years of working with exotics in several areas throughout the world, will be included.

BRUCE J. ZOBEL
GERRIT VAN WYK
PER STAHL

Raleigh, North Carolina
Pretoria, South Africa
Bangkok, Thailand
April 1987

ACKNOWLEDGMENTS

The authors obtained extensive help in the preparation of the book *Growing Exotic Forests*. Each chapter was edited by several different persons; to each of these we owe a special debt of gratitude. We know how much time, effort, and dedication was required. Others contributed photographs and relevant literature, which add greatly to the value of the book.

We can only recognize those persons who contributed to the success of the book, as listed alphabetically below. Thanks to each one.

Jeanne Adams, Cary Office Services, Cary, NC

Richard Barnes, Oxford Forestry Institute, Oxford, U.K.

Paul Bolstad, Monterrey Forestal, Zambrano, Colombia

Sheryl Brown Bolstad, Monterrey Forestal, Zambrano, Colombia

Leopoldo Brandão, Aracruz Florestal, Rio de Janeiro, Brazil

Edgard Campinhos, Aracruz Florestal, Aracruz, E.S., Brazil

Mary Conway, John Wiley & Sons, New York, NY

Charles Davey, School of Forest Resources, N.C. State University, Raleigh, NC

Gary De Barr, U.S. Forest Service, Athens, GA

Derek Donald, Stellenbosch University, South Africa

William Dvorak, CAMCORE Cooperative, N.C. State University, Raleigh, NC

Teoboldo Eguiluz, Univ. Autonomo Chapingo, Chapingo, Mexico

Emile Falkenhagen, South African Forest Research Institute, Pretoria, South Africa

Carlos Gallegos, Agency for International Development, Washington, DC

Denham Grey, South African Forestry Research Institute, George, South Africa

David Harcharik, U.S. Forest Service, Washington, DC

Yara Ikemori, Aracruz Florestal, Aracruz, E.S., Brazil

Michael Kane, CAMCORE Cooperative, N.C. State University, Raleigh, NC

William Ladrach, Zobel Forestry Associates Inc., Raleigh, NC

Clem Lambeth, Cartón de Colombia, Cali, Colombia

Phil Larson, U.S. Forest Service, Rhinelander, WI

Roger Lines, Forestry Commission, Northern Research Station, Roslin, Scotland

Gladys Ladrach Lopez, Zobel Forestry Associates Inc., Raleigh, NC

Ted Miller, N.C. State University (retired), Raleigh, NC

Garth Nikles, Queensland Forest Service, Brisbane, Australia

Ted Palmer, Tropical Products Institute, London, U.K.

Ron Pearson, School of Forest Resources, N.C. State University, Raleigh, NC

Flavio Pereira, Jari Company, Rio de Janeiro, Brazil

Jesse Perry, Rockefeller Foundation (retired), Hertferd, NC

Anders Persson, Royal College of Forestry, Garpenberg, Sweden

Hubert Polge, Centre National de Rechérches Forestéres, Nancy, France

Richard Poynton, South African Forest Research Institute, Pretoria, South Africa

Beatriz Redko, Jari Company, Mt. Dourado, Pa., Brazil

Ken Roeder, School of Forest Resources, N.C. State University, Raleigh, NC

Claes Rosengren, Swedish Forest Service, Falun, Sweden

Ola Rosvall, Institute of Forest Improvement, Savar, Sweden

Dolf Schönau, Institute for Commercial Forestry Research, Pietermaritzburg, South Africa

Chris Schutz, South African Forest Research Institute, Sabie, South Africa

Veikko Silander, Finnish Forest Research Institute, Helsinki, Finland

Bent Soegaard, Royal Arboretum, Horsholm, Denmark

Erik Ståhl, Royal College of Forestry, Garpenberg, Sweden

Fred Taylor, Mississippi Forest Products Laboratory, Mississippi State University, State College, MS

Ricardo Umaña, Pizano Co. (formerly), Bogota, Colombia
Hans Van Buijtenen, Texas A & M University, College Station, TX
Hank Van der Sijde, South African Forestry Research Institute, Pretoria, South Africa
Frank Wadsworth, ISTF, Bethesda, MD

CONTENTS

1

EXOTICS—GENERAL CONCEPTS

1.1 DEFINITION OF EXOTIC

It is essential to understand just what is meant by exotic. There are many definitions, some vague, some contradictory, and some specialized. For simplicity and clarity, in this book the authors will use the term *exotic* to apply to trees that are growing in an area in which they do not naturally occur (Zobel and Talbert, 1984). This definition is similar to that of Webster and Mc-Ketchnie (1980): "an exotic is a plant that is not native." Although Wright (1976) states that an exotic is strictly defined as "an introduction from a foreign country," he points out the difficulties of this definition and feels that an exotic is "one which is grown outside the limits of its natural range." Morandini (1964) also states that exotic "applies to a species grown outside its natural habitat." Thus, all four of the definitions quoted are essentially in agreement.

Everyone will agree that *Eucalyptus* grown in Brazil is an exotic, as is *Pinus radiata* (Monterey or radiata pine) when grown in New Zealand or Australia. Most would agree that Douglas-fir (*Pseudotsuga menziesii*) is an exotic when grown in the eastern United States. But is *Pinus elliottii* (slash pine), which is indigenous to South Carolina, an exotic when grown in North Carolina, where it does not naturally occur? By our definition it is. Actually, it really does not matter whether or not slash pine is technically considered to be an exotic under these circumstances, because all of the principles regarding management of exotics will apply to slash pine when grown outside its natural range.

1

1.2 WHY EXOTICS ARE USED

Exotic species are utilized to supplement or replace the local indigenous forests that cannot, or do not, produce the desired quantity and quality of forest products when the local forests have been destroyed or when suitable trees are not present, such as in the scrub-brushlands or grasslands. As Ciancio et al. (1982) stated in their book describing the use of exotics in Italy, "foresters find in the cultivation of exotic forest species a very interesting and reliable means of rapidly obtaining satisfying and profitable results." They go on to point out that the main advantage of the introduction of new species was to increase the number of species from which to choose, which will increase the desired wood production in a short time.

In the tropics and subtropics there is often a great need for coniferous timbers, since the indigenous forests frequently do not contain this type of wood and exotic plantations have been widely used to fill this need (Fig. 1.1). According to Simoes et al. (1976), special emphasis on exotic species used in the tropics is in the pines and eucalypts; the eucalypts are the most widely planted exotics in the world, as stated by Pryor (1978b).

Exotics are used for many reasons, some legitimate and some not really well founded. It is important to be aware that the term *exotic* has a large degree of fascination for some laymen and foresters alike. Just like *hybrid* or *tissue culture,* it sometimes brings forth the picture of something extraordi-

Figure 1.1. There are many incentives for using exotics. One major reason is to produce coniferous wood. Although this indigenous forest in South America contains wonderful species, the need for coniferous wood requires planting some exotics.

nary, and highly superior to indigenous trees. This feeling sometimes carries over very strongly into the area of support and financing. Researchers and many foresters are aware that it frequently is much easier to obtain funds for work on exotics than on the indigenous species; it is not unusual for the word *exotic* to be the deciding factor as to which species will be emphasized.

The increasing need for wood products,[1] the increased use of the better forestlands for agriculture, the destruction of indigenous forests by shifting agriculture, indiscriminate logging, and the difficulty in managing tropical hardwoods in fragile ecosystems have all led to the feeling that the proper use of plantation forestry, primarily using exotics, is the only way to avoid a shortage of wood in the near future (Brandão, 1981; Jabil, 1984). Added to this is the greatly increasing need for wood for industrial energy and firewood, much of which will be supplied by tropical species from genera such as *Leucaena* (Anon., 1977; Anon., 1978a) or *Eucalyptus* (Hillis and Brown, 1978; Pryor, 1978b).

As Sedjo (1983) emphasizes, plantation forestry must play a rapidly expanding role in the production of forest products, and many plantations will be made using exotics; for example, in 1984 Brazil planted 350,000 hectares, almost all from exotic species (Fig. 1.2). In 1983, Sedjo estimated that good sites in the tropics will easily have a growth rate of 15 to 20 cubic meters per hectare per year, and that 140 million hectares, or 5.0% of the world's for-

Figure 1.2. Very large plantations of exotics are made in the tropics and subtropics. Shown is a planting of *Pinus elliottii* in southern Brazil which is the basis of a thriving wood products industry.

[1]It is reported that the demand for wood products will double by the year 2000 (Hair, 1974; Keays, 1975).

estland, would meet the world wood demands in 1998 if only 10 cubic meters per hectare per year were grown. Expressed in another way, McDonald (1983) states that in industrial programs in the tropics in Brazil, Colombia, and the Philippines the indigenous forests being cut are growing at 0.5 m³/ha/yr while the exotic plantations that will replace them are growing at 25 to 30 m³/ha/yr. Added to the increased wood production per se, the fast growth rate results in a lowering of rotation ages and, thus, increased economic returns; it is a major incentive to the establishment of exotic plantations.

In many parts of the tropics there is no option except to use exotic conifers or hardwoods because suitable indigenous species do not exist (Zobel, 1961, 1964, 1979). This has led to the widespread use of exotics over a long time in countries such as South Africa, where the first commercial plantation of eucalypyts was made in 1876 (Nordin, 1984). South Africa now has over 1.1 million hectares of exotic plantations, is self-sufficient in softwood timber, and exports many kinds of wood products from exotic plantations. Additionally, tropical hardwood forests are so variable and difficult to manage ecologically that, on suitable sites, foresters generally prefer to use species that are more uniform and whose products are known and accepted. Often the numerous different genera of the tropical hardwoods with the most desirable wood are also slow growing or are hard to establish in plantations (Jabil, 1984) and plantations of indigenous species are rare. Current knowledge is generally lacking as to how the indigenous species should best be managed. Foresters are usually trained to handle the exotic species and do not feel competent to work with the indigenous species. Therefore, exotics are commonly chosen as the basis of the forestry enterprise in many tropical and subtropical areas.

In the temperate zones, exotics are not as widely used as in the tropics and subtropics, but some have great local importance. They are of primary interest because they provide a chance to increase growth rate and enable a broadening of the species base available to the forester, sometimes supplying a useful species where a suitable indigenous one is not available (Ciancio et al., 1982; Edwards, 1963). The use of exotics in the temperate forest regions is particularly heavy where the indigenous species are few, such as in northern Europe (Edwards, 1963; Zobel and Talbert, 1984). Often they give quite superior yields over the indigenous species (Schober, 1963). For example, as shown by Krutzsch (1974), suitable provenances of *Pinus contorta* (lodgepole pine) produce 30% greater volume after 40 years' growth than do the indigenous *Picea abies* (Norway spruce) and *Pinus sylvestris* (Scots pine). Yet persons such as Kiellander (1963) caution against the use of exotics in Sweden unless there are special problems, such as diseases or other pests that attack the indigenous species. He especially mentions the susceptibility of exotics like Douglas-fir to damage by rabbits and elk, which negates their general use (Fig. 1.3).

The usual movement of species in the temperate areas is from the West Coast of North America to Europe and to Asia. In addition, there has been considerable use of the temperate species such as *Pinus taeda* (loblolly pine) as an exotic in the temperate and subtropical areas of the Southern Hemi-

Figure 1.3. Despite their advantages, exotics have many problems. Usually these are diseases, insects, adverse weather, or poor soils. Not uncommonly, problems are also caused by indigenous animals; this is evident for *Pinus taeda* that is several years old and constantly grazed by antelope in South Africa.

sphere, such as in South Africa, Brazil, and Argentina (Zobel and Dorman, 1973). Excellent species such as Douglas-fir, Sitka spruce (*Picea sitchensis*), and loblolly pine are commonly used as exotics. Other genera in the pines, hemlocks, and larches from the temperate areas also have been and are being used as exotics. One species being used on a large scale in Scotland, Ireland, and Scandinavia is lodgepole pine, which is performing better than the indigenous species in Sweden (Hagner, 1979; Anon., 1980b; Nellbeck, 1982; Stahl, 1982). Although not yet extensively grown in the temperate areas, the opportunity for the use of Asiatic trees like the larches (*Larix* spp.), firs (*Abies* spp.), and pines is large and may increase with time.

Generally, movement of forest tree species from Europe to North America as exotics has not been very successful, although there are major exceptions in the Christmas tree industry, where exotics are widely used both in the north-central and northeastern United States. Not many exotic forest tree species grow timber better than do the indigenous species in the northeastern United States, although some, such as Norway spruce and larch, have potential (Carter et al., 1981). As pointed out by Wright (1981), the widespread use of exotics for timber in the northeastern United States lost favor when a series of un-suited seed sources were planted that either grew poorly, had poor tree form, or were attacked by pests. As so often happens, this negatively influenced interest in planting exotics. However, in general, exotics are less often used and less necessary in the temperate than in the tropical and subtropical areas.

There is no unanimity that exotics are good. This is pointed out by Morandini (1964), who states:

There is no complete agreement about the importance of exotic trees in the forest economy. A swing of opinion against exotics has arisen in the past because of disappointments from certain introductions, too optimistic an evaluation of the possibilities of some species and, chiefly, too early a passage from the experimental phase to large-scale plantations.

Since Morandini wrote that, criticism has been aimed at exotics by environmentalists who fear site degradation, environmental upset, and monoculture. In numerous instances, the term *exotic* raises suspicion, skepticism, and the fear of introducing something that is dangerous to the indigenous forests or local environment. For example, as early as 1883, Tanaka warned that caution is needed in the use of exotics and that there is no urgent need to introduce them when many useful indigenous species were available in Japan. Many foresters are conservative and satisfied with what they have, so are less than enthusiastic about the introduction of something that is new, not well known, and sometimes considered to be dangerous.

In an early paper, Jacobs (1964) presented a number of arguments for the use of exotics. He stated that to be successful, an exotic must have the ability to grow on bare land without shelter, should have early rapid growth and high-volume production, be well adapted to take advantage of the exotic environment, and have multinodal branching habits and indefinite shoots that will continue to produce leaves and extend in length as long as suitable growth conditions exist. Jacobs emphasized that successful exotics possess a large amount of variability and are especially useful when the trees can be reproduced vegetatively, will grow well in the nursery, and provide a plentiful supply of seed.

The most important reasons for using exotics were summarized by Zobel and Talbert (1984) and are briefly discussed below.

1. In many parts of the world, where none now exist or where the indigenous conifers grow poorly or do not respond well to intensive forest management, there is an urgent need for coniferous woods for use both for fibers and for solid wood products. Because of their broad adaptability and utility, members of the genus *Pinus* are among the most widely planted exotics, although several other conifers are also used, but on a less extensive scale. Even when the wood of the indigenous species may be of a high quality for certain products, it often is less adaptable for general utility purposes than the pines. Since the forest industries often do not know how best to utilize woods from many indigenous species, they prefer to use the familiar wood of exotic conifers.

2. One of the most frequently cited reasons for planting exotics is that they grow much faster than indigenous species. For example, it is not unusual

to find rotation ages as low as four to seven years in hardwoods like *Euca-lyptus* and *Gmelina* when grown in the tropics (Fig. 1.4). The reasons behind the slow growth of indigenous species is that throughout the eons they have become adapted for their ability to survive and reproduce and not necessarily for fast growth, good tree form, or high wood yields. These attributes in the indigenous populations are not necessarily advantageous in an operational forestry program, so exotics sometimes are used to replace indigenous species because of rapid cellulose production. This is particularly true in the semi-desert climates.

3.   In the tropics and subtropics the indigenous species are more difficult to manage silviculturally than the exotics. Management is a special problem with tropical hardwoods that have only a few desirable trees among the many different species on each hectare. In his discussion of the tropical wood resource, Chudnoff (1973) emphasizes the large number of species in the indigenous forest (500 in Surinam and Nigeria, 1000 in West Maylasia). Despite this large number of species, 90% of the wood used comes from only 5 or 6 species or species groupings. Chudnoff states that to avoid this, "some tropical forest managers are clearing off the natural growth in order to establish plantations of short-rotation, fast-growing, 'utility' species." Most of these are exotics. The local species are largely wasted because they are available only in small volumes, many species are intermixed, many species have high-density

Figure 1.4. Under good conditions, some exotics grow very rapidly and are harvestable at short rotations. Shown in a 2.5-year-old planting of *Gmelina* in coastal Colombia that will be harvested at 4 years.

wood, and there is a lack of knowledge about how to handle the species silviculturally.

4. Of great importance, foresters frequently do not know the biology of the indigenous species, even if the species has the potential to grow in plantations and produce good wood on short rotations. Often, such basic things as how to collect, store, and germinate seed, how to produce seedlings in the nursery, and how to outplant and manage them in the forest are not known. Rather than doing the studies necessary for the management of indigenous species, many foresters prefer to work exclusively with exotic species, which they know best.

5. Availability of suitable seed is a key to success in any plantation forestry program. The seeds of indigenous species are sometimes hard to obtain because knowledge about how to collect and store them is not available. Oppositely, some exotic species have been developed into improved genetic stock, resulting in better-quality and more uniform trees for which seed are easily available.

6. Much of the land area where exotics are grown is grassland or scrub-forestland. Frequently, the exotic species are more suited biologically to these marginal forestlands than are the species indigenous to the better forest sites in the same general geographic region. Additionally, exotics are frequently especially successful in forestland that has degenerated due to past poor management.

7. Especially in the tropics and subtropics, it is frequently necessary to develop local forest industries to improve the balance of trade by reducing the need for imported wood products. Knowledge of markets and manufacturing technology currently favors the use of the wood of exotics such as pine or *Eucalyptus*. This econo-political need is sometimes of key importance when a decision is made to produce exotic forests.

8. Occasionally, exotics are used to replace indigenous species that are very susceptible to diseases or insects and cannot be grown profitably.

Sometimes exotics are used that are not necessarily the best for overall wood production or growth, but because they have some special use, silviculturally or product wise, or for their potential for environmental purposes, which is as yet unproven. Examples of these are *Leucaena leucocephala* (Anon., 1977), where the species is described as containing the amino acid mimsine, which is toxic to nonruminate animals when it makes up as much as 10% of their diet. This species also has a bad name because of the widespread use of the aggressive shrubby types rather than those with good forest tree form. A special use of *Cordia alliodora* in Colombia and Costa Rica is for shade trees for coffee (De las Salas, 1980). General reforestation with this species, often called salmonwood, is promising in the tropics. Many of the *Acacias* have specialty uses for erosion control on poor sites and even for competing with imperata grass. *Acacia auriculiformis* was one especially noted by Wiersum and Ramlan (1982).

1.3 WHEN EXOTICS SHOULD NOT BE USED

An exotic should never be used until it has been thoroughly proven by testing in the area in which it is to be grown. This ideal situation requires an extended period of testing that should encompass the complete rotation length; in practice, an assessment after a half-rotation has usually been found to be satisfactory. But so many forestry programs are so politically motivated or their economic foundations are so unstable that immediate large-scale planting is demanded and therefore done. Often, such crash programs without prior testing end in catastrophic failures that give exotics a bad reputation, as will be explained in later chapters (Wright, 1981).

One of the major problems related to the use of exotics is that they are often used when and where indigenous species would be more suitable. In addition to the pest problems limiting the use of exotics, as is outlined in Chapter 4, there are other general reasons why exotics should not be used in some areas where they are currently planted or are being considered for use.

Exotics are often planted with the belief that they will be pest free and thus will continue to produce at the very high rate observed in the first few years after plantation establishment. This is not correct because pests of different types will appear; therefore, exotics should not be used as a result of the supposition that they will remain pest free (see Chapter 4).

Exotics are rarely best in areas containing good and diverse species. For example, in the southeastern United States, exotics have been extensively tried, but none have proven to be widely useful (Zobel et al., 1956). According to Grigsby (1969), the best performers among the 140 species he tried in the southern United States were the indigenous pines and hardwoods. However, in trials of exotics in the same general area of the United States, Franklin (1978) found that in parts of Florida *Eucalyptus grandis* and *E. robusta* grew satisfactorily. Farther north, European black alder (*Alnus glutinosa*) has shown good cold hardiness and rapid growth on very adverse sites (Fig. 1.5). Its ability to fix nitrogen is also beneficial. As mentioned earlier, somewhat similar results have been found in the northeastern United States, where exotics of European origin were widely planted in the early years, but where now the indigenous species are primarily used for certain specialties such as Christmas trees. In the western parts of the United States, no exotics have been found to be as good as the many indigenous species except in the semi-desert areas. In some tropical and subtropical areas, exotics have been almost exclusively used and often the indigenous trees have never been suitably tested (Zobel and Talbert, 1984).

Although the indigenous species have the advantage of being well adapted

Figure 1.5. Alder (*Alnus glutinosa*) is one of the few exotics that is used operationally in the southeastern United States. It grows rapidly; these trees shown in northern Alabama, are two years of age. Alder is grown on poor sites where its nitrogen-fixing ability is advantageous.

to the local climate, if intensive forestry is practiced they may not be as well adapted to the changed site as is the exotic species because of the effects of intensive site preparation, fertilization, release from competition, and other management practices that change the environment in which the trees will be grown.

In all instances care must be used when making a decision as to the use of exotics. An example is the genus *Leucaena*, which has been widely championed as a "miracle tree" suitable for supplying wood, fodder, food, and nitrogen to the soil (Anon., 1978a). Despite the good qualities of *Leucaena* there are limitations in its use that are sometimes overlooked. For example, Benge (1982) states:

> What people tend to forget is that marginal lands that will not sustain continued cultivation with agricultural crops will not sustain continued cropping with trees either. Trees require fertilizer, water, soil amendments, site preparation, etc. to reach maximum production and sustained yield. This is true of all trees, including *Leucaena,* despite its reputation as a miracle tree.

One of the greatest dangers is to become so enthusiastic about the potential of exotics that common sense and biological information are not followed, resulting in the use of exotics where they should not be planted.

1.4 DEFINITIONS OF TEMPERATE, TROPICAL, AND SUBTROPICAL AREAS

There are numerous definitions of what constitutes the tropical, subtropical, and temperate zones, many similar to the one used by Lugo and Brown (1981).

We define the tropics as the area encompassed by the Tropics of Cancer and Capricorn. However, ecosystems with tropical attributes may be found beyond these geographic limits. Because lowland tropical species are not frost-resistant, we also use the frost-free line as a secondary indicator of tropical environments.

They go on to describe a number of definitions of tropics given by others; Lugo and Brown favor use of the Holdridge Life Zone System (Holdridge et al., 1971), which will be described later. Because of the great overlap of the definitions, it is nearly impossible to develop a clear-cut one to apply to the use of exotics that will not be challenged. It is especially difficult to differentiate among tropical, subtropical, and temperate because numerous species, like *Pinus patula, P. taeda, P. elliottii,* several of the eucalypts, and some other species, will grow in both the subtropical and milder portions of temperate regions; other species, like *P. caribaea* and many eucalypts, grow in both tropical and subtropical areas. Therefore, in this book the differentiation among the three types of climates will be arbitrary and one of utility rather than strict adherence to any set of definitions.

The most clear-cut differences are relative latitudes and the presence of killing frosts. The reformed classification of Köppen, as described by Rudloff (1981), can be consulted if definitions are desired. According to this classification, most of the land area in the Southern Hemisphere, except the areas classified as dry steppe climates in Australia, Africa, and South America (where forest trees usually do not grow), is classified as tropical or subtropical. North of the equator, the eastern parts of Asia, the Middle East, the southern "fringes" of continental Europe bordering the Mediterranean Sea, Central America, and the southern portion of the southeastern United States would fall into one or both of these climatic categories.

Plantation forestry with exotics in the tropics and subtropics will include all countries listed by Evans (1984), but may also include parts of the countries north and south of 27 degrees north and south latitude, respectively, which were excluded by his descriptions. Analogous to equating the "tropics" with "bananas," the expanded area of subtropical plantation forestry may refer to climates "where *Eucalyptus grandis* will grow."

Within the broad areas of subtropical climates, many areas may be found that could be described as warm or mild temperate, especially where light winter frosts are common. For the purpose of this book, all mildly temperate areas where "overlapping" species might be grown and which could be called subtropical and the truly tropical forestry zones will be referred to as being tropical.

A definition for temperate zones was given for New Zealand by Sweet and Thulin (1963) based upon the number of days each year that the daily temperature exceeded 42°F (6°C). The dictionary definition of *temperate* as "neither very hot nor very cold, as related to climate" (Webster and McKetchnie, 1980) is not very helpful. As far as growing exotics is concerned, it is easiest to not differentiate between tropical and subtropical zones and to refer to all other areas as temperate, although some exotics, such as *Pinus contorta* and *Larix sibirica* (Siberian larch), are grown in areas with very cold climates that would technically be called subarctic.

In fact, any definition of temperate or tropical will never be satisfactory because there are many special combinations that do not easily fit into any one. For example, Kaul (1970) emphasizes the problems of arid sites that range from extremely cold to hot in Indo-Pakistan. He states that exotic plantations must be very carefully planned in these extreme conditions and that failures occur "by attempting afforestation on a large scale on sites where Nature intended no trees to grow."

1.5 DONOR AND RECEPTOR COUNTRIES

The major emphasis in discussions about exotics usually relates to the species and countries in which they will be grown. However, to be successful, the source of the exotic material must also be studied and protected in its indigenous habitat, and this is too rarely done. The gene complexes of the species to be used in exotic plantings must be preserved on the species, provenance, ecotype, and individual mother tree level. Genetic base populations with many different genotypes ensure broadly adapted breeding populations for future generations.

It is evident that some countries are primarily users of exotics and others are suppliers. Although artificial, a good classification is to make a separation into the *donor* countries or areas from which exotic species are obtained, and the *receptor* areas that use the exotics in their operational programs. Even when a donor area has limited wood production potential, its contribution to world forestry may be huge because of the value of the species supplied. As much effort needs to be expended on the donor areas as is expended on the areas where the trees are to be planted as exotics. If this is not done, exotic forestry will seriously suffer. What happens in the donor countries will determine the future of exotic forestry in the receptor countries.

Prime examples of donor areas are Central America and Mexico, which are exceedingly rich in species diversity, adaptability, growth, and wood characteristics. Species from these areas are widely used in receptor areas such as South America, Africa, Asia, Australia, and elsewhere. Because of its political isolation, Cuba is often overlooked as an important donor country. However, as outlined by Almirall (1982), the four pine species growing in Cuba have great potential for wider usage as plantation trees; only one, *P. caribaea* var. *caribaea,* is well known (Fig. 1.6).

The Guatemalan conifers will be used as an example. As described by Veblen (1978), no other area of equally low latitude—approximately 14 to 16 degrees north—has as great a variety of coniferous taxa. Veblen lists seven coniferous genera found in Guatemala, namely, *Abies, Cupressus* (cypress), *Juniperus* (juniper), *Pinus, Podocarpus, Taxodium* (cypress), and *Taxus* (yew). Many authors, such as Din (1958), Molina (1964), and Zobel (1964), discuss the species diversity in this region, and Mirov (1967) feels that the highlands of Mexico and Central America are a secondary center of evolution for the genus *Pinus.* Mirov and Larsen (1958) state that Mexico and Guatemala, which have many species in common, possess more species of the genus *Pinus* than any other region of comparable size. This area is an exceedingly rich source of genetic material for use in world reforestation because of the pronounced interspecific and intraspecific variation and the extensive hybridization, backcrossing, and introgression that occurs there (Loock, 1950; Aguilar, 1961). It is for this reason that the international organizations such as CAMCORE, CFI (now OFI), DANIDA, FAO[2] and others have concentrated collection efforts in Central America and Mexico; Dvorak (1984) points out that a number of species and provenances are only 5 to 10 years away from being reduced to

Figure 1.6. Many potentially good species for use as exotics are not well tested. For example, of the four pine species growing in Cuba, only *P. caribaea* var. *caribaea* (shown growing on poor sites in Venezuela) has been widely tested or used. This variety makes a very fine exotic.

[2]See the appendix for definition of the acronyms.

genetically high-graded stands of little value, with many valuable genotypes on the verge of extinction. Forest plantations as such are restricted in the Central American and Mexican group of donor countries, but enough natural stands are present from which good exotic programs can be developed.

Some donor regions produce large amounts of timber; examples are the West Coast of the United States and Canada and parts of Australia. The West Coast supplies exotics widely planted in Europe, Asia, Africa, Australia, and South America, and the chief donor country from which *Eucalyptus* arises is Australia. Although a major donor for the eucalypts, Australia also is a receptor country, extensively using exotic conifers such as *Pinus radiata* and *Pseudotsuga menziesii.*

Some areas use few exotics but contribute species used as exotics elsewhere and are also important timber producers; examples are the southern United States, the northeastern portion of North America, and northern Europe. Few conifers are used as exotics in the southeastern United States, but some hardwoods such as *Eucalyptus* and *Alnus* are planted (Franklin, 1978). In Europe, a number of conifers are used as exotics, but Europe also contributes species such as *Pinus sylvestris* and *Picea abies,* which are important exotics elsewhere. A number of tropical areas also fit into this category, especially for hardwoods, although the diversity of plant material obtained from tropical areas is still limited. With time, some tropical forest regions will also develop into important donor areas.

Figure 1.7. Some provenances of species valuable for exotics are being endangered. Shown is logging on one island of the Bahamas where the species *Pinus caribaea* var. *bahamensis* is very badly depleted because fires following the logging operation destroyed almost all tree growth.

It is essential that forestry in the donor regions be given more emphasis to avoid restrictions to the production of exotic trees throughout the world. As emphasized by Wood (1982), the problem of loss in the donor countries is not primarily of species themselves but of the varieties or provenances of species (Fig. 1.7). This concern was the driving force behind the formation of CAM-CORE (Dvorak, 1981a). The species, provenance, and individual tree variability present in the donor countries are all necessary to establish successful exotic forestry.

Although only a generality, it appears that the donor regions in which intensive forestry is not widely practiced are the ones most needing attention to preserve the available useful genetic material for the receptor regions. For example, an important difference between Central America and western North America is that the latter area has an established forestry tradition and environmental management, which more or less guarantees that most of the important genetic material is kept fairly well intact. Regrettably, this is not the situation in many of the developing countries. Through neglect, much good material has been, or is being, lost or the best has not been used. Recently, foresters in some receptor areas have realized the stake they have in trees from the donor countries and have helped to keep material available, as will be described in more detail in Chapter 8.

1.6 THE SPECIAL SITUATION IN THE TROPICS AND SUBTROPICS

One of the reasons commonly cited for the need for exotics is to reforest tropical and subtropical hardwood forest areas that have been destroyed by cutting and burning that results from shifting agriculture, firewood harvesting, logging, or numerous other reasons. According to Sedjo (1983), the worldwide shift of forest production is southward, mostly into the tropics and subtropics. Such cutting often results in the elimination of the most desirable indigenous species (Eckholm, 1978). To get the forests back to a productive state will require a large planting job, since often there is no longer an opportunity for natural regeneration (Wood, 1982).

Many of the plantations will be made with exotic species. The problem of regenerating these areas is made much more severe by secondary vegetation such as imperata grass (*Imperata cyllindrica*), which follows shifting agriculture (Soenianegara, 1980). Eradication of this grass and its control as a competitor with planted exotic trees is a most difficult and severe problem; as Ladrach (1985b) shows, "the growing problem in Central and South America is the invasion of toxic weeds and inedible grasses of large areas of cattle ranches cleared from virgin forests" (Fig. 1.8).

Although not a suitable subject for in-depth discussion in this book, the extent and severity of the damage caused by deforestation and regeneration in the tropics and subtropics has been and is still being hotly, and too emotionally, debated with, many statements not based on fact but on hearsay or

Figure 1.8. Conversion of grasslands that replace forests and then are abandoned is most difficult and expensive. Shown is an attempt to get trees established in a heavy grass sod in a former pasture in South America. Pine is usually the best exotic under such circumstances.

on some preconceived opinion. Better data are becoming available yearly, as shown by many new publications.

It is evident to those of us working in these areas that the subtropics, which usually have the highest population density, are more severely deforested than the tropics. Vast areas have reverted to scrub-brushland that are covered with a heavy regrowth of mostly worthless, slow-growing or poor-quality vegetation which must be removed prior to planting forest trees.

In his article describing the problems of tropical forestry, Wood (1982) pointed out that as recently as 1970 the immense volumes of wood present in tropical and subtropical forests were estimated to last for several centuries. Wood indicates that a large percentage of the forestland is degraded; this can only be brought back to productivity through planting, in which exotics will play a major role (Gallegos et al., 1982). But the limitations of the tropical resource and its current status cause concern, not only for the wood supply, but because of other accompanying problems such as the oxygen balance and the greenhouse effect from forest removal (Kellogg, 1978).

Whether one takes the extreme optimistic or pessimistic viewpoint about the rate and severity of deforestation, it is evident that there are valid and major reasons why exotics are needed and often preferred in the tropics and subtropics.

One of the main perceived problems in growing exotics are the adverse soils often considered to be general in tropical areas. Sometimes this is true, sometimes not; nevertheless, overlooking the true characteristics of the soils is a serious problem restricting the use of exotics. The idea that all tropical soils are fragile and that they are unsuited to forest management has been grossly overemphasized and has led to efforts to use species of trees that are not the best suited to the area.

Especially misleading have been statements concerning the extent of the very difficult-to-handle lateritic soils that are found in the tropics. Where these soil types, which set hard and irreversibly when exposed following forest removal, do occur, they must be absolutely avoided for exotic plantations. However, as Sanchez and Buol (1975) state, less than 10% of the forest soils in the tropics are laterites. It is evident to those of us working in the tropics and subtropics that many of the soils there can be handled in a manner similar to those of temperate regions such as the Piedmont of the southern United States. On soils of this kind, exotic forestry activities are suitable and not too difficult.

Based upon our experience in the tropics in South America, it appears that about 50% of the tropical forest area has soils suitable to support exotic plantation forestry, with little adverse ecological impact. The areas on which it is intended to plant exotics should be surveyed as to soil characteristics and only the suitable soils planted. The authors foresee tropical plantation forestry in the future to consist of natural regeneration on the more fragile and difficult soils, with plantations only on the operable sites using indigenous species as well as exotics. It is clearly evident that for all exotics, not only those used in the tropics, good soil information must be available before widespread planting is done.

The variability of the species composition in the tropics is a cause of problems that exotic forests avoid. There are often over 100 indigenous species on a hectare, making them difficult to handle silviculturally. Also of key importance, some indigenous forests have highly variable woods. One organization in the Amazon uses only 10 of the many species for solid-wood products; another, in Colombia, only uses 2. In Africa, Steenberg (1983) reported that out of 100 species exported, 3 accounted for 80% of the total export timber. The complexities and problems created by so many diverse species in the tropics is a major reason for a shift to exotics. As stated by Guppy (1984): "The very plethora of varieties is an embarrassment when demand in the timber trade is for standard raw materials with which to make uniform products at the cheapest possible price."

1.6.1 Where Exotics Are Grown in the Tropics

Although there has been a recent recognition of the "facts of life" about growing exotics in the tropics, the general impression still exists that they are planted mostly after harvesting the tropical high forest. In fact, it is the grasslands and scrub-brushlands that are primarily used; examples of the grasslands are the llanos of the Orinoco Basin in Venezuela and Colombia, the western side of the Fiji Islands, and in East Central Africa (Fig. 1.9). Scrub-brushlands

Figure 1.9. Many exotics are planted in the grasslands where indigenous trees are not found. These sites are severe but will grow specially chosen exotics such as the pines in the grasslands of the Orinoco Basin in Venezuela.

occur in Africa, in numerous places in Asia, central Brazil, Colombia, Chile, and many other areas. As Lanly (1982) states:

> The majority of reforestation programs are not carried out where deforestation takes place . . . almost all Brazilian plantations are concentrated in the south of the country. [This is where much of the grasslands and scrub-brushlands occur.] We have to note a much higher acceleration in clearing of unproductive forests compared to productive forests [Fig. 1.10].

Although afforestation of brushland and grasslands in Africa, Brazil, and Venezuela has produced quite acceptable yields of wood (Sedjo, 1983), planting in the grass or scrub-brushlands is not done because the climate or land is better or more productive, but for various other reasons. Actually, growth conditions are frequently marginal for wood production because of insufficient rainfall or adverse patterns of moisture availability, which result in severe soil moisture deficits for several months of the year. Also, the soils are not always the most desirable, since they frequently are deficient in nutrients or have poor structure. Some soils are deep droughty sands, while others are heavy textured, difficult to manage, and often have excess moisture during the wet season, which limits operability. It is usual in the tropics that phosphorus is deficient, and sometimes lack of other elements, such as boron, zinc, or copper, seriously limits tree growth. Despite all of these problems the grasslands and scrub-brushland sites are widely used in exotic tropical forest plantings for the following reasons.

Figure 1.10. Use of wood for charcoal for energizing industry is done on a very large scale. So much of the indigenous forests have been depleted for this purpose, as illustrated, that a major objective is growing wood specifically for energy. Usually exotic species are used.

1.   Clearing and site preparation in the scrub-brushlands and grasslands are simple and inexpensive and competition from regrowth with the planted trees is less severe than from tropical forested areas. Conifers often can compete with the grass and scrub-brush, but release from competition is still necessary for the eucalypts and most hardwoods. It is difficult to convert a tropical hardwood high forest to a plantation. Costs are high both for removing the trees from the planting site and because of the need to intensively release the planted trees from competition after planting. When planting is done in the grass and low brushlands, many of these problems do not occur.

2.   Sites can be prepared without using or removing the wood present in the indigenous high forest. Woods of some tropical species are excellent and some are marginal; usually they are not well known and markets for them are limited. Even when markets are available, the wood from only a part of the species can be economically utilized and the remaining wood must be disposed of, sometimes by burning or other methods, with considerable expense. The destruction of the undesired wood in tropical forests cannot be tolerated by society, yet the wood must be removed if intensive forest plantation management is to be practiced. The result is that many of the more productive tropical hardwood forest sites are not used for plantation establishment.

3.   Generally, the grassland and scrub-brushland are available for planting immediately since much of it has been tried for agriculture and has been found

not suitable for growing crops economically or for grazing. Land prices are reasonable and the need to "salvage" the land back to a productive state is evident to all (Gallegos et al., 1982). Actually, currently much of the grasslands and scrub-brushland is not being used at all, so tree planting is possible. No matter how unsuitable for agriculture the land is, however, it is sometimes difficult to plant trees on it because of political considerations; even though the farmers are obviously living at a subsistence level, farming is still the best method of living they have and their only known way to survive. There is sometimes real resistance to tree planting.

4.   Strong ecological and political reasons are frequently cited for growing exotics in the scrub-brushland and grasslands instead of the tropical high forests. If the needed wood can be grown in these accessible, available, and generally low-productive agricultural areas, it takes the pressure off the ecologically fragile tropical hardwood forests (Wadsworth, 1965).

The very high productivity of the exotic species grown in the tropics, which are estimated to produce 4 to 10 times more wood than the indigenous forests (Gladstone, 1980), enables a restricted area of grassland or scrub-brushland to produce a volume of wood equivalent to a much larger area of poorly managed tropical forest. The same concept was covered by Lugo and Brown (1981) when discussing the popular misconceptions about tropical lands. They emphasized that the faster growth of the exotic species can satisfy the increasing demand for wood and even contribute to reducing deforestation because plantations are more productive than natural forests by a two- to tenfold factor. When used in this way, the exotic plantings are called "replacement or compensatory" plantations, and are being strongly advocated by many foresters and ecologists [Johnson (U.S. Congress, 1980, p. 289) and Wood (1982)]. Sedjo (1983) emphasizes how agro-forestry and replacement forests can reduce the pressures on the natural forests. He goes on to say that if the wood needs of local people are not met, the efforts to conserve forests are doomed.

The popularity of the replacement forest concept to reduce pressures on the indigenous forests is rapidly increasing; nearly all replacement forests are planted using exotics. On a world level there is a definite shift from hardwood plantations for sawlogs of slow or average growth to hardwood and softwood plantations of fast-growing exotic species (Lanly, 1982).

Myers (U.S. Congress, 1980) emphasizes that the number one cause of tropical forest destruction is the 200 million shifting cultivators, and Sedjo (1983) states that direct conversion of natural forests to plantations is only a minuscule percentage of the total amount of tropical deforestation. In theory, tree planting of the degraded farms will be with indigenous species, but in practice much of it will entail the use of exotic species. The care necessary to choose the correct exotics is often not taken. This was stressed by Ladrach (U.S. Congress, 1980, p. 275) for a number of species, and by Kalish (U.S. Congress, 1980, p. 434) for *Gmelina*.

1.7 EXOTICS FOR "NONCONVENTIONAL" FORESTRY USES

Exotics are being increasingly used for what might be termed "nonconventional" forestry purposes. These activities are also sometimes described as social forestry (Wood, 1982). Nonconventional forestry, which relies heavily on the use of exotic species has many facets; one of primary current importance is the production of firewood, especially in the developing countries (Chittenden and Breag, 1980). There is a desperate need for fuelwood in many parts of the tropics, according to Eckholm (1975) and Sedjo (1983). As expressed by Burley (1980):

> In the current world situation of diminishing, irreplaceable fossil fuels, trees planted for fuelwood, charcoal or derived chemical fuels offer a partial solution to a crisis that, depending on the country, already exists or is very near.

Firewood use is widespread; it is estimated that from 20% to over half the wood harvested in the world is used for firewood. Some countries are as much as 90% dependent on wood for energy (Evensen, 1981), and Harker et al. (1982) state that one-third of the human population depends upon wood for cooking and heating. In 1985, Nor estimated that on a global basis 80% of the wood harvested is used for fuel, 70% of the world's population depends on wood for energy, and 68 of the 98 so-called developing countries have a shortage of fuel. Nor further states that current tree-planting programs comprise only 1% of what is required for a continued wood supply. This was also the theme of a publication by the National Academy of Sciences (1983), which contains an extended list of species suggested for use as firewood, mostly when grown as exotics.

It is estimated that by the year 2000, if the rate of deforestation is not slowed and better forestry practices are not adopted, well over 200 million people will not have enough fuelwood to meet their necessary cooking and heating requirements. In addition, the philanthropic organization CARE states in one of its flyers: "By the year 2000, just 17 years away, fuelwood requirements will exceed the available supply by 25%." New plantations of 50 million hectares will be required each year until the year 2000 if a reasonable degree of world self-sufficiency for firewood is to be achieved (World Bank, 1980). Spears (1978) states that a continuation of the current rate of plantation establishment will produce less than one-tenth of the projected firewood requirements. The average fuel and wood needs for a person in the humid tropics is 0.3 to 0.5 hectare of farm woodlot; for a family, 2 to 3 hectares. Thus, a major planting program, based mostly on exotics, is required.

Well-adapted exotic species will be needed if the requirements are to be met. This need was summarized in IBPGR (1982) by the following statement:

> The main emphasis has been directed toward fuelwood species in areas receiving less than 500 mm of rainfall and in dry tropical regions with six or more rainless

months per year. Lack of firewood in these areas is critical, and many people often go hungry, not for lack of food, but for lack of fuel in the form of wood to cook it. Much of the food consists of grain and roots such as rice and cassava which cannot be consumed without cooking. In these areas wood is the only fuel source as other fuels are unavailable or too expensive.

In an attempt to help satisfy the need for firewood, selections are being made of dry-zone species for use as fuel (Hughes, 1984). The CFI (OFI) has collected the seed of 25 species from Central America based upon the success of nonindustrial species such as *Calliandra callothyrsus, Prosopis* spp., and *Leucaena* spp. The dry-zone species are getting rare in areas and many potentially valuable species have been ignored or are being lost.

Although there are often indigenous tree species in the energy-poor regions that can be used, exotic species are frequently preferred for the reasons enumerated earlier: they are more easily handled, usually grow faster, and seed is available. Burley (1980) lists characteristics of trees suitable for supplying energy. In addition to having good survival, resistance to adverse factors, and fast growth, the wood of species used should be suitable for heating, have low sparking, good growth, and ease of cutting. It is beneficial if they can also supply shade, shelter, food, fodder, soil stabilization and enrichment, and supply some poles and timber. Species that have a good ability to coppice are particularly desired.

A primary exotic for firewood is *Eucalyptus,* but many other species, mostly hardwoods, are also being used. For example, Boland and Turnbull (1981) suggest several Australian genera such as *Acacia, Casuarina, Grevillea, Terminalea,* and *Trema* in addition to the eucalypts, all of which are used as exotics. The International Board of Plant Genetic Resources, associated with FAO and the United Nations in Rome, has published six manuals on *Acacia* and *Prosopis* in 1983 for firewood production. The IBPGR/FAO organization is cooperating with other world organizations in the collection and testing of seed for this special purpose. The United States National Academy of Sciences is producing a series of bulletins on various species that might be of use; an example is the booklet on *Calliandra callothyrsus* (Anon., 1983b). Also, the publication about *Leucaena leucocephala* (Anon., 1978) is very helpful to persons interested in use of exotics for energy. These are supplemented by specific information on the handling of useful species, such as the one on *Leucaena leucocephala* by Ahmad and Ng (1981).

The knowledge and use of exotic hardwoods for energy production, especially in dry climates, are limited, but activities in this area are increasing. Exotics such as *Acacia mangium* from Australia are available for fuel from wetter areas (Nicholson, 1981). Publications such as the one by Harker et al. (1982) show the calorific values and a bibliography for many species of trees that can be helpful in making decisions as to which exotic should be preferred. References are too numerous to list, but many like *Firewood Crops: Shrub and Tree Species for Energy Production* (National Academy of Sciences, 1983) are a good place to obtain information.

Plantations of exotics will be established for nonconventional forest uses other than for firewood. For example, Pohjonen and Nasi (1983) discuss the combination of growing trees for wood biomass for fuel along with wet biomass (leaves) for animal feed. They cite, for example, that the nutritional value of the leaves from cultivated *Salix* (willow) is high, especially when collected in the autumn.

Perhaps the largest use of exotics for energy is the production of charcoal for the steel industry in Brazil, where nearly 100,000 hectares are planted each year, most of them used for the production of energy. Wood is also being used in other tropical areas for the production of energy on a commercial scale (White, 1977; Smith, 1981). Energy plantations seem to be spreading very rapidly and special efforts have been made to develop forests for energy production in short-rotation energy plantations (Steinbeck and Brown, 1975; Schneider, 1977; Land, 1980). Ultimately, many species will be grown to supply industrial energy, and many trees so used will be exotics. As so clearly put at the meeting in Nairobi (Anon., 1980c), "wood will be maintained as a major fuel in developing countries."

Also becoming more important, and perhaps of key value if petroleum prices increase again, is the use of wood for organic chemicals. The methodology has been developed, and if the economic picture shifts, this use of trees, many of which will be exotics, will greatly expand (Goldstein, 1980a; Zobel, 1980a; and many others.) There is considerable enthusiasm about the potential for trees in the future to supply energy and chemicals (Ek and Dawson, 1976).

Another different, but important, use for exotics is for Christmas trees. It is safe to say that a great deal of our knowledge about the introduction and handling of exotics came from horticultural efforts and the widespread planting of Christmas trees, rather than through the efforts of conventional foresters (Wright, 1976).

Another common, but nonconventional use is to help restore badly eroded or exhausted lands by planting very hardy exotic species or species whose roots have symbionts that can fix air nitrogen such as *Alnus, Casuarina, Leucaena, Robinia* and many others, especially the legumes. As stated by OTS (1984): "For many degraded sites, the species need to be those that can add nitrogen to the soil." Wasteland reforestation and watershed protection, such as control of drifting sand by *Casuarina* or in developing windbreaks, are both major uses for exotics. Usually, exotics are relied upon in the more extreme environments; often the indigenous species are totally unsuited to the drastically changed environments created by man (Gallegos, 1980b).

Although fast-growing exotic species are nearly always emphasized for energy or nonconventional uses of forestry, this is not always true. For example, Hoskins (1985), when quoting myths regarding social forestry, states that one of the myths is that "Fast-growing exotic species are always the only trees of interest to local populations." She emphasizes the desirability of indigenous species and the difficulty of establishing village woodlots. The current trend is for successful indigenous species to become more widely used, especially under the most severe environments.

1.8 NECESSITIES FOR A SUCCESSFUL PROGRAM BASED UPON EXOTICS

The question is sometimes asked: "What does it take to make a successful exotic?" As outlined, Gallegos (1980b), in the North Carolina State Tropical Tree Improvement Short Course, stated that a successful exotic must meet the following criteria for timber production [compare these with comments by Jacobs (1964) in Section 1.2 of this chapter]:

1. It must grow well.
2. It must produce the desired products.
3. It must grow on bare ground without shelter.
4. It must have rapid early growth.
5. It must grow well in plantations.
6. It must be physiologically suited to take advantage of favorable growing periods in the new environment.
7. It must be acceptable environmentally.

The preceding criteria will be discussed and expanded throughout the book, supplemented by a listing of species that fulfill them. Some foresters feel, as expressed in Nairobi (Anon., 1980c), that reforestation efforts should be concentrated in the subhumid and semiarid zones rather than in the wet tropics.

There are some broad general rules that must be followed when an exotic program is to be started if it is to be successful:

1. Decide *what the objective is, what product is desired, and where the product will be used* (Ladrach, 1985b). It is sad, but true, that many programs establishing exotic forests are done as a whim, a hobby of some powerful person or for some perceived political advantage. Such programs nearly always fail, either in the establishment phase or when the timber is to be harvested. A few examples will illustrate this. In several countries, large acreages have been planted to exotic pines, often stimulated by subsidy payments, without any forethought as to what is to be done with the wood produced. Now there exist huge volumes of low-quality juvenile pine that cannot be used profitably. As a result, the exotic forestry programs are in serious danger of being abandoned (Fig. 1.11). A second example is a program in one country where the decision was made that, for political purposes, each administrative unit in

Figure 1.11. Large plantations of exotics are made with no plans for utilization; that is the situation with some pine plantations such as the one shown, located in South America. As a result, many people lose interest in planting trees when they see wastage and loss of established plantings.

the country would have approximately the same area of plantations. The timber grew beautifully and is of high quality, but it is going to waste because none of the plantings are large enough to support an economically profitable mill. The long haul distances, railroads with differing gauges and general lack of infrastructure prevent the concentration of timber to a central mill site even though the total timber available is enough to support several efficient-size mills. As a result, the timber from the exotics is not being utilized.

2.   Once a program is started, it *must be continued each year* to assure a *continuous supply of timber*. It cannot be turned on and off for convenience of finance or as political attitudes change (Fig. 1.12), which creates a timber imbalance. Several countries that have rather large timber inventories of exotics are unable to lure industries to build manufacturing facilities because of the lack of assurance of a suitable timber supply to continually produce a desired quality product because of fluctuating policies relative to forestry. Success of any forest-product manufacturer is dependent on a reliable and continuous timber supply of the desired quality. Changes in species composition or timber age make this impossible.

3.   Do not initiate a program with exotics unless there is *assurance* of *adequate funding* to keep the program *continuously operating*. This is the most common cause of failure of exotic programs promoted by governments, which

Figure 1.12. If exotic forestry is to be successful, there must be a continuous source of supply of wood. Frequently this does not occur. Shown is a mature stand of trees in the background and young seedlings in the foreground. In this instance, due to government policy which restricted planting for 15 years, few trees are available in the intermediate age classes.

often leads to the disenchantment of the local populace with the potentials of forestry (Anon., 1980c). Too often a political party in power favors forestry, but the one that replaces it does not, so the program is either terminated or so reduced that it fails when governments change. The same failure results when forestry incentive programs are started and then are abruptly terminated. Tax incentives should lead to the planting of already deforested and degraded areas rather than encouraging clearing, burning, and plantation establishment in indigenous forests (Anon., 1980c).

4.   In the operational program, *proceed* with the *best available knowledge about provenances and species, but immediately establish additional tests for better species, geographic sources, and land races.* Rarely is the first material used found to be the best in the long run. Have someone with wide experience advise on the best possible species or sources to use. It is amazing how often their suggestions are correct or at least direct a program into the "ballpark" to start. Land races should be established as soon as possible.

5.   Have *one or two species as secondary species* in case the primary species fails. Pests or problems always occur when exotics are grown, and sometimes they are serious enough so that the source or species being used must be abandoned.

6.   Use all possible *international cooperation* for an exchange of information and plant materials (Nikles and Burley, 1977).

Although frequently not included in a list of what makes a suitable exotic, one requirement is that it not develop into a pest species (see Chapter 4). This need before classifying an exotic as satisfactory was pointed out by Franklin (1978). Certainly one does not want to bring in a species that will grow wild and take over indigenous vegetation, as has occurred in parts of South Africa, New Zealand, and numerous other areas of the world. In their recommendations for use of exotics, the National Academy of Sciences (1983) warns against the indiscriminate use of invasive exotics which can become weeds.

1.9 SOME BIOLOGICAL CONCEPTS RELATED TO THE PRODUCTION OF EXOTICS

The idea has generally been accepted that exotics will produce a great deal more wood in a given time on a given hectare than will indigenous species. To some extent, and under some circumstances, this is true, but there is a limit to productivity no matter what the source of the genetic material used.

1.9.1 The Law of Limiting Factors

Productivity of any site has limitations for various reasons—this is often stated as the *Law of Limiting Factors*. Simplified for forestry, this basic biological concept generalizes that a given hectare can produce only a given amount of wood before some factor, or combination of factors, becomes limiting, thus restricting further expansion in production. Although this statement may not be strictly scientifically correct, it is a good working hypothesis and one that all foresters should recognize. It is especially important when growing exotics, because sometimes production expectations or claims are well above the biological possibilities. Especially on the poorer sites, such as eroded areas, grasslands, or scrub-brushlands that may be deficient in moisture or certain nutrients, even the best exotics may not be productive because of the limiting factors.

What are the limiting factors? There are many, most of which are touched upon throughout this book. It is sufficient to mention a few of them here.

1. *Moisture, amount and distribution pattern.* Where exotics are used, such as in the tropics and subtropics, frequently rainfall is very low. When it becomes less than 1000 mm/yr, moisture becomes critical and greatly restricts growth. Few forest crops can be successfully grown where there is less than 700 mm of rainfall per annum, although species are available for fuelwood production where rainfall may fall below 500 mm annually (IBPGR, 1982). The distribution pattern is of key importance; that is, does the rain come in a few very hard showers or is it evenly distributed throughout the year? Does it come during the cool or warm period of the year? Is there too much at any given time? All of these can become severe limiting factors for growing exotics. The importance of water as a limiting factor was especially emphasized

by Nambiar et al. (1984). They state: "In many such cases growth rates are limited primarily by shortages of soil resources, particularly water and nutrients." The authors discuss how other supposed limiting factors such as nutrients are frequently grossly affected by the moisture supply.

2. *Temperature extremes.*   Cold and hot temperatures are commonly recognized as being limiting to tree growth; for example, most of the best *Eucalyptus* cannot stand freezing weather. Again the sequence is important; some species that can stand low temperatures when there is a gradual hardening off will be damaged by temperatures just below freezing if the cold is immediately preceded by a warm spell. This is one of the major items to look for when selecting provenances for exotics. Unfortunately, the temperature fluctuations are often not known, and one is often lucky to obtain even monthly averages. Temperature extremes are also cyclical and a major reason for losses in exotic plantings.

3. *Nutrient deficiencies or excesses.*   It is very common on the marginal lands used to plant exotics that one or several necessary chemicals are in short supply. These can be many; in the tropics most commonly it is phosphorus, boron, zinc, or a combination. Sometimes nitrogen is limiting. The nutrient status of the soil must *always* be assessed before exotics are planted. Sometimes there are excesses, such as of aluminum, which frequently greatly restricts growth. As stated by Cianco et al. (1982) regarding work with exotics in Italy, growing exotics successfully "presupposes a rigorous and precise diagnosis of site characteristics in relation to the needs of the exotic species."

4. *Pests.*   Commonly, the productive potential of an exotic is curtailed by attacks by insects or diseases. These, like all other factors listed, can either be so limiting as to kill the exotic or, more commonly and more seriously, to reduce its productivity greatly below the potential. As pointed out in Chapter 4, there are many pests in addition to insects and diseases. In fact, too frequently, the greatest pests becoming a limiting factor are humans.

5. *Genetic potential for overcoming limiting factors.*   One of the most frequent limiting factors, not widely recognized until recently, is the restricted genetic potential of the trees used. Often they are not capable of using the available resources, so production is limited. The basis of tree improvement is to develop trees that more successfully use the resources and convert them into the most valuable product.

There are essentially two ways to overcome environmental conditions limiting the productivity in exotic forestry. First, the forester can help to reduce the limiting factors of the environment through use of better forest management and silviculture. This has been, and for a long time will continue to be, the easiest and most common method to increase forest productivity. However, the second option of using the best sources and strains of exotic trees to overcome severely limiting environmental factors is becoming increasingly important. Care in choice and breeding of exotics has already made some forestry operations profitable on land that had been considered marginal or sub-marginal for economic forest production. How to overcome some of the limiting factors by breeding were well covered by Christiansen and Lewis (1982) in their book *Breeding Plants for Less Favorable Environments*. As pointed out by them, most problems are directly related to the law of limiting factors; the improved strains can grow satisfactorily where environments (like drought) would normally be limiting.

From a practical standpoint, the only economic way of overcoming limitations in moisture and temperature is to breed strains of trees that are able to grow under adverse conditions. Although fertilization can sometimes be used to improve nutrients, often the best strategy is to develop genetic types that grow well with less nutrients. Similarly, the genetic method is quite often the best to overcome serious pests.

As so strongly emphasized by Zobel and Talbert (1984), the development of trees especially suitable for marginal sites is long-term in nature but will result in substantial benefits as pressures for forestland use gains in intensity. Use of marginal lands for growing exotics is increasing, which is moving forestry operations from the more productive sites to areas that were previously considered to be marginal or useless for timber production. As a result, large amounts of suitable seed are needed quickly for exotics that are specifically developed to grow on the vast areas that are currently marginal or submarginal for economic forest or agricultural production.

Potential gains from breeding exotic species for adaptability to marginal sites are great, but forest managers must be constantly aware of the basic biological constraints on the full productive potential of a given area of land. Because of the limiting factors, exotic forestry without commensurate intensive forest management will fail. There must be a union between the kind of trees used and good culture to restrict limiting factors if maximum gains from either are to be achieved. This combination of the best plants and culture has been shown many times to be essential in agriculture.

A concept that dictates problems over the long term are ongoing climatic changes, as was stressed by Hepting (1960). He presented the view that some of the major reasons for the decline of tree species is the warming trend in the Northern Hemisphere that has been constant since 1900, resulting in changed growth patterns and the predominance of previously innocuous pests. Environmental changes, no matter what the cause, frequently result in the decline of what otherwise had been considered a good exotic.

1.10 THE LITERATURE ON EXOTICS

Stated conservatively, the literature related to exotic forestry is voluminous. There is no practical way to cover even a significant part of it in this book. The authors have therefore chosen references to show the breadth of the work done in various areas on various species under differing environments.

The huge number of publications is somewhat misleading, however. Many are in the form of progress reports on how different species or geographic sources within species have performed after only a year or two, and sometimes even on their performance in the nursery bed. Such information is of very limited value at best, for reasons outlined in Chapter 2. Another large group of papers reports on studies of specific provenances, or geographic areas, so are of value only for a limited audience. These categories of publications will not be generally covered in any detail in this book; as possible, the publications that will be cited are related to more general concepts and principles. Occasionally, specific studies will be used to illustrate how the general principles have worked out under actual situations.

It is particularly frustrating to try to locate important studies that are contained in proceedings of meetings or are published internally by companies or other organizations; these are often not generally referenced or available. Despite the difficulties in citing them, in a few instances we have cited such work if it is of special value. Good detective work is sometimes required to obtain the desired information. A number of excellent references are contained in short courses, many of which also have limited publication or distribution. These are also difficult to cite by the standard methods.

Most publications are in English or have English summaries that enable the English-language reader to assess the value of the article sufficiently to make a decision as to whether to have it translated in whole or in part. This is particularly true of publications from the Scandinavian countries, the Spanish-speaking countries, and to some extent the German publications. Many French, Portuguese, Russian, and East European publications, and many of the older Japanese ones, do not have English summaries and the language barrier creates a severe loss of information exchange and sometimes considerable amounts of duplication when summaries are not given in more than one language. To aid with the Japanese, Toda (1970, 1972) published English summaries of Japanese articles in two volumes covering the time from before 1880 through 1945 and entitled *Abstracts of Japanese Literature in Forest Genetics and Related Fields*. One finds in these pages many references to exotics, some published hundreds of years ago. Many of the concepts outlined by the Japanese are currently being "rediscovered"—a major duplication that would not have occurred except for the language barrier.

The group of publications by the Commonwealth Forestry Institute (OFI), Oxford University, Oxford, England, has several numbers covering the silviculture and breeding of several species used extensively as exotics. Two of these [the one on *Pinus caribaea* (Greaves, 1978) and one on *P. oocarpa* (Greaves, 1979)] have been listed in the list of references at the back of this book. CFI (OFI) also puts out a series of very informative releases called Tropical Forestry Papers; an example is No. 18, on *Pinus caribaea* and *P. oocarpa*. A publication covering *Pinus contorta* from Sweden and one on *Cupressus lusitanica* by FAO illustrate the type of publications that are available for certain species. A series of publications by FAO (Rome) entitled *Forest Genetic*

Resources and another set entitled *Plant Genetic Resources* are most helpful in keeping up to date on collections and sources of seeds for exotics. The series of Technical Notes published by the Department of Forestry in Queensland are most useful; an example is Tech. Note No. 5, by Nicholson (1981), on *Acacia mangium,* a species suitable for wet sites, or one on *Acacia auruculiformis,* a species planted widely as an exotic and especially adapted to grow on impoverished soil and which will compete with imperata grass.

Numerous symposia, like those on *P. radiata* in New Zealand (Burdon and Thulin, 1966), carry information of great value to those interested in growing exotics, and publications by the Commonweath Scientific Industrial Research Organization (CSIRO) in Australia give much information on the eucalypts and other trees used as exotics. Similar excellent information is available from the Proceedings of the Representatives of the Australian Forestry Council (for example, *Proc. 6th Meet., Forest Genetics,* Research Working Group #1 at Coffs Harbour, New South Wales, 1978, 209 pp.). Methods to use and develop exotics that are quite sophisticated are described in "A National Exotic Forest Description System" by Butler et al. (1985). It is only recently that forestry has developed methodologies suited specifically for exotics.

Without doubt, some of the best sources of information on obtaining seed for, growing, and managing exotics are in proceedings of the World Consultations on Forest Genetics and Tree Improvement. These conferences, sponsored by FAO and IUFRO, have been held in Stockholm, Sweden (1963), Washington, D.C. (1969), and Canberra, Australia (1977). In addition, proceedings from a number of international meetings and symposia sponsored by FAO and IUFRO contain a vast amount of important information.

The literature is filled with large and sometimes quite meaningless acronyms, letters representing various organizations, both in English and other languages. It is impossible for the reader to remember all of these—at least it is for the authors of this book. Therefore, an appendix was prepared to cover a few of the more common acronyms found in the literature.

2

SPECIES, VARIETIES, AND GEOGRAPHIC VARIATION IN EXOTIC FORESTRY

2.1 PROVENANCE (GEOGRAPHIC SOURCE) AND ITS RELATIONSHIP TO EXOTICS

It is not possible to discuss exotics without at the same time considering geographic variation, or, as it is commonly called, provenance variation. The success of an exotic forestry program is dependent upon using the correct provenances of the species being planted; Steenberg (1983) states that plantations in the developing countries often are failures because of the lack of research on provenances. As pointed out by Squillace (1966), genetic gains from growing exotics are determined by the quality of the geographic race or the seed source used. Eldridge (1978) emphasizes that after a decision as to which species to plant is made, the next step is to identify the best provenance.

Without any question, the most frequent cause for failure of exotic forestry programs is the use of the wrong species or provenance, either through lack of knowledge or the inability to obtain the proper seed in sufficient quantities. Many examples could be given, especially in tropical pines and eucalypts, where species have been grown under conditions for which they were not biologically suited, or the wrong provenances were assessed (Figs. 2.1 and 2.2.). Therefore, a knowledge of geographic variation, its causes and uses, is just as mandatory as knowing other causes for variation, such as individual tree differences (Boland, 1978).

It is of key importance to take the necessary action to procure, or to produce, the desired quantities of seed of the best provenances. A complete coverage of provenance research is not suitable to this book, but the relationship of provenance to exotic forestry will be dealt with. As it is so positively stated

Figure 2.1. Exotics are extremely sensitive to the use of the wrong provenance. When the correct provenance is not used, the trees may die or have dieback. Frequently they grow well, as shown above for slash pine in Colombia, but their form is totally unacceptable. Diameters and heights of the plantation shown are good, but the tree form is hopeless. (Photo courtesy of John Wiley & Sons.)

Figure 2.2. Most *Eucalyptus* species show marked provenance variation, especially species such as *E. camaldulensis,* shown in the photograph. Note the large height growth differences of two sources when grown on a sandy soil in South America.

by Yeatman (1976), the key point in forest planting is to know the true origin of seed and seedlings that are to be used.

It is necessary that the reader understands the meaning of provenance, geographic source, geographic race, and seed source. For convenience, the definitions used by Zobel and Talbert (1984) are repeated below:

1. *Provenance, geographic source or geographic race:*   These denote the original geographic area from which seed or other propagules were obtained (Callaham, 1964; Jones and Burley, 1973). If, for example, seed of *Eucalyptus grandis* were obtained from Coff's Harbour, New South Wales, Australia, and grown in Zimbabwe, they would be classified as the Coff's Harbour provenance (or geographic source or geographic race).

2. *Seed source:*   If seed from the trees grown in Zimbabwe were harvested and planted in Brazil, they would be referred to as the Zimbabwe seed source and the Coff's Harbour provenance. The term "origin" is used by Barner (1966) in the same way as seed source. When the difference between provenance and seed source is not recognized, large and costly planting errors may be made. Seed source will be used very specifically throughout this book while the terms provenance, geographic source and geographic race will be used interchangeably.

In the short course given in Kenya in 1974, Barner recognized five sources of seed including provenance, stands, seed production areas, individual trees, and seed orchards. Although classifying seed in the donor country helps, Turnbull (1978) brings out the point that no matter how seed is classified in the donor country, the receptor country should make its own assessment as to whether the exotic will meet the conditions in the new environment.

Many small and some huge provenance tests of exotics have been made in species such as *Pinus sylvestris, P. caribaea, P. contorta, Pseudotsuga menziesii, Picea abies, Picea sitchensis, Populus* spp., *Tectona grandis, Eucalyptus* spp. and many others. Some of these studies are old enough so that good results are now available (Fig. 2.3). As an example of a very large test, one on Douglas-fir in Germany contained 111 different provenances from British Columbia to Oregon, California, and Mexico, as well as from German seed sources, which were used to confirm and/or supplement older European provenance tests. It was found that provenances from under 600 m elevation in British Columbia, Washington, or Oregon were the best in the German Federal Republic. They also showed large differences between the so-called east and west side geographic sources, separated by the ridge line of the Cascade Mountains in Washington and Oregon (Kleinschmit et al., 1974). Another very large test, on *Pinus sylvestris,* was established with 122 origins in the north-central United States. Major source differences were found, and the species was divided into 14 geographic ecotypes (Wright and Bull, 1963).

Eucalyptus camaldulensis is reported to be the most widely planted exotic forest tree species, but we have also heard the same for *Pinus radiata*. With the current emphasis, *P. caribaea* and *Eucalyptus grandis* will soon be com-

Figure 2.3. A vast amount of information is becoming available on provenance differences in species used as exotics, especially for the eucalypts and tropical pines. Very large differences occur among sources shown for four-year-old *Eucalyptus nitens* tested in Australia. Such differences are magnified when trees are grown in a new exotic environment.

petitors for this title. The predominance of recent provenance studies in *Pinus caribaea* and *P. oocarpa* in the tropical conifers and *Eucalyptus* spp. in the hardwoods indicates the use and importance of, and the wide variability in, provenances in these very widely used genera.

We also have heard that the poplars (*Populus* spp.) are the most widely planted exotics. Although not all poplars are grown as exotics, many are, or are partly exotics via hybridization. The literature on the poplars is huge and specialized and can only be recognized in this book. For example, Noh et al. (1984) published a long article regarding poplar breeding, cultivation, exploitation, and utilization in Korea. Their paper includes much data and lists 75 papers on poplars published in Korea alone. It is unfortunate that the specialized and well-developed work on poplars cannot be fully included in this book with other exotics, since many of the general principles outlined do apply to growing poplars as well as to other exotics.

When considering the use of exotics, it is impossible to proceed efficiently without the inclusion of the general principles applied to provenance testing and choice of sources. Some of the principles have been summarized by Larsen (1954), Callaham (1964), Lacaze (1978) and Zobel and Talbert (1984). One important concept that is often overlooked is that *provenance differences which exist within the natural range of a species usually become more evident (and important) when a species is grown as an exotic.* This was clearly shown for *Pinus taeda* in southern Brazil, using the work by Shimizu and Higa (1981) as just one example.

Provenance variation studies were started a long time ago, but their application to exotics is generally more recent. Studies by Wright et al. (1970) for Douglas-fir (*Pseudotsuga menziesii*) in Argentina showed that making plantings based upon simple provenance tests could probably increase productivity by more than 50%, as they had in Michigan and Nebraska. The authors rightfully emphasize, however, that results of tests in the United States cannot be directly applied in Argentina. Only tests there will give the correct answers because one of the major unknowns in working with provenances and exotics is the magnitude of the interaction between provenance and the environment. This interaction has been discussed by many authors (Callaham, 1964; Burley and Nikles, 1973b) and summarized by Zobel and Talbert (1984).

All degrees of interaction have been observed, but generally little or no significant provenance × environment interaction is found. A number of papers are quoted on this subject in Chapter 3. To illustrate, one study on *Pinus pinaster* (maritime pine), by Matziris (1982), showed the best provenances were superior in all seven locations where the tests were made. Provenance × environment interaction has been given so much emphasis because no matter how sophisticated the breeding techniques, the largest, cheapest, and fastest gains in forestry can be made by assuring use of the proper geographic source for a specific site within a species. This is especially true with exotics.

Despite all the work that has been done, there still is great ignorance about the size and importance of geographic variation in some species used as exotics. Anderson's 1966 statement is very relevant:

> A reliable provenance would be one producing a decent forest crop with 90% probability rather than an outstanding crop 50% of the time. A usable provenance is one from which seed are readily and economically available as needed.

Lessons have been learned about how difficult it is to define seed or planting zones in areas with complex physiography. Some general rules as to what should and should not be done are now well accepted, including the major finding that there is no single rule that can be applied to all species in all areas. Alerted to the importance of seed source, foresters working with exotics are now more careful about shipping seed indiscriminately over long distances and make it a rule to obtain seed from proven provenances or to test new sources as thoroughly as possible before making large-scale plantings.

Ideally, decisions as to which is the best source of seed for exotic plantings should not be made until extensive testing has been carried out for the greater part of the rotation period, although this is often not possible to do. The hoped-for gains from using an unproven source must be weighed against the risks involved. Unfortunately, the risks can only be assessed after a period of testing long enough to yield reliable results (Fig. 2.4). The most common prob-

Figure 2.4. Growing exotics can be risky even after a long period of testing. Sometimes unexpected pests and/or adverse weather will destroy them, as occurred with this stand of *Cupressus lusitanica* in Colombia. For well over 20 years, the insect *Glena bisulca* was no problem, but it suddenly became epidemic and a killer.

lems related to use of different provenances in planting exotics is to have good initial performance followed by a later slowdown, lack of vigor, dieback, poor form, resin streaks in the wood, or even death.

An exotic must be assessed on its performance relative to the indigenous species when such is possible. An example of this was given by Martinsson and Lundh (1981), where they reported great differences in the lack of root stability within provenances of *Pinus contorta* but found general stability with the local *P. sylvestris*. Choosing the proper exotic is much different when there are no indigenous species, as opposed to the situation where good species are already available and the exotic must outperform them.

Although tree form is less affected by provenance than is growth, sometimes differences in form are related to provenance. One example is the foxtailing (lack of limb production) in the tropical pines. As shown by Das and Stephan (1982), the amount of foxtailing varied greatly among provenances of *Pinus caribaea* var. *hondurensis* as well as among the three varieties of *Pinus caribaea,* var. *hondurensis,* var. *caribaea,* and var. *bahamensis.* The problem of foxtailing is more thoroughly covered in Chapter 4.

Those working with exotics are aware that geographic races occur most often in species that have a wide natural range and are growing in a number of diverse environments. They may differ relative to latitude, altitude, rainfall amount and patterns, temperature, or other environmental conditions (Holzer, 1965; Axelrod, 1967). Although nearly all forest species have distinct geographic races, those species that contain the largest racial divergence afford the best opportunity for gains through provenance selection when growing exotics. This concept was stressed by Jacobs (1964), who showed that many successful exotics have a wide natural latitudinal occurrence, although there are exceptions such as *Pinus radiata*. The wide-ranging species are the ones with which the grower of exotics must exercise the greatest caution to assure that the proper geographic sources are used.

Many specific results could be cited of excellent in-depth studies of variation among sources within a species range; examples are reports on *Pinus caribaea* by Greaves (1978) and *P. oocarpa* (Greaves, 1979). The within-species provenance variability was discussed for plants in general by Clausen and Hiesey (1958). In-depth studies have great importance when selecting the proper provenance, as shown by Sorensen (1983) for Douglas-fir in the western Siskiyou Mountains of Oregon. Another example of a detailed study of the natural range of a species which makes possible good provenance studies is one in the Sunda Isles by Martin and Cossalter (1976). It covers the species *Eucalyptus alba* and *E. urophylla,* two eucalypts growing naturally outside Australia. When available, studies such as these should be used as the starting point when making exotic introductions.

It is not unusual for differences in growth, adaptability, or wood properties to be less between species than between geographic races within a given species that occurs over widely differing environments. This is most evident in the pines from Mexico, where sometimes the differences between high- and low-elevation material within one species will be greater than that between two species growing on similar environments at the same elevation. Similarly, in Scandinavia, differences between *P. contorta* var. *latifolia* and var. *contorta* are usually greater than the differences between var. *latifolia* and *P. sylvestris.*

It is important to understand that when two species occupy the same or similar ranges, races may develop within each species that are quite similar physiologically (Kung and Wright, 1972). For example, most high-latitude or high-elevation sources grow slowly but have better tree form with straighter stems and smaller limbs than do those from lower elevations or lower latitudes (Hermann and Lavendar, 1968). [The same results were shown by Falkenhagen (1979) even for a tropical species.] In addition, they can withstand cold weather that will kill or injure trees adapted to lower elevations and latitudes. The three characteristics of slow growth, good form, and good resistance to cold are common to most high-elevation and high-latitude provenances regardless of the species involved. In his summary paper, Wright (1970) noted that the theoretical generalizations that sources from warm climates grow faster and sources from cold climates were hardier were usually true, but that there are notable exceptions. Those persons searching for sources for exotic planting need to use this kind of information.

As emphasized by Bialobok (1967) and Zobel and Talbert (1984), a deter-

Figure 2.5. Some areas, such as the one in Guatemala shown here, are particularly conducive to the development of many provenances. The environments differ greatly and change rapidly, producing ideal conditions for species and provenance differentiation.

mination of the boundaries of a geographic race may be difficult. The differences can be abrupt and clear when there are gaps in the species range such as when there is a separation by deserts, bodies of water, or mountains, or they can be gradual when the species occurs continuously from south to north, from dry to wet sites, or from low to high elevations (Koski, 1974) (Fig. 2.5).

Actually, the determination of the exact boundaries of a provenance is not as important as an understanding of the patterns of variation and how these can be used in choosing populations of trees for use as exotics. Although this concept does not apply to exotics, it is true that usually the indigenous source of a species is best until proven otherwise (Bingham, 1965). For exotics, the situation where the donor and receptor environments are the most similar should be used until sources from different environments are proven to be better.

2.2 DEVELOPMENT OF TREES SUITABLE FOR EXOTICS

A field of great interest relates to how species and individual trees suitable for exotic use have been developed over time under natural conditions. A detailed treatment of this subject is beyond the scope of this book, but speciation and evolution in forest trees must be well understood if one is to work intelligently with exotics. Especially helpful are books, such as Parsons (1983), or articles, such as Bannister (1965), on the evolutionary biology and genetics of colonizing species. One publication dealing especially with the development in the eucalypts (Pryor, 1959) describes genetically controlled clines within the species. Examples he gives are frost resistance and slow growth of high-elevation sources even when grown at low elevations. A whole series of books is related to the development of natural populations: Huxley (1938), Mettler and Gregg (1969), Stebbins (1950), Hawkes et al. (1983, Sect B), and Zobel and Talbert (1984). These books, which are listed in References, are only a few of the many available on the subject. According to Shepherd (1978), there is agreement that evolution is still occurring, forming subspecies and species that account for the diversity of organisms. It is greatly speeded up when man interferes through selection programs, and the end point of a desirable land race can be achieved very quickly.

When selecting provenances to use as exotics, often the physiological characteristics are of greater importance than the morphological ones (Langlet, 1936). This means that the choice of a source based on tree phenotype alone will often lead to incorrect results without follow-up intensive testing. The physiological characteristics usually are related to survival, growth, and adaptability and thus are key in determining which geographic race of a species should be used in an operational exotic planting program. Sometimes it is possible to make a wrong judgment. For example, with *Pinus taeda* in Texas, a small island of trees is growing in the very severe climate of Caldwell Co. in the brushlands. This area has very low rainfall. The opinion naturally was that these trees would be drought hardy. Much to our surprise, they were not particularly so. Upon study of the natural stands it was evident that only two age classes occurred, and these matched the years of unusually high rainfall which enabled the trees to become established. Since the trees were growing on Carrizo sands with a relatively high water table, once established, moisture was not limiting for tree growth, so drought resistance was not especially beneficial.

Individual trees within a given geographic source are somewhat similar from past heritage or selection pressures, but they are by no means genetically identical. Usually, great individual differences in phenotype and often in genotype occur among trees within each provenance. This heterogeneity enables individual tree selection within sources to be used effectively by those growing exotics; thus, selection of provenance and individual tree within provenance to produce a land race will give good gains, especially in tree quality characteristics. It is possible, for example, to obtain straight or crooked trees from either the higher-latitude seed sources or from the lower latitudes, although there are more straight individuals in the high latitudes.

A very practical example of the importance of major ecological variability on provenance formation can be found in Guatemala. As reported by Loock (1950), Mittak (1978), Veblen (1978), Gallegos (1980b), and many others, this area of Central America is a "paradise" for selection for use as exotics. The greatly varied soils and climate, the volcanic activity, the huge differences in elevation and land stewardship have all created a set of environmental conditions that has resulted in the development of many differing races, species, and hybrids. In the highland regions of the country it is sometimes difficult to accurately field-identify pine specimens because of the many intermediate hybrid forms that exist. In an attempt to clarify the species from this area, a book is being written by Perry (in press) for use by laymen.

2.2.1 Which Species and Varieties to Use

It is, of course, axiomatic that the first necessity in using exotics is to choose the correct species. Geographic differences within species are usually so overpowering, however, that the main discussions in this chapter have related to them, although the rules for making a choice are essentially the same for species as for provenances. Although stated earlier, it is essential to reemphasize that only a few of the provenances and species tried will be successful. This was clearly stated by Ciancio et al. (1982) in Italy:

> after a second period of 20 years . . . only about 10 conifers of the over 50 species experimentally introduced were of some interest to Italian silviculture, and of these only four or five as fast growing species. . . .

In the hardwoods only *Eucalyptus, Populus,* and *Quercus* were of potential value.

One cannot always predict how a species will respond based on the conditions in its indigenous range (Laurie, 1962). Some species with wide ranges are most difficult to adapt to an exotic environment because they have such well-defined provenances that grow best only on a specific environment. Other species are "plastic," that is, they are not divided into discrete provenances but can grow fairly well on a wide range of environments. These can arise naturally within a narrow geographic and ecological range and would not be expected to have the wide adaptability they actually exhibit. Wright (1962) emphasizes that the best clue to the potential usefulness of a species in a new but similar habitat is its performance in its native habitat. A number of species with narrow ranges have done well when widely planted as exotics because of wide areas suitable for growth of the species (that is, similar to the native conditions) in the exotic habitat (Wright, 1976).

There are occasional exceptions in which species with large plasticity seem to defy all the rules, and infrequently the species will also grow well on environments that differ from its native environment. Species such as *Pinus caribaea, P. radiata, P. elliottii, Acacia auriculiformus, Eucalyptus grandis,* and *Gmelina arborea* have the plasticity to grow well under a wide range of conditions in the new and different environments. This has been particularly evident in the eucalypts, where some species from restricted ranges have performed well in varied environments. As described by Pryor (1959):

"Eucalyptus is extremely sensitive ecologically in its natural environment, and this maintains barriers between populations.'' When moved and grown as an exotic, sensitivity sometimes is no longer so apparent.

The adaptability of *Pinus radiata* to numerous soils and rainfall regimes is legendary. *Larix leptolepis* (Japanese larch), now used widely as an exotic, is only found on a few mountains in Japan but grows well in many conditions (Wright, 1962). Another species with a narrow indigenous range but somewhat wide adaptability is *Pinus elliottii,* although its plasticity is not as broad as that of some other species.

As outlined in Chapter 1, there is a strong move toward using fast-growing hardwood species in addition to the eucalypts in the tropical regions. Most of these have shown a tolerance to degraded sites such as worn-out agricultural lands. Some, like *Acacia mangium,* are also successful in the most competitive herbaceous vegetation in the humid tropics, such as Imperata grass (Anon., 1983a). The statement was made by D. I. Nicholson, who introduced *A. mangium* for use in plantations, that such species will usher in a new resource for the tropics because of their ability to withstand many different growing conditions.

Another hardwood species that seems to have considerable promise is *Cordia alliodora,* as outlined by Stead (1979, 1980). It is considered to be suitable for large-scale plantations and has desirable wood; its performance is not yet well documented, however. As is common for so many tropical hardwoods, initial growth is rapid but long-term growth rates in plantations is still unknown. There are numerous literature citations of new species under test, especially for dry-zone areas (Hughes, 1984), with emphasis on multipurpose trees (Bonkoungou, 1985). For example, *Acacia albida* is described as ideal for agroforestry because it drops its leaves during the rainy season, letting interplanted crops grow, and forms dense shade during the hot, dry season. A whole new literature has been built up in the area of dry-land and multipurpose trees, many of whom are exotic species.

It is obvious that there are considerable differences among the various coniferous and hardwood species used as exotics. Further, several of the more important species have been separated into varieties, which can be of the greatest importance when establishing exotic plantations; a prime example of this are the three varieties of *Pinus caribaea,* var. *hondurensis,* var. *bahamensis,* and var. *caribaea* (Lamb, 1973). Some genera, like *Eucalyptus,* contain hundreds of species. In others, like the genus *Populus,* species have become badly blurred with hybrid production, some of which have been given specific names. Especially in the Mexican pines, species have become taxonomically confused. An example is *Pinus oocarpa.* It has a var. *ochoterenai* that is sometimes called *Patula* var. *longipedunculata* and now *P. tecunumanii* or *P. patula* subs. *tecunumanii* (Barnes and Styles, 1983; Robbins and Hughes, 1983). The switching among varieties and species makes for mass confusion.

Only a sampling of available species comparisons can be listed, as has been done in Table 2.1. Many publications such as *Silvicultura* 30 (1983) list whole

TABLE 2.1. Comparative Performance of Some Species When Used as Exotics[a]

Species Compared	Author(s)	Country	Comments
		Conifers	
Pinus rudis *P. hartwegii* *P. michoacana* *P. oocarpa* *P. montezumae* *P. pseudostrobus*	Debazac 1964	France	Only *P. rudis* and *P. hartwegii* survived winters in northern France after 3 yr; *P. michoacana, P. oocarpa, P. montezumae, P. patula* and *P. pseudostrobus* only survived in southern France.
P. caribaea *P. elliottii*	Lückhoff 1964	South Africa	In summer rainfall areas *P. caribaea* grows twice as fast as *P. elliottii.*
Pinus caribaea *P. patula* *P. oocarpa* *P. douglasiana* *P. taeda* *P. elliottii*	Barrett 1969	Argentina	After 5 yr, best growth in warm humid areas was from *P. caribaea, P. patula, P. oocarpa,* and *P. douglasiana.* In colder climates these were hurt by frosts. They all grew better than *P. elliottii* and *P. taeda,* which, however, were more uniform.
Pinus caribaea *P. oocarpa* *P. patula* *P. pseudostrobus* *P. durangensis* *P. leiophylla* *P. teocote*	Mullin 1969	Rhodesia (Zim- babwe)	*P. oocarpa* is promising, as is *P. patula* and *P. pseudostrobus.* At high elevations, *P. durangensis, P. leiophylla,* and *P. teocote* do well; the first is moderate in growth but very straight; the latter two are faster growing but not so well formed.
Pinus patula *P. teocote* *P. leiophylla* *P. douglasiana* *P. tenuifolia* *(P. maximinoi)* *P. pseudostrobus*	Olesen 1971	Malawi	One of the most promising species is *P. leiophylla;* it grows fast and produces good timber but generally has poor form. Other promising species are *P. douglasiana, P. pseudostrobus,* and *P. tenuifolia. P. patula* is best on high ridges that have the most rain.
Pinus caribaea *P. merkusii* *Cupressus lusitanica*	Geary & Briscoe 1972	Puerto Rico	*P. caribaea* grew well on all sites and survived better than any conifer tested. *C. lusitanica* was susceptible to windthrow. *P. merkusii* was not acceptable.
Pinus caribaea *P. elliottii* *P. oocarpa* *P. kesiya*	Lamb 1973	General	*P. caribaea* var. *hondurensis* is best for hot lowland coastal plains up to 18° from the equator. On drier sites *P. oocarpa* can flourish as

TABLE 2.1. Continued

Species Compared	Author(s)	Country	Comments
P. merkusii			low as 300 m and P. kesiya can be grown above 700 m. P. merkusii needs form improvement and frequently has a juvenile "grass stage."
Pinus oocarpa P. patula P. leiophylla P. hartwegii P. michoacana P. rudis P. tenuifolia (P. maximinoi) P. teocote P. pseudostrobus	Whitesell 1974	Hawaii	P. oocarpa was frost damaged, P. patula and P. leiophylla were damaged by wind. Height growth for the rest were impressive. Some species, like P. teocote, are good for erosion control. P. patula is susceptible to attack by caterpillars.
Pinus caribaea P. oocarpa	Greaves & Kemp 1977	General	On all tropical sites where P. caribaea can be grown, trials of P. oocarpa should be made; on most sites where the best provenances of both have been made, P. oocarpa has been superior.
26 coniferous species	Harvey 1977	Australia (Queensland)	Best species are Pinus radiata, P. patula, P. caribaea var. bahamensis, and P. taeda. The first two mentioned are not the best on certain sites.
Pinus caribaea P. oocarpa	Greaves 1979	Uganda	Honduras origins of P. oocarpa grew as well or better than P. caribaea. P. oocarpa is genetically adapted to grow on degraded sites.
P. elliottii P. caribaea	van Altena 1979	Australia	Caribbean pine was the best grower and produceu ..1ore merchantable volume except on wet sites.
Pinus banksiana P. rigida P. sylvestris P. ponderosa P. jeffreyi	Shote et al. 1982	Japan	P. banksiana grew best. P. rigida and P. sylvestris also grew well, while P. ponderosa and P. jeffreyi were poorest. P. banksiana and P. sylvestris had crooked stems.
Pinus merkusii P. kesiya P. caribaea	de Barros & Brandi 1983	Brasil	P. merkusii is very poor after 7.5 yr. 3 of the P. kesiya sources were as good as P. caribaea in both height and diameter. The poorest P. kesiya was 24% poorer than the best.

(continued)

TABLE 2.1. Continued

Species Compared	Author(s)	Country	Comments
Picea sitchensis *Pinus contorta*	Cannell et al. 1983	Scotland	At age 8, Sitka spruce produced 44% more stemwood per unit needle area than did lodgepole pine.
Pinus patula *P. pringlei* *P. greggii* *P. teocote* *P. chiapensis*	Darrow & Coetzee 1983	South Africa	*P. patula* had superior volume growth. *P. pringlei* grew well in the cooler temperate zones and had higher wood density. In cooler, higher elevations *P. greggii* and *P. teocote* showed potential. *P. chiapensis* grew well and had light, fine-grained wood. Most species were partially resistant to aphids.
Larix laricina *L. eurolepis*	Reed et al. 1983	United States	The 12-yr-old European larch were about the same size as 16- to 18-yr-old indigenous tamarack (*L. laricina*).
Pinus oocarpa *P. caribaea*	Brigden et al. 1984	Australia	At one location, *P. caribaea* was better than *P. oocarpa;* at the other, they were equal. This disagrees with those who say that good provenances of *P. oocarpa* are better than *P. caribaea.*
P. caribaea *P. oocarpa*	Barrett 1984	Argentina	*P. caribaea* var. *caribea* is planted most extensively. It grows well only in the province of Corrientes; the risk of damage from cold in the other "suitable" areas is too great. It outgrows *P. elliottii* (after 20 yr) by 31 m^3/ha/yr to 18 m^3.
Pinus kesiya *P. caribaea* *P. patula* *P. radiata*	Chagala 1984	Kenya	*P. kesiya* was better than *P. radiata, P. patula,* or *P. caribaea* after 12 yr. *P. kesiya* has a thick bark, is more resistant to fire, and is suited to shallow, poor, and droughty soils.
Pinus caribaea *P. kesiya* Other tropical pines	Das & Stephan 1984a	India	*P. caribaea* and *P. kesiya* are the best of the tropical pines.
Larix laricina *L. Leptolepis* *L. sibirica*	Hall 1984	Canada (Newfoundland)	The Siberian larch was very poor and the local tamarack the best. The tamarack is gradually outgrowing the Japanese larch.

TABLE 2.1. Continued

Species Compared	Author(s)	Country	Comments
Pinus kesiya *P. oocarpa* *P. caribaea* *P. pseudostrobus*	Halos & Abarquez 1984	Philippines	6 species (27 provenances) were tested for shoot moth infestation. *P. caribaea* was least infested, while *P. pseudostrobus* showed the greatest infestation; *P. kesiya* and *P. oocarpa* were intermediate. *P. caribaea* var. *bahamensis* was chosen as the most desirable species.
Pinus caribaea *P. oocarpa* 12 other species	Ladrach 1984d	Colombia	In the llanos, at the end of 4 yr only *P. caribaea* and *P. oocarpa* had acceptable survival and growth. The test included 6 broad-leaved species, none of which were good.
Pinus caribaea *P. oocarpa*	Liegel 1984a	Puerto Rico	Results on 16 *P. caribaea* and 15 *P. oocarpa* sources at one location showed the latter to be the best. It had more variability in height, diameter, form, and frequency of forking. *P. caribaea* was more variable in stem straightness, conelet production, and internode length.
Pinus caribaea *P. oocarpa*	Liegel 1984b	Puerto Rico	At 6 sites, 16 provenances of *P. oocarpa* and 13 *P. caribaea* var. *hondurensis* were tested. Blowdown was 6 times worse for *P. oocarpa* and mortality and total damage was twice as bad. Coastal *P. caribaea* was more resistant to wind than inland sources. The fastest-growing *P. oocarpa* had the worst blow-down.
Pinus kesiya *P. elliottii* *P. patula*	Morris 1984	Swaziland	After 10 yr at low altitudes *P. kesiya* was much superior to *P. elliottii*. At high altitudes *P. patula* was slightly better.
Pinus merkusii *P. kesiya*	Mubita 1984	Zambia	The stem quality of *P. merkusii* is much superior to *P. kesiya*.
Pinus oocarpa *P. kesiya* *P. pseudostrobus* *P. caribaea* *P. maximinoi* *P. montezumae*	Nicolielo & Bertolani 1984	Brazil	In a subtropical environment *P. caribaea* var. *hondurensis* was superior, followed by *P. kesiya* and *P. oocarpa,* which grew equally well, and then *P. maximinoi, P. montezumae,* and *P. pseudostrobus*.

(continued)

TABLE 2.1. Continued

Species Compared	Author(s)	Country	Comments
Pinus kesiya *P. tenuifolia* *(P. maximinoi)* *P. patula* *P. oocarpa* *P. pseudostrobus* *P. taeda*	Ladrach 1985a	Colombia	73 provenances and sources of 14 species were tested for 5 yr on 3 farms in the Andean region of Colombia. Best are: at 1400 m, *P. kesiya* and *P. tenuifolia;* at 1750 m, *P. patula, P. kesiya,* and *P. oocarpa;* at 2500 m, *P. patula, P. pseudostrobus. P. taeda* grew well at the highest elevation.
Pinus chiapensis	Dvorak & Brouard 1986	General	Plantings from the 1960s and 1970s have grown well in Brazil, Colombia, New Zealand, South Africa, Zimbabwe, and elsewhere. It will produce more than 20 m^3/ha/yr; wood specific gravity values are 0.342 to 0.351. It does well on proper sites.

Hardwoods

Species Compared	Author(s)	Country	Comments
Swietenia *macrophylla* *S. humilis* *S. mahagoni*	Geary et al. 1973	Puerto Rico Virgin Islands	*S. macrophylla* is the fastest grower but the most drought susceptible. *S. mahagoni* was resistant to shoot borer attack.
Gmelina arborea *Eucalyptus degulpta* *Pinus caribaea*	Woessner 1980	Brazil	The pines will produce about 25 m^3/ha/yr on a 12-yr rotation, while the hardwood will produce about 40 m^3/ha/yr harvested at 6 yr.
Toona ciliata *(Cedrela toona)* *Fraxinus uhdei* *Grevillea robusta* *Eucalyptus* *microcorys* *E. pilularis* *E. robusta* *E. saligna*	Buck & Imoto 1982	Hawaii	11 major species were assessed over 21 yr for growth (7 hardwoods). Results by species are given. Australian toon, tropical ash, and silky oak can be managed for sawlogs. The growth of the eucalypts was good on a variety of sites; sawtimber trees can be produced; the best was *E. robusta.*
Eucalyptus viminalis *E. deanei* *E. macarthurii* *E. grandis*	Anon. 1983b	South Africa	*E. deanei* was best overall on both good and poor sites. *E. viminalis* and *E. macarthurii* were best on poor sites. *E. macarthurii* was most cold tolerant, *E. grandis* most susceptible. The wood of *E. grandis* is superior.

TABLE 2.1. Continued

Species Compared	Author(s)	Country	Comments
Eucalyptus urophylla *E. grandis* *E. saligna*	Darrow & Roeder 1983	South Africa	The volume of *E. urophylla* was smaller than that of *E. grandis*, but higher wood density made it better than *E. saligna* and equal to *E. grandis*.
Alnus glutinosa *A. cordata* *A. incana*	Genys & Hall 1983	United States	After 1 yr, the best *A. glutinosa* was much larger than the best *A. incana*. The *A. cordata* was intermediate.
Eucalyptus saligna *E. grandis* *E. deanei*	Wilcox et al. 1983a	New Zealand	*E. saligna* grows better and is less affected by the *Eucalyptus* tortoise beetle (*Paropsis charybdis*) than the other two species.
Acacia mearnsii *A. decurrens* *A. dealbata*	Anon. 1984a	South Africa	Green (*A. decurrens*) and silver (*A. dealbata*) wattle were highly inferior to the black (*A. mearnsii*) wattle. Survival and form of the green and silver wattle were very poor.
Gmelina arborea *Cassia siamea* *Bombacopsis quinata* *Hura crepitans* *Tabebuia rosea* *Cordia gerascanthus* *Eucalyptus tereticornis*	Ladrach 1984b	Colombia	After 4 yr, *Gmelina* had 120 m³/ha; *Cassia,* 41; *Bombacopsis,* 40; *Hura,* 21; *Tabebuia,* 19; *Eucalyptus,* 11; and *Cordia,* 7.
Eucalyptus camaldulensis *E. tereticornis* *E. cloeziana* *E. citriodora*	Massavan- hane & Rudin 1984	Mozambique	Under conditions in Mozambique *E. camaldulensis* was best, *E. tereticornis* was second.
Eucalyptus grandis *E. saligna*	Darrow 1986	South Africa	At 8 yr, *E. grandis* was highly superior to most *E. saligna* in volume and stem form, but *E. saligna* had higher wood density.

[a]Full references are shown in the reference list at the end of the book. Details of age, site, and other test conditions can be found in the reference articles. The aim of this table is to give some idea of the scope of the work done. A number of comparisons of other species, like *Pinus contorta* and *P. sylvestris,* are discussed in the text.

series of tropical species that are now being studied, many of which are exotics. Although we attempted to get comparisons of species used as exotics from different areas, most of them listed are from the tropics and subtropics. Especially in the conifers, we have concentrated upon the Mexican and Caribbean pines; areas such as Guatemala were emphasized by Veblen (1978) as one of the few tropical highland regions (along with Mexico and Honduras) in which conifers are well represented. Results for many of these pines are not clear because often the provenances used were not well defined. Some general observations and conclusions about species based upon the literature, Table 2.1, and our own experiences follow:

1. In the hot coastal tropical lowlands, *P. caribaea* does well. However, under most conditions, the correct geographic source of *P. oocarpa* is as good or better than *P. caribaea*. *P. oocarpa* has better tree form, smaller limbs, and better wood overall than does *P. caribaea,* but *P. oocarpa* is not suited to areas with strong winds, such as along the seacoasts. The very heavy emphasis on the use and testing of *P. caribaea* and *P. oocarpa* is evident from the mass of references in Table 2.1.

2. *Pinus contorta* is usually quite superior to *P. sylvestris* when grown in n. Europe, although it is less windfirm.

3. *Eucalyptus grandis* is generally the best species among those tested when placed on suitable sites. However, *E. urophylla* will grow nearly as well and has similar wood; it also is less sensitive to the *Eucalyptus* bole canker disease (*Cryphonectria cubensis*). In some environments, especially where the canker is not present, *E. saligna* is best. *E. deglupta* is an exceedingly fast grower with suitable but somewhat low-density wood and grows best on heavier, wet clay soils in tropical conditions; provenance is also important in this species.

4. From the host of Mexican and Caribbean pines, *P. patula* has been most widely used at the higher elevations (Barnes and Styles, 1983). Many other species have been tried, but usually on a restricted scale and often without proper attention to provenance. *Pinus chiapensis* (*P. strobus* var. *chiapensis*) (Dvorak and Brouard, 1986) is an excellent grower and produces a light, high-quality wood. Species like *P. pseudostrobus* and *P. maximinoi* can be used with *P. patula* and *Cupressus lusitanica* (Ladrach, 1984c). Although normally not formally recognized, species like the Mexican and Caribbean pines intergrade so much that they have been grouped into complexes or groups of related species. This was done by Barnes and Styles (1983) for the closed-cone pines, which include the species *P. patula, P. oocarpa, P. greggii, P. tecunumanii,* and *P. pringlei*. The authors state that this group of pines could someday be the most widely planted conifers in the tropics.

5. Many of the Asiatic pines, especially the Chinese, have potential, but they have not been well tried and their provenances are essentially unknown. They have proven to be very susceptible to pine aphids when grown in South Africa.

6. Many good members of the genus *Populus* exist, but *P. deltoides* has proven to be one of the best both as a pure species and in hybrid combinations.

7. The best-performing species of the mahoganies is *Swietenia macrophylla,* although some hybrids have potential (Geary et al., 1973).

8. *Pinus elliottii,* which has been so widely planted as an exotic, may do well but usually is not as good as *Pinus taeda* if the correct provenance of the latter is used.

9. *Gmelina arborea* is a very rapid grower and several good provenances are available. Its wood is an excellent hardwood and it will nearly always outgrow any other species on a suitable site when the proper provenance is used.

10. Many of the tropical hardwoods can be grown successfully, but they usually are slow growers—examples of genera are *Tabebuia, Cordia,* and *Hura.* Others like *Toona, Tectona,* and *Bombacopsis* grow well enough to make profitable plantations both in their indigenous ranges and as exotics.

11. A number of temperate species are widely used as exotics; one most used is *Pseudotsuga menziesii* (Fig. 2.6). It has many differing and distinctive provenances, as do *Pinus taeda, Pinus contorta, Picea abies,* and others.

The best starting point from which to choose a species is to consult summaries or symposia in which all available data about the species are summarized. There are a number of these; a few have been listed in Table 2.2.

Figure 2.6. Douglas-fir (*Pseudotsuga menziesii*) is a major temperate climate species used as an exotic. It can grow excellently when the correct provenance is available, as in New Zealand, shown here, but it can be very poor if an incorrect provenance is used.

TABLE 2.2. Some Important Summaries or Symposia about Species Used as Exotics[a]

Species	Author(s)	General Results
	Hardwoods	
Eucalyptus camaldulensis	Eldridge 1975	Several of the many papers on this species were reviewed and summarized.
Australian Acacias	1975–1982	Leaflets on a number of Australian *Acacias* were published over the years. They are available from CSIRO, Canberra, Australia. Sixteen species are described.
Eucalyptus spp.	Gutiérrez 1976–1982	This is a 5-volume compendium of all aspects of the eucalypts—very complete.
Eucalyptus spp.	Hillis & Brown 1978	The book gives complete coverage on the eucalypts with considerable information of value for their use as exotics.
Eucalypts	Poynton 1979	Poynton's book provides excellent coverage of the use of *Eucalyptus* as an exotic in southern Africa.
Cordia alliodora	Stead 1979	This species, widespread from Argentina to Mexico and the Caribbean islands, is wind firm, has good form, and has no known pests. It appears to grow well in plantations.
Eucalyptus urophylla	Martin & Cossalter 1976	A complete coverage of *E. urophylla* is given.
Species other than *Eucalyptus* in Australia	Boland & Turnbull 1981	6 *Acacia* species, *Casuarina equisetifolia* (and other species in the genus), *Grevillia robusta, Terminalia catalpa,* and *T. orientalis* all are covered for use as fuelwood in the developing countries. Also, some eucalypts are mentioned. The appendix covers 13 *Casuarina* species.
Gmelina arborea	Greaves 1982b	The complete bibliography on *Gmelina* covers the literature from 1921 to 1981.
Leucaena leucocephala	Anon. 1982b	The publication is a compilation of 32 papers on all aspects of *Leucaena*, emphasizing both its advantages and limitations.
Many dry-zone species	Hughes 1984	The report contains a list of 25 dry-zone species and locality of collection in Central America.

TABLE 2.2. Continued

Species	Author(s)	General Results
	Conifers	
Pinus caribaea	Lückhoff 1964	An excellent description of the species, with its three varieties in their natural range, is given.
Pinus radiata	Burdon & Thulin 1966	A series of papers given at a symposium on radiata pine, covering all aspects of growth and utilization of the species, is included.
Pinus merkusii	Cooling 1968	The book carries a good description of the species, its sources and variation within species and its uses.
Pinus caribaea	Lamb 1973	A complete survey of the history, development, and taxonomy of the species is covered.
Pinus taeda	Zobel & Dorman 1973	This paper outlines the use of *P. taeda* as an exotic in the tropics and subtropics.
Pinus spp.	Poynton 1979	This volume thoroughly covers the use of pines as exotics in southern Africa.
Pinus contorta	Persson 1980	*Pinus contorta* and its use as an exotic species is covered.
Pinus oocarpa	Greaves 1982a	This publication is an annotated bibliography of publications related to the species.
Pinus caribaea	Robbins 1983	Various aspects of the species are very well covered through seed and regeneration.
Southern pines	McDonald & Krugman 1985	The 11 species of the southern pines (including *P. caribaea, P. cubensis, P. occidentalis*) are among the most widely planted trees. They are used as exotics in South America and Africa. In the Asia–Pacific region they comprise 60% of the exotics, and in China, most of the exotics.

[a]Full references are given in the reference list.

2.2.1.1 Importance of Varieties and Hybrids. The subspecific categories of varieties are one step above provenance. It is not always clear why in some instances, such as in *Pinus caribaea,* varieties are named and in others, like for Douglas-fir, which contains huge provenance differences, varieties are not commonly used. Although some people disagree, Douglas-fir has recently had some sources differentiated on a varietal status, but officially *Pseudotsuga menziesii* is generally regarded as a species with numerous provenances.

It is immediately evident that the most-studied varieties are those of *P. caribaea* (var. *hondurensis,* var. *caribaea,* and var. *bahamensis*). Some general facts emerge from nearly all studies regarding these three varieties, although there are occasional exceptions in very different environments.

1.   Variety *hondurensis* is the fastest grower, but when not genetically improved, it sometimes has very poor form and a high incidence of foxtailing. It is somewhat sensitive to site differences, but is overall a rather plastic variety that is capable of growing well under some quite widely differing conditions. *Hondurensis* is best in the lowland tropics, but above 1000 m the *bahamensis* is better in form. Both varieties are easily killed by frost. Variation in stem and branch form within *hondurensis* is much greater than within the other two varieties.

2.   Variety *caribaea* is frequently the slowest grower but has the best stem and limb form. It rarely has foxtails. It is quite drought hardy and does well at higher elevations, being more resistant to frost than the other two varieties.

3.   Variety *bahamensis* is nearly as good in form as *caribaea* and grows slightly faster. It is frequently planted on more basic soils than the other two varieties. It sometimes is more drought resistant than *hondurensis.*

Varietal studies have been made with other exotics (Critchfield, 1978). In Finland, the continental source *Pinus contorta* var. *latifolia* had better survival than the coastal var. *contorta* or the Sierra Nevada var. *murrayana.* Many of the coastal provenances were killed outright; survival ranged from 8 to 100%. After eight years all 43 provenances of variety *latifolia* exceeded the best Scots pine provenance by as much as 20%; the other two varieties were shorter than Scots pine. Similar results are available from Sweden.

Natural hybridization, followed by introgression and backcrossing, or by the production of hybrid swarms, gives a large number of "new" or different genetic combinations, some of which are especially suitable for exotic environments (see Chapter 3). A prime development of this type is among the Caribbean pines, where complexes of intergrading types have developed (Styles et al., 1982).

Similarly, *Eucalyptus* has a great amount of variability resulting from hybridization and introgression (Clifford, 1954; Pryor, 1978a). Another genus with a very broad gene pool for selection is *Quercus* (oaks), where an almost unbelievable number of natural hybrids and introgressants have been formed. Some of the hybrids and introgressants in species used for exotics have gene combinations with the ability to grow on unique exotic sites; they are especially useful when vegetative propagation is used to establish operational forests.

2.2.2 Which Provenances to Use

A general summary of the conditions most conducive to obtaining provenances that will be of interest for use as exotics is given next. It is evident that most exotic species require international cooperation if tests are to be successful (Martin, 1983).

1. One can work with species that have wide ranges over diverse environments, but they should be from similar latitudes. As an example, Skroppa and Dietrichson (1978) found that in Norway, the northern sources of *Pinus contorta* grew best; they defined 54 degrees to 56 degrees north latitude as northern. Experience in Sweden shows that the even more northerly sources up to 63 degrees north latitude are very good. In Great Britain, where most forest trees are exotics, Eldridge (1978) uses the example that vigorous forests can all be obtained from *Pinus sylvestris, P. contorta,* and *Picea sitchensis* by collecting seed from about 50 degrees north latitude, similar to that of Britain. Seed from the more northern and more southern latitudes did not produce acceptable plantations. But this "same latitude" rule often breaks down. For example, Eldridge (1978) mentions species like *Picea abies* and *Larix decidua* where seeds imported from more southern latitudes are by far the best.

2. Examples of wide-ranging species with great provenance differences are *Pseudotsuga menziesii, Pinus banksiana, P. sylvestris, P. contorta, P. ponderosa, P. caribaea* (where varieties are recognized), *P. oocarpa, P. taeda, Picea abies,* some of the eucalypts, and *Tectona grandis.* It appears, however, that a few wide-ranging species do not have strong racial development; for example, it is suspected that the very widespread aspen *Populus tremuloides* has limited geographic variability throughout its range (Fig. 2.7).

3. Species growing over a wide but continuous geographic range develop provenances that intergrade one into the other, making a good differentiation of provenances impossible. There are many examples of such intergradation in the Mexican and Central American pines, where some species even have no distinct separations between them (Caballero, 1966; Perry, in press). Adding to the difficulty of determining provenances is the variability resulting from hybridization and introgression in which intermediate individuals are formed. Such a confusing pattern is evident for many eucalypts (Clifford, 1954; Pryor, 1951) and in the Mexican pines (Styles and Hughes, 1983; Perry, in press). When hybridization, backcrossing, and hybrid swarm formation occur, it becomes totally impossible to definitely separate provenances (and even species) from one another.

4. Provenance differences in survival and growth attributable to geographic variation can be very large but often intergrade from provenance to provenance, as shown for yellow poplar (*Liriodendron tulipifera*) by Kellison (1967). Another well-documented example is the intergrading characteristics from altitudinal differences that are present in ponderosa pine in the Sierra Nevada Mountains in California (Callaham and Liddicoet, 1961).

Figure 2.7. Aspen has a very wide distribution, but some persons feel that it has relatively little geographic variation. The species grows very rapidly, as shown by this vigorous 17-year-old stand in Saskatchewan, Canada, but aspen is not widely used for planting.

5.   Species that occur in regions with greatly diverse soils, soil moisture, slope, or aspect can develop very distinct geographic race differences even though they may be at similar elevations or latitudes (Squillace and Silen, 1962; Antonovics, 1971). A good example of widely differing soil environments adjacent to each other are the granitic and serpentine soils in the Sierra Nevada Mountains of California, where sometimes distinct provenances are found. This is also true for the greatly varying environments on the west and east sides of the Cascade Mountain Range in Oregon and Washington, where in relatively short distances natural selection caused by the differing soil and rainfall patterns has resulted in major provenance differences within species such as Douglas-fir.

There have been many attempts to delineate provenances within an area as an aid to persons collecting seed for exotics. One example is Robbins and Hughes (1983), who designated provenance regions for *Pinus caribaea* and *P. oocarpa* in Honduras. Sometimes such attempts are successful, sometimes they are not too helpful.

One should never overlook the potential of trying provenances that have already been proven good in other exotic locations. This has worked well with *Pinus caribaea* (Nikles, 1984a). In a paper on the value of such importations,

Mullin and Denison (1983) list five reasons why proven provenances are successful; these include correct provenances, similar environments, selection already done, well-defined quarantine procedures, and the availability of detailed records. This point was also emphasized by Wilcox (1983); he mentioned exchanges having worked well in the poplars, eucalypts, *Pinus radiata,* and *P. caribaea.* He said that the imported material must be truly genetically improved if it is to be of value. Too frequently, developed provenances of material from other areas are overlooked.

One type of intergradation among provenances is of the clinal variety (see Stebbins, 1950). Clinal variation is usually associated with an environmental gradient, and it is not possible to indicate definitive provenances (Langlet, 1959b). As examples, clines in frost resistance have been reported by Eldridge (1968) for *Eucalyptus regnans;* Larsen (1965) found clines with latitude in *E. citriodora;* clines associated with continentality, or distance from the sea, are suggested in the eucalypts by Pryor (1976). It is sufficient to say that one person's description and limitation of a provenance can be quite different from another person's and part of the problem results from clinal variation and intergradation associated with changing environments.

2.2.3 Some Examples and Results of Provenance Tests with Exotics

Using the correct provenance is the basis for success in an exotic forestry program. It is necessary to develop the best land races, the ultimate need requirement if one is to be successful with exotics. It is our objective to list in Tables 2.3 and 2.4 a few of the many thousands of studies that have been made on the provenance performance of exotics. The references shown were chosen for being somewhat representative and covering various species, regions, and conditions. But a look at the tables shows an imbalance; for example, there is a disproportionate number of reports related to the pines of the Caribbean region and Mexico and to the eucalypts. This simply reflects the emphasis of provenance work in these species.

A vast amount of literature is available on provenance tests—certainly several hundred on *Pinus caribaea* alone. Luckily, many of these have been summarized in books, like the one by Burley and Nikles (1973b), which contains 138 papers relating to provenance, 27 of which are about *Pinus caribaea.* Some excellent papers are included in Burley and Nikles' book; most are not shown in Tables 2.3 and 2.4 because they are available in the book. Similarly, the four numbers of *Silvicultura* (29–32, 1983) contain hundreds of references dealing with exotics. Tables 2.3 and 2.4 are therefore incomplete, but those references shown were chosen to give some idea of the diversity of species and areas where provenances of exotics are tested.

The most striking thing about Tables 2.3 and 2.4 is the lack of reported *failures* in exotic testing (Fig. 2.8). Basically, few persons report failures since it does not make for very exciting publications. But a very distorted picture is painted when the reader gets the impression that most provenance tests are

TABLE 2.3. Performance of Provenances and Seed Sources of Exotic Conifers[a]

Species	Author(s)	Age	Country	General Results
Pinus sylvestris	Wright & Baldwin 1957	Varied	United States	Scots pine is very variable, with some sources being nearly worthless; others grew well and had satisfactory form.
Picea abies	Gathy 1960	20	Belgium	Spruce from Poland and the Balkans is the best.
Pseudotsuga taxifolia (menziesii)	Gathy 1961	7	Belgium	The best area for Douglas-fir for both low (100 m) and middle (500 m) elevations are from less than 200 m on the west side of the Cascades in Washington near the ocean.
Pinus khasya (kesiya)	Shelbourne 1963	Varied (to 30)	N. Rhodesia (Zambia)	Tests of 5 different provenances at 6 different stations showed the Assam and Burma sources much superior in growth to the Philippine and S. Vietnam sources, but they were not as good in stem form and branch habit.
Pinus nigra	Miller & Thulin 1967a	9	New Zealand	46 provenances were tested. Sources from the west were better than those from the east.
Pinus sylvestris	Klein 1971	10	Canada	10 sources from Russia and the Ukraine were tested. Best growth was from the southernmost sources; western sources were better than those from farther east.
Pinus contorta	Miller 1971	6	New Zealand	Height of coastal sources was 8.3 ft, the transition 6.5 ft, and inland sources 3.6 ft grown at 17 sites from 300 to 3000 m. Stem lean was greatest in coastal sources. *P. contorta* is a

TABLE 2.3. Continued

Species	Author(s)	Age	Country	General Results
				suitable species for severe sites.
Larix leptolepis	Farnsworth et al. 1972	13	United States	There was a 25% difference in growth rate between the fastest- and slowest-growing origins. There were also differences in stem form and damage by cold and insects.
Pinus elliottii *P. taeda*	Barrett 1973	5	Argentina	38 sources of *P. elliottii* and 29 of *P. taeda* were planted on 20 different sites. *P. elliottii* showed little source difference, the southern source being a little better; large differences in *P. taeda* were evident, with southern sources best.
Cupressus lusitanica	Raunio 1973	4	Tanzania	Ugandan sources were better in height, diameter, and canker resistance than those from Tanzania and Kenya. One Kenyan progeny was best overall; next two best were Ugandan.
Pseudotsuga menziesii	Kleinschmit et al. 1974	3	Germany	Provenances from southwestern British Columbia and elevations below 600 m in Oregon and Washington were best for the German Federal Republic.
Pinus ponderosa	La Farge 1974	10	United States	Taper differed strongly between the coastal source, which was more cylindrical, and the interior variety scopulorum, which was more conical.
Pinus contorta	Lindgren et al. 1976	5	Sweden	83 provenances were tried in 13 plantations north of 60°N latitude in Sweden *(continued)*

TABLE 2.3. Continued

Species	Author(s)	Age	Country	General Results
				den, planted in 1971. The more southern the origin, the higher was the mortality. Provenances originating south of latitude 51°N had poor height growth.
Pinus patula	Barrett 1977	5	Argentina	The fastest-growing origin was 20% taller than the slowest.
Pinus caribaea	Cracium 1977	4	Australia	There are real differences in performance by provenance. The author recommends sources for differing sites.
Pinus oocarpa	Diabate 1977a	5	Ivory Coast	2 trials were made with 4 sources. 2 (Mountain Pine Ridge [Belize] and Zacapa [Guatemala]) are good; the other 2, from Mexico, are very poor.
Pinus caribaea	Diabate 1977b	6	Ivory Coast	Provenances from Belize and Guatemala have the most forked trees. There is little difference in growth among sources.
Pinus elliottii *P. taeda*	Fishwick 1977	9	Brazil	Total wood production and form varied by 25% from best to poorest sources.
Pinus caribaea	Granhof 1977	3	Thailand	Faster-growing provenances are less stable in form than slow growers; the exception is the Alimacamba source.
Pinus caribaea	Greaves & Kemp 1977	Varied	Lowland tropics	Mountain Pine Ridge, Poptun, and Alamicamba sources were best in lowland conditions.
Pinus oocarpa	Kageyama et al. 1977a	4	Brazil	Differences were numerous; an empiric selection index was developed to assess all characteristics among provenances.

TABLE 2.3 Continued

Species	Author(s)	Age	Country	General Results
Picea rubens P. sitchensis	Khalil 1977	10	Canada	Sitka spruce varied, with some being damaged by winter desiccation. Red spruce had large intra-provenance variation; all provenances were resistant to winter damage.
Pinus caribaea	Nikles 1977	7	Australia	Coastal Nicaragua and Honduras provenances are promising compared to those from Mountain Pine Ridge from Belize.
Pinus oocarpa	Wood & Greaves 1977	10	General	P. oocarpa shows great diversity of response to exotic environments, depending upon the source of seed, with great differences after 2 yr. Best provenances have good growth combined with good form after 10 yr.
Pinus caribaea	Falken-hagen 1977	General	South Africa	Deals with provenance variation in P. caribaea relative to growth, wood density, and wood qualities and their interaction with the environment.
Pinus contorta	Persson 1980	Varied	Scandinavia	The uses, problems, and predictions for future use of P. contorta in Scandinavia are outlined. It has responded well as an exotic.
Pinus caribaea	Venegas 1981	2	Colombia	In the llanos, there were great differences among provenances. The Guanaja Island (Honduras) provenance is best.
Pinus muricata	Shelbourne et al. 1982	10	New Zealand	The Sonoma County green and Mendocino blue sources were the best in New Zealand.
Picea sitchensis	Delaporte 1983	Young	France	Interprovenance variability is more important than (continued)

TABLE 2.3. Continued

Species	Author(s)	Age	Country	General Results
				intraprovenance. Growth cessation in the autumn is correlated with the latitude of seed origin.
Pinus caribaea *P. oocarpa*	Greaves 1983	Varied	Many	36 provenances of *Pinus caribaea* and 46 provenances of *P. oocarpa* were tested in 49 and 35 tests, respectively. 4 *caribaea* and 4 *oocarpa* provenances were outstanding.
Pinus strobus	Han & Lee 1983	15	Korea	There was a positive correlation between volume growth and latitude of source. One land race from Italy and one provenance from North Carolina were best.
Agathis macrophylla *A. robusta*	Karani 1983	15	Uganda	Growth starts slowly but speeds up. Form of stem and self-pruning are excellent.
Araucaria spp.	Karani & Chaudhry 1983	20	Uganda	Some sources start well but slow down after 10 to 15 yr. There has been no seed production after 20 yr.
Pinus taeda	Ladrach 1983a	5	Colombia	Good family differences were found; growth was greatest for the most southerly provenances from the coastal plain.
Pinus caribaea	Nikles et al. 1983	8	Australia (Queensland)	Mainland coastal provenances were the most resistant to windthrow. The local land race was best.
Pinus caribaea	Robbins 1983	General	Several	The inland provenances produce more needleless shoots and dieback when planted on wet sites. Coastal sources tend to have more foxtails. A

TABLE 2.3. Continued

Species	Author(s)	Age	Country	General Results
				large proportion of the total variation is among trees within provenance rather than among provenances.
Pinus patula	Barnes & Mullin 1984	7	Zimbabwe	There were significant differences among provenances for all traits.
Pinus oocarpa	Brigden et al. 1984	10	Australia	Considerable provenance differences were found; the Mountain Pine Ridge from Belize was best.
Pinus kesiya	Chagala 1984	12	Kenya	Provenances from the Philippines were best as were the seed sources from Zambia.
Pinus oocarpa	Chagala & Gibson 1984	8	Kenya	15 provenances were tested. The best provenance was more than twice as productive as the poorest.
Pinus caribaea	Das & Stephan 1984a	9	India	Stem form and foxtail frequency varied greatly among the 8 provenances studied.
Pinus kesiya	Das & Stephan 1984b	11	India	The differences among 12 provenances were small and not significant.
Pinus kesiya	Granhoff 1984	9	Thailand	18 sources from the natural range in Thailand, the Philippines, Vietnam, and Assam were tested. Best growth was from 4 sources from Thailand.
Pinus banksiana	Han & Ryu 1984	10	Korea	10 provenances from the U.S. and Canada were tested. There were height differences among provenances; these were strongly negatively correlated with latitude and

(continued)

TABLE 2.3. Continued

Species	Author(s)	Age	Country	General Results
				positively related with longitude. The best provenance is 12 to 20% better than the native *P. densiflora*.
Picea abies	Han et al. 1984b	8	Korea	Significant differences in height were present among provenances within a plantation. 24 provenances were tested at 10 locations. The West German sources were best.
Pinus taeda	Kraus et al. 1984	Many	United States	*P. taeda* from west of the Mississippi grow more slowly than from the east. The species is adapted to a wide variety of sites. Provenance variation plays a large part in the success of this species as an exotic.
Pinus pseudostrobus	Ladrach 1984c	5	Colombia	*P. pseudostrobus* had a lot of geographic variation. All provenances forked, but it was most evident in the slow growers. 3 lots (slow growers) had over 20% foxtailing.
Pinus caribaea	Liegel 1984a	10	Puerto Rico	Differences between the fastest- and slowest-growing provenances were 2 to 5 m in height and 5 to 9 cm in diameter. Forking was most evident in the slow growers.
Pinus oocarpa	Liegel 1984d	6	Puerto Rico	15 sources were tested in 8 sites; 4 were very good. All were sensitive to wind damage but varied by provenance.
Pinus merkusii	Madoffe et al. 1984	10	Tanzania	5 provenances were assessed. 1 from Java was outstanding, except for

TABLE 2.3. Continued

Species	Author(s)	Age	Country	General Results
				leaning and forking. The second-best provenance was from Thailand.
Pinus kesiya	Mondeil 1984	10	Madagascar	Great differences were evident. Some of the sources from the Philippines grew well, but 6 of the 8 provenances had terrible form.
Pinus merkusii	Mubita 1984	9	Zambia	The stem form of the continental sources was better than the insular sources, but vigor was less.
Pinus kesiya	Mullin et al. 1984	12	Zimbabwe	There were significant differences among provenances in straightness, basic density, and diameter and height growth. There was a strong correlation between provenance and wood density.
Pinus taeda	Mushi & Madoffe 1984	19	Tanzania	The southern sources were superior in growth, the northern ones inferior, with some having complete mortality. The southern sources were crooked and heavy limbed.
Pinus kesiya	Tozer & Robertson 1984	9	Australia	Few traits showed provenance differences. Growth decline because of poor adaptability restricts provenance differences.
Cupressus lusitanica	Vélez 1984	5	Colombia	Costa Rican and Kenyan seed sources were better than those from Mexico, Portugal, and Italy. Family heights of Costa Rican sources were best in Colombia.

(continued)

65

TABLE 2.3. Continued

Species	Author(s)	Age	Country	General Results
Pinus attenuata	Brown & Doran 1985	12	Australia	Differences in growth and branches were substantial. Provenances from California from less than 1000 m elevation grew the best.

Note: In Nikles et al. (1978) there are 25 papers on provenances of *P. caribaea*, 13 on *P. oocarpa*, 5 on *P. merkusii*, 5 on *P. kesiya*, and 3 on *P. patula*.
[a]Full references are found in the reference list.

TABLE 2.4. Performance of Provenances of Exotic Hardwoods[a]

Species	Author(s)	Age	Country	General Results
Eucalyptus camaldulensis	Barrett & Carter 1970	2	Rhodesia (Zimbabwe)	Differences in performance were not significant among sources.
Swietenia macrophylla *S. humilis*	Geary et al. 1973	7	Puerto Rico & Virgin Islands	Within species there was considerable variation in survival with seed source. On wetter sites there were statistical differences among sources of *S. macrophylla* from both northern & southern collections. On dry sites there was variation among sources of *S. humilis*. Collections were from 18 sources planted at 13 locations.
Tectona grandis	Delaunay 1979	6	Ivory Coast	15 origins were tested. Great differences were found in forking. The best-formed trees were from plantations from Africa. Provenance selection and individual tree variation will result in good gains.
Leucaena leucocephala	Brewbaker & Hutton 1979	Varied	Many	Varies from seedy shrubs to "giant" varieties, with the highest recorded wood yields from

TABLE 2.4. Continued

Species	Author(s)	Age	Country	General Results
				exotics credited to this species.
Cordia alliodora	Stead 1979	Varied	Many	This paper summarizes work that has been done on this species, including provenance differences.
Tectona grandis	Keogh 1980	Varied	Puerto Rico	Seed source is important for teak. It is used in the Caribbean, Central America, Venezuela, and Colombia.
Toona ciliata	Ledoux 1980	8	Amazon Zone	This species is now being tried in plantations at 8 yr of age. It looks good but is too variable. The wood is excellent.
Eucalyptus citriodora	Roeder 1980a	3	South Africa	No significant differences were found for height, diameter breast height, or volume by provenance after 3 yr when grown in 6 locations.
Eucalyptus grandis *E. saligna*	Roeder 1980b	4	South Africa	*E. grandis* from Coffs Harbour, Australia, is consistently good. *E. saligna* was not as good as *E. grandis,* with the exception of one New South Wales provenance.
Eucalyptus regnans	Wilcox 1982a	2	New Zealand	Highly significant frost resistance, height, and resistance to leaf blotch disease (*Mycosphaerella*) was evident among 36 seedlots from 2 sites.
Eucalyptus nitens	Anon. 1983b	8	South Africa	6 provenances were tested by mother trees. Highly significant differences were found among provenances and families within provenance. Provenances from northern New South Wales were best.

(continued)

TABLE 2.4. Continued

Species	Author(s)	Age	Country	General Results
Eucalyptus camaldulensis	El Dafei 1983	12	Sudan	Certain provenances were outstanding and better than seed collected from local stands.
Gmelina arborea	Egenti 1983a	2	Nigeria	No provenance differences of any size were found.
Tectona grandis	Egenti 1983b	6.5	Nigeria	At 6.5 yr the Asian provenances were better than the Nigerian or Ghanaian seed sources.
Alnus glutinosa	Genys & Hall 1983	1	United States	Sources from 123 areas were tested in the nursery. Huge differences of 9.7 cm (from Finland) to 40.1 cm (from Ireland) were found.
Eucalyptus camaldulensis	Grunwald & Karschon 1983	6	Israel	The 31 sources from northern Australia varied from 49 m³/ha/yr to 4 m³/ha/yr. Provenance variance in this species is large and tends toward two drainage divisions.
Tectona grandis	Woessner 1983b	5	Brazil	There were no really outstanding provenances.
Cordia alliodora	Boshier 1984	7	Costa Rica	Few real differences were found between provenances because of great differences within provenance. One provenance was highly susceptible to canker and there were smooth and rough bark types; smooth was associated with wet-zone provenances.
Liquidambar styraciflua	Hughes & McCarter 1984	Varied	Several	For the first time, range-wide collections were made, including Guatemala and Honduras. The southern provenances are frost sensitive. The species has performed well in Brazil and South Africa. All

TABLE 2.4 Continued

Species	Author(s)	Age	Country	General Results
				sources are considered to be *L. styraciflua.*
Tectona grandis *Gmelina arborea*	Keiding et al. 1984	10	Many	21 teak and 30 *Gmelina* trials were tested at 10 yr of age for teak and 3 to 6 yr for *Gmelina.* There were large provenance differences among both the teak and *Gmelina* sources.
Leucaena *leucocephala*	Ladrach 1984a	3	Colombia	After 3 yr there were large differences in survival among provenances, as well as in growth, wood density, and forking. Good provenances are from Mexico, El Salvador, and Honduras.
Cordia alliodora	Neil 1984	4	Brazil	Few provenance differences were noted.
Eucalyptus *camaldulensis*	Moura 1984	3	Brazil	Differences in the 10 provenances were great for both height and diameter. The Queensland sources were highly superior.
Gmelina arborea	Ladrach 1986a	5	Colombia	Large individual tree and site differences were found, but no significant differences were found among provenances.

Note: In Nikles et al. (1978) there are 11 papers on provenance of *Tectona grandis,* 10 on *Eucalyptus* spp., and 11 on other tropical hardwood species.
*a*Full references are found in reference list.

successful, when the truth is that the *bulk of the provenance tests result in failure.* This is no surprise, and failures should be reported. The nature of provenance studies is such that failures are to be expected and a good provenance assessment program will always have failures. The adverse thing about not reporting failures is that the same mistakes and tests resulting in failures are done over and over simply because of a lack of awareness that previous failures have resulted.

Certain trends related to species performances are common and a few of

Figure 2.8. A major feature related to the literature on provenance tests is the lack of reported failures, such as the one shown here, of *Gmelina* in a test in South America. The fact is that most provenance tests are unsatisfactory. It is the rare success that foresters are looking for.

them are summarized in the following paragraphs based partially on Tables 2.3 and 2.4 and on our own observations.

Conifers

1.   The Mexican and Caribbean pine species usually contain very large provenance differences. These species are thus difficult to work with because wrong decisions about species are frequently made as a result of incomplete provenance assessment. Despite the wide testing on the Mexican pines, their geographic variation patterns are not well known, except for a few species.

2.   Very serious errors have been made in the use of *Pinus oocarpa* because of the lack of plasticity within a given provenance and the huge provenance differences that are evident. To add to this, there is confusion as to the taxonomy of *P. oocarpa* and some related species, as described earlier.

3.   One of the oldest, best known, and most intensively tested exotics is *Pinus sylvestris*. It is a very variable species with some excellent and some very poor sources. In the early years the source was essentially ignored, and some poor sources were planted that to this day give this species a bad reputation, especially in the United States.

4.   The species with currently the greatest emphasis on provenance test-

ing in northern Europe is *Pinus contorta.* The coastal provenances are hopeless in cold climates; some of the inland and more northern sources are doing well in Scandinavia, Ireland, and Scotland. This variable species is remarkably hardy and frequently grows much better than the indigenous *P. sylvestris.* Some coastal sources have performed well in climates like New Zealand. Symposia and books have been published on the use of *P. contorta.*

5.   Two of the southern pines (*P. taeda* and *P. elliottii*) have been extensively tested as exotics. They do well in the subtropical areas and at higher elevations. *Pinus taeda* has many geographic sources that are so greatly different that they hardly seem to represent the same species. Poor initial choice of provenance has resulted in *P. taeda* being rejected as a species in many areas. *Pinus elliottii* has few diverse provenances, with the species being plastic and easy to manage. Generally, if the correct source of *P. taeda* is used, it will outproduce *P. elliottii.* Currently, because of its silvicultural characteristics and ease of handling, *P. elliottii* is being widely used as an exotic.

6.   Many recent publications deal with *Pinus caribaea,* which is a widely planted exotic. Growth is rapid but, depending on source, form can be good or terrible. The presence of the three varieties (see Section 2.2.1 for a discussion of these) has complicated the use and assessment of this species. Frequently, when *P. caribaea* is mentioned, it is the widely planted var. *hondurensis.* This variety is plastic but also has very large provenance differences. One of the most serious current errors with operational use of *P. caribaea* is ignoring provenance, and some awful plantings have resulted. Much within-provenance variability also occurs in this species.

7.   Many tests are done with the Mexican and Central American pines, but large plantings are only being made of a few of them other than *P. caribaea.*

(a)   *Pinus oocarpa* is a marvelous species whose utility has suffered greatly from lack of recognition or use of wrong provenances. When proper provenances are recognized, the inability to obtain proper seed has been a serious restriction. *Pinus oocarpa* has many provenances with extremes of adaptability. In many instances, the correct sources will outgrow *P. caribaea* (see Table 2.1). Too often *P. oocarpa* used as check lots has come from the higher elevations and is highly inferior to *P. caribaea* in the lowlands. The wood of *P. oocarpa* is excellent. The tree has a root system that makes it sensitive to windthrow. This species will have much wider usage as provenances become better known and seed becomes available.

(b)   *Pinus patula* has been widely tested, especially in South Africa, Zimbabwe, and east-central Africa. Large provenance differences were found—in Argentina, the best origin grew 20% faster than the slowest. Breeding work with this species is well advanced in several parts of the world.

8.   *Cupressus lusitanica,* used as an exotic primarily in east-central Africa and in South America, has had a relatively large amount of work done on it. Large provenance and within-provenance differences are present.

9. A species with huge provenance variation is *Pseudotsuga menziesii.* Differences are so large that some persons prefer to call them subspecies or varieties. Before planting Douglas-fir as an exotic, extreme care must be taken to obtain the proper provenance.

10. Two of the tropical pines, *P. merkusii* and *P. kesiya,* show very large provenance differences, some of which, such as a grass stage, make certain sources unusable. In general, *P. merkusii* has not been very successful as an exotic, but *P. kesiya* is more widely planted.

11. Sitka spruce (*Picea sitchensis*) is becoming more widely used. Provenance differences are surprisingly large despite the relative restriction of the species in its indigenous range.

12. *Picea abies* is widely planted as an exotic mainly in Western Europe. The species has an enormous amount of variation. Currently, widely based studies are being made on the variable *Pinus contorta.* This species is specially covered in Chapter 7.

Hardwoods

1. The emphasis on hardwood provenance variation is in the eucalypts; there are hundreds of references that could be cited. Most species that have been intensively studied show from large to very large provenance differences. One of the most variable is *E. camaldulensis,* although one report showed only small differences with source. *E. grandis, E. nitens,* and *E. urophylla* show great variability by source of seed. It is safe to say that with only a few exceptions, provenance differences are large and of great importance in the eucalypts and must be a prime consideration before exotic forestry programs are developed.

2. The importance of provenance has not always been recognized in the genus *Populus,* but provenance can be well developed in species like *P. deltoides.* Much of the provenance difference has been lost in the hybrids and frequently the provenance of the parent trees are not considered before a hybrid is produced.

3. A surprising number of studies of source of seed have been made on *Leucaena leucocephala.* Large differences occur, with tree form varying from seedy shrubs to large trees (Fig. 2.9).

4. Other tropical hardwoods such as *Swietenia, Tectona,* and *Gmelina* show important provenance differences based on considerable testing, some on an international level. For example, Keiding et al. (1984) and others report on a series of teak (*Tectona grandis*) and *Gmelina arborea* provenance trials. There was considerable between-provenance variation within site for teak. We have also seen large differences in *Gmelina;* even wood density differences among provenances were evident. *Swietenia* also shows large provenance differences. Some stable provenances are found in the tropical hardwoods, and local land races generally are superior. Similar studies on provenance for trop-

Figure 2.9. Some species have received a lot of publicity about their value as exotics. Although this may be true with certain provenances and on certain sites, sometimes they turn out to be multistem bushy trees of limited value, such as this seven-year-old *Leucaena* planting in Brazil.

ical species used as exotics have been made for species such as *Cordia allio-dora,* where provenance differences were not large.

2.3 HOW AND WHERE TO CHOOSE PROVENANCES TO TEST

Perhaps the most difficult job of the forester interested in growing exotics is to decide where and how to obtain the plant material to be tested and, hopefully, to be ultimately used operationally. The first reaction is to go to areas that have environments similar to the area where exotics will be grown (Kung and Wright, 1972; Nienstaedt, 1975; Wright, 1976). This theory of matching the environment of the species or provenance with the one where the plantation will be established is good and many helpful methods have been developed such as the zoning of northeastern Brazil by Golfari and Caser (1977);

they made a search in countries rich in the desired species and that had similar climates. Yet, generally it is not possible to match environments exactly. This was expressed well by Ciancio et al. (1982): "Since it is impossible to introduce exotic species in areas with an identical environment, many species undergo changes that reduced . . . their biological functionality." As a result, the exotic may lack competitive ability in the new environment.

All sorts of systems have been developed to help estimate what may be the best provenance. For northern Sweden, Eriksson et al. (1980) developed what they called a "severity index," that is, the expected percentage of plant mortality in the population during the first 20 years after establishment of the plantation. They found that each degree of latitude transfer southward meant an increase in survival of *Pinus sylvestris* of 10.8%; every 100 m of downward transfer in elevation meant an increase in survival of 3%. Such a system might be useful for exotics in extreme environments. For the exotic *Pinus contorta*, Lindgren et al. (1976) report that latitude is by far the most important single factor when provenances are chosen. In tests of *Pinus caribaea* in South Africa, Falkenhagen (1979) found that provenances from the higher latitudes produce less volume and have better tree form; the reverse was true related to the longitude of origin.

Very useful information is available to help make decisions concerning the selection of provenances as exotics. For example, the pioneering method of Thornthwaite (1948) and later work such as Thornthwaite and Mather (1963) have changed and modified the original concepts to show, especially in tropical areas, the growth potential of a site based upon evapotranspiration and water balance, which some foresters feel is more important in the tropics than the usually cited latitude and longitude location. The water balance is obtained by determining the difference between moisture available to plants and the evapotranspiration. The latter is defined as "the amount of moisture that would be transferred by evaporation and transpiration from a vegetation covered soil, if it were constantly available in optimum quantity" (Wilm and Thornthwaite, 1945–46). A moisture deficiency develops when the amount of evapotranspiration plus water losses due to percolation and runoff exceed the moisture available from rainfall and/or groundwater. This description of a climate, which takes into account the effectiveness of the rainfall received over a 12-month period with regard to seasonal distribution as well as mean monthly temperatures, may be used to compare the known habitat of a species with that of the site to be planted, as was done by Golfari and Caser (1977).

The water balance, along with other information, was used by Golfari (1963, 1974, 1975a) to develop a scheme of ecological zones for Brazil that would be of value as a guide for choosing exotics. He also developed a scheme to compare locations in Australia and Brazil for planting *Eucalyptus grandis* (Golfari, 1983). Water balance was emphasized. The method works fairly well, but there are some notable exceptions.

Other helpful methods of dealing with soils, such as those by Buol and Sanchez (1978), have been developed. Although less common, climatic zones in temperate areas suitable for use of specific exotics have been developed. One by FAO (Anon., 1959) contains regions and lists of suitable species in Burma, India, and Pakistan.

The preceding points up that no one environment or location parameter is sufficient to make assessments as to where it is best to obtain trees to use as exotics. In truth, every bit of information must be employed before making the choice. As emphasized elsewhere, especially in Section 2.3.1 of this chapter and in Chapter 4, the matching of environments is of minimal value without a matching of extremes and sequences of these extremes.

However, the decision of where to collect seed is more difficult than simply matching environments, although rapid screening for similar environments is certainly the first step. The final step relates to the suitability of survival, growth, form, adaptability, and wood qualities of the exotic when grown in the new exotic environment. This requires testing, ideally for a full rotation and certainly for a long enough period of time to obtain sound indications as to the usefulness of the exotic, especially including wood quality.

Although sometimes listed as a necessity, the ability to reproduce or produce seed in the new environment is not mandatory for exotic plantation forestry when seeds can be obtained from seed orchards or seed stands established elsewhere. For example, *Pinus caribaea* and *P. oocarpa* will grow very well in some lowland areas near the equator, but the species do not produce abundant seed in this environment, so seed must be obtained elsewhere.

The major consideration concerns how seeds are collected to represent a provenance. Although there is an increased recognition of the importance of provenance differences, the best is sometimes not selected because of a lack of knowledge or through false economies that result in suboptimal sources being used (Barnes and Gibson, 1984). Collections are often from roadside trees, from originally poor provenances, from the poorest phenotypes that happen to have seed, from thinnings, and, much too often, from only one or two trees that represent the provenance. A few trees usually are quite nonrepresentative of a provenance. This can be avoided by collecting the seed of mother trees and then using the best trees of the best families to represent the provenance (see Chapter 3).

In no area of forestry is the need for international cooperation greater than in obtaining provenance material for testing for exotics; this was emphasized by Burley and Nikles (1973b), Slee (1977b), and Wood and Greaves (1977). Very extensive and expensive seed source studies have been made possible by cooperation among governments and industry. Especially helpful have been international organizations such as IUFRO (International Union of Forest Research Organizations) and FAO of the United Nations. Specific groups like the CFI (Commonwealth Forestry Institute) OFI (Oxford Forestry Institute)— now from Oxford, England, DANIDA (from Denmark), CAMCORE (U.S.), and CSIRO (Australia) have been instrumental in organizing numerous large-scale collections. Many governmental organizations, such as the Department of Forestry in Queensland, Australia, have spearheaded the international exchange of seed. Coalitions of industry and government, like the CAMCORE (Central America and Mexico Coniferous Resources) Cooperative, have had a major influence on international seed collection and the testing of exotics.

2.3.1 Environmental Assessment

A range of exotics may be found that will grow on a certain site. However, only a few will be most productive on that site. Therefore, a knowledge of site factors and their relationship to the requirements of different species should be the ultimate objective of matching species to site to attain most economic timber production. Thus, a quantification of site factors is important, and this field of study is getting more attention in exotic forestry. (This is also covered in Chapter 4.)

Where a wide variety of soils with widely differing characteristics exists, the soil series, together with factors such as moisture regime and effective soil depth categories, provides a systematic and useful way to group soils with similar tree production potential (Schönau and Fitzpatrick, 1981). Where topographical and detailed soil series maps are available, these should be consulted in addition to studying soil profiles in the field. A commonly known fact is that most exotic tree species will grow best on the lower slopes and on valley bottoms with deep, well-drained soils with a relatively high nutrient status. However, such knowledge must be combined with other environmental parameters, especially drainage of cold air, moisture regimes, accessibility, and management objectives.

Different methods of site classification exist, such as ecological approaches to ecosystem classification (Barnes, 1984) and terrain classification (Loeffler, 1984). Barnes states that ecological site classification will focus on the interrelationship and interaction of physical site factors and organisms. One system used in the American tropics and found to be very satisfactory, and which has been relatively widely accepted, is the one developed by Holdridge et al. (1971).

Ecological classification involves gathering information on the important components of ecosystems and studying their functional interrelationships and interactions so that landscape units of appropriate scale are identified. Barnes (1984b) feels that "such ecological classification is a key to, and a necessary prerequisite for, evaluating economic opportunities offered by investment in plantation forestry." A simplified example is the use of "indicator species" that indicate the nutrient status of the site or are associated with other soil factors. For example, *Urtica dioica* and *Digitalis purpurea* typically indicate a high nitrate content in soil (Champion and Brasnett, 1958). Similarly, the presence of pronounced calciphiles on soils that show no free lime to the eye may indicate a high base status, permitting the planting of species which require that particular pH.

The differences in environment are largely due to differences in climate, although soils and topography play an important role in some instances. They affect the growth rate and pattern by controlling the pattern of physiological development. As one example of this, Mikola (1982) used the phenology of bud-set to indicate climatic adaptation of Scots pine. A strong association between timing of bud-set and geographic source of seed was found, indicating that the variation in nursery-stage growth rhythm reflects genetic differences in hardiness and adaptation. Eventually, this type of information will be very helpful in matching potential exotics to their new environment.

In his "Report on the Natal Forests," published in 1889, Fourcade put forward the original suggestion that climate exercises a much greater influence on trees than does the soil, pointing out that many species which will "thrive in almost any soil and with varying supplies of moisture" will only succeed in "a zone with certain definite conditions of temperature." Expanding his philosophy, he continued:

> There is for each species a central climate where it flourishes best, the fertility of the soil and the supply of moisture being otherwise equal; as it recedes from this central climate, either through changed latitude or elevation, it becomes gradually more stunted and scarce; and finally disappears beyond certain limits which determine the geographical and altitudinal range of the species.

He observed that the two principal elements of climate that need to be taken into consideration are temperature and rainfall.

Each species has its own latitudinal and altitudinal limits, with one or possibly more optimum zones within this range. Other circumstances being favorable, a species can be expected to thrive in a new environment where mean and seasonal temperatures approximate those in its natural habitat, particularly if these are near the optima. As far as rainfall is concerned, both the total amount and the distribution of the precipitation are important.

In their book *Choice of Species,* Champion and Brasnett (1958) also classify precipitation—amount, distribution, and quality—and temperature—mean annual, mean monthly maximum/minimum, and absolute maximum/minimum—as most influential in making decisions regarding species or provenance choices.

However correct the admonition to "test before you use an exotic" may be, it is not always possible to follow it. Often there are economic or political pressures that require planting exotics before they have been tested (see Chapter 10). Therefore, it is essential to provide some general rules as a guide for anyone who needs to choose an exotic for testing or, if it absolutely cannot be avoided, to operationally plant an exotic before it has been sufficiently tested.

Among the attempts to assess the environment in which the exotic species will grow and compare it with its indigenous environment is one by LeCam (1983). He describes a methodology, based upon a number of criteria, for selecting from among 118 provenances of *Pinus contorta* in its natural range so it will be best adapted to the northwest of France.

As was earlier mentioned, Golfari and Caser (1977), Golfari (1975a) and

Golfari et al. (1978) attempted to match ecological conditions and, on the basis of these, recommend which species would be most useful in different parts of Brazil. To do this, Brazil was divided into regions according to climate, vegetation type, elevation, temperature, amount and distribution of rainfall, water deficit, and frost occurrence. Twenty-six bioclimatic zones were developed, for each of which species of eucalypts and conifers were recommended. The system was partially successful; the authors state that more knowledge based on better experimentation is necessary to give a better base for introductions.

The key environmental information that must be sought about the donor and receptor areas relates to unusual environments, weather extremes, and large fluctuations or unusual sequences of weather. Natural selection does not operate on averages; it operates on the extremes. It may be the one day in the one year of the life of the natural stand or plantation that will result in death or injury from something like cold weather. Alternatively, it may be the one dry period out of 50 years that will kill from drought. It is these conditions that shape the donor forests through the eons and will determine which of the new exotic plantations will survive. Therefore, information on climatic averages is usually of limited value. For example, Jacobs (1964) points out that total rainfall is not a good way to compare climates, but that its distribution between the cooler and warmer periods is of key importance.

In forestry, reliable weather data often are not available either for the donor region or for the receptor area where the exotic will be planted; when available, they usually describe yearly averages and rarely monthly or daily figures. This presents a severe handicap, and the person needing such information then must ask people who have lived in the area for a long time. Such information can be very useful, accurate, and helpful, but sometimes one must wonder at the accuracy of the memory of the locals. The senior author, for example, asked such questions about ice storms in a given area in the southeastern United States. Everyone questioned said there never had been any ice storms. Yet five years after planting the exotic, there were two severe ice storms, and two years later there was another. We have experienced the same for droughts and floods; in one instance, the "100-year flood" has occurred at least six times within 10 years.

In the plantations in the receptor areas, the extremes do not occur yearly, but perhaps only once or twice during the lifetime of a given plantation. Thus, meaningful testing of the suitability of species and provenances cannot really take place until the trees have grown for a full rotation or have had a chance to encounter the extremes. Sometimes that is not even long enough, as, for example, a "40-year freeze" may occur only once in several rotations.

Although a knowledge of environmental extremes is very helpful when choosing exotics, even this information is not sufficient. The key is the environmental sequence prior to or following the extremes; for example, does cold weather occur gradually, so the plants have a chance to harden off, or does the cold spell come immediately following a period of warm weather. Plant responses to these two conditions will vary greatly, and differing provenances may be necessary to allow normal establishment and growth of the exotic under the two sequences.

Some general rules can be formulated relative to obtaining provenances for use as exotics:

1. *Do not obtain seed from high-elevation or high-latitude sources to plant in low elevations or low latitudes,* or the reverse. Growth differences can be considerable, as reported by Miller (1971) for *Pinus contorta* in New Zealand, where a close correlation was found with elevation of a provenance and height growth, the seed from the lower elevations producing the taller trees. High-latitude and high-elevation sources are usually slow growing but of good form, while lower-elevation and low-latitude sources produce faster-growing trees which frequently have heavy limbs and crooked boles (Hermann and Lavender, 1968; Kung and Wright, 1972). The preceding rules do not always hold. For example, the inland provenances of *P. caribaea* var. *hondurensis* tend to produce trees with larger limbs and more crooked boles than do those from the coastal region, which are straight and have better form.

High-elevation provenances from low latitudes can often be used successfully in lower elevations at higher latitudes and vice versa. Usually the interest relates to movement from lower to higher elevations or from lower to higher latitudes in order to take advantage of the greater growth rate. When such moves are made, adaptability problems often occur and a major decision must be made as to whether the gain from the move is great enough to justify the risk from the poorer adaptability.

Differences in latitude involve daylength and temperature, which become increasingly important at high latitudes and elevations. A species such as *Pinus caribaea,* when moved from higher to lower latitudes, must be able to adjust to large physiological changes. In 1973, Slee proposed a method for predicting the importance of temperature and daylength variation; he used the product of the mean monthly temperature and mean monthly daylight in the donor and receptor areas to give a possible method for predicting species performance, especially flowering.

2. *Provenances from a maritime climate should never be used in a continental climate;* it is not as dangerous to move seed from continental to Mediterranean areas. This rule also holds for coastal versus inland climates. As reported by Krutzsch (1974), the coastal provenances of *Pinus contorta* are completely unfit, while those from interior sources are well suited to Swedish conditions. In the New Zealand conditions, Miller (1971) found that the best coastal provenance of *Pinus contorta* were 8.3 ft tall in six years, while the inland sources were only 3.6 ft tall. Miller concluded that the clearly superior vigor of the coastal source makes it the logical prospect for New Zealand even though it has more crooked stems and larger limbs.

The seasonal periods of moisture and temperature differ greatly between maritime and continental climates, and only rarely will a source developed where there are cool, wet winters and warm (hot), dry summers do well where the cool seasons are dry and the warm periods are wet or where rainfall is uniform year round (Kiellander, 1960). Failures are common when species are moved between areas with winter rains and those with winter drought or between those with summer rains and those with summer drought conditions (Hillis and Brown, 1978). Put another way, Jacobs (1964) states that provenances or species moved from a summer to a winter rainfall area are more likely to succeed than those moved from a winter to a summer rainfall area. Sometimes trees from areas with long dry seasons can be moved to those with uniform year-round rainfall, but often this is only partially successful.

3. *Species coming from milder climates usually grow well* unless there is a risk of freezing. In their work with *Pinus banksiana* in New Zealand, Sweet and Thulin (1963) found that trees from milder climates were taller, showed less yellow color in winter, and were more likely to set cones at an early age than those from severe climates. The same pattern of rapid growth from mild-climate sources was reported in New Zealand by Sweet (1963) for *Pinus resinosa*. Additionally, species or provenances from an area where the atmospheric humidity is low tend to be unhealthy where the humidity is high.

4. *Do not move trees from areas of uniform climates, where minor fluctuations in rainfall and temperature occur, to those with severe and large fluctuations,* even though the annual averages may be similar. Most trees require preconditioning before they can tolerate extreme environments and are susceptible to damage without this conditioning period. What is actually a severe environment may not at first appear to be so until the climatic patterns are closely studied. For example, the climate in the southeastern United States is not generally considered to be severe based on the extremes, but it is not suitable for most exotic trees because of wildly fluctuating wet and dry spells and particularly because temperatures can vary in one day from 80°F (27°C) to 15°F (-8°C). It is not uncommon in midwinter to have several days of 80°F followed immediately by several days when the temperature will drop below 10°F (-12°C). Because of such large fluctuations in climatic environment, most exotics have proven to be failures in the southeastern United States (Zobel et al., 1956; Grigsby, 1969). Species can be easily moved from cool climates to areas that are less cold; however, when moved to areas of higher temperatures or subjected to strong drying winds, these trees are often deformed, though not necessarily killed (Jacobs, 1964).

Only a few forest trees can tolerate large and quick fluctuations in the environment, although with proper preconditioning they can easily withstand the absolute temperature extremes. Coldhardy species such as *Pinus resinosa, P. contorta,* or *P. banksiana,* which can stand temperatures of -30°F (-34°C) or even lower when properly and gradually preconditioned, will often freeze at 10°F (-12°C) following a warm spell without the proper preconditioning (Zobel et al., 1956).

Certain species, such as some of the eucalypts, are particularly sensitive to environmental extremes because they never seem to develop a real period of dormancy. Such species start growth during warm spells in midwinter and then are killed or damaged when cold weather follows (Hunt and Zobel, 1978).

5. Be careful *not to choose trees that originate in basic soils for growing on acid soils or vice versa.* Movement from clay to sand or sand to clay soils should also be done carefully. If, for example, *Pinus pinaster* or *P. clausa,* which grow well on deep sands, are transferred to heavy clays, their roots never develop correctly and grow just under the soil surface with no tap root, even though the trees grow well. Ultimately, many of the trees will lean or fall over following heavy rains and wind, and most die.

The literature concerning where and how to select species for testing or to obtain seed is voluminous. One example of a very complete development is by Martin and Cossalter (1976–77) for *Eucalyptus urophylla,* which is now being widely tested. They have published detailed information of inestimable value to persons interested in provenances of this species, regarding its range, characteristics in its natural range, response when planted as an exotic, and wood properties.

It is fascinating to compare a species like *P. radiata,* which comes from a narrow environmental range but grows well under a wide range of environments, with those like *P. taeda* or *Pseudotsuga menziesii,* which grow naturally in many different environments. Although overall the latter two species have a wide range of adaptability, each individual provenance has a relatively narrow range of adaptability and *use of the proper provenance is mandatory.* Without care in choosing provenances for species such as these, large errors will be made.

One of the most difficult problems for one who wants to obtain seed for provenance studies is where to obtain seed that ensures reliable studies and accurate selections. Although certainly not general, unfortunately, many seed merchants are not reliable. The best strategy is to collect the seed yourself, but often this is not possible—although it is being done more frequently for northern species in the developed countries. The next best approach is to get seed from a reliable friend(s) or researcher(s), but again this usually is not possible. One reliable method is to get seed from groups who specialize in making international cooperative studies, such as CFI (OFI), DANIDA, and CAMCORE, or to rely on FAO. The latter publishes a series of *Forest Genetic Information* booklets listing seeds and provenances available and how to get them. For example, Information No. 12, from 1983, lists a number of available species. Copies of *Forest Genetic Information* can be obtained from Publications Division, FAO, Via delle Terme de Caracalla 00100, Rome, Italy. This publication was first put out in 1973.

2.3.2 Choose from the Center or Fringes of a Species Range?

An ongoing argument is whether one should choose provenances for use as exotics from the center or the fringe of the species range. Discussions of this kind revolve about the so-called center of origin of a species (Stebbins, 1950) or the "gene center theory" of Vavilov (1926). Relating to fruit trees, Zagaja (1983) emphasizes the importance of centers of diversity but questions whether these are always also the centers of origin, as proposed by Vavilov. Zagaja points out from the crop improvement standpoint the special value of knowing the centers of diversity (Fig. 2.10). These authors state that the richest genetic pool is present in the center of the species range, with limited but more specialized genes in the fringe areas.

The concept of centers of diversity was discussed by Muller (1959) and developed by van Buijtenen and Stern (1967), who mention that marginal populations occupy ecological niches that are not available for central populations. They state:

> It seems to be very common that a species undergoes high selection pressure from intraspecific and interspecific competition within the central part of its range, whereas marginal populations of the same species are mainly selected for survival under extreme conditions for one or more factors of the physical environment.

In addition to the preceding, Bialobok (1967) reported that definite ecotypes exist on the periphery of a species range, and Bannister (1965) stated that new genetic types generally evolve on the edge of a species range, especially when the species is growing under unfavorable conditions. This was con-

Figure 2.10. One center of diversity for pines is in Central America and Mexico. Many species and intergrades are found on areas with large environmental variations, such as the highlands of Guatemala, shown here. Such an area is ideal for provenance and species selection.

firmed by Mergen et al. (1974), who found that adaptability was greater for provenances near the center of the natural distribution.

Marginal populations can be totally isolated outside the main range of the species or only partially isolated near the border of a continuously distributed species adapted to a clinal variation of environmental factors. The isolated populations will have very divergent ecotypes from the combined effects of isolation, small population sizes, and high selection intensities. The contiguous populations will have less well-developed provenances because of gene exchange.

When sources are chosen to try as exotics, the fringe or nontypical areas should be considered along with the major part of the species range. For example, in *Pinus radiata,* a species widely used as an exotic, Libby (1978) found that trees from the outlier populations on Cedrus and the Guadalupe Islands have about 40% of the taxon level of variability in that species. He suggests that there are some useful alleles present on these islands that are not found in the three main populations. Trees from these two outliers differ from each other and are very different from those of the main populations.

The needs of the exotic must be the determining factor regarding which provenances should be tried. There can be no totally correct answer to the questions of how and where to select. If one is seeking a population of trees for introduction into some specific or extreme environment, then the fringe populations will often be best if the environments in which they are growing resemble those where the exotics will be planted. The population may have limited total variability, but may possess the specially needed adaptability. If one is going to plant the introduced trees in a nonextreme environment and wishes the maximum genetic variability, then it is best to select from the center of the species range, where genetic variation usually is the greatest.

A knowledge of the history and geology of a region is also essential. For example, Gallegos (1980b) states that pines migrated south down the Pacific coast, east to the eastern United States and to Europe. The pine areas in Mexico and Central America are important secondary centers of speciation, where highly variable environments have led to the formation of new species and varieties (provenances) of pines and other forest trees. Knowing this pattern is a great help in making decisions about where provenances should be obtained for testing.

2.3.3 Summary: Steps Suggested for Selecting Provenances to Use for Exotics

In choosing the best provenances to use for exotics, we cannot overstate the value of experience and the use of common sense. After one works with a species for a long time, one gets a "feel" for where it will prosper and where it will fail. It is best to have seen or worked with similar species and environmental conditions elsewhere. Most of the early plantings in severe environments have been made in this way. Certainly, mistakes have been and will be made! This is inevitable, but it is amazing how well an experienced and alert forester will be able to suggest a source of seed that later tests confirm was best. The key to success in making such recommendations is close observation, knowing the species being considered for use, and having a good knowledge of the environment, especially the magnitude and sequences of extremes in the exotic environment. Some suggested steps are:

1.   Make a decision about the objective of the plantings and the products desired. Then determine the category of trees (for example, pines or hardwoods) that will best fulfill the objective.

2.   Obtain all information possible, both from the literature and from plantations or tests that may be available. This informational phase should include visiting areas with environments and species similar to those that will be used and on which plantations will be established.

3.   Survey the area to be used for any plantations of the desired species that may be available. Immediately develop land races through selection of the best trees from these plantations for use as an immediate source of seed, unless the provenance of the plantation is obviously very unsuitable.

4.   Make a systematic investigation through planting trials of potential species and provenances, to determine their growth and variation patterns. Obtain seed from the best trees from these plantings to use as a good land race. Obtain improved stock through additional testing and seed orchard establishment to develop a permanent seed supply for operational planting.

5.   Operationally, use seed from the initial land race or best potential provenance while better genetic material is being developed through a tree-improvement program.

2.4 HOW TO TEST PROVENANCES AND SPECIES FOR USE AS EXOTICS

A number of persons have published on the essentials of testing for exotics; most are similar in overall methodology, although details vary greatly with individual researchers. The methods were summarized in short course outlines by Gallegos (1980b) and FAO–DANIDA (1980) and in the book by Burley and Wood (1976) entitled *A Manual on Species and Provenance Research with Particular Reference to the Tropics,* which is specifically related to the introduction of exotics. We will not attempt to describe and compare the different methods that have been suggested and used, but we will summarize and paraphrase them. Most of the topics discussed relative to testing are nothing but common sense, but it is amazing how often the most simple things that are essential for success are overlooked.

One important early decision is whether to test by bulk collections or by individual, selected mother tree collections. The former is by far the simplest, but no knowledge is gained relative to the genetic potential among families and individual trees within the provenance. (This is discussed more fully in Chapter 3.) In short, despite the extra work and greater complexity, many persons (Dvorak, 1984, for example) prefer to collect seed by mother trees within a provenance, grow the progeny separately, and then select a land race consisting of the best trees of the best families for seed production. This gives an estimate of the worth of the provenance as well as the value of select unrelated trees.

The selection method recommended by Kemp (1978) is to use random selection; this was also the suggestion of Burley and Wood (1976). This attitude was summarized by Greaves (1979) as follows:

> Seed for provenance trials must be representative of the full genetic variation in populations from which it is collected. The frequent assumption that the seed should come only from the best phenotypes is therefore, not valid.

Oppositely, Zobel (1978) points out the fallacy of the common misconception that good phenotypes within a provenance show less adaptability than poor phenotypes from the same population. The decision of whether it is best to mass select or to select good phenotypes is one to be made by each organization.

The danger of picking genetically related trees from a general mass collection is very great. As reported by Zobel et al. (1972), strong general combiners always are present in a population of trees, and if a number of good trees are selected from a plantation of mixed parents, the chances of the best trees being related is good. Mass selection of the best individuals with parents unknown always carries the risk of relatedness.

Certain steps should be taken if one wants to grow exotics in a new area in which no previous testing has been done. Although this situation may not appear to be common, in fact it happens quite frequently that exotics are to be grown under totally new conditions such as grasslands or scrub-brushlands. The general concepts outlined are also valid when a program is already under way, although the methods to be followed would be somewhat different if considerable information were available from previous testing. When such information is available, an immediate start should be made on development of a land race, as described in the next chapter. Even then, one needs to continue testing for more suitable species and sources of exotics to supplement those currently in use.

There is often need for a decision, after only a few years of testing, regarding which provenances or species are suitable for use. The problem of too short a test period is critical for all exotics. There is no immediate answer to this problem other than to use experience combined with common sense (Langlet, 1959a; Rohmeder, 1959). For long-term reliable answers on growth rates, tests need to be conducted for at least half-rotation age and preferably for a full rotation (Wells and Wakeley, 1966).

After a species or provenance has been designated for trial, its introduction should follow the general approach suggested below. If reliable results are desired, representative seed samples are needed. Only a couple of trees representing a seed source can give very misleading answers. The following sequence should be followed:

1.   Make *small observational plot trials;* these are frequently referred to as *arboretum plantings* (Gallegos, 1980b; Ladrach, 1980a). The arboretum tests are small, containing a block of perhaps 25 to 36 trees which are planted on the site where there is interest in making operational plantings. Frequently the trials are planted simply as rows rather than as blocks with no replications. Although the ideal is to run the trials to near rotation age, this is rarely possible. Almost always an early judgment of performance must be made; this carries some real dangers because frequently a species or provenance can look good initially, but when subjected to several years of the exotic environment, may be found to be ill adapted.

The main value of the arboretum plantings is that they allow one to distinguish and reject the poorest species or provenances immediately. Further study of the best species and provenances can then be conducted in statistically sound experiments replicated at several different sites over several years. The greatest danger in arboretum testing is that not enough provenances have been chosen to be representative, and one or two poor provenances may result in the rejection of a whole species. There have been many examples of this; one is *Eucalyptus cloeziana* in South Africa, where some sources are outstanding and others are hopeless. Another is in South America, where the wrong sources of *Eucalyptus camaldulensis* and *E. grandis* were tried and both species were rejected. The most outstanding example is *Pinus oocarpa,* where the easily obtained higher-latitude and higher-elevation sources were tried and found inferior; the Central American sources are excellent, but they were not tried. No species should be totally rejected until sufficiently representative provenances have been tested as arboretum plantings.

No definite span of years to keep observational tests can be recommended because it depends on the species and the severity of the exotic environment as well as the product desired and the age of tree necessary to supply it. For example, *Eucalyptus* to be used for pulpwood and planted in a rather uniform environment can be assessed in 2 to 3 years, while for pine used for pulpwood in the tropics, 5 years is about as early as a reasonable assessment can be made. In cold climates the waiting period before eliminating species or sources must be 10 years or more. If solid-wood products are desired, the time must be great enough to see if the trees approach the proper size and wood properties for the end product.

2.   Plant the desired species and provenances in statistically sound *plot performance tests* to narrow the choices for subsequent larger pilot plant or crop performance tests. An alternative and, in our opinion, a better design is to test individual mother trees separately within provenance blocks, usually

by a group of mother-tree row plots which together constitute a provenance block. This design is standard for CAMCORE and is sometimes used by CFI and others.

The provenance tests with a mixture of mother trees should always be made as block plantings, such as 7 × 7, or 8 × 8 tree plots, with the internal 25 to 36 trees being measured. (One row around the edge of each plot serves as a buffer.) Row plots or single tree plots for gross provenances (i.e., not with mother trees) should never be used for the plot performance tests. It is important to assess the trees of a provenance in competition with each other just as they will be grown operationally. Rarely are provenances or species grown in mixtures, and the information needed is how well the trees do in competition with those with which they will be grown operationally.

(a) Never use less than four replications for any test; six are preferable.

(b) Establish tests on each major soil type where operational planting is being considered.

(c) Assess these tests in a time frame similar to that for the arboretum plantings described earlier.

3. Establish *pilot plant or crop performance tests* of the three or four very best species or geographic sources as found in the plot performance tests on the major planting areas. These should be at least two hectares in size and preferably four hectares or greater. They will need to have as broad a genetic base as possible because they will be used for:

(a) Making initial selections for a greatly improved land race, as described in the next chapter.

(b) Learning how best to handle and manage the species or provenance for operational planting: If several management methods are to be tried (fertilizer, site preparation, bare-root vs. containerized seedlings, etc.), the plantings can be broken into separate one-half- to one-hectare blocks for each treatment. *Do not* try to *superimpose several* treatments on top of each other; failure to significantly differentiate any differences is almost always the result. The objective is to know generally how best to grow the provenance or species; refinements of things such as stocking density can be made later.

(c) Obtaining *yield measurements* is a primary objective of the crop performance stage. Sufficiently large and uniform plantings are needed to be able to estimate with reasonable accuracy volume growth and tree quality. This means that the length of the test period should be at least half-rotation age before a final decision is made about which will be the primary species provenance and which will be the secondary one (ones) (Zobel and Talbert, 1984).

(d) Make an assessment of the wood properties and their utility, as spelled out in Chapter 9. No large-scale planting of exotics should ever be done until the suitability of the wood produced in the new environment has been determined.

Although it is impossible to generalize about the tests that should be made on exotics as a group, certain characteristics are of key importance. For example, there are many attempts to use members of the genus *Eucalyptus* at the higher latitudes or elevations, where cold weather is a factor. Literally hundreds of tests have been made to assess cold hardiness in the eucalypts, and groups have been organized to exchange information and experience in this area; an excellent collection of 46 papers on cold resistance of *Eucalyptus* was presented at the IUFRO Symposium (1983b), which summarized information to that date. Individual papers, such as those by Wilcox (1982b) on *Eucalyptus fastigata* in New Zealand or the ones by Boden (1958) or Hunt and Zobel (1978), all have dealt with peculiar problems of the sensitivity of the eucalypts to cold and proposed actions to overcome this situation.

Other species groups, like the tropical pines, are very sensitive to high soil pH and to the absence of mycorrhizae, and such major factors must always be of primary consideration when testing provenances.

2.5 SEED MOVEMENT

When exotic plantations are established, the question is always raised of how far seed can be moved to sites other than where it was tested. This question has no answer other than "It depends," until one actually tests the seed in the new environment. There is a strong tendency by some people to test a provenance and, if it works, to plant it in similar, and even different, environments elsewhere. Also, sometimes closely related sources or provenances are used without testing under the assumption that the apparently slightly different source will be satisfactory. Despite apparent similarities, sometimes the second source is not at all adapted to the exotic environment in which the first source grows well.

It is not always possible to test the exact location of each source of seed to be used. However, if there is any doubt about the suitability of a source, it must be tested in the exotic environment, despite the following general rules for seed movement:

1. The closer the source of seed is to the edge of the range of the species, the more care must be taken (Wells and Wakeley, 1966). Elevational or latitudinal effects become more severe near the edges of the range of a species. Also, the harsher the planting site, the greater is the risk when moving seed long distances (Adams and Campbell, 1981). Sometimes the rare or extreme conditions do not become evident until late in a rotation. These authors emphasize that it may even take several decades for poor adaptation to become evident. They found for Douglas-fir that seed zone differences are related to about two-thirds of the genetic variation, indicating that seed zone guidelines will be moderately successful in delineating environmentally homogeneous areas.

2. Care in elevational changes is always a major consideration. Rehfeldt (1980) suggests that it is safe to use seed from an area approximately 230 m (750 ft) above and below a given area for movement of *Pinus ponderosa* seed in Idaho, but claims in another publication (Rehfeldt, 1979) that there is no source limit for elevation for *Pinus monticola.*

In an early publication, Shirley (1937) quotes the principle developed in Europe that it is not safe to move seed more than 300 ft in elevation. Currently, the idea has become generally accepted that it is safe to move seed approximately 300 m (1000 ft) in elevation before problems arise. No one is quite sure from where this rule arose, but certainly it does not hold near the edges of the species distribution and, as clearly shown by the preceding examples, it varies greatly with the species used. In Guatemala, we have seen that near the bottom of the species range of *Pinus oocarpa,* where the environment rapidly changes towards desert conditions, even a few meters of elevational change make a great difference in the characteristics of the trees and that here the 300-m rule would be totally unacceptable. Shirley (1937) explains that trees moved from a low elevation to a high elevation tend to grow late in the fall and are often killed back by early fall frosts, while trees from high elevations moved to low elevations start active growth during the first few days in the spring and are often injured by late spring frosts.

3. Another major concern is the movement of seed latitudinally. In this case, a rule that it is safe to move seed 160 km (100 mi) in latitude is often quoted; Shirley (1937) states that European workers used 1 degree in latitude as a safe distance. Again, such a rule must be followed with great caution because the differences with a given change of latitude are usually much more severe at the higher latitudes—that is, as one proceeds towards the poles, a given change in latitude has a greater influence on development of provenances. As is well illustrated by *Pinus contorta,* it can work to move seed to higher latitudes if compensated for by lower elevations. Seed of *Pinus contorta* from 60 degrees north in Canada is used successfully at lower elevations when grown at 65 degrees north in Sweden. For ponderosa pine Rehfeldt (1980) lists 0.7 degrees in latitude and 1.2 degrees in longitude as realistic values for safe seed movement, while he feels that for Idaho white pine there need be no concern with either latitude or longitude. Changes in latitude have causes and effects similar to those in elevation; this was pointed out by Shirley (1937).

4. Great care must be taken in moving seed between greatly differing soils. Sometimes ecotypes have been formed with soil type that are different, even though they may be very close to one another geographically.

There have been many reports concerning safe distances to move seed for specific species in a given area. For example, Wakeley (1963) and Wells (1983) have developed some rather specific rules for the southern pines. But general rules for movement of seed within a species range usually are not very useful for exotics except perhaps for the general lead given by Wiersma (1963) that a displacement of one degree in latitude is equivalent to 100 m in elevation; this, however, must be tested more widely before being accepted.

According to Yeatman (1976), development of seed source zones, based on field testing and ecological criteria, is the key step in determining safe seed movement. But even these are only good as a general guide, and Yeatman emphasizes they need to be under constant review and modification. Movement of seed is especially troublesome near the equator, where latitude, longitude, and other environmental characteristics become superseded by the moisture patterns and extreme soil differences in the tropics. Here seed zones are more closely tied with soil and moisture changes as well as with elevation. Publications such as those by Golfari (1974) and Golfari et al. (1978) can be used as the basis to determine seed zones.

As information is obtained and experience gained, seed zones can be designated. A number of these are in use for different species, as shown for Douglas-fir by Adams and Campbell (1981). These are helpful for designating where collections for exotics should be made. Sometimes greater seed movement is possible than would be expected. For example, Lambeth et al. (1984) found that coastal North Carolina *Pinus taeda* does very well in the quite different environment in Arkansas.

The "safest rules" are to use common sense and experience and to use more care near the edge of a species range or where environmental gradients are steep or abrupt. The seed of interest must ultimately be tested in the new environment; that is the only sure way to assess the safe distance for movement of seed.

2.6 PREDICTION OF LATER GROWTH FROM EARLY GROWTH

In all of forestry, but especially for exotics, there is a great need to predict the response of the trees being tested at the earliest possible age. There is always a hurry, and forestry programs are frequently under pressure to go operational before species and provenance tests have matured to the age where reliable data, especially for growth and resistance to pests and temperature extremes, are available.

As emphasized by Zobel and Talbert (1984), many mistakes are made by premature selection of individual tree performance as well as by premature provenance and species selection. As one example, Clausen (1982) found that height at ages 1 or 2 was totally unreliable as a predictor of height at ages 16 and 17 in *Juglans nigra* and *Fraxinus americana*. Similarly, for Douglas-fir, Lambeth et al. (1982) found only a weak correlation in height between family performance in the phytotron and performance after 6 years' growth in the field, but they did find a better relationship for total dry weight. Relating their comments to Douglas-fir, Namkoong et al. (1972) discussed reasons why a tree's growth pattern might vary with age. They stated that the genetic control of apical growth changes during a tree's lifetime. Growth patterns evident in the juvenile period change as competition increases. The authors stated that the added physiological requirements when cone production starts (at about 15 years of age) imposes restrictions on height growth.

There is considerable confusion about the use of juvenile-to-mature correlations in a breeding program where quick generation turnover will allow the use of low correlations; the final gains may be good. But to use low correlations in developing plants for extensive planting, correlations must be much higher or heavy losses will be sustained. Most of the comments in this chapter refer to the correlations for production populations summarized by Zobel and Talbert (1984), that about one half-rotation age is required to obtain reasonably safe juvenile-to-mature correlations for use in large-scale operational planting.

Unfortunately, juvenile-to-mature correlations for volume and many other characteristics in individual forest trees are nearly always poor except for very short rotation ages (Kageyama, 1984). Kageyama found for the eucalypts that selection at age two was better than at age one. Using age two (for 6- or 7-year rotations), he obtained a good estimation of gain. He also stated that very early growth is genetically different from growth at a later age.

The importance of juvenile-to-mature correlations in short-rotation eucalypts was stressed by Grunwald and Karschon (1983). Even at later years, considerable change in ranking can occur, as reported for two *Eucalyptus* species by Darrow (1986). He found that even between 4 and 8 years there were major changes in ranking of seedlots. He states: "It may be unwise to select superior seedlots at a young age. . . . ." Similar results were found by others where there were essentially no correlations among several factors in *E. grandis* at age 3, and for some characteristics the relationship disappeared at 6 months. For the same species, Borges and Brune (1983) found that height in the nursery had some correlation with height at age 6 months but none with height at later ages.

Longer rotations have demonstrated poor early-to-mature growth correlations in species used for exotics such as loblolly pine (Wakeley, 1971; LaFarge, 1972), ponderosa pine (Steinhoff, 1974; Namkoong and Conkle, 1976), Douglas-fir (Namkoong et al., 1972), slash pine (Squillace and Gansel, 1974), and various of the hybrid poplars (Wilkinson, 1973). In *Pinus contorta* planted in Finland, the coastal and southern provenances (varieties) grew best initially, but after the second growing season the inland source material grew faster and continued to increase its superiority up to 8 years of age.

Correlations of growth performance at very young ages, say, age 3 or less, with performance at mature ages are usually poor, but they improve progressively as the first assessment time becomes closer to the mature age. Such results were reported by Chagala and Gibson (1984) on *Pinus oocarpa* where the rankings were found to be variable the first four years, but in the fifth year a clear picture emerged regarding provenance superiority. Similarly, Eisemann et al. (1984) found small differences among provenances of *P. caribaea,* but at 8 to 10 years of age there was a more pronounced change in provenance performance. They report that the changes observed would not be predictable from early growth. Also, on *P. oocarpa* and *P. caribaea,* Liegel (1984a) found that rankings between the ages of 6 and 10 years in *P. caribaea* were not good, with sources changing by four to six ranks. However, the top-ranking sources of *P. oocarpa* had little position change. Liegel (1984c) also says that ranking of provenance tests of *Pinus caribaea* may change with age and he recommends that assessment should not be made before 10 years. In *P. caribaea,* changes in relative positions in the height and diameter of provenances were great between year 1 and year 11. Most changes occurred before the ninth year. The best time to select appears to be about the seventh year.

There is a real danger of making mistakes by premature selections within provenances. For example, Barnes and Schweppenhauser (1978) found no correlation of seedling height at 1 and 12 months for *Pinus patula.* In South Africa *Eucalyptus grandis* measured at 6 years of age showed one family the best through 15 years of age, but another family, which was second best at 6, was last when harvested at 15 (Anon., 1983b). The authors state that "early ranking does not necessarily agree with that at harvesting." This lack of relationship was expressed for provenances of tropical pines by Barnes and Gibson (1984b) as follows:

> Each parameter assessed at a different age is a different trait and may be controlled by a different set of genes—the eighth year is probably the most significant point as it is half a normal pulp and quarter of a normal sawtimber rotation; it is also the point where thinning is imminent.

Although the caution about premature selection is frequently expressed, not all scientists agree with it. For example, Nixon (1974) reports for black wattle (*Acacia mearnsii*) that selections at 5 years of age gave good indications of ranking at maturity. She therefore recommends reducing the length of time taken for progeny trials from 10 to 5 years. For *Pinus caribaea,* Falkenhagen (1979) found that growth traits could be selected as early as 8 years of age. In Korea, Han and Ryu (1984) reported strong correlations among heights at ages 3, 5, and 10. Likewise, Lambeth (1980) feels that ranking of *Pinus taeda* at 4 years gives a good indication of older performance, although rankings were not reliable at earlier ages. Previously, for *P. taeda,* 8 years was thought to be the earliest reliable date at which to obtain good growth correlations for 12-year-old trees (Paschke, 1979).

When assessing the results of early selection, it must again be emphasized that juvenile-to-mature correlations among provenances are usually better than for individual trees or families within a provenance. This is especially true for provenances that originate in very different environments. Therefore, it is sometimes possible to make predictions of mature performance from performance at a young age when comparing provenances grown in exotic environments. This is so because the physiology of the provenance is such that it may have the same effect at all ages. For example, a high-elevation source is slow growing at all ages, and this is readily evident when the trees are young.

Numerous studies report generally good predictability of older performance of a provenance from young trees. For *Pinus contorta* in New Zealand, Miller (1971) found tree heights of provenances at 6 months of age were closely correlated with those at 3 years. Also, height growth at 3 years was very highly correlated ($r = 0.90$) with volume production of provenances of *Pinus taeda* at 35 years of age in trials described by Falkenhagen (1978). But there is an inherent danger when correlations are made among provenances only a few years old or when only small age differences exist. Although these are often very close, they may not hold when young provenances are compared to older ones.

Sometimes provenances show considerable changes in relative performance over time. For example, Namkoong and Conkle (1976) found that some adaptations in ponderosa pine were not expressed until after age 20. Thus, premature growth predictions relative to adaptability were misleading since the general patterns developed slowly. Namkoong and Conkle found that juvenile-to-mature correlations dropped considerably with greater age.

As Callaham and Liddicoet (1961) show, after some years, environmental factors can greatly change the relative performance of provenances. They found that, initially, the middle-elevation sources grow best the first 12 years regardless of the elevation of planting, but after 20 years the sources from each elevation generally grow best when planted back at elevations of 960, 2730, and 5650 ft, (290, 830, and 1710 m), from where they originated.

The potential for a change in provenance performance of exotics is always present and assessments of the best provenance must be made carefully. This was stated rather well by Heybroek (1974) when he said that:

> many tree breeders tacitly assume for their testing and experimentation that populations growing faster than others in their youth will continue to do so later; in other words, that the species has only one uniform growth-rhythm. This is not generally true.

2.7 SECONDARY, OR RESERVE, SPECIES

A concept of key importance in any forestry program, but of special importance with exotics, is to have secondary, or reserve, species that can be used if the preferred exotic fails. As is pointed out strongly in Chapter 4, pests and adverse environments always ultimately affect exotics, although the extent of the losses may not be apparent for many years. Usually the pests or adverse environments are not so serious that they cannot be handled through silvicultural manipulation, selecting and breeding for tolerance, or use of different provenances within the desired species. But occasionally the pest is so destructive that the exotic species cannot be managed profitably. This situation occurs frequently enough *so that all forestry programs based on exotics must have one, or preferably two, secondary, or reserve, species* that can be used in case of a catastrophe with the primary species. The reserve species should ultimately be thoroughly researched and tested, nearly as intensively as the primary species. This includes determining the best seed sources, trying different management techniques, and ascertaining their utility in the desired product. Following are some general rules for handling secondary species once preliminary tests have indicated that it (they) is suitable enough to warrant trials:

1.   Make trial plantings of the potentially best provenances on all the sites where operational planting might be done. This can be through bulk plantings or by seed from selected mother trees. The key here is to have a broad enough genetic base represented so that initial selections for land race development will be possible.

2.   Make small "mill runs" of the wood to assure yourself as well as the user that the wood is suitable for the desired product. It is mandatory that this be done because wood of a species can change drastically with a different environment (Zobel and van Buijtenen, 1987) (see Chapter 9). The wood of the reserve species must be assessed in the environment in which it will be grown as an exotic.

3.   After the best sources have become evident (this cannot be decided much prior to half-rotation age), select the best trees in the best provenances and use these in a seed orchard to produce the desired land race. Seed from the orchard will be used for small annual plantings of the reserve species.

4.   Progeny test the trees so that their genetic worth can be assessed and a bank of genetic material will be available for immediate use once a decision is made to do further work with the species.

5.   Annually plant about 5 to 10% of the operational forestry program from the best apparent seed source of the reserve species and ultimately from the land race developed for the reserve species. These plantings need to be done so the foresters will know how best to handle seed, grow trees in the nursery, outplant, and efficiently manage the plantations.

It is shocking how often the basic requirement of having a reserve species is ignored. There are numerous examples of complete loss of a species to a pest; one prime example is the damage caused by *Dothistroma* fungus on *Pinus radiata* in several parts of the world. In certain environments this disease has totally decimated the exotic radiata pine forests, making the use of another species mandatory. Similar experiences have occurred with some *Eucalyptus,* where droughts or unexpected freezes have destroyed the exotic plantations. Another example is wind damage on some coastal plantings of *Pinus oocarpa.* (More examples need not be given here because this subject is handled more completely in Chapter 4.) The important point is that frequently a secondary species is necessary and should *always* be ready in case of an emergency. In some instances, a different provenance will serve in place of a secondary species, but if so used, the new provenance must be genetically very different from the one that has failed.

3

GENETIC IMPROVEMENT OF EXOTICS— DEVELOPING AND USING LAND RACES— GENOTYPE × ENVIRONMENT INTERACTION

3.1 INTRODUCTION

In no forestry operation is genetic improvement more greatly needed than when exotics are grown. As emphasized in Chapter 2, provenances used for exotics frequently consist of very few original trees, which restricts variability and the potential for genetic gain. An extreme example is cited by Bawa (1976): " . . . in many areas where teak has been introduced, all of the seeds may have originated initially from a single tree." The exotic species is usually not well adapted to the new environment and improvements in adaptability are always needed (Fig. 3.1). To do this a broad genetic base is essential.

Although an attempt may be made to get the best provenances of the best species for use as an exotic, further genetic improvements are necessary within the chosen provenance. As Morandini (1964) emphasized, genetic work should be done both in the country of origin and in the country where the exotic is planted. He points out the importance of the plasticity of a species (that is, its ability to grow well in diverse environments) if it is to be a good exotic.

Genetic gains in addition to those from using the best provenance are possible by selecting the best individuals within provenances because of the very large variability within forest tree species (Wood and Greaves, 1977) (Fig. 3.2). This was stated by Guries (1984) as follows:

Most forest trees contain . . . higher degrees of heterozygosity than observed in most organisms. As a result, the bulk of the gene diversity contained within a species resides within populations. . . . levels of variation for some hardwoods appear comparable to those noted for conifers.

Figure 3.1. A major problem with establishing exotics is lack of adaptability that may show up as the plantations age. Shown is a planting of *Pinus caribaea* on sandy soils that grew satisfactorily until a dry year occurred. Only a few trees of the provenance used were adapted to drought conditions; from these a land race was developed. (Photo courtesy of John Wiley & Sons.)

In a similar vein, Conkle (1980) found that, compared with herbacious plants, conifers rank among the most variable plants studied by the use of isozymes. As an example of the magnitude of individual tree variability, Marquestant et al. (1977) reported that in southern France the largest eucalypts are five times as large as the smallest ones. He explained this as resulting from a lack of man's selection on the Australian forests from which the seed were obtained. There are always exceptions; for example, there are some essentially monomorphic species with little internal variability, such as Torrey pine (*P. torreyana*) and red pine (*P. resinosa*), as described by Ledig and Conkle (1983) and Fowler and Morris (1977).

Large amounts of seed are often required for exotic plantings, necessitating large-scale seed collections from wild populations. Since wild stands from which seed are collected have often been badly degraded, the plantations from seed of wild forests are often extremely nonuniform and of poor quality and thus are badly in need of additional genetic improvement (Fig. 3.3).

One very important concept related to genetic improvement is to understand the relationship among different characteristics of the tree. Most fortunately, in forestry many of the important characteristics are partially or almost totally genetically independent of one another. Thus, it is possible to have fast-growing trees that are straight or crooked or straight trees that have

Figure 3.2. Forest trees generally have a great deal of variability within a species. Individual tree variation can be large, as illustrated by the different limb form of *Pinus strobus*. Determination of the cause and use of such variation is a key to success in growing exotics. (Photo courtesy of John Wiley & Sons.)

Figure 3.3. A major problem with exotics is that frequently seed has been collected from degraded stands. Shown is a stand of pine in Guatemala that has been badly degraded by firewood cutters. This stand had previously been a good source of seed for planting in South America.

small limbs or large limbs because the characteristics of growth rate, bole straightness, and limb size are not closely related genetically. As always, there are exceptions to any general rule. For example, Shelbourne and Thulin (1974) found a strong correlation between growth rate and branch diameter in rooted cuttings; it was difficult to select small-branched but fast-growing clones. Another example is Scots pine (Squillace et al., 1975) in Holland, where rate of height growth and needle cast damage were strongly correlated.

Another usually low correlation in most exotic conifers is that between growth rate and wood specific gravity (Zobel and van Buijtenen, 1987). As usual, there are major exceptions to this independence between characters; one was described by Cotterill and Cameron (1984). They report strong negative correlations between growth rate and wood density in radiata pine in Australia and describe breeding methods that attempt to overcome this problem. Other notable exceptions with negative correlations between growth rate and wood density occur in the spruces and soft pines. In most hard pines, Douglas-fir, and diffuse porous hardwoods there usually is only a small relationship between growth rate and wood properties.

The lack of correlation of adaptive versus economically important form and growth characteristics is of key importance to one growing exotics (Fig. 3.4). This makes it *possible to breed intensively for broadening the adaptive genetic base* (against diseases, insects, adverse sites, or adverse weather) *and at the same time breed strongly for greater uniformity in tree form and quality and wood or other properties* (Zobel and Talbert, 1984). This potential to develop well-adapted strains of trees that also have desired economic characteristics is vitally important in exotic forestry. This was shown by Wilcox (1982b) for *Eucalyptus fastigata*. He reported the absence of any major adverse correlation between frost hardiness and growth rate. It is often claimed for the eucalypts that the faster growers are more sensitive to cold damage; when this occurs, the faster growers tend to be more forked as a result of the frost damage.

Imagine the frustration if, for example, trees that were drought tolerant all had crooked stems. Luckily this is not so and we can breed drought-tolerant trees that have either straight or crooked boles, as we desire. When a lack of genetic correlation occurs between adaptive and morphological characteristics, rapid gains in tree improvement[1] are possible, and it is an absolute blessing when breeding tree species used as exotics.

One major consideration in working with exotics relates to whether provenance assessment is to be made by bulk seed collections or with seed from selected mother trees. As pointed out by Barnes and Gibson (1984b), bulk seed lots are easier and more convenient to work with, but they give little information on family and within-family variation (Fig. 3.5). This knowledge is

---

[1]Although there is a technical difference between "tree improvement," "tree breeding," and "forest genetics" (see Zobel and Talbert, 1984, p. 6), for purpose of simplification we will refer to them interchangeably in this book.

Figure 3.4. It is possible to have trees with a broad genetic adaptability but with a narrow genetic base for desired characteristics. This is a *Pinus caribaea* var. *caribaea* of outstanding form adapted to a very severe site in Venezuela. Good form and tolerance to bad site are often independently inherited, so it is possible to breed for desired combinations.

essential; as Barnes and Gibson (1984b) found, the best phenotypes in one provenance may be nearly twice as productive as those in another with the same mean performance. If it is not possible to keep seed from mother trees separate, it is essential to include a minimum of 30 to 50 parents in the bulk lot in order to sample the range of variation within the provenance. For those interested in detailed strategies for testing provenances, Nikles (1984a) discusses three methods that may be used to genetically improve exotic species.

Because of the opportunity to obtain larger gains and the good response of some exotic species to vegetative propagation, a special section in Chapter 5 is devoted to clarifying how vegetative propagation can be used to obtain early and large genetic gains in exotic forest tree species.

Figure 3.5. Family information is vital to provenance assessment. Shown to the right are four trees from a good mother and, to the left, four from a poor mother. The test, made by Aracruz Florestal, shows huge family differences in *Eucalyptus grandis* within a provenance.

3.2 GENETIC IMPROVEMENT OF EXOTICS

The methodology of genetically improving exotic forest trees is basically the same as for indigenous species, although sometimes the emphasis will be somewhat different (Shepherd, 1978; Brune and Zobel, 1981; Namkoong, 1984a; Nikles, 1984a). In some instances, advanced generation breeding programs have been started for exotics such as for *Pinus radiata* (Cameron et al., 1984). Suggestions for advanced multiple population breeding for exotics in Zimbabwe were made by Barnes (1984); these publications are most helpful for those nearing the completion of their first-generation programs. The potential breeding strategies using multiple small breeding populations with an emphasis on the need for international cooperation was covered by Namkoong et al. (1983).

When different provenances are involved, the question always arises if the better ones should be kept separate or combined in the breeding program. Brune (1983) makes suggestions as how to use both methods. For greatest operational gains, we have found it best to use the very best genotypes regardless of their original provenance.

This chapter will not repeat the methods used to genetically improve forest trees; these have been adequately covered by many persons, such as Wright (1976) and Zobel and Talbert (1984). However, a number of publications deal specifically with genetic problems of specific exotics. Some of these, such as *Tropical Trees—Variation, Breeding and Conservation,* by Burley and Styles (1976), and *Progress and Problems of Genetic Improvement in Tropical Forest Trees,* by Nikles et al. (1978), contain a number of chapters dealing with breeding methodology with trees commonly used as exotics, such as the eucalypts, teak, pine, and others. Numerous articles in Burley and Nikles (1973a) cover the methodology of breeding tropical forest trees. This book contains one whole section on breeding methodology (pp. 148–456), including advanced generation breeding. Many of the papers deal with exotic species, with a preponderance on *Pinus caribaea.* The general concepts are applicable to most exotic forest tree species.

Similarly, the book by Barnes and Gibson (1984a) has much information on breeding philosophy. In 1983, Matheson and Brown published the *Radiata Pine Breeding Manual,* which contains 11 chapters on various aspects of tree breeding contributed by six different authors. As stated in the preface, "The purpose of this manual is to provide up-to-date information on how to go about the genetic improvement of radiata pine." It is a most valuable reference that can also be helpful with other species.

The emphasis here will be to describe the peculiar needs of and methodology to apply to exotic species and to state the importance of certain approaches to genetic improvement as well as some of the results obtained. As pointed out by Libby (1973), as exotic tree improvement becomes more intensive, the species or provenances being worked with change from essentially wild populations to domesticated species. This change is well along with a few exotic species.

The first stage, and the one often giving the greatest gains in genetic improvement in exotic forest trees, is the choice of proper species and the best provenances within them; these key aspects have been covered in the previous chapters and will not be repeated. In this chapter we will discuss genetic improvement within the provenances and species that have already been found to be most desirable (Fig. 3.6). In their article about testing provenances, Barnes and Gibson (1984b) emphasize that land races should be included. They discuss measurement schedules and point out that the most important measurements are at one-half the pulpwood and one-quarter the sawtimber rotation ages.

It is clear that genetic improvements and genetic gains are greater when one is working with a species as an exotic than for the same species in its indigenous environment. Because of extreme and different growth conditions, the trees seem to have a greater response to genetic manipulation, resulting in greater genetic gains. Added to this is the smaller number of pests associated with some exotic species, at least initially.

Forest trees are among the most variable of all living organisms; trees have a high level of heterozygosity (Hamerick et al., 1979; Guries, 1984; Namkoong, 1984b). This large amount of variation is very beneficial to the tree breeder, but it tends to obscure differences between provenances or treatments (Barnes

Figure 3.6. Breeding better trees within provenances is essential. This select tree is to be used as a basis for a breeding program in *Pinus caribaea* in South America. Such trees, combined as a land race, give great improvements in addition to the gains from using better provenances.

et al., 1983). Although some of this variability is environmentally caused, a great deal has a genetic basis. According to Barnes et al. (1983), quantitative traits are under less genetic control (as expressed by provenances) than are qualitative traits. Fortunately, the genetic variability is mostly of a type which responds to selection and breeding and is reasonably strong (Wright, 1976; Zobel and Talbert, 1984). The gain from a selection program is determined by the heritability (the strength of inheritance) and the selection differential (the amount of variation between the select and base populations). (To state it as a simplified formula: $G = h^2 \times SD$, with G = gain, h^2 = heritability, and SD = selection differential.)

One section of the Third World Consultation on Forest Tree Breeding in Canberra, Australia, in 1977 was devoted to genetic improvement of forest trees, most of which were exotics (FAO, IUFRO, and CSIRO, 1977, pp. 475–749). Papers covered many species, such as the eucalypts (Eldridge, Van Wyk, Chaperon, and others); *Casuarina* (Badran and El-Lakany); *Pinus caribaea* (Chaperon and Dvorak); *Pinus patula, P. elliottii,* and *P. taeda* (Barnes, Kellison, and Dinus); *P. pinaster* (Butcher); *P. radiata* (Eldridge et al., Pederick and Griffin); *Tectona grandis* (Muniswani, Harahap, and Soerianegara); *Acacia mearnsii* (Nixon); and *Picea* (Enescu and Popescu). In general, strong genetic control exists, especially for form, adaptability, and pest resistance. Effective and rather quick gains are possible for some characteristics. Volume improvement was good but not as rapid as for quality and adaptability traits. The results in many parts of the world with many species is that genetic improvement, both on a population basis (as provenances) and with individual trees within provenances, is a major method of improving exotics and must be included in any exotic forest tree program.

3.2.1 Making Genetic Tests

In general, testing procedures for exotics are the same as for indigenous species, but there are a few differences in emphasis. In all instances, simple randomization and replication of tests is best (Zobel and Talbert, 1984) and fancy or complicated test designs frequently fail. Based upon extensive tests in many areas with many species, for most characteristics, we have found that the tests must be large enough so that at least 30 trees per test unit (family, provenance, or other) are measurable at the end of the experiment. Not all researchers report this; for example, Cotterill (1984) finds that 20, or even 10, are enough. Only for wood density with full-sib families have we found that so few entries are satisfactory.

If several different sites are to be used to plant the exotics, tests must be replicated in space that represents these areas. Because of the sometimes extreme environments in which exotics are frequently grown, it is also usually essential to replicate in time, that is, repeat the test in a given area preferably for three years (Zobel and Talbert, 1984). For exotics, replications in time are often more important than replications in space because of the huge year-to-year differences in environment that occur. This *most important need to test over time is usually overlooked when exotics are grown.* As a result, many of the genetic test and progeny test results are misleading or downright incorrect.

Few people recognize the importance of replicating in time, but Schrum and Gerhold (1970), testing Scots pine in the northeastern United States, where yearly fluctuations are rather predictable, state, "Replication in time may be equivalent to replication in space for some traits." Because of the long-lasting results from stress (see the section on competition and stress), an adverse environment one year can still be observed in plant performance many years after the stress has been removed. Certainly, disease or insect infestation that is dependent on cycles or on a specific environment that may only occur occasionally cannot be fairly assessed in only one year's planting in an adverse exotic environment.

One key to establishing tests is to get the field-test layout so that it is sound. This was discussed for provenances in many publications, for example, Burley and Wood (1976) and Nikles et al. (1978), both of which cover many papers dealing with tests with tropical and exotic trees.

The mating designs that should be used differ with species and condition. Normally, designs are employed that give a good estimate of general and specific combining abilities, like variations of the half-diallel [see Zobel and Talbert (1984), Chapter 8, for details]. With some exotics the ideal often cannot be met because of the difficulty of obtaining seed or of making control pollinations. This is especially difficult with some tropical species that are insect or animal pollinated. Except for the well-known genera like the pines or eucalypts, it is necessary to learn the biology of the species before developing mating designs.

No genetic program can be successful in exotics without extra care being exercised in choice of both mating and testing designs. These in turn are dictated by the biology of the species, the environment in which the tests are to be made, or the objectives of the tests. Within limits, the best possible advice is to attempt to achieve the maximum of simplicity in both mating and testing methods.

3.2.2 The Problems with Hardwoods

Working with the genetics of exotic hardwoods is generally difficult, particularly with those that are not wind pollinated. In fact, the amount of work done with them is limited; as emphasized by Bawa (1976): "The breeding systems of tropical forest trees are not well investigated." Because of the several reasons he discusses, Bawa feels that the local races are more similar genetically than are most wind-pollinated hardwoods. Special care is therefore required in the design and selection for an exotic-tree improvement program. Although details are not warranted here, a few of the problems that must be faced when breeding exotic hardwoods are summarized below:

1.   Some species are dioecious (i.e., there are male and female plants that bear reproductive structures separately) (Bawa and Opler, 1975). In some ways this makes crossing programs easier because emasculation is not necessary. But it makes for real difficulties in the design of seed orchards where the sex of the tree to be placed in the seed orchard must be known. How many females should be used for each male and how they are to be deployed in the orchard are questions for which good answers are not available. How to tell the sex of a plant before it flowers is also difficult, and the program must be delayed until this is known.

2.   Many species are insect or animal pollinated. Some are pollinated only by a single insect and sometimes, especially in some tropical species, the flower is shaped so that only a specific insect, bird, or bat can do the pollinating (Frankie, 1976; Start and Marshall, 1976). Many of these species are not yet planted as exotics but have potential for such use. One reason they are not used more now is that foresters have not yet learned to manipulate their difficult pollination systems.

3.   Flowers of hardwoods are often perfect, so emasculation of the anthers must be performed when control pollination is attempted. This can be accomplished rather simply for some eucalypts (Eldridge, 1976; Pryor, 1976), but an efficient methodology is not yet known for many species.

4.   For some genera, such as *Quercus,* or species such as *Tectona grandis* and *Gmelina arborea* (Bawa, 1976), only one or a few fruits or seeds are formed per pollination. This discourages any breeding designs requiring two-parent pedigree crossings.

5.   Some species have unusual floral forms with the fertilization patterns essentially unknown. One example is *Cordia goeldiana,* a species with excellent timber, fast growth, a straight bole, high survival, and good adaptability to plantation conditions. It has heterostyly, having flowers with short styles and long stamens, long styles with short stamens, and an intermediate form. The pollination compatibility patterns are complex and not well known (Kanashiro and Martins, 1984), and sound seed set is erratic.

6.   Seed are often fragile, with transient viability, and must be germinated immediately or viability is lost. Seed of temperate species such as the poplars have transient viability, and many of the tropical hardwoods such as *Shorea robusta* (Troup, 1921) lose their viability rapidly. Some have extremely hard seed coats and are difficult to germinate without special treatment. To illustrate the importance of knowing how to handle seed, Bawa (1976) states that "in the initial establishment of gene or clone banks, the main concern would be the problems of seed viability, germination and predation rather than appropriate mating designs."

7.   Because of their scattered locations as individual trees in mixed stands (Fig. 3.7), and sometimes because of their tendency towards insect pollination, selfing or inbreeding is frequently common (Frankie, 1976; Van Wyk, 1977b). The seriousness of this problem is not always known. Sometimes there is a wholesale excision of flowers in some tropical hardwoods even if good flower crops were formed, resulting in a shortage of good seeds (Bawa, 1976; Kanashiro and Martins, 1984).

3.2.3 Genetic Studies with Exotics

Exotic species respond well to genetic manipulation and give large gains for tree form, wood qualities, adaptability, and pest resistance. Growth characteristics are less responsive to breeding programs. Rather than discuss in detail the type and magnitude of genetic studies and gains that have been achieved in exotics, Tables 3.1 and 3.2 provide samplings of the genetic work and gains achieved in breeding exotics. These gains are additional to those from proper provenance selection. Actual details of the genetic improvements that have been obtained cannot be listed because of the many pages this would require. Genetic gains of the species in their indigenous habitats are not listed in these tables unless there is need to illustrate some special situation.

It is obvious from Tables 3.1 and 3.2 that the genetic patterns for exotics are quite similar to those for species grown in their indigenous environments. It is striking how few genetic studies have been completed on exotics in the exotic environment, with the notable exceptions of *Pinus radiata,* members of

Figure 3.7. Mixed tropical hardwoods sometimes have complex genetic interrelationships because the trees may be scattered, insect pollinated, or dioecious. This jungle in the Amazon may have a single species occur only infrequently on each hectare.

the genus *Populus,* a few *Eucalyptus* species, *Pinus sylvestris,* and species, such as Douglas-fir and the larches, which have been used as exotics for a long time.

Much relevant information is available from proceedings and symposia on genetics of exotics such as the recent ''Work Conference on Provenance and Genetic Improvement Strategies in Tropical Forest Trees'' (IUFRO, 1984), and the symposium on fast growing trees (IUFRO, 1980).

It is not possible to cover genetic results on exotic species in any detail in this chapter. However, based upon the varied genera and studies made in different parts of the world, some of which were described in Tables 3.1 and 3.2, it is evident that:

1. Heritabilities for most growth and form characteristics are of such a magnitude that a tree improvement program is justified. Especially good heritabilities occur for height growth and are usually low for diameter growth. Heritabilities for adaptiveness and pest resistance are usually high. An intensive forest management program on exotic forest tree species will fall short of its potential without an accompanying tree improvement program to exploit the genetic variation.

2. Most genetic improvement has resulted from following classical breeding techniques, although with some use of specific combining abilities (specific

TABLE 3.1. Genetic and Breeding Activities with Some Selected Exotic Conifer Species[a,b]

Species	Author(s)	Country	General Results
Larix spp.	Nilsson 1959	Sweden	Some clones (3 of 9) are completely self-sterile; one was self-fertile. Inbred plants are inferior. Very strong additive variance was found, and some of the trees were very good general combiners.
Pinus radiata	Bannister 1962	New Zealand	A multiple-factor system influences the number of branch clusters. The gene combinations form a series of genotype classes.
Larix spp.	Keiding & Olsen 1965	Denmark	Variation of trees within progenies was greater than grafts within a clone. There was large progeny-to-progeny variation.
Pinus patula	Armitage & Burrows 1966	Zimbabwe	Plus tree selection is appropriate for a tree improvement program. Estimates of broad sense heritability were 0.53 for height.
Picea sitchensis	Burley 1966	Great Britain	There was little genetic variation in rate of growth, but variation in time of bud formation was related to variation in height.
Pinus radiata	Bannister 1969	New Zealand	At 7 yr, there were large differences between individuals and families for many characteristics. The h^2 of the number of branch clusters was 0.45.
Pinus radiata *P. elliotti*	Nikles 1970	Australia	An increased net economic yield of about 30% to age 15 resulted from establishment and culling of seed orchards.
Pinus sylvestris	Schrum & Gerhold 1970	United States	Heritabililty for 7 traits in the northeastern U.S. were reported; h^2 was 0.50 for height, 0.33 for branch length, 0.26 for branch angle, and 0.25 for number of branches.
Pinus radiata	Burdon 1971	New Zealand	Clonal repeatabilities for clonally propagated material within sites were high (0.50–0.75) for height, stem straightness, and branch fre-

(continued)

TABLE 3.1. Continued

Species	Author(s)	Country	General Results
			quency, but very variable for diameter growth.
Pinus radiata	Shelbourne 1971	New Zealand	The heritability of height growth was surprisingly high; that for diameter was low. Heritability of butt sweep and stem sinuosity was lower than expected. Considerable gain in volume is possible and the time to reach a certain size can be reduced.
Pinus patula	Barnes 1973	Zimbabwe	A rather complete genetic assessment was made based on recurrent selection. A good portion of the variability was under additive genetic control. Maternal effects were not important.
Pinus patula	Denison 1973	South Africa	Two seedling seed orchards were assessed. Large enough family differences were found to indicate good gains from tree improvement. Selection will yield the greatest improvement within an environment similar to that in which the population is destined to grow.
Pinus radiata	Eldridge 1974	Australia	The progeny trials show conclusively that a large amount of genetic variation exists in radiata pine; the potential for genetic gain is evident in all progeny trials—initial gain was 11% in volume.
Pinus sylvestris	Squillace et al. 1975	Holland	500 trees were tested in 6 localities in Holland. The strongest genetic effect was height growth. Volume gain estimates were 14% for seedling seed orchards and 28% for clonal seed orchards from parents chosen on the basis of progeny tests.
Pinus caribaea	Chaperon 1977	Congo	Classical breeding strategy was used. Good heritability for form and low heritability for growth occurred. High specific combining ability was found.

TABLE 3.1. Continued

Species	Author(s)	Country	General Results
Cupressus lusitanica	Dyson & Raunio 1977	East Africa	Heritability varied from 0.26 to 0.87 for height, from 0 to 0.93 for diameter, from 0.11 to 0.70 for stem form, and from 0 to 0.90 for the stem canker disease. Different values were obtained from different trials. No change of heritability values was found with age up to 10 yr.
Pinus patula	Kageyama et al. 1977b	Brazil	Genetic variation was evident for all characteristics studied. Heritability was estimated for several characteristics.
Several pine species	Ladrach 1977	Colombia	Average height gain of the selected progeny was 25% over the commercial checks.
Picea sitchensis	Samuel & Johnstone 1979	Great Britain	116 open-pollinated families were studied. There is doubt about the system of phenotypic forest selection, but progeny selection should be used for growth estimates.
Pinus caribaea	Ledig & Whitmore 1981	Puerto Rico	Height had a heritability of 0.04–0.53; volume, 0.11; bark thickness, 0.53. The heritability for foxtailing was 0.17.
Pinus caribaea	Gibson 1982	Many	Bark percentage was under strong genetic control, as was branch angle and stem form.
Pinus radiata	Anon. 1983d	Australia	This working party report summarizes much genetic information about *P. radiata*. Gains, inheritance, and provenance results are all covered. This report is of great value for those interested in the genetics of the species.
Picea sitchensis *Pinus contorta*	Cannell et al. 1983	Scotland	Sparsely branched clones were the most efficient stemwood producers; at ages 6–8, both species produced 1.5–2.0 times as much stemwood per unit needle mass as heavily branched clones. Large gains in volume could be made by selecting simultaneously for rapid growth and a high foliage efficiency.

(continued)

TABLE 3.1. Continued

Species	Author(s)	Country	General Results
Pinus caribaea	Kageyama et al. 1983	Brazil	Genetic variation was found among young progenies from plus trees selected in Australia for height, foxtail percentage, and survival, but none for forking. Heritability for height was 0.36.
Cupressus lusitanica	Ladrach 1983c	Colombia	Progeny from select trees were 13% better in height and 50% better in volume than the commercial check after 3 yr in the field. Progeny of select trees were straighter.
Pinus caribaea	Long & Dykstra 1983	Indonesia	Variation among half-sib progeny was more distinct among trees from different progenies. Choice of the 10% best gives a 12% improvement in height above the commercial checks.
Pinus caribaea	Nikles et al. 1983	Australia	There were significant differences among provenances in windfirmness. Some of the tallest were also the most windfirm. Windfirmness is closely related to straightness.
Pinus caribaea	Sato & Brune 1983	Australia	Narrow-sense heritabilities for foxtailing varied form 0.40 to 0.75; for height, from 0.06 to 0.70; and for diameter, from 0.13 to 0.71.
Pinus radiata	Anon. 1984a	New Zealand	Tests of 104 long-internode parents showed at 10 yr an internode score 15% higher than the controls; the score of the best 20 progenies was 25% higher.
Pinus patula	Barnes & Mullin 1984	Zimbabwe	Stem straightness and height were under the greatest genetic control for provenances; wood density was the least.
Pinus caribaea	Brigden & Williams 1984	Australia	Family heritabilities for height, diameter, and volume were 0.86, 0.89, and 0.86, respectively; individual tree heritabilities were 0.30, 0.33, and 0.35, respectively.
Pinus radiata	Cameron et al. 1984	Australia	Individual selection gave gains of volume (10.5%), straightness (16.1%), branches (7.9%), and

TABLE 3.1. Continued

Species	Author(s)	Country	General Results
			wood density (0.6%). Family selection gave gains of 13.1% for volume, 24.0% for straightness, 9.5% for branch quality, and 0.7% for wood density.
Pinus kesiya	Chagala 1984	Kenya	Cone production showed very strong genetic control; 38% of the differences were related to provenance.
Pinus oocarpa	Chagala & Gibson 1984	Kenya	The best is to test provenances as half-sib families based on phenotypic selection. This gives information about co-relatedness and lets one choose the best trees of the best families.
Pinus rigida	Han et al. 1984	Korea	There were differences in both specific and general combining ability among clones for height. Some parents showed high general combining ability and some crosses had high specific combining ability.
Pinus rigida	Han et al. 1984a	Korea	Volume increase by selection of the 5 best provenances was 77%; by selection of best families within provenances was 17%.
Pinus radiata	Matheson & Raymond 1984b	Australia	Heritability estimates were larger for stands thinned selectively than for row thinning. The method employed for thinning has a major effect on additive variance.
Pinus merkusii	Pousujja 1984	Thailand	Differences in height and diameter were highly significant in 12-yr tests. No difference was found in survival. All provenances were attacked by shoot borers, but the Vietnam source was the least damaged. Foxtailing is limited to the continental provenances, which also have a grass stage.
Pinus rigida	Ryu et al. 1984a	Korea	Narrow-sense heritability for early flowering was 0.5. A considerable change in flowering time is possible.

(continued)

TABLE 3.1. Continued

Species	Author(s)	Country	General Results
Cupressus lusitanica	Velez 1984	Colombia	Large family differences were found, with height roughly from 4.5 to 10.6 m after 5 yr; 3 mother trees were outstandingly good.

[a]Full references are shown in the reference list.
[b]Generally does not include genetic studies on wood, pests, or adaptability that are covered in other chapters.

TABLE 3.2. A Sampling of Genetic Studies of Exotic Hardwood Species in Their New Environment[a,b,c]

Species	Author(s)	Country	General Results
Dalbergia sissoo	Vidakovíc & Ashan 1970	Pakistan	Stem straightness is strongly inherited, with heritabilities from 0.42 to 0.65. Height and diameter are much more affected by site differences than is straightness.
Eucalyptus grandis	Hodgson 1976	South Africa	Self-pollinations produced less than half the seeds compared to control pollination. There is strong evidence for selective fertilization in favor of cross-pollination.
Eucalyptus grandis	Van Wyk 1976, 1977a,b	United States	Full-sib families grown in the greenhouse and in the field (Florida) showed large genetic variation. Nonadditive variance was often as high or higher than additive variance.
Casuarina spp.	Badran & El-Lakany 1977	Egypt	Limited genetic work has been done with several species in this genus for shelterbelts and windbreaks. The species has good drought resistance and salt tolerance.
Tectona grandis	Harahap & Soerianegara 1977	Indonesia	Heritabilities (broad sense) of height, clear bole, diameter, and stem form were 0.67, 0.69, 0.87, and 0.94, respectively.
Castanea mollissima	Keys et el. 1977	United States	Four 25-yr-old open-pollinated families of Chinese chestnut in West Virginia varied in form, disease resistance, height, and diameter both within and among families.
Tectona grandis	Muniswami 1977	India	Contains a good and complete summary of teak, its distribution, characteristics, and the genetic work

TABLE 3.2. Continued

Species	Author(s)	Country	General Results
			done on it. Many countries have undertaken teak tree improvement when it is used as an exotic.
Eucalyptus spp.	Boland 1978	General	The large variation among individuals within provenances is emphasized; frequently, variation within populations is greater than between provenances. Sometimes the different individuals are given varietal status.
Eucalyptus robusta	Dvorak 1981b	United States	An intense breeding program into the third generation was carried out. Species and hybrids show dramatic gains.
Gmelina arborea	Bolstad & Bawa 1982	Costa Rica	The species is self-incompatible and pollinated by bees.
Leucaena leucocephala	Brewbaker 1982	Hawaii	Trees are self-fertilized and polyploid. Breeders should concentrate on selfed lines. Multiline breeding is recommended. Other species of *Leucaena* are cross-fertilized and diploid.
Eucalyptus fastigata	Wilcox 1982b	New Zealand	Genetic variation was evident in several form and growth characteristics as well as frost tolerance. 79% of the latter is due to provenance differences, 21% to family differences within provenance.
Eucalyptus grandis	Brune 1983	Brazil	Narrow-sense heritabilities varied from 0.33 to 0.59 for height. Heritability for resistance to eucalyptus canker was 0.65 and 0.77 in 2 different areas.
Eucalyptus camaldulensis	Grunwald & Karschon 1983	Israel	There was large variation between families from the same origin; good gains by selection of parent trees are indicated.
Eucalyptus grandis	Van Wyk 1983a	South Africa	Large family variation for full-sib families at 5 yr was reported. Gain predictions for volume growth varied from 6 to 77% depending upon the level of genetic improvement and breeding strategy.

(continued)

TABLE 3.2. Continued

Species	Author(s)	Country	General Results
Eucalyptus grandis	Van Wyk 1983b	South Africa	Selfing and full-sib matings are undesirable. The difference between half-sib and outcrosses is less evident.
Eucalyptus grandis	Van Wyk 1983c	South Africa	Gains of 26 and 62% in volume production and stem form, respectively, should be obtained from seed orchard seed. Using vegetative propagation, gain could be increased to 51%.
Eucalyptus citriodora	Yeh et al. 1983	Brazil	As much as 14% of the seed is self-fertilized, with a high inbreeding coefficient (0.205). Mature trees were highly heterozygous; selection against homozygotes may occur in the eucalypts.
Eucalyptus grandis	Kageyama 1984	Brazil	Height was under stronger genetic control than volume. There was a decreased heritability with age, with a strong decrease from years 1 to 2 and a gradual decrease from years 2 to 5.
Acacia mangium	Pettersson & Havmöller 1984	Philippines	Although there were only small differences among provenances, differences among progenies within provenances were evident for height, stem form, and branching habit.
Eucalyptus camaldulensis	Quaile & Mullin 1984	Zimbabwe	Growth rate and stem straightness are under strong genetic control. The more northerly sources were the best performers.

[a]Full references are shown in the reference list.
[b]References for *Populus* are not included because there are so many that have been brought together in several symposia.
[c]Does not include genetic studies on wood, pests, or adaptability that are covered in other chapters.

combinations) it is possible to achieve greatly increased gains with some species and characteristics. The use of vegetative propagation is very helpful in capturing more of the potential gains and is becoming more widely used.

3. Gains in most characteristics studied are surprisingly large. However, most of these are obtained from young trees, so real care must be taken to avoid overestimations. Several studies reported no decrease and even an increase in inheritance with tree age. This is a most encouraging trend. Further, Nikles (1970) feels that assessment of young tests has some advantages and

states: "Details of young tests are important not only because they often forecast what will follow, but because more rapid early growth can be of value per se, for example in quick suppression of weeds, even if it is not sustained." However, the general rule is to use early gains cautiously, especially when expressed as percentages. It is obvious that the base on which percentage estimates are made changes with time, which will in turn affect the percentage value.

4. Most work on conifers is on the pines, Douglas-fir, and the spruces. However, a surprising amount of work has been done on *Cupressus lusitanica* despite its relatively minor importance. In hardwoods, significant results have been obtained for the genera *Gmelina, Tectona, Swietenia,* and *Leucaena.* Only scattered information is available for genetics of other exotic hardwoods, except for *Populus* and *Eucalyptus,* which have an extensive literature and have been extensively studied genetically. Few of the *Populus* results have been included in this chapter because they are so voluminous and so well documented elsewhere.

5. The grower of exotics faces the problem of whether to use genetics to produce the same amount of wood in less time or to produce more wood in the same amount of time. The shorter time is most beneficial from an economic standpoint, based on the compound interest curve, but has the disadvantage of a higher proportion of juvenile wood, which is not desired for some products (Laarman and Dvorak, 1985).

6. Genetic gains are better in quality improvement than in volume. The size of gains necessary to make a tree improvement program worthwhile is in the order of 5% for volume at time of harvest (Nikles, 1970).

3.3 THE PLACE OF HYBRIDS IN EXOTIC FORESTRY

Whenever exotics are discussed, the question arises about the utility of hybrids. The fact is that hybrids can have great utility as exotics. They have a distinct advantage because the tree breeder can create different gene combinations (Piatnitsky, 1960) that may not occur in nature; sometimes genotypes well suited for an exotic environment can be produced in hybrids. By developing hybrids the breeder can bring together desirable characteristics of the parents and "tailor make" trees not otherwise present in nature such as the pitch × loblolly hybrid in Korea (Hyun, 1976). This was the specific objective of the "Popularis" hybrid (Weiying and Yongchang, 1984), a cross of *Populus simonii* with mixed pollens of *P. pyramidalis* and *Salix matsudana* to create a hybrid suitable for the unfavorable environment in the north and northwest regions of China. Ten of the best progeny were selected to form a cultivar called Popularis. The individuals produced were fast growing, photosynthetically efficient, tolerant to alkaline soil, drought tolerant, and resistant to the diseases *Cytospora* and *Dothiorella.* The wood was of high quality.

Despite the advantages and potential value of hybrids, they generally have been used only sparingly in exotic forestry programs, except where vegetative methods are used in regeneration. The key to how much the use of hybrids as exotics will grow depends partially on the degree to which vegetative propagation can be used operationally, since mass hybrid seed production is usually difficult and costly. Hybrids have been used extensively in exotic species relatively easy to reproduce vegetatively, such as the poplars and willows (Stout et al., 1927; Hunziker, 1958; Schreiner, 1965).

The use of hybrids as exotics is rapidly expanding as better propagation techniques are developed, and hybrid programs such as the ones for *Eucalyptus* in Brazil (Campinhos, 1980) and in the Congo (Delwaulle, 1985) have shown great promise (Fig. 3.8). For example, Brigatti et al. (1983) report that in São Paulo state in Brazil the *E. saligna* × *E. grandis* hybrid is best. Different hybrid combinations have been widely reported as superior in the eucalypts (Martin, 1982). The particular combination that is best depends upon the region where the hybrid is grown and upon the genetic quality of the specific parents used to create the hybrid. Mass production of hybrids from seed has been successful in only a few instances. One noticeable success has been the pitch pine (*P. rigida*) × loblolly pine (*P. taeda*) hybrid in Korea (Hyun, 1976). For this same hybrid, Ryu et al. (1984a) were able to select early-flow-

Figure 3.8. Sometimes hybrids made with exotics are outstanding, as evidenced by this 7-year-old natural eucalypt hybrid on lands of Aracruz Florestal, Espirito Santo, Brazil. Outstanding trees like this are used in the company's vegetative propagation program. (Photo courtesy of John Wiley & Sons.)

ering clones of *Pinus rigida* to establish a seed orchard, which enabled a more efficient method to produce hybrid seed.

It is important to know what the word *hybrid* means. To most foresters a hybrid is a cross between two species. To others, especially those working with exotics, the term *hybrid* also includes crosses between different geographic races within a species (Scamoni, 1950; Nilsson, 1963; Wright, 1964; Howcroft, 1974). Many botanists define a hybrid as a cross between any two unlike genotypes; this is similar to the definition by Snyder (1972), that "a hybrid is the offspring of genetically different parents." If this definition is followed, nearly every cross made between forest trees would technically be a hybrid. In this book we will use *hybrid* to refer to crosses between species and sometimes between quite different provenances within a species.

Hybrids inherit the characteristics of their parents, usually in an intermediate manner. If hybridization is to successfully produce a better exotic with improved growth, form, adaptability, or pest resistance, the individuals used as parents of the hybrid must be carefully chosen to provide the desired characteristics. It is a common belief that only the desirable characteristics of the parental species will be evident in the hybrid; however, the worst characteristics of each parent can also appear in the hybrid progeny. Differences in hybrids between the same two species were reported by Eifler (1960) to depend upon the particular parental combinations that were used. Ways to assure good parental combinations have been discussed by Conkle (1969); the importance of using good parents is also emphasized by Miller and Thulin (1967b) in producing hybrid larch in New Zealand. The hybrid was superior to both the European and Japanese parents. The importance of parents in hybrid performance was similarly stressed by Dimpflmeier (1959), also for larch. Methods used to hybridize numerous species, including choice of parents, are outlined in one chapter of the book by Wright (1962).

Often the first crosses to produce hybrid exotic trees are made on park or arboretum trees or those on which the flowers are easy to reach. Because the number of the parental trees used in such crosses is limited and their variability may be restricted, the hybrid trees may be of low quality. Hybrids produced from arboreta usually are not the best for exotics and actually may give a distorted view of the potential of what otherwise might be a good hybrid. When assessing the potential of hybrids for exotics, it is absolutely essential to assure the good characteristics of their parents.

Although the hybrid usually has characteristics intermediate between its parents, occasionally the hybrid will have a desired characteristic of one of the parents and not show intermediacy. For example, the loblolly × shortleaf pine (*P. taeda* × *P. echinata*) hybrid is nearly resistant to fusiform rust, similar to the shortleaf parent, even though the cross is otherwise intermediate (Sluder, 1970). Sometimes hybrid crosses produce rare individuals that have characteristics outside the range of both parental species. Such individuals can be quite remarkable and have great potential value, especially when vegetative propagation can exploit the unusual and desirable genotypes.

Sometimes hybrids within exotic species or provenances exhibit what is called *hybrid vigor* or *heterosis* (Chiba, 1968), in which the hybrid is superior to both parents (Györfey, 1960); hybrid vigor is sometimes defined as the hybrid being superior to the mean of the two parents (Snyder, 1972). Usually heterosis is defined in terms of growth, but, technically, hybrid vigor can be shown in many different characteristics. For example, early flowering in eucalypt hybrids frequently occurs (Venkatesh and Sharma, 1976), so, technically, hybrid vigor is shown. Commonly, however, hybrid vigor usually is equated to volume, height growth, or general vigor. In this book we will usually refer to hybrid vigor in relation to size and growth traits, unless otherwise stated.

There is a difference of opinion about the extent and importance of hybrid vigor in forestry. Generally, hybrid vigor in forest trees is rare or not dramatic, and it usually is not present in meaningful amounts (Van Buijtenen, 1969). Others express the same view; Fowler (1978), for example, states that "heterosis or hybrid vigor in species and provenance hybrids is the exception rather than the rule." He explains this partially as being the result of crossing highly adapted parental species, which may produce hybrids less well adapted to the habitats in which the parents are growing. For pines, Little and Somes (1951) report little exceptional vigor in hybrids involving pitch pine, which is sometimes used as an exotic. In fact, however, hybrids with intermediate characteristics may be best for certain exotic environments.

There have been a number of reports of hybrid vigor occurring in the poplars and willows that are frequently used as exotics (Stout et al., 1927; Pauley, 1956; Schreiner, 1965; Chiba, 1968). Significant superior vigor in hybrids in species used for exotics has been reported in *Eucalyptus* (Chaperon, 1976; Venkatesh and Vakshasya, 1977; Wang, 1971), spruce (Hoffman and Kleinschmit, 1979), and larch intraspecific hybrids (Nilsson, 1963) (Fig. 3.9). In one recent example cited by Meskimen and Franklin (1984), hybrids with *Eucalyptus grandis* were superior to the pure species. The hybrids outperformed the pure *E. grandis* in growth, cold tolerance, and coppicing ability. Generally, however, hybrids have historically had more value as a source of new combinations of genes rather than for extra vigor, but this may change with more experience and wider crossing.

One must be very careful in assessing hybrid vigor since both age of hybrids and location where they are grown are important. Hybrids can express vigor at one stage of their development while showing none at other stages, or under certain environmental conditions and not under others (Johnson, 1955). Another problem in definition of hybrid vigor for exotics occurs when the hybrid is planted in a habitat where only it and one parent can survive and grow but the other parent may not grow well or even die. Such a situation occurs with the pitch × loblolly pine hybrid (Little and Trew, 1976); when grown on cold, poor sites, the hybrid pine does well and often surpasses the pitch pine, while the loblobby parent is killed or severely stunted by cold. Therefore, does the

Figure 3.9. One genera in which there appears to be considerable hybrid vigor is in *Larix*. Shown is a hybrid Dunkeld larch, a cross between Japanese larch and European larch. This hybrid produces a fast-growing, desirable tree.

pitch × loblolly pine have hybrid vigor? Based upon the definition we are following, it does since it is outperforming both parents.

Hybrids can either be developed by the forester or they can occur naturally; natural hybrids are particularly common in the eucalypts (Pryor, 1976) and pines of Mexico and the Caribbean (Boland, 1978). Both types of hybrids can be of importance in exotic forestry. Natural hybrids are a problem in provenance selection or individual tree selection in the donor country, since hybrids do not breed true when crossed but produce progeny with characteristics varying from one parent to the other. When hybrid seeds are included in the selection from wild stands, the resulting plantations are not uniform and hybrid individuals accidentally selected for land races produce variable progeny.

There have been several attempts to produce F_2 hybrids by crossing F_1 hybrid parents, as outlined by Nikles (1981) for *P. caribaea* × *P. elliottii* and Hyun (1976) for the *P. rigida* × *P. taeda* cross. This attempt is somewhat surprising because, generally, F_1 crosses produce nonuniform progeny that vary from one parent to the other with degrees of hybridization between. Nikles, in fact, recognizes that a very considerable amount of segregation is evident in the F_2 progeny; adverse results from crossing F_1s was also reported in *Eucalyptus* by Meskimen and Franklin (1984), who state that "hybrid progenies of F_1 mother trees displayed wide segregation and generally inferior performance except in coppice traits."

Natural hybrids can be very difficult to identify, especially when the parents are quite similar. The problems involved in identifying hybridity of *Casuarina* grown in Taiwan were discussed by Wang et al. (1984). Seven morphological traits were used. Much work has been done on how to recognize natural hybrids; each species is different. Occasionally, however, they are easier to distinguish because of their intermediacy between two differing species (Boland, 1978). The more intensively natural populations of forest trees are studied, the more hybrids that are found. But care needs to be taken; just because a tree differs considerably from its "type" species, it is not necessarily a hybrid. The most difficult job in working with hybrids is to delineate between hybrids and normal variants within a species. To add to the confusion, often the hybrids cross back to the parental species creating a group of backcross intergrading individuals, and it becomes nearly impossible to accurately determine as to whether the individuals are hybrids, backcrosses or species variants. The newly developed biochemical methods, such as the use of isozymes (Conkle and Adams, 1977), or the older methods using resinous substances (Mirov, 1958) often have been found to be most helpful in differentiating hybrids.

Hybrids quite frequently occur when exotics are brought together. This is common when the trees are grown in arboreta where species which never occur together in nature are grown together so that gene exchange is possible (Marien and Thibout, 1978). A classic for this involves *Eucalyptus* in the arboretum at Rio Claro, Brazil, from which numerous hybrids have arisen (Brune and Zobel, 1981).

Certain groups of species used as exotics hybridize freely. One of the most studied is the eucalypts (Kirkpatrick, 1971). Intensive studies of hybrids have been made within the genus *Eucalyptus* by researchers such as Pryor (1951, 1978b) and Clifford (1954). Certain species in this genus hybridize easily and the number of actual species in *Eucalyptus* varies greatly depending upon the individual taxonomist. Many so-called species may in fact be hybrids. As mentioned earlier, *Eucalyptus* hybrids are used operationally in Africa, Europe, and South America, especially when combined with vegetative propagation (Lacaze, 1978; Campinhos, 1980; Delwaulle, 1985).

Another major group of species in which hybridization in natural stands is of key importance is the pines in Mexico and Central America. It is common to identify one species at the bottom of a mountain that gradually intergrades up the mountain until it is called another species at the top. Some workers divide such groups of interrelated and intergrading species into *complexes* that contain one to several species which frequently hybridize. Many of these hybrids are used as exotics.

A third group of species commonly used as exotics that hybridize freely is comprised of members of the genus *Populus* (Einspahr and Joranson, 1960). When material is obtained to use as exotics, areas in which hybridization occurs give a rich choice of genetic types, but it is difficult to classify the trees strictly into species or provenances.

Producing hybrids artificially is sometimes done in exotics, but the effort is not widespread except in *Eucalyptus* and *Populus.* The major obstacle to widespread use of hybrids in exotic forestry is the difficulty of producing hybrid seed in quantity. In some instances, as in Korea, where labor is cheap, this has been partially overcome by control pollinating to produce the hybrid *Pinus rigida* × *P. taeda* by hand on a mass scale (Hyun, 1976). Attempts have been made to produce hybrids using supplemental mass pollination techniques for a number of species (Hadders, 1977; Bridgwater and Trew, 1981). This method distributes large quantities of pollen from one of the desired species to the receptive female structures of the other. Attempts to isolate large groups of flowers in tentlike structures and then to mass pollinate within this isolation zone generally have not been successful, although this method is sometimes used in *Alnus* and *Betula.*

One method used successfully to produce hybrid *Eucalyptus* in Florida and Brazil consists of establishing an orchard of one species within which individuals of another species are planted at wide spacing and from which hybrid seed will be collected (Campinhos, 1980; Dvorak, 1981b). A similar approach is used in Sweden to produce *Larix decidua* × *L. leptolepis* hybrids. The individuals from which seeds are collected must be isolated and relatively or completely self-incompatible. This method also works well for dioecious species used as exotics where interplanting compatible species that flower in synchrony has resulted in an easy production of large amounts of hybrid seed.

There is no point to listing the many hybrids that are used or may have use as exotics, but a sample is given in Table 3.3. As is evident from the table,

TABLE 3.3. Some Hybrids Between Species or Provenances Used in Exotic Forestry[a]

Cross	Author(s)	Location	Comments
Cupressus macrocarpa × *Chamaecyparis nootkatensis*	Jackson & Dallimore 1926	England	This generic cross has been named *Cupressus leylandi.* It is reported to have potential in operational forestry in several countries.
Pinus rigida × *P. taeda* *P. echinata* × *P. rigida*	Little & Somes 1951	United States	None of the hybrids tested showed exceptional vigor, but the pitch × loblolly has some value because of good survival. The trees are large limbed.
Eucalyptus camaldulensis × *E. viminalis*	Franclet 1957	France	Successful hybrids were produced. Methods to hybridize up to 12 m from the ground were described.
Larix hybrids	Nilsson 1959	Sweden	The quality of hybrids is closely related to the quality of the parents; hybrids grew better than the parent species.
Eucalyptus viminalis × *E. globulus*	Giordano 1960	Italy	There are many crosses, some used as exotics. The hybrid occurs naturally. This wide cross between Globulares

(*continued*)

TABLE 3.3. Continued

Cross	Author(s)	Location	Comments
			and Viminales has real potential for use in Italy.
Larix decidua × L. leptolepis	Miller & Thulin 1967b	New Zealand	Hybrid larch (L. eurolepis) is clearly superior to the parental species in both height and survival.
Larix decidua × L. leptolepis	Keiding 1968	Denmark	Good results were obtained from the hybrids (L. eurolepis), which grew 10 to 20% faster than the parents.
Liquidambar orientalis × L. styraciflua L. orientalis × L. formosana	Santamour 1972	United States	L. orientalis × L. formosana had inferior progeny. All crosses had good germination and gave good yields of hybrid seed. Only one tree of each species was involved.
Interprovenance crosses within Picea abies & Pinus sylvestris	Nilsson 1973	Sweden	There was superiority in interprovenance crosses in spruce, but none in pine. The natural European spruce grew best; the Swedish spruce was frost hardy.
Pinus griffithii × P. strobus	Zsuffa 1975b	Canada	Hybrid trees were intermediate and had moderately high heritabilities.
Eucalyptus spp.	Chaperon 1976	Congo	Several eucalypt hybrids have proven to be very good and are used on a large operational scale.
Pinus rigida × P. taeda	Hyun 1976	Korea	Millions of hybrids were produced that grow better and have better form than P. rigida and were hardier than P. taeda.
Eucalyptus camaldulensis × E. tereticornis	Venkatesh & Vakshasya 1977	India	The selfs were taller than the hybrids in the nursery, but the hybrids grew faster than either selfs or outcrosses in the field. Heterosis increased with age.
Crosses within Picea	Kleinschmit 1979a	Germany	Out of 1260 possible spruce hybrid combinations only 156 have been reported; some are of great potential value as exotics.
Eucalyptus grandis × E. urophylla	Campinhos 1980	Brazil	The hybrid performs extremely well. It has good growth, form, and disease resistance.
Pinus caribaea × P. elliottii	Nikles 1981	Australia	The hybrid is especially good on swamp sites to which neither parent is well adapted.
Sylvestres pines	Furukoshi & Sasaki 1982	Japan	28 interspecific hybrids were produced. All had viable seeds, but some produced only a few seeds.

TABLE 3.3. Continued

Cross	Author(s)	Location	Comments
Pinus radiata (× Guadalupe source)	Anon. 1983d	New Zealand	Alone, the Guadalupe source is not good, but when hybridized with regular *P. radiata* the trees are healthy, vigorous, with straight stems and intermediate wood density.
Eucalyptus grandis × *E. robusta* *E. grandis* × *E. camaldulensis*	Meskimen & Franklin 1984	United States	The mother trees in Florida had 14% hybrid progenies compared to 5% in seed from Australia. Hybrids from pure *E. grandis* mothers were good, but F_1 crosses had inferior performance.
Pinus caribaea × *P. elliottii*	Nikles 1984b	Australia	There was some nonuniformity, but the best F_2 crosses were as good as or better than the F_1 parents.
Populus species and hybrids	Khalil 1984	Canada	Rooting ability and growth show a strong inheritance pattern. Hybrids show heterosis in growth.
Eucalyptus hybrids	Delwaulle 1985	Congo	Over 600 hybrids of several kinds have been selected. Each is tested by at least 25 ramets. Clonal tests are rated as to tons of pulp/ha/yr and also include wood properties.
Pine hybrids	Van der Sijde & Roelofsen 1986	South Africa	Many pine hybrids, mostly *P. elliottii* × *P. caribaea,* are reported. Gains of up to 50% are expected from the *P. elliottii* × *P. caribaea* hybrid versus pure *P. elliottii.*

[a]Full references are given in the reference list.

most hybrids are in the pines, the eucalypts, the poplars, the larches, and the spruces. All of these are now being used to some extent in exotic plantations.

Hybrids have great potential value as exotics, since trees can be developed for specific environments, marginal environments, desired wood, or resistance to pests by proper selection of parents and crossing (Giordano, 1960; Diller and Clapper, 1969). They are particularly useful in "hybrid-habitats" as described by Nikles (1981); these are environments intermediate to those that are optimum for the parental species.

A great deal of confusion was caused by hybrids having been called species, as was extensively done in the eucalypts, poplars, some pines, and larches. Hybrids are not species; this concept was discussed by Zobel and Talbert (1984, pp. 364–365). There are several correct ways to name hybrids; the authors prefer a hybrid, as, for example, between radiata and knobcone pine, to be called *P. radiata* × *P. attenuata* rather than × *P. attenuradiata.*

3.4 THE LAND RACE CONCEPT

A land race can be defined as *"a population of individuals which has become adapted to a specific environment in which it has been planted."* The term is usually applied to exotic species where man has intensified the selection and chosen the trees most suitable for a given habitat and which also have the most desired characteristics. The concept of a land race is simple and of key importance when working with exotics and provenances planted outside their normal environment (Marsh, 1969; Pellate, 1969; Zobel and Talbert, 1984).

In exotics, the land race is usually developed by choosing the best trees of the best available provenances, letting the selected trees intermate, and using their seed, or propagules, in operational forest programs. This is a point of some disagreement. The authors prefer to choose and combine the best trees of the best several provenances within a species for a given area. We feel that the important thing is that the selected trees are well adapted to grow in the exotic environment. The major restriction is that the trees must flower in synchronization. Others, however, state that land races should only be selected from individual provenances and not be combined. For example, in FAO (1982), the editor notes: "In the case of exotics . . . the principle is that all the ortets represented in a seed orchard should generally be of the same provenance." We see no need for such a restriction if flowering time permits crossing among provenances.

Put simply, the land race is developed by planting the exotic trees in the new environment, letting nature sort them out according to their adaptability through natural selection, then choosing the best of the naturally selected trees and using them as a source of seed or propagules to replant the area. Normal plantation management with silvicultural thinnings also produces a land race. The group of best-adapted individuals with desirable growth and form are then collectively referred to as a *land race*. Land race selection can be done after a single generation, but the best results occur following several generations of growth and selection in the new environment.

Frequently, the most suitable individuals from indigenous stands are called land races, but this usage is less common. The end point is somewhat the same, but not altogether. For example, natural selection requires that a species or provenance which is to become predominant in an area have the ability to *grow* and to *reproduce*. Quite often the growth form or rate is not what the forester might desire even though the species or provenance may be well adapted to the site. It takes eons of selection to produce the best-adapted race in indigenous species because of the low selection intensity; furthermore, nature frequently does not select for characteristics desired by the forester. Such a population of trees is normally referred to as a provenance, or sometimes an ecotype, rather than a land race.

The ability to produce seeds or to reproduce otherwise is not necessary in an exotic land race; frequently it will not reproduce well, or even at all, in the new environment. A prime example is *Pinus caribaea*, which grows very well in the lowland tropics and is much desired by the forester but frequently will not produce seed in this environment (Gallegos, 1983). Under natural conditions a land race would not be formed, but through man's intervention, and producing seed elsewhere, a land race can be selected and the needed seed produced.

For our purposes, we will refer to land races as something developed by foresters for the desired adaptability, growth, form, and disease resistance in an exotic environment. Whether or not the land race that is chosen can reproduce naturally in the new environment is not vitally important.

It is now widely recognized that the development of land races can be *the easiest and best way of making quick and large genetic gains* in exotic forestry. There are numerous examples where land races have performed well above the level expected or hoped, and they frequently perform better than any newly imported sources of the species. For example, Owino (1977a) found that, for *P. patula* and *Cupressus lusitanica* in Kenya, the advanced "land race" selections were highly superior. For northwestern Europe, Edwards (1963) stated that great advances can be made when seed of exotic species can be collected from stands of plus trees growing in the exotic environment; distinctions between native and exotic species may then disappear. Keiding et al. (1984) found, for *Tectona grandis* and *Gmelina arborea,* that the local selections from earlier introductions grow well and are healthy and usually better than or equal to the average of recently introduced provenances. They state: " . . . local provenances after one or more generations in the new environment have adapted themselves." In New Zealand, Miller and Thulin (1967a) found that seed collected from local pine plantations compared favorably with the best provenances from natural stands. As mentioned by Burley (1976), seed sources already growing in the region (in Malawi) produced *Pinus elliottii* and *P. taeda* that was more productive for at least eight years than any of 24 and 30, respectively, introduced provenances.

Table 3.4 lists a few of the studies in which the land race concept has been observed in exotic forestry. In most, but not all, instances of the numerous species listed in the table, the local selections from the exotic plantations were better than the new provenances brought from the indigenous range of the exotic. This general finding was spelled out clearly by Owino (1977a), who determined that second- and third-generation land races were highly superior. However, oppositely, Mullin et al. (1981) found certain provenances of several eucalypt species that were better than selections from local plantations. This result will often occur when an inherently unsuitable provenance has been used initially, but even then it is remarkable how often the few outstanding individuals of a mediocre provenance will produce a desirable land race.

Frequently, the situation occurs when a political decision has been made that an exotic forestry program will be immediately initiated on a large scale. There often is no option but to act immediately, and a planting program will be initiated whether or not the forester feels it is a wise decision. If plantations of the desired species can be found in the area, seed for a land race should be

TABLE 3.4. Some Studies Showing Results of Land Race Development[a]

Species	Author(s)	Study Age (years)	Country	General Results
Exotic species	Edwards 1963	General	Northwest Europe	A great advance can be made when seed of exotic species can be collected from plus trees in their new home.
Pinus nigra	Miller & Thulin 1967a	9	New Zealand	The selections from local plantations were equal to the best provenances from natural stands.
Pinus radiata	Eccher 1969	Young	Italy	Italian seed sources were better than New Zealand provenances for survival and juvenile growth. There is optimism about developing land races even on environments greatly different from those optimum for the species.
Pinus patula	Denison 1973	5	South Africa	For growth characteristics, the South African seed source was superior because it was better adapted to the environment at the test locations.
Pseudotsuga taxifolia (menziesii)	Kleinschmit et al. 1974	3	Germany	Progenies from German stands show outstanding growth and low frost sensitivity.
Pinus sylvestris	Squillace et al. 1975	Several ages	Holland	Progenies from stands within Holland grew the fastest and had the least needle-cast damage.
Pinus patula *Cupressus lusitanica*	Owino 1977a	Mature	East Africa	Selections from second- and third-generation exotic plantations were far superior to the best provenances newly introduced from the natural range of the species.
Pinus contorta	Hahl 1978	8	Finland	All sources collected from Finnish plantations had the best growth along with those collected from latitudes 53.5 to 56.5°N.
Pinus caribaea	Hawkins et al. 1978	19	Australia	Progeny of local superior trees are much straighter, more windfirm, and have less fox-

Species	Author(s)	Study Age (years)	Country	General Results
				tails than from imported seed.
Eucalyptus grandis *E. saligna*	Roeder 1980b	4	South Africa	The Coff's Harbour source outperformed the locally selected seed orchard stock. The South African land race was better in stem form.
Eucalyptus (several species)	Mullin et al. 1981	9	Zimbabwe	In some cases, local breeding material is inferior to new imports.
Eucalpytus regnans	Wilcox 1982a	3	New Zealand	A New Zealand exotic source performed well compared to imported Australian sources.
Eucalyptus nitens	Anon. 1983b	8	South Africa	The local land race was as good as the best imported provenances and better than most. Luckily, the original provenance was the best.
Alnus glutinosa	Hall & Miller 1983	8	United States	Initial improvement of the species should be based upon land race development from existing provenance tests.
Pinus patula	Barnes & Mullin 1984	8	Zimbabwe	The Zimbabwe source was greatly superior in height growth and stem straightness. New provenances from Mexico were of no value for direct operational use.
Pinus caribaea	Eiseman & Nikles 1984	General	Australia	Introduction of improved material was successful; top-class families from local material were the same as top-class families from introduced material.
Pinus elliottii *P. taeda*	Ingram 1984	7	Malawi	In *P. elliottii*, the local race was not as good as imported ones, but the local *P. taeda* was very good throughout.
Acacia mangium	Liang 1984	General	Malaysia	Local seed, although derived from a narrow genetic base, is well adapted to local conditions and outperforms the

(*continued*)

TABLE 3.4. Continued

Species	Author(s)	Study Age (years)	Country	General Results
				new imports. It is the best to use.
Pinus merkusii	Mubita 1984	9	Zambia	A local source outperformed all other provenances; its height was 59% above the population mean and its diameter was as good as the best. Local sources were used for operational planting.
Pinus kesiya	Mullin et al. 1984	12	Zimbabwe	The local material ranked near the top in growth and best in form but was the lowest in wood density.
Gmelina arborea	Sim & Jones 1984	2	Malaysia	New populations developed from current stands were markedly better in tree form than new imports.
Pinus caribaea *P. oocarpa*	Thompson & Nelson 1984	14	Jamaica	Locally collected seed gave as good growth as the best provenances.

[a]Full references are shown in the reference list.

immediately selected even if the original seed source is not the best. At the same time, or as soon as possible, a series of species and provenance studies should be initiated (Burley and Nikles, 1972, 1973a, b; Nikles et al., 1978). These will provide the information and plant material necessary to develop a base for future selections for an improved land race.

Many exotic programs have been scrapped because planting was delayed because a suitable provenance was not available. Making operational plantings before proper information or proven plant materials are at hand will result in inefficiency; this is a penalty that must be absorbed to accommodate the political pressures and time needs. *Any* type of *crash program* is *inefficient;* this is especially true in exotic forestry. However, if one is faced with establishing a crash program because of needs and political considerations, drastic failures can be avoided when all the experience and common sense available are drawn upon. Then, as rapidly as possible, conditions should be set up so that a land race can be developed or selected from whatever plantations might be available.

3.4.1 Developing Land Races

When a species or provenance is introduced into a new (exotic) environment, it rarely is fully adapted to the new environment and sometimes is quite poorly adapted. As individuals of the exotic grow in the new environment, the most well adapted will survive and perform the best (Fig. 3.10). When the best trees are selected from these for use as a source of propagules for planting for the next generation, either through seed or vegetative propagation, the performance of the new forest will often be from moderately to much better than the stand from which the trees were chosen. This will depend upon the quality of the original trees, the selection intensity, population size, breadth of the genetic base, and the severity of the new environment. As previously mentioned, the developed land race, even from a moderately well-adapted source, may outperform any other provenance of the same species planted directly in the exotic environment, indicating that selection can be very effective within a broadly based, large, moderately well-adapted population.

Because of this potential, the first thing to look for when starting a large exotic forestry program is previously established plantations of the desired species. When such exist, occasional outstanding individuals may be found even though the plantations may overall be rather poor. Seed from these in-

Figure 3.10. Establishing tests from which land races can be developed is essential. The test plantation of CVRD in the Carajas region of the Amazon will be used to select an outstanding land race. Note the complete failure of some sources tested and the good growth of others.

dividuals can be used in operational plantings while seed orchards of the best land race parents are being established and further introductions and tests are being made.

If applied intensively, the land race approach will lead to the development of new strains of a species with great utility in the new environments. In the southern United States, for example, a cold-tolerant land race of eucalypt is being developed by planting the exotic *Eucalyptus viminalis,* selecting the best of the trees that survive the local freezing weather and bringing these together as a seed source to grow *Eucalyptus* in a region where it previously could not be grown operationally (Hunt and Zobel, 1978). (Note: since 1978, two "100-year freezes" occurred and severely damaged even members of the cold-hardy *E. viminalis.*)

As land races are developed in one region, they often will also be useful in other, similar regions (Nikles and Burley, 1977). For example, seed from the land race of *Eucalyptus grandis* developed in Zimbabwe from the Coff's Harbour, New South Wales, provenance grows much better in several parts of Brazil than when seed are imported directly from Coff's Harbour. A good example of the development of a land race is the apparent good adaptability of the greatly improved *P. caribaea* var. *hondurensis* developed in Queensland, Australia. The Queensland land race has performed very well in Fiji, New Caledonia, Vietnam, parts of Brazil, Zambia, and other countries (Nikles, 1979).

To be most successful, the following situations should occur when land races are used (the following is paraphrased from Zobel and Talbert, 1984):

1.   The original provenance must be reasonably well adapted to the environment in which it will be planted. If the provenance is too poorly adapted for the area, such as using a southern source of *Pinus contorta* in Sweden, an east-side (of the Cascades) source of *Pseudostuga menziesii* in Western Europe, or a high-elevation source of *Pinus oocarpa* in lowland Venezuela, there will not be enough good individuals in the plantations to form a suitable land race.

2.   The populations from which the land race trees will be selected must have a broad genetic base. Usually, several hundred parent trees should contribute seed to the plantation from which the land race selections are to be made. As is now being more commonly done, it is best to establish tests from individual mother-tree seed collections from which land race individuals will be chosen. When the best trees of the best families are selected for the land race, based on a broad base of unrelated individuals, the long-term use of the land race can be assured because relatedness will be avoided. Some foresters do not appreciate the fact that if outstanding, closely related individuals are brought together in a land race, growth of their progeny may be poor, seed nonviable, or seed will not even be produced as a result of the relatedness.

3.   The plantations from which selections for a land race will be made should be reasonably large, generally on the order of 400 h (1000 acres) or more. This is not always possible, but plantations that are too small will not have enough trees to give a reasonably high selection intensity or a broad enough genetic base to produce the best land races. Many small plantations used for initial land races are from very restricted genetic bases, so the land race will not perform well.

4.   Enough plus trees need to be selected as the basis of the land race. As few as 30 can be used for a short-term production seed orchard, but 300 to 400 or more will be needed for a long-term breeding program. When breeding for improvement of the land race, small populations will soon lead to troubles from related matings and will restrict advanced generation development. The selected land race individuals will form the basis for an ongoing breeding program, which should be supplemented by well-adapted individuals from outside sources. The latter should be used only following testing in the exotic environment involved (Fig. 3.11).

5.   The selection system used to choose parents for the land race must be well devised and rigorous enough to assure choosing only the most outstanding trees. As for all selection programs, gain is dependent upon a large selection differential, so selection must be very intensive.

Figure 3.11. Land race development is essential for success with exotics. This two-year-old test of *Pinus oocarpa* is part of the CAMCORE cooperative tests of Carton de Colombia. An outstanding seed source will be developed from this and other tests.

3.4.2 Competition and Stress

When trees are planted as exotics, they are almost always under stress because they are not well adapted to the new exotic environment. Trees under stress are more sensitive to the vagaries of weather and to pest attack. The only way to reduce the stress within an otherwise satisfactory provenance is to produce a land race that is better adapted. This is possible because natural populations have a great deal of variability. Although the population as a whole may not be well adapted, there will always be a few trees that are better suited to the new environment. It is these that are chosen to produce seed or propagules for the new land race.

When there is a problem with adaptation, some of the poorly adapted exotics may die immediately, but the rest will grow normally until they come under a period of severe stress caused by extreme environmental fluctuations or pest attack. At that time many trees will develop leader and branch dieback, or they may even die, and only those that are reasonably well adapted will survive and grow normally. These few best-adapted individuals are used to develop the land race with better adaptability and with the assumption that most are superior genotypes and that their morphological superiority is not due primarily to chance or favorable environments.

Throughout the world, wherever unimproved trees are planted on stress environments, such as the llanos (grasslands) of the Orinoco Basin in Colombia and Venezuela, dieback will occur in one form or another at some time in the life of the stand. Stress increases following drought or as the trees become larger and come into severe competition with one another for the available moisture and nutrients. Dieback is often a response to stress, and after the stress situation is alleviated the trees that have not died will recover to some extent. When stressed again, the trees will go through the same cycle; the amount of deformity and death will increase with each cycle, unless modified by silvicultural practices such as thinning, which reduces the stress for moisture or nutrients and removes the poorly adapted individuals.

Thinning is one way of reducing stress damage in exotic plantations. The timing of when thinning should be done is critical and if delayed too long, the stressed trees may never fully recover. The ability to recover well from stress varies widely with species; for example, *Pinus taeda* has a great potential to recover, while *P. elliottii* does not. Some species, such as several of the eucalypts, are extremely sensitive and never do recover to grow normally following a period of severe stress. To be safe, the rule should be never to let exotics come under strong stress from competition. Another essential is, immediately after plantation establishment, to control competition from other vegetation that uses scarce resources such as water. This can be done using intensive site preparation before planting by mechanical methods such as disk harrows, by the use of herbicides, or by hand.

Most useful for exotics is to develop fast-growing trees that quickly suppress the grass, weeds, and brush, so they "capture" the site early, kill out the competition, and thus reduce stress (Nikles, 1970). After the trees begin to compete seriously among themselves, thinning must be done to reduce the stress. An objective when working with exotics is to develop a land race that grows better under stress and competition than does the original introduction, because no matter how good the forest management is, unusual environmental conditions will occasionally cause stress.

Stress is a natural part of silviculture. For example, it is necessary to "harden off" and stress seedlings in the nursery to make them survive and grow better when field planted. Such nursery stressing must be done, but it must be done carefully. One of the most serious errors made in exotic forestry is to overstress the seedlings in a nursery; this is especially true for the eucalypts. Although they may survive better, they do not grow normally later. The authors have observed this error commonly in pines and eucalypts in the tropics, where hardening off has been stopped just short of seedling death. In fact, a lack of appreciation of the long-range adverse effects of severe stress, either in the nursery or in the plantation, is one of the most serious professional errors of many foresters.

3.4.3 How Much Wood Can an Area Produce?

Although the subject of the productivity of forested areas is most appropriate in a silviculture, silvics, or physiology book, it is important to consider it briefly here as an indication of how the forester can grow the best exotics. It is also discussed in Chapter 6.

Although it is not strictly true, for general consideration it is realistic to consider that a given area of land (an acre or hectare) is essentially capable of producing only a given amount of biomass. How, when, and in what form this biomass will be produced depends upon the desires and silvicultural skills of the forester. For example, if a quick fulfillment of the productive potential of an area is desired, trees can be planted in a very close spacing. Numerous tests have shown that the cubic volume potential of an area is obtained quicker at closer spacings. However, the drawback to this approach, including exotic forest trees, is that the costs of establishing many trees per unit area are very high and the size of trees harvested will be very small. Additionally, the costs of harvest will be large while bark percentage is high and wood quality is often reduced. With very few exceptions, the option of very high initial stocking with very early harvest has not been accepted by operational foresters as being the best way to obtain the potential productivity from forest land. If a proper thinning regime is followed, then high initial stocking may be satisfactory.

Thus, the problem of the forester becomes one of deciding how much less volume and how much more time should be taken to optimize monetary returns from the plantation, which is always different from optimizing the biological productive potential of the area. Different methods to control costs and returns are available; for example, if large trees are desired, one option is to plant at wide spacings, not thin, and then make a final harvest of large trees. This has definite advantages because the costs of stand establishment will be low and there is no need to harvest small stems as thinnings, but it has the major disadvantage that the land is partially unproductive for a part of the rotation because of understocking. It also has the disadvantage that, although the trees may be large, they may be rough with large limbs because of free growth (lack of competition) early in the life of the stand. This option of wide spacing becomes increasingly feasible as better genetic stock is available, assuring the desired number of prime trees per hectare at time of harvest. A suitable pruning regime can yield the same results.

Another option is to plant at a closer spacing and thin at the proper time. This has the advantage of fuller utilization of the site and the capturing of what would be mortality in the trees removed in thinning. It also results in better self-pruning plus an earlier control of weed competition, thereby reducing the number of times this must be done mechanically or with chemicals. It has the major disadvantage of requiring the removal of many small, low-quality trees with a high proportion of juvenile wood (Zobel and Kellison, 1984) at a relatively high cost and sometimes with considerable damage to the residual stand, unless the greatest care is used.

The decision of how to handle the stands to best utilize the productive potential of the forestland is a major one for the forester growing exotics. Of course, the product desired has a heavy bearing on the forester's judgment of what is best to do. The decision is especially critical for most exotics when sites are frequently poor because of low moisture content, nutrient deficiency, or other causes. Thinning is a very crucial operation that must be done just at the right time; frequently there is only a two- or three-year correct time-frame. Too often—we will say commonly—thinning is done too late or too lightly. Sometimes it is not done at all, resulting in stagnated stands that essentially cease to grow or grow "negatively," that is, more wood is lost through tree mortality than is produced by the residual trees.

3.5 GENOTYPE × ENVIRONMENT INTERACTION

A most important concept is that sometimes individual trees will respond differentially relative to each other in different environments (Barnes et al., 1982). This is called *genotype × environment interaction* (GEI), which means that the relative performance of clones, families, provenances, or species differs relative to others when grown in different environments. This may involve an actual change in rank, which is the most important type of interaction, or may only involve a change in productivity from one environment to the other, with no change in rank (Fig. 3.12). According to Shelbourne (1972), GEI is very important in developing a tree improvement program. He states that GEI is usually small, but where it is important it is more often associated with edaphic than with climatic factors. Shelbourne goes on to say: "The identification of

Figure 3.12. Genotype × environment interaction is sometimes so evident that there is a change in ranking in different environments as shown by families 3 and 2. At other times there are smaller differences, such as between families 1 and 3, but no change in ranking. This lesser type of GEI may or may not be important, depending on the magnitude of the difference.

highly productive, well adapted, stable provenances for base populations is—an important first step in tree improvement.'' The need to alter breeding strategies to use GEI with fast-growing trees was covered by Barnes (1984).

Genotype × environment interaction has been most studied in provenances of exotics (El-Lakany, 1983; Lindgren, 1984; Van Wyk and Falkenhagen, 1984) but is also prevalent in family or clonal performance, where it is not unusual to find the winner in one site only moderately good, or even mediocre, in a different environment. Oppositely, as Nikles et al. (1977) found, some families always ranked in the top third for each of 11 sites where *Pinus caribaea* var. *hondurensis* was planted in Queensland, Australia, and GEI was not important because ranking was more stable. Trees from the clone bank from selected parents were generally superior. Van Wyk and Falkenhagen (1984) reported that *Pinus patula* and *P. kesiya* were relatively stable for growth, but branch size showed large GEI effects and bole straightness had no GEI component. In Indonesia, Long and Dykstra (1983) found site × genotype interactions were negligible for growth of *P. caribaea*.

Although it is generally referred to in broad general terms, GEI is often quite different for different characteristics within the same group of plants. Thus, for six-year-old Douglas-fir, Lambeth et al. (1982) found rather strong genotype × environment interactions for height while ranking for total dry weights was relatively the same from one environment to the next, showing little interaction. GEI is most pronounced for growth characteristics but often is less pronounced for tree morphological characteristics or for wood density unless the environments are drastically different; then very large GEI interactions may occur.

In a study of GEI by provenances of nine *Pinus caribaea* provenances in five locations, some provenances showed little GEI while others were very reactive to differing sites (Liegel, 1984a). In *Eucalyptus grandis* in Florida, Rockwood and Geary (1982) found that progeny performance relative to biomass yields was stable on two very different soils. Similarly, *Eucalyptus camaldulensis* has exhibited very stable provenances in wood quality when grown in France (Sesbou, 1981). In South Africa, Darrow (1986) found a moderate GEI interaction for *E. grandis*. Although affected by extremes, wood properties tend to show less genotype × environment interactions than do growth characteristics.

Many large genetic differences have been found for many species among trees originating in different parts of a species range, but a source that grows well at one location will not necessarily grow well at another. However, there are exceptions; for example, Wright (1970) made studies on *Pinus resinosa* that have shown only small variations when grown in several different environments. Northern white cedar (*Thuja occidentalis*) also appears to follow the same pattern of having little provenance variation. In India, *P. caribaea* is also reported to show little interaction (Tavitayga, 1984); similar noninteraction in *P. caribaea* was reported for Indonesia (Long and Dykstra, 1983). Yet in Zimbabwe, Mullin et al. (1983b) found that "there was significant provenance × locality interaction in all traits but stem form."

When present, genotype × environment interaction has been a great source of concern to all plant breeders as it strongly influences development of strains for operational planting. Its importance was evidenced by a special conference on genotype × environment interaction by the Nordic Group of Forest Tree Breeders (1984). The forester working with exotics is faced with similar choices relative to GEI. Generally, the decision has been to develop trees that are adaptable on a series of different environments, rather than excelling on just one (Zobel and Talbert, 1984). This trend was emphasized by Burley et al. (1984) in their discussion of multipurpose trees. An exception to the broad-adaptability approach is where extreme environments or serious pests occur and it is sometimes necessary to develop trees especially for the particular adverse situation. In general, the GEI reversals in ranking take place at the environmental extremes, as Gibson et al. (1983) found for *Pinus caribaea*. Similarly, *P. oocarpa* had some provenances with little interaction, but a number showed differential performance on the three sites tested (Mullin, 1984).

Genotype × environment interaction is of interest for individual genotypes, clones, or families and is of equal importance for provenances used in exotic forestry. A 1984 paper by Matheson and Raymond (1984a) covered provenance × environment interaction, its detection and importance in exotic forestry. The authors emphasized that where the genetic resources of a species are still being explored, it is essential to discriminate between stable and sporadic high-yielding provenances and to assess the real importance of GEI. They summarize as follows: " . . . in general, provenance × environment interactions are often statistically significant but rarely have a great effect on the gains made from provenances." But they concede that occasionally provenances are found that perform well in many environments and would be the ones to grow widely.

The subject of provenance × environment interaction was well covered by Gibson (1982) for *Pinus caribaea*. Fifteen trials of the International Provenance Test were chosen and assessed on the basis of 10 traits. Growth and volume traits showed significant GEI. Characteristics such as bark percentage and branch number showed little interaction; this was also true for stem form. Cone production had a strong GEI. Often provenances showed little differences over sites, even though there were large provenance differences within sites.

Another example was reported by Bird (1984). He showed that *Pinus caribaea* and *P. oocarpa* in Costa Rica had no significant provenance × environment interaction for any of the tree traits he studied. A similar result for *P. caribaea* was reported by Eisemann and Nikles (1984); they found in Australia that interactions were limited and relative performance was generally consistent across sites. Brigden et al. (1984) showed little differences in rank among *P. oocarpa* grown in Australia; this is similar to the report by Nikles and Newton (1984). Mullin et al. (1984) also found negligible site × provenance interaction.

Lack of GEI was evident for *P. elliottii* in Malawi, where the order of ranking by height and basal area was very similar on all 11 sites Ingram (1984) assessed. This result (little interaction) was also reported by Brigden and Williams (1984) in 5.5-year-old *P. caribaea* var. *hondurensis* tests on two sites. Haines and Tozer (1984) found a good correlation ($r = 0.73$) between two different sites for *P. oocarpa* grown in Australia; in South Africa, Van der Sijde (1983) found good correlation, and provenance × site interactions were small in *P. oocarpa*. On *P. caribaea,* Falkenhagen (1979) reported no significant provenance by test site interaction. In Scots pine, Squillace et al. (1975) reported that genotype × planting site interaction in Holland was not significant.

In contrast, GEI is sometimes very important; genotypes may have very little stability, as reported for *Pinus caribaea* in Australia by Eisemann et al. (1984). They found definite provenance × site interaction for growth. Most of the interaction occurred at the extremes of the latitudinal range, a common observation. They also found the correlation of relative provenance performance between trials to be 0.5 for *P. kesiya.* A good example of the interaction effect at the provenance level was shown for loblolly pine by Fuentes (1972), who collected seeds from both wet and dry sites and backplanted the trees in both sites. He found a strong interaction for both tree diameter and height between planting site and seed source.

In his work with *Picea sitchensis,* Burley (1966) found that "there is broad interaction of genotype with environment that should be evaluated before planting the species at any given site." Severe clone × site interactions were reported by Burdon (1971) because of the ability of certain clones to tolerate a low soil phosphate status. GEI may be modest, as reported by Moura (1984) for *Eucalyptus camaldulensis*. He found GEI to be present when the species was placed on many differing sites, but it contributed only one-third as much to the total variance as did provenance. Further, almost all the GEI in Moura's study resulted from one provenance that was superior on the poorest sites but ranked low on the best sites. Brune (1983) reported a significant GEI for most characteristics for *E. grandis* grown in two locations in Brazil.

Sometimes GEI is very low, as Lindgren et al. (1976) found for *Pinus contorta* in Sweden. Similarly, rather limited GEI was evident for *Pinus sylvestris* when grown for Christmas trees in the northeastern United States. In their study of teak and *Gmelina*, Keiding et al. (1984) feel that interactions are important, but if larger tests are made, stable provenances may be found.

Most often the interaction with provenances and environment involves growth, but sometimes, as Barnes and Mullin (1984) report for *Pinus patula* in Zimbabwe, some genotype × environment interaction occurred for stem straightness (along with height), but it was not large.

Considerable error and confusion occur in an exotic testing program when provenances respond differently to differing environments. It is a complicating factor in growing exotics that must be recognized, adjusted for, and used. A species' ability to grow especially well in a specific environment can be of great benefit when maximum gains are desired in that particular environment, but the interaction can be a formidable barrier when broadly adapted provenances suited to several different environments are sought.

The *only* way to assess the provenance × site interaction effect is to test in more than one environment; when tests are established in one location, no interaction can occur, so it cannot be detected. Different environments may consist of different locations, different years, or different site preparation or management treatments. Environments can be macroenvironmental factors such as temperature or rainfall patterns, physiographic differences, or differing soils. Generally, the experience of the forester is the best way to differentiate environments. No matter how well environments are delimited, unpredictable environmental factors such as large year-to-year climatic changes can cause varied results. Foresters testing exotics are thus often faced with a large environmental variation that might cause an interaction no matter how well the normal environmental fluctuations have been assessed.

Generally, the desire is to select for provenances that perform well and show little interaction over a wide variety of environmental conditions. For example, Wray and Promnitz (1976) found that 7 *Populus* clones out of the 25 tested produced greater volume irrespective of environment. These consistent producers were recommended for operational use. This approach has received much attention from foresters in recent years, and several different statistics used to estimate general adaptability (stability) have been developed (Finlay and Wilkinson, 1963; Eberhardt and Russell, 1966) and used in exotic forestry programs. For example, Morgenstern and Teich (1969) used genotypic stability parameters in an investigation of genotype × environment interaction of Jack pine provenances. A series of papers by Owino and colleagues (Owino, 1975, 1977b; Owino and Zobel, 1977) dealt with stability in *Pinus taeda* and the potential to find families well adapted to many environments. These extensive studies again indicated that some families are stable (i.e., perform relatively equally in diverse environments) and others are relatively good on some sites and poor on others.

When GEI is ignored, large production losses in exotic forestry will result. Losses may be either from death or from reduced growth or quality. The former is easily recognized, but it takes close observation to assess the importance of the latter. Interaction is most prevalent for growth characteristics, but occasionally quality characteristics can be more interactive than growth traits.

Although the emphasis on genotype × environment interaction is usually concentrated on families, individuals, and provenances, it can also be applied to species. For example, many examples of the effect of interaction resulting in loss of growth and quality for species and provenances have been cited by Binet (1963) and King (1965).

Much effort in exotic forestry is required in the determination of gross genotype × environment interactions. Results indicate that some species, such as *Pinus elliotti* and *P. radiata,* have wide adaptability. These have few provenances but show plasticity and grow well in differing environmental conditions. Other species that have many provenances are very variable but have low plasticity within provenances and thus require specific environmental conditions to grow well (Suassuna, 1977). *Pinus taeda, P. oocarpa,* and *Pseudotsuga menziesii* fit the category of species with many differing provenances but little "within-provenance" plasticity.

Determination of the environmental conditions to which a provenance is adapted is the first essential step if an exotic forestry program is to be successful. However, the identification of an adapted provenance does not completely solve the problem, because there is always the danger of "off-site" planting as an exotic forestry program is expanded to include different sites. It is absolutely necessary to assess the adaptability and possible interaction of any species, provenance, or land race for the different environments in which they may be grown, be they in space or time.

There is no general rule about which species, sources, or families will show GEI for which characteristics. Sources that do consistently well on differing environments are most beneficial for exotic forestry, as reported for *Pinus radiata,* which had a group of stable, high-yielding genotypes in Australia (Eldridge, 1974). Also, for Japanese larch, Farnsworth et al. (1972) found that some sources grew relatively slowly in one area and rapidly in another. It was not possible to predict when interactions would occur. The use of GEI was well expressed by Goddard (1977):

GE interaction can be dealt with in breeding programs by (1) utilizing stable genetic lines of good mean value which do not contribute strongly to GE interaction and eliminating the . . . lines that interact most or (2) by taking advantage of GE interactions by developing two or more breeding programs for specific adaptation to two or more identifiable environments.

Despite the generally bad connotation about genotype × environment interaction, it can also be used to advantage for special or unusual conditions with careful selection and testing. As pointed out by Kurinobu (1984) for Japanese larch (*Larix leptolepis*), even though the genotype × environment interactions were large for all 12 traits assessed, gains were increased by using knowledge of GEI.

A special warning is needed about the use of GEI: it refers *only* to change in relative positioning or ranking. When a species, source, or family grows well on one site and poorly on another, this is not genotype × environment interaction; it is only a response to differing environments. To assess GEI, there must be at least two biological entities (such as families) and at least two environments involved. Genotype × environment interaction only occurs when the performances of the entities differ relative to one another when grown in different environments. The most extreme form of GEI is when the biological entities change ranking in the different environments, but this is not the usual case.

4

LIMITATIONS TO PRODUCTION IN AND UNUSUAL PROBLEMS WITH EXOTIC FORESTS

4.1 GENERAL CONCEPTS

Working with exotics can be difficult and sometimes actually dangerous from a production standpoint. In general, the limitations to production of desired wood can be broadly classified as environmental difficulties and pest attacks; these can be modified or made worse by genotype × environmental interactions that affect growth and wood properties as described in Chapter 3. Although a book could be written on the limitations to production in exotics, this chapter will cover only briefly the mass of information available.

Many persons have described the problems related to growing exotics; for example, Sedjo (1983) suggests that problems in exotic forestry that must be avoided are site degradation, pests, and diseases. He relates these to the two most important exotic plantation genera (*Eucalyptus* and *Pinus*) now being used. It was the opinion of McNabb et al. (1980) that the drastic modifications of the environment that accompany short-rotation tree crops used in exotic forestry drastically affect the interaction of host and parasite, resulting in damage to forest trees. This concept was also stressed by Shea (1971), who concluded that diseases and insects will become more destructive with monoculture planting. However, this concept is not accepted by Burdon (1982) and many others.

The layman usually hears about the wonders of growing exotics but not so much about their problems and frequent failures. Visits to areas where exotics are grown are usually channeled through the best and most successful plantations, and the observer often ends up with an enthusiasm about growing exotics that is totally unrealistic. In this chapter we will show the other side of the situation and, as realistically as possible, discuss some of the difficulties related to exotic forestry. We are not emphasizing "gloom and doom" about growing exotic forests (far from it, because exotics have a tremendous potential), but it is important for those working with exotics to realize that there are limitations involved and that there have been many more failures than successes.

One frequently hears of, and occasionally sees, figures describing fantastic production from exotic plantations. Because of good growth patterns, good genetic stock, favorable weather, lack of pests, and excellent forest management, it is sometimes possible to obtain very high wood production when using exotics, as, for example, has been obtained by Aracruz Florestal, in Espirito Santo, Brazil (Campinhos, 1980) (Fig. 4.1). In just a few years, productivity of *Eucalyptus* has been increased from 33 to 70 m³/ha/yr, on a 6- to 7-year rotation, as described by Brandão (1984). Now available, and currently being planted on a large scale, are clones that are producing over 100 m³/ha/yr. Such a great increase in growth over such a short time is fantastic but far from standard for all exotics. More common is production from 15 to 30 m³/ha/yr.

Exotic trees are subject to the same pests and growth limitations common to other planted forests and will respond or fail for the same reasons. They are subject to the law of limiting factors in which growth increases are restricted by the factor that is in short supply. There is frequently an interaction

Figure 4.1. Under ideal conditions, the growth rate of exotics can be very rapid, as shown by this five-year-old plantation on the lands of Aracruz Florestal in Espirito Santo, Brazil. The trees are over 30 m tall.

among factors that causes one to be limiting because another is in short supply or in excess; this is common for soil characteristics. For example, extra-high or -low pH makes certain chemicals in the soil inaccessible to the trees, even though a plentiful amount of the desired chemical may be present in the soil.

There are many types of limiting factors. One of major importance is the lack of genetic potential of a geographic source, or individual tree, to produce wood according to the potential of the site. Frequently, factors of the environment, such as excess or lack of soil moisture, nutrient lack or excess, soil structure or texture, cold and heat, or other factors, cause limitations in growth or wood quality.

Foresters working with exotics must soon determine the limiting factors, be they environmental, genetic, or pests. These may be evident immediately, such as cold or drought, but other limiting factors may not become evident for years. An example is a marginal soil pH in which the tree survives for a number of years but is so stressed it eventually dies back or succumbs either to the limiting factor of improper soil acidity or to pests that attack the weakened plant. As stressed by many authors, and especially by Zobel and Talbert (1984), it is usually not the average environmental condition that causes limitations in growth or the demise of the exotic, but the occasional extreme or sequence of extremes that results in a loss of productivity. For example, the extremely cold winters of 1984–1985 killed many of the French and southern United States plantations of *Eucalyptus*. The important aspect of environmental extremes was covered in Chapter 3, dealing with stress and the development of land races.

There are many kinds of enemies of exotic forests, including diseases, insects, environmental problems, and miscellaneous. Miscellaneous includes such factors as animals, parasites, and man. Some problems encountered in growing exotics are caused by man; air pollution and acid rain are examples. One of the worst is degradation of the site from man's activities; these and a partial approach to solve them were covered by Gallegos et al. (1982).

Despite the many specific causes of trouble, difficulties with exotics can be categorized into four general reaction types. These were discussed in detail by Zobel and Talbert (1984) and are summarized and paraphrased as follows:

1. *Immediate failure of the plantation.* Severe damage or death of plantations is obvious. Although many complete failures occur, one rarely hears about them because such negative results usually are not published.

2. *Delayed failure* is more common and can occur in several forms:

(a) Initially there is good survival and growth, but the trees do not develop into a useful forest. This occurs when high-elevation or high-latitude sources are planted at low elevations or low latitudes or when trees from Mediterranean or maritime climates are planted in a continental climate. Delayed failure causes severe loss, but the mistake is often recognized early enough to stop continued long-term planting of the wrong source.

(b)   There is good survival and growth rate but the wood is not suitable (Fig. 4.2). Many examples exist of exotics producing poor wood, especially when temperate species are planted in tropical or subtropical climates. A serious error is to plant large plantations before the quality of the wood that will be produced has been determined.

(c)   The exotic trees initially have good survival and growth but are later attacked by pests or damaged by adverse environmental conditions. This loss is extensive and long-term and is a frequent cause of failure of exotic plantations.

3.   The exotics have a *continued substandard performance,* resulting in low production and poor quality. This problem causes the greatest losses when species or provenances are planted off site. The inferior production can approach 50% of the site potential; it is subtle and cannot be assessed without a comparison with the suitable sources and the best species. The forester is often quite unaware of the poor performance of the exotic, since there is nothing to compare with the planted trees. When this kind of error is made, inferior sources may be used on a large scale in exotic plantations.

4.   *Growth is unsatisfactory due to a shortage or absence of suitable mycorrhizae.* This has been a major problem with many exotic plantings, especially in the tropics, but the importance of mycorrhizae is now becoming gen-

Figure 4.2. Good growth and form of an exotic tree is not enough—it must also have good wood. Some species lika *Pinus caribaea* frequently have their wood changed by the exotic environment, as is shown by this beautiful plantation, which has extra-low wood density. (Photo courtesy of John Wiley & Sons.)

erally recognized. The soils in the exotic environment often are marginal for survival and growth of the proper mycorrhizal fungi.

The objective here is not to go into great detail relative to tree growth and limitations with environmental, pest, and genetic characteristics but to alert those working with exotics that the potential of exotics is often limited by these factors. In many ways, growing exotics requires more skill than growing indigenous species because of the marginal qualities of many sites and climates where exotics are grown, which in turn imposes massive limiting factors on the productive potential of exotic plantations.

The most common error in growing exotics is to make a decision too early about the growth potential and quality of exotics. Frequently, decisions are made after only a few years. Despite the criticisms of many researchers, the senior author discounts the early results when an exotic is tested by 30% for long-term projections, because it is almost inevitable that some pest or adverse condition will reduce the initial optimistic growth assessments.

When dealing with factors that are adverse to exotic forests, a term often used is *resistance. As pointed out by Zobel and Talbert (1984), true resistance is rare; tolerance* is the more realistic and useful term. It indicates that the trees may be affected by an adverse factor and still grow and retain a degree of economic worth. Damage to exotic plantations appears to be becoming more frequent and severe. This is partially the result of closer observation by the forester as well as greater concern about intensive forest management of exotics. Under this situation, problems that were formerly overlooked or considered to be minor suddenly become important.

Sometimes the greater incidence of problems when growing exotics results from more intensive forest management or from the establishment of trees with restricted genotypes over large contiguous areas. Although this concern is sometimes overemphasized, it is important. Large plantings of a single species do not present a serious hazard or loss unless the genotypes used are so uniform that a true monoculture results. This danger was emphasized by Heybroek (1980), who showed the advantages of mixing genotypes to discourage damage. The mixing of genotypes should be done consciously but can only be effective after a good knowledge has been obtained about both the host tree and the factor doing the damage. There is a special danger of damage when vegetative propagules of restricted genetic background are used for operational planting. Vegetative propagation in itself is not hazardous if a broad enough genetic base is assured through use of several different genotypes.

As mentioned earlier, there is *always* a trade-off between *gain* and *risk* when growing exotics. This is especially evident when pests or adverse environments are involved. Decisions must be made about obtaining greater gain from the use of better exotics with more intensive management. Only when tolerant strains of trees are used can exotic forestry come close to optimal production of desired products. Full gains from tolerant trees can only occur if forest management is synchronized with control of the damaging factors. This type of activity is particularly critical for the success of exotic forestry.

4.2 SOIL LIMITATIONS TO THE SUCCESSFUL GROWTH OF EXOTICS

Edaphic, or soil, problems can be a major source of difficulty when growing exotics. Although the following sections cover specific soils aspects, the problem is not at all simple since each characteristic interacts with the other. Sometimes the failure of an exotic occurs, even when all environmental and soil factors seem to be satisfactory. This may result from obscure interactions among pH, nutrients, and soil types. Such interactions are most difficult to assess when they result in an exotic not growing well or even not surviving. All soil properties also interact with the climate, and often it is a given weather pattern in combination with soil deficiencies that causes problems in growing exotics.

The importance of soils when exotics are grown was covered by Mew (1981), who developed plans for obtaining and using soil information to better grow exotic forest plantations. He emphasized this need because exotic forests are mainly planted on soils that are marginal and considered to be of little value for agriculture. One action too rarely taken before exotics are planted is to get a good soil-type map. It need not be complex, fancy, or costly, but it is essential if an exotic forestry program is to be totally successful.

The influence of the exotic on the soil is of special concern and will be covered in Chapter 10. One example is the study of Lundmark et al. (1982) in which the soils under *Pinus contorta* and *P. sylvestris* plantations were compared. It was found that there was a larger needle fall with a higher nitrogen content in stands of *P. contorta* compared to *P. sylvestris*. The litter broke down more rapidly for *P. sylvestris* and the pH was a little higher under a *P. contorta* stand. The problem of declining productivity with successive rotations is dealt with in several places in this book. As Evans (1983) states: "There is no evidence yet of declining productivity with successive rotations in tropical plantations." Yet he warns that only limited data are available and describes the great need for well-established long-term studies.

4.2.1 The Problem of Soil Acidity

Although all soil factors are of importance in determining the utility of exotics, one that often is especially restricting is the acidity of the soil, or the soil pH. Soils on which exotic forests are planted vary greatly, from highly acid, with a pH of 4.0 or less, to very basic, with a pH of 8.0 or more. Some species are very restricted in their tolerance to pH of the soil and are quite incapable of growing on soils with the wrong pH. Planting on soils with an unsuitable pH has resulted in the failure of large plantation programs; one prime example is the planting of tropical pines on high-pH soils. Although most tropical pine species will survive and grow at pHs ranging from 4.5 to 6.5, many will not survive when the pH is outside these limits.

Some species are very tolerant of high pH; for example, red ceiba (*Bombacopsis quinata*) grows well at a pH of over 7.0 and seems to grow normally when the pH is over 8.5. Most hardwoods will not tolerate a low pH and conifers usually do not grow well on high-pH soils. As usual, there are some exceptions to this general rule. The ability to tolerate different pHs varies. There are numerous direct and indirect studies in which trees, sources, or species have been found that are especially adapted to acid or basic soils. For example, Lacaze (1963) tested the ability of several species of *Eucalyptus* to grow in basic and acid soils. In pine, there are species such as *P. serotina* that grow well in soils with a pH below 4.0. There are also indications that certain families of *P. taeda* will grow satisfactorily at this low pH, although the species in general does much better at considerably higher pH values (Williams and Bridgwater, 1981).

It is fair to state that the most common cause of failures in establishing exotics (either death or poor growth), apart from using the wrong source of seed, results from planting a species, or provenance, on soils with an unsuitable pH. There can be no question that *the first step in an exotic forestry program is to determine whether a species,* or a source within a species, *can survive and grow well at the soil pH existing where the exotic will be planted.* It is amazing how often this fundamental step is overlooked.

4.2.2 Soil Nutrients

Although the importance of the effect of soil pH on the growth and survival of exotics is not well enough understood, considerably more information is available about the deficiencies or excesses of certain chemical properties in the soil. Such information is especially needed because of the heavy nutrient use by exotics that grow with great vigor in the absence of pests. The very fast growth is likely to deplete soil nutrients more rapidly than in the case of slower-growing forests. One example of the limitation of the use of an exotic is the deficiency of phosphorus and nitrogen for *Cupressus lusitanica* in Colombia. On poor sites, growth increased from 4 to 12 m^3/ha/yr when fertilized; on medium sites the increase was from 10 to 18 m^3/ha/yr (Anon., 1972).

The ability of different species, or individuals within species, to tolerate chemical shortages or excesses are well known and well documented; one example concerns trees that will grow with little boron (Zobel and Talbert, 1984) (Fig. 4.3). McCormick and Steiner (1978) found that the poplars and some eucalypts are particularly sensitive to high aluminum content of the soil. Some species have the ability to take up nutrients from very diverse kinds of soils. For example, Oppenheimer and Halfon-Meiri (1959) obtained similar calcium, potassium, magnesium, and phosphorous contents in the leaves and needles of oak and pine grown under extremely varying soil conditions.

Figure 4.3. Occasionally trees are found to be resistant to serious soil deficiencies, such as the *Pinus radiata* growing in boron-deficient soils in Chile. It is often possible to develop land races tolerant to nutrient deficiencies. (Photo courtesy of John Wiley & Sons.)

Nitrogen is quite commonly deficient in areas where exotics are grown. Particularly troublesome in the subtropics and tropics are phosphorus and boron deficiency and aluminum excess, which causes toxicity. The typical diebacks caused by these deficiencies or excesses tend to intergrade and it becomes difficult to separate them.

In New Zealand, Ballard (1978) reported the first commercial use of phosphate fertilizers for radiata pine in the mid-1960s. As of that time, 6000 ha of newly established plantations were fertilized with phosphorus each year. Boron and sulfur deficiency symptoms in *Pinus radiata* were described by Gentle (1970). Boron is used to fertilize radiata pine on specific sites in New Zealand (Ballard, 1978). Windsor et al. (1970) found differences in tolerances to sulfur and boron deficiency among clones in a Monterey pine seed orchard, with one clone highly superior. They observed that one sulfur-deficient soil, the progeny of the best sulfur-tolerant clone grew well and those from sulfur-sensitive parents grew poorly.

There are nearly always instances in exotic forestry when one or several of the many nutrients are not present in proper or balanced quantities. Therefore, a *basic rule in growing exotics is to obtain soil samples* to determine the excesses or deficiencies in soil chemistry (Leaf and Madgwick, 1960). One example where zinc was deficient was described for *Pinus kesiya* and *P. caribaea* in Madagascar, where severe top-dieback occurred. The Philippine source of

P. kesiya was much less affected than the Malagasy provenances (46 compared to 84%) (Mondeil, 1984). Height-growth decline and sometimes death accompanied the dieback. Most substances are too expensive to apply in large amounts as soil amendments (the major exceptions are boron, zinc, copper, and sometimes phosphorus), so generally it is necessary to find or genetically develop species, sources, or families that will grow satisfactorily despite the imbalanced soil chemistry.

Studies indicate that different species take up and use different amounts of nutrients. For example, Shibata et al. (1970) found that varying mineral contents were found in the species *Pinus densiflora, P. thunbergii,* and their hybrids. They also observed differences related to soil; for example, trees grown on granitic soils had more calcium and magnesium than did those from high-pH black soils. Similar species responses were found by Zobel and Roberds (1970), who reported some large genotype × fertilizer interactions, which indicates that some individuals can withstand more severe nutrient shortages and still grow well than can others. Large variations were found among families of *Pinus taeda* in growth response to nitrogen (Roberds et al., 1976). Similar results were reported by Goddard et al. (1976) for loblolly and slash pines. In teak plantations in Nigeria, Nwoboshi (1984) studied the nutrient requirements and accumulations. His results indicate that nutrient immobilization in teak plantings is high compared to the natural tropical forest or tropical pine plantations.

Of particular interest are trees that are more efficient in the uptake of phosphorus, since this substance is often limiting where exotics are used. For example, Forrest and Ovington (1971) found that some clones of *Pinus radiata* accumulated much more phosphorus than others. Similar individual tree differences in phosphorus response were found for *Eucalyptus* by Groves (1967), for slash pine progenies by Walker and Hatcher (1965), and for *Pinus virginiana* by Scott et al. (1975). In a phosphate fertilizer test, Goddard (1969) found that some clones grew well with no fertilizer while others grew well only when phosphorus was added to the soil.

Similar large clonal differences in phosphorus requirements were found by Fielding and Brown (1961) for *Pinus radiata;* clones grown on phosphate-deficient sites differed strikingly in their ability to survive and grow. It is of interest that Patrick (1977) found that phosphorus availability is usually increased as a result of flooding while nitrogen becomes less available. The kind of phosphorus used can be very important in exotic species, as reported by Mattos and Maciel (1984) for *Eucalyptus grandis* in Brazil. Both the performance following the use of soluble and natural phosphates (rock phosphate) and the relative costs must be assessed.

Different seed sources within a species may take up different amounts of minerals; this was reported for jack pine by Mergen and Worral (1965), for Scots pine by Steinbeck (1966), and for *Picea abies* by Giertych and Fober (1967).

The situation relative to soil chemistry is most complex because of the interactions among chemicals. Sometimes soil tests will show a sufficiency of the needed chemicals yet the plants cannot obtain them from the soil. Usually this is related to high or low pH values, but it takes one experienced in soil interactions to predict whether or not good tree growth is possible (Sanchez, 1976; Beek, 1978; Sanchez and Uehara, 1980).

Toxic substances, like aluminum, that are a problem on well-drained soils are less serious in wetlands; however, reducing conditions in wet sites may result in the production of toxic materials, such as hydrogen sulfide, which do not exist under well-drained conditions.

After trees are planted, they must be closely monitored to observe whether sufficient chemical nutrients are available to the plant, regardless of the soil analysis. There are several methods that the novice can use to assess mineral shortages in growing plants; Hacskaylo et al. (1969) and Sucoff (1961) made complete descriptions of plant deficiency symptoms. Although symptoms differ somewhat among species, their general appearance for a shortage of a given nutrient is usually similar.

A sufficiency of soil nutrients is of particular concern in the tropics. As so clearly described by Garcia and Beronilla (1979), the tropical rain forest has a closed nutrient cycle. No matter how luxuriant rain forest vegetation may appear, it does not always indicate highly fertile soils (Fig. 4.4). In actuality, some rain forests thrive on a small nutrient budget and survive only by maintaining an almost closed nutrient cycle, which means that nutrients and minerals are held and recycled in the vegetation and not in the soil. This is a major condition for sustained functioning in certain, but not all, tropical rain forest ecosystems.

Such a complex and fragile ecosystem poses problems in exotic forest management relative to a continually sustained production. This theme was dis-

Figure 4.4. Luxurious jungle growth does not necessarily indicate rich soils. Sometimes soils on which tropical hardwoods grow well, such as the stand in the Amazon shown above, are very fragile. A careful choice of sites is necessary if exotics are to be successfully grown in the tropical hardwood zones.

cussed for the Amazon Basin by Herrera et al. (1978), who assessed the differences in the productivity of the ecosystems based upon the color of the water of the rivers and the nutrients contained in them. They feel that factors such as the color, and thus richness, of the water in the rivers should be taken into account when the growing of exotics in tropical rain forests is considered.

4.2.3 Other Soil Properties

Numerous soil properties other than nutrients are limiting to the growth of exotic forest trees. Most foresters commonly understand that differences in soil structure and soil texture can greatly affect tree growth. Some species have wide adaptability and can grow equally well on sandy and clay soils, or on well-drained or compacted soils. However, most species can only grow well on soils with specific physical soil properties and great care must be taken to determine this before an exotic species is operationally planted. Although in many ways soil structure and soil texture are most important in limiting the growth of exotics, they will not be covered further here because of the complexity of the situation. But before one grows exotics successfully it is essential to make sure that hardpans are absent and the physical soil properties are satisfactory for growth of the exotic. A common adverse result is that the exotic will grow well for a few years, then growth will slow with dieback occurring, sometimes followed by death if planted on the wrong soil.

One characteristic of many soils on which exotics are grown, especially in the tropics and in semidesert conditions, is the presence of a high salt content. This problem is often closely related to pH extremes and drought. Trees that do not have considerable tolerance to high salt concentrations in the soil should not be grown where high salt content frequently occurs, such as in semidesert conditions where moisture is limited (Monk and Weibe, 1961). Many windbreak plantings of exotic species are established in soils with high salts, like the alkaline lands or among sand dunes near the sea-coast. Certain generally tolerant genera, such as *Tamarix* and *Casuarina* sometimes show a remarkable ability to grow in such sites and are among some of the most widely used exotics planted for amenity purposes in the semi-desert regions.

Salt tolerance can vary greatly between and within species. For example, Monk and Wiebe (1961) found that *Pinus ponderosa* and *Fraxinus pennsylvanica,* which are sometimes used as exotics, have a moderate amount of salt tolerance. In laboratory tests using different salt concentrations, Monk and Peterson (1962) found that *Pseudotsuga menziesii* and *Picea pungens,* also often used as exotics, had essentially no salt tolerance and were killed at relatively low concentrations of salt in the soil. Species such as *Pinus thunbergii* and some sources of *P. elliottii* have a great deal of salt tolerance.

Salt tolerance is frequently of key importance in areas where irrigation is practiced, as in Israel. A test of salt tolerance of species under these conditions was done by Kaplan (1983), who found that *Eucalyptus camaldulensis* is highly tolerant to salinity and flooding with saline water. The tolerance is directly related to the environmental conditions prevailing at the seed origin in Australia. *E. occidentalis* is also highly tolerant and *E. viminalis* varies in tolerance related to place of seed origin.

Some species grow naturally in environments with a high concentration of salts. According to Stern and Voight (1959), red mangrove (*Rhizophora mangle*) trees grew best in successively higher salt concentrations up to those approximating seawater. They concluded from their studies that at least the early development of mangrove is favored by high salt concentration. In addition, some species are tolerant to salt sprays (like *Pinus thunbergii*). Of increasing importance for roadside planting in cold climates are species that are tolerant to both soil and foliage salt deposited after roads are treated to reduce ice accumulation.

Interplanting of species to improve the fertility of the soil by nitrogen fixation or for nurse trees is frequently discussed but less frequently used in exotic forestry. Leguminous genera like *Leucaena* have been suggested and tried, but with only moderate success; members of the genera *Alnus, Acacia,* and various other legumes have been used. In general, the nitrogen fixers do not produce a significant excess of N until the plant dies, releasing it into the soil. Yet, in Indonesia, *Calliandra* is being interplanted with *Pinus merkusii* and *Eucalyptus deglupta* and sometimes as nurse trees for teak (O.T.S., 1984). The interplanted trees produce firewood along with shade, in addition to nitrogen for better growth of the teak.

4.2.4 The Need for Mycorrhizae

Although the mycorrhizal association between the tree and the fungus certainly is not a soil property, it is so closely related to soils and nutrient relations, and the lack of mycorrhizae has been so important in limiting production of exotics, that it is discussed here along with soil properties. In the early years of establishing exotics a major source of confusion and bad decisions in the choice of species and provenances was the lack of proper mycorrhizae (Fig. 4.5). Since mycorrhizae are necessary for most species as an aid in the uptake of nutrients from the soil, they are absolutely essential for normal tree growth. Without them growth is slow, leaves become yellow and stunted, and frequently the plant is so stressed that it dies following weather extremes. One sometimes gets the impression that there are only a few mycorrhizae. But there are a number of different species; for example, nine different genera of mycorrhizae were found in exotic forest plantations in Colombia (Cielo, 1980).

Nearly all forest trees require mycorrhizae; they occur as the external type (ectomycorrhizae) or the internal type (endomycorrhizae). The "ectos," as they are often called, occur on most, but not all, conifers. The spores are wind disseminated so that they spread and colonize an area quickly. Their location on the roots usually can be seen without the aid of magnification. Anderson and Cordell (1979) published a small pamphlet showing roots infected with mycorrhizae and their form and appearance in a series of color photographs

Figure 4.5. The dramatic results from proper mycorrhizal infection on the roots of exotics is shown for pine in central Brazil. The trees near the men in the foreground were not inoculated with mycorrhizae. They are the same age as the tall, inoculated ones in the background.

that are very helpful. The lack of mycorrhizae is of particular importance when conifers are grown in tropical hardwood areas, brushlands, or grasslands where no conifers exist. A successful conifer exotic forestry program will be impossible in these areas without the introduction of ectomycorrhizae; this is usually done by infecting the seedlings in the nursery.

Two important groups of hardwoods also are associated with ectomycorrhizae, namely, *Eucalyptus* and *Quercus* (oaks). The mycorrhizae are not so easily seen on the roots of these hardwoods as on the conifers. Most of the other hardwoods important as exotics have endomycorrhizae that cannot be seen without special treatment of the roots followed by staining. These are much more common in the tropical areas and occur on many crop species. But the spores are not airborne. Usually, nursery beds do not need to be inoculated, because they are already in the soil in which the trees are planted.

There has been much research on the ectomycorrhizae relative to infecting conifers used as exotics. The mycorrhiza *Pisolithus tinctorius* has been used to infect nursery seedlings (Cordell and Webb, 1980; Cordell and Marx, 1983); this was done by Filho and Krugner (1980) in Brazil, where the common *Thelephora terrestris* as well as *Pisolithus tinctorius* were used in fumigated soil. Both produced improved seedling growth (total dry weight of seedlings increased by 87%). In Puerto Rico, Vozzo and Hacskaylo (1971) tried pure cultures of several kinds of mycorrhizae. The infected seedlings all grew better than those not infected. They found that surface soil from established plantations provided a very effective inoculum. Usually, the most efficient source of mycorrhizal inoculum is the duff and thin soil layer near the surface. Soil inoculum can be obtained from soil and duff collections under established plantations or, as is frequently done, from special "mycorrhizal nurseries" established by planting trees with infected roots in conjunction with forest nurseries. The duff and surface soil layer are then collected and used on the nursery beds or in nursery containers.

There have been several studies to determine which of the many species of mycorrhizae are best for specific conditions, or if different provenances of a species require different mycorrhizae. One study, by Linneman (1960) on Douglas-fir in Germany, showed that of the three "races" of this species, *viridis* had the most, *glauca* the least, and *caesia* an intermediate number of mycorrhizally infected roots. These results were based upon 30- to 60-year-old trees and 2-year-old seedlings with seven trial series on different soils. For the tropical lowland pines, Yvory (1983) reports that particular fungi vary in their effectiveness, either for a specific host or particular environmental conditions. For example, in Ceylon, Muytiah (1972) showed a change in mycorrhizal form and growth of *Pinus caribaea* resulting from a severe drought. He reported a favorable type of mycorrhiza (*Boletus*) was partially replaced by a less favorable one (*Cenococcum*) as a result of the dry conditions. In an attempt to obtain tolerance to limestone in *Eucalyptus delegatensis,* Lapeyrie and Brucket (1982) tested ectomycorrhizae in France that are adapted to a high pH and to tolerate and reject a high concentration of calcium. Such work with the potential of different mycorrhizae is really just beginning in exotic forest trees. However, the results from a lack of proper mycorrhizae in *Eucalyptus,* such as chlorosis and lack of vigor, were described many years ago by Pryor (1956).

It is not unusual to hear comments to the effect that pests (mycorrhizal fungi) attack the roots of exotics and therefore exotics should not be used (see Chapter 10). Certainly the situation is just the opposite and exotic trees without mycorrhizae rarely grow satisfactorily.

4.3 WEATHER LIMITATIONS FOR EXOTICS

One of the most frequent causes of failure of exotics is adverse weather. Damage is usually directly related to heat or moisture stress which weakens the plant, making it susceptible to other pests. As reported by Stahl (1968), the defense mechanism of *Pinus radiata* to *Diplodia pinea* breaks down under these stresses so that the fungus will invade tissue not usually susceptible. Stahl concludes that *Diplodia* occurs only under climatic conditions unfavorable for growth of the host.

As mentioned earlier, extremes of weather result in loss in growth and quality, or even in death of the exotic plantations. But the sequences prior to and following the extremes are usually most critical. For example, some eucalypts

Figure 4.6. Periods of extreme weather frequently cause heavy losses in exotics. Shown is a stand of *Eucalyptus* that had grown well for many years in South Africa and then was severely damaged by a drought.

and tropical pines can tolerate quite low temperatures without damage if the temperatures drop slowly and are maintained. But the same trees will be killed back or badly deformed if there are alternative warm and very cold temperatures (Fig. 4.6). The trees will respond to a period of "hardening off" enabling them to survive what might otherwise be damaging conditions.

The primary problem with weather damage and growth of exotics is the cyclical nature of the adverse weather situations. Extreme weather may not occur for many years and then be present several times in a single year. The so-called 100-year storms can be primary limiting factors to the growth of exotics, but, unfortunately, this cannot be determined until the unique weather conditions actually occur. This concept was expressed by Adams and Campbell (1981), who pointed out that in milder climates, the detrimental effect of seed transfer of Douglas-fir depends on the occurrence of rare climatic extremes and the gradual accumulation of small damages that may not become evident until late in a rotation.

The long-term changes in weather, as described by Hepting (1960), will have a major effect on exotics. He reports a worldwide warming trend since 1900 (2°F in the Temperate Zone, 5°F in the Arctic). Hepting postulates that some of the recent epidemic tree diseases (that also affect exotics) have been set in motion by this warming trend. He notes that all the worst diseases of this type have their origin below the ground line.

4.3.1 Drought and Cold

One major adverse weather condition limiting the growth of exotics is drought. Many exotics are grown in climates where rainfall amount and distribution are marginal at best and which, in some years, become critical. For such an exotic to be totally successful it must be able to withstand occasional extreme periods of low moisture, usually combined with high temperatures, hard winds, and low relative humidities.

Sometimes varieties, provenances, or individuals are found within desired species that show a great ability to withstand drought and still grow well (Fig. 4.7). Numerous studies have examined why this is so. They vary widely, from root development (Brix, 1959) to morpho-physiological characteristics (Van Buijtenen et al., 1976). Differences are very clear for *Pinus caribaea,* where var. *caribaea* is more drought hardy than var. *hondurensis* (Venator, 1976). Venator also found a couple of provenances of var. *hondurensis* that were quite drought hardy. In the CAMCORE cooperative, Dvorak (1984) divided collections into dry- and moist-site sources. Results have shown that some sources are specifically capable of growing better in conditions of moisture extremes. Also in Douglas-fir, Ferrell and Woodard (1966) found considerable differences in drought tolerance from different seed origins.

The foregoing discussion dealt with the ability to withstand a shortage of moisture. Of equal importance for many exotics is the ability to tolerate an

Figure 4.7. It is possible to develop hardy land races. Shown is a good-growing *Pinus caribaea* on very deep, droughty sands in Venezuela, where most trees did not survive or did not grow. Enough trees were found as good as the one shown to enable the development of a "deep-sand-tolerant" land race.

excess of moisture. The same patterns that have been described for drought tolerance are found for moisture tolerance. It is of equal importance to use an exotic that will survive and grow in an excess of moisture as it is to find those that will grow in a deficiency of moisture.

The brevity of this section on moisture extremes in no way reduces the importance of moisture when growing exotics. Results are so commonly known and recognized that a detailed discussion is not needed. Unfortunately, the most moisture-tolerant species and sources are frequently also slow growers. Because of this there has been considerable effort to develop land races that are tolerant to both moisture extremes and have a reasonable growth rate.

Destruction or damage by cold weather is another common and major reason for the inferior performance of exotics, and perhaps lack of cold tolerance can be considered the most severe restriction on the use of numerous exotics that would otherwise grow well in a given area. Certain genera, like the eucalypts, and many other tropical species, such as *Pinus caribaea,* simply are not adapted to withstand below-freezing weather. Attempts to grow them in colder climates result in frequent failures. Many species, such as *Gmelina arborea* (Lamb, 1968), are restricted as to where they grow because cold weather either kills or deforms them. The relatively cold-tolerant *Eucalyptus nitens* had one provenance (Errinundra) that was particularly cold sensitive in frost pockets (Anon., 1983b). In their studies of *Eucalyptus* in Florida, Franklin and Meskimen (1975) put special emphasis on cold hardiness because subtropical Florida occasionally has severe frosts.

Sometimes land races can be developed for the cooler conditions. For example, Hunt and Zobel (1978) were able to develop land races of *Eucalyptus viminalis* in the southeastern United States that could withstand temperatures as low as 10°F (−12°C) and also grew well. But sources were not found to tolerate the occasional temperatures down to 5 or 6°F; these temperatures killed back the tops and deformed the trees. Working with the same material, Jahromi (1983) found, for the 98 seed lots of *E. viminalis* tested, that fluctuation, duration, and time of frost occurrence were more damaging than absolute minimum temperature. Within the species there were great differences among the provenances and seed sources. There was no correlation between growth rate and frost tolerance, but several provenances were good in both. One of the most intensive research efforts involving exotics is to develop more cold hardiness in *Eucalyptus* (Boden, 1958). Special seminars and symposia have been held in which cold hardiness was the central theme (IUFRO, 1983b). The IUFRO publication contains 29 papers on cold-hardiness aspects related to the eucalypts in cold winter rainfall climates, in cold temperate climates, and in cold summer rainfall climates. This set of papers is so voluminous that it cannot be reported here, but it is invaluable to anyone interested in cold hardiness within the genus *Eucalyptus.*

As more cold-hardy strains are developed, *Eucalyptus* will become even more important as an exotic. The large number of excellent papers indicates the importance of cold hardiness in the eucalypts and the efforts being made to develop suitable land races. Much less concentration has been made on methods to improve cold hardiness in conifers.

Techniques have been developed to choose cold-hardy individuals at a young age (Schultz, 1979; Marien, 1980). Methods for Scots pine and lodgepole pine are described by, respectively, Ericsson (1984) and Jonsson et al. (1980). In New Zealand, Wilcox et al. (1983b) tested 18 provenances of *Eucalyptus fastigata* under artificial frosts in controlled-environment rooms. The most hardy sources were from the higher altitudes or more inland sources. Winter frosts of −9°C were endured by most seedlings of the hardiest provenances while −6°C caused severe damage to the least hardy. *E. regnans* included in the test were more frost sensitive than *E. fastigata*.

Even in colder-climate species, frost hardiness of exotics often is limiting (Bates, 1930, on Norway pine [red pine] and Schummann and Hoffman, 1968, on spruce). The cycle of growth and development, time of bud burst, and time of hardening off can be critical for so-called cold-tolerant exotics like Douglas-fir and will frequently determine the success or failure of an exotic plantation (Szöny and Nagy, 1968). This type of information frequently is not available from conditions in the indigenous range of a species and can only be determined from tests. Efforts to locate more cold-tolerant sources are not always successful. For example, *Pinus radiata* can stand some cold, although it is easily damaged, but, as reported by Hood and Libby (1980), little genetic variation in cold tolerance has been evident within the species.

Studies such as the one by Dormling (1982) on *Picea abies* attempt to determine the cause of differential cold damage. She reported that freezing occurred in the developing shoot and trees of all origins froze when tested at the same flushing stage. The degree of hardiness was related to the earliness of flushing, with the more northern and higher-elevation trees flushing earlier, depending on the temperature sum needed to induce flushing. The result is that the northern sources are much more damaged by late spring frosts than the southern ones, often resulting in stunted growth. Because of this, the Belorussian spruce provenances, which are very late flushers, are used in Sweden, south of 60 to 61 degrees north latitude. At more northern sites, the later cessation of growth in the fall of the southern sources limits their use, as this process is induced by increasing night length (Personal communication, Anders Persson, College of Forestry, Garpenberg, Sweden).

Cold hardiness is sometimes obtained by creating hybrids. In Hyun's (1976) study of hybrids with pitch and loblolly pines, the hybrid was found to be much more cold hardy than the loblolly pine parent; the same results were obtained by Buchert (1983). Although breeding of especially cold-hardy hybrids has a great potential, this approach has hardly been started, primarily because of the difficulty of mass-producing the hybrids. The advent of better methods of vegetative propagation will make the use of cold-hardy hybrids more feasible.

Although emphasis usually is on cold tolerance, frequently excessively high temperatures, especially high night temperatures, will cause an exotic species to fail. Sources from high latitudes and high elevations will often continue to respire too rapidly during warm nights, so the photosynthate produced during the day simply is not adequate to keep the plant alive, healthy, and putting on growth. Many attempts to move desired species from cooler to warmer climates have failed, not because the day temperatures were too high but because the night temperatures did not drop low enough to keep the plant healthy.

A remarkable number of researchers have reported on the similarity of the physiology within the plant for resistance to drought and to cold. This was discussed by Shirley (1937), Pisek and Larcher (1954), and Schönbach et al. (1966) for different species and conditions. The damaging effects to the plant are somewhat similar, and cold damage is often a result of desiccation resulting from a combination of low temperatures and low relative humidities, the same as desiccation from low moisture, high temperatures, and low relative humidities.

4.3.2 Violent Weather

Not much can be done to escape destruction by violent storms and winds other than to try to use species or provenances that are less susceptible to wind damage, ice, and rain. In extreme environments, such as growing lodgepole pine in Sweden, severe weather can be more important than diseases or insects. For example, Hägglund (1982) stated that, in his judgment, the risk of snow and wind damage is great and lodgepole pine is a more risky alternative than the indigenous Scots pine and Norway spruce at most sites.

It is well known that *Pinus oocarpa* is much more susceptible to windthrow than is *P. caribaea,* as reported in Puerto Rico by Liegel (1984b). He found that five- to six-year-old *P. caribaea* had 22% damage while *P. oocarpa* of the same age had 52% damage; mortality from blowdown was 2% for *P. caribaea* and 13% for *P. oocarpa.* This knowledge must be used to avoid planting *P. oocarpa* in windy areas or along coasts with constant or heavy winds. In Fiji, Bell (1977) also reported that *P. oocarpa* is more prone to windthrow than is *P. caribaea* when hurricanes occur; this is the usual observation when these two species are subjected to hard winds.

Sometimes individual trees within species are found that resist high winds. For example, in 1972 Kerr reported on loblolly pine trees that resisted a severe hurricane in the southern United States. Although such information is available, little has been done with it. It might, for example, be possible to develop wind-stress-resistant land races, but storms are so unpredictable and infrequent that this has not been a high priority in working with exotics. However, Nikles (1981) developed the *Pinus elliottii* × *P. caribaea* hybrid and selected successfully for windfirmness.

4.4 PESTS AND GROWING EXOTICS

Although it is a loose usage of the term, *pests* may refer to insects, diseases, animals, and even to humans (Zobel and Talbert, 1984). This definition was followed by Browne (1968) in his book on pests of plantations grown in the British Commonwealth. He lists animals, pathogenic viruses, bacteria, fungi, and higher plants as all constituting major pests of forest trees. Conditions adverse to forest growth, such as fume damage, salt deposits, or other conditions caused by humans, are sometimes referred to as pests. No matter how a pest is defined, the results are poor productivity, poor tree and wood quality, and even mortality.

Questions frequently arise about controlling pests by chemicals. Although this method has been extensively recommended, frequently tested, and occasionally used [such as for *Dothistroma* needle blight (Gilmour and Noorderhaven, 1972)], artificial control in plantations is generally ineffective. Elliott (1976) found that sprays readily controlled the *Dothistroma* disease, but the high cost made it impractical. Usually, any kind of silvicultural control is too difficult, expensive, or uncertain (Zobel and Talbert, 1984).

Ultimately, development of tolerant trees must be resorted to, as described for *Dothistroma* by Ivory and Patterson (1970) and Wilcox (1982c). This concept of breeding for pest tolerance is widely accepted and widely practiced. Much is known about pest tolerance in exotics. Many papers relating to the resistance of trees to both insects and diseases were published in *Breeding Pest-resistant Trees,* by Gerhold et al. (1966). This book emphasized genetic improvement in disease and insect tolerance in forest trees; papers also dealt with the variation of genetics of the pest and how to develop tolerance breeding programs. Always associated with a pest-resistance breeding program, or with control of pests by chemicals, is the possibility of developing pests that are resistant to, or overcome, the controlling chemicals or the tolerance developed in the improved trees.

A most common statement related to exotics is that they are more susceptible to pests than are indigenous species (see Chapter 10). This may border on the truth when exotics are planted as large blocks of single species with limited genetic variation—that is, in monocultures, which are frequently grown on marginal land. It also happens too frequently that seed used to make the plantings comes from restricted sources or from small numbers of parents. Usually, the exotic is not initially well adapted to its new environment, so the trees in the new forests are growing under considerable stress, making them more susceptible to pest attack (O.T.S., 1984). In their discussion on controlling pests in forest trees, Schultz and Baldwin (1982) emphasize the necessity of maintaining physiological and genetic variability.

As Burdon (1982) points out, the argument that establishing a species outside its natural habitat (i.e., as an exotic) increases its susceptibility to pests has not been proven. Some diseases may be encouraged, but others will be discouraged. Growing a species as an exotic may actually release that species from its natural pests and thus improve its health and performance. This was well stated by Pryor (1978b) when he said that "one of the reasons for fast growth when they [the eucalypts] are planted as exotics is the absence generally of the widely prevalent leaf-eating insects which abound in their natural habitat." Burdon (1982) explains how this has worked for *Pinus radiata* and some of the *Eucalyptus* grown in New Zealand; it is also true for *Pinus contorta* in Scandinavia. This concept was also mentioned by Sedjo (1983), who says that part of the success of exotics can be attributed to escaping from native pests and diseases. Generally, natural and biological control agents are not present when pests do occur in exotic plantations. Because of this the stand appears to be more susceptible, since it suffers heavily under the initial pest attack.

In an opposite context O.T.S. (1984) states that native pests and diseases tend to switch to plantation crops, where resources are more uniform and abundant. Despite this, the risks will continue to be taken because of the greatly increased yields. This idea was also espoused by Sedjo (1983), who stated: "Yet there is also danger for exotics in that pests and diseases to which they are susceptible and for which they have not developed resistance may be at their new site."

The newly established exotic may be initially pest free, but it rarely fails that some pest will sooner or later attack it. The situation is especially insidious because the exotic often grows so well in the early years and appears to be pest free in its new environment. This often leads to an incorrect assumption about the productive potential of an exotic (Martinsson, 1970; Zobel, 1980b). As an example, Karlman (1982) states:

> In the central parts of northern Sweden most provenances of *Pinus contorta* are less attacked by pathogens than the indigenous *Pinus sylvestris*. . . . Here also the superior productivity, more than 50% better, of *Pinus contorta* in comparison with *Pinus sylvestris* is probably due to escape from natural pathogens.

Even though it may take 1 year or it may take 10, it rarely fails that pests of some type, frequently serious, will attack an exotic plantation. This recognition of the potential of an attack by pests is critical to foresters involved in exotic forestry.

The pest attack will frequently result from the severe stresses that often occur where exotics are grown. The poor physiological condition of the trees under these stresses enhances the spread and damage by pests that may have been previously unknown or which were considered to be of only minor importance or only a nuisance. Many large exotic programs have failed because pest attacks were not anticipated.

One prime example is the large *Pinus radiata* plantations which have been destroyed by *Dothistroma pini* in several parts of the world, including Brazil, Zimbabwe (Rhodesia), New Zealand and East-Central Africa. As a result of plantation damage from this disease (Fig. 4.8), a major loss of confidence in forestry has occurred in some of these areas. The losses could have been pre-

Figure 4.8. Sometimes exotics are seriously damaged by pests. One of the worst of these is *Dothistroma pini*. The plantation shown was five years old and nearly completely destroyed. Somehow this disease moved from its indigenous range in California to where the exotic had been planted in New Zealand.

vented and millions of dollars could have been saved if those who established the exotic *P. radiata* had heeded the advice of those who warned that *Dothistroma* probably would become severe in radiata pine plantations established where there are warm and moist summers. It is a puzzle how *Dothistroma,* present on *P. radiata* in its indigenous range in California (where the disease is primarily considered only a nuisance), has become established in such widely separated regions throughout the world, where it becomes a killer. *Dothistroma* is capable of spreading to other areas with the warm, wet summers suitable for development of the disease.

But the preceding concept of greater destruction by pests in exotic plantations is not fully endorsed by everyone. Bawa (1976) says that exotic plantations have a better "track record" than monocultures of plantations of indigenous species. He cites the lack of natural enemies, but further states that:

> most of them [exotics] comprise tree species that are naturally found in pure stands. . . . It could be argued that the native pests will eventually catch up with these exotic plantations. Yet while this is likely to be true, it is just as likely that pests will damage indigenous forests. Pest outbreaks in artificially established stands are no more common than they are in natural forests.

Frequently, the pest will not kill the exotic but is harmful because it deforms the tree, reducing its value to low-quality products. A good example of such deformation is the cypress stem canker on *Cupressus* planted in Colombia, Kenya, and elsewhere (Fig. 4.9). Stem deformation can be so severe that the only suitable use of the tree is for fiber products, and the good-quality solid-wood products for which many of the plantations were established will not be produced.

The appearance of pests makes it essential for the person growing exotics to have one or more secondary, or reserve, species (see Chapter 2). This was stated clearly by Darrow and Coetzee (1983) in South Africa:

> The introduction of several insect pests, notably the pine woolly aphid, calls into serious question the policy of depending upon so few species for more than 90% of the coniferous wood supplies of the region.

Even if the species used are not lost, damage to them on marginal sites restricts the area for afforestation and will reduce productivity of the trees that survive.

There are numerous publications and pamphlets about exotics that contain information about pests (insects and diseases) that can attack exotic plantations (Table 4.1). Nearly every publication related to exotic forestry mentions pests of one type or another.

Figure 4.9. Not only do diseases kill trees and reduce growth but they cause deformation that reduces the value of the wood. The large logs of cypress with the fluted outline were deformed by the cypress canker. This disease occurs in *Cupressus lusitanica* in as widely separated plantings as northern South America and East-Central Africa.

TABLE 4.1. A Sampling of Bibliographic Publications That Deal with Pests of Exotic Forest Species[a]

Author	Date	Subject Matter Covered
Björkman	1964	A summary of major points related to breeding for resistance in forest trees, very applicable to exotics, is presented.
Callaham	1966	He discusses resistance and escape and the difficulty of predictions for tolerance because trees may become more resistant or susceptible with age, environmental changes, or silvicultural manipulations.
Hare	1966	This is a good review of the physiological aspects of disease resistance.
Gerhold et al.	1966	This comprehensive summary covers pest-resistance breeding for a large number of species used as exotics.
Hodges et al.	1971	This is an excellent summary of the literature on *Fomes annosus* (now called *Heterobasidium annosum*) from 1960 to 1970.
Day	1972	A most helpful summary discussion is given of the genetics of rust fungi, and how complex it is dealing with genetic systems of both host and parasite.
Stern	1972	The basis and theory of testing for rust resistance is covered, especially as to the co-evolution of host and parasite and how a balance between them is maintained.
Morris et al.	1975	The authors list many insects and diseases that attack cottonwood (*Populus deltoides*). This gives some indication of the susceptibility of the genus *Populus* to pests.
Zsuffa	1975a	Approaches and problems encountered in breeding for pest resistance are outlined.
Reis & Hodges	1976	The authors name and describe diseases and insects in Latin America that are a major influence in exotic forestry.
Waters & Cowling	1976	The importance of integrated pest management and methodologies that may be used to achieve the objectives are covered.
Schmidt	1978	The importance of diversity in forest ecosystems, and its effects relative to pests, is stressed.
Cielo	1980	27 fungal genera were found that attack exotic plantings of *Cupressus, Pinus,* and *Eucalyptus* in Colombia.
Horsfall & Cowling	1980	This comprehensive book covers plant diseases, their control and disease management; concepts outlined are applicable to exotics.

TABLE 4.1. Continued

Author	Date	Subject Matter Covered
Nelson	1980	A general coverage is given of host–parasite interactions and how to breed for resistance.
Anonymous (16 authors)	1981a	Individual pamphlets deal mostly with insects (1 paper on diseases), heavily oriented to aphids, termites, and beetles that attack South African forests.
Kelley & Cordell	1984	Different diseases affecting forest tree nurseries through damping off, stem diseases, root rots, and foliage diseases are discussed.

*a*Full references are given in the reference list at the back of the book.

4.4.1 Where Do Pests of Exotics Come from?

It is frequently stated that because an exotic is growing in a totally different environment, it will be free of pests from its indigenous range (Boland and Turnbull, 1981) and local pests will not attack it because it is so different. This feeling was expressed by Burdon (1982) as one reason why *Pinus radiata,* which has been grown extensively as an exotic, has not been generally damaged by pests, except for *Dothistroma.*

But the general situation does not seem to support a concept of exotics being pest free. As stated earlier, somehow, some way, pests will appear in exotic plantations; it may happen soon or it may take many years. Pests of exotics will come from three major sources:

1. Those that are indigenous to the area in which the exotic tree is planted but never before were in association with the exotic. Pests of this kind can become a major destructive force after they adjust to and favor the exotic. This type of pest adaptation to the exotic is of rather common occurrence, especially with leaf-eating beetles and worms, but also with diseases. It is very common with animal pests. As one example, several species of insects have become major defoliators of eucalypts in Brazil and New Zealand (Fig. 4.10). In several instances, the indigenous pest newly established on the exotic has become so serious that it has made impossible the successful management of a species in the exotic environment.

2. Pests of the exotic in the exotic's indigenous range appear in the area where the new species is planted. One of the most well-known examples of this is *Dothistroma pini* on *P. radiata. Dothistroma* seems to have followed *P. radiata* wherever it has been planted in environments suitable to the development of the disease. Its destructiveness, frequently causing heavy mortality, would not be expected because it is not a major pest in California, where it came from. Another example is the black pine aphid on *Pinus taeda* in southern Africa.

3. A pest not indigenous to the area where the exotic is planted and also not indigenous to the home environment of the exotic—that is, exotic pests

Figure 4.10. Insects are particularly serious on the eucalypts. Beetles such as the one shown become major defoliators that frequently make it impossible to grow the exotic. (Photo courtesy of Mike Carson, F.R.I., New Zealand.)

attacking exotic trees can develop as a major pest of exotics. One example of this is the insect *Sirex,* which attacks radiata pine and can be a serious cause of mortality (Fig. 4.11).

Sometimes pests attacking the indigenous species make the use of exotics desirable. Kiellander (1963) cites the example in Sweden where *Fomes annosus* (*Heterobasidium annosum*) is widespread and very injurious to *Picea abies,* especially on calcareous soils and old fields; on sandy soils *Pinus sylvestris* is

Figure 4.11. A major insect pest attacking pine in Australia is *Sirex*. Shown are dead trees in a radiata pine plantation after the living trees have been removed.

also attacked. Kiellander states that on soils such as these, exotics are of special interest if they are reasonably tolerant to *Fomes*. But the chance of finding a *Fomes*-resistant tree is very small because the disease attacks such a broad spectrum of species. However, some species are less susceptible than are others.

An additional danger related to exotics is the potential of importing a pest that may be only minor on the exotic but can become a killer on species indigenous to where the exotic will be grown. There are a number of such possibilities, although, luckily, few are serious at this time.

The question is often asked, "How does the pest get to the new environment in which the exotic is grown?" It is sometimes hard to know, but usually it is brought in "illegally" on plant material that should have gone through quarantine or inspection. With today's means of transportation it is almost impossible to prohibit the entry of pests. It is the responsibility of those handling the plant materials to assure that proper care has been taken. The problem is especially critical now that vegetative propagation has such a wide acceptance in forestry. The danger of bringing in a pest and the need to prevent its introduction is much greater with vegetative material than with seeds, although the latter should also be imported with care. Perhaps we will never be totally successful in preventing the import of pests, but we must do the very best we can.

In the long term, persons such as Hepting (1963) feel that global climatic changes are causing changes in disease problems. For example, he states that a continuation of the recent warming trend accentuates the northward movement of tropical and subtropical organisms such as *Phytophthora cinnamomi*. In the short term, Hepting says, the severity of rusts, foliage diseases caused by rusts, the *Phytophthoras,* and the *Pythiums* are directly related to individual-year weather fluctuations. This concept applies especially to trees planted as exotics in environments to which they are not completely adapted.

4.4.2 Diseases of Exotics

Many different kinds of diseases attack exotic forests. They range all the way from a nuisance, causing quality and some growth loss to deformers and killers. Some of the worst diseases are like *Dothistroma pini,* which somehow came from the indigenous range of *Pinus radiata* to attack it and many other hard pines in many parts of the world. *Dothistroma* does not exist in the indigenous range of many species it attacks vigorously when they are planted as exotics. This disease is so important that the Forest Research Institute of New Zealand put out a special bulletin on its control (Kershaw et al., 1982). In a test of annually sprayed and unsprayed stands of radiata pine in New Zealand for the control of *Dothistroma,* it was found that after five years the sprayed stands grew 6.0 m^2/ha basal area more than the unsprayed stand. The standard spraying at a 25% level of green crown infection was not effective, as judged by basal area increment (Woolens and Hayward, 1984). In another study, Van der Pas et al. (1984) found that "The data suggest that in the experimental plots spraying was not justified on purely financial criteria."

Another serious disease of *P. radiata, P. patula,* and other species in New Zealand is *Diplodia pinea* (Burdon et al., 1982). Observations indicated that some trees are resistant; tests of selected progeny confirmed this. The selection method was only marginally effective. The authors suggest regular inoculation screening to obtain strains of trees tolerant to *Diplodia.*

A disease that has caused a great deal of concern on exotics is *Eucalyptus* canker (*Cryphonectria cubensis,* formerly called *Diaporthe cubensis*) (Hodges, 1980). According to Hodges et al. (1979), this disease has become very widespread and is a major pest in some environments and on certain species. The disease is completely described, from its discovery to its symptoms, in the FAO bulletin on planting eucalypts (FAO, 1979). It not only affects the growing tree but, when coppiced, canker-infected trees have their sprouts infected, which die or grow poorly (Ferreira et al., 1977).

One kind of disease that causes real concern about its potential to become a major pest in exotic environments is pine rust in Guatemala (tentatively identified as a form of *Cronartium quercum* f. sp. *fusiforme*) (Webb, 1984). Is it a danger in South America? The oak (*Quercus* spp.) alternate host to this fungus occurs only in a part of the area where exotic pines are planted, but closely related genera also can act as the alternate host for the disease. Therefore, we feel it is only prudent to ensure that this disease is not inadvertently introduced from the donor area into areas where Central American pines are extensively grown as exotics.

New diseases are constantly being found. For example, Gibson (1980) reported two new needle fungi (*Meloderma desmazierii* and *Scirrhia acicola*) on several pine species in Colombia.

The danger of diseases attacking exotic forest plantings is constantly emphasized, and rightly so. For example, Martinsson (1978) discusses the possible dangers from disease with the introduction of exotics; he uses *Pinus contorta* as a prime example. Martinsson spent considerable time studying the pests of *P. contorta* in its indigenous range. He is particularly concerned about gall rust (*Endocronartium harknessii*), which is widespread wherever lodgepole pine grows naturally. This disease also seriously damages the indigenous Scots pine in Sweden, which causes great concern among foresters. It is especially worrisome because it does not require an alternate host to complete its life cycle. However, lodgepole pine growing in Sweden is surprisingly free of parasites. Martinsson hypothesizes that the absence of parasites contributes to the superiority of *P. contorta* over *P. sylvestris.*

Working with diseases on exotics is not simple because of the interaction of the disease with the environment and the health (stress) of the host tree. It becomes even more difficult when variations in the disease and variations in the host occur together. This effect of the interaction of the environment and the disease has been stressed by Schreiner (1963) as well as by many others. Schreiner illustrated such effects on clones in the genus *Populus,* which he considers one of the most disease-prone genera in forestry.

Many foresters attempt to predict what will happen relative to disease incidence in exotics, but their predictions are often upset by unforeseen or unexplained interactions. Added to this is pseudoresistance, as referred to by Callaham (1966), which is an apparent resistance to or escape from the disease resulting from a particular environment, age, or silvicultural operations employed. Because of this, apparently disease-free exotics may suddenly become infected for no obvious reason. Callaham emphasizes that to be successful the exotic must be tolerant over its various developmental stages.

Tolerance to disease among species is well known and documented. Similar patterns occur among provenances within species used for exotics. In Douglas-fir, for example, Stephan (1973) found that different sources varied greatly in susceptibility to *Rhabdocline pseudotsugae,* with southern sources being the most susceptible. When Douglas-fir was grown in Europe, the same disease was found to be much more severe on the Rocky Mountain sources. Those from the dry continental climates were both disease susceptible and grew poorly. The only satisfactory provenances that were not harmed by disease were from the moister areas, such as the west slopes of the Cascade Mountains. We have observed that *Eucalyptus grandis* from some sources are much more damaged by canker than are others; for example, the sources from Zimbabwe are more resistant in Brazil than are several others. In *Pinus contorta,* Martinsson (1980) found that different geographic sources of lodgepole pine showed great differences in resistance to needle cast disease and stem rusts. In *Populus,* Thielges and Adams (1975) found large differences in susceptibility to *Melampsora* spp. leaf rust among provenances. Many more examples could be cited, but the preceding are sufficient to illustrate that sometimes provenance is an important factor in whether or not an exotic will become diseased.

A vast literature exists on diseases and tolerance for individual trees or families, as well as for provenances. There is not space enough to mention them in this book other than to illustrate a few in Table 4.2. Some, such as Gibson (1979), deal with pines grown as exotics in the tropics and the Southern Hemisphere. The diseases, their occurrence, and details of hosts, life cycles, damage caused, and methods of control are included. Another publication, by Browne (1968), annotates diseases associated with principal tree species found in the British Commonwealth. Many of the species are exotics. Some diseases are very specific to given geographic areas or seed sources, but others, such as the root diseases *Fomes annosus* (*Heterobasidium annosum*), and *Phytophthora cinnamomi,* are widespread and occur in many parts of the world on many species, including both conifers and hardwoods.

4.4.3 The Impact of Insects upon Exotic Forestry

It is sometimes debated, rather pointlessly, whether insects are a more serious pest on exotics than are diseases. It is sufficient to say that insects can have a devastating effect and, when epidemic, can either restrict production or destroy exotic plantations in a hurry. Insects are particularly hard to work with

TABLE 4.2. A Partial Listing of Some Publications Dealing with Diseases of Exotics[a]

Species	Author(s)	Comments
Populus spp.	Schreiner 1959	Great differences in susceptibility to *Melampsora* leaf rust were evident.
Populus spp.	Chiba 1964	Successful breeding has been done against leaf diseases in poplars.
Many species	Baxter 1967	Although the title of the book is *Diseases of Plantations,* the author lists all early exotic planting in the northeastern U.S. starting about 1850. Pests that attacked these are described, along with the history and success of the introductions.
Pinus radiata *P. attenuata* *P. nigra* *P. ponderosa*	Gilmour 1976	The author deals with the impact and control of *Dothistroma pini* on several exotic pine species in New Zealand.
Pinus sylvestris	Dietrichson 1968	Large differences in tolerance to *Scleroderris* were found, with the northern sources being the most tolerant. Cold resistance and disease resistance were related.
Gmelina arborea	Lamb 1968	A number of diseases attack *Gmelina.* In waterlogged soils in India and Pakistan, it is attacked by *Poria rhizomorpha.* Other root rots of *Gmelina* are *Fomes lignosus* and *Armillarea mellea.*
Pinus radiata	Libby et al. 1968	The trees from Cedrus and the Guadelupe Islands are much more tolerant to *Dothistroma pini* than the mainland Monterrey pine.
Pinus radiata	Stahl 1968	The author disputes that hail damage is related to infection by *Diplodia pinea,* as usually claimed. Stahl found the disease on trees, but none entered through hail wound damage in A.C.T., Australia.
Ulmus parvifolia	Filer & Mc-Cracken 1969	48 Chinese elm trees were infected with *Clitocybe tabescens* in the north-central U.S. Small branches died first, then large branches died, and later 22 trees died.
Pinus patula	Mullin 1969	*P. patula* is very susceptible to attack by defoliating caterpillars, and alternative species are desirable in Zimbabwe.
Thuja spp.	Soegaard 1969	Described is one of the few examples of single-gene inheritance for disease resistance in forest trees.
Exotic conifers	Ivory 1972	Diseases of seedbeds, nurseries, and plantations of 6 conifers grown in West Malaysia are described.

TABLE 4.2. Continued

Species	Author(s)	Comments
Pinus sylvestris	Squillace et al. 1975	Strong genetic control was found for tolerance to *Lophodermium* needle cast in Holland. Height growth and needle-cast damage were highly correlated.
Eucalyptus spp.	Ferreira et al. 1976	In Brazil, infection by *Eucalpytus* canker starts at 3–5 months after planting and kills young trees and damages larger ones.
Several pines *Araucaria* spp.	Hodges 1976a	Most pines and *Araucaria* species grown in Brazil are attacked by the root disease *Cylindrocladium clavatum;* no pine has shown resistance. The roots become resin soaked and the foliage wilts and reddens rapidly.
Tropical pines	Hodges 1976b	*Cylindrocladium pteridis* attacks young pine needles only in the tropical areas. Sometimes as much as 80% infection occurs.
Pinus radiata	Carson 1977	Good tolerance has been found against *Dothistroma pini* in radiata pine.
Populus spp.	Palmberg 1977	Large differences in melampsora rust (*Melampsora* spp.) were found among clones of *Populus deltoides* and *P. nigra* tested in Australia. The rust, discovered in 1972, shows the importance of having many clones under test.
Several eucalypts	Hodges et al. 1979	*Eucalyptus* canker disease (*Diaporthe cubensis* or *Cryphonectria cubensis*) occurs over a widespread area, such as in Florida, Hawaii, and Puerto Rico as well as in South America.
Pinus resinosa	Nicholls 1979	Red pine is not disease free. The species has restricted genetic diversity and shows little resistance to pest outbreaks.
Ulmus spp.	Elgersma 1980	Dutch elm disease destroys many exotics. Resistance mechanisms have been found and described.
Pinus contorta	Martinsson 1980	In North America, lodgepole pine is subject to many pathogens. These are discussed along with the risks of transferring them to Europe or to other exotic plantings.
Pinus radiata *P. patula* *P. elliottii*	Ramirez 1981	The brown spot needle blight (*Scirrhia acicola*) has been found on radiata, patula, and slash pines.
Pinus radiata	Van der Pas 1981	Spraying copper compounds for control of *Dothistroma* is too expensive. The disease causes reduced early growth rates.

(continued)

TABLE 4.2. Continued

Species	Author(s)	Comments
Pinus radiata	Franich et al. 1982	The monoterpene composition of the foliage does not have a simple relationship to mature tree resistance to *Dothistroma pini*.
Pinus oocarpa	Greaves 1982a	A series of papers on diseases of *P. oocarpa* are abstracted. Part of these refer directly to exotics.
Many pine species *P. attenuata*	Kershaw et al. 1982	This booklet contains a complete description of *Dothistroma pini* disease, its infection, damage, and treatment. A list shows the relative susceptibility of various pine species. *P. attenuata* is most severely damaged.
Pinus contorta	Martinsson 1982a	So far, when grown in Sweden, this exotic has been essentially free of, or only lightly attacked by, the common diseases of pine. The author states "the introduction of lodgepole pine into Sweden must be considered a success as seen from a pathological . . . view."
Pinus radiata	Wilcox 1982c	There is high heritability for tolerance to *Dothistroma*. It is inherited in such a way that it can be reduced through use of seed orchards.
Guatemalan pines	Anderson et al. 1983	All 5 species tested are apparently susceptible to and show symptoms of fusiform rust (*Cronartium quercum* f. sp. *fusiforme*), which attacks the southern pines of the U.S.
Eucalyptus nitens	Anon. 1983b	Sources that maintain juvenile leaves, such as the Macalester provenance, are badly attacked by a leaf-spotting fungus in South Africa.
Acer platanoides	Wittberg 1983	Norway maples are found that are tolerant to *Verticillium* wilt. Resistant trees have lower vessel and vessel group densities than susceptible trees. This characteristic appears to be heritable.
Pinus banksiana *P. contorta*	Hunt & Van Sickle 1984	When measured on 62 provenances of *P. banksiana* and 77 provenances of *P. contorta,* it was found that the infection percentage of *Cronartium comptoniae* varied among provenances in both species. Provenances from outside the range of the alternate host *Myrica* were most susceptible.
Pinus attenuata	Brown & Doran 1985	Some provenances were little affected by *Dothistroma* and, even though there was considerable loss of foliage, growth ranking after 20 yr was only a little altered.

[a]Full references are shown in the reference list.

because of their mobility and the inability to predict where and when an attack will occur. Furthermore, there generally is a major lack of knowledge as to the genetics of the insect and of tolerance of the host. Too often it is not possible to cause forced attacks by the insect, which is so necessary in all types of resistance studies. Because of their presence and mobility, insects are often more noticed by, and hold a fascination for, the layman; epidemic insect build-ups are rapid and very dependent on environmental fluctuations.

Some insect pests are better known than others and new ones are always being found. For example, in Chile, the tip moth *Rhyacionia buoliana* has been found on *Pinus radiata;* it was introduced from Argentina. There is considerable concern about its potential damage to radiata pine plantations. Those that defoliate are always most evident, while the bark beetles also cause very visible damage. This has occurred in Queensland, Australia, where the southern pine engraver beetle (*Ips grandicolis*) was introduced from North America with imported pine timber that contained some bark. The insect is now widespread in exotic pine plantations in southern Queensland.

The sucking insects and those that damage the wood or those that operate underground like the termites cause less visible damage, although such insects can be devastating to the growth and quality of exotic plantations (Lamb, 1968). Insects can cause the loss of most valuable exotics; examples are *Cedrela odorata* and *Swietenia macrophylla,* which are damaged by the shoot borer *Hypsipyla grandella* (Ledoux, 1980). Loss of these two species, both of which otherwise would make fine exotics, is serious. Other species, like *Toona ciliata* (*Cedrela toona*), that resist the insect may be able partially to replace the unusable exotics.

As for diseases, there is no point in listing all the insects that attack exotic forest trees. Therefore, Table 4.3 has been prepared to indicate some insect pests and to give an idea of how diverse the insect damage problem on exotics may be. A number of summary publications list insect enemies of the forests, such as the worldwide survey by Morris (1983) describing the potential insect pests for *Alnus, Salix,* and *Populus,* some of which are used in exotic plantations. He includes tables of host tree species by region, the common and scientific names of the insects, the part of the tree attacked and the importance of the damage, country of occurrence, and natural controls. Another table includes host tree species, scientific names, and country of occurrence.

4.4.3.1 A Few Examples of Insect Tolerance. Although many foresters believe that tolerance of forest trees to insects is not large, this is not necessarily so. In his review article, Soegaard (1964) makes it clear that some species of both conifers and hardwoods have shown considerable tolerance to insect attack. In recent years, this information has greatly increased (see Table 4.3).

Currently, attempts are being made to determine a resistance pattern, even for the very destructive bark beetles (Waring and Pitman, 1980). Resin quality is a major factor in tolerance to bark beetles; especially important is the vapor toxicity of the monoterpenes of ponderosa pine (Smith, 1966). Smith con-

TABLE 4.3. Some Publications Dealing with Insects that Attack Exotics[a]

Species	Author(s)	Comments
Pines in general	Perry 1951	Discusses the bark beetles of pines in the donor areas. These have a potential to be transferred to the species that are used as exotics.
Eucalypts	Golfari 1963b	The insect pest *Cephisus siccifolias* occurs from Mexico to Argentina. It was especially studied in Misiones, Argentina.
Robinia pseudoacacia	Soegaard 1964	The widely used black locust shows variability in resistance to the locust borer (*Cullene robiniae*).
Pinus sylvestris	Wright et al. 1967	European sawfly (*Neodiprion sertifer*) attacked test plantings of Scots pine in southern Michigan. Northern sources were lightly attacked (less than 6%); central European sources were attacked 12–26%.
Gmelina arborea	Lamb 1968	The leaf-feeding insect *Calapepla leayana* so severely attacked limbs, leaves, and twigs in India that 4- to 6-yr-old trees were killed.
Pinus spp.	Henson et al. 1970	The pine sawflies are general in both exotic and indigenous pines and are often serious pests. It is possible to find provenances and individuals that have some tolerance.
Salix spp.	Randall 1971	There were differences in susceptibility within willows to the cottonwood leaf beetle (*Chrysomela scripta*).
Larix leptolepis	Farnsworth et al. 1972	There were significant between-origin differences to two different insects (larch sawfly, *Pristiphora enrichsoni,* and larch case borer, *Coleophora laricella*).
Pinus strobus *P. peuce*	Heimburger & Sullivan 1972	*P. peuce* showed more attack by the white pine weevil (*Pissodes strobi*) than *P. strobus* but had fewer leaders killed. Morphological characteristics of leaders and resin flow apparently affect tolerance.
Pinus sylvestris	Wright & Wilson 1972	The root collar weevil caused up to 69% mortality in rapidly growing sources from central Europe and up to 19% for western and southern sources.
Swietenia macrophylla *S. humulis* *S. mahogani*	Geary et al. 1973	*S. macrophylla* was heavily attacked by the shoot borer, *S. humilis* less, and *S. mahogani* was not attacked.
Picea spp. *P. abies* *P. sitchensis*	Mitchell et al. 1974	10 spruce species were studied to determine their susceptibility to white pine weevil (*Pissodes strobi). P. abies* was much more resistant.

TABLE 4.3. Continued

Species	Author(s)	Comments
		than the indigenous Sitka spruce in the northwestern U.S.
Toona ciliata	Grijpoma 1976	*Hypsipyla* is a very destructive shoot borer to *Toona ciliata,* but tolerant trees are sometimes found.
Populus spp.	Myers et al. 1976	Defoliating insects and aphids account for most of the insect problems that occur under intensive culture.
Larix leptolepis	Blada 1980	A number of larch clones were tested and showed considerable variation in resistance to *Adelges laricio.*
Ulmus pumila	Cunningham & Dix 1983	Windbreaks of Siberian elm are often severely defoliated by the spring cankerworm (*Paleacrita vernata*). Resistant trees occur. Percentage defoliation was greatest for trees with thicker leaves; tolerant trees started growth 2 weeks later than susceptible ones.
Pinus taeda and others	Darrow & Coetzee 1983	The 3 imported aphids, black pine aphid (*Cinara cronartii*), pine needle aphid (*Eulachnus rileyi*), and the pine woolly aphid (*Pineus pini*), are creating severe problems with several species of exotic pines grown in South Africa. Some other species of pine are tolerant to the insect.
Pinus contorta	LeCam 1983	All provenances of *P. contorta* were susceptible to the stinging insect *Evetrya;* most vigorous trees were the most susceptible.
Eucalyptus saligna *E. grandis* *E. deanei*	Wilcox et al. 1983a	*E. saligna* is far more tolerant to the *Eucalyptus* tortoise beetle (*Paropsis charybdis*) than are *E. grandis* or *E. deanei.*
Cedrela spp. *Swietenia* spp.	Ladrach 1984e	The *Hypsipyla* shoot borer of the Meliaceae has no known control; because of this, *Cedrela* and *Swietenia* are not planted commercially in many areas to which they are otherwise suited.
Pinus oocarpa *P. kesiya* *P. caribaea*	Halos & Abarquez 1984	Two shoot moth species (*Dioryctria rubella* and *Petrova cristata*) attacked all species 100%. However, *P. kesiya* was the most damaged and *P. caribaea* the least.

[a]Full references are shown in the reference list.

cludes: "Host specificity of bark beetles, particularly on hard pines, can be associated with resin vapors."

Similarly, Harris et al. (1983) found that the monoterpene profile is important as an indicator of the tolerance of *Picea sitchensis* to the white pine weevil (*Pissodes strobi*). Bark beetles are becoming increasingly important as exotic conifers are planted over large areas, especially on marginal sites. Using tolerance to sawflies (*Neodiprion*) as an example, Henson et al. (1970) expressed the opinion that trees can be developed with comparatively low susceptibility to insect damage.

One group of insects, the shoot moths, which belong to *Rhyacionia,* are widespread and destructive. Usually, host tolerance to them is not considered, but Holst (1963) found some tolerance by species. Similarly, the webworm and tip moth attacks so destructive to pines in the southern United States show differences in degree of attack related to seed source.

The aphids are another group of insects that do widespread damage to exotics. On Douglas-fir, Meinartowicz and Szmidt (1978) found plantations infected from 0 to 94%, with those sources of Douglas-fir from east of the Cascades being most tolerant. They concluded that the differences appear to be under genetic control. In South Africa and Zimbabwe, the black pine aphid (*Cinara cronartii*) on *Pinus taeda* has greatly reduced the utility of that species; it causes growth loss, death, and a major change in wood properties through the stimulation of compressionlike wood (Barnes et al., 1976; Darrow and Coetzee, 1983; Van der Sijde et al., 1985). Excessive compression-like wood is formed following attack by the black pine aphid. Results are so severe that planting of *Pinus taeda* has been stopped until enough tolerant families have been found. The pine woolly aphid (*Pineus pini*) introduced into Zimbabwe (Rhodesia) in 1962 has spread to all forested areas in southern Africa. *Pinus sylvestris* is most susceptible, the Mexican pines are more tolerant, all white pines are resistant. Pines under stress are particularly susceptible. Merrifield and Howcroft (1975) describe the damage of the red wax scale (*Ceroplastic rubens*) on *Pinus caribaea:* a check showed that the scale was found on 6 of the 13 species of pine studied in Papua, New Guinea. Dense sooty-molds made the crowns dark and height increment was reduced.

In the authors' opinion, the use of chemical sprays must be viewed as the very last resort to keeping the forest intact until tolerant strains of the best exotics and/or biological control of the insects have been achieved. After this has occurred, there will be a drastic reduction in the potentially deleterious effects of pesticides on the environment. If an insect pest occurs in exotic forests, it is sometimes contained by introducing biological control, that is, parasites from the native range of the species, as was done in South Africa with the control of *Eucalyptus* snout-beetle (*Gonipterus scuttellatus*) by a parasite wasp (von Rensburg, 1984).

4.4.3.2 The Special Situation of Ants, Termites, and Pine Wood Nematodes.
In some tropical and subtropical areas, the most serious restriction to growing exotics are the so-called leaf-cutting ants. These pests are widespread and trem-

endously destructive, making successful exotic forestry where they occur impossible without their control. There are several kinds, chief of which are those of the genera *Atta* and *Acromyrmex,* which defoliate both young and old trees, conifers and hardwoods. (A review of the status of leaf-cutting ants was given by Cherrett and Peregrine in 1976.) There is a species preference, but when the ants are bad, few trees escape. Foliage is cut, transported to underground nests, where fungi are grown for the ants to feed upon.

Control of leaf-cutting ants is difficult, but some applied chemicals, such as Myrex and methyl bromide (to name a few), or chemically treated baits are being used successfully. Under the latter conditions the ants transport the baits, which can be treated with chemicals or other fungi, to the nests, where either the food supply is destroyed or the ants that eat the food supply are poisoned. A group studying ant control in Brazil reports often on joint studies. One such report, by S. Alves, discusses the effects of introducing the fungus *Metharizium anisopliae* into an artificial ant hill. Leaf-cutting activity was reduced one hour after application, and after 60 days the ant population was significantly reduced (Filho and Pacheco, 1985). In Minas Gerais, Brazil, Santos et al. (1979) used pure diesel oil, which decomposes at high temperature and asphyxiates the ants by exhaust gases with less than 50% efficiency. Heptachlor (12%) killed 100% of *Atta laevigata.*

One of the most encouraging aspects of ant control is the apparent success of baits instead of the potentially dangerous chemicals that have been used in the past. For example, Naccarata (1983) tested eight different baits; those from orange pulp were most attractive to the ants. The baits were impregnated with different chemicals and kept in plastic bags. Baits using Myrex were the most effective. In Brazil, pineapple rind, eucalypt leaves, rice straw, and peanut shells were preferred in decreasing order (Filho and Pacheco, 1985). As such baits are being developed, however, it is necessary to use chemicals, because without ant control, plantation establishment will be a failure.

Another potentially exciting development is that of apparently ant-tolerant exotic individual trees. In Espirito Santo, Brazil, a number of *Eucalyptus grandis* trees have been selected that were bypassed by ants. The trees appear to be untouched in stands that have otherwise been completely defoliated (Fig. 4.12). In their report from Brazil, Filho and Pacheco (1985) showed that there were differences in provenance preference within species. In Venezuela we have noticed that the pines with thin, flexible needles are greatly preferred by the ants to those with thick, heavy needles. It appears possible, then, to overcome the ant problem by the two-pronged attack of biological control of the ant and development of tolerance in the host.

A great deal of study has been done on the life cycle and control of leaf-cutting ants. For example, Fowler et al. (1984) studied the spread and establishment of the leaf-cutting ant *Atta capiguara.* They found that elimination of ant colonies by poison baits led to a higher success rate of subsequent colony founding than when mature ant colonies were present. In Venezuela, Naccarata (1983) studied the biology of the very serious leaf-cutting ants *Acromyrex laevigata* and *A. landolti.* It was found that only small populations of

Figure 4.12. In an area of *Eucalyptus* completely defoliated by leaf-cutting ants, an occasional tree is not touched, as shown. These are being tested in Brazil to determine if usable ant tolerance is present. Current studies are encouraging.

A. laevigata were found in the savanna (where trees are to be planted), but the population exploded in the pine plantations and did serious damage. Nacarrata cites a number of studies in Brazil and elsewhere where ant control by baits has been tried. In Brazil, Filho and Pacheco (1985) showed that the leaf-cutting ant *Atta sexdens rubropilosa* preferred young leaves of *Eucalyptus grandis* to older leaves. Leaves of the species *E. tereticornis* were most preferred, and those of *E. grandis* the least.

Termites can do widespread damage on many species of trees. Sometimes trees like *Gmelina arborea* are tolerant, while at other times in different environments they are damaged. Termite damage is so severe in some tropical areas that profitable exotic forest tree crops cannot be grown. Efficient controls for termites are not known. More commonly, subterranean termites cause great damage to sound, seasoned timber, as do the dry-wood termites (Yale and Wylie, 1983).

Another organism with great potential for destruction of exotics is the pine wood nematode (*Bursaphelenchus xylophilus*), which causes severe damage and pine wilt in Japan (Wingfield et al., 1982). The nematode is also found in the United States and Canada. The authors state that monocultures, off-site plantings, and the introduction of effective vectors could result in heavy nematode damage; exotics are frequently attacked. There are definite differences in species susceptibility. In Japan, *Pinus densiflora* is least sensitive, although there are no differences among provenances. Exotic species such as *P. oocarpa* are severely infested. The nematode is apparently spread by Japanese pine sawyers (*Monochamus alternatus*) (Ohba, 1984). Ohba warns of the adverse consequences if the nematode and its vector are introduced into areas of heavy exotic pine production. Furukoshi and Sasaki (1982) show that certain hybrids made with exotics have a strong tolerance to the nematode;

among these are *P. densiflora* × *P. nigra, P. thunbergii* × *P. massoniana,* and *P. thunbergii* × *P. nigra.*

4.4.4 Miscellaneous Pests of Exotics

In addition to insects and diseases, other destructive pests cause major problems with exotics. Frequently, animals or birds cause damage, and it is not unusual for the exotic to be a preferred food source (Radwan, 1972). This preference was reported by Krutzsch (1974) for lodgepole pine in Sweden. He stated: "It is a very welcome addition to our mammals' natural dishes, and even some insects show a preference for lodgepole pine." Similar problems in Sweden were cited by Kiellander (1963), who noted that exotics were especially palatable to roe deer, elk, and rabbits. It is so serious a problem that sometimes special fencing is required, but fencing against elk and rabbits is not very effective.

As discussed in more detail in later chapters, humans and associated animals are a major source of preventing regeneration after forests have been cut. Especially destructive in the semiarid areas are sheep and goats. As was stated by Thirgood (1983), "Goats and forests do not mix," and several researchers have found that, of those commonly found where many exotics species are used, goats and sheep are the worst enemies of the forest. Although animal damage is widespread on natural regeneration of indigenous forests, it also is most applicable to exotic forest plantations, which are frequently destroyed by indiscriminate grazing.

4.5 UNUSUAL PROBLEMS WITH GROWING EXOTIC FORESTS

It was earlier stated that numerous enemies of exotic forests do not fit neatly into the category of soil, weather, or pests. Some of these can be very important and a few of them will now be treated as miscellaneous enemies.

4.5.1 Poisoning of the Soil by Trees—Allelopathy

One factor limiting growth of exotics is very hard to categorize. It results when a tree "poisons" the soil, resulting in poor growth for itself or for other species (Fisher, 1980). The technical term used to describe this phenomenon is *allelopathy,* which is the influence of plants, other than microorganisms, upon each other, arising from the products of their metabolism. A simple definition of allelopathy was given by Webster and McKetchnie (1980), as "the reputed influence of one living plant upon another due to secretion of toxic substances." A great deal has been written about allelopathy in agriculture and, recently, in forestry. Much of it is summarized by Rice (1984), including the newest information on forest trees. Rice states that, unfortunately, in forestry most studies of allelopathy have been made on very young trees.

Some species poison the environment, so that they cannot be grown in pure plantations. Allelopathy is present among tropical and subtropical forest trees, as reported for *Grevillia robusta* by Webb et al. (1967), who found that the roots of this rain forest species produced a toxic substance. The best-known species in the temperate area to be allelopathic is *Juglans nigra* (walnut) (Gabriel, 1975), which produces the toxic substance juglone. When, for example, pines are planted where walnuts have been grown, they often die or are stunted. A similar allelopathic reaction was found by DeBell (1971) for cherrybark oak (*Quercus pagodafolia*). Many exotic species, such as those in *Eucalyptus,* and even some pines, appear to have mild to severe "allelopathic" effects because of changes they cause in the soil environment.

It is suspected that the problems encountered when growing some tropical hardwoods in pure plantations may have an allelopathic cause. Of major importance to the forester growing exotics, many weed species and grasses are strongly allelopathic, resulting in damage and growth retardation greater than that caused by simple competition.

4.5.2 Fume Damage and Acid Rain

In parts of the world, especially in the Northern Hemisphere, exotics are sometimes grown where the indigenous species show adverse effects from fumes or acid rain. However, most exotics, especially the eucalypts, are injured just as much as the indigenous species. It is not suitable to cover the problem of acid rain and fume damage at length in relation to exotics, but these destructive environmental factors certainly are becoming of increasing importance when growing exotics (Cowling, 1979). Their potential to limit production must be recognized, as well as the occasional instances where exotics can be used to overcome the problem (Fig. 4.13).

The subject of air pollution and acid rain as they affect forest tree growth

Figure 4.13. Fume damage is a cause of growth decline and sometimes death in exotics. Shown are two *Pinus taeda* in North Carolina, one killed and one uninjured, to illustrate the huge differential susceptibility to this type of damage. (Photo courtesy of John Wiley & Sons.)

was covered in some detail by Zobel and Talbert (1984). Since forest trees obtain part of their essential nutrients, such as carbon dioxide, nitrogen, and sulfur, as well as an important part of the minor mineral elements from the air (Witwer and Buckovac, 1969), toxic substances that occur as gases or fine particles (such as in smoke or smog) can be very important. Sometimes trees are killed or are deformed or sustain a loss in growth (Berry, 1973).

The most widespread and serious problem from fume damage is loss of growth, but this often goes unnoticed or is ignored by the forester. Another serious problem is the increase in susceptibility to other pests by the pollutant-weakened trees; frequently the fumes cause a loss in vigor that enables a normally nondestructive pest to become important (Treshow, 1980). This has been the case for attack by beetles on spruce and pine in Europe and on *Eucalyptus* in Brazil, both of which have resulted in serious losses when fume weakened trees have been damaged. The pollutants can modify the physiology of the host tree, or even physically damage it, thus increasing the potential for infection of the host plant by pests. However, air pollutants can inhibit parisitism by acting directly on the fungus or bacteria, and sometimes the changes in the host by pollutants can make it less susceptible to pests (Treshow, 1980).

Perhaps the most intensive studies on exotics and air pollutants have been on the poplars because they are frequently grown near population centers (Patton, 1981). As a result of the increased awareness now developing, and since much more needs to be learned of damage potential, symposia such as the proceedings edited by Bialobok (1980) cover what is known about chemical problems and potential methods to avoid losses. Concern for chemical damage applies to exotics as well as to indigenous species, but it is becoming greater for exotics as population centers expand into areas where exotics are grown.

Although acid precipitation is a threat to exotic forest plantings, the precise seriousness and damage is not yet well understood. The effects of acid precipitation on forests is still so uncertain, the variability among forest trees and soils is so great, and the growth responses are so long-term that the actual effects of acid precipitation on growth of exotics have not yet been generally quantified (Cowling and Davey, 1981; Hornbeck, 1981). A number of researchers have hypothesized about how acid precipitation might affect the trees. Some of these would be of major concern to persons growing exotics on marginal sites. For example, Shriner (1976) feels that erosion of the protective waxes on leaves causes problems related to drought hardiness and pest resistance, while Ulrich et al. (1980) blame the killing of feeder roots by acid-mobilized aluminum. Fume damage, such as from ozone, seems to be greater in trees also subjected to acid rain. No matter how it operates, air pollution predisposes the weakened trees to attack by insects, particularly bark beetles.

As industrialization increases in areas where exotics are grown, acid rain and fume damage will become a major factor. It is possible to develop strains of trees more tolerant to fumes and it is possible to develop trees that will grow with nutrient deficiencies such as would occur from acid precipitation (Van Buijtenen and Isbell, 1970). These threats to productivity of exotic forestry are now just developing and much is yet to be learned. There is even concern about the effects of a greater carbon dioxide concentration on exotic forests and their having a modifying effect (Woodwell et al., 1983).

4.5.3 Abnormal Growth and Tree Form

Sometimes the exotic does not grow normally in its new environment. For example, it frequently happens that near the equator some conifers lose strong apical dominance and grow very crooked or have multiple tops. Provenance differences in this response are great, but it is an adverse response that cannot be exactly predicted. Many stands of trees, especially *Pinus caribaea, P. elliottii, P. taeda,* and *P. kesiya,* are prone to wavy bole growth in exotic environments. Even though growth may be good, much of the wood is of low quality because of a high amount of compression wood (see Chapter 9).

One of the most bizarre abnormal growth patterns common to several exotic pine species is the production of what are commonly called "foxtail" pines, which produce only a central stem and few or no limbs (Fig. 4.14). Such trees put on excellent height growth, but as they get older they tend to lean and to have sweep in the bole. Many individuals produce the foxtail form for three to five years and then resume branch production. If a main leader is then formed, the tree will develop normally thereafter. Frequently, however, a

Figure 4.14. A common response when subtropical or temperate pines are moved into tropical environments is for them to form foxtails. This is illustrated for *P. caribaea* growing in the grasslands of the Meta River Basin in Colombia. Few or no side branches are formed or they are formed late.

"basket top" of many leaders is formed, which makes the tree top-heavy so that it develops an accentuated lean. Most foxtailing occurs in *Pinus caribaea* var. *hondurensis* (it is much less prevalent in the varieties *bahamensis* and *caribaea*) and *P. kesiya*. It is much less frequent in *P. patula* and *P. oocarpa* and will occur occasionally in species such as *P. taeda* or *P. elliottii* or other pines grown in tropical environments.

Foxtailing varies greatly by provenance within species; for example, in India, Das and Stephan (1984a) found great differences in foxtailing among provenances of *Pinus caribaea* var. *hondurensis; P. pseudostrobus* also has poor form and many foxtails. In South Africa, Lückhoff (1964) found similar results, as did Falkenhagen (1979).

In a study of the genetics of foxtails, Ledig and Whitmore (1981) determined that there was a strong enough inheritance pattern so that selecting against foxtailing would be effective. In Brazil, Kageyama et al. (1984) found that the selected normal trees produced progeny with many fewer foxtails than the commercial control. Genetic variation in foxtailing was observed among families, with a narrow-sense heritability of individual trees of $h^2 = 0.62$. They summarize that their studies confirm the strong genetic control for foxtailing; similar strong inheritance for the presence of foxtailing was found for *P. caribaea* in Brazil by Sato and Brune (1983). We have observed that one generation of selection could reduce foxtailing in *Pinus caribaea* var. *hondurensis* by more than 30%. In Queensland, Australia, in Colombia, and in many other areas, seed collection following intensive selection against foxtailing has produced plants that were very low in this deformity. Such results were reported by Hawkins et al. (1978) when they found in Queensland that land races of local superior trees had fewer foxtails than stock from imported or local routine sources.

Foxtailing is stimulated by certain environments. It may be as high as 85% or none may occur, depending upon the species and the environment where it is grown. Bell (1977) reports it as related to boron deficiency. In his studies of the relationships of foxtails to soils, Liegel (1981b) related this deformity to a higher nutrient status in the soils around foxtailed trees; foliage element concentrations in foxtails were usually higher than for normal-branched trees. Granhoff (1977) seems to agree when he states that better growth conditions tend to induce more foxtails. He also observes that the fastest-growing provenances of *P. caribaea* var. *hondurensis* have more foxtails. Similarly, Golfari (1972) found for *P. caribaea* var. *hondurensis* that foxtail growth occurs most frequently on sites with a low or no water deficit and decreases where the deficit is more pronounced. One thing is certain, foxtailing is more frequent the closer the exotic is planted to the equator at lower elevations. Regardless of its cause, it is necessary for a specific environment to be combined with the genetic potential for foxtailing to occur.

Heights of foxtails are greater than normal-limbed trees at all ages, but not so diameters at the older ages (nine years) (Whyte et al., 1981). In an earlier paper, Whyte et al. (1980a) suggest that foxtails are not particularly bad. A similar sentiment was expressed by Woods et al. (1979). Despite this, most foresters grade strongly against foxtails, many of which take on rather bizarre form, producing abnormal wood as they grow older. Those trees that foxtail early and then develop a normal growth pattern seem to produce normal wood.

Another undesirable form of many conifers in tropical plantations is the production of multiple-branched tops without a definite leader. These often develop into top-heavy trees which lean, resulting in large amounts of compression wood, ring shake, and resin deposition. This defect appears to be easily overcome by intensive selection for form as land races are developed. Not too much has been reported about the genetics of branch characteristics of exotics. As discussed in Chapter 2, high-elevation and high-latitude sources frequently have small limbs with a flat branch angle and the more tropical sources have less desirable limbs. For *Pinus attenuata* in Australia, Brown and Doran (1985) found that some sources, such as those from the California Coast Range, at altitudes of less than 1000 m had very vigorous growth and relatively small limbs.

4.5.4 Weed Competition

Although normally not listed in the category of a pest, weed competition can be a serious deterrent to growth of exotics. For example, Wilde et al. (1968) stress how the consumption of water by weeds depresses growth. On good soils *Pinus resinosa* plantations consumed about 500 kg of water to produce 1 kg of dry matter. Heavy blueberry, sweet fern, and heath plants can cause more than 50% loss in the volume of mature timber. This is covered in more detail in Chapter 6, where the severe effects of weed competition in the tropics and subtropics are discussed. Lack of control of weedy vegetation (pests) can cause total failure of the tree crop. The importance of weeds as a pest limiting growth of exotic forest trees cannot be overemphasized.

4.6 EXOTICS AS PESTS

Too little thought is usually given to the aggressive characteristics of some tree species that, when used as exotics, grow so well that they become weeds that crowd out desired indigenous species. Although not much discussed or recognized in print, the problem of a species used as an exotic becoming a pest is widespread. In some areas, the exotic pines become such a pest that pastures must be periodically mowed to keep grass production from being reduced by the heavy growth of tree seedlings. In South Africa, New Zealand, and other areas, exotic pines such as *P. pinaster, P. patula, P. strobus,* and *P. radiata* are taking over the natural forests and suppressing the indigenous species. This is especially frustrating in parks and plant reserves whose botanical values are ruined by the aggressive exotic competitors (Fig. 4.15).

The problem of exotics competing with and overcoming indigenous vegetation is becoming more severe. It has strong political overtones and is often

Figure 4.15. One of the greatest dangers in growing exotics is that they may escape and essentially become a weed, as shown in this photo from southern Africa, where the exotic pines are destroying much of the indigenous vegetation.

cited as a reason why exotics should be banned (see Chapter 11). A publication on firewood by the National Academy of Sciences (1983) has a special warning section that reads as follows:

> Because of the severity of the firewood crisis, the panel has selected trees and shrubs that are aggressive and grow rapidly. These seem appropriate for cultivation in areas of extreme fuel shortage, particularly when climates and soil conditions are harsh. . . . such potentially invasive plants should be introduced only with great care and with serious consideration for the threat posed by their weediness.

Such invasion by *Leucaena* and *Acacia* is evident in a number of places in the tropical and subtropical areas of the world. For example, *Cassia siamea* is so widespread that it is considered to be indigenous in parts of Colombia, although historically it apparently was an exotic.

Among one of the most insidious exotics "gone wild" in parts of North America is the "Tree-of-Heaven" (*Ailanthus altissima*). It is a super-hardy tree, resistant to smoke, fumes, and dust, is drought hardy, and will grow on shallow soils and where other trees will not (Baxter, 1967). But it is a very aggressive tree and a real pest on some good sites in prime hardwood forests. It seems to have few enemies other than foresters. Another tree that has become somewhat of a pest in certain areas is the mulberry (*Morus* spp.). Causing great concern in the southeastern United States are the two Australian species *Melaleuca quinquenervia* and *Casuarina glauca;* these have become widely spread, the former through seed and the latter by root suckers (Vietmeyer 1986a,b). In South Africa, 8 of the 19 species of acacias are from Australia and are most aggressive following fire, invading and suppressing indigenous vegetation (Berg, 1977). Another species causing similar problems in South Africa is *Hakea suaveolens* (Boland and Turnbull, 1981). The Brazilian peppertree (*Schinus terebinthifolia*) has strongly invaded the Everglades in Florida. No control has proven to be effective (Toops, 1986).

Many species grown as exotics have the potential to become a pest. Real care must be taken when working with exotics so that a bigger problem is not created than is being solved by introducing an overly aggressive species.

4.6.1 Effects of Exotics on Soil and Water

The subject of the so-called adverse effects of exotics in relation to political considerations is thoroughly covered in Chapter 10. It is sufficient to state here that there are many adverse effects ascribed to exotics, some of which are true, many of which are not. Few really good studies have been made; one exception is by Lundmark et al. (1982), who reported results for paired stands of Scots and lodgepole pines that were 25 to 50 years old. Some differences were found, such as more litter fall with higher nitrogen content and lower pH values under lodgepole pine than under the Scots pine stands. In the Scots pine, the rate of decomposition of the litter was faster than for lodgepole pine. In Spain, Temes et al. (1985) compared soils under *Eucalyptus globulus, Pinus pinaster,* and *Quercus robur.* The flora under the three species and the physical condition of the soils were about the same. Similar results were reported by Bard (1984).

In his dissertation on soil and nutrient cycling under natural and plantation forests in Tanzania, Lundgren (1978) summarizes as follows:

> Without special soil conservation measures, the conversion of natural vegetation (forest or bush) to man-made forests, with the management techniques normally used today, and continued cropping of plantations, will inevitably result in soil deterioration in the form of decreased soil organic matter and nutrient levels, and loss of topsoil structure and porosity. The magnitude and speed of this deterioration will depend on: a. *Initial soil conditions.* . . . b. *Climatic conditions.* . . . c. *Management practices.* . . . d. *Species used.* . . .

One of the most commonly mentioned problems is that exotics change the quality and amount of the water supply that drains from the forest. One study in New Zealand on *Pinus radiata* (Dyck and Cooke, 1981) showed that nutrient losses from draining water was less from the pine plantation than from an adjacent pasture. The nutrients in the forest were cycled rather than leached off.

4.7 LIMITING THE RISKS

The subject of avoiding the risks outlined in the preceding sections is too complex and broad to cover in detail, but it can be summarized as follows:

1. Take care not to reduce too greatly the genetic variability of the exotics used. Even though most trees are very heterozygous, it is generally felt that

about 30 unrelated individuals should be used in an operational program, while 400 or more are needed in a longer-term breeding program. Since, too frequently, seed of exotics are obtained from a few trees (sometimes from only one tree), the often related item of keeping the genetic base broad enough has often been ignored. This error must be corrected! The danger is always there. If, for example, seed were collected from 400 trees and 10,000 ha were established as an exotic plantation, one would assume that selections of the best 30 trees from this large plantation would be safe. But this is not necessarily so! If, as usually happens, 1 or 2 of the 400 parents were very strong general combiners, essentially all 30 selections would be either half- or full-sibs and thus totally unsuited for a long-term breeding program. That is why (see Chapter 3) we so strongly urge that pedigrees be known before selections are made.

2.   Use care when planting exotics in marginal environments. Even the best of exotics have their environmental limitations beyond which performance is not satisfactory. Off-site planting is common and contributes a great deal to the failures of, and attack by pests on, exotics. At best, one is working on the edge of adaptability with exotics, as discussed in Chapter 3. When conditions are known or suspected to be dangerously adverse, avoid widespread planting of the exotic.

3.   When seed or vegetative material is transferred, use the strictest sanitary precautions to prevent importing a pest that will attack the exotic, and perhaps also the indigenous species. Rules are sometimes cumbersome and frequently administered so bureaucratically that the urge is to bypass the whole process. This is dangerous indeed, especially with "green tissue" used for grafting or rooting.

4.   Do not permit the import of unbarked logs. Pests are frequently present (or brooding) under the bark and many pests have been transferred in this manner. In a similar vein, be very careful of using exotics near harbors or where timber imports take place.

5.   Make sure the soils are suitable for exotics. Frequently, nutrient deficiencies, such as of phosphorus or boron, occur where exotics are planted. Equally serious, pH values fluctuate widely in different environments, and numerous failures have resulted from not taking these differences into account.

6.   Try to avoid areas with environments that occasionally exceed the tolerance of the exotic. Lack of knowledge about weather fluctuations is a common problem, but sometimes, even when suspected, it is ignored. Knowing the species used as an exotic is key—for example, one would never plant *Pinus oocarpa* in an area subject to high winds, or eucalypts where extreme cold temperature fluctuations occur.

7.   Make certain the plants are properly mycorrhizal. It is not generally known by many foresters, for example, that some hardwoods, such as *Eucalyptus* and *Quercus,* are ectomycorrhizal like most conifers and that some conifers are endomycorrhizal.

8.   Be sure that the species is not allelopathic when using it in plantations. If the planting area is subject to fume damage, make sure a species is used that has reasonable tolerance.

9.   Initiate an aggressive breeding program to combat the pests that cannot be handled silviculturally by developing tolerant land races.

10.   Use care that the exotic itself does not become a major pest.

5

SEED PRODUCTION, SEED CERTIFICATION, VEGETATIVE PROPAGATION, AND MONOCULTURE

5.1 SEED PRODUCTION OF EXOTICS

For an exotic program to be successful, sufficient seed of good quality must be available from the desired seed source. For some species used as exotics, such as *Cupressus lusitanica, Pinus taeda,* and *P. elliottii,* good seed are available. Enough suitable seed can also be obtained for some of the eucalypts and for certain seed sources for species like *Pinus caribaea* and *Pinus contorta.* But, unfortunately, one of the most adverse phases of exotic forestry is a general lack of desired seed at a reasonable cost. As a result, more frequently than not, improper seed are used, thus limiting the productivity of exotic forests. Therefore, a major effort must revolve around developing a reliable seed supply. But this is not always a simple and straightforward matter, because seed production is sometimes not satisfactory in the exotic environment.

The changes in flowering and seed production with movement of a species to an exotic environment have been ascribed to many causes, some related to latitude or elevation and others independent of these factors. Rainfall, its amount and timing, is often given as a reason for the observed flowering patterns. More directly, temperature and its sequences have an obvious effect on either preventing the triggering of the flowering response, preventing the proper development of the reproductive structures, or, where cold is severe, actually killing the reproductive structures of the exotic.

In a paper that includes a discussion of poor seed production in *Pinus caribaea,* Slee (1977a) states: "Suggested causes are a failure of the pollen supply due to rainfall and high humidity—or breakdown of pollen development due to high temperatures." Another environmental factor affecting flowering is soil; it is commonly observed that seed production is much better on some soils than on others, such as on sands versus clays.

Drought stress is an important aspect of the frequency of flowering as well as the fruit and seed production of trees. Soil texture and climate (rainfall distribution) are two key components that affect drought stress. Well-drained, sandy-loam soils are generally conducive to seed production. Weather patterns that produce reduced rainfall during flower initiation also favor reproductive growth, at least in the hard pines. Assessment of local weather patterns and soil conditions can help in the selection of sites that are best suited for seed production. Excessively wet or well-drained sites should be avoided. The "drought day" concept, used by Gallegos (1977), is a convenient measure for determining the effect of soil physical characteristics and moisture availability (climate) on seed production.

A unique problem occurs with *Larix sibirica,* which produces good seed in its indigenous continental climate but fails in seed production when moved to a maritime climate in Sweden. The meiosis in the male strobili is susceptible to low temperatures. It is therefore important that pollen formation is stopped during the winter. It should not start developing until the risk of cold spells is over and the temperatures become reliably warm. In a continental climate ιhis does not happen until spring, but in a maritime climate there frequently are a few mild days in the middle of winter when the pollen will start to develop. The following cold kills the pollen that has started to grow (Ekberg and Eriksson, 1967; Stern and Roche, 1974).

In exotics there are some unusual problems related to flowering. Occasionally, especially in the tropical pines, the exotic does not produce seed even though strobili production is heavy, or it produces cones that have essentially no sound seed. This creates some major shortages of seed and sometimes prevents the use of the local land race in an area. Sometimes, flowering times vary greatly, even among populations and individuals of the same species. As an example, Bawa (1976) reports that adjoining populations of *Gmelina arborea* have two to three weeks' difference in time of flowering. Sound seed production may be delayed in some genera. In Zambia, Geary (1984) reports that the eucalypts do not flower for five years after planting and "inadequate flowering limits the ability to genetically improve *Eucalyptus* spp. in Zambia. Five years is a substantial part of the rotation age . . . imported seeds may be required for many years." Generally, however, most hardwoods will flower in the exotic environment.

Although some exotics have delayed or no seed production, others, especially some of the eucalypts and tropical pines, have flowering stimulated in certain exotic environments so that they have both heavy and early seed production (Fig. 5.1). When this happens, it gives a unique advantage to exotic forestry and opens up the possibility of growing seed as an economic crop for other areas, as is being done in South Africa (Smith, 1975).

The principles related to seed production in exotic species are essentially the same as for indigenous species in that they are responsive to fertilizers,

Figure 5.1. Early seed production is essential for development of exotic forestry. This photograph shows a *Eucalyptus grandis* seed production area that produces early and heavy crops. Sometimes, exotics produce flowers but little sound seed.

especially nitrogen, and to temperature; full sunlight is generally needed for best flowering. They are also responsive to use of growth regulators, girdling, or other management practices, as used on larch by Melchior (1960) and Bonnet-Masimbert (1982); to exogenous growth substances on Scots pine (Brown and Sauvé, 1975); to gibberellins on *Picea abies* and many other species (Hashizume, 1975; Pharis, 1976; Dunberg, 1980); to thinning in radiata pine (Eldridge, 1966); and many other methods too numerous to mention.

The subject of factors affecting cone and flower initiation were reviewed by Nienstaedt (1961), Wareing and Longman (1960), and Lee (1979). Climatological control of flowering in forest trees was covered by Sarvas (1967). He stresses the importance of temperature when it is assessed as "temperature sums" in the colder climates. The importance of heat and light were also stressed in Giertych's 1977 review of flowering of forest trees.

One complex factor affecting flowering is the response of the exotic to light. According to Christiansen and Lewis (1982), light-mediated systems determine when the plant shifts from a vegetative to a generative stage. Most plants require a certain number of days or weeks of the proper combination of temperature and light before flowering is induced. In agriculture, it has been possible to breed strains for a broad tolerance to environmental triggering of flowering; we are not aware of any such effort in forestry, although the individual variations in time, precocity, and heaviness of flowering within populations of exotic species are enormous and inheritance in flowering capacity is large (Chaves et al., 1983).

Despite the complexity, in its simplest state, flowering in most plants is regulated by the daily light–dark cycle, according to Christiansen and Lewis, (1982). It is our opinion that upsetting this cycle has a major effect on flowering in exotics. Although not intensively studied, especially for exotic forest trees, light intensity and light quality as related to the latitude and elevation where exotics are established probably have major influences on flowering.

Frequently there is a lack of knowledge about how best to handle and store seed of exotics. There are several broad-based publications on this subject such as those by Schopmeyer (1974) and Willan (1984). Handling and storage characteristics of seeds of exotics and treatment for germination are covered for many species in publications of this kind. Some exotics are not widely used because of difficulties of seed storage or transport. An example is *Araucaria hunsteinii* from New Guinea. Although there is definite interest in this species for exotic plantations, Howcroft (1983) states that "serious losses in seed viability, during storage and transportation, have restricted its use as an exotic species for large scale plantations, and prevented the establishment of provenance trials."

A few publications related to flowering in exotics are listed in Table 5.1 to give the reader some idea of the problems involved.

5.1.1 Production of Abnormal Flowers or Seed

As mentioned earlier, exotic species frequently either do not produce flowers, fruits, or cones or they have a low seed set; many seeds fail to germinate. There are numerous causes for this but they all relate to moving the trees so that they are out of synchronization with the environment, upsetting the normal physiological flowering processes. One rather common response, especially in the tropical pines, is that the trees produce catkins and conelets throughout the year, but not necessarily in synchronization. This has been observed by the authors in many places, such as Fiji, Brazil, and French Guiana, and seems to be a common response in the tropical areas when exotics are grown near the equator.

One adverse and frustrating result with seed production in exotics, especially in the cold climates, is to have what appears to be normal flowering and seed production but to find that the embryos in the seed are only partially developed and will not germinate or germinate only very weakly (Ryynänen, 1982). Such a problem plagued the tree improvement people in northern Europe, and seed orchards established in the colder climates were often of only limited value (Sarvas, 1962). This problem has been one major stimulus to moving seed orchards into the warmer climates, as is now commonly done in the Scandinavian countries.

Exotic species sometimes have greatly delayed seed production, or only one kind of reproductive structure is produced. This occurred for *Araucaria hunsteinii* when grown in Uganda. At 20 years of age, few trees have produced flowers, and those that have done so have only male and no female structures (Howcroft, 1983).

Perhaps the most common problem with seed production of exotics is to move them into an environment where they will grow but where the weather sequence is such that the flowers usually freeze. This has been a major problem

TABLE 5.1. Some Flowering and Seed Production Studies for Exotic Species[a]

Species	Author(s)	General Results
7 Eucalypt species	Moggi 1958	A 24-month developmental cycle is described in Italy that is divided into 6 stages. Inflorescences were initiated in May; buds developed slowly for 1 yr and flowering occurred in July. The last seeds were shed in April.
Eucalyptus camaldulensis	Zucconi 1958	The paper gives an account of the development, morphology, and embryology of ovaries, etc. Studying the 11 chromosomes in this species is not too difficult.
Liriodendron tulipifera	Taft 1962	Honeybees did not significantly affect the viability of yellow poplar in North Carolina. Control pollinations were very successful.
Eucalyptus regnans	Eldridge 1963	Increasing the bee population did not affect seed production. Only one-tenth of all ovules per bud formed viable seed in Australia.
Gmelina arborea	Lamb 1968	Trees flower as young as 3 or 4 yr; flowering is regular and usually plentiful each year. Germination power is high for fresh seed, but some viability is lost when seed are stored.
Tectona grandis	Bryndum & Hedegart 1969	The flowering period of an individual tree is 1 day. Emasculation and isolation can be carried out for 1 hr after the flower is fully opened. Insects are the primary pollinators, but some wind pollination may occur.
Eucalyptus camaldulensis	Panetsos 1969	Flowering in Greece was from mid-May to July, 1 yr after initiation of the inflorescences. In September, capsules had seed with 95% germination.
Eucalyptus camaldulensis	Barrett & Carter 1970	Flowering was observed in all provenances at 2.5 yr of age. Northern warmer sources flowered more heavily than the southern sources when grown in Zimbabwe.
Larix leptolepis	Fransworth et al. 1972	There were strong genetic differences as well as genotype × plantation interactions in production of female flowers in the north-central U.S.
Eucalyptus camaldulensis	Doull 1973	The author discusses pollination of eucalypts by honeybees in Australia, mostly by the European honeybee introduced in 1826.
Pinus caribaea var. *hondurensis*	Slee 1973	A temperature–daylength ratio was determined to help in prediction of climates where pine would flower and set seed. A range in this ratio is necessary for seed production, if not for flower production.

(continued)

TABLE 5.1. Continued

Species	Author(s)	General Results
Eucalyptus grandis	Hodgson 1976	Three stages in floral development are recognized. Flower buds take 4 months to anthesis and capsules mature after 5 months. Flowers are insect (mostly honeybee) pollinated. Little seed was produced by self-pollination, but varied from 3 to 47%. Degrade in vigor from self-pollination was 8% compared to outcrossing.
Pinus caribaea var. *hondurensis*	Drew & Cole 1977	A reconnaissance was made in Brazil. Reduced cone production occurred at higher latitudes and elevations. Best seed production was at low elevations (200 m or less) near latitude 13°.
Pseudotsuga menziesii	Enescu et al. 1977	All clones in a seed orchard in Romania responded in both male and female flower production to fertilizer treatments, but there were strong clonal × environment interactions.
Pinus caribaea var. *hondurensis*	Ibraham 1977	In the humid tropics there is almost no production of seed from exotic pine species. Little pollen is produced. Cones averaged only 3 to 6 seed/cone in *P. caribaea*. Control pollinations were not successful.
Pinus caribaea var. *hondurensis*	Slee 1977b	Development of strobili in Malaysia is abnormal compared to Queensland. Pollen may be shed any time of the year and shedding from a single cluster may spread over several months rather than the usual 2-week period.
Pinus caribaea var. *hondurensis*	Ng 1983	In Malaysia, *P. caribaea* seeds reliably only near the sea and on mountain ridges, but seed yields still are low compared to Queensland.
Pinus caribaea var. *hondurensis*	Greaves 1978	Inland provenances flower at an earlier age and produce more conelets than coastal provenances.
Gmelina arborea	Bowen & Eusebio 1983	Self-pollination in unlikely, but control self-pollinated flowers produce full-size fruits. There are two flowering peaks, and mature fruit is present about 1 month after flowering. There are large tree-to-tree differences in amount and time of seed production.
Pinus caribaea var. *hondurensis* *P. oocarpa*	Chaves et al. 1983	There is a large flowering difference among clones and a strong genetic control for flowering. Broad-sense heritabilities are 63 and 53% for female and 53 and 47% for male flowering in *hondurensis* and *P. oocarpa*. No correlation was found between flowering and vegetative growth.

TABLE 5.1. Continued

Species	Author(s)	General Results
Eucalyptus deglupta	Davidson 1983	Flowers are pollinated by insects and birds; bees are important. It is possible to emasculate, bag, and obtain sound seed. No selfs have yet been obtained.
Pinus caribaea var. *hondurensis*	Gallegos 1983	A world survey shows that the optimum environment for seed production is between 9 and 27° latitude N and S. No flowering occurs at high elevations, except between 9° N and S and latitude.
Pinus caribaea var. *hondurensis*	Gibson et al. 1983	Great provenance differences in flowering were found. The upland provenances were particularly prolific.
Cupressus lusitanica	Ladrach 1983b	Both flower and cone production were greatly increased in 2-yr-old grafts in Colombia.
Pinus caribaea var. *hondurensis*	Roberts et al. 1983	Flowering times were later the more tropical the location, with up to 6 weeks' difference recorded. At Darwin, Australia, there was some loss of coincidence of pollen flight and conelet receptivity.
General	Duryea & Brown 1984	A compendium of seed quality, physiology, and germination is included in the book.
Eucalyptus saligna E. *cloeziana*	Geary 1984	It is dangerous to make a species generalization about flowering. For example, one seed source of E. *saligna* did not flower, while 62% of another did. None of the E. *cloeziana* flowered in Zambia.
Larix leptolepis	Jo et al. 1984	In a 16-yr-old larch seed orchard in Korea, pollen density rapidly decreased to a distance of 40 m from the pollen source. Pollen captured varied greatly by wind direction from 63 to 7%. 43% of the ovules had one or more pollen grains; 71% of these developed to fertilization.
Pinus rigida × *taeda*	Park et al. 1984	Early cone collection in Korea produced seed with low germination. Specific gravity of cones (0.80) and moisture content (50%) were best indicators of cone ripeness and seed maturity.
Pinus rigida	Ryu et al. 1984a	Cones at lower nodes produced more seed. In Korea no difference was found in the percentage of fertile scales and full seeds between upper and lower nodes.

(continued)

TABLE 5.1. Continued

Species	Author(s)	General Results
Pinus rigida	Ryu et al. 1984b	Early- and late-flowering clones were present with a variation of 2 days in Korea. The h^2 for flowering dates is 0.5. Trees from northern provenances flowered early.
Pinus caribaea var. *hondurensis*	Spidy 1984	In Queensland, Australia, heavy flowering and seed production occurs, except in southeast Queensland. Regular and heavy flowering occurs at 7 yr on seedlings, 4 yr on grafts.
Tectona grandis	Keiding 1985	Covers flowering, seed production, and seed handling of teak. A good summary of all work on teak, including its natural distribution.
Pinus patula	Ladrach 1985c	Fertilization using nitrogen and boron increased male flower production in Colombia. Ringing branches and subsoiling had no effect.

[a]Full references are shown in the reference list.

in developing a land race of *Eucalyptus* in the southeastern United States (Hunt and Zobel, 1978). In this case, *E. viminalis* flowers heavily but they are produced in midwinter and nearly always freeze. A similar situation occurs when *P. elliottii* is moved north of its indigenous range. It flowers as it did farther south and the conelets are usually killed or the pollen is frozen during development, so that it is nonviable and few good seeds are formed.

Sometimes there are ways of overcoming poor seed production. One common method to increase flowering, frequently used by the forester, is to move trees from high latitudes or high elevations to warmer climates, where they often flower earlier and more heavily as exotics than they did in their indigenous environments. This reaction is a very practical one and is used to speed up production of genetically improved seed. For example, several seed orchards with clones from the southeastern United States have been established in South Africa to produce loblolly and slash pine seed for second-generation orchards (Smith, 1975). Seed quality is very high and seed production is early. The same principle has also been used in Europe and northern North America, where northern species are moved south to warmer climates to enhance seed production (Johnson et al., 1953; Vidacovíc, 1962; Schmidtling, 1978).

Selfing within *Eucalyptus* is varied. For example, Claudot (1963) found that seedlings from selfed seed of *E. camaldulensis* were uniform but only half the height of normal seedlings; an occasional selfed tree was very tall. In another study on *E. camaldulensis,* Mendoza (1970) reported that in Argentina the effects of self-pollination were not severe. Selfed trees had poorer germination (49–84%) and more abnormal seedlings (30–50%); those selfs that survived grew about as well as the control-pollinated progenies. In *E. grandis,* Van Wyk

(1981a) states that selfing is very detrimental to growth performance; full-sib mating is not desirable. On the same species, Hodgson (1976) mentioned that the greatest effect of inbreeding was on height, but that bole straightness was also affected. Yield of sound seed was seriously reduced in the selfs. In India, control pollination showed *E. tereticornis* and *E. camaldulensis* to be self-fertile (Venkatesh et al., 1973). In a series of three papers, Hodgson (1976) reported on the selfing ability of *E. grandis*. Although selfing was generally low, it graded as high as 47% on some individuals and over 80% in trees that had off-season flowering. Some species of eucalypts will not self.

It is sufficient to note for all exotic species that it is necessary to know the ability to self so that breeding, regeneration, and testing plans can be designed accordingly and proper seed orchards can be established.

5.1.2 Failure to Produce Viable Seeds—the *Pinus caribaea* Example

It will become immediately evident from Table 5.1 that the bulk of the references on the flowering patterns of conifers and lack of production of viable seeds is for *Pinus caribaea* var. *hondurensis.* Problems in seed production also occur for varieties *bahamensis* and *caribaea* as well as for several other tropical species, such as *P. oocarpa, P. kesiya,* and *P. patula,* when grown in exotic environments. To illustrate the failure of seed production of a species used as an exotic, we will use *P. caribaea* var. *hondurensis.*

The seriousness of the problem is emphasized by Ibrahim (1977), who worked with *P. caribaea* var. *hondurensis,* when he states: "In the humid tropics, there is almost no production of seed from exotic pine species." Even control-pollination attempts were unsuccessful. Gallegos (1983) found that this species does not produce viable seed at low latitudes (9°N–9°S), but Delwaulle (1982) states that there are exceptions such as the Congo, Kenya, and Tanzania. Varying climates, like the dry season in the Congo, result in considerable seed production, which is used in reforestation. Delwaulle says: "I am strongly of the opinion that climatic factors, rather than latitude *per se,* are limiting in . . . seed production of *P. caribaea* var. *hondurensis."* In Nigeria at latitudes 4 to 10 degrees north, both male and female strobili are formed and a satisfactory number of seed are produced (Okoro, 1985).

The seed supply situation in Honduran pine is critical. Many of the indigenous stands are now gone or so badly degraded that seed from them is not desirable. In his collections for the CAMCORE Cooperative, Dvorak (1981a) stresses the disintegration of quality and outright destruction of many of the indigenous stands of *Pinus caribaea* var. *hondurensis,* especially the best provenances. Since most of the planting with this species is as an exotic, seed must be obtained from some indigenous source.

Many stands of *P. caribaea* var. *hondurensis* grown as an exotic are of seed-producing age. Sometimes large crops of viable seed are produced, such as in central Brazil, Queensland, and the Fiji highlands. But in other areas, mostly lowlands near the equator, this species produces very many strobili and conelets which hang on the tree and mature but which contain very few seeds, most of which are empty (Fig. 5.2). Because of the large demand and small supply, especially for genetically improved seed or seed of the desired provenances, the cost of seed of *P. caribaea* var. *hondurensis* has greatly increased, and frequently plantings are made with incorrect provenances simply because seeds from the desired ones are too expensive or are not available.

The cause of the failure of *P. caribaea* to produce good seed in the warm, humid tropics near the equator is not definitely known. There are many ideas and theories (see Table 5.1 for a few examples), some of which are:

1.   There is a shortage of pollen or it is produced out of synchronization with the receptive stage of the conelet, especially at the lower latitudes and altitudes (Gibson et al., 1983).

2.   There are heavy rains during pollination, so pollen never gets to the conelets (Nikles, 1973; Teunissen and Voorhoeve, 1973).

3.   The temperatures, especially night temperatures, are so high that the pollen does not germinate and the pollen tube does not grow well enough to effect fertilization (Slee, 1973; Shim, 1974; Slee, 1977b). In their analyses of many areas, Gibson et al. (1983) found that strobilus production was low or nonexistent in subtropical areas where the mean temperature was about 21°C,

Figure 5.2. *Pinus caribaea* has particularly severe problems related to seed production. Shown is a good tree in a seed production area at low elevation near the equator. Many cones are formed but only a few (one to five) sound seeds are produced per cone. It is necessary to produce seed of this species in a different environment from where it is grown in this planting.

the mean temperature for the hottest month 26°C, and for the coldest month 17.5°C.

4. Dieback of branch ends destroys many of the potential conelets (Slee, 1977a).

5. Photoperiod and the environment near the equator limit seed formation (Gallegos, 1980b).

Whatever the cause, the usually observed situation is that plentiful pollen is formed and many of the conelets stay on the trees and develop, but are small and abnormal. (Usually, unless at least some fertilization occurs, the conelet soon dries up and dehisces.) In some areas, most of the conelets are shed during the first year following pollination. Those that do mature have essentially no sound seed, or at least too few to make an economic collection. The only "cure" to the lack of seed production now known is to move seed orchards to higher latitudes or elevations or more inland, where definite seasons occur. A number of organizations are doing this. Too-high elevations or too-severe environments also are not conducive to seed production. Gallegos (1980b) states that the best seed production for *P. caribaea* var. *hondurensis* is between latitudes 9 to 27 degrees north and south.

Even though most publications about lack of seed production refer to *P. caribaea,* the seed situation in the tropical areas can be as severe with *P. oocarpa, P. patula,* and *P. kesiya* (Fig. 5.3). As a result, these species are planted less than they would be otherwise because, although they often grow very well, seed are not available. Therefore, the usual method of getting a temporary source of seed as a land race from exotic plantations, by collecting from individual trees or from seed production areas, cannot be practiced. It is safe to say that *limitation* of *seed production* in the exotic environment is *one of the most serious problems in exotic pine forestry,* especially in the tropics, as illustrated earlier for Honduran pine.

Figure 5.3. A seed orchard of *Pinus patula* established at the wrong elevation near the equator is illustrated. Although the trees grow very well, essentially no sound seed are produced.

5.1.3 Production of Early and Heavy Seed Crops

As just discussed, some exotic species fail to flower or produce a reasonable number of viable seeds in the new environment. But sometimes the physiological response to the exotic environment is just the opposite and the exotic species flowers very heavily and early in the new environment. This occurs for several species. For example, seed crops are very heavy and early in *Pinus taeda* and *P. elliottii* when grown in South Africa, Zimbabwe, and in parts of Brazil. Because of this, a number of advanced-generation orchards of these two species have been established and are now producing considerable quantities of seed. The economic potential for this practice, along with some of its restrictions, were outlined by Smith (1975). It is not unusual for flowering to be so heavy that small seed orchards can supply large amounts of seed. Early and heavy seed production is commonly found for some species of *Eucalyptus* in exotic environments. In Brazil, for example, it is not unusual to find flowers on *E. grandis* at 6 to 10 months of age, much earlier than this species flowers in its indigenous range. For several temperate species, such as *Pinus taeda* and *P. elliottii,* movement from higher to lower latitudes will stimulate flowering (Schmidtling, 1978). A number of seed orchards have been established using this principle; it also works to move from higher to lower elevations for some species.

In some instances, species other than the eucalypts flower heavily and early as exotics. For example, *P. caribaea* produces large amounts of seed at an early age near the coast in the state of Espirito Santo in Brazil. Some temperate or subtropical species other than the pines also flower early as exotics; one example is several of the members of the genus *Cupressus* in South America. In our opinion, the knowledge about early and heavy flowering of exotics in certain environments is too frequently overlooked.

When working with exotics, it is important to observe changes in floral patterns. But just because an exotic tree produces flowers, cones, or seed does not mean the seed will be sound or germinate well. This was expressed by Gibson et al. (1983) when he stated that "the presence of strobili must not be taken to be indicative of potential seed production."

For the convenience of the reader, Table 5.2 was prepared to indicate a few of the many sources of seed for species that may be used as exotics. Most supply seed primarily for research studies, but some produce seed on a commercial scale. Commercial seed dealers have not been included in the list.

5.2 SEED CERTIFICATION

It is especially critical that the seed used for tests be from a known source of seed that can be relocated. We have seen tests from a given source (of *Pinus oocarpa* in Brazil, for example) that grew beautifully. The next year seed were obtained from the same dealer, nominally from the same source and stand of

TABLE 5.2. List of Organizations That Cooperate in the Collection, Storage, and Sale of Seed of Exotic Trees[a]

Acronym[b]	Headquarters	Contribution
BANSEFOR	Guatemala	Seed for tropical pine species are available upon request.
BLSF	Costa Rica	The seed bank had 600 accessions of 210 species in 1985. Special collections were made of *Calliandra callothyrsus* and *Gliricidia sepium,* especially for fuelwood.
CAFMA	Brazil	Genetically improved tropical pine seed are available for testing and for commercial use.
CAMCORE	United States	Collection and testing of seed of endangered conifer and hardwood species from donor countries is made. Testing and preservation is done both in the receptor and donor countries.
Carton de Colombia	Colombia	Seed of several species of eucalypts and pines, and especially *Cupressus lusitanica,* are available in research quantities. Commercial seed are also available.
CATIE	Costa Rica	Collecting hardwood species, including those of special use for fuelwood is done.
CFI(OFI)	Grat Britain	Collection, storage, and testing of many species, confiers and hardwoods, from throughout the world, mostly tropical is done.
COHDEFOR	Honduras	Seed from Honduras are collected and made available.
CSIRO	Australia	Collection and testing of species used as exotics are made. Emphasis is on the eucalypts.
CTFT	France	Collections of seed of tropical hardwoods, including seed of *Acadia* from West Africa are made.
DANIDA	Denmark	Collection and storage of both conifers and hardwoods from throughout the world, mostly of tropical species is done.
DANISH-FAO[c]	Denmark	Concentrates on the Southeast Asian area to obtain improved seed for plantations in the tropical and subtropical area.
ESNACIFOR	Honduras	Seed of both conifers and hardwoods are supplied upon request.
FAO	Italy	Advisory and funding in seed collection, storage, and dissemination of seed. FAO publishes many helpful booklets for persons using exotics.
IBPGR	Italy	Consultative on genetic resources; publishes books on seed technology for gene banks.

(continued)

TABLE 5.2. Continued

Acronym[b]	Headquarters	Contribution
IUBS	France	Aid and recommendations regarding seed problems related to seeds of exotics.
Mondi Forests	South Africa	Seed is available for research purposes or on an operational scale.
NTSL	United States	Collection and sending of small lots of seed or cuttings from many species are made, both nationally and internationally.
Queensland Forestry Department	Australia	Genetically improved seed are available, mostly for research tests and provenance trials.
SAFRI	South Africa	Seed of conifers and hardwoods are available for trial or research purposes.
SEPASAT	Great Britain (Royal Botanic Garden, Kew)	Collecting seed for IBPGR, FAO, and others for research and conservation.

[a]The list does not include commercial seed dealers.
[b]The meaning of the acronyms are shown in the Appendix.
[c]Barner and Keiding, 1983.

trees; these were planted across the road and were terrible. One planting was straight, small limbed, and fast growing while the second, although described as being an identical seed lot, was crooked, slow growing, and large limbed. Similarly, in Europe we have seen Douglas-fir "from the same elevation of the same source" that turned out to be the "grey" and the "green" strains of this very diverse species.

Any successful large exotic program is totally dependent on having a reliable source of seed that has been proven to be the best and is reproducible. Similarly, it is necessary that the source tested and found to be good be labeled correctly. Great concern about the proper labeling of provenances and seed sources, and the confusion that occurs when this is improperly done, has been stressed by Jones and Burley (1973).

Because of the difficulties in collecting seed in some donor countries and because some seed dealers are not reliable, a number of foresters favor seed certification on an international level (Barner, 1963). In fact, seed certification, in which species and sites suitable for collections were determined and license cards were issued before seed could be collected and used, has been used in forestry for a long time (Doi, 1903). International seed certification has been in effect for many years in some European countries, but it is not always used and sometimes is not even respected. The need for reliable seed certification for exotics has been emphasized by many persons, for example, Rudolf (1966) and Kemp (1971).

There is no general agreement either about the need for seed certification or what should be certified; discussions sometimes become quite emotional (Cech et al., 1962). This is partially because many persons feel that certification is something that should be voluntary within the profession and rigid rules controlled by governments will not work. Others note the many times that seed turns out differently from what was desired and feel there should be some protection for the purchaser. As Banks (1967) stated: "Tree seed certification must provide a guard against the collection of seed from single trees and from trees of suspect genetical quality."

In a survey made by the Society of American Foresters, Horning (1961) found that 97% of the replies favored some sort of seed certification and 47% felt this need was urgent. But it was significant that 93% of the respondents favored voluntary certification by nonprofit, nongovernmental agencies. In his recommendations, Mathews (1963) stated that certification should make available to the forester material that is true to name and source and which satisfies certain standards of quality. He mentioned that four categories of certification should be used in international trade: minus or *unclassified;* normal or *source identified;* plus or *selected;* elite or *certified.* Others, such as Rudolf (1963), feel that the term *certified* should be used only for trees of proven genetic superiority. Other qualities of purity, seeds/kilogram, seed size, etc., must be known, but these come under the term *labeling.*

What should be certified—therein lies the major disagreement. Banks (1967) feels that the objective of tree seed certification is to give a complete description of a seed lot. Some persons, such as Eliason (1963) and Barber (1969), state that it should be restricted to trees of known parental origin, as contrasted to a geographic source. Barner (1963) outlined in general terms what he felt should be minimum standards for seed certification:

> (1) The progeny of the seed source must either be known to be suitable for the purpose stated or the features of the seed source and its site and climate must be such as to render this probable. . . . (2) The origin of the seed source . . . and its size must justify its utilization as a seed collection unit. . . . (3) The seed lot must represent the desired source. . . . (4) The origin and location of the seed source must be unambiguously declared. . . . (5) The origin . . . must be certified by a recognized agency.

According to Barner (1968), a forester's definition of seed certification is "To maintain and make available to the public, forest tree seeds properly identified as *to species* or *origin.*" It is essential to recognize that seed certification deals with the origin of the seed, the number of parents involved, any testing which may have been done, etc. Seed certification cannot in any way guarantee performance in the new habitat.

Seed certification related to exotic forestry almost always involves international exchange. Several organizations are active in handling certification of forest tree seed on an international scale. In 1963, members of FAO and IUFRO discussed with OECD (Organization for Economic Cooperation and Development) setting up an international procedure for certifying forest tree seed. The scheme was similar to, and compatible with, the ICIA (International Crop Improvement Association) minimum standards (Rudolf, 1966). The ICIA recognizes four categories of certification for agricultural seed which are to be followed in forestry (Banks, 1967). Others, such as Horning (1961), feel that international forest seed certification should be tied to ICIA, but with a revision of standards to include wild seed. Another organization, the ISTA (International Seed Testing Association), has a forest seed committee that has improved specifications for forest seed, and most of the seed-testing stations are members.

A number of examples could be cited of seed certification programs related to exotics. For example, Piesch and Stevenson (1976) report that Canada is a member of OECD along with several European countries that purchase Canadian seed. These countries insist on adhering to OECD standards that seriously affect the export seed business of several seed companies in British Columbia. The Tree Seed Association in Britain sponsors certification schemes and favors a percentage increase over normal prices for certified seed (Larsen, 1960).

A type of seed certification results from activities of international organizations and seed collection centers, usually operated by governments and often funded partially by FAO. A list of species and provenances available from these centers is made available by FAO (Larsen, 1969). In Germany an international board (German Federal Board of Variety Testing) is used for certification (Langner, 1963). He emphasizes that progeny tests are needed because, in plantations, few conclusions can be drawn from only the phenotype.

In a country like Zimbabwe, Banks and Barrett (1973) point out the great need for a tree seed certification service. Properly handled, such an organization will pay its way. In Zimbabwe, poor documentation and little attention to parentage or provenance were evident from early plantings. Now the country grows seed for export and a need for international standards is very urgent. Growing seed in one country to supply another is becoming more widespread. Dunn (1965) published a report regarding the potential of radiata pine seed as an export to over 20 countries. The seed were certified in terms of bulk collections, seed from especially good phenotypes, and plus-stand seed collections.

Although it is not precisely the subject matter of this chapter, it is essential to alert the user and supplier of exotic forest seed that many difficulties occur. For example, sanitary certificates or special treatments are required. Unless carefully done, the treatments sometimes result in dead seed. Since every country has different rules, it is sufficient to warn both the seller and buyer to be aware of restrictions, permits, and other requirements. Much seed, time, and money is lost if this is not done. This is referred to by Palmberg (1983b), who gives four major points for ordering seed. The actual procedures for preparing for international shipment of seeds and cuttings is described by Karrfalt (1985).

As exotics are used more, international seed certification will be urgently needed to assure the buyer that the provenance desired is in fact the one sent. Needless to say, international cooperation is essential but can be very difficult to achieve in some countries. Turnbull (1978) summarized seed certification as follows: "Make it as simple as possible, but make sure that the scheme is framed for further development and that terms used are in accordance with international nomenclature." He emphasizes the need for international cooperation through organizations such as OECD.

5.3 VEGETATIVE PROPAGATION FOR QUICK AND LARGE GENETIC GAINS

The subject of vegetative propagation is complex. We will cover enough of it here to briefly illustrate its use to expand and put improved exotic trees to operational use quickly and more fully than is possible through the use of seeds. Vegetative propagation is not a breeding method and genetic improvements are not developed by it. It is a method of rapidly multiplying desired genetic material and of capturing more of the genetic potential. This was clearly pointed out by Van Wyk (1985b), who stated that:

> while gains from vegetative propagation may far exceed gains from sexual breeding, the former is "one-off" in nature. Unless new genotypes with superior characteristics are created the gains obtained from clonal forestry will become stagnant.

When vegetative propagation is used, most of the genetic potential, including the nonadditive variance (Chaperon et al., 1983), can be transferred to the new plant, not just part of it, as when seed are used in which genetic segregation and recombination occur and only a portion of the desired qualities can then be found in the new plant (Chaperon, 1979).

Numerous aspects of vegetative propagation were described in Chapter 12 of Wright's (1962) book, and a whole series of papers on the methodology and use of vegetative propagation, with many on the eucalypts, is included in *Silvicultura* 32 (1983), pp. 770–801. There are literally hundreds of papers listing specific techniques used to propagate different species; these will not be covered in this book. Special emphasis is needed for species that have seed in short supply and have not yet had their rooting techniques developed. Examples are *Albizia falcataria, Araucaria cunninghamia,* and *A. hunsteinii* (De Muckadell, 1985).

The need of and emphasis on the use of vegetative propagation in exotic forestry is great and, as emphasized by Chaperon (1984), the breeding strategy for exotics should take into account the possible use of vegetative propagation, the methodology of which is being rapidly developed. In our opinion, it is the fastest developing and most revolutionary aspect of forest research currently taking place. It is especially valuable where hybrids are used (Geary, 1984) and already has widespread use for exotics.

Vegetative propagation is not a newly discovered technique, as it has been used successfully for several centuries. There are records in the literature of using rooted cuttings of *Cryptomeria japonica* for planting during the nineteenth century (Ono, 1882) and commercial planting of cuttings has been standard practice for this species for many years. The older practices as well as new methodologies are being increasingly applied in forestry programs (Toda, 1974; Rauter, 1979; Zobel, 1981a; Libby and Rauter, 1984). However, aside from a few genera commonly used for exotics, such as *Eucalyptus, Populus, Salix, Cryptomeria,* and *Picea,* vegetative propagation has not been used extensively in operational exotic forest planting programs. Much study has also been done with radiata pine; a number of aspects were summarized by Cameron (1968) (Fig. 5.4).

There is special interest in the use of vegetative propagation in exotics because a number of species respond well to this type of regeneration. Notable are the poplars and the eucalypts as well as some tropical hardwoods (Fig. 5.5). It is dangerous to generalize, however. A number of eucalypt species root easily and the general attitude is that all species of eucalypts will root well. This is not so, and some are most difficult; for example, in South Africa, *Eucalyptus nitens* roots with great difficulty and the cuttings either rot or callous without root production (Anon., 1983c).

There are a number of different kinds of vegetative propagation, but most emphasis will be on rooted cuttings, which are currently of primary operational use. There is continued interest in in vitro production of plantlets that serve as a good source of mother trees supplying the necessary material for

Figure 5.4. The ideal would be if conifers could be rooted. Some work has been done on *Pinus radiata* in New Zealand and Australia. The uniformity within one clone of rooted cuttings from Australia is illustrated. (Photo courtesy of John Wiley & Sons.)

Figure 5.5. Some species, such as some of the eucalypts, root so well that they are used in operational planting. Shown are rooted cuttings of *Eucalyptus* from Aracruz Florestal in Brazil ready for outplanting. Improved containers and mechanization have greatly reduced the cost of producing rooted cuttings.

mass production. This form of vegetative propagation, called tissue culture or organo-culture, appears to have promise for the future. Great emphasis is now being placed on improving tissue culture, but at the time of this writing it cannot be considered operational in forest regeneration, although it is serving some important research functions. As stated by Chaperon et al. (1982): '' . . . the high production costs are still prohibiting its use for reforestation.'' Grafting is of course employed widely in clone banks and seed orchards, but is little used for operational planting.

Along with its advantages, vegetative propagation raises some unique and serious questions. It is the objective of this short section to point out the uses and advantages along with the restraints and dangers of using vegetative propagation in exotic forestry.

5.3.1 Vegetative Propagation with Exotics

Operational use of vegetative propagation in species used as exotics, such as the southern pines (Van Buijtenen et al., 1975), spruce (Birot and Nepveu, 1979; Rauter, 1979), radiata pine (Thulin and Faulds, 1968), *Eucalyptus* (Campinhos and Ikemori, 1980; Destremau et al., 1980; Hartney, 1980; Zobel et al., 1983), is so new that there still are many questions about how best to employ it. Some of the new techniques have not yet been tried extensively, but this is one of the most intensive areas of current research. Vegetative propagation of species most used, such as radiata pine and *Eucalyptus grandis,* is described by Cameron (1968) and Burgess (1973).

To be effective, information must be available on the performance of vegetative propagules compared to trees grown from seed. Such tests are often not made or are generally inadequate. Occasional studies list similarities and differences between rooted cuttings and seedlings in growth rate and form (Fielding, 1970; Sweet and Wells, 1974; Roulund, 1978a; and Jiang, 1982). For example, Alazard and Kadio (1983) found that the initial growth from cuttings was less than from seedlings of *Pinus pinaster,* but the trend reversed after several years. Sometimes cuttings from older trees grow more slowly than seedlings as well as being harder to root. According to West (1984), seedlings and cuttings of radiata pine had similar height growth through five years, but seedlings had a 1.0–2.4-cm diameter advantage over the cuttings.

If done correctly and if obtained from the proper part of the donor plant (Roulund, 1978a), with similar physiological age, generally the performance of trees from seed and vegetative origin are quite similar, although distinct growth pattern and form differences are found. But, as Chaperon et al. (1983) note, poor techniques of vegetative propagation can lead to intraclonal variability and even a decline in the performance of the clone. He outlines the best methodology for obtaining propagules that will grow normally. The differences in growth characteristics of cuttings taken from different parts of the tree were analyzed by Alazard and Kadio (1983). They state that "the homogeneity and juvenile growth of cuttings from clones has yet to be improved." A common observation is that rooted cuttings have a better tree form and frequently smaller branches than seedlings. In Australia, Matheson and Eldridge (1982) report that radiata pine cuttings made from two-year-old plants grow as fast and have better form than seedlings. They find that cuttings made from trees up to six years of age are satisfactory in rooting and growth.

Although it is not necessary to wait for seed production before producing vegetative propagules for operational planting, the tested desirable tree usually cannot be used directly in operational vegetative-propagation reforestation programs. Although this is possible for some species in the genus *Populus,* where cuttings from older trees can be readily rooted, cuttings from physiologically mature trees of most species are difficult or impossible to root. In sprouting species, such as in the eucalypts, the stump sprouts formed following felling of the tree are physiologically juvenile, so they root just like juvenile material.

Even when rooting is easy, it takes several years to develop the "clonal reproduction area" that is necessary to produce the large number of cuttings necessary for operational planting (Fig. 5.6). In species that root with difficulty, it is sometimes necessary to undertake expensive and detailed procedures to maintain the rooting ability of the juvenile material. As an example, the rooting ability in some species can be maintained by keeping the trees in a juvenile stage through hedging, where the trees are pruned at a young age and kept pruned so that the new shoots can be used for rooting (Libby et al., 1972; Van Buijtenen et al., 1975; Gantry, 1983).

If vegetative propagules of exotics can be produced at a reasonable cost, the uniformity of growth, form, and wood properties of plantations will be greatly improved. Vegetative propagation thus can produce exotic forests where

Figure 5.6. Going operational in a vegetative propagation program takes some time and much effort. Once a good clone has been found, it must be placed in a clonal reproduction area to produce the large number of sprouts needed for operational planting. A clonal reproduction area of *Eucalyptus* that supplies sprouts for an operational program is shown.

variability among trees is minimized, a major improvement when established in an operational forestry program.

5.3.2 Problems with Using Rooted Cuttings for Exotic Forestry

Many problems are associated with vegetative propagation. Some of these were listed by Kleinschmit (1977) as aging, early testing, interaction with environments where grown, and genetic variation. These will now be briefly covered.

A major deterrent to using rooted cuttings is that young trees will often root readily but the same trees may be almost impossible to root when they become older (Ducci and Locci, 1978). The problem was summarized by Franclet (1979), who stated that "there is a progressive loss with age of the aptitude for vegetative propagation." Physiologically mature tissue has a lower rooting percentage, takes longer to initiate roots, and develops fewer roots than does physiologically juvenile material. This difficulty with older trees is particularly frustrating in exotic forestry, where there is a need to work with proven provenances and desirable trees from land races. Because trees must be left to grow long enough to prove their worth, it is then usually too late to root them operationally. Additionally, trees that are rooted from older trees usually grow more slowly than those taken from younger trees.

Another problem with using rooted cuttings from older trees is that the propagules sometimes do not grow into a normal tree form and develop what is called plagiotropic growth. When this happens, nominally genetically identical propagules will grow differently, depending on where they are obtained from the donor tree and the age when the propagule is taken. When plagiotropic growth occurs, the cutting does not assume tree form but rather continues the growth form of its origin, that is, like a branch. The differential in growth and form development when plagiotropism occurs can be catastrophic to an applied program. Even though the cuttings are identical in the sense that they have the same genotype, they do not respond the same way in a given environment. Plagiotropic growth is most common in genera such as *Abies, Picea, Araucaria,* and *Sequoia* and is found to a lesser extent in *Pseudotsuga.* Plagiotropism is not common in *Pinus,* or in most hardwoods.

Another deterrent to achieving maximum gains using rooted cuttings in exotic plantations is the very large clonal variability in rooting ability; this is especially strong in some species. Variation in rootability will determine what trees are available to a planting program (Hyun, 1967; Shelbourne and Thulin, 1974; Kleinschmit and Schmidt, 1977). Clonal variation in rooting occurs no matter what species or provenance one works with. The percentage of clones that propagate satisfactorily is vital, and in some species so few parent trees respond well enough to rooting that an initially broad genetic potential may be reduced to an alarming degree. Improved techniques will help some, but losses of large numbers of otherwise excellent genotypes in desired provenances is one of the most serious obstacles to operational use of rooted cuttings. Satisfactory rooting percentages will vary; for example, for *Eucalyptus* in Aracruz, Brazil, a 75% rooting success is considered minimal for use in the planting program (Campinhos and Ikemori, 1980; Anon., 1984a).

If rooted cuttings are to be used more widely with exotics, methods of developing juvenility, as outlined by Franclet (1979), or maintaining juvenility by some method such as hedging (Libby and Hood, 1976; Brix and Van Driessche, 1977) must be perfected. Although many hardwoods produce stump sprouts that are juvenile, pines rarely do so, although some pines, such as *P. oocarpa, P. canariensis,* and *P. serotina,* produce abundant sprouts. Initial tests of rooting these pine sprouts have been successful; this was shown for *P. rigida* by Santamour (1965) and by studies by the authors on *P. oocarpa.* Thus, there is an as yet unused opportunity for a greater utilization of rooted cuttings in conifers that would be of special value in exotic species with insufficient seed supply of the proper source, such as some tropical species or particularly valuable hybrids. Rooting young trees is used to mass-produce species that have a very light seed set, such as spruce in Sweden, or for hybrids where few seeds are available.

5.3.3 Using Vegetative Reproduction Operationally in Exotic Forestry

When the advantages and problems of vegetative programs are assessed, they all must be judged by how much risk can be tolerated to obtain the extra gain that can be achieved through using this method. Relative gain-to-risk is widely argued but rarely decided because of the different emphases on the relative risks by various organizations; commonly, there is a lack of knowledge about the gains that are achievable. There is no way to come to a consensus, but the important thing is to be aware of the relative gains and risks and then to make a conscious decision about their importance. This must be done before an operational vegetative propagation program is undertaken. The decision must include biological, operational, economic, policy, and political considerations.

A major biological concern is the danger of planting large areas with the same or similar genotypes. As will be mentioned in the next section, this represents a dangerous monoculture. Yet, if handled correctly, the danger, which frequently is blown out of perspective, can be minimized, as has been done in agriculture with its widespread use of crops with very narrow genetic bases. Yet the situation here is different, since a dangerous monoculture can have more serious long-term consequences in forestry than in agriculture (see Zobel and Talbert, 1984).

A common misunderstanding is that members of one specific clone will be adapted only to a very narrow range of environmental conditions. Certainly, clones are less broadly adapted than mixtures of full- or half-sib seedlings since each member of a clone has the same genotype. However, the ramet of a given clone can possess considerable ability for adaptation to different pests or to adverse environments. Thus, it is quite possible to choose clones that have greater (internal) adaptability than that possessed by the average seedling. The danger with large exotic plantations is that if the adaptability of the clone used is exceeded by adverse conditions or pests, the result will be that all trees of the clone will be subject to damage or death. Within-clone adaptability seems to be less to attacks by pests, especially pests that have come from outside the natural range of the exotic species, than to weather extremes. Also, some clones may not be able to utilize the full capacity of a site because of uniform root depth or other. The genetic diversity in clonal forestry was well discussed by Libby and Rauter (1984).

A first consideration relates to how many different clones should be used in an operational rooted-cutting program. There is no "correct" answer, although experience and knowledge of the variation in the species or provenance should be used as a guide. The objective is to plant only the best clones while still maintaining enough variability to limit the risks of destructive losses to an acceptable level. The answer to the question as to what number of clones is correct is usually, "It all depends upon rotation age, on intensity of forest management, on genetic variability of the species and clones involved, the likely risks and the acceptable loss levels" (Libby, 1981; Zobel and Talbert, 1984).

Clonal mixtures are usually assumed to be best (expressed as early as 1918 by Hirasiro), and some governments have laws requiring the intermixture of hundreds of clones. Biologically, hundreds of clones are not required, as the more cautious advise. As an example, 100 to 500 intermixed clones have been suggested by politicians in Germany (Kleinschmit, 1977; Muhs, 1982). Muhs emphasizes the difficulty of legislating the number of clones and that there is sometimes a conflict between laws and breeding practices. He illustrates this by the laws and rules of the Federal Republic of Germany and concludes that, although laws and rules are a handicap for the breeders, the contradictory opinions of scientists help to stimulate such legislation.

The optimal clone number will vary with the species used, yet this is often overlooked by the legislators. Further, for example, if 100 clones are considered to be the correct number, the legislator "prefers safety and he takes 500 instead of 100 clones for species to be grown on large areas." Muhs (1982) does suggest the use of differing clonal mixtures over large areas. Similarly, Martin (1982) recommends a number of intermixed clones for *Eucalyptus* in the Congo.

Many persons do not agree that clonal mixtures are best operationally, although they recognize that a number of different clones are needed. The problem then becomes how the clones should be deployed. It is operationally unsuitable and biologically disadvantageous to plant complete clonal mixtures, despite the frequent recommendation to do so. Heybroek (1982) stresses that although the use of diverse genotypes spreads the risks, a mosaic of pure stands of single genotypes may be adequate under certain circumstances. In fact, Libby (1981) states that mosaics of monoclonal plantings are the best. The arguments favoring operational planting by clonal blocks of limited size in operational forestry were detailed by Zobel and Talbert (1984) and are paraphrased below:

1.   Each clone will have a different growth curve and developmental pattern (Fig. 5.7). Some clones will be severely suppressed by competition from

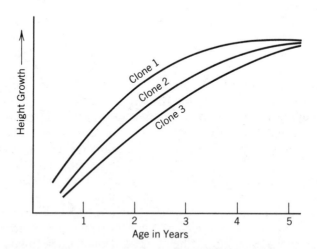

Figure 5.7. Growth curve differences make interplanting of clones unsatisfactory. The fast starters will suppress the slow starters even if at a given time they would all be about the same size if left free to grow. For example, clones 1, 2, and 3 might all be the same size at year 5 if left free to grow, but in mixture, clone 1 would suppress clones 2 and 3 before they had a chance to express themselves. Thus, stocking is reduced and some clones are essentially lost becuase of differential competition.

other, faster-starting clones and never be able to develop properly in mixture. At the very least there will be differences in size and quality of trees in the intermixed plantings, reducing one of the greatest advantages from vegetative propagation, greater uniformity.

2.   Planting and "nursery" operations are much simplified when planting by clonal blocks.

3.   Wood uniformity among trees is maximum within a block of trees from the same clone. Trees from different blocks can be used for special products, such as plywood, sawtimber, or special qualities of paper.

4.   If a really serious problem develops within a given clone, a whole block can be harvested and replaced to keep the forest in maximum productivity. It is not possible to efficiently salvage an individual clone from individual clonal mixtures; but even if it could be done, the missing trees cannot be replaced and the result is a forest with below-desired stocking. Often a salvage operation causes more damage to the residuals than the net return from the salvage operation.

There is no question that a single clone, as suggested by a few, will entail too much risk. As a generalized guide, based upon the variation pattern of most forest tree species, we agree with Libby's (1983) recommendation that 7 to 25 differing clones appear to be a safe and reasonable number. Some persons feel strongly that 25 clones should be the very minimum number used.

Although many others could be selected, the work of Aracruz Florestal on *Eucalyptus* in Brazil will be used as an example of a successful use of vegetative propagation in exotic forestry. (Although the example is for *Eucalyptus* for pulp, there is great potential for vegetative propagation to develop high-quality tropical hardwoods, some of which root with ease.) The Aracruz program has been described in a number of publications (Campinhos, 1980; Zobel et al., 1982, 1983; Anon., 1984c). Of the initial 5000 selections made, the best 100 clones nearly doubled the production over the planting of unimproved stock (see Fig. 4.1). The best 15 clones were chosen for each of the six different environments with which the company works; the same best clones were not suitable for all environments, so a total of about 50 clones are used. It is felt that the danger of using 15 clones per site is not excessive for the variation present and for the short-rotation crops of five to seven years.

Although the question about clonal distribution must be settled through trials rather than merely by an expression of opinion, most large exotic vegetative-propagation operations such as the one by Aracruz are currently maximizing gains by block plantings. For variable species and those with short-rotation ages, the recommendations generally are for 10- to 20-ha monoclonal blocks. Some persons feel these may be too large, but blocks smaller than 10 ha are inefficient to operate. This recommendation may change with experience, but now it appears that 10- to 20-ha blocks are satisfactory both operationally and from a risk standpoint.

A major error often made relative to the use of rooted cuttings, especially in exotics, is to assess the propagules at too young an age. An early assessment can be especially dangerous for growth characteristics. The time needed to test the performance of vegetative propagules for a given rotation age is little different than when testing seedlings. For the latter there are occasional reports of good juvenile–mature correlations for volume or height growth, but for most species a reliable estimate of mature performance cannot be obtained until about one-half rotation age (Wakeley, 1971; Franklin, 1979). Some persons are less conservative; for families of *Pinus taeda,* Lambeth (1979) feels that an assessment at age 6 to 8 years is the most economical and is reasonably accurate for a 30-year rotation. This problem is less serious with exotics that are grown on shorter rotations, although bad errors have been made by judging poplars by 1 year's growth in the nursery even though the rotation age is only 6 years. Yet Rone (1982), working with Norway spruce in Russia, found that young tree selection produced greater height and frost resistance in 6-year-old trees. A 50%-intensity nursery selection increased height up to 30%. Individual clone selection was difficult because of the strong genotype × environment interaction.

Some of us are very concerned about bad decisions currently being made from premature assessments in exotic species used in vegetative propagation programs because of the major need in some species to have physiologically young material for rooting and to avoid plagiotropism. Some foresters assume that if a cutting is superior when very young, or if it is taken from a good-looking seedling, it will be superior at rotation age. Such an assumption about early assessments is not correct and currently constitutes a most serious error related to using vegetative propagation in growing exotics.

Sometimes within-clone variation will be found after several generations; this can occur from virus infections, internal physiological changes in the tree, or poor root development. Vegetative propagules are generally more expensive than seedlings, but with proper equipment and planning, costs of vegetative propagules can be greatly reduced (Kleinschmit and Schmidt, 1977) and under special circumstances need not be greater than seedlings (Campinhos and Ikemori, 1980). An additional cost per planted tree will be insignificant when assessed on cost-per-hectare and gain-per-hectare bases, and a couple of percentage points of improvement from using rooted cuttings can more than justify an increased cost of getting the propagules established in the field.

5.4 PLANT UNIFORMITY AND MONOCULTURE—A SUMMARY

Perhaps the most widely used word regarding exotics is *monoculture.* It frequently is presented as the Achilles' heel of exotic forestry, a potential source of trouble and, in some extreme opinions, a reason why exotic forestry should not be practiced (Zobel, 1972; Burdon, 1982; Will, 1984). There is much emotion related to the subject, with false claims being made on both sides. Looked at realistically, it is an assessment of gain versus risk—that is, how much additional risk is one willing to take for a given amount of added gain. This decision is one that has to be made by all organizations faced with the concept of monoculture. The following sections are intended to help explain and clarify the situation regarding monoculture and exotics with some reference to perceived gains and risks.

5.4.1 What Is Monoculture?

It is essential that a term so widely used as *monoculture* be understood. To the layman, it is often synonymous with planting large areas with a single species (Glasgow, 1975) (Fig. 5.8). To the forester concerned with growing exotics, the concern is mainly with the amount of genetic uniformity, regardless of whether it is within or between species (Feret, 1975). Depending on the source and kind of regenerative material and its built-in genetic diversity, the single-species plantation can be either a dangerous monoculture (i.e., it is an economic risk) or a safe plantation. A single-species plantation will become vulnerable if one source with few parents is involved, but when it is very diverse genetically, there may be greater genetic variability within a single-species planting than between two different species.

Monoculture is covered in this chapter and is also discussed in other chapters because it either contributed to problems in growing exotics or it is blamed for the problems whether or not it truly is a contributing factor. The concern is illustrated by Tucker (1975), who stated that growing relatively similar genotypes over large areas worries many foresters. In his paper, Heybroek (1980) compares growing trees in monoculture versus in mixture and covers any potential dangers involved. In a paper on monoculture and site productivity, Will

Figure 5.8. The photo is of a large monoculture planting of *Pinus radiata* in Chile. Whether or not such a monoculture is dangerous depends upon how heterozygous is the genetic base used in the planting. Some monocultures are vulnerable biologically, others are not.

(1984) well covers the subject of monoculture in both the temperate and tropical regions, especially as related to soil deterioration. He states that the dire predictions about monocultures effects on site productivity have not occurred. Where problems have occurred, it is due to poor forest management practices. He lists methods necessary to maintaining productivity when monocultural silviculture is used. These are (1) conserving nutrients by avoidance of practices such as litter raking or poor use of fire, (2) replacement of fertilizers removed in harvest, and (3) control of weed competition.

The term *monoculture* has been popularized, and even politicized, to the point that it really has lost much of its meaning (see Chapter 10). Yet, biologically, monoculture is a key concept that has special significance to the future and long-term productivity of exotic forests. Although monocultures frequently occur with exotics, true, biologically dangerous monocultures are not as prevalent as would appear from many publications and the popular press.

The exact definition of monoculture would not be of importance except that layman and even most foresters often make monoculture synonymous with potential trouble because of a reduced genetic base. When defined as being the plantations of a single species, then a huge misunderstanding of the dangers of a monoculture occurs.

Webster's New Twentieth Century Dictionary (1980) defines *monoculture* as the "cultivation of a single crop or product without using the land for other purposes," while other authors define it as growing a crop of closely related individuals (Zobel and Talbert, 1984). Still others, such as Glasgow (1975), consider that growing even-aged stands of one or a very limited number of species in blocks large enough to have an ecological impact is a monoculture. Since the general public embraces the first and third definitions, it is best to use them. Therefore, essentially all forest tree plantations are monocultures. Some persons differentiate "mixed genotype" plantations, "single genotype" plantations, and "single genotype plantations in a mosaic of stands" when monocultures are considered.

The key point to understand is that only the monocultures (stands) with restricted genetic bases are vulnerable, and a monoculture by the dictionary or layman's definition is not necessarily dangerous. The dictionary definition of monoculture as being a single crop says nothing about its being good or bad. It is the heterogeneity of the gene base that is important to the one growing the plantation (Zobel, 1972).

The real key to the forester working with exotics concerns how genetically uniform the planting is, whether it consists of one or several species. Single-species plantings can have a very broad genetic base if developed and planned for this purpose, such as seedlings from seed orchards in which the basic objective is to use very diverse genetic individuals as parents. This was expressed by Feret (1975), who emphasizes that planting a single species does not necessarily make a dangerous monoculture, but everything depends on how uniform the species is. For example, *Pinus resinosa* (red pine) is very uniform genetically (Fowler, 1961, 1964), and a plantation of this species (Fig. 5.9)

Figure 5.9. When species with limited genetic variability are planted such as *Pinus resinosa,* shown in Canada, a potentially dangerous monoculture results. Yet this species grows naturally in mono-cultures and has been widely grown in plantations with few destructive pests.

must be considered a vulnerable monoculture while a plantation of loblolly pine (*P. taeda*) from parents widely selected for adaptability is not a dangerous monoculture (Zobel and Talbert, 1984).

The forester has a great advantage over the agriculturist because of the general broad genetic independence of desired economic characteristics (such as straightness of stem) along with adaptive characteristics (such as disease resistance). This genetic independence enables a narrowing of the genetic base for the desired product while at the same time broadening the base for adaptability to different pests or adverse environments. We would, in effect, have in a plantation which is a monoculture with a restricted genetic base for straightness but one with a broad base for adaptability. In growing exotics, the loss of adaptability is the concern of the forester, not whether a large area is planted to a single species with straight stems.

It is obvious that large monoclonal plantings are the most extreme example of a dangerous monoculture. Dangerous monocultures will become more prevalent in exotic forestry because a number of species are now being established from rooted cuttings, some on a large scale (Rauter and Hood, 1980; Libby, 1981; Zobel, 1981a; Anon., 1984c).

5.4.2 The Dangers from Developing a Restricted Genetic Base When Using Exotics

Stated simply, the dangers from using too restricted a genetic base in exotic forestry are great. Yet this is a daily fact of life. Humans have used only about 5000 plant species for food and fiber, and presently only about 50 are used extensively. Of these, 3 species supply over half of all human energy requirements. These greatly used species should be the focus of attention regarding gene diversity (Anon., 1982c).

One of the special problems of exotic forest trees is that frequently, known or unknown by the forester, some provenances are originally represented by very few parents, sometimes by only one tree (Larsen and Cromer, 1970; Turnbull, 1978). When this happens, there is no way to prevent a dangerous monoculture. A typical example was a study of cold-tolerant eucalypts in South Africa (Anon., 1983c) in which the following statement is made:

> The seed sources of the plantations are not recorded but information from some of the older growers and managers suggests that seed from only a few trees may have been used to establish extensive areas. If this is the case, selections could be closely related.

Such a quotation could be made numerous times relative to exotic forestry work outlined by Brune and Zobel (1981) in Brazil, where most of the original eucalypt parents came from an arboretum at Rio Claro. Seed sources from arboreta are especially undesirable, because of both the small genetic base and the opportunity for hybridization (Fig. 5.10). Frequently a species in an arboretum is represented by a single female parent.

A second danger is that, even though enough different parents were originally selected to make safe plantations, there are not enough individuals to go into advanced generations without developing relatedness or without reducing the genetic base so much that an ongoing, long-term breeding program will not be successful. Both, or either, of these are critical and can cause failure in an exotic forestry program. For an immediate use (not a long-term program) it is felt that at least 15 nonrelated, diverse parental genotypes are necessary to lessen risks associated with a restricted genetic base. For a long-term program, 300 to 400 breeding parents are essential and more are greatly desired. Few exotic programs have that many original unrelated and diverse genotypes,

Figure 5.10. A classic example of a poor result from obtaining seed of exotics from an arboretum is the "Brazil source" of *Eucalyptus grandis* originally from Rio Claro. There is much related mating and hybridization, which results in very nonuniform and low-quality plantations.

so if a long-range exotic tree improvement program is desired, a genetic enrichment program will be necessary to avoid eventual relatedness and a vulnerable monoculture.

The danger from too restricted a genetic base in exotic forestry is greater than in using exotic crop plants and is of considerable concern among foresters (Tucker, 1975). In agriculture, environmental manipulation to reduce dangers of heavy losses is much easier and more easily economically justified than in forestry. Because of the nature of forest environments and the relatively long rotation ages of trees, plantations will be subjected to all manner of uncontrollable stresses during their lifetime, not just part of one season, as in most crop plants. If a plantation is damaged or destroyed, many years of productivity is lost.

We are often asked, "When is a genetic base too restricted?" The desired answer usually lies in the number of genotypes used. A pat answer is not possible because it depends both on the variability within the species and the ability to control the environment where the exotic is planted and the length of the rotation. The usual objective of tree breeders is to narrow the genetic base for economic characteristics and to broaden the base for adaptability and pest resistance. The true answer to when the genetic base is too small (but one that still defies a general definition because of our lack of knowledge both in biology and economics) is, "When the risk becomes greater than the gains achieved."

We still cannot accurately assess either the gains or risks in exotic forestry. Thus, when *Pinus contorta* is grown in the northern spruce and pine forests, some foresters think it is worth the risk to get the gains, others do not (Krutzsch, 1974). Similar debate rages in nearly every instance when exotics are used, with wild claims sometimes made for potential gains and just as wild predictions of losses from using exotics. The risk factor can be greatly reduced when growing exotics by maintaining a broad genetic breeding base.

In addition to the variability of the base population from which trees have been obtained (Fowler, 1961), the kind of regeneration used is also of key importance. For example, the problem is different if one uses monoclonal plantations where all the trees are genetically similar or seed regeneration from a seed orchard where a broad genetic base has been established.

As was stressed in Chapter 4, pests will appear sooner or later in all plantations, whether of exotics or indigenous species. Bain (1979) emphasizes that this will happen whether or not pure stands of a species are used. He warns that he is not saying that monocultures of radiata pine are not at risk. His point is that *they are at no greater risk* than other alternatives would present and that the risks that do exist can be greatly reduced by planting the right species on the right site and carefully tending it.

The point of view of a pathologist is given by Chou (1979), who defines *monoculture* as the large-scale establishment of even-aged pure stands and states that a critical review of the literature showed little support for increased disease and pest risks. He cites instances of serious outbreaks of diseases in mixed as well as pure stands and says there is no clear evidence that outbreaks of diseases in pure stands can be ascribed to lack of species diversity. Chou even questions the theoretical basis of such a view. He challenges the concept that any departure from "nature" must increase disease hazards.

It is evident that the planting of pure species (monoculture) need not entail the sacrificing of tree-to-tree genetic variation necessary for protection from major disease losses (Chou, 1979). He says that "there is a tendency to exaggerate the advantages of diversifying into a range of major production species to the point of ignoring its advantages, difficulties and its sheer practical realities in some countries." Chou explains that if a great number of added species are required in an exotic forestry program, it will create greater disease hazards than from using fewer, well-adapted species.

Certainly there are differing opinions. For example, Boyce (1954) categorically states that pure stands are more susceptible to diseases, especially those caused by introduced pests, than are mixed stands. He feels that a pure stand is ideal for a pathogen to build up to epidemic proportions, and the most hazardous are pure, even-aged stands such as commonly occur in exotics. Specific illustrations of these concepts were made by Cowling (1978) and De Gryse (1955) using radiata pine. Statements made by them indicate that the extreme vulnerability of the extensive monocultures of this species is challenging all the laws of nature. The large-scale replacement of genetically diverse native forests with plantations of exotic pines has drastically increased the genetic vulnerability of the genetic resource. Yet, no major disaster has occurred in New Zealand, which has large monocultures of *Pinus radiata* (Burdon, 1982).

Many more examples could be listed, both pro and con, relative to the dangers of monoculture in exotic forestry. Are the dangers of single-species plantations real and proven or do they represent unproven theory? Foresters have spent much effort to diversify because of the supposed reduction of risks from absent or unknown pathogens. But, according to both Chou (1979) and Bain (1979), such risks exist more in theory than in fact. In a recent review on forest monocultures as a precursor to pests and diseases, Gibson and Jones (1977) stated that:

> such arguments have frequently been overstated to the point of asserting that all attempts to develop forest crops using intensive management systems on a large scale are doomed to failure. Indeed, it is surprising how these views have persisted despite the evident success of tree farming in most places where it has been tried.

The potential adverse results of growing a restricted number of genotypes of forest trees over large acreages hardly needs documentation. Disasters from using restricted *Cryptomeria* or *Populus* clones have resulted in death, decline, or reduced growth and quality. Troubles with seed-propagated exotics are less commonly documented than those where vegetative propagation has been used, largely because adverse results are decline rather than death. However, growth losses from a narrowed genetic base for adaptability are more widespread than is usually recognized. The difficult job is to accurately assess whether death or decline resulted from off-site planting or has been caused by a narrowed genetic base.

One real danger in using exotics is to use a species or source that is obviously under severe stress yet outproduces any other source or species. Here it is better to forego the added production and work with a better-adapted source; trees under stress are especially susceptible to attacks by pests or damage by adverse environments. This has been a major problem with *Pinus radiata* in some areas as well as for species such as *Eucalyptus grandis,* where we have heard it said, "We don't care if the trees are half-sick; they are outproducing anything else and we will continue to use them."

Monocultures must be looked at realistically, not from a popular or emotional viewpoint. Bain (1979) was concerned with the safety of monocultures from an entomologist's point of view. He explains that the expected damage does not occur because of lack of natural enemies for the exotic trees and because the species used as exotics are normally found in pure stands. Bain summarizes by saying that the "widely held belief that forest monocultures are courting disaster because of their extreme vulnerability, is refuted." However, this depends upon the species. For example, Nicholls (1979) stresses the danger of monoculture in red pine (*P. resinosa*), a species that contains very little variability. Large plantings of this species would constitute a vulnerable monoculture and little resistance is present in pest attacks. Yet, for many years this species has been grown in pure stands, both in natural populations and in plantations, and is one of the more pest-free conifers.

5.4.3 Summary: Exotics and Monoculture

There is no doubt that monoculture is a major consideration when growing exotics. Nearly all exotic plantations are monocultures by definition, and some of them are vulnerable monocultures. A major task of foresters is to limit and reduce this trend. But the true situation needs to be assessed.

A common misunderstanding occurs with exotics when destruction by pests, poor growth, or poor survival resulting from using the wrong provenance is blamed on monoculture or "planting pure stands of the same species." Examples are numerous, especially in the eucalypts and for species like *Pinus radiata* and *Pseudotsuga menziesii.* For example, problems such as those resulting from using radiata pine in the southeastern United States or in central Brazil were caused by a lack of species adaptability and were not related to the claims that the decline of the plantations resulted from planting monocultures. Likewise, poor growth or even death of an eastern Cascade source of Douglas-fir planted in eastern Canada should fall under the category of carelessness and not be blamed on the adverse effects of growing the trees in pure stands. The trees would have grown no better if they had been mixed with other seed sources. *The concern with monoculture* by the forester growing exotics must be *related to the dangers from having a reduced genetic base of an otherwise well-adapted species.*

Recently, Sweet and Burdon (1985) wrote a detailed article about experiences gained over many years with monoculture in radiata pine and an examination of its ideologies. They emphasize that the supposed ecological risks of disease and insect epidemics, climatic injury, and soil degradation have not been evident. They come to the conclusion that large-scale use of monoculture does not necessarily entail greater risks than arise in natural forests or in mixed or uneven-aged forest tree crops. They state that departing from radiata pine monoculture might reduce the scale of risks but could incur others that might be far more serious. They obviously view the gains to be achieved from monoculture plantings certainly worth the risks involved.

Statements are commonly made, similar to the one in the UNEP Report (Anon., 1980c), that monoculture in exotic forestry in the tropics leads to increased susceptibility to pests and degradation of soil fertility. This was refuted by Burdon (1982), who states that it is not true that "artificial stands established with exotic species are at much greater risk than natural forests." The grower of exotics needs to know what such statements mean and what dangers are really involved in any plantation forestry program, whether exotic or indigenous species are used. Burdon strongly points out, based on a systematic evaluation of the risks associated with monocultures (mostly with *Pinus radiata*), that:

1. The critical study has failed to confirm that pure, even-aged stands (and thus monocultures) are at more risk than mixed stands.

2. Most outbreaks of pests can be explained as the result of growing the wrong species on the wrong site or from the use of poor silviculture rather than from having monocultures of exotic species.

Any decision related to exotics and monoculture comes down to *gain* versus *risk*. The question to be faced and answered is, "How much risk am I willing to take in order to obtain a given amount of gain?" As pointed out by Zobel and Talbert (1984), this is a most difficult decision. If one is too conservative and "plays it safe," gains are greatly reduced; if one does not understand or take into account the risks involved and goes mainly for gain, catastrophic results may be obtained. So there is no answer regarding what is too much risk. It depends on the organization, species, product, rotation age, and many other factors. The key, however, is to know and appreciate the potential dangers and to weigh them against achievable gains. Thus, a dangerous monoculture to one may be an acceptable plantation to another.

We like the sentence summarizing monoculture in the book by Zobel and Talbert (1984):

Great care needs to be taken in invoking the horrors of a too restricted genetic base, but it can be a horror if ignored. The forester must always be cognizant of both the potential gains and dangers from establishing plantations with a restricted genetic base.

6

GROWING EXOTIC FOREST TREES IN THE TROPICS AND SUBTROPICS

6.1 GENERAL CONCEPTS

The bulk of this book deals with general principles and concepts related to growing exotics, both in tropical and temperate climates. This chapter discusses how exotics are grown in the tropics and subtropics and how the general principles are applied. Problems encountered and special techniques that have been developed to grow exotics under the unique environments of the tropics and subtropics will be emphasized.

The definitions of tropics and subtropics have already been covered in Chapter 1 and will be followed in this chapter. All countries listed by Evans (1984) will be included as tropical or subtropical. Also included will be areas north and south of 27 degrees north and south latitude, respectively, that were excluded by Evans descriptions but fit our definition of tropical and subtropical.

Within the broad definition of subtropical climates, areas are found that are really warm or mild temperate, especially where light winter frosts are common. Often species that are grown in the subtropics can be grown in these areas—for example, *Pinus radiata, Pinus elliottii,* or even *Eucalyptus grandis.* For this chapter, all mildly temperate areas where such "overlapping" species can be grown will be regarded as subtropical. Generally, however, for ease of reference in this book, the *tropical and subtropical forestry zones will be referred to as the tropics* unless a specific separation is needed.

6.1.1 Forest Resources in the Tropics

In Chapter 1 the requirements for a successful exotic were covered. Also discussed were the most important reasons for using exotics, chief of which were rapid growth, adaptability, and desirable wood. Although forest plantations constitute only a small percentage (less than 4%) of the world area, the high productivity from the tropical plantations is currently having a major impact on world timber production and the importance of plantation forestry is rapidly increasing. Most of the plantations in the tropics are established with exotic species.

Timber yields in temperate forestry plantations rarely reach 10 m³/ha/yr and may average as low as 1.0 in Canada, 3.3 in Sweden, or 2.6 in the northern United States according to Evans (1984). In contrast, yields from tropical plantations usually are not below 15 m³/ha/yr, and many reports of 50 or more and even up to 100 m³/ha/yr have been published (Brandão, 1984).

The total area of forest tree plantations in the tropics is estimated to be about 18 million hectares (Evans, 1984). This differs from the data cited by Lanly (1983), who reported 11.5 million hectares. However, Evans included 103 countries in his survey, while Lanly included only 76 countries. Also, Evans' report included China, which has an estimated plantation area of more than 4 million hectares. Regardless of the exact area, it is easy to understand why exotic tropical forestry is becoming more important because the present timber yields from plantations in this area are 400 million or more cubic meters per annum.

The importance of tropical plantation forestry and increased productivity through proper management of exotics is stressed by Lanly (1983). He states that in the 76 countries studied, only "one hectare of plantation will be created for each 10 hectares of closed or open tree formation that will be cleared." The United Nations Environmental Program stated that the decline of natural forests is not being compensated for by the addition of planted forest land. In a country like Brazil, which has the most extensive plantations in the tropics, the area of plantations makes up only an insignificant portion of the forest land.

The correct choice of species, efficient silvicultural practices, improvement of yields through breeding and vegetative propagation, and proper management of exotics will ensure that tropical plantation forestry will play an ever increasing role in world timber supplies. The value of exotic plantations is especially great when used as replacement forests reducing pressures on the harvesting of the indigenous forests.

6.1.2 Species Considerations

Tropical exotic forestry must include the proper choice of species and provenances as described in Chapter 2. From these, the trees that are most suitable for the local site conditions and management objectives are chosen to form local land races. The importance of species, provenances, and land races have been covered in several chapters in this book.

The most widely planted exotic pine species in the tropics and subtropics are *Pinus caribaea, P. taeda, P. patula, P. radiata, P. elliottii, P. oocarpa, P. pinaster, and P. kesiya* along with several additional Mexican pines (Fig. 6.1). Among the cypress species, *Cupressus lusitanica* has been planted on large areas, with some *Cupressus macrocarpa* also being used. Many publications are available that show how best to grow conifers as exotics; one of the earliest was by Hiley (1959), on the cultivation of conifers in South Africa.

The most extensively planted hardwoods are *Eucalyptus globulus* and *E.*

Figure 6.1. Shown is a fine 19-year-old stand of *Pinus caribaea* var. *hondurensis* in South Africa. Such stands are often used as a source of seed obtained from developed land races. (Courtesy S.A.F.R.I.)

grandis (and rubber trees, *Hevea* spp.). Other species, such as *E. camaldulensis, E. tereticornis, E. urophylla,* and *E. deglupta,* have all proved to be valuable exotics in the tropics. Wattle (*Acacia* spp.), teak (*Tectona grandis*), mahogany (*Swietenia* spp., although several genera are sometimes called mahogany), and *Gmelina arborea* plantations are successfully grown in large tropical forest plantations.

More complete descriptions of exotic species and experience with their cultivation are given in several FAO publications, such as FAO (1979). Detailed descriptions were given by Hiley (1956), Streets (1962), and Evans (1984). Both conifers and *Eucalyptus* are well covered in the extensive descriptions in the two volumes by Poynton (1979). For special products, such as energy production, publications such as the one by Mariani et al. (1978) give details and procedures about how to cultivate various exotic tree species. Many books have been specifically written for *Eucalyptus,* such as Penfold and Willis (1961), and Hillis and Brown (1978). Additionally, there are numerous published papers, such as the one by Poynton (1983), on the silvicultural treatment of eucalypt plantations.

One of the best sources of information on forest management of exotics is the two-volume *Symposium on Site and Productivity of Fast Growing Plantations* held in 1984 in South Africa (Grey et al., 1984). Numerous subjects in this chapter refer directly to the papers covered in this publication, and anyone interested in having a reference to management of fast-growing plantations should have these two volumes available.

6.2 SITE REQUIREMENTS

Success in growing tropical and subtropical exotic forest trees is largely determined by a choice of the suitable environmental conditions as well as by the forest management applied and the use of the correct genetic stock. Environmental conditions can be referred to as "macro," or broad, site characteristics when they include the climatic variations determined by rainfall, light characteristics, and temperature. This agrees with the classification of world climates by Köppen, cited and further described by Rudloff (1981). Within these broad macroclimates, large variations in environments exist which result in specific conditions affecting forest establishment and growth.

"Specific" site characteristics of macroclimates include rainfall amount and timing, temperature fluctuations, and soil physical properties and nutrient levels. Also important are the physiographic variables that include, among others, altitude, slope, and aspect.

The specific environments play an important role in determining species suitability and their performance (Fig. 6.2). Many papers on this subject could be cited; one good example is Golfari (1972), who relates the responses of a number of tropical and subtropical conifers to the large variations in site conditions within Brazil. Consideration of only the broad macroclimates or undue

Figure 6.2. Planting a given provenance on the wrong site can have "fatal" results, as shown by this *Pinus oocarpa* planted on too cold a site. The resulting plantation is nearly useless. (Courtesy S.A.F.R.I.)

concern for certain specific site requirements such as frequency of killing frosts or depth of soil may lead to disastrous effects when establishing exotic species. Due to their evolutionary development (Chapters 2 and 3), most species have become generally site specific and careful consideration must be given to matching species to the overall site characteristics of the new environment.

6.2.1 Precipitation and Temperature

Macroclimates are always a major consideration when establishing exotics. A good example of how these have been handled can be obtained from the experiences in South Africa. Due to its limited natural timber resources, South Africa was one of the first countries to pioneer exotic plantation forestry. Much of the success in South Africa can be attributed to the foresight of Fourcade and Hutchins, two British foresters who made firm proposals for afforestation of the provinces of Natal and Transvaal based upon macroenvironments. Their contributions in the late 1800s were described by Poynton (1979), who stated:

> To Fourcade belongs the distinction of having been among the very first to recognize the importance, when introducing forest trees from abroad, of choosing species from parts of the world which experience a climate similar to that of the area in which planting is to be undertaken.

With this principle as a basis, Fourcade compiled an annotated list of tree species recommended for planting in Natal. However, he failed to distinguish between the macroclimates designated as of the Mediterranean type and those in which the greater part of the annual rainfall is received during the warmer months of the year. From his observation he noted that *"Pinus insignis (P. radiata)* has been found to be the fastest growing conifer . . . in Natal," and concluded (incorrectly, as it later turned out) that "there appears to be no reason why [this species] should not be grown as the dominant species in Natal plantations." Fourcade came closer to the mark, however, when he suggested that unquestionably "the best hardwoods for profitable culture are the gums of Australia."

Fourteen years later Hutchins (1903) published his *Transvaal Forest Report,* which showed an appreciation of the necessity of concentrating upon species well adapted to the local climate. Poynton (1979) says:

> His view, like that of Fourcade, was that the species most likely to thrive in a particular region are those naturally best adapted to the prevailing macro-climatic conditions. This innate suitability he termed "climatic fitness." Above all, Hutchins cautioned against the practice, common at the time and condoned by Fourcade, of cultivating species in the summer rainfall area that were introduced from parts of the world with a Mediterranean climate. He showed extraordinary insight in forecasting that this practice must sooner or later result in failure. He presented a catalogue of species proposed for trial in the Transvaal and formulated an approach well in advance of his time when he wrote: "Climatic fitness is the crux of the list, and on that every care has been bestowed."

Elaborating on this theme, Troup (1932) summarized, for exotics grown in South Africa, that successful acclimatization depends primarily upon securing favorable macroclimatic conditions for the species introduced. This entails an adequate knowledge of the climate both in the natural habitat of the species and in the proposed country of introduction. Nine broad thermal regions and three main rainfall types were recognized in the so-called tropical portions of the British Empire by Troup. He subdivided these into cool summers, cold winters; warm summers, cold winters; hot summers, cold winters; warm summers, cool winters; hot summers, cool winters; hot summers, warm winters; cold at all seasons; cool to warm at all seasons; hot at all seasons. The three rainfall types he discerned were pronounced summer rainfall, pronounced winter rainfall, and well-distributed rainfall (including snowfall), with varying seasonal preponderances that were subdivided into temperate and tropical (Poynton, 1979).

In discussing the source of species to use in the tropics, Evans (1984) refers to the importance of *total annual precipitation* and *rainfall distribution*. Species are mentioned, such as *Eucalyptus deglupta,* that will not grow in areas with only 500 mm of rainfall but require rainfall ranging from 2000 to 5000 mm/yr even though temperatures may be similar to the area of natural distribution. Conversely, drought-hardy species found in regions of low rainfall, such as *Acacia arabica, Azadiracta indica,* and *Prosopis juliflora,* will not grow in humid conditions. Evans produced a table of five broad classes of annual rainfall upon which a "first simple division of species" can be made according to moisture requirement (Table 6.1).

With reference to *rainfall distribution* in the tropics, climates were classified into three simple groups by Landsberg et al. (1963): tropical rainy climates with only short dry periods and humid for more than 9½ months of the year; monsoonal and alternately wet and dry climates with distinct long dry periods, with 4½ to 9½ humid months; and arid climates with fewer than 4½ humid months.

Exotic tree species usually show a definite preference for specific rainfall patterns. This was shown by Golfari (1963a) for both tropical and subtropical conifers. Teak was cited by Evans (1984) as a species that will survive in uni-

TABLE 6.1. Classification of Tropical Climates According to Amount of Rainfall with Examples of Suitable Species[a]

Annual Rainfall (mm)	Class Description (with W. African zonation)	Examples of Species Suitable for Planting
Less than 200	Arid, desert	None except possibly *Acacia tortilis* and a few *Prosopis* spp. Irrigation necessary for tree planting.
200–600	Semiarid, Sahelian zone	*Prosopis* spp., several Acacias, *Azadiracta indica*
600–1000	Dry tropical, Sudan zone	*Eucalyptus camaldulensis, Cassia siamea*
1000–1800	Semihumid tropical, Guinea zone	*Eucalyptus grandis, Gmelina arborea, Tectona grandis, Pinus caribaea*
More than 1800	Humid tropical, equatorial region	*Swietenia macrophylla, Pinus merkusii, Eucalyptus deglupta*

[a]From Evans (1984).

formly moist tropical climates, but grows best where there is also a dry season of three to four months. He also states that *Pinus patula* grows best in summer rainfall areas even though total rainfall may be lower than in other areas such as Papua New Guinea, where there is little seasonality. Evans feels that both *P. elliottii* and *P. taeda* will grow well in both summer and uniform-rainfall areas. For *P. elliottii,* this was confirmed by good growth obtained in the Southern Cape Province of South Africa, where uniform rainfall prevails.

6.2.2 Specific Site Factors

While it is becoming generally recognized that climates should be matched when making a choice of species, the mistake often made in the tropics is to match climates based only upon macro site requirements. The choice certainly is dependent on the broad classifications (Rudloff, 1981), but the decision maker must concentrate on the actual and specific site(s) where the exotic is to be planted. This requires a consideration of the specific local climate and related edaphic, biotic, and topographic factors.

Sometimes exotic plantation forestry in the tropics is practiced on large tracts of land with more or less uniform climatic and soil conditions, as exemplified by the coastal plains of Brazil. More often they are on very variable topography where environmental conditions change within very short distances within a small region such as a district or county (e.g., in Colombia, Chile, Swaziland). Under these conditions rainfall and temperature are very important, but soil factors can become primary. The combination of moisture, temperature, and soil properties will ultimately determine whether a species will be well enough adapted to be sufficiently productive to enable the development of a land race. The higher the productivity, the more justification there is for intensive timber management.

Accurate classification of site is difficult but mandatory. An example of determination of site index and species productivity was given by Male (1981) for four species in the variable soils of the granite belt in Queensland; the effect of good site preparation was great. In an attempt to classify site in the grasslands of Venezuela, Vincent (1978) found that moisture, rather than nutrients, was predominant for site quality classification.

6.2.2.1 The Forest Site (General). When growing exotics, timber management should be concentrated on *productive* sites (Grey, 1978). Good sites produce a greater quantity, and usually a better quality, of timber yield. They produce trees of acceptable dimensions more quickly, so rotation ages are shorter, compound interest on investment is minimized, and economic returns are greater. Additionally, it is usually the good sites that are most responsive to forest management practices. The trees that give the highest economic returns often require the best sites, for example, blackwood *(Acacia melanoxylon)*, poplars *(Populus* spp.), and some eucalypts.

Plantation foresters are (belatedly) becoming more aware of the importance of the forest site when establishing exotic plantations. Many mistakes have been made in the past, and are still being made, with "off-site" planting on a large scale. Management and harvesting practices can enhance or reduce the site productivity as succeeding rotations are grown.

6.2.2.2 Forest Soils. A knowledge of soil conditions in the indigenous habitat of a species will help in site selection of an exotic environment. As pointed out by Troup (1932), most species will grow well on moist loams with moderate fertility, but afforestation or reforestation in the tropics is usually not undertaken on such fertile soils; commonly, planting is done on worn-out land, arid land, or on land that is otherwise unfit for successful agriculture. According to Champion and Brasnett (1958), soil depth, permeability, water relations, aeration, the nature of the subsoil, humus conditions, and base status are most important factors to consider for new species introductions.

Soil depth determines the success of root penetration and must be considered as being of first importance since hardpans at shallow depths are common in the tropics (Fig. 6.3). Growing conditions can be very severe (Evans, 1984) where a given soil may oscillate between swampy in the wet season and very arid in the dry. This makes for poor conditions for root growth and lessens a tree's stability and resistance to drought. Also, the small volume of soil available to the roots may lead to nutrient shortages. A survey of potential root

Figure 6.3. Otherwise apparently productive sites can be very poor because of impenetrable layers, or hardpans, near the soil surface. Shown is a densely packed stone layer that prevents root penetration. The resulting shallow roots cause unstable trees and, in droughty years, loss from moisture shortage. (Courtesy S.A.F.R.I.)

depth and possible means of overcoming depth limitations caused by pans by use of subsoiling or plowing must be considered before site preparation is started. Soil should be at least 45 cm deep and easily penetrable by roots for successful afforestation, according to King (1951). Marsh (1978) feels that soils that shallow would be acceptable only if there is an even rainfall distribution. For optimum production of fast-growing exotics, the rooting depth should be greater than 90 cm and the soil should contain sufficient macro- and micropores to ensure good but not excessive drainage and aeration.

All trees, including exotics, do best on soils of moderate texture such as sandy loams, loams, or clay loams, with more than 30% silt and 10 to 35% clay. These foster adequate moisture and nutrient retention capacities (Grey, 1983). In South Africa, most commercial afforestation takes place on clays and sandy clays with a clay content in excess of 35% and less than 20% silt. Contrary to what some foresters expected, the heavy clays proved to be well suited to tree growth because of their well-developed microaggregate structure. Heavy clay soils may be more fertile than sandy soils but often have poor drainage, which leads to waterlogging or, if exposed, to hardening and cracking under conditions of alternate wetting and drying (Evans, 1984). Few tree species grow well under such conditions, though in the Sudan *Acacia seyal* grows well on heavy clays, and in coastal Colombia *Gmelina* and *Bombacopsis quinata* grow well on heavy soils. Some of the best soils for tree growth found in many Central American countries are clays, but they are well aggregated and have good internal drainage. The growth differential of differing soils was dramatic for *Eucalyptus deglupta* in Brazil (Woessner, 1983a). After 1 year, heights varied from 2.0 to 5.9 m, depending on chemical and physical soil properties. Yet some of the best growth was found on soils with pH as varied as 4.6 and 7.5. The determination of growth response to soils is dependent on interactions among a number of soil characteristics.

In North Auckland, New Zealand, early afforestation was done on difficult clay soils in areas of cleared forest, but later the podzolized pumice soils of the central volcanic plateau of North Island, to which *Pinus radiata* was well adapted, became of major importance for exotic forestry. Although they are sandy, these soils hold moisture fairly well (Weston, 1957), in contrast to the deep sands found in some of the grasslands, such as in the Orinoco Basin in South America. Generally, the sandy soils are infertile and freely draining, so Evans (1984) suggests that an undemanding species like *Pinus caribaea* var. *hondurensis* should be planted on sands in the lowland tropics.

Site surveys before establishing plantations are very important. Such surveys, even if done extensively, should identify problem areas such as shallow soils or soils with hardpans or poor structure. For instance, not commonly known are thixotropic, or shock-sensitive, soils, which have the ability to flow under stress and often turn into a "liquid phase" after a single passage of a vehicle (Fitzpatrick, 1980). These unusual and hard-to-handle soils were described by D. Grey (personal communication) as "forming a dense layer following shock which restricts root penetration." Costly delays in harvesting occur on such soils. Thixotropism is a topsoil property associated with wind-fall in young trees (2 to 4 m tall) and with excessive compaction from forest operations (Fig. 6.4).

High soil fertility is not as important for growing trees as it is for agricultural crops. But good soil fertility will make trees grow better, especially the hardwoods. For example, the eucalypts generally must be fertilized at time of planting. Since forestry usually has second priority to agriculture in tropical countries, the less suitable soils are used for tree planting. These are often low in nutrients, especially phosphorus, boron, or copper.

However, if nutrient lack is not too extreme, nutrient-deficient soils often support quite good pine plantations. In southern Africa, Australia, and South America, reasonable productivity is obtained on soils somewhat low in phosphate content. An example are the soils in the llanos of Venezuela in the Orinoco Basin. According to Salas (1976), the soils are low in nitrogen, phosphorus, and potassium. Rainfall is also low and very seasonal. Salas concludes that in this area water, rather than the low nutrient content of the soil, is the limiting factor to growth. A knowledge of fertility levels will contribute to improved productivity, and some tropical soils are so deficient that fertilization is essential. For example, in parts of Chile the trace element boron is deficient, as is boron for eucalypts in parts of Africa, zinc in pines in Australia, and manganese in *P. radiata* in South Africa. These types of deficiencies

Figure 6.4. Sometimes special soils in the tropics, such as the thixotropic, or shock-sensitive, soils, make plantation operations difficult. Shown is the rutting that results from the soils that "flow" following shaking in the logging operation. (Courtesy S.A.F.R.I.)

can be rectified once they are identified, and this normally leads to an improvement in productivity.

Soil acidity problems are not common, according to Evans (1984). However, in South America soil pH is a major factor controlling tree growth and determines the species that can be used. Soil acidity is important because it influences the availability of nutrients and because some exotic species are sensitive to extremes of pH. Pines generally only grow well on moderately acid soils with a pH 3.5–6.5, but even this genus shows variation. *P. caribaea* var. *hondurensis* grows very poorly on alkaline soils, but var. *bahamensis* is more tolerant and, indeed, in Jamaica this variety is specifically planted on the calcareous soils. *Azadiracta indica* (Neem) is a species requiring neutral to alkaline soils and will not grow well where the pH is less than 6 (Laurie, 1974). In parts of South America, some hardwood species, such as red ceiba (*Bombacopsis quinata*) and *Gmelina arborea,* grow with a pH as high as 8.5. Frequently, the correct pH is a major determining factor of what can be grown in tropical areas.

When consideration is given to choice of tropical species with regard to soil reaction as well as other site factors, the publication by Webb et al. (1980) is most helpful. They produced a listing of 125 species and varieties that could be accessed by computer. By entering the relevant variables, the computer program will select several species that might be suitable for a particular site.

6.2.2.3 Local Climate.   In contrast to the closed forests of tropical central Africa or the Amazon, much tropical plantation forestry is practiced on open grassland or scrub-brushland. The fact that the climax vegetation is grass indicates that high forest conditions are not ecologically normal. Where plantations now exist on such areas, it is evident that forests can abruptly change from productive plantations to low-quality, poor-growing trees within a few kilometers or sometimes even a few meters.

The local rainfall pattern, including amount and distribution, and temperature are influenced by local conditions, most commonly a mountain range or other topographic feature. These interact with soil conditions. A change in topography and elevation creates ecological niches where the magnitude of variation is often as great as between macroclimates. Tree species used as exotics that come from complex ecosystems, like many of the Australian eucalypts, respond to small changes in the exotic environment. In subtropical mountainous or hilly country, foresters sometimes complain that they cannot plant a particular species in certain valley bottoms or on hilltops where it otherwise grows well in the general area. Poor air drainage creates frost or cold-air hollows, which requires the use of a different species or provenances if productive plantations are to be grown. Windy areas in relationship with shallow soils will frequently cause plantation losses.

6.2.2.4 Quantification of Site Factors.   All exotic plantations, including those in the tropics, need a classification of site factors. As an example, in a study of *P. radiata* in Chile, Schlatter and Gerding (1984) reported that growth is mainly influenced by soil factors and states that a climatic assessment restricted to the measurement of average annual rainfall is of minor importance. He found that factors related to soil fertility in the top 15 cm had the greatest influence on site index for radiata pine. Available moisture capacity, drainage, and nutrient reserves explain the major portion of the variation in growth. Soil texture was the single most important variable.

In a study of one district representing a relatively uniform climate with little change in parent materials and vegetation, Grey (1978) found that, for *Pinus patula,* altitude, relative distance from the ridge crest, and land surface unit (an index of land surface with 1 being "poorest" and 6 the "best" land unit) are the most important site factors for maximum productivity. In a wider context, however, *Pinus patula* should not be grown at low altitudes (below 100 m) in a warm climate where the risk of fungus attack by *Diplodea pinea* is high after hailstorms. Grey (1978) also lists four other studies that indicated that nutrients within the A horizon (for radiata pine), moisture and temperature (for wattle), altitude, relative distance from ridge top to valley bottom, slope percentage, phosphorus in the subsoil, and potassium near the soil surface are most important factors for site classification in patula pine.

An intensive study on the influence of site factors on the growth of *Pinus patula, P. elliottii,* and *P. taeda* in the eastern Transvaal in South Africa has been undertaken by Schutz (1985). He found *P. patula* to be the most site demanding, followed by *P. taeda,* with *P. elliottii* the most tolerant. From numerous variables investigated, the most important site factors affecting site indices of *P. patula* are soil parent material (geology), depth to a stoneline, calcium of the A horizon, percentage of stones present in the B horizon, altitude, topographic position, and percentage of fine sand in the A horizon (Fig. 6.5). These variables appear in a model explaining 86% of the total variation in site index of *P. patula.* In this area, *P. patula* has also proved to be sensitive to wet soil conditions, preferring red subsoils to yellow subsoils, and growing less well in very high rainfall areas. An excess of boron was found in soils derived from quartzite rock that adversely affected *P. patula* growth. Whereas this species is unaffected by the high manganese levels typical of dolomite soils, *P. elliottii* is adversely affected.

In a study on *P. radiata* in New Zealand relating productivity to site factors, soil phosphorus, mycorrhizal infection, drainage, and soil pH appeared to be the most important (Ballard, 1971). Turner (1984) also mentions several other studies relating productivity to site factors, but admits that using many characteristics is not efficient for plantation selection, especially since some factors interact with each other.

Soil and site surveys are essential for maximum productivity when growing exotics in the tropics. This was well stated by Stone (1982) as follows:

If an organization cannot afford the low cost (per ha) insurance provided by good soil mapping and map interpretation, it probably cannot afford the risk of investing in plantation establishment without such guidance.

Figure 6.5. Soil characteristics usually determine the success of an exotic. Such things as depth to a hardpan, soil chemistry, and physical characteristics of the soil are critical. When starting an exotic tree program it is necessary to obtain soil profiles, such as the one shown, before final decisions are made. (Courtesy S.A.F.R.I.)

When afforestation in the grasslands is to be undertaken, Carmean's (1984) site evaluation system is very appropriate. His general approach can be summarized as follows: (1) subdivide the country into "site regions" based on broad climatic, topographic, and soil differences; (2) for each site region construct a general "first approximation" site evaluation system based on obvious features such as topographic position, soil depth, texture, stone content, and drainage; (3) initiate research designed to convert the general "first approximation" into more precise quantitative site evaluation systems—research will require many measurements from existing plantations (when such exist) for use in site curve and soil-site regression analyses; and (4) quantitative systems of site evaluation must be linked to growth and yield measurements from local plantations, and to tables expressing growth and yield for each species used for fuelwood as well as timber management for other forest products.

6.3 SILVICULTURE

The amount of information related to the silviculture of exotics in the tropics is voluminous. Even the proceedings and symposia are too numerous to cite here; we have chosen to cover in a general way specific silvicultural operations, with only an occasional reference for illustrative purposes. As examples of symposia, the two-volume *Symposium on Site Productivity of Fast Growing Plantations,* taken from the symposium held in 1984 in South Africa and edited by Grey et al., has numerous excellent references in many of the areas of silviculture. Another is the IUFRO symposium on "Fast-Growing Trees" held in Brazil and published in numbers 29–32 of *Silvicultura.* Many articles summarize various silvicultural aspects of growing exotics. Similar symposia are available specifically for the eucalypts.

6.3.1 Nurseries

Detailed explanations of how to produce seedlings in nurseries is not the objective of this chapter—they are described in publications such as those by Denison (1980), Napier and Willan (1983), Davey (1984), and many others. Special nursery techniques for different species are available, such as the one by Chanshaima (1984) for *Eucalyptus* in Tanzania. He reported, for example, that nitrogen fertilizer lowered survival while root pruning and potassium improved it; root growth was related to potassium. Root pruning was the most important nursery treatment.

A tree seedling can be grown in any kind of container, be it a jam tin, paper pot, or plastic bag, or in a nursery bed. But to grow *healthy* plants efficiently and most *economically* requires careful planning, management, and control of the forest nursery. It must be emphasized that raising the tree seedlings is not just a matter of simply growing a large number of single plants, but it involves a *system.* The objective of this system is to supply good-quality tree seedlings at the proper time in the desired quantities at the lowest possible cost. The following emphasizes this concept for the tropical areas.

Plantation forestry in the tropics must include a much more sophisticated approach to raising seedlings than has been done in the past. Nursery practices vary widely and no "single best system" exists whereby plants of all species in all areas should be grown. Management objectives and size of operation dictate the nursery system to be used, and improved techniques may cause a complete change in existing, well-established nurseries. A prime example of this for pine in the tropics is the move towards the use of bare-root seedlings in large operations and the less common use of plastic bags when containerized seedlings are produced.

Many exotics have been established by direct sowing in the past, a practice that was quite popular with *Acacia* spp., *Cassia* spp., *Prosopis* spp., *Gmelina arborea,* and others. For this practice, seed must be available in large quantities, especially when broadcast sowing is practiced. Many seeds are lost to birds and rodents. The large quantities of seed needed were normally obtained from seed merchants from bulk collections, and little control was exercised over the origin and quality of the seed. Now most exotic forest trees in the tropics are produced in nurseries as seedlings or rooted cuttings, especially related to the shortage of improved seed.

Nursery practice varies with the climate. In tropical areas seedlings are normally kept in the nursery for less than one year, often only three to four months. This is a major difference compared to nurseries in the temperate regions, where seedlings may remain in the nurseries as long as four years except when grown in greenhouses. Because of their rapid development, care and hardening off of seedlings are particularly difficult in the tropics, and if not done well, a high mortality of transplants and poor growth may result.

Many early nurseries produced seedlings on beds using manual root pruning with spades, with later field planting of so-called open-root (or bare-root) plants. Others used treated wooden boxes (also called nursery trays) with soil in them; these normally held 30 or 36 plants and weighed from 11 to 15 kg when filled with moist soil. A third method commonly employed involved single containers having a size and shape which varied with almost every nursery or species being grown. For many years the most popular container was the plastic (polyethylene) bag or tube filled with soil. These have been losing favor and in many areas are now being replaced with polystyrene trays called planter flats or other solid plastic containers and the use of a growing media other than soil. With this change has come mechanization in the filling of the containers, along with their sowing, watering, fertilizing, and transport.

6.3.1.1 Nursery Systems. The objective of the nursery system is to supply good-quality seedlings cheaply and quickly at the proper time for outplanting. To achieve this objective, a total nursery system should include careful plans for the selection of site, type of nursery, proper establishment, and intensive management, which requires good maintenance and protection. Before a new nursery is built, full consideration must be given to management objectives. These include choice of species, number of plants required, and thus size and type of nursery required.

Sometimes the decision must be made that more than one nursery is required because of different species. Different species in the same nursery, especially if both conifers and hardwoods are grown, will require contrasting growing conditions and different nutrient regimes, different spacings, different watering schedules, and often bare-root versus containerized systems.

The selection of a nursery site is a key and difficult job, but one that is often done with too little care. Obviously, the layout of the nursery must be such that there is a smooth flow of suitable plants at the desired time with a minimum amount of handling.

6.3.1.2 Open- or Bare-root Nurseries. The term *open root* or *bare root* refers to plants grown in beds and lifted and transported to the planting site with roots not in soil or other medium. The bare-root nursery method is coming into wide usage in the tropical and subtropical areas, especially for the pines (Fig. 6.6). At one time, containerized seedlings were primarily produced, but this is now rapidly changing. As one example, Morales (1983) covers in detail the methods used for producing bare-root *Pinus caribaea*. His discussion is based on a nursery that will produce 10 million plants annually.

The roots of bare-root seedlings must be carefully handled to prevent the seedlings from developing large taproots growing deep into the beds, with poor secondary root systems. Of key importance, the seedlings must be hardened off; if not, they will be in a succulent condition and cannot successfully withstand planting shock if weather conditions are not ideally cool and moist. A hardy seedling must have a well-developed fibrous root system. This is done through root wrenching or undercutting and side pruning of the seedling roots. Having the seedlings well hardened off before planting is essential for all situations, but is especially critical in the tropical areas, where there is a short

Figure 6.6. One of the methods of growing exotic seedlings in the tropics is to use open- or bare-root nurseries. This method, as shown, works well for some species. There has been controversy about its suitability, but the use of bare-root nurseries is increasing rapidly. The netting is to protect the seedlings from hail. (Courtesy Stellenbosch University, South Africa).

rainy season followed by a long, severe dry season with constant winds and low relative humidities. Planting success is totally dependent on getting physiologically suitable seedlings planted at the proper time.

Mechanized bare-root nurseries can be justified when more than one million plants are needed annually. The initial capital cost is high, but thereafter annual direct nursery costs are much lower than for other nursery systems. On an 1.8-m-wide bed, 12 rows of seedlings can be raised, yielding a total plant capacity of 300 per meter length of bed (Denison, 1980). Another rule for proper stocking, emphasized by all with experience with nurseries, is to avoid overstocking, a most common error. Densities of about 150 plantable seedlings per square meter are about correct, but the density should never exceed 200 trees per square meter (Davey, 1984). With the very fast-growing tropical pines, overdensity in the nursery results in a very poor shoot-to-root ratio with resultant poor survival and poor growth following outplanting.

All operations can be mechanized using as few as two laborers per day, except when lifting seedlings; in some nurseries the lifting is done mechanically. In the tropical areas for pine, usually 2 vertical and 5 horizontal wrenchings are adequate to produce the desired plants, but this varies greatly with nursery from a low of 3 to as many as 11 undercuts without vertical pruning. *P. elliottii, P. taeda, P. radiata,* and *P. caribaea* all respond well to this system and develop hardy, well-conditioned plants. *P. patula* is also responsive but, although it develops a good root system, it is more sensitive to planting shock than the other species and survival may be low unless very good planting conditions exist.

Conditioned seedlings that are dormant can be stored for several weeks at temperatures around 1–3°C and still survive well at planting (Denison, 1980). To store seedlings satisfactorily, Denison states that the foliage must be free of moisture; this can be done by sealing fresh seedlings with dry foliage in thick, laminated, brown paper bags coated on the inside with polyethylene, enabling transport of seedlings over long distances.

Eucalypts are more sensitive than pines to planting shock, and it is generally accepted that they should be produced in containers. However, Barrett (1978) reported good success with open-root eucalypt nurseries and some trials have been made in Venezuela; open-root methods have also been tried with *Eucalyptus* in New Zealand, where a technique has been developed in which trees are lifted a month after two fortnightly wrenchings. They are then bundled and heeled in; then they are given a series of wrenches by lifting a little every four to five weeks, with each wrenching being accompanied by copious watering (Weston, 1957). Poor stock is heavily culled and no trees are planted until white rootlets are well developed. The planting stock has its roots dipped into a clay slurry; planting is done during wet weather. A recent report by Revell and Van Dorsser (1983) in New Zealand showed that if proper care is taken in the nursery and in planting, winter and early spring planting gave survivals over 90%. Seedlings are produced in the nursery using techniques similar to radiata pine. (However, the standard is still to raise eucalypts in containers.)

A common question relates to the kind of soil that is best for a nursery. Although it varies greatly by species and condition, for conifers Davey (1984) suggests a fine sand to sandy loam to a depth of at least 25 cm before finer-textured soil is encountered. The best pH is 5.2 to 6.2; soils over pH 7.0 give problems with the conifers.

One variation of open-root nurseries is the production of striplings and stumping. A *stripling* is an oversize seedling (2 to 2½ m tall) from which the aerial shoot is stripped of leaves before field planting. As much as possible of the root system is saved when lifting. This sytem was developed in West Africa with the objective of getting the growing tip of hardwoods out of reach of small browsing buck and above low weed competition. The size of these plants requires large planting holes, and the cost of this system is prohibitive for general commercial forest plantations. For tropical hardwoods, which are much sought after for furniture, and when labor is abundant and cheap, the cost of stripling production might be offset by the high value return.

Stumping refers to production of stumps from large nursery plants 1 to 2 m high and 1 to 3 cm in diameter. The plants are cut back to about 15 to 25 cm when lifted. Side roots are also pruned back. Many tropical hardwoods such as *Gmelina arborea* sprout readily if planted in the form of stumps. Species from the following genera are adaptable to stumping: *Afzelia, Cassia, Chlorophora, Entandrophragma, Gmelina, Khaya, Lovoa, Pterocarpus, Tectona, Terminalia, Triplochiton,* and even some *Eucalyptus* (Parry, 1956).

Parry reports that stumps are easy to raise, cheap to transport, and almost foolproof to plant with unskilled labor. They are relatively unaffected by dry spells because new roots develop deep at the tip of the stump. Normally they are more successful in sandy than in clay soil. Stumps are sometimes attacked by termites. Teak (*Tectona grandis*) is commonly grown from stumps because fairly thin stumps (optimum 1 to 2 cm) work well. They are easily raised by sowing thinly in the nursery bed and harvesting the largest ones by pulling the seedlings when they reach the desired size (usually after about one year). The smaller ones are left to develop, often for another year, before lifting. This is a very simple nursery technique, particularly where the seed can be germinated and grown without shade, as is possible with teak (Parry, 1956).

6.3.1.3 Containerized Nurseries.
Although used in other parts of the world, such as Canada and northern Europe, container nursery stock has been particularly used in the tropics because of a lack of good bare-root nursery sites, fast growth, lack of preplanning for nurseries, and because some widely used species such as the eucalypts do not respond well to bare-root nursery methods.

Container stock is defined as being raised and planted as a unit with the root system isolated from the root systems of other plants. Numerous kinds of containers have been developed and used, (Fig. 6.7), especially where labor was plentiful, although mechanized systems are now being developed. Some of the classical types of containers are banana leaves laid across each other at

Figure 6.7. The standard method used in the tropics has been to produce seedlings in one of many different types of containers. The MELFERT container, used by A.F.O.C.E.L., France, allows roots to freely penetrate the container walls. Root binding is a common problem with containerized seedling systems. (Courtesy S.A.F.R.I.)

right angles and the four ends turned up vertically and bound into position; banana fiber pots made from fiber pulled from the bole of the banana tree; baked clay tubes that are cracked at planting; bamboo tubes made from two split halves bound together but with binding broken at time of planting; baskets; rolled-up roofing felt or tar paper; wood veneer; tin plate; polyethylene bags or tubes; and many others. Different sizes of polyethylene containers and their characteristics as used in 12 countries are listed in a table by Napier and Willan (1983).

A composite container used in many forest nurseries is the creosoted box or nursery tray. This is filled with soil and contains 30 to 36 plants. At time of planting, these boxes are taken into the field and the seedlings are planted *supposedly* with soil still adhering to the root system. Such boxes require a lot of soil, are heavy and cumbersome, and close supervision is necessary at planting. Transport costs for such containers are high.

For many years the polyethylene bags, with holes in the sides and bottom or in the form of a tube, was most popular. These are filled with pure topsoil, with soil mixtures with or without fertilizers added, with soil substitutes like powdered bark or vermiculite, or even with subsoil. Fertilizer is sometimes added in the irrigation water. This container system was used because it was claimed that planting stock could be produced that was of exceptional vigor, uniformity, and size and would withstand shock better than other plants. Furthermore, plants could be easily transported over long distances, and planting operations are not so dependent upon good weather conditions. The system lends itself to establishment of trees in unfavorable areas such as droughty conditions or where weed competition is severe.

Some of the advantages just listed are debatable, and containers have some distinct disadvantages. An important one is that they require a lot of soil that may be scarce and needs to be transported a long way; they are labor intensive, and root circling and strangling occurs if the root ball is not cut at the time of planting. In the early years (and, quite unbelievably, even today) trees were sometimes planted with plastic bags left on the roots, the idea being that the roots would penetrate the drainage holes, rupture the bag, and grow normally. This they do not do and trees planted with plastic bags on the roots have unbalanced root systems and the trees often lean or actually fall over (Fig. 6.8). Variations of plastic tubes have been developed with the use of woven paper sleeves and using soil-less media like old pine bark.

The most advanced containerized systems being adopted by most progressive organizations are the polystyrene trays (planter flats) or individual plastic containers carried in styrofoam trays—the plug or Hawaiian dibbling tube or many variations thereof. These systems lend themselves to mechanization because the flats or trays form units that can be filled with growing media and can be mechanically sown much easier than the polyethylene bags. These systems also use soil-less media—pine bark, bark and compost mixtures, or nonorganic media such as vermiculite. The forms or tubes usually have vertical ribs that prevent root spiraling and the ends of the roots are air pruned.

The capital layout of such a modern nursery is higher than one with polyethylene bags, but the operational costs are reduced and the containers can be used numerous times. Usually the light planter flats are put on racks built of timber and taut wire to facilitate aerial root pruning. Alternatively, the carrying trays (for Hawaiian dibbling tube) are high enough to let the tube hang above ground level and also effect air root pruning. Nutrients are supplied in the irrigation water and are varied according to the shoot and root development required for the seedlings. As opposed to transporting polyethylene bags with plants, the seedlings from these containers are pulled out with the root plug intact and then packed in containers (coated paper bags or boxes) and transported in very much the same way as open-root seedlings. The seedlings from such containers can be used in planting machines. Small containers are only good under ideal planting conditions, but under the usual harsh condi-

Figure 6.8. It is commonly recognized that containerized seedlings must have the roots freed before planting. Despite this, some trees are still being planted with the plastic bag left on. Root deformation, as shown for this pine, results in an unstable tree. (Courtesy S.A.F.R.I.)

tions in the tropics larger containers with well-developed root systems and good top-to-root ratios must be used.

The scope of this chapter does not allow further discussion of different types of nurseries, so a comparison summary is given in Table 6.2.

6.3.1.4 Growing Rooted Cuttings. Vegetative propagation, particularly the growing of rooted cuttings, has been thoroughly described in Chapter 5. It requires special preparation of the material, which makes it more complex than producing trees from seed. The first "preparation" necessary is to select clones for their rooting ability. This is easily done by comparing cuttings of roughly similar physiological age and condition from different ortets under the same environmental conditions. As emphasized earlier, the age of cutting is important. For the eucalypts, cuttings are harvested from coppice shoots

TABLE 6.2. Comparison Between Container and Bare-root Methods of Raising Seedlings[a]

	Container System	Bare-root system
Materials	Need as many containers as seedlings. Supply of good soil for potting mix.	Nursery site with easily worked soil suitable for bed cultivation.
Equipment	Container filling device, soil-sieving screen. Tubing shed.	Tractor and several implements for ploughing, rotovating, bed formation, seed sowing, undercutting, lifting, etc.
Labor	Labor intensive, not easily mechanized. Much labor needed for container filling, seed sowing, weeding, and container removal at planting. Typically, 10–20 men are needed per million seedlings produced.	Well suited to mechanization. Most labor-intensive component is lifting and packaging, but even these may become mechanized in the future. At Beerburrum, Queensland, 2–3 men raise 1.4 million seedlings per year.
Transport	Bulky and heavy to transport, costly over long distances but not so easily damaged.	Plants easy to transport over long distances if carefully packed.
Silviculture	Excellent survival at planting. Overgrown plants become pot bound and suffer serious root deformation and, later, instability.	Good survival depends on careful timing of lifting and planting, to coincide with wet weather, and adequate conditioning of plants. Gives poorer results where climate is unreliable. Coating roots with a clay slurry is helpful.
Supervision	Easier to grow satisfactorily, timing of operations not too critical, but may suffer more from casual neglect of watering and shading. If left too long, they get root bound.	Requires a high degree of supervision to ensure proper timing and regularity of operations.
Protection	Fresh soil in every container reduces chance of buildup of pathogens or soil pests. Diseased seedlings easily isolated and discarded. Weed control tedious.	Reuse of same soil may lead to buildup of pathogens or soil pests. Pests and diseases more likely to affect all seedlings in a bed.

(*continued*)

TABLE 6.2. Continued

	Container System	Bare-root system
Cost	High labor intensity results in more costly seedlings.	Capital intensive, but at high levels of output unit costs are low.
Suitability	All smaller nurseries and especially: (1) for better survival in arid conditions, (2) when many different species are raised, (3) where plants are distributed to the public and postplanting care is likely to be poor.	(1) Large production nurseries raising only a few species and where climate is dependable, (2) raising "stump" plants and as a cheap method for hardy species.

*A partial summary after Evans (1984).

that should not be older than 80 days, even though they may still appear to be small. Coppice shoots harvested from stumps of selected trees in the field will vary in physiological condition, but this will be improved in a clone bank or clonal reproduction area, where the health of the sprouts is improved by fertilization and possibly by irrigation. This produces more uniform cuttings that are more efficiently handled and usually root better.

Planter flats are suitable for growing cuttings, but plastic tubes like the Hawaiian dibbling tube or variations thereof, such as the wedge-shaped square tubes now used in South Africa, are more popular because they are easier to handle and sort; furthermore, the root plug easily slips out of the container, yielding an intact root plug. Growing media may vary, but vermiculite has given the best results. The growing medium must be well aerated but also have a good water-holding capacity.

It is important that nurserymen producing rooted cuttings (also called *estacas* or stecklings) do not try to "reinvent the wheel" by trying all kinds of methods, media, and regimes that others have already found do not work. They need to learn through experience how to grow *estacas* commercially under their particular conditions. Do not use commercial production as a method of experimenting. Techniques for growing rooted cuttings have been well documented by Campinhos and Ikemori (1980), Durand-Creswell et al. (1982), Zobel et al. (1983), and many others. Growing cuttings usually is more expensive than growing seedlings, but the extra expense is justified by the higher yields that will be obtained; with experience and mechanization, cuttings can be produced as cheaply as or cheaper than seedlings (Zobel et al., 1983). Psychologically, field personnel tend to take better care of rooted cuttings because they know that the material is more valuable and they expect them to perform better. This awareness is very valuable in an applied vegetative propagation program.

6.3.1.5 Nursery Sites. Location of nursery sites in the tropics is sometimes difficult. Needed is proximity to and an adequate supply of suitable water. Soil must have proper physical characteristics and, of key importance, should have the correct pH. Soil or water with an undesirable pH or excess chemical concentration is a major problem when locating nurseries in the tropics. Water requirement will vary with the growing medium and nursery type being used, but will be between 2,000 and 14,000 liters per 100,000 plants (Barrett, 1978; Marsh, 1978). Water must also be free of contamination by fungal spores. Exact requirements for nursery soil nutrients are listed by numerous authors (Barrett, 1978; Denison, 1980; Marsh, 1978; Napier and Willan, 1983; Davey, 1984; and many others). In addition, the nursery must be accessible by all-weather roads. To the forester establishing a nursery, the same advice given to couples about to marry is relevant: "Do it in haste, repent at leisure." Improper choice of nursery sites is one of the most common and serious problems encountered in tropical forestry.

Of special importance in tropical nurseries is to assure that the seedlings become suitably mycorrhizal. Mycorrhizae are important in all nurseries but are of special importance in nurseries using soil-less media. If nurseries are situated adjacent to plantations, inoculation with ectotrophic mycorrhizae occurs freely; this condition occurs with most conifers and the eucalypts. But the endotrophic mycorrhizae, required by most hardwoods and *Cupressus,* are soilborne and spread with more difficulty.

Many organizations establish "mycorrhizal nurseries" of pines which serve as a source of inoculum to put in the nursery soil. This is easily done by mixing some duff and topsoil from plantations into the nursery soil mixture. Lack of suitable mycorrhizae has been one of the most frequent reasons for failure of exotic tropical plantations, and the mycorrhizae must be supplied in the nursery for growth there and for later development in the plantation.

In all nurseries, but especially in the tropics, regular inspections and observations are essential. Failure to observe for as little as two days may be disastrous because fungal diseases, lack of water, or a heat wave can kill many plants very quickly. In subtropical areas, the nursery site should be on a slight slope (say, 5 degrees) to have free drainage of water and cold air. No subtropical forest area is guaranteed the absence of occasional frosts and frost pockets caused by surrounding hills, buildings, or dense vegetation that will hinder cold-air drainage. These frequently are detrimental to seedling production.

6.3.1.6 Growing and Managing Seedlings. Poor germination of seed is common with some exotic species used in the tropics. It can be caused by empty seed, partial dormancy, hard seed coats, chemical inhibitors, or other seed phenomena. One common cause of loss in viability is too severe or careless treatment with chemicals like methyl bromide for seed imported from other countries; equally frequent are losses from long storage times under unsuitable conditions while the seed are awaiting clearance or inspection through customs. Empty seed are of special importance in species such as *Pinus caribaea, P. oocarpa,* and other tropical pines. Especially at low elevations and low latitudes (near the equator) these species produce abundant reproductive structures and mature cones which contain few seeds, many of which are in turn hollow. The causes of this problem are discussed in Chapter 5, but poor seed quality of the tropical pines is a plague to the nurserymen.

The need for seed stratification occurs with some of the pines such as *P. elliottii, P. patula, P. taeda, P. radiata,* and *P. pinaster.* A successful treatment is to soak the seed in water for 8 to 24 hours and then store them at 2–4°C for four to seven weeks (cold stratification). Sowing should be done soon after stratification because species such as *P. elliottii* may lose the advantage of stratification or may even lose germinative capacity if allowed to dry after treatment (Daniels and Van der Sijde, 1975).

Tropical pine species do not need stratification. For some hardwoods, germination can be very erratic unless seed pretreatment is applied. Hot soaking or dipping in hot water (90°C) for two minutes will improve germination of some hard-coated seeds like those of species of *Albizzia* and *Acacia.* For some species, for example, *Acacia nilotica,* acid soaking may be required. For teak, "no universally reliable pre-treatment method" has been achieved (Evans, 1984).

Sowing and germination are done in various ways in different nurseries. Direct sowing by hand is mostly practiced in large bare-root nurseries, although use of machines has recently become more common. Poor seed germination, unless adjusted for, can cause an underutilization of the nursery capacity with resulting increased costs. Good seed germination tests are a prerequisite for direct sowing, especially where precision sowers are used in large beds.

In some container nurseries the effect of poor germination is overcome by sowing two to three or more seeds in the same container and subsequently thinning out the excess germinants. In most tropical areas, a most common cause of poor stocking in nurseries is the extremely hard and heavy rain showers that occur and wash seed from the nursery soil. A common practice still used in many nurseries is to broadcast sow seed in germination boxes or beds and to "prick the seedlings out" (transplant) when very small into individual containers or into nursery beds. This is a labor-intensive and tedious task that requires good supervision and training or numerous J roots will be formed. A J root results when the taproot is bent upward while transplanting the seedling, a situation that happens easily when seedlings are too large before pricking out. The resulting distorted root systems produce unstable trees after field planting. However, hand transplanting into nursery beds assures having the proper density and utilizes the nursery to its fullest.

Seedlings grown in the tropics often are produced under favorable conditions and are so luxuriant that they are not suitable to plant directly in the field unless site and weather conditions are ideal—that is, well-prepared sites and cool, moist or rainy weather on planting days. Such conditions are rare!

For good survival and subsequent growth, seedlings must be *conditioned* (hardened off) before planting, whether they are grown in open-root nurseries or containers. Seedlings in polyethylene tubes must be root pruned by lifting containers regularly or undercutting them with a taut wire. Watering is reduced to harden off plants before field planting, but sometimes rains prevent this. Nutrients are changed; nitrogen is reduced and potassium fertilizers are used in the hardening-off process.

The best success in bare-root nurseries is obtained by conditioning seedlings through regular wrenchings or undercutting. These treatments inhibit shoot growth, stimulate tertiary and fibrous root production, and increase root-to-shoot ratios. Wrenching causes plant dormancy and therefore induces morphological and physiological changes in the seedlings that are most suitable for field planting. Wrenching stress causes the stomata to close and photosynthesis to be reduced. The result is reduced translocation of photosynthates to the roots (Denison, 1980).

It takes eight to ten days after wrenching for the plant to regain its original turgor. As photosynthesis strengthens, massive root proliferation occurs. Repeated wrenchings at 10- to 14-day intervals enhance stomatal resistance in the pine needles (Denison, 1980, 1981). During the conditioning period, nutrition in the form of fertilizers is essential and promotes the accumulation of carbohydrates in the plant, but nitrogen should be avoided during the hardening-off period. The well-conditioned seedling has a dryish, hardened, brownish shoot and the loss of chlorophyl sometimes makes its foliage appear to be somewhat chlorotic.

Care must be taken in hardening off that the stress conditions are not so severe as to cause permanent loss of vigor. All species will respond adversely to excess stress, but some hardwoods, especially the eucalypts, are particularly sensitive. An overstressed eucalypt will never grow normally, no matter how ideal the following environmental conditions.

Lifting and packing seedlings is an important phase of the nursery operations in the tropics. It is particularly critical because of the intensity of the sun, low relative humidities, and winds that often blow during the planting period. All seedlings, container or bare root, must be protected against drying. For the open-root nursery, a short period from lifting to planting is mandatory. Lifting should be done in the early morning or at night, when soil and air temperatures are low and the turgor within the plant is high. On some of the more severe planting situations, such as the grasslands in South America, both lifting and planting are sometimes done at night. Systems must be developed to provide the necessary care in lifting and packing seedlings, whether done mechanically or manually.

Although plants can be "stored" in the container until planting, open-root seedlings must be held in cold storage; they are stored in sealed containers in cold rooms at 2–4°C. If pine seedlings are lifted before dormancy or after height growth is rapid, they do not store well, and seedlings in a stage of active growth have a physiological status such that storage for more than a few days is not recommended (Denison, 1981). Dormant, well hardened-off seedlings may be stored satisfactorily for up to three months (Denison, 1981; Davey, 1984), although the storage time should be shorter if possible.

A close coordination must exist between the nurseryman and forester responsible for field planting. This is particularly critical in the tropics with short wet seasons and long, severe dry spells. It is of no use for the nursery to produce good-quality seedlings that are not ready for planting at the beginning of the wet season. Numerous studies have shown that the key to planting success is to get the trees in the ground early in the wet season so that they can become established before the drought occurs. Special care in planting is essential when there are alternating wet and dry seasons, and a quality control system is necessary whereby quality of the seedlings, weather conditions on planting day, planting methods, and an estimation of subsequent weather conditions (up to 14 days after planting) are all taken into account. Records of these are assessed by the nurseryman as an evaluation of the quality of the nursery stock produced (Denison, 1980). Such a record-keeping system is often overlooked in tropical forestry operations, but it is the key to continued success.

6.3.2 Site Preparation

Very few domestic crops will grow satisfactorily on uncultivated land. This is also true for forest trees, especially hardwoods grown as exotics. Often this critical aspect of exotic forestry is neglected (Fig. 6.9). The main arguments for such neglect is that the cost incurred at the beginning of the plantation accrues compound interest, so it must be kept as low as possible. Although this is a true economic fact, any forestry enterprise must assess the economic benefits derived from proper site preparation.

A large proportion of world exotic forestry consists of short-rotation hardwoods, especially with the eucalypts. Usually the end product dictates the dimensions at harvest, such as mining timbers, pulpwood, or poles. Uniformity with respect to diameter growth, straightness, and wood density is of special importance for industry. Stand uniformity leads to higher efficiency in logging and transport and results in higher utilization per unit area of timber. Proper management can help in stand uniformity, especially with the trend towards clonal forestry. But the potential for improved and uniform growth rate is lost if competition suppresses the trees!

In most tropical forest areas weed growth is very luxuriant and competes strongly with young trees. The importance of competition depends upon the species planted as well as on the weed species. This, combined with local climatic conditions, causes confusion among foresters as to the intensity of site preparation required. Too often a single method is followed for all conditions and all species, resulting in either severe growth loss or excessive cleaning costs.

In many tropical countries forest planting follows shifting cultivation. The inhabitants clear patches of land, cultivate it for two to four years, and then

Figure 6.9. The method of site preparation is of key importance in the success of exotic plantations. Intensive site preparation is best. Shown are 5½-year-old *Eucalyptus grandis;* the tall trees had complete ploughing for site preparation, the smaller trees had only pitting for preparation. (Courtesy, Institute for Commercial Forestry Research, South Africa.)

move to a new area. Forestry is best established by planting trees on the degraded lands before the last agricultural crops are grown. This is one form of agroforestry, known by the Burmese word *taungya,* and works well in some countries because the forest trees benefit from the complete cultivation given to the crops. Sometimes legumes like beans, soybeans, or groundnuts (peanuts) are used; they improve the nutrient status of the soil through their nitrogen-fixing capacity.

The *taungya* system can also be used in replanting following forest harvest. Indigenous and exotic weeds quickly colonize clearfelled stands, but if not controlled, they will develop into dense competing vegetation among young trees. Cultivation and planting legumes among these young trees has substantially increased growth of *Gmelina* and *Eucalyptus grandis* in South Africa. The *taungya* system is becoming increasingly important in growing exotics in the tropics.

There is not room for a discussion of the methods of site preparation. There are many publications dealing with this. One of the most recent is a symposium covering land clearing in the tropics (Lal et al., 1985). Land-clearing methods and relationships to ecology are covered in the several papers.

6.3.2.1 Burning. The use of heavy machinery on large tracts of land contrasts with the *taungya* system. The clearing may include logging of merchantable trees, uprooting and crushing small trees and shrubs, followed by burning once the debris is dry enough. Burning is widely practiced and is the cheapest way of getting rid of unwanted debris. Fires that are too hot may affect the soil and kill soil fauna near the surface, but this is rare; most well-controlled burns consume only the dry organic material above the soil surface. The ash layer following burning is rich in nutrients, with exchangeable bases being increased by 25% and usable P_2O_5 by as much as 400%.

Burning must be done with care in areas prone to erosion. Heavy thundershowers are prevalent in the tropics and can wash away large amounts of the topsoil and the ash layer. When rainfall is seasonal, burning should be done early in the dry season because of danger of fire escape during the peak dry season. Some countries prohibit controlled burns during the dry season, especially if burns are done in harvested stands where slash piles are to be removed before planting.

Although burning is cheap and effective in clearing land, it is not always satisfactory or may even be impossible. Mountain grassland in Africa usually is dry in the dry season and burns easily, but the kikuyu grass covering large areas in the mountains of Colombia, for instance, will not be killed by fires. The fire and ash stimulates its growth and the area again becomes grass-covered shortly after the burning has been done. Some grass species like *Setaria chevaleiri* are stimulated by fire and grow and spread very prolifically after fire and are very detrimental, especially where species like the eucalypts are to be used. It is clear that where grassy growth is heavy, as is common in the tropics, burning must be followed by other means of site preparation.

Occasionally, burning stimulates growth of fungi such as *Rhizina undulata* that may attack and kill *Pinus* seedlings. *Pinus patula* is very susceptible to this fungus and should never be planted soon after burning (Anon., 1981a). In Swaziland, up to 80% mortality has occurred from this pathogen (Germishuizen and Marais, 1981). When the area is burnt about six months before planting at the beginning of the dry season, the risk of seedling mortality from fungi is reduced. If left unplanted this long, the advantage of cleared land is lost because weed species colonize the burnt area very rapidly.

Although still not generally employed in the tropics, use of fire as a silvicultural tool is increasing. As reported by Fahnestock (1983) for pine plantations in Venezuela, even prescribed burning is technically and biologically feasible as a management practice in *Pinus caribaea*. Much more needs to be done in this area, but it is evident that prescribed fire in pine plantations will become an increasingly important tool of silviculture in addition to the use of fire for site preparation.

6.3.2.2 Herbicides. Herbicides are one of the most effective and safest ecological ways of preparing land for planting in the tropics. They are especially effective on sprouts following fire or after mechanical site preparation. Herbicide use is frequently combined with some form of cultivation.

The benefit of using herbicides is clearly illustrated in a simple trial laid out in *Eucalyptus grandis*. The four treatments applied were total spray of the area with glyphosate, spot spraying and spot hoeing of 1-m diameter around each tree, and a control with no weed elimination. The trees were planted with no special care and no fertilizer. After 37 months the trees planted after total spraying of the area had 25% more height growth and 78% more volume production than the control trees; these in turn were better than those that received spot hoeing. The difference in mortality between the "total spray" and "spot hoe" treatments would be enough to offset the cost of the chemical (Anon., 1984a). The allelopathic (poison) effect sometimes related to grass competition disappears quickly when the grass is killed by herbicides. That is why hoeing around a tree is not always most effective even if the grass that returns is not tall.

6.3.2.3 Intensity of Cultivation. Minimum cultivation consists of making a planting hole with a spade, hoe, or dibble without further tilling the soil. This is cheap and fast, but unless climatic and soil conditions are favorable and weed competition is at a minimum, the lack of site preparation will lead to slow growth response and often to heavy mortality.

The most common site preparation in hilly areas is spot preparation whereby each planting spot is cultivated individually, usually by hand because rough terrain prevents the use of machinery. It is also popular on flatter lands because foresters believe that it is cheaper than strip or total cultivation, but this is not always true. Spot preparation consists of clearing a one square meter patch. A hole about 50 cm in diameter and 30 cm deep is dug. The loose soil should be replaced in the hole and allowed to settle somewhat during subsequent rainfall, although holes are sometimes left open to ensure better quality control. Spot preparation is difficult and expensive where weed cover is dense or where thick grass needs to be removed, such as the kikuyu grass in Colombia. If herbicides are used, the spots can be sprayed in advance and as soon as the grass is dead it is raked away before planting. Chemical control of grass lasts longer before the grass invades the planting spot than does manual preparation, because the systemic chemicals kill the grass roots. One common error of spot planting on steep slopes is to dig out a hole with the topsoil being allowed to go down the slope. The tree is planted in the excavated hole, often in shallow topsoil or even in subsoil. Making "convenience" cleanings of this type results in poor survival and poor growth.

The next, more intensive cultivation is strip preparation, by ploughing, ripping, or disking a strip; this cannot be done on steep slopes and must never be done up or down the slope. Spraying of herbicide on both sides of the strip is very beneficial. Subsoiling or ripping the planting line with a single tine is usually a very effective site preparation and leads to good growth due to improved root penetration and water retention. The use of a subsoiler is also often beneficial because shallow stone layers or hardpans on old agricultural fields are broken up. Ripping is effective on shales, except that tunnels left by rip lines sometimes facilitate activity of rodents. Ripping is recommended on soils with clay content exceeding 35% or where small surface rocks are abundant or hardpans are present.

Complete cultivation is possible only on relatively flat terrain without obstructions such as rocks and large stumps. The cost of complete cultivation is high but results in increased survival and initial growth and sometimes eliminates the need for weeding after planting. This was shown in a series of trials comparing various site preparation treatments by Schönau and Boden (1982), where complete preparation and intensive cultivation was most beneficial for *Eucalyptus grandis*. However, complete cultivation will stimulate rhizomatous grasses like kikuyu and *Imperata cylindrica* unless they are killed by herbicides.

A prime example of the benefit of intensive site preparation is the operation of Aracruz Florestal in Brazil for clonal plantations of eucalypts (Brandão, 1984). After clearfelling, weeds and sprouts are herbicided and then the residue is burnt. Trees are cut close to the ground, allowing bedding ploughs to make a ridge of topsoil over the stumps which prevents coppice sprouting. A preemergent herbicide is applied at planting time to the ridges and the land is cultivated between the ridges. The practice of ridging, or bedding, is becoming widely used. This method of site preparation is strongly recommended by Male (1981), who suggests its use on both wet and dry sites. He lists six reasons why mounding is beneficial, including improvement of soil moisture, aeration, soil structure, infiltration rate, soil depth, the roots' ability to use soil, and mineralization of nutrients. Similar benefits from bedding are cited by numerous foresters. In Tanzania, for example, Chanshaima (1984) reported growth of *Eucalyptus* was best on disked and bedded land.

It is essential to control competition by intensive site preparation for most hardwoods and cypress. Some pines, such as *P. patula* and *P. elliottii,* are somewhat more tolerant to weed competition, but others, like *P. kesiya* and *P. merkusii,* are very sensitive to competition.

6.3.3 Plantation Establishment

Even if *good-quality* seedlings and *proper* site preparation are used in plantation establishment, close attention must be paid to the actual planting operation. Therefore, preparing the site, using healthy plants, and proper planting are all needed to form an integral plantation establishment system.

The cheapest method of "plantation" establishment is by direct sowing from the ground or by aircraft. Techniques are available for coating seed with oxygen-generating substances that are rich in nutrients and slightly toxic or repulsive to predators and contain mineral clays with high water-absorption capacities (Letourneux, 1957). Seed for direct seeding is expensive if obtained from a tree improvement program, so direct sowing has not been common. Good-quality nursery plants will usually outperform the direct-seeded plants and stocking control is obtained through planting; thus, planting is the usual method used. Almost always, those who do direct seeding sow for the "bad" year, and thus the forest is commonly overstocked. Overstocking is just as adverse to commercial wood production as is understocking.

6.3.3.1 Planting Season and Weather Conditions.

In most tropical countries planting is done at the start of the rainy season, never near the end. No planting should be done before good soaking rains (more than 100 mm) have restored soil moisture levels to field capacity. Early, heavy thundershowers may be followed by long dry spells, so any planting program must be programmed with due consideration of the weather patterns. Occasionally, out-of-season planting, such as winter planting of pines in summer rainfall areas, has been practiced successfully in southern Africa. This is possible in areas where mist occurs and well hardened off seedlings are used. Seedlings must still be dormant and preferably should be watered and/or mulched when planted (Denison, 1980, 1981). The advantage of such off-season planting is that trees are well established by the time the rainy season starts and will fare better against the weed competition than seedlings planted during the rainy season.

Better success can be obtained with winter planting than with summer planting in tropical areas with definite seasons where sandy soils and scorching heat occur, such as on the coastal plains of Zululand, South Africa, or the deep sands of the Orinoco Basin in Venezuela. Even if rainfall is heavy and frequent, a short hot spell with dry soils can be fatal to newly planted seedlings.

Planting must be done during cool and preferably cloudy weather. Planting operations can well be carried out in rainy weather, enabling a goot root–soil contact to be obtained; as mentioned earlier, night planting is sometimes done.

6.3.3.2 Planting Techniques.

The tree rows should be oriented at right angles to harvesting roads when possible. Where land is prepared by pitting, planting spots will be clearly visible, but on completely cultivated land, planting spots must be specially selected to have rows that facilitate harvesting. Nursery stock must be culled before planting so that only good-quality seedlings are used. If roads are poor and likely to become slippery during wet weather, seedlings should be transported to points close to the planting site shortly before the rainy season starts. Although watering must be continued, it should be reduced a few weeks prior to planting to harden off the plants against planting shock. However, seedlings should be well watered immediately before planting.

Planting must be done with care under thorough supervision. Use of contract planters often results in failure because a hasty worker intent on a large daily production will not do the job properly. Sometimes the workers plant multiples at one spot or even put numbers of trees in stump holes to make numbers. Particularly, plant spacing must be watched with contract planters.

Plastic bags or tubes must be removed by cutting on at least two sides. This is very important; vertical cuts on both sides will break up spiraling roots, insuring stable trees. Old seedlings may be cut back for ease of handling or dry conditions; deep planting is good for many species. For instance, a 15-cm plant could be "buried" so that only 5 cm will be above ground, ensuring that roots are closer to the soil moisture and transpiration from excessive foliage is checked. Deep planting is particularly effective on sandy soils, but too-deep planting must be avoided on heavy clays. Seedlings must be firmed down at planting to ensure that roots come into contact with the soil. Care must be taken that the soil (especially clays) is not overly compacted, because this will impare drainage and aeration.

There are four reasons for stress at time of planting: loss of fine roots when seedlings are lifted, desiccation during transport and storage, poor root-to-soil contact after transplanting, and lack of moisture, low humidity, and winds at and immediately after planting. These problems were described for *Pinus radiata* seedlings by Sands (1984).

When mortality is more than 10%, filling in the missing spaces (also called blanking or beating) should be done within one month after planting for eucalypts or within the same planting season for pines. Done any later, the replacement trees will become suppressed and never grow right. Interplanting has been assessed by many persons. Usually, interplanting of *Eucalyptus grandis* in coppice growth adds additional volume only if there is more than 60% failure. Interplanting after some months in reasonably well-stocked stands is a most misused operation, because rarely do the interplants grow to become merchantable-size stems.

Planting operations are becoming increasingly mechanized on accessible terrain. Containerized plants, as well as bare-root ones, are suitable for mechanized planting, and under harsh conditions planting machines can be set to plant seedlings deep. Experience has shown that if done correctly, machine-planted seedlings can survive better and grow faster than hand-planted ones because of the subsoiling effect of the planting foot when such is present on the planting machine.

6.3.3.3 Coppice Regeneration.

Although some pines like *P. oocarpa* and *P. canariensis* produce stump sprouts, sprouting is mainly a feature of hardwoods. It is commonly used as a method of regeneration. Coppice is simple because planting costs are eliminated, but it costs to reduce the sprouts to the desired number. Coppice is not the utopia often visualized.

Coppice sprouts need management just like plants. With the eucalypts, some foresters reduce coppice sprouts to four per stump, and when these reach 4–6 cm in diameter, two of them are harvested for fencing, binding laths, or other uses in construction. The remaining two sprouts are allowed to grow until they reach a size suitable for use as fencing or building posts. At this time one of the two sprouts is harvested and the other is left to develop into the final crop, usually poles, mining timber, pulp, or even sawtimber. If no market exists for these intermediate thinnings and if the objective is growing pulpwood, a management method using only one or two sprouts is followed. A description of management of coppice crops for *E. grandis* was given by Stubbings and Schönau (1980). Time of cleaning (reducing) the sprouts was described by Pereira and Rezende (1983) for eucalypts in Minas Gerais, Brazil. Among different methods used, no differences in vigor were found, but cleaning should be a regular silvicultural operation about 30 days after the harvest cut. Fire was not useful. A study on the best stump size for *E. urophylla* (Pereira et al., 1983) indicated that stumps about 18 cm in diameter produced the best and healthiest sprouts. The greatest percentage of stumps sprouted occurred on stumps 15–20 cm high. The best sprouts were halfway up the stump (Pereira et al., 1984). Sometimes application of chemicals like ethrel is used to stimulate coppicing, as reported by Brune and De Paiva (1983) for *E. saligna*.

It is important for coppice regeneration that the original stocking be high and that the release be carefully done (Fig. 6.10). About 5–15% of the stumps are lost from damage or lack of sprouting ability during harvesting, and if the

Figure 6.10. Use of coppice regeneration in some exotic hardwoods is becoming widespread, but it must be done carefully or results such as shown can occur. One must manage coppice as intensively as seedlings. (Courtesy, Stellenbosch University, South Africa.)

original stocking is low, the loss of stocking after two to three rotations of coppice regeneration will be too much to accept. When rooted cuttings of known sprouting ability are used, less loss is encountered following coppicing.

One disadvantage of coppice is that the sprouts are genetically identical to trees originally planted. If greatly improved genetic stock is available, the amount of genetic improvement of seedlings available for planting must be weighed against the savings in planting cost if coppice regeneration is used. With a rapid recurrent selection program of *Eucalyptus grandis,* for instance, three to four generations of selection can be done during the life of a stand that is regenerated once with coppice sprouts. Seedlings then available will be greatly superior to the sprouts.

There have been some questions about the wood produced by coppice. Generally, it is similar to the tree from which the coppice arose. The largest shoots tend to have the highest specific gravity within the 23 coppice clones of *Eucalyptus saligna* tested in Hawaii (King, 1980). King reports: "The specific gravity of coppice wood was similar in value to similarly-aged tree wood of this species."

6.3.4 Fertilization

Fertilization has not been standard in forestry. However, tropical plantations frequently require fertilization because of short rotations and soil nutrient deficiencies. Under tropical conditions conifers and especially hardwoods like the eucalypts are grown on such short rotations that the investment in fertilizers becomes more feasible because of the short time before harvest. Much has been learned about forest nutrition and tree response on different sites to both macro- and micronutrients. Although successful plantations are grown on tropical forest soils without fertilizers, recent results indicate that greater success usually results with the use of fertilizers. Many times exotics have failed because of a lack of knowledge about nutrient deficiencies.

There has been much controversy about fertilizer use in growing exotics, but it is becoming more evident that it is generally advantageous. Frequently, it is mandatory for the eucalypts and will play an increasing role in conifer silviculture (Crane, 1984). A similar review for broad-leaved species was given by Schönau (1984). He summarizes: "Fertilization is shown to be one of the most efficient ways of increasing land productivity and is highly profitable." A number of authors, such as Malvos (1983), point out the futility of fertilizing if competing vegetation is not controlled.

Lack of soil nutrients reduces growth and vigor and thus increases sensitivity to pests or adverse weather. It often results in discoloration of the foliage and sometimes causes deformities. Most species will respond to the application of fertilizers; Schutz (1976), reviewing the literature, listed species that had improved volume growth up to 100% (even 1300% in one instance) following fertilization. Examples given were: *P. taeda,* 85% height increase at 5 years, 70% volume increase at 19 years; *P. elliottii,* 300% volume increase at 7 years;

P. patula, 31% volume increase at 7 years; *P. radiata,* 138% height increase at 5 years; *P. pinaster,* 36% height increase at 5 years; *E. globulus,* 200% wood production increase at 2 years; and *E. grandis,* with volume increases of 100% or more. Schutz also listed the fertilizer requirements of each species for maximum economic returns.

The effect of fertilizers varies according to the rate of application, species, site, soil factors, and nutrient deficiencies. Many factors influence fertilizer response and the interaction among them makes responses difficult to interpret or predict. Generally, fertilizer effects last to the end of the rotation for conifers but are not as pronounced as for hardwoods, especially for eucalypts grown on short rotations. For *E. grandis,* Schönau (1977, 1984) concluded that response to fertilizers is maintained until the end of short rotations (10 years or less) and that fertilization is, "beyond doubt," economically justifiable.

The economic justification for fertilization cannot be determined as just an increase in volume production since it is also part of establishment along with site preparation. The effect of fertilization will disappear or be reduced on poorly prepared sites, especially in the tropics, where weed competition utilizes the nutrients. Weeds also compete for moisture, which immobilizes fertilizers, as well as compete for the fertilizer itself. Grasses are especially responsive to nitrogen fertilizers. For *Pinus taeda,* Schutz (1976) states that of the 30% gain in volume at seven years, 9% was due to cultivation, the rest to fertilizers.

Use of fertilizers can reduce the need for weeding, as much as four to one in eucalypt stands. Fertilizers also increase stand uniformity, tree form, survival, and even frost resistance; an example is boron on eucalypts (Schutz, 1976; Schönau, 1984). Research on the time of fertilization shows that an early single application (at or soon after planting) in eucalypt plantations lasts until the end of the short rotations; longer rotations need repeated applications (Schönau, 1984). Repeated applications of fertilizer when eucalypt trees are 50 cm tall can be beneficial, according to Schönau and Boden (1982).

The rate of application of fertilizers varies according to the growing conditions. The best hand application is in a ring 30 cm from the tree with the fertilizer worked into the soil. Sometimes it is best to leave it in a hole because if rains do not follow fertilizing, on some soils the phosphorus becomes fixed rapidly and is basically lost to the plant. Sometimes soil fertility is improved by aerial topdressing. Problems are encountered with an uneven spread of the fertilizer, but good results can be obtained through the use of a helicopter and an electronic guidance system and with larger than normal fertilizer granules (Anon., 1982a).

Nutrient deficiencies are common in tropical soils, often being very low in phosphate and the micronutrients boron and copper, especially in Africa and South America. Copper deficiency occurs in parts of Queensland and zinc in South Australia (Evans, 1984). The interaction of nutrients with each other is generally more important than a single element. For instance, when nitrogen alone was added to a phosphorus-deficient soil, growth of *Pinus radiata* dropped behind the control. However, maximum growth improvement was obtained when the nitrogen to phosphorus ratio was between 0.9 and 2.0 (Schutz, 1976).

Assessment of nutrient requirements for a particular species on a particular site is not easy (see Chapter 4). Assessment of the nutrient status can be included in site surveys, but trials are needed to provide information on growth responses. Although trials are slow and expensive, they are the key to determining nutrient status. Foliar analysis is also used to determine nutrient levels, but only when objectives are clearly defined (Schutz, 1976; Lambert, 1984). Results need to be interpreted in relation to stand age and whether age produces soil changes or physiological changes in the plant.

Soil chemical analyses are useful to assess fertilizer requirements for fertilization of new land at time of planting. However, there are problems with soil analyses which include lack of standardization in techniques, poor selection of representative soil samples, and the complicating role of mycorrhizae. Soil analyses give a good starting point, but refinements are necessary.

It is not the purpose here to include the technical details and the pros and cons of fertilization. We wish to emphasize that fertilization under tropical conditions usually is beneficial and economical, and often essential. Tree species, especially the hardwoods, often respond to fertilizers, and fertilization must be a part of the silvicultural system, especially with short-rotation crops. If applied at an intermediate time in established stands, fertilization combined with thinning is needed to obtain the maximum response. This was reported by Mead et al. (1985). They found that the increase in dry-matter production after fertilization was related to an increase in foliage amount rather than to changes in foliar efficiency.

6.3.5 Maintenance and Cleaning

Proper site preparation and good planting practices will ensure a healthy start for seedlings. In tropical areas care must be taken not to neglect the plantations after establishment, since many factors can contribute to seedling mortality or slow growth. Post-planting care is essential to obtain a healthy, well-stocked stand.

A survey of survival should be made within one to two months after planting. Reasons for mortality should be determined and immediate remedial action taken to try and eliminate the cause and to replant spots where dead seedlings occur. Strong plants held over in the nursery for this purpose should be used. Experience has shown that if replanting is delayed too long, such as into the next season, it will be unsuccessful. The interplants become suppressed early and never develop into usable trees.

The most common cause of tree mortality and growth retardation is weed competition. Proper site preparation, use of strong plants, and good planting practices are important. The better the site preparation, the less severe will be the weed competition immediately after planting. Weeding young trees is difficult. Up to now, most weeding has been done by hand or with machinery, but herbicides are coming into wider use. Incorrect chemical sprays can affect tree growth, and chemicals should be used only after their success has been proven. Many of the new herbicides are effective and safe. Selective chemicals are now available that kill all weeds and grass but do not harm conifers; others are available that do not harm trees and kill only grass. Since these are all systemics, they give long-term control of competing perennial vegetation. Also available are effective preemergence herbicides that are used just prior to planting and give control from two to four months or more.

Hand weeding can be very costly. For example, repeated manual slashings before pruning and thinning can reduce net discounted plantation revenue by as much as 5% and can amount to roughly double the cost of pruning stands for sawtimber production (Wessels et al., 1983). Comparative advantages of mechanical and chemical cleaning are being tested and evaluated by many organizations. Obviously, results depend upon species, site, kind of competition, and other factors. As one example, Otarola et al. (1983) report for *Eucalyptus camaldulensis* in Nicaragua that control of competing vegetation was effective for height growth. The best control was from use of chemicals followed by mechanical treatment around the tree.

Weeds are very aggressive under tropical conditions and can colonize a site very rapidly (Fig. 6.11). This is especially true for grasses or weeds with seed carried by birds. Many grasses (e.g., *Setaria chevalieri*) may remain under trees in latent form since they are not killed by suppression, although they do not spread under closed canopies. However, as soon as a stand is clearfelled and receives full sunlight, the grasses grow very prolifically (Fig. 6.12).

It is important to understand the biology of competitive species. Grass can be a particularly severe competitor; many grasses have an allelopathic effect upon tree growth. For example, five-year-old *Pinus radiata* trees were 30% taller after five years of growth merely from having grass controlled for one year (West, 1984). Some grasses are stimulated by slashing and spread and become more aggressive following treatment. Competition by rhizomatous grass can become severe soon after planting, even though good spot preparation has been done beforehand. Moisture competition is a major result of weed competition. As Sands and Nambiar (1984) report for radiata pine, the severity of moisture stress caused by weeds decreases with tree age. Most seriously damaged were transplanted seedlings with poorly developed root systems; seedlings in the second and third year extracted water from a depth of at least 2 m. Early growth of radiata pine can be increased greatly if weeds are controlled, limiting the amount of moisture stress.

In some environments, climbers invade and often smother trees. Taylor (1982) mentions that lianas should be cut at two levels, near the ground and at man height, because some liana stems cut near the ground send out adventitious roots into the soil and continue to live. With shifting cultivation, some of the trees of original forests are left and become a nuisance either by smothering a young plantation or causing damage upon falling. Such trees should

Figure 6.11. Some competitive vegetation can colonize a new plantation very rapidly. One of the worst in South Africa is bugweed (*Solanum mauritianum*), as shown. It can grow into an impenetrable thicket in a very short time. (Courtesy, S.A.F.R.I.)

be killed by girdling, but Letourneux (1957) reports that some tropical hardwoods are very hard to kill. This is especially so with aggressive woody weeds such as unwanted bamboo, acacias, or eucalypts.

The best action is preventative control to minimize weeding operations. No matter what means of weed control is practiced, it is costly and difficult after a stand has been established but is necessary if the trees are to survive and grow normally. The use of selective herbicides is the most encouraging method of competition control. However, public response to the use of herbicides is often unfavorable and political problems can develop.

Sometimes the suitability of a species as an exotic depends upon its ability to suppress competition. For example, *Gmelina* develops a large crown early and, combined with fast growth, shades out the competing vegetation quickly. Some eucalypts, like *E. pellita,* have a dense shade-forming crown, while other

Figure 6.12. Most serious competition in exotic plantations comes from the grasses. Shown is one of the most aggressive and serious grass competitors in South Africa, *Setaria chevalieri.* If not controlled, plantation failures will occur. (Courtesy, S.A.F.R.I.)

species, like *E. camaldulensis,* have thin crowns that are ineffective in shading out competition. In selecting clones of *E. grandis* the dense-crowned clones are often preferred because of their control of understory competition. For mahogany, Geary et al. (1973) raise the question of whether this narrow-crowned tree is suitable for use as an exotic because of its inability to suppress competition. The crown characteristics of exotics certainly are of importance in determining the ease of competition control and establishing subsequent rotations.

6.3.6 Spacing

Spacing obviously affects intertree competition, with competition established early at close spacings and later at wider spacing (Harvey, 1983). Plantation forestry in the tropics initially employed high stocking densities, but experience and economic considerations have led to an increase in espacement. Early stand densities for pines and eucalypts ranged from 1700 to 6900 stems per hectare (s/ha), seldom falling below 2000 s/ha. A high initial stocking yields the maximum timber over short rotations, but above a certain limit the standing merchantable volume will decline (Bredenkamp, 1980). Higher-value timber can only be obtained at lower initial stand densities or through use of proper thinning regimes. Currently, only short rotations for fiber production or for special dimension stock such as poles or mine props are grown at densities over 1500 s/ha. Some companies in South America grow eucalypt plantations at a stocking as low as 1100 s/ha. One concept often overlooked is that stocking affects tree form and thus standard yield tables often give biased estimates (Vanclay and Anderson, 1982).

Although planting patterns vary, square patterns are traditionally used that vary from 1.2 × 1.2 m (4 × 4 ft) to 3.7 × 3.7 m (12 × 12 ft). The most common espacements for pines and eucalypts are 2.4 × 2.4 m (8 × 8 ft) and 2.7 × 2.7 m (9 × 9 ft); Whitmore and Liegel (1980) prefer 2.1 × 2.1 m (7 × 7 ft) to 3.0 × 3.0 m (10 × 10 ft) for *P. caribaea* in Puerto Rico. *Eucalyptus* is normally planted at 2.7 × 2.7 m (9 × 9 ft) or 3 × 3 m (10 × 10 ft) and the standard for pine is 3 × 2 m (10 × 6.6 ft) or 2.5 × 2.5 m (8.3 × 8.3 ft). Rectangular planting patterns such as 3 × 2 m (10 × 6.6 ft) are gaining in popularity, especially since evidence suggests that such patterns will not increase stem ellipticity (Daniels and Schutz, 1975; Bredenkamp, 1982) and volume growth will be the same whether rectangular or square spacing is used. Rectangular spacings are more efficient when mechanical methods are used.

Plantation spacing is determined by the site, the species, the objectives of management, and harvesting variables (Marsh, 1978). In steep and inaccessible terrain intermediate harvests are not economical and initial wide espacements are often adopted. Normally, pulpwood plantations and short-rotation crops for mining timbers, charcoal production, and pole production are grown at close spacings while sawtimber plantations are established at wider espacements. These vary according to the genetic quality of the seed stock. High initial stocking using unimproved trees has sometimes been favored, so poor-quality individuals can be removed in thinnings to leave enough high-quality trees at time of final harvest. This argument was used for *P. caribaea, P. montezumae,* and *P. pseudostrobus* in South Africa by Poynton (1979).

Improved genetic material results in more uniform stands, reducing the need for early removal of poor-quality stock. Because of the availability of good stock and use of vegetative propagation a wide espacement of 3.5 × 3.5 m (12 × 12 ft) has been adopted by the Forestry Branch in South Africa for planting *E. grandis* for the production of sawtimber. For slash pine from genetically improved stock in Queensland, Australia, a 3.0 × 3.0 m (10 × 10 ft) initial spacing is used.

In an intensive spacing study varying from 4.5 to 25.0 m² per tree, Aracruz Florestal obtained the results shown in Table 6.3. Note that the best stocking for very fast-growing clones on a good site at four years of age is an approximate 3 m × 3 m (10 × 10 ft) spacing.

Since harvesting is the most expensive operation in forestry, other operations must be planned to reduce this expense as much as possible. Rectangular spacing facilitates entrance of vehicles and equipment between rows. Large stumps develop, for example, if eucalypts are grown for up to four rotations on the same stump. Therefore, initial planning is required so that straight rows at regular spacing are planted at right angles to harvesting roads.

Plantations with too dense stocking soon develop unstable trees of varying size, often susceptible to diseases and insects. The dynamics of stand growth

TABLE 6.3. A Spacing Trial in Rooted Cuttings of *Eucalyptus* After Four Years[a]

| Spacing (Meters) | Square Meters/Tree | Diam. (cm) | Height (m) | Basal Area (m²/ha/yr) | Growth (m³/ha/yr) | | Total Solid Vol. (m³/ha) |
					Current Annual	Mean Annual	
2.1 × 2.1	4.5	20.7	20.7	27.1	62	59	236
3.0 × 2.0	6.0	22.5	22.5	26.3	77	62	248
3.0 × 3.0	9.0	23.4	23.4	23.1	78	57	228
4.0 × 3.0	12.0	23.0	23.0	20.1	67	49	194
3.9 × 3.9	15.0	23.9	23.9	19.3	71	48	193
4.0 × 5.0	20.0	24.3	24.3	16.0	64	41	163
5.0 × 5.0	25.0	25.3	25.3	14.5	62	39	154

[a]Data courtesy of Aracruz Florestal, Espirito Santo, Brazil.

has been discussed by Evans (1984), who shows the large differences between trees with different degrees of dominance and crown classes. Codominant and subdominant trees of *P. patula* start lagging behind dominant trees in volume growth as early as eight years after planting. Competition for light is very important for light-demanding species such as the eucalypts. This is why more than one clone in a clonal mixture will yield less timber than a monoclonal stand, unless all clones maintain exactly the same growth rate. When one clone lags in growth, competition by the stronger clone will result in suppression of 50% of the stand in the case of a two-clone mixture. The concept of crown competition with resultant variation in stem diameter is very important.

When left too long, high stand densities can result in serious loss from wind damage (Cremer et al. 1982). Trees become whippy and unstable and stem strength is reduced due to suppression in stem diameters. Height growth is not much influenced within normal limits of stocking, but diameter growth, crown size, and root development result in suppressed trees that can also easily be broken or uprooted by strong winds. The importance of stocking was stressed by Cremer et al. (1982) as follows:

(1) The benefits of growth at low stocking during the early years are permanent. Stands raised at low stocking do not attain height/diameter (H/D) values as high as those raised at high stocking, no matter how long they are left unthinned. (2) The trends in H/D values emphasize the paramount importance of growing space early in the stand's life (before 20m height in *P. radiata*). . . . The earlier the thinning, the more effective it will be in keeping risk [of wind damage] low.

Experimental results in South Africa illustrate the importance of spacing in eucalypt and pine stands. The Correlated Curve Trend (CCT) trials of O'Connor laid the basis for scientific approaches with respect to spacing and thinning practices in exotic tree stands (Bredenkamp, 1984). Important results from the CCT trials are: (1) The height/dbh (diameter breast height) and form factor/dbh relationship are affected by stocking. (2) In free-growing trees, ring width for any one year remains even at all heights, but in suppressed trees it increases with increasing height. (3) Current annual increment varies with stocking. The striking effect of stand density on mean tree volume with increasing age is illustrated in Fig. 6.13. Results from a CCT experiment on *Eucalyptus grandis* in Zululand show that even small increases in growing space result in real differences in mean tree volume (Anon., 1984a).

6.3.7 Thinning

Thinning is a silvicultural operation aimed at removal of poor trees so that the best remaining trees are allowed more growing space in which to develop. *The objective of thinning is never to obtain inexpensive wood; it is to improve the residual stand.* Stress that is built up from competition is partially

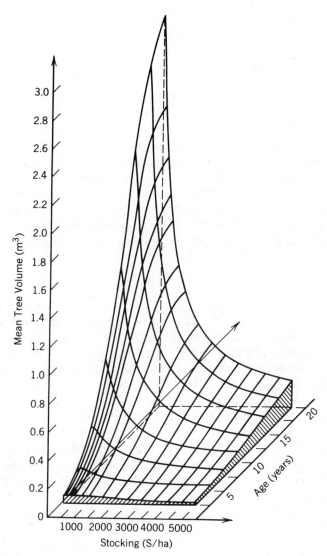

Figure 6.13. The relationship between mean tree volume, age, and stocking is shown for *Eucalyptus grandis*. See the text, section 6.3.6, Spacing. (From S.A.F.R.I. Research Review, 1983/1984).

released by thinning. Understanding stand dynamics and the concept of competition is of prime importance for thinning schedules for long-rotation crops. This is not easy; O'Connor's words in 1935, when he introduced his CCT concept, are apt: "After 30 years of observation and discussion, and inquiry into the matter, I have come to the conclusion that I know nothing about thinning" (Bredenkamp, 1984). He wanted "a complete exposition of the ef-

fects on the development of trees of the growing space provided for them.'
In the pine CCT experiments, espacements ranging from 125 to 3000 s/ha were
planted, and in *Eucalyptus grandis* espacements ranged from 30 to 6700 s/ha,
enabling evaluation of the effects of any planting espacement and thinning
degree within this range. It is now possible to determine in advance what initial
espacement and thinning regime will best serve a specific objective of management (Marsh, 1978).

A pioneer in thinning, pruning, and management studies was I. J. Craib.
With his 1939 publication Craib put forward a new approach to silviculture
with the novel concept of early, heavy thinnings prescribed on a strictly nu-
merical basis (Poynton, 1979). (This was modified in 1947 in the light of further experience). The aim was to improve the financial return by producing
logs of acceptable diameter without unduly long rotations. Poynton discusses
some thinning regimes in southern Africa based on Craib's recommendations,
which formed the basis for early tropical plantation forestry in the British
Commonwealth.

Fast growth of trees results in a large juvenile wood core with properties
different from mature timber, especially for pines (see Chapter 9). One idea
was that dense stocking would reduce the juvenile core and that systematic
thinnings could then produce a constant rate of growth in diameter, thereby
improving the quality of sawn timber. Even if this were possible, a very dense
initial stocking is required with high establishment costs. The timber of the
dominant trees left after thinning is normally not influenced by early espacement, as mentioned by Evans (1984). He showed that the difference in mean
diameter between a thinned plot of 25½-year-old *Araucaria cunninghamia* and
the 10 largest trees in an *unthinned* plot was only 8 cm, while the means of
the plots differed by nearly 20 cm.

The stability factor (height/diameter [H/D] ratio) described by Cremer et
al. (1982) for assessing stocking and thinning effects on wind damage was used
in South Africa to develop thinning schedules. Cremer et al. found that thinning is unlikely to reduce H/D values once they have reached high levels. Thinning clearly is beneficial in release from competition, which results in low mortality, deeper crowns on remaining trees, and crown expansion, leading to
diameter growth increase (Evans, 1984). According to Mead et al. (1985), thinning increased the fraction of dry matter allocated to crowns in the year after
treatment in radiata pine.

Although the effect of thinning has been known for a long time and experimental results indicate which thinning regimes should be followed, the regimes vary from country to country. No single schedule can ever be prescribed
for all species and environments (Wessels et al., 1983). A compilation on economics and techniques of thinning by Griffith (1982) included practices on
steep terrain interacting with silviculture and future developments and their
likely influence. Many aspects of thinning have been discussed at the Meeting
on the Economics and Harvesting of Thinnings held in Australia and New

Zealand [see *New Zealand Journal of Forestry Science* **6**(2) (1976)] and at two other symposia on pruning and thinning practice held in 1963 and 1970. Thinning research in South Africa has been discussed by Van Laar (1974).

A survey in New Zealand revealed nearly 70 differing silvicultural methods, but current trends favor lower initial stocking and earlier and fewer thinnings. On steep terrain there is a reduction in frequency of thinnings or no thinning at all. Mechanized thinning systems have been developed. Row thinnings are done, but they are less preferred than access row combined with silvicultural thinning. Consideration is given to site factors, especially where mechanized systems are used (Griffith, 1982).

Short-rotation crops normally are not thinned, especially hardwoods that are grown on a rotation of less than 10 years. For pines with longer rotations, care must be taken not to leave the stands too long before thinning, because they come under stress and become susceptible to insects, diseases, and windthrow. If large genetic variation exists in the stand, a loss of up to 20% will be obtained due to under- or oversized trees. Under such conditions it has been shown that a mid-rotation thinning will not significantly change clear-felling yields of *Eucalyptus grandis,* although 25% fewer stems are left to harvest (Bredenkamp and Schutz, 1984).

There are numerous papers that report the results from thinning experiments in exotics, such as the one by De Graaf (1978) on Caribbean pine in Surinam. As would be expected, results differ somewhat in magnitude but there is a general trend:

1. A combination of row removal for access plus silvicultural thinning between access rows is best (Fig. 6.14). In patula pine in Colombia, Ladrach (1980b) found greater tree diameters on the thinned plots, and the silviculturally thinned area had better diameters than when row thinning was used.

2. At the first thinning, approximately the poorest half of the trees should be removed, which will take about 40% of the volume. One restriction is that no more than two trees are left adjacent no matter how good they are. This system has been used by the senior author for many species in many areas with great success.

3. Most thinning in the tropics is too light to result in much improvement.

4. Short-rotation and pulp crops should be planted at a spacing so they need not be thinned.

5. Care in thinning is critical, or more harm than good can be done to the residual stand.

6. Thinning with heavy equipment, especially on wet soils, can cause soil compaction and root damage that reduces the productivity of the residual stand (Froehlich, 1976).

7. The objective of thinning is to improve the residual stand, not to obtain

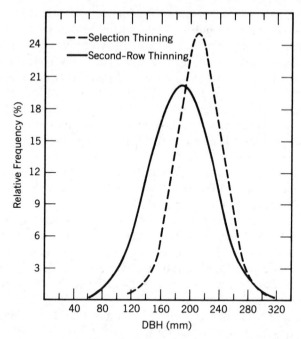

Figure 6.14. There are many different methods of thinning. Most successful is often some combination of silvicultural and row thinning. Shown are diameter distributions following row and silvicultural thinning of *Pinus taeda* grown in South Africa.

cheap wood. If one can just break even on the cost of thinning, the economic benefits will often be great. Wood obtained by thinning is usually expensive wood.

8. Precommercial thinning is sometimes preferred in dense plantings and where poor genetic stock is used. In a study on Caribbean pine, Anderson et al. (1981) found that precommercial thinning maximized financial returns while repeated commercial thinnings did not.

In summary, thinning is an important silvicultural tool in managing exotics, but it must be done correctly and carefully and great skill is required by the forester.

6.3.8 Pruning

Production of sawtimber is important in most tropical countries. The objective often is to produce logs with the highest value, so silvicultural schedules must be designed to produce high-quality timber. Sawn timber from unpruned trees is knotty. Even with timber having high density and thus high strength, the value of structural timber is affected by the degree of knottiness (Bryant,

1984). It is obvious why a high amount of clear timber in structural or sawn lumber is highly valued by the end user. Despite the potential value of pruning, more harm than good will result if done carelessly. Correct methodology is all important (Fig. 6.15).

The first objective of pruning is to produce the maximum clear timber. As Fenton (1977) reported for radiata pine, pruning increased the percentage of clear lumber and taper was not affected. This requires restriction of the knotty core. It is important that the clear timber over the knotty core be sufficient in quantity and quality to offset the costs of pruning. Craib (1939) has shown that the clear timber must be at least 10 cm thick to be economically justifiable. To obtain this for pruning as high as 7 m, the mean dbh over bark would

Figure 6.15. Careless pruning causes serious defects. Shown are the results of tearing bark by incorrect cutting technique on *Pinus radiata*. The value of pruning is lost. (Courtesy, Stellenbosch University, South Africa.)

need to be at least 45 cm for most pines (Marsh, 1978). Rotation length must be adjusted to allow for such diameter growth; pruning will be less feasible on poorer sites that require longer rotations to attain the desired dimension. Craib (1939) showed that for rotations used at that time, thinning on poor sites was not feasible because of the low production of clear timber.

The second objective of pruning is to avoid dead knots, which degrade structural timber. If a market for knotty timber exists, pruning may even be justified if the required amount of clear timber is not produced. Pruning is also done to facilitate access in pine stands for fire protection or weed and pest control in tropical environments.

Restriction of a large juvenile wood core is not economically justifiable through dense initial stocking. It is, however, possible, to restrict the core by heavy pruning. Also, heavy early pruning sometimes results in an increase in latewood percentage, density, and fiber length while grain spirality may be reduced (Gerischer and De Villiers, 1963). Heavy pruning means removal of live branches, which results in tight knots. Any increase in wood quality must be weighed against the costs and the loss in volume production that may occur from heavy and early pruning.

Studies on the effect of pruning on growth have shown that removal of 25% of the living crown of *P. elliottii, P. patula,* and *P. taeda* gives a temporary depression in diameter growth per se but no significant effect on either the mean diameter or mean height of the stand. However, 50 and 75% removal of the live crown has a significant reduction on diameter growth, while height was significantly reduced only for the 75% pruning. Recovery of normal increment was rapid and usually regained by the fourth year, even after severe pruning. The loss in volume tended to be permanent, particularly for the heaviest pruning, and will probably not be regained (Lückhoff, 1949). These results were partially confirmed by Sutton and Crowe (1975) with trials on *Pinus radiata.* They found some loss of height with all pruning treatments. The size of the knotty core decreased with an increase in both the severity and the frequency of pruning. Pruning *P. radiata* too high and too early causes development of an excessive number (but not size) of epicormic shoots, which degrades timber quality (Hinze, 1984). The season of pruning has no effect on the number of epicormic shoots.

Pruning schedules vary according to management objectives. Most growers of sawlogs prune 40–50% of the living crown in three to five times (Wessels et al., 1983; Poynton, 1979; Sutton and Crowe, 1975; Griffith, 1982). When possible, pruning should coincide with thinning to allow the pruned trees to respond to thinning, thereby compensating for a possible loss in increment from pruning. It may be necessary to prune all stems the first time to allow for a more efficient selection of stems where early and few thinnings are proposed (Sutton, 1974; Bredenkamp et al., 1983a). Site factors may determine where to prune, as in New Zealand and Chile, where varying schedules will be used on different slopes.

Commonly, it is felt that pruning in excess of 7 m in height cannot be justified (Craib, 1939). However, (Lückhoff, 1956) felt that pruning up to 11 m should yield enough increase in the value of the timber to justify the cost. This was also reported by Sutton (1974), where the more profitable "direct thinning regime" included pruning to 11-m height while the comparative regime only included a 6.1-m pruning. Generally, high pruning—up to 7 m— is not justifiable on poor sites; before pruning is undertaken on poor sites consideration should rather be given to extra-high pruning (10–12 m) on the best sites.

Most hardwoods grown for sawtimber will need pruning, except the eucalypts, which are mostly self-pruned and seldom need more than having the dead branches knocked off. Some eucalypts, such as *E. cloeziana* and *E. saligna,* grown for poles, may be pruned to obtain occluded branch stubs and a smooth surface to prevent entry of fungi or termites into the heartwood, which is not easily penetrated by preservatives. A study on the pruning of *E. grandis* in Zululand showed no effect on growth rate but essentially no gain in knot-free timber; also, there was little degrade from pruning. Essentially, it is of no value to prune *E. grandis* (Brendenkamp et al., 1983a).

6.4 PLANTATION HARVESTING

Forest management cannot be divorced from silviculture. All forestry operations—from site preparation to harvesting—must be planned for efficiency of the succeeding operations. For example, trees are planted (an early operation) in rows at right angles to roads to facilitate harvesting (a late operation).

6.4.1 Objectives

The objective of growing plantations is to produce timber for fiber, solid-wood products, or other products such as energy. Great diversification exists among each industry, so proper planning is needed to deliver the required raw material efficiently for the end product. Several decades ago managers were primarily preoccupied with getting land planted, but this is now changing to the need for improvements to obtain optimum production of the most desired wood per unit of land area.

6.4.2 Rotation (Harvest) Age

Rotation in forestry refers to the planned period between plantation establishment and harvesting. The rotation determines the age of felling; it also plays a major role in financial decision making, which is not always understood. It is generally accepted that short rotations are the most profitable, but this sometimes leads to the use of rotations that are too short because the length of the rotation affects the end product desired. Normally, the technical, biological, and financial rotations are key in tropical forestry.

In a biological (or technical) rotation, the manager aims at producing the desired quality of timber. For example, mining timber is mainly used in the form of so-called matpacks, which are stacked to supply support against sagging rock ceilings in mine tunnels. For these matpacks, timber dimensions must be uniform and not oversized so that they are not too heavy to handle. Sawtimber must be grown to a minimum size for profitable utilization and acceptable quality. Naturally, the silvicultural operations, especially spacing, thinning, and pruning, are important to ensure the maximum return on investment when such technical rotations are adopted.

Financial rotations aim at the highest possible financial return and may differ from biological or technical rotations. When timber dimensions are of lesser importance, as for pulpwood, economic analyses determine how to optimize return on investment. When Schönau (1982) considered rotation for maximum income, rotation for maximum yield, and rotation for maximum turnover, he showed that no justification exists for the very short rotations often adopted in South Africa for growing *Eucalyptus grandis.* All decision criteria indicate rotations of 11 years or more, except under unusually favorable circumstances such as very highly productive sites and high prices for small timber. In other areas, such as coastal Brazil, rotation ages in the eucalypts of six to seven years are best for pulp, while four years is good for *Gmelina.*

The rotation should be used that produces the maximum volume yields, the greatest annual output of timber, and realizes the full growth potential of a species on a given site (Evans, 1984). This rotation requires comparison of current annual increment (CAI) and mean annual increment (MAI). Initially, CAI is much higher than MAI, but as a stand matures, a point will be reached where CAI is equal to MAI and this is often considered to be the best harvest age.

Other things that may influence rotation length are the market situation, unequal age-class distribution, accessibility for harvesting, and even amenity considerations (Evans, 1984). Although a rotation may be discussed separately, all items must be taken into account. Flexibility must be maintained, enabling the use of a management regime which will include a combination of rotations.

6.4.3 Stand Regulation and Normality

It is difficult to ensure continued maximum output from plantations. One important decision is how soon a sustained yield and normality in the timber supply must be obtained. Some tropical countries rely heavily, if not exclusively, on the supply of timber from natural forests; these would only be interested in plantation forestry to overcome a future shortfall. Such countries afforest large areas of savannah for needed timber. No matter what the current situation, companies must ultimately have a sustained supply of timber from plantations as their objective.

Yield tables are needed to enable predictions about a particular species on a particular site. Early planning and management was based mainly on growth averages and tedious compilations of maps indicating areas to be clearfelled, regenerated, thinned, pruned, and so on. Modern management, however, makes full use of technological advances such as computers. Linear programming techniques are used to develop stand growth models and commercial accounting systems, and even computerized maps are drawn. Computerized systems such as COMPAS, described by Wessels and Kassier (1985), and SIL-MOD, by Whiteside and Sutton (1983), are powerful tools with accurate predictive capabilities and very versatile applications that, with time, will be more widely adopted in tropical forestry.

6.4.4 Harvesting

Timber harvesting usually also includes transport, that is, movement of the wood to the processing plant; it is in this context that it will be discussed in this section. Transport costs must also be included in the cost of harvest, and they are becoming increasingly important. Harvesting systems whereby whole-tree processing, like field chipping, is used are not yet common in tropical plantations, but they are becoming more widely used.

Harvesting is the most expensive of all forestry operations, and careful planning and management is required if it is to be cost-effective. Since transport cost forms a major component of harvesting expenses, it is clear that plantations should be as close as possible to the processing plant. Sometimes afforestation of average or marginal land close to processing facilities may be more profitable than highly productive land a long distance away. Land location is key in planning land purchase in an exotic forestry enterprise. An example of the "law of cost efficiency" is the practice of "thinning to waste." Unless the processing plant is nearby, small-size timber is not worth transporting and is usually left in the forest.

A discussion of the numerous harvesting techniques available is beyond the scope of this book. Generally, short-rotation crops will be extracted in relatively short log lengths with diameters varying from 4 to 30 cm. Hand labor and light machinery is used to fell and process the logs, especially on relatively flat terrain. On steeper terrain, cable systems are becoming more widely used. Timber grown on longer rotations for construction or veneer logs is more difficult to handle and longer log lengths are desirable. This requires use of heavier and more sophisticated harvesting equipment. More detailed discussions of harvesting systems are made by Taylor (1983), who also lists advantages and disadvantages of systems for different timber sizes. Another useful reference, with many illustrations, covering safety aspects as well as concepts necessary for those not experienced in logging, has been prepared by Zaremba (1976).

Heavy equipment usually has an adverse effect on soils. Even sandy soils may be affected to such an extent that very uneven future tree growth will be obtained. Soils are either compacted, disturbed, or removed along extraction roads that may accelerate subsequent erosion. Damage to stumps by extraction equipment in eucalypt plantations to be regenerated through coppice leads to a reduction in the stocking of the resulting stand. Harvesting techniques and equipment must be adjusted according to local conditions.

Efficiency in harvesting is key to keeping costs low no matter what techniques and equipment are used. Efficiency is needed to get logs to the sawmill quickly, to reduce loss of timber through excessive splitting, as for eucalypt sawtimber, or blue staining of pine. Usually, efficiency can be improved through studies whereby desired norms are laid down for all tasks to be performed in harvesting. Experience has shown that good planning is essential to keep production high. Perhaps even more important is the skill of the worker performing the tasks, especially in harvesting operations where workers handle very expensive equipment. Thorough training to obtain maximum proficiency for performing harvesting tasks cannot be overemphasized.

6.5 FOREST PROTECTION

6.5.1 Insects

The occurrence and damage caused by insects in exotic plantations have been covered in Chapter 4. Exotics in their new environments may initially enjoy freedom from insect attacks, leading to high productivity even where silvicultural treatments have not been the best. For instance, *Eucalyptus* grows very well outside Australia and usually does not suffer from insect attacks. In Australia, however, most eucalypt species are so severely attacked by insects that it is often hard to find undamaged botanical leaf specimens (Pryor, 1978b). The damage to the leaves results in reduced growth.

Insect attack often is very frightening because the plantations may appear to be totally destroyed. Defoliators may leave large areas of pine without any green needles on the trees, as happens with attacks by the caterpillar of the pine brown-tail moth (*Euproctis terminalis*) on *Pinus patula*. Normally, the trees are defoliated one year and not attacked for several of the following years. Although growth loss for much of one season may occur, trees normally recover the next season with no apparent sign of damage. The same kind of cyclical effect occurs with attacks by insects like the different pine aphids. However, bark beetles have a more devastating effect and trees may be killed. Such beetles also carry fungi, often causing such rapid damage to the wood that very little salvage value remains.

A timber defect suspected of being associated with insect attack is the reaction wood in *Pinus taeda* that has a completely different anatomy from the usual compression wood, even though the appearance to the eye is very similar. This reaction wood forms continuous bands around the tree, in contrast with compression wood, which normally forms on the lower side of a leaning conifer tree. The reaction wood is often so severe that it will jam saws in the mill, making conversion to lumber impossible. Although not finally proven, the black pine aphid (*Cinara cronartii*) is strongly suspected to be the cause of this reaction wood (Herman, 1985; Van der Sijde et al., 1985).

Different pine species are attacked by aphids with different degrees of severity. Often the initial appearance may seem severe, but over two to three seasons the severity may decrease. Unless an outright kill of trees over large areas is observed, plantation managers should not panic, especially when variation in attack is observed within a plantation. Drastic steps like clearfelling or spraying should not be taken hastily. Rather, the natural variation in resistance among trees should be utilized. Thinning and salvaging damaged trees should be done. Biological control, which can be very effective, should be considered. Examples are the control of the *Eucalyptus* snout beetle (*Gonipterus scutellatus*) in South Africa by an egg parasite and the apparent success of controlling three aphid species by introducing parasites.

6.5.2 Diseases

Countries that pioneered in tropical exotic forestry have been relatively fortunate in that few serious diseases initially occur. However, serious outbreaks of diseases like *Dothistroma pini* and *Diplodea pinea* (now called *Sphaeropsis sapinea*) are becoming more frequent in countries such as Kenya, Brazil, New Zealand, and South Africa.

Tropical climates are conducive to infection by pathogens (see Chapter 4). An awareness of this by foresters along with the knowledge that diseases spread rapidly under tropical conditions has generally prevented serious disease problems. Precautions by plant quarantine have been taken when plant materials were moved between countries, or sometimes even within countries.

Increasing populations, better communication, and increased stresses on forestry land play a role in the more frequent appearance of diseases. Foresters should be especially careful with movement of plant material and be selective with regard to species, site, and other environmental factors. Diseases are normally not easily transported with seed. The worldwide trend towards vegetative propagation and movement of propagules must be carefully monitored or diseases will spread rapidly. The best method to combat disease will always be preventive measures. Hygiene in nurseries will help in preventing the spread of diseases like *Phytophthora cinnamomi* to plantation areas.

A knowledge about the pathogens, their spread and the susceptibility of tree species, will aid in avoiding disease. For example, *Diplodea pinea* normally enters plants through wounds caused by insects, hail, or pruning. Under favorable conditions this pathogen will kill whole forests, especially of *P. patula* and *P. radiata*. But a change in altitude to slightly cooler conditions will get susceptible trees out of the "danger" zone where the disease develops most rapidly. Another example of avoiding disease is not to plant *P. patula* seedlings too soon after burning, to avoid attack of *Rhizina undulata,* which will kill seedlings.

Early identification of forest diseases is important and attempts must be made to determine all environmental factors that may be associated with them. Many diseases are not easily controlled, even by using fungicides. For example, the best practical control measures for *Diplodia* are to plant *Diplodia*-resistant species where damage may occur, such as in hail belts, and to eliminate stress conditions. Trees suffering from stress become susceptible to both disease and insect attacks. Often diseases are associated with insect attacks, such as the occurrence of *Diplodia pinea* following bark beetle or even aphid attacks.

6.5.3 Weed Competition and Its Control

Weeding soon after planting always is important, as has been described in Section 6.3.5. The effect of weed competition on young seedlings in the tropics is so intense that it often causes failure. Weed competition can also be very adverse in older plantations. In older trees the competition is for moisture and nutrients. Tree growth will be retarded due to a combination of factors, including the allelopathic effects of weed species.

The effects of weed competition in older plantations has not been well studied and is not easy to quantify. Usually, competition studies relate to establishment success and most trials are terminated by the time canopy closure occurs. Frequently, the results are projected to mature trees, especially for short-rotation crops. This was done in South Africa on the trial of *Eucalyptus grandis* shown in Fig. 6.16, where the projected loss in volume due to weed competition was 23% at the age of eight years.

It is commonly believed that weed competition in older stands is not severe because trees are considered to be deep rooted and competition for nutrients and moisture is at different soil depths than the competitors. However, most of the feeder roots of forest trees are right below the soil surface. During periods of good rainfall there are no problems, but during droughts, which are common in many tropical regions, dense competing vegetation creates stress situations for moisture, especially on shallow soils.

The tendency now is toward too little weeding of young plantations because of rising costs. Studies like those of Geary and Zambrana (1972) were made to determine the least amount of weeding that is required for pine for good survival and reasonable growth. All studies show the adverse effects of weed competition, and the key is to determine the point of diminishing returns where the added cost of additional weeding is not compensated for by the added growth or quality. Conifers in general can withstand some weed competition and grow normally, but most hardwoods, especially the eucalypts, must be kept weed free up to a given point to grow normally. For example, Briscoe and Ybarra-Coronado (1971) found that the best way to increase the growth rate of teak plantations was to remove competition. Some organizations have

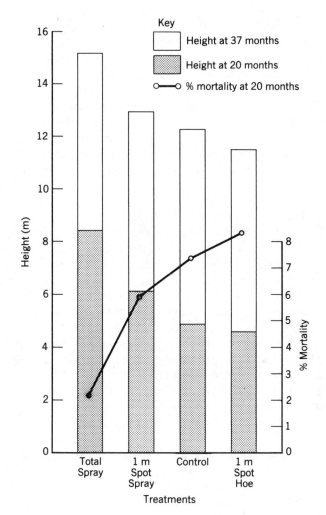

Figure 6.16. Both growth and survival are affected by the method of competition release used. Shown are the effects of different weed control methods on the height growth and survival of *Eucalyptus grandis* in South Africa. (From S.A.F.R.I. Research Review, 1983/1984.)

a tendency to continue weeding beyond the point where the trees are totally dominant and have captured the site. Much money is wasted by overweeding.

Weed competition increases variation in diameter apart from increasing mortality. It is usually not realized how much timber has been lost because of missing or nonusable trees. The small trees are either thinned to waste or do not contribute very much to yield, so the total loss from competition is not appreciated or even measurable. A wider initial spacing, good weed control, and a later thinning will yield uniform, merchantable timber from the first thinning that should be profitable.

Perhaps the most serious competition in tropical plantations, especially following site preparation, is provided by the various types of grasses. Some of these are very aggressive, fierce competitors that cause poor survival and poor growth and frequently result in the failure of a plantation. The effects of grass competition on survival and growth of radiata pine was clearly shown by Balneaves (1982). He found the control radiata pine trees were 8.5 cm dbh and 5.5 m tall after eight years while trees with 15 months of weed control were 17.9 cm dbh and 8.5 m tall. Nothing is gained by mentioning all the different grasses that cause trouble, because these are many, but a first priority of competition control must be grass control. Grasses not only use moisture and nutrients, but many are allelopathic and poison the soil, inhibiting the growth of trees, particularly the eucalypts.

Weeds will always be a problem in tropical plantations. Dense weed growth limits access to plantations and hampers normal forestry operations such as pruning, thinning, and especially fire fighting. Species such as bugweed (*Solanum mauritianum*), bramble (*Rubus* spp.), Mauritius thorn (*Caesalpinea sepiario*), *Lantana camara,* and thorny *Acacias* can very quickly develop such dense covers that a plantation becomes impenetrable without specialized equipment. It is good policy to fight large weed patches systematically, and eradicate small patches as soon as they appear. It is often argued that small patches are not a problem and eradication should be concentrated on large invasions. But a program of limited weed control can easily lead to small patches rapidly spreading out of control.

It is very important to follow up on weed control. Once the forest is invaded by weed species, a systematic approach must be adopted. Normally, a certain area is cleaned in one year; the next year a new area is tackled, but all of the area from the previous year should be covered again; the following year another new area is cleaned along with all of the area of the previous two years; and so on. This will effectively control seedlings and vegetative sprouts that normally appear after the initial control.

Weed control methods are varied. They include manual, mechanical, chemical, and even biological techniques and the success of each depends on many factors, such as climatic conditions, sites, species, and so on. A variety of herbicides is available and the effectiveness of each is dependent on various factors. Details on weed control techniques and the use of equipment and herbicides cannot be covered in this book, but the reader is referred to publications like the Weed Control Handbook (cited by Evans, 1984) and Haigh (1983).

6.5.4 Miscellaneous Pests and Problems

Forest protection problems have been classified into two groups by Evans (1984). First, inorganic and man-caused damage, which includes fire, climatic extremes, domestic animals, and theft; and, second, organic damage through factors such as fungi, insects, wild animals, or microorganisms. Problems caused by theft, mostly for fuel, squatting on land set aside for afforestation, and grazing of domestic animals concern social problems that make them difficult to control. Such problems are mostly localized and solutions must be found for them.

Browsing by wild or domestic animals can be a serious problem in tropical plantations. The animals often feed on pines, especially *P. oocarpa,* retarding growth. Usually such pines recover well and develop normally, but growth for at least one season is lost. In South Africa, damage of one- to two-year-old *P. oocarpa* trees has also resulted from baboons uprooting the trees to eat the thick bark of the roots, especially the young taproot. The thick bark on the roots of *P. oocarpa* also attracts bush pig (common in Africa), which will damage even the roots of older trees. Provenance variation of the source of tree seed in such damage has been observed. Relatively severe damage to young *P. patula* has also been caused by bush pigeons landing on the tops of the young trees and snapping the leader, causing malformed stems.

Browsing of hardwoods by animals normally is even more serious than in pines. Plantations of *Gmelina arborea, Chukrasia tabularis,* and *Khaya nyassica* in South Africa have been damaged to such an extent that controlled removal of the animals as well as fencing of planted areas sometimes has to be done. Fencing is so expensive that it is often not feasible. Since establishment of hardwoods requires good site preparation, the young trees often are the main source of food for animals. One attempt to overcome the browsing problem in West Africa consisted of planting striplings.

A major threat to tropical plantations is fire caused by lightning or by man through accidental fires from burning firebreaks or land clearing, by honey hunters, or sometimes by arsonists. Tropical indigenous forests grow under moist conditions, so they do not burn well; however, many tropical plantations are established on savannas, where a fire climax vegetation exists. Climatic conditions vary and wet periods are followed by dry, hot spells with accompanying dry winds that create extreme fire danger.

Protection from forest fires should consist of two actions: preventive and direct control. Preventive action includes the establishment of firebreaks by clearing strips through removal of combustible material, either by ploughing, raking, or disking or by controlled burns. Controlled burns are also undertaken in older plantations, especially with species that can withstand fire, such as *P. caribaea* or *P. elliottii.*

Good fire-fighting equipment is essential along with proper training so that the equipment can be handled efficiently. A communication network of fire lookout towers linked to each other and to control centers with two-way radios or telephones is essential. Access is important to all points within a plantation, and the existence of poor trails must be compensated for by using four-wheel-drive vehicles. Water storage at strategic places in the plantation is essential. Speed is important because fires spread very rapidly under weather conditions conducive to burning. Patrolling burned areas is very important because experience has shown that many forest fires start from reignition of burned areas thought to have been controlled.

6.6 POTENTIAL YIELDS

Exact productivity values from tropical plantations cannot be quoted because they vary by species, site, seed source, climate, nutrients, silviculture, and other factors. Therefore, the following values are only generalities. In the temperate zones a mean annual increment (MAI) below 10 m³/ha is common while tropical plantations normally produce an MAI above 15 m³/ha, unless they are grown on very poor sites. Generally, pines in New Zealand, South Africa, and Chile produce over 20 m³/ha/yr, but this can vary greatly, as shown by Gewald (1980) for *Pinus caribaea* in Panama, where growth of 7- to 11-year-old stands fluctuated from 5 to 23 m³/ha/yr, with an average of 11. In many areas the same production is obtained from the eucalypts, but good silviculture and tree improvement have raised the yields to above 40 m³/ha/yr. Intensive tree selection and the more recent application of vegetative propagation have increased the MAI in countries like Brazil to more than 60 m³/ha/yr, with the highest yields being over 100 m³/ha/yr (Brandão, 1984).

Yield tables are essential for the planning and management of plantations and must be prepared for each situation. Examples of yield tables for both sawtimber and pulpwood have been published by Loveday (1983) and Ladrach (1978). In developing growth predictions and yields for *Pinus patula*, Córdoba (1985) discusses the steps necessary for meaningful estimates. From height-age relationships, yield equations for volume and green weight are developed. By means of growth equations for basal area, prediction equations for yields are developed. Site-index curves must be established. There are many references that describe how to develop growth and yield prediction equations, but which are not suitable to cite here. It is important, however, to know that such equations must be developed for species grown as exotics because the standard tables usually do not suffice. For example, Mohd et al. (1981) describe how to develop volume tables for *Pinus caribaea* var. *hondurensis* in Malaysia. Many such tables are now being constructed to fit exotics grown in various environments.

One major caution needs to be given about the interpretation of growth values for exotics. In addition to using different methods to measure growth, frequently there is confusion about whether growth consists of wood only (inside bark) or wood plus bark (outside bark). In the temperate zones, almost all growth data are inside bark. Many of the large growth values reported in the tropics are outside bark. Especially in young pines, bark is thick; for example Gewald (1980) reported 45% volume was bark in 11-year-old *P. caribaea* var. *hondurensis; Eucalyptus* has about 10% bark at time of harvest

(Delwaulle, 1985). The first clarification needed when analyzing growth and yield is whether wood alone or wood plus bark is included (Delwaulle, 1985).

Although a subject unto itself, it is of importance to determine the growth patterns and yields of exotics. Equally important is whether yields are measured as volume or weight of wood produced. Some are exceptionally fast starters but slow down quickly. As one example, Ladrach (1986b) showed that the mean annual increment of four pine species he was working with in Colombia culminated by the eighth year. *Pinus patula* and *P. oocarpa* actually reached the biological culmination of growth by the ninth year. When weight of wood (as tons/hectare) was used, three of the species showed an increase and only *P. oocarpa* slowed down, but it still had not reached its culmination in height growth at 10 years of age. Prediction or estimation of yields is very difficult because it is so dependent on the biology of the trees, methods of measurement, and characteristics of the site.

6.6.1 Economics of Exotic Plantations in the Tropics

Returns from exotic plantations are complex to assess and will be covered only briefly here. Some general concepts and ideas were covered by Sutton (1984). He makes the point that essentially all fast-grown plantations are exotics and that "plantations are expensive but can be profitable." The value of fast-grown plantations will increase as wood values rise, the current trend. It is often assumed that at time of harvest the plantation has reached a normal sustained yield, so that the MAI is the amount of timber harvested annually, but normal yield is virtually never reached in practice. Problems related to economic assessment of plantations include standardization of cost recording, inflation rates, fluctuation in market trends, and many others. Put simply, in too many instances the growth that has been achieved or the growth potential of a provenance on a specific site simply is not known. Many more studies like those of Silva and Arellano (1982) and Silva et al. (1982), on volume tables and inventory methods for *Pinus caribaea* in Venezuela, respectively, need to be available to the operational forester.

Despite these restrictions, economists have devised ways to calculate profitability of exotic forest plantations. Early work on the economics of plantations was done by Craib (1939) and Hiley (1956). In 1986, the Internal Rate of Return (IRR) in New Zealand generally is from 8 to 10% (Sutton, 1984), but profitability is much affected by marketing. For instance, IRR for the export log trade in New Zealand has been calculated as 11.2–12.8% and at 6.7–7.4% for a "normal" sawlog regime (Fenton and Justin, 1972; Fenton, 1972). Since the inflation rate varies from country to country, real values are difficult to determine. The current rate of return for pine is from 12.8 to 19.2% and for eucalypts from 15.7 to 20.7%, as reported by Rusk et al. (1983) in South Africa. Many factors influence profitability of plantations; for example, long transport distances and market fluctuations will seriously affect profits.

Despite all the unknowns and variables, there is general concensus that tropical forestry is profitable. Profitability can be increased through better silvicultural techniques, use of genetically improved seed, better matching of species to site, and so on. The importance of forest tree breeding in aiding economic returns in exotics was emphasized by Van Wyk and Van der Sijde (1983). The return-to-cost ratio is very favorable. Rusk (1983) reported that the implementation of a standard forestry cost-recording system has led to "enormous increases in profitability of plantations" of members of the South African Timber Growers Association (SATGA) simply because growers started comparing their figures with those of others and attempted to improve their own profits.

Tropical exotic plantation forestry will become more profitable in the future because of dwindling natural forest resources. The yield and quality of overexploited indigenous forests will become so poor and the exploitation cost so high that felling will almost cease (Sutton, 1984). Eventually the cost of management of regenerated natural forests will equal that of plantations. More plantations will be established because all indications are that the price of timber must rise. Sutton states that countries with fast-growing plantations should be assured of a profitable export market in the long term, especially for high-quality sawtimber. The concept of replacement forests (as covered in Chapters 1, and 10) is important here, as tropical plantations will take the pressure off the exploitation of indigenous forests.

7

GROWING EXOTIC FOREST TREES IN TEMPERATE CLIMATES

7.1 INTRODUCTION

This book concentrates on the growing of exotics in the tropics and subtropics. This would be expected, since the tropics and subtropics comprise the parts of the world where today most of the work with exotics is being carried out and where the success has been most outstanding.

However, it would be a great error not to cover the situation of exotic forestry in the temperate and boreal zones, because that is where exotic forestry began. In many countries in this part of the world large forestry programs are based upon exotic species and exotics there are very important.

In this chapter, after a short historical explanation, we will discuss some important differences between the use of exotics in the warm and cool areas of the world, explore the use of exotics region by region in the temperate areas, and describe in some detail one of the larger exotic programs in temperate and boreal zone forestry in which *Pinus contorta* is used.

7.2 HISTORY OF EXOTICS IN THE TEMPERATE AND BOREAL AREAS

We depend upon exotic plants and animals for our lives and accept this situation without question. Most persons are not aware that the most important agricultural crops used today are mainly exotics, with only the rare species being indigenous (Table 7.1). The art of using exotics is well developed.

The success of exotics in agriculture can be explained by the fact that man

TABLE 7.1. Some Important Agricultural Crops Used Outside the Continents Where They Originated[a]

Crop	Native Continent	Percentage Outside Usage
Potato	South America	95
Wheat	Asia	90
Corn	South America	88
Cotton	South America	88
Sugar cane	Asia	78
Coffee	Africa	77
Banana	Africa	67
Rice	Asia	52
Tea	Asia	51

[a]From FAO, 1981c.

has been cultivating, naturalizing, and improving the species concerned for millennia. Of course, there have been numerous failures and even disasters. The classic example is the potato blight that originated in Belgium in 1845 and then swept over Europe, resulting in widespread hunger and starvation and poverty among farmers. It was one of the main causes for the large emigration of people from Europe to the new world in the middle of the nineteenth century. To feed a hungry world we have to accept such risks from using exotics because we must continue relying upon them for the bulk of food and fiber crops produced throughout the world.

The need for more and better forest trees and wood has not been as pronounced as the need for food, but in parts of the temperate region the history of tree introduction is long. As seen in Table 7.2, which summarizes several studies (e.g., Cajander, 1914, 1917; Ilvessalo, 1926; Lanier, 1981), potato and corn were probably not introduced into Europe much earlier than the first exotic tree species. Evelyne was already familiar with a number of exotic trees when writing his *Sylva* around 1700.

The history of exotic forestry is oldest in countries with a long maritime tradition and overseas colonies, such as England, Holland, and France. It seems certain that many of the colonists also took tree seeds with them when they left their homes, but this is not well documented. Usually, the introductions were first used as ornamentals and park trees, but the fastest-growing and better-formed trees were then used as forest trees.

The gain from use of exotic forest trees has been very much reduced because of the often haphazard methods of introduction. Many early failures have given a bad name to forestry using exotic trees and success in some countries has also been very limited. Lähde et al. (1984), for instance, lists and describes trials with more than 50 different exotic conifers in Finland. Of these, only

TABLE 7.2. Year of Introduction for a Few Park and Forest Tree Species into Europe

Year	Species
1534	*Thuja occidentalis*
1553	*Pinus strobus*
1600	*Robinia pseudoacacia*
1629	*Juglans nigra*
	Carya alba
	Prunus serotina
	Prunus virginiana
1636	*Platanus acerifolia*
1640	*Taxodium distichum*
1664	*Juniperus virginiana*
1668	*Liquidambar styraciflua*
1700	*Picea glauca*

one, *Larix sibirica,* has so far been successful enough to be planted commercially, and this species is not used on a large scale.

Only during the latter part of the past century has there been a somewhat scientific approach to the introduction and trial of exotic trees. And, indeed, before Darwin's *The Origin of Species,* which first appeared in 1859, and Mendel's studies became accepted in the beginning of the twentieth century, there was not much theory on which to base such introduction trials. There are some early examples, however. The Swedish Admiralty in 1749 issued a regulation about the choice of seed source for oak plantations. The more northern seed sources produced the best-quality trees.

A classic example is De Vilmorin's provenance studies with Scots pine in France. The trials were planted in the early 1820s and Vilmorin reported results in 1857. He could demonstrate a substantial inherited variation and showed that pine from the Baltic states produced a superior-quality wood. These studies caused researchers in a number of European countries to start experimenting with geographic variation. Results indicated the care necessary when making introductions of exotic seed sources. This must be seen as a starting point for a more scientific approach to forest tree introductions. Similar early work on provenances and the introduction of exotics was done in Japan by researchers such as Tanaka (1883).

7.3 DIFFERENCES BETWEEN EXOTIC FORESTRY IN TROPICAL AND TEMPERATE OR BOREAL CLIMATES

There are a number of differences, both biological and nonbiological, between exotic forestry in tropical and temperate conditions.

7.3.1 Biological Differences

7.3.1.1 Diversity of the Flora. The wealth of species in many tropical and sub-tropical forests has always fascinated botanists, but at the same time it is a source of many problems for foresters. It is not uncommon to find as many as 700 different tree species in 100 ha of tropical rain forest. As a result of this complexity, it is easy to understand why the tropical forester would rather plant and manage a forest with a single species, which is usually an exotic. There are forests in the tropics with a simple composition, but these usually occur in environments with poor growing conditions.

The temperate and boreal forests have a much simpler composition, with only one or a few tree species dominating. These species are well known to the foresters of the area and to the industry. If there is no problem with the indigenous trees, an exotic species must have obvious advantages before there is interest in growing it.

The decreasing number of tree species at the higher latitudes has been explained in many different ways by Pianka (1966). One of the most important has to do with time: the number of species in a plant community tends to increase with its age. The temperate and boreal forests are relatively poor as a result of recent glaciations and short-term fluctuations in the climate. The species have either not had time to migrate or return since the last change of climate or the time has been too short to permit the evolution of new species.

The history of forests since the latest ice age is very different in the different temperate areas. In North America the major mountain chains all have a north–south direction, which made it possible for the flora to retreat to the south in front of the ice and to reinvade as the climate improved. The Carpathians, Alps, and Pyrenees in Europe are oriented east–west, so they were formidable obstacles over which species were lost and across which it has been difficult to return. This is an explanation of the richness of species in the North American forests compared to the situation in northern Europe, where only a few indigenous species occur.

Another interesting comparison is made by Stern and Roche (1974), who point out that the forests of Siberian Asia are largely made up of mixed forests of larch, pine, spruce, birch, and aspen, compared to the distribution of the species in northern Europe and northern North America, which occur as a mosaic depending on site factors. From a forester's point of view, this latter situation is much to be preferred.

The effect of glaciation is demonstrated in Fig. 7.1, showing where Norway spruce existed through the last glaciation and the routes by which it returned to northern Europe. There are several species such as *Picea omorika* and *Aesculus hippocastanum* which are hardy enough for the climate of central Scandinavia but which were never able to return north from the Balkans, where they survived the ice age.

Exotics are obviously most useful in areas where the native flora is deficient. Northern Europe has a relatively poor flora, with only 5 natural coni-

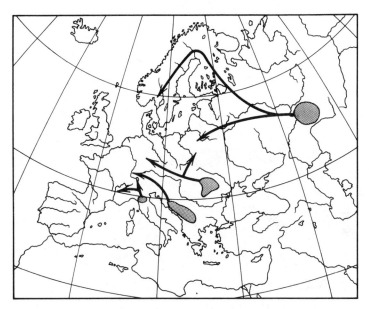

Figure 7.1 The postglacial history of the migration of Norway spruce is shown for northern Europe (after Schmidt-Vogt, 1977).

ferous tree species north of the Alps; Japan, for instance, has approximately 25 species. The British Isles have only one native conifer of economic importance, Scots pine, and Denmark not a single one.

7.3.1.2 Adaptation of the Native Trees.

The time of occupancy of many temperate tree species in their present environment is often short compared to an average tree generation. For example, Beech (*Fagus silvatica*) only reappeared in southern Sweden and Denmark 5000 years ago. And Norway spruce reached southern Sweden and western Norway much later than that, perhaps only some hundreds of years ago, as demonstrated in Fig. 7.2.

If one assumes an average generation as short as 100 years for a species (and that is a low estimate for most temperate species), the present trees at a given site would only be in the fifth to fiftieth generations. This is too short a time to develop good adaptivity to the local environment, particularly since the climate continues to vary since the reestablishment of the species. The time in northern Europe has certainly been too short for the evolution of any new species.

Many of the temperate species have used migration patterns after the last ice age that have cost them much of their genetic variability. Norway spruce will again serve as an example. As is evident from Figs. 7.1 and 7.2, it reached the Scandinavian peninsula from the north. Most of the genotypes adapted to milder climates from forests in the south were lost during the passage through

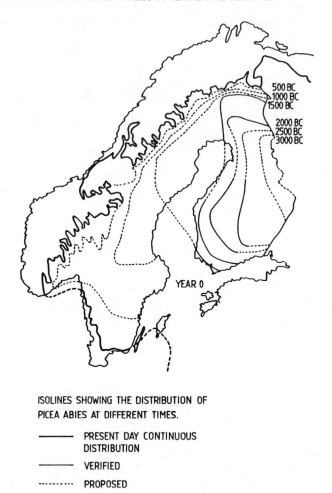

ISOLINES SHOWING THE DISTRIBUTION OF
PICEA ABIES AT DIFFERENT TIMES.

———— PRESENT DAY CONTINUOUS
DISTRIBUTION

———— VERIFIED

·········· PROPOSED

Figure 7.2 Present and past distribution of Norway spruce in Fenno-Scandia is illustrated from 3000 B.C. to the present range (after Moe, 1970).

the very harsh climate of Lapland before they again moved south into Scandinavia to more mild climates. Thus, one finds indigenous trees not as well adapted to southern Scandinavia as those from some outside environments.

In temperate and cold climates the plants must be adapted to make optimal use of the short growing season and endure the unfavorable winter weather, particularly the low temperatures. To survive this difficult period most perennial plants cease growth and winter in a dormant state. The physiological changes that make it possible for the plants to do this are very complex and still not fully known (Lyr et al., 1967).

Initiation of shoot growth in spring is primarily triggered by a critical "temperature sum," which is the duration of preceding temperatures above a certain threshold value. Shoot-growth cessation and hardening is often controlled by a certain critical night length or a combination of temperature and night length (Dormling, 1977). The reason for this probably is that photoperiod is the only environmental factor varying in exactly the same way each year. At high latitudes it is important to choose trees that make optimum use of the growing season. The trees should start growing as soon as the risk from spring frosts is over, but they must also stop growing in time to harden off before the first severe autumn frosts.

The situation becomes even more complicated because of the fluctuations of most temperate and boreal climates. At a given location, year-to-year variation in rainfall, minimum winter temperature, or length of growing season is usually much greater than the variation between long-term averages of these variables observed in widely different locations. With rotation ages often as long as 100 years, it must be expected that during the lifetime of the forest extreme environmental conditions will occur.

Since growth initiation and cessation is controlled by temperature and changes in day length, both of which vary with latitude, problems are created when foresters make long north–south movements of trees. In the Northern Hemisphere, a tree adapted to the cold north will normally start growing early in the year when moved to the south since it gets the critical temperature sum earlier in the warmer climate. If a late frost then occurs, the northern source will be damaged or killed. A source moved north will, on the other hand, encounter long nights and short days earlier, which will cause it to stop growing too early and not fully utilize the growing season. A plant moved north will start growing too late in the spring and will continue to grow too long in the autumn.

In the southern part of the temperate zone, drought often becomes restricting to growth, such as in parts of the Mediterranean region or the prairies of North America and in Asia. The total precipitation is important, but even more critical is its distribution over the year. Where much of the precipitation comes in the form of snow which melts and runs off during a few short spring weeks, the total amount of moisture is of little significance.

7.3.1.3 Productivity and Rotation Length. The climatic conditions of the boreal and temperate areas, with lower temperatures and no or little growth during the winters, result in lower production than is obtained in the tropics. This is not compensated for by the longer summer daylight hours of the north or less drought stress or often higher nutrient levels in the soils. The lower productivity results in longer rotations.

Tropical plantations yield several times the quantity of wood per hectare than do those in the temperate and boreal regions (see Table 7.3). A main reason for growing exotics in the colder climates is to reduce this discrepancy as much as possible.

TABLE 7.3. Comparison of Growth Rates and Rotation Ages in Managed Forests and Plantations in Temperate and Tropical Areas

Region	Yield m^3/ha/yr	Rotation (yr)
Siberia	1–1.5	100–100+
Sweden	3.2	60–120
United Kingdom (conifers)	10	40–70
New Zealand (pines)	15–30	20–40
Tropical pine plantations	15–45	10–30
Subtropical *Eucalyptus*	5–30	8–25
Tropical *Eucalyptus*	10–60	6–20

7.3.1.4 Diseases and Pests. It is sometimes stated that tropical plantations are more affected by diseases and other pests than are those in temperate regions (Bassus, 1979; Uhlig, 1979). This sounds plausible, especially for diseases, since it is assumed most diseases develop best in the warm and often humid tropical climate very suitable for growth and reproduction. However, this is not the general situation and the difference between risks from pests for tropical and temperate plantations must not be overrated. It is easy to find examples of successful pest attacks on exotics from both regions. There are, in fact, several reasons for extra caution about pests in the temperate and boreal zones:

1.   Many introductions into colder climates are moved into environments where close relatives are already living naturally. This situation is certainly true for most of the exotic conifer plantations in Europe, North America, and northern Asia. The risk of having a pest of a close relative, perhaps from the same genus or closely related species, attacking an introduced species is much higher than an attack from a pest from a nonrelated species.

2.   The relatively long rotations in the temperate plantations give the pathogens more time to adapt to the new host. It may take some time before a pest will attack an exotic, but this almost always happens (see Chapter 4).

3.   Frost damage often sufficiently weakens the exotic to reduce its resistance to pests, even when the frost damage itself is not fatal or even visible.

4.   There is always the risk of introducing exotic pathogens with exotic trees which can attack the native species. Often-cited examples are the risk of introducing the North American rust fungi *Endocronartium harknessii* or *Cronartium comptoniae* to Europe when *Pinus contorta* is introduced as an exotic. Both of these diseases would be serious threats to the native European Scots pine. It is of utmost importance to use strict sanitary precautions to prevent pathogens from accompanying the exotic to its new environment, not only to

permit the exotic to flourish but also to protect the indigenous species in the area.

Two classic examples of diseases on exotic trees in the temperate zone are *Rhabdocline pseudotsugae* on Douglas-fir and *Cronartium ribicola* on Weymouth or eastern white pine. The effect of the diseases on the future of the two tree species as exotics has been so different that an examination is warranted.

Douglas-fir was introduced to central Europe around 1830 but did not become really popular until the end of the century. Large trials with many different provenances were planted around 1885–95, mainly in Germany. It was generally thought of as an unusually healthy and extremely productive species until the early 1920s, when the first rhabdocline attacks took place. The disease spread rapidly over central Europe, probably from infected seedlings. The damage was so serious that all planting of the *glauca* and *caesia* (but not the *viridis*) varieties had to be stopped (Schenk, 1939). Another disease, *Adelopus gaumannii,* also struck, but again the var. *viridis* was not seriously injured. By 1939 the situation was so bad that the forestry authorities in Germany were considering a ban on the species and Schenk wrote: "In the observed area a continued cultivation of Douglas-fir is without any prospect of success, if we continue as we have been doing and do not take into special consideration resistance to fungal diseases."

However, today probably 15% of the forest plantations in West Germany are again established with Douglas-fir, and in certain areas it makes up as much as 40% (Weissenberg, 1982, Kleinschmit, 1984). The most probable explanation is that the diseases did not strike until Douglas-fir had been cultivated as an exotic for many years over large areas and good trials had been established and had reached a meaningful age. This made it possible to evaluate the situation relative to source of seed and to make a decision to continue to work with the *viridis* variety.

Pinus strobus was introduced to continental Europe in the early eighteenth century and rapidly became popular, both as a park and forest tree. The early plantations were established in areas outside those that contained native soft pine, so white pine did not reach the areas where the *Cronartium ribicola* existed until 1850. Then the disease spread rapidly to all areas where Weymouth pine was cultivated (see Table 7.4). (A major tragedy was, of course, that the disease also reached North America.) The damage was devastating in northern Europe, and even though many stands survived in fairly good condition (Schmitt, 1972), all cultivation of the species ceased.

Why did this reaction occur and not have the same results as with Douglas-fir since white pine had been just as good a species before the blister rust occurred. Weissenberg (1982) suggests the very interesting explanation that the main difference between the two species was that for Weymouth pine there was very little information on where the seed of the plantations came from. The seed had come to Europe before anyone was interested in or even knew

TABLE 7.4. Spread of White Pine Blister Rust in Europe[a]

1850	The Baltic States
1861	Finland
1880	Sweden
1885	Holland
1889	France
1892	England
1895	Switzerland

[a]From Liro, 1908; Fassi, 1960.

about the importance of provenances. The foresters and researchers therefore had no clues as to where to find more tolerant material. Another possible explanation is that there seems to be very little resistance to rust in *Pinus strobus* and that the remaining stands may have been exposed only to light infection accidentally.

The two examples show the importance of knowing the origin of exotic material. It is necessary to obtain a fairly complete sample of the genetic variability of interesting exotics. This will make it possible to evaluate the seriousness of pests and will also permit countermeasures to be planned with sound background information so that the species can continue to be used.

Although the examples described were for disease attacks, other pests, especially insects, are severe on exotics in the temperate region. Some of these were described in Chapter 4. No matter what the pest, it is essential to remember that exotics can stay healthy for very long periods and then be hit by devastating attacks. An excellent source of information on the risks of pests with exotics, particularly in the boreal areas, is Karlman's thesis (1984).

7.3.2 Nonbiological Differences Between Temperate and Tropical Areas

7.3.2.1 Importance of the Forests. Almost without exception, forestry is of high importance to temperate zone countries. In many countries the forests form a solid base for a forest industry or for benefits other than wood production that also have great importance. Of increasing importance is the use of forests for biomass production. Much testing is being performed in this field of forestry. For example, a report was published in Sweden listing 27 genera (23 deciduous and 4 conifers) with 288 species that might be of value for biomass production in the Northern Hemisphere (Anon., 1981b).

Countries like Finland and Sweden rely almost entirely upon forests planted or reestablished by foresters in other ways. The value of the forests to these nations cannot be overemphasized. Other countries with a large forest industry, such as Canada and the Soviet Union, have such vast forests that they have based much of their industry on the natural forests. Plantation forestry and the use of exotics is still new in these countries. With increased transport distances between the natural forests and the industries and an increasing competition for the wood, the interest in intensive forestry and the use of exotics is rapidly increasing in these regions.

Central and southern European countries are densely populated and heavily industrialized. Even when a forest industry exists, recreational use of the limited forest area is very important. It has even been argued, by Richardson (1970), for instance, that the recreational value of the forests in certain European countries is of greater significance in economic terms than is cellulose production.

Many countries in the temperate zone, such as Great Britain, Ireland, Portugal, Spain, Greece, and Turkey, are increasing their forest area, as unproductive and degraded agricultural land is restored by forest plantings, largely with exotic species. These new forests will provide raw material for industry and better areas for recreation, and they will also help control erosion.

Planting in the temperate regions is, however, not increasing nearly as fast as in the tropics, where the area of forest plantations has tripled between 1965 and 1980 (Evans, 1984).

7.3.2.2 The Long History of Plantation Forestry in the Temperate Regions. It
is a fact that intensive forestry started in the temperate zone. During the 200 to 250 years that have passed since organized forestry became important in central Europe, extensive experience has been gained about forestry, especially about the use of exotics.

The general reason for the early activity in forestry was that the natural forests were no longer able to satisfy the demand for wood products for a growing population. Wood use in Europe in those days was similar to that in the tropics today: firewood, charcoal, and building material. Linnaeus and other travelers in central Sweden during the second half of the eighteenth century all mentioned the heavy demand for wood and charcoal for industry. Forests had largely disappeared in the mining areas and around the cities. Although land transportation in those days was difficult, it is interesting that a substantial part of the firewood used in Stockholm was brought in by ship from Finland. This is hard to believe for visitors to the well-forested central Sweden of today. With industrialization came increased needs for raw material for the pulp and paper industry and for lumber.

As industrialization spread, so did plantation forestry. The general trend has been for an increase of coniferous species, both native and exotic. In West Germany, for instance, the percentage of conifers in the growing stock increased from 30% at the end of the last century to approximately 70% in 1960 (FAO, 1967). Larches and hardwoods have been replaced mainly by Norway and Sitka spruce and Douglas-fir.

During two and a half centuries much experience and knowledge have been gained about plantation forestry and exotics. Much of the forestry practice of the temperate zone today is quite conservative and bound by tradition. Plantation forestry is well accepted even if there is some concern among environmentalists that not enough natural forests are saved and that too much emphasis is put on high productivity. And some forestry practices necessary for the efficient management of exotics as well as indigenous species, such as the use of herbicides, are being protested. Forestry in the tropics is often more open to new ideas and to the trial and use of exotics.

Forestry research and education also have long traditions in much of the temperate zone. Trial plantations with large numbers of provenances and species are available. Many trials have also reached the age that it is possible to make conclusions about the long-term effects of spacing, thinning systems, repeated fertilization, and other aspects of intensive forest management.

Well-accepted forestry laws exist in most temperate zone countries. Not only are they accepted by the general public but also among most forestry owners, who often must accept considerable restrictions on how they can use their land. The laws aim at maintaining or, if possible, increasing both the forest area and forest productivity while at the same time stressing the importance of multiple use of the forests. Protection of the natural forest is done by setting aside protected areas, national parks, and nature reserves. In most temperate zone countries, well-established forest services or similar organizations exist with the task of enforcing the forestry laws, managing publicly owned land, and providing assistance and advice to the private land owners. The organizations are usually responsible for the control of the seed trade and in charge of seed certification, with a large emphasis on sources of seed to be used as exotics.

7.3.2.3 Degree of Economic Development. The tropics are generally in the early stages of development, although there are major anomalies, such as parts of highly developed Australia, South Africa, and Brazil. The less developed countries of the Middle East and northern Africa fall partly within the temperate zone.

In the developing countries, more than half of the population still lives in rural areas and earn their living from some form of agriculture. In some areas, the high population pressure has caused a shortage of land available for agriculture and the forests, often on soils sensitive to erosion and degradation, are being cleared for firewood and then for farming. The need for wood is great. For example, 85% of all the wood used in the developing countries is for firewood (FAO, 1984).

In the developed countries the situation is quite different. The forests have primarily become sources of raw material for industry and providers of secondary benefits for the largely urban population. The use of forest products by the rural population is little more than that of the people in the cities. Most of the energy generated from wood (8% of Sweden's energy and 15% of Finland's) is produced by the lumber and the pulp and paper industry, which burn

TABLE 7.5. Important Factors in Species Choice for Various End Uses[a]

Characteristic	Fuelwood	Woodpulp	Lumber	Plywood/Veneer
Growth and silviculture	Fast growth with early culmination of maximum growth rate. Large tree size unimportant or disadvantageous. Tree shape unimportant. Should be easy and cheap to grow. Coppicing ability desirable.	As for fuelwood, but straight stems are important to aid rapid debarking and efficient harvesting and avoid reaction wood.	Moderate to fast growth with ability to grow to large size. Good form important, ease of pruning and freedom from butt rots highly desirable. Limb characteristics are important.	As for lumber, but growth to very large size important. Good natural pruning with rapid wound occulsion desirable.
Wood properties	Quick drying with low ash content. Burn readily without smell or sparks. Moderate density.	Fiber length, color, extractives content, and wood density are primary papermaking qualities that are important.	Strength, dimensional stability, wood uniformity, along with good seasoning, preservation, working, and finishing properties are essential.	Peeling or slicing ability. Figure is important, as is being knot free. Good adhesive bonding for plywood. Good burning characteristics for matches.

[a]After Evans, 1984.

bark and waste to generate steam and electricity (National Academy of Sciences, 1983).

Competition for land no longer seems to be acute in most developed countries. In Western Europe, for example, the forested area has increased by approximately 10% during the last 15 years (FAO, 1981c). Major conflicts with other potential users of the land are uncommon.

One major disadvantage of industrialization has been increased pollution. Chemical air pollution is a major threat to the forests of the industrialized world. Widespread damage has occurred in central Europe (West and East Germany and Czechoslovakia), and also in the northeastern United States and adjacent parts of Canada. In central Europe the very existence of a species such as *Abies alba* may be in danger. If it is lost, it will be necessary to look for a replacement, perhaps a more resistant exotic species. Hopefully, the many pollution countermeasures already implemented or planned will make this unnecessary, but exotic usage has been stimulated by the pollution problem.

7.3.2.4 Desirable Characteristics of Species and End Uses. The desirable characteristics for an exotic species vary for different end uses. Some of the most critical factors are described in Table 7.5. The main end uses for industrial wood vary, not only between the tropics and the temperate zones but within the zones. In the warmer parts of the temperate zones, just as in the tropics, plantations are usually established for high-volume production, mainly to produce wood fiber. In the colder regions, with their lower productivity, the economically most important products are often high-quality lumber and plywood or veneer, produced with long rotations.

The salary levels are normally higher in the industrialized countries of the temperate zone than in the tropics. This has resulted in more mechanization of the forestry operations. Also, a rather stereotyped management has developed, which is a major disadvantage. The usually better training of the forestry personnel from the temperate zones tends to result in better forestry.

7.4 REGIONAL USE OF EXOTICS

It is rather well known which exotics should be used for the temperate and boreal zones, particularly for countries which have a long forest history. But if this is not known, no matter how well one may succeed in matching environments and using general information, the only absolute way to find out how well a tree species will perform in a new area is to plant it and keep it under observation.

For the colder parts of the temperate zone, by far the most important donor region is northwestern North America. In this region there are a number of valuable species, especially conifers, which have proven to be widely useful. Of greatest importance are species like Douglas-fir, Sitka spruce, and lodgepole pine, all of which have performed well in much of Europe. These are also of interest in the Soviet Union and other areas in Europe, in Asia, and in the temperate zones of the Southern Hemisphere such as in Chile or New Zealand.

Douglas-fir has been especially widely tried. For example, Schober (1963) relates in some detail the experiences with this species in Europe. He discusses sources to use and those to avoid and covers the *viridis* and *glauca* strains; he states that only Douglas-fir from the moister climates do well in Europe. Wright et al. (1971) cover the usage of the Rocky Mountain source of Douglas-fir. They state: "The present data indicate that a grower in the Eastern U.S. will obtain no advantage . . . with seed collected from a particular elevational zone, aspect or soil type. . . . ." This differs greatly from the more western sources, where all aspects of the environment are important. Another study, in France (Michaud, 1978), tested 184 Douglas-fir sources. Height differences were already evident in the nursery. In the test area the best provenances were from the western part of the species range and from under 800 m elevation. Sitka spruce also has been widely tested, as reported by O'Driscoll (1978) in an international provenance trial of the species.

Northern Japan is also an important donor country, but the species native to this area have not yet been as thoroughly tried as those from western North America, except for species, such as Japanese larch, which has been widely planted.

For the warmer parts of the temperate zones, trees from Australia (*Eucalyptus*), the southeastern United States, and California (pines) are of major importance. One of the most outstanding exotics is Norway spruce, which comes from species-poor Europe, the main receptor area for temperate exotics. It is widely planted in Europe outside its natural distribution and is also promising in northeastern North America and northern Japan (Wright, 1976).

The main temperate and boreal receptor areas are Europe, New Zealand, parts of Asia, southern South America, and southern Australia and New Zealand. In the Southern Hemisphere, most of the exotic planting programs are concentrated in the warm northern parts of the temperate zone. In the Northern Hemisphere, the use of exotics extends north to the tundra and up to the alpine tree limit.

A great deal of information about the use of exotics in the temperate zone has been published. It is impossible to list more than a fraction of it, but the publications by Streets (1962), Edwards (1963), FAO (1981d), Hall (1982), and Larsen (1983) serve as good summaries. Specific papers are available by the hundreds; a few examples are Doran (1978), on *Pinus radiata,* and Sweet and Thulin (1963), on *Pinus banksiana.* Many papers have been published on *Pinus contorta,* such as Dietrichson (1970) and Skroppa and Dietrichson (1978) for Norway. Other publications related to this species are available for Sweden, as covered at the end of this chapter.

Several examples of the use of exotic species in the temperate zone will now be given. No attempt has been made to cover more than a small part of the activities or to give complete references.

Northern Scandinavia. The natural forest in the region is floristically rather simple, with Norway spruce and Scots pine as the major commercial species. Trials with exotics have been numerous and have been planted as far north as forests exist (Kiellander, 1963; Lähde et al., 1984).

So far, the use of exotics is rather limited in production plantations: Siberian larch mainly in Finland; Norway spruce, Sitka spruce, and the hybrid between Sitka and white spruce in Norway north of the natural distribution of Norway spruce; and lodgepole pine in Sweden and Norway. The Swedish lodgepole pine plantations consist of 35,000 ha planted each year. They are by far the most important in the region and will be described in some detail. New trials with a number of species (*Picea mariana, P. glauca, Abies lasiocarpa, A. sibirica,* and *Larix sibirica*) plus the native species and lodgepole pine are being made in Sweden. The most northern sources are being tested to see if any can be found that will survive and grow better than the indigenous species in the very extreme climates at the tree limit of the mountains in northern Sweden. A report of the 15-year performance of a number of North American species tried in Sweden was made by Johnsson (1957). He reported that *Pinus contorta* was greatly superior in growth to the other species tried. The wood of all species tried was similar and acceptable.

Southern Scandinavia. More species have been tried in the south than in the north. Even though many species survive and grow well, few are superior to the native Norway spruce and Scots pine. Only Sitka spruce is used for commercial planting, and then only on the best sites in areas with a maritime climate.

Most of the Norway spruce planted in the southern part of the Scandinavian peninsula is from foreign provenances. In the warmer zones, Romanian provenances are superior while for the rest of the area White Russian or east Polish spruce is the best. The overall superiority for White Russian provenances in 23 different Swedish trials was 11% better than the local controls (Dietrichson, 1970). The superiority of the exotic provenances apparently results from a better utilization of the growing season. This is explained by the migration route around the Gulf of Bothnia which had been followed by the native spruce (see Fig. 7.1). The superiority of the foreign provenances would not have been predicted using similarity of climates as the major basis for comparison.

Denmark. The situation in Denmark is quite different from neighboring southern Sweden and Norway. Denmark has no native coniferous trees of commercial importance, so most of the production forests are planted with exotic material. The most important are Norway and Sitka spruce, a number of *Abies* species, Japanese larch, and Douglas-fir.

The Danish hardwood forests consist mainly of two native species, oak (*Quercus robur*) and beech (*Fagus silvatica*). However, seed from foreign provenances is used to a large extent for both these species.

Iceland. Located in the middle of the North Atlantic Ocean, Iceland has no natural forests. A number of trials with trees from northern regions have been planted. The most successful seems to be Siberian larch from the Archangelsk region in the Soviet Union. Some species from northwestern North America are also showing some promise.

Great Britain and Ireland. This is another area with a very limited indigenous coniferous flora, with the only native species of any importance, Scots pine, being confined to a small area. Forestry is now based on large plantations of exotics and only to a small degree on the management of a few native hardwoods.

Great Britain probably has more and longer experience with exotic plantation forestry than any other northern country except Japan. Streets (1962) provides much information of interest about the very impressive introduction program that has been followed there. The information about exotics in Great Britain shown in Table 7.6, was kindly supplied by Lines (personal communication 1984); it indicates the rather large amount of exotic plantations in a relatively small country. The forestry situation in Ireland is similar to Great Britain, although plantings are not on the same scale and some different species are used.

TABLE 7.6. The Area and Percentage Distribution of Forestry Commission High Forest in Great Britain as of March 31, 1981

Species	Total Area (1,000 of ha)	% of all Species
Scots pine	100.9	12.0
Corsican pine	35.7	4.2
Lodgepole pine	101.8	12.1
Sitka spruce	380.7	45.2
Norway spruce	67.5	8.0
Larches	72.0	8.5
Douglas-fir	25.4	3.0
Other conifers	19.8	2.4
Mixed conifers	1.8	0.2
All conifers	805.5	95.7
Oak	12.9	1.5
Beech	15.7	1.9
Other broad-leaved	6.8	0.8
Mixed broad-leaved	1.2	0.1
All broad-leaved	36.6	4.3
All species	842.1	100.0

Some of the northernmost eucalypt plantations and trials exist in this region. Evans (1980) and Evans et al. (1983) describe the British situation and conclude that there is evidence that some eucalypt species have adequate cold tolerance and fast enough early growth to be of potential interest for British forestry. After the winter of 1981–82, when Britain experienced the coldest weather ever recorded, a number of species survived temperatures down to −10°C. A few hardy provenances of *E. gunnii,* one of the more promising species, survived −16°C, but only high-altitude provenances of *E. niphophila* and *E. debeuzevillei* survived temperatures as low as −23°C. The effect of freezing depends not only upon the minimum temperature but also upon a suitable period of hardening off, which makes trees much less sensitive to frosts than if a rapid drop in temperature occurs following warm weather.

Central Europe. Throughout central Europe the establishment of man-made forests has resulted in a substantially increased area under coniferous trees, both native and exotic. Hardwoods such as beech and oak, along with the native larch and Scots pine, are being replaced by the exotic Norway and Sitka spruces and Corsican pine. Douglas-fir and the hybrid larch (*L. decidua* × *L. leptolepis*) is faster growing than the native European larch and has higher resistance to the larch cancer *Daysyscypha willkommii.*

Some exotic hardwoods are also planted, not always primarily for wood production. Hungary, for instance, has plantations of *Robinia pseudoacacia* for multiple purposes, including honey production and landscaping (Keresztesi, 1970).

In Holland and adjacent countries, intensive forest management mainly concerns exotic poplars, often in row plantings along roads and canals. These produce high-value wood on short rotations. Traditional plantations with *Quercus rubra* also exist.

Soviet Union. It is difficult to assess Russian forestry, since so little is published about it or summarized in other languages. Most of the country's forestry concerns the management and utilization of the vast native coniferous forests of Norway spruce, Siberian larch, Siberian fir, and pines. There is, however, also a certain interest in exotic species (Kalutskii et al., 1981a,b).

In the Soviet Union, particular attention has recently been given to the introduction of fast-growing exotics. From the north to the south, the following species seem to be the most promising: *Pinus contorta; Abies balsamea; Pseudotsuga menziesii; Abies fraseri; Abies concolor;* and *Picea pungens.*

Several of the species, particularly Douglas-fir, appear to perform well in several climatic zones. Parallel to these introduction trials there is much activity in tree improvement and provenance trials of indigenous trees like Scots pine and Norway spruce. Trials with larch hybrids are also promising. So far, the only exotic hardwood with potential is *Quercus rubra.*

Foresters in the Soviet Union have been experimenting with eucalypts for at least 150 years. At one time, as much as 10,000 ha were planted in Georgia and other southern areas of Russia. However, most were killed in the winter of 1949–50, when temperatures in the region fell to −30°C, including, for example, 70-year-old trees of *E. viminalis* (Linnard, 1969). The interest in eucalypts has never developed again, and the area now growing eucalypts is small. The Russian experience with *Eucalyptus* is a prime example of the difficulty of growing exotics where delayed pests or weather extremes can make a once promising species or source undesirable.

Mediterranean Area and Southeastern Europe. Throughout the Mediterranean area a number of very active reforestation programs are under way, many of which rely on the use of exotics.

On the Iberian peninsula there are large eucalypt plantations, mainly with *E. globulus* and *E. camaldulensis.* Spain actually ranks third in the world after Brazil and India in total area planted to *Eucalyptus.* (FAO, 1981c). Other important plantation species are *Pinus radiata* along with the native *P. pinaster* and *P. halepensis.* Pines from the southeastern United States are now being evaluated, with some promising results.

Eucalypts are planted on a large scale in southern Italy, France, Portugal, and on the islands of the Mediterranean. The same species are grown as on the Iberian peninsula, and *E. occidentalis* and *E. viminalis* are also used.

Poplars are very important in Italy. In 1967, they occupied only 6% of the forest area but provided 40% of the industrial wood (FAO, 1967). Most of these poplar plantings, as well as others in southern and central Europe, the northeastern United States, and Argentina, involve hybrids that qualify as exotics. The usual hybrid parents are European black poplar (*Populus nigra*) and American eastern cottonwood (*P. deltoides*) (Wright, 1976).

In the Balkan countries and farther east, most of the plantations are established with native trees. In the colder parts, some use is made of the same exotics that are used in central Europe. In Romania, there is still a certain interest in Weymouth pine (Radu, 1974). Both Greece and Turkey have areas planted with eucalypts, mainly *E. camaldulensis,* and other exotics such as *Pinus radiata* are used.

Northeastern North America. There are a number of excellent native species in this part of the world, and they satisfy most industrial needs. Large numbers of trials with exotics have been planted, but with only limited effects on forestry. Many species have become popular park trees and ornamentals and the important Christmas tree industry uses a number of exotics, such as Douglas-fir and Scots pine. Results indicate that for plantation forestry there may be some future for European and Japanese larch, larch hybrids, and perhaps also Norway spruce (Hall, 1982; Carter et al., 1981; Einspahr et al., 1984).

Southeastern United States. This region has a very unique climate with hot summers, while the winters, although mainly moderate, sometimes have sudden periods of very cold weather with dramatic fluctuations in temperature over a short period. Very few exotics have been able to withstand such a climate and still grow well enough to compete with the native trees, which include species such as loblolly and slash pine, themselves widely used as exotics. One possible exception is European black alder, which is used in restoring strip-mined areas and grows very rapidly on poor sites. Possibly some eucalypts will also be able to grow satisfactorily along the Gulf of Mexico and in Florida (Hunt and Zobel, 1978), but severe freezes in recent years have reduced interest in developing suitable cold-hardy land races of eucalypts.

Northwestern North America. As was mentioned several times, northwestern North American is a major donor region for the temperate zone, the home of many outstanding species such as Douglas-fir, Sitka spruce, and lodgepole pine. The superb native species outgrow all of the exotics that have been tried and there is very little interest in making trials with exotics.

Southwestern North America. Generally, exotics have not been successful when compared to the native trees, but many have been tried. Some, like the eucalypts, have been widely planted for wood production, but most exotics like *Acacia* have been used mainly for ornamentals or for urban or conservation purposes. Several exotic genera, such as *Acacia* and *Tamarix,* have become serious pests. Radiata pine, the most widely planted of all exotic pines, is native to the California coast. A number of other species from this area have limited use as exotics throughout the world.

Northern Japan. Hokkaido, the most northern of Japan's main islands, has a climate similar to the northeastern United States, and a very large number of indigenous tree species, both conifers and broad-leaves. In spite of this, several exotic species such as Norway spruce and white pine have been superior in introduction trials and are widely planted on the island.

Northern China and Korea. Very extensive forest plantations have been established in this part of the world. Although most of them have been with native species, which are numerous, several hybrid as well as exotic poplars are used. Farther south, the Chinese are using various *Eucalyptus,* including *E. exserta* and *E. citriodora* (Matthews, 1979), and are widely testing several species from North America, such as *Pinus taeda* and *P. elliottii.* The number of exotic species tried by the Chinese is very large, but it is difficult to determine which of these are really of importance in operational forestry.

In Korea, the hybrid of two exotic pines, loblolly and pitch pine, is planted on a large scale. The F_1 hybrids were produced by controlled pollination made possible by low-cost labor. On poor sites with severe frost, a common situation in Korea, the hybrids grow better than pitch pine and are less damaged by frost than loblolly pine (Hyun, 1976; Little and Trew, 1976) (Fig. 7.3). F_2 and later hybrids have also been produced; they are fast growing and reasonably

Figure 7.3 The pitch × loblolly hybrid grows well on environments too severe for the loblolly parent. Exact parents used to make the cross are important. Shown is a good hybrid of pitch × loblolly pine grown on a severe site in West Virginia.

uniform (Wright, 1976). Numerous other exotics have been grown in Korea, such as the poplars and even radiata pine, but the one most noted is the hybrid pine, *P. rigida* × *P. taeda*.

New Zealand, South Africa, and parts of Australia. New Zealand still has a large area of natural forest, which is mainly found in inaccessible mountains and usually consists of mixed hardwoods. There are no fast-growing indigenous conifers. Very large plantations of exotic forests have been established in recent years, mainly in the north. More than 85% of the plantations are in a single highly successful exotic species, radiata pine, but numerous other conifers and eucalypts also grow well.

Similarly, a great many exotic species can grow well in the cooler and higher-elevation portions of South Africa and Australia. Like parts of New Zealand, these regions are in the "gray zone" between temperate and subtropical climates. As a result, numerous exotic species from the milder climates grow well, some extraordinarily fast with good form. It is in these areas where the person growing exotics is hard-pressed to choose the best.

Foresters in these areas are well aware of the risks and dangers of monocultures (see Chapter 5). Regardless, as in New Zealand, they see no real alternatives to growing mainly radiata pine. The situation is explained and defended by Burdon (1982), who gives several reasons why disasters will not occur. Among Burdon's explanations are: radiata pine occurs naturally in even-aged stands; it is very well adapted to New Zealand conditions; it is so productive and economically important that it can carry expensive protection measures; strict quarantine restrictions are possible and have been enforced; intensive management and short rotations will make it easier to check diseases and insects; a full range of the genetic variation within radiata pine is available; and vegetative propagation methods and tree improvement are well advanced and can be used to develop and multiply resistant strains if necessary. If a disaster should occur in radiata pine, a number of other species have shown potential. The best of these are Douglas-fir, Corsican pine, and ponderosa pine; their growth is promising, but they have not been as healthy as radiata pine. Trials of numerous alternative species are ongoing. *Eucalyptus* has been more widely tried and has potentials in the cooler, higher areas as well as being extensively used in the more subtropical climates.

Southern South America. Argentina, southern Brazil, and Chile have large-scale exotic plantation forestry, but mainly in the more subtropical northern regions. Radiata pine, slash pine, and loblolly pine are widely planted and trials with Mexican and Central American species exist. A number of eucalypts and poplars are also grown. Conditions here are very similar to those outlined earlier for New Zealand, South Africa, and Australia. A host of exotic species can be grown in the very wide variety of generally favorable climates in the area. Suitable environments are available in which a large number of exotics can be grown. For example, some of the fastest growth of pine anywhere is found in Chile. It is a paradise for foresters interested in growing exotic forest tree species.

7.5 LODGEPOLE PINE IN SWEDEN: A CASE EXAMPLE

Lodgepole pine was probably first introduced to Sweden around 1875. A number of plantations were established during the first 40 years of this century. Most were regular plantations, usually with seed from unknown origins; however, some plantings were made to compare a few known provenances. For a number of years after that, the interest in lodgepole pine in Sweden waned.

Evaluations of the early trials in the 1960s showed how fast growing the species was and resulted in large-scale production plantations being established from 1967 onward (Fig. 7.4). As of 1986, the annual planting of lodgepole pine was around 35,000 ha, all in the northern part of the country, from 60 degrees north latitude up. Since around 1965, research on the species has been intensive. Numerous papers and books have been published covering the use of lodgepole pine as an exotic, such as by the International Workshop on Lodgepole Pine, along with those, such as Martinsson (1983), that discuss the problems and potentials for use of lodgepole pine in Sweden.

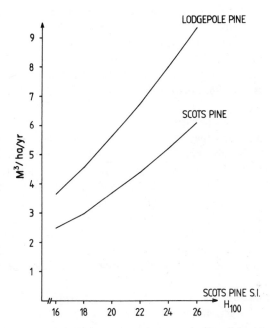

YIELD CAPACITY OF SCOTS PINE AND LODGEPOLE PINE ON GIVEN SITE INDICES IN INTERIOR NORTHERN SWEDEN.

Figure 7.4 Growth of lodgepole pine (*P. contorta*) as compared to Scots pine (*P. sylvestris*) in northern Sweden is shown. Note the superiority of the exotic (From Zobel and Talbert, 1984).

7.5.1 Site Factors

Pinus contorta has an unusual ecological amplitude with regard to both climate and soils. It grows from Baja California (31°N) to the Yukon (64°N), from sea level to almost 4000-m altitude in the Sierra Nevada (Critchfield, 1978). It is not surprising that a species with such a widespread distribution is highly variable. In fact, Critchfield distinguishes five different subspecies. Of these, the subsp. *latifolia* from interior British Columbia and the Yukon is the important one for planting in Sweden. The only other subspecies included in many Swedish trials, subsp. *contorta* (shore pine from the Pacific coast), has not been successful. When not stated otherwise, lodgepole pine and *P. contorta* will refer to the subsp. *latifolia*.

The forests in the main areas of interest, where seed will be collected, in interior British Columbia and the Yukon to a large extent contain virgin timber. Man, or at least the forester, has had very little to do with their development. Only rather recently has lodgepole pine become an important raw material for industry, and in most of the northern parts of its distribution there are few people and very little forest industry. It is difficult to find lodgepole pine plantations older than 25 years, and there are probably more seedlings of the species produced and planted in Sweden than in Canada.

Picea mariana and *P. glauca,* together with jack and lodgepole pines, dominate the forest regions in North America where lodgepole pine occurs just as Norway spruce and Scots pine do in Sweden. Much of the flora, from lichen and mosses through bushes and trees, are similar or identical in Canada, Alaska, and Sweden. As an example, the floral symbol for Yukon, fireweed (*Epilobium angustifolium*), also colors most Swedish clear-cuts every summer.

7.5.1.1 Climate. The areas of interest in Canada have a climate similar to that in central and northern Sweden. Although the annual average temperatures are similar, the differences between summer and winter temperatures are larger, that is, the climate is more continental in Canada. Precipitation in much of British Columbia is similar to northern Sweden, being about 600 mm per annum. However, there are areas, mainly in the Yukon, which are much drier and receive only 250–300 mm of rainfall per year. Whereas Sweden often gets considerable heavy, wet snow, most of the pine's native area only has a little light and dry snow. The western slopes of the Rocky Mountains have much higher precipitation than the rest of the area where lodgepole pine occurs.

7.5.1.2 Soil. The soils of the donor and receptor areas are quite similar. In the river valleys, lodgepole pine is dominant on the often extensive sandy sediments just as Scots pine is in Sweden. In both countries there are also large, flat, and dry pine moors. Sandy-loamy moraine is the most common soil in both countries, and here spruce forests dominate. On the moister sites, often a thick humus layer is produced. In parts of northern Canada deep permafrost is common.

7.5.1.3 Forest Fires. Forest fires are an essential part of the ecology of the native lodgepole pine forests in Canada. Without fire, the pines are usually suppressed by the spruces after 100–150 years. On heavier soils, permafrost starts to appear once the spruces have shaded the ground, and this will result in the decline of the pines.

Particularly in drier areas, fires are relatively common. The pine has managed to adapt to this. It starts producing seed when it is only 5–10 years old. Most cones are serotinous and adhere to the branches for many years, and they will only open to release their seed after having been exposed to high temperatures, such as when fires sweep through the stands. Large quantities of seed then fall to a very suitable germination environment, also provided by the fire, and very dense regeneration results. It is often so dense that it prevents normal tree development.

Forest fires are today very much more common and burn much more of the forests every year in Canada than in Sweden. This partly results from the sparser human population, who do not have the potential of controlling the fires effectively. However, the more humid climate in much of Sweden probably explains most of the difference in fire occurrence.

7.5.2 Provenance Effects

The provenances used for the earliest plantations in Sweden were often unknown or were obtained too far south. A high frequency of both climate-related and other damages occur in these plantations. It became clear about 1975 that for northern Sweden, seed should not be collected much farther south in Canada than 55 degrees north latitude.

To illustrate the very strong effect of provenance on growth, survival, and plant health in Sweden we have chosen a test from an extreme northern trial, in Nattavaara (66°47'N, 425 m above sea level), as reported by Rosvall (1984) and illustrated in Fig. 7.5. The Nattavaara trial was planted in June 1974, after manual patch scarification, on an area clear-cut in 1971. Four replications, each with 8 × 8 one-year-old containerized seedlings of a number of lodgepole and Scots pine provenances were planted. Data were collected in 1982. Sur-

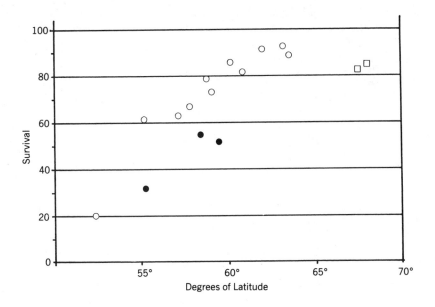

○ *Pinus contorta* var. *latifolia*   ● *P. contorta* var. *contorta*   □ *P. sylvestris*

Figure 7.5 The relationship between origin and survival eight years after planting for *Pinus contorta* var. *latifolia*, *P. contorta* var. *contorta*, and *P. sylvestris* at Nattavaara, Sweden (66°47'N, 425 m asl), is shown. Note the inferiority of the var. *contorta* and the better survival of the more northerly sources.

vival figures refer to survival among plants living the fall of the planting season, which avoids nursery and planting effects.

The very clear differences in this trial of Scots and lodgepole pine are rather typical for trials this far north. The most northern sources of the exotic were best for all of the characteristics that were observed. The survival data shown in Fig. 7.6 can serve as a basis for recommendations for provenance selection. The superiority of the subsp. *latifolia* over subsp. *contorta* is also clearly indicated in the figure.

The next question after survival is how well the lodgepole pine grows compared to the best Scots pine provenances; this is illustrated in Fig. 7.6, along with survival and frequency of leaning trees for the two species. The Scots pine values are the average of the two best provenances and the lodgepole pine value is the average for the three northernmost lodgepole pine provenances. It is of importance that one only rarely can find Scots pine seed to use in areas this far north.

Lodgepole pine had both better growth and better survival than the native Scots pine. However, the frequency of leaning trees was higher for the exotic. This seems to be true in many trials and plantations and probably results from the normally smaller root system of lodgepole pine.

Diseases, climate-caused damage, and other pests were also checked and evaluated. The results from the Nattavaara trial will be discussed after a general presentation of pests, diseases, and other threats that occur in growing lodgepole pine as an exotic.

A series of provenance tests similar to the one described have been widely planted and evaluated and complemented with other studies (Stahl, 1982). The

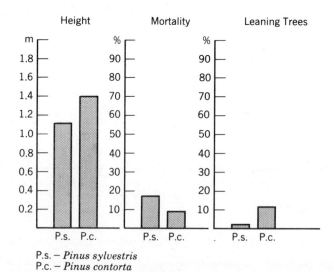

P.s. – *Pinus sylvestris*
P.c. – *Pinus contorta*

Figure 7.6 The comparison between survival, height, and frequency of leaning trees for *Pinus contorta* and *Pinus sylvestris* at Nattavaara, Sweden (66°47'N, 425 m asl), are shown. Note that the exotic was taller and had less mortality, but more lean, than the indigenous Scots pine.

present recommendations are summarized in Fig. 7.7. Seed collection areas with provenances which show similar characteristics when tested in Sweden are marked on a map of northwestern Canada. Planting sites in Sweden are defined by their latitude and elevation, two factors that give a general indication of the environment. The best provenance areas in Canada for use in each planting area in Sweden are indicated.

7.5.3 Pests: Diseases, Insects, and Other

The general health situation for lodgepole pine in Sweden has been described by Karlman (1984). The following is a very brief summary of her concepts.

Weather damage has caused only minor damage to provenances that are

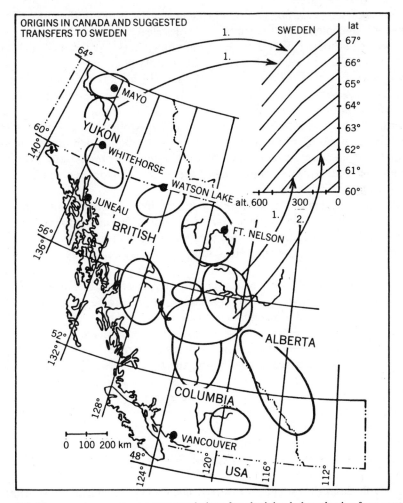

Figure 7.7 The present provenance recommendations for obtaining lodgepole pine from western North America to use in Sweden are illustrated in this map.

well adapted to their sites. In extreme sites or when provenances are not hardy, several kinds of damage have been observed. The most serious result of weather damage is that it predisposes the trees to infections by secondary pathogens, mainly *Gremmeniella abietina*. Additionally, the more bushy branches of the exotic make it more prone to top and branch breakage when the trees become covered with heavy snow or ice. Also, the dense crowns combined with a relatively small root system make *Pinus contorta* sensitive to windthrow. This may well become quite serious when the plantations grow taller and are more exposed to strong winds (Martinsson, 1982b).

Insect damage to the exotic lodgepole pine is limited even though 60 different species of insects have been found on it in the Nordic countries. Neither in Finland (Annila et al., 1983) nor in Sweden (Eidmann, 1982) are insects seen as a serious threat.

Vole damage, caused by two small rodent species, is one of the more serious risks for lodgepole pine plantations. The voles clearly prefer lodgepole to Scots pine and cause damage by debarking the young trees. At times of high vole populations, Scots pine is also eaten. Lodgepole pine has a relatively good capacity to recover from even severe attacks, which Scots pine normally does not. Damage is most severe on sites with dense grass. Severe infection by *Gremmeniella* may follow on the trees weakened by vole attack.

Moose browse less on lodgepole than on Scots pine. On the other hand, they debark stems and branches of the exotic by rubbing their antlers against them; lodgepole pine seems to be preferred. The denser moose and deer populations of southern Sweden are one of the reasons why lodgepole pine is not planted more widely there.

Most of the fungi that attack *Pinus sylvestris* have also been found on *Pinus contorta*. However, the exotic so far seems not to be susceptible to the two major Scots pine diseases, the *Melampsora pinitorqua* rust and the *Lophodermella sulcigena* needle cast. How long this nonsusceptibility will last is a most important question.

Snow blight (*Phacidium infestans*) is the most severe problem for Scots pine regeneration in northern Sweden. This disease appears to be a less severe threat to lodgepole pine plantations, mainly because of their rapid early growth. Snow blight only attacks the plant parts that are covered by snow.

Gremmeniella abietina is a secondary parasite on pines and spruces, causing dieback, cankers, and sometimes killing the trees. Normally, it only attacks trees already weakened by other agents, frost, snow blight, or voles. In many trials of lodgepole pine there seems to be a tendency for severe damage by both *Gremmeniella* and *Phacidium* to decrease with an increasing latitude and altitude of the seed origin.

Some results from pests in the Nattavaara trial are shown in Fig. 7.8. The comparison is made between the two best Scots pine and the three best lodgepole pine provenances.

The vole damage is similar for the two species. However, experience enables us to predict that more of the damaged Scots pines will die from the vole

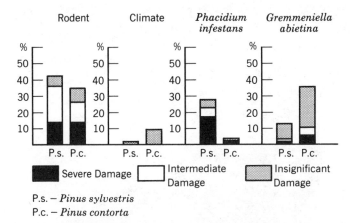

Figure 7.8 Relative damage by pests of *Pinus sylvestris* and *Pinus contorta* at Nattavaara, Sweden (66°47'N, 425 m asl), is illustrated. Note how the exotic is more tolerant to two pests and more susceptible to one pest.

damage. The higher frequency of climate-caused damage and *Gremmeniella* attack on lodgepole pine is somewhat worrying and should serve as a caution in its use. It may be that there will be problems in the future on extremely severe sites, such as at Nattavaara. Perhaps not even the hardiest provenances will be a success there. Only the future will give the answer. The severe snow blight damage to Scots pine explains most of the mortality in this species. The northernmost lodgepole pine provenances are only slightly damaged (Fig. 7.9). On a site such as this, with much snow and long winters, snow blight is certainly of critical importance for reforestation success, and the exotic species has a major advantage.

7.5.4 Silvicultural Characteristics

7.5.4.1 Growth and Yield. *Pinus contorta* is capable of 40–60% higher yield than the native pine, depending upon site quality (Hägglund et al., 1979).Remröd (1977) suggests that optimum rotations for lodgepole pine may be 15–20 years shorter than for Scots pine. The superior growth of the exotic is shown in Fig. 7.4. Very little land in northern Sweden has a Scots pine site index higher than H_{100} 24 m. On the very best sites and on much land farther south, where the average site quality is higher, Norway spruce can probably compete successfully with lodgepole pine.

The excellent growth and the possibility to work with shorter rotations is a strong temptation for Swedish forestry, which is faced with a severe shortage of mature forests in the early twenty-first century. This is definitely the main reason for the interest in planting the exotic lodgepole pine.

Figure 7.9 Very clear provenance differences can be found in extreme climates. The picture shows lodgepole pine at Nattavaara, Sweden (66°47'N, 425 m above sea level). To the left is a tree from a suitable provenance, West Summit Lake, Yukon (63°03'N, 740 m asl), and to the right a too southern and not hardy provenance from Blueberry River, B.C. (56°35'N, 860 m above sea level).

7.5.4.2 Tree Size and Form. Lodgepole pine is not a big tree, rarely 30 m tall, and quite slender. How much of this is caused by the often very dense natural stands is hard to say; 5,000–10,000 stems per ha in older stands is not uncommon. Very little information is available from Canada on the growth of lodgepole pine in planted and thinned stands. What little there is and the few older stands in Scandinavia seem to indicate a normal response to wider spacing with an increase in diameter and denser crowns. The trees maintain their straight stems and relatively narrow crowns under plantation conditions. How much tree diameter can be increased by controlled stocking is not known, but it is considerable.

7.5.4.3 Response to Silvicultural Treatments. It is an advantage when the exotic can be treated similarly to the native species. Lodgepole pine in Sweden is managed in much the same way as Norway spruce and Scots pine. Nursery procedures, planting methods, and spacing and thinning intensity are all similar. As more experience is gained, this will probably change to silvicultural manipulation especially suited to the exotic.

The stability of the trees to wind, snow, and ice is an example of conditions that may make changes necessary. As previously mentioned, lodgepole pine is somewhat unstable. The easiest way to avoid windthrow is not to plant the exotic in areas that are particularly exposed to hard winds or where heavy snow or icing often occurs. Soil texture and depth also influence root growth and stability, so the prudent forester would not plant lodgepole pine on soils with a fine texture or on shallow soils. Plants produced from direct seeding have a better-developed root system than do planted seedlings. One can then use direct seeding instead of planting, or develop a new plant system, which will enable lodgepole pine to develop a better root system, resulting in more stable plantations.

There is genetic variation as to how well root systems develop. Martinsson (1982b) indicates that there are provenance differences in root characteristics, and this could certainly be utilized. The selection of individual superior genotypes that also have the desired root pattern is complicated but feasible.

New scarification or site preparation methods can perhaps be developed that will result in greater stability. An environment that is advantageous to the production of a more stable root system can be created. A number of other changes such as the timing and intensity of thinnings, rotation length (the taller the tree, the more storm exposed), pruning to limit crown size, and the like, would also be possible to help stabilize lodgepole pine. Not until more information on the actual risk becomes available will it be known how much new research and development will be needed and justified to prevent the blowing over or leaning of trees.

Lodgepole pine, like many good exotics, responds strongly to more intensive silvicultural treatment, as shown by a trial with different site preparation methods (Lundmark, 1984). The trial site is extremely difficult (67.6°N, 300 m asl), with poor soil, cold, and exposed. Lodgepole and Scots pines were planted on three increasingly intensive site preparations: unscarified soil, mounding (planting in a small mound of upturned soil), and on a ridge created with a heavy forest plow. Both soil temperature and availability of plant nutrients increase with the increase in site preparation intensity. One of the results is shown in Fig. 7.10. Both species respond when the site preparation intensity increases, but the exotic's response is much greater.

7.5.5 Wood Characteristics

Rapid tree growth or good health and survival are not enough for an exotic to be successful. It must also produce the kind of wood desired. A major problem is that the quality of the wood often cannot be determined until the

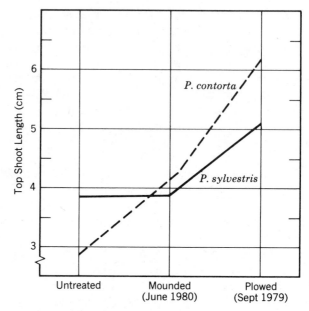

Figure 7.10 Top shoot length in 1983 for two years is shown after plantings where three different site preparation treatments were used. Note the height superiority of the exotic on the intensively prepared site and its inferiority where site preparation was minimal.

trees have reached a considerable age or size. Larch in Sweden is a good example of an exotic which, in spite of acceptable growth and good health, has never become popular because its wood is difficult both to saw and to pulp.

Most of the present knowledge about exotic lodgepole pine wood properties has been summarized by Persson (1985). Results are mainly based on trees from 35- to 50-year-old Swedish plantations. Wood information from native pines in Canada is of very little value. The very dense and slow-growing stands there produce a wood much different from that of the vigorous, rather open-grown plantations in Sweden.

As far as pulpwood is concerned, the following comparisons between lodgepole and Scots pines can be made when grown in Sweden:

Wood density is similar.

Knot content is higher in lodgepole pine.

Pulp yield in the sulfate process is similar.

Pulp quality is similar.

Lodgepole pine seems to provide a suitable raw material for thermomechanical pulp; Scots pine does not.

The economy of Swedish forestry depends heavily on the production of quality lumber. Andersson made studies in 1976 comparing the lumber of the two pines of similar age (35–50 years) and established that the two species produce similar-quality boards. In both instances the quality from the plantations was very low compared to what is presently cut from natural old-growth stands. The young age and small size of the trees provide only a part of the explanation for this difference. The main reason is the very open stands in which the trees had grown, with rapid early growth and little natural pruning.

The best-grown provenances of lodgepole pine produce thicker and more crooked stems, a similar frequency of double leaders and spike knots, and branches of approximately the same diameter as Scots pine under the same growth conditions. The strength properties of the lumber are slightly lower for the exotic while the permeability for wood preservatives is similar. It is obvious that the trees used for the sawing studies are very young, but the information is the best available.

Artificial pruning makes it possible to produce higher-quality sawn wood on young trees. The higher productivity and shorter rotations of the exotic should make the economy of pruning better for lodgepole than for Scots pine. Pruning trials with the exotic have given mixed results, sometimes very good but other times there has been excessive resin flow and fungal infection. More research is under way on the feasibility of pruning.

7.5.6 Seed Availability and Production

For at least another 10 years all or at least most of the *Pinus contorta* seed used in Sweden will have to be imported from Canada. Three major seed suppliers collect and process the 600–700 kg of seed needed each year. The cones are collected from felled trees or from squirrel caches. The Canadian Forest Service controls the origin of the seed and issues certificates according to OECD regulations. OECD certificates are required for all seed imported into Sweden. So far, no major problems have occurred.

Future demand for higher-quality seed will have to be met by seed production in Swedish seed orchards. Three forest companies have already established around 30 ha of seed orchards using either vegetative material from plus trees in Canada or from young Swedish plantations. For phytosanitary reasons green material can no longer be imported from Canada into Sweden.

The Swedish Forest Service, the National Board of Forestry, and several companies are also cooperating in the establishment of almost 100 ha of new seed orchards. Seedling seed orchards will be established for each of six climatic zones in northern Sweden. The seed was collected from a number of good parent trees in six zones in British Columbia and the Yukon. The program is described in detail by Rosvall (1982) from parent tree selection and orchard design, via testing, to seed production. As the Swedish plantations grow older, a regular tree improvement program with plus tree selection will be started.

One of the major disadvantages of the indigenous Scots pine in northern Sweden is its poor seed production. Many years pass between good seed crops.

This makes natural regeneration via seed trees a slow and unreliable method. It also makes it very hard to collect and store enough seed for seedling production. Scots pine seed orchards have been established since the 1950s, but they will not supply enough seed for the extreme north for many years. The possibility of obtaining seed from Canada and the expectation of early Swedish orchard seed production, plus the fact that lodgepole pine starts flowering at a younger age than Scots pine, all increase the interest of the Swedish foresters in the exotic.

7.5.7 Conclusion of the Lodgepole Pine Example

A number of reasons exist for the Swedish fondness for the exotic lodgepole pine. Its superior growth, good survival, and the possibility to obtain seed are the most important. Another essential reason is that with three, rather than two, coniferous species, the foresters will be able to utilize more completely the whole spectrum of site conditions.

Doubts remain, based upon the general uncertainty of what can happen to an exotic from diseases or pests. The problem of the stability of the trees and their relatively small root system will need to be resolved. The authors would be very surprised if a silvicultural or genetic solution to this problem could not be found. A final uncertainty applies to the plantations where there are extremely difficult climates. The experience there is still too limited.

Present forestry legislation in Sweden restricts the total annual *Pinus contorta* plantations to 35,000 ha per annum. Recommendations are given regarding where to plant the species, and planting is prohibited in the southern part of the country.

The future for lodgepole pine is bright in northern Sweden. As more experience is gained and if no catastrophic event occurs, current restrictions will be reduced. More trials will show if this exotic has a future in the south. Norway spruce is a very strong competitor there, and several possible diseases and insects, plus dense populations of moose and deer, make the future of lodgepole pine hard to predict in the southern part of Sweden.

8

GENE CONSERVATION
AND EXOTIC FORESTRY

8.1 THE NEED TO MAINTAIN VARIATION

Foresters that grow exotics must develop their species in two directions. On the one hand, there is a need to improve quality and reduce variation in economically important properties such as good growth, desirable wood, and good tree form. Gains result from having a more uniform product, and the industry is striving to achieve that goal both through increasing uniformity among forest trees as well as by developing better manufacturing technology.

On the other hand, diversity must be maintained in the tree's ability to adjust to different climates, pests, and silvicultural manipulations that will be encountered in the new environment; it also means retaining the ability to grow different phenotypes (Fig. 8.1). Without sufficient diversity a long-range and efficient exotic forestry program established in many different environments and for many different products will fail. As emphasized by Wilcox (1982) "Diversity is the key to maintaining the functional integrity of natural ecosystems and thus their capacity to provide resources on a sustainable basis." He goes on to discuss the three main problems related to preserving biological diversity. This need for diversity is especially true where the imported genetic material may be only marginally adapted to the new site. As emphasized by Brune and Zobel (1981) for *Eucalyptus* in Brazil, "To make the desired type gains for either the short or long term, a proper gene base is needed." Speaking about gene conservation in general terms, Namkoong (1984b) emphasizes its need in well-studied and widely used species but also in currently unimportant species that may ultimately become useful, supply needed genes, or be a part of an important supporting ecosystem.

Figure 8.1. Variability must be maintained through gene conservation. Although it now has little economic value, the "globe spruce" shown might someday be desired. These unique Norway spruce growing in Norway develop into small, rounded bushes.

How can both these objectives be achieved? It is, of course, obvious to even the most casual observer that perfection will never be obtained and that improvement in some traits will be made at the expense of improvement in others. But, as so strongly emphasized by Zobel and Talbert (1984), it is possible to come closer to the ideal in forest trees than in most organisms because of the relative genetic independence of major traits, especially those for economic characteristics and those for adaptability and pest resistance. This enables the forester to incorporate desired characteristics, such as fast growth or straightness of tree bole, into well-adapted populations. It is possible, for example, to develop straight pines that are also drought tolerant, or fast-growing eucalypts that are resistant to bole canker. This "independent" inheritance of important tree characteristics enables one to tailor-make the type of tree desirable for the short term and for the specific conditions needed to grow it as a successful exotic in the long term.

The long-run situation is complex, however, and to be successful, *variation in characteristics* needs to be maintained even above and beyond those that have immediate value, especially for adaptability. For example, it is hard to visualize why there would be a need to preserve the characteristics for crooked tree growth if straight trees are available. But it is very evident that there is need to preserve gene complexes that allow the species to adjust to changing environments or pests, either those that are now known and occur naturally or those that are the result of man's or nature's actions and have not yet appeared. It is sufficient to say that it is essential to preserve available genetic components for possible later needs.

The need for conservation has been emphasized by many persons. For example, in the book *Tropical Trees*, edited by Burley and Styles (1976), there is a whole section on exploration and conservation, with five papers covering various aspects related to tropical trees. Although only a few of the species involved are now used as exotics, more will be; the problems and concepts covered apply to gene conservation in places other than the tropics. The need is best summarized by Holdridge (1976) relative to the situation in Central America:

> . . . man appears about ready to start exerting a strong force to eliminate tree species. . . . Shifting cultivation is widespread . . . as stimulated by rising export prices for beef, a widespread elimination of forests and their replacement by grasslands [will occur] in a broad range of climates and on an extensive spectrum of soils.

The biological concepts of conservation were covered by Wilcox (1982) in a symposium held in Georgia and entitled "Natural Diversity and Forest Ecosystems."

The effort to preserve genetic material is called *gene conservation* or, by some, *gene preservation*. If exotic forestry is to continue to make progress, it is necessary both to preserve the genetic material now present and, by astute breeding, to increase variability. Foresters and laymen usually use the term *gene conservation*, but this is somewhat misleading. Almost all economically important tree characteristics are controlled by different alleles often found at several gene loci. An important characteristic of forest trees may occasionally be under the control of a single gene, but this is the exception. The most common examples of single gene control are tolerance to diseases; an example is tolerance to the leaf blight *Didymascella thujina* in *Thuja* (Soegaard, 1969). In fact, the so-called gene conservation efforts usually involve conservation of the *gene complexes* that make a tree economically desirable and adaptable (Zobel, 1978). The gene complex *does not* equate to the genotype of the individual; it relates to the combined gene action or actions that determine specific traits. *The conservation and use of gene complexes is the key to progress in exotic forestry.*

Conservation often is used in a broad context, such as preserving provenances. For example, in FAO Bulletin No. 12, *Forest Genetic Resources* (1983), the need to preserve provenance material is emphasized. It is urged to "take steps for safeguarding all stands from which provenance collections are made." In India, for example, a directive has been given to demarcate all the valuable sources on the ground and ensure that the gene resource is conserved properly for future use.

Efforts in gene conservation have been under way for many years in agriculture. Much of this work has been summarized in five separate chapters by Hawkes et al. (1983) in their bibliography of crop genetic resources. Some of the general concepts and methodologies they describe are of considerable interest to foresters.

It is necessary to preserve genetically variable material for possible future use, as outlined earlier. But often overlooked is the other major objective of keeping a broad genetic base: to prevent relatedness as a tree improvement program matures. Almost all studies have shown that high relatedness is associated with low seed production and/or germinability, low vigor of the trees produced, and sometimes with the loss of the ability to withstand severe environments.

The need to maintain genetic variability, when added to the need to avoid relatedness, makes gene or gene complex preservation a most important function. In the past, the attention of conservationists has focused mainly on the preservation of ecosystems and endangered species. Conservation of within-species and within-provenance genetic diversity has often been neglected (Davidson, 1983b) but is of critical importance.

Agricultural literature is replete with methods and attempts to preserve genetic material; an example is *Collection of Crop Germplasm—The First Ten Years (1974–1984)* by IBPGR (1985) (International Board for Plant Genetic Resources). Emphasis of this kind for gene conservation in forest trees is relatively new and small scale by comparison with agricultural crops. Two recent publications by IBPGR (1985) will be helpful to those interested in gene conservation. The first volume covers principles and methodologies and the second has specific seed germination information and test recommendations. Although primarily for agricultural crops the techniques will be helpful to the forester, especially for tropical trees. For forest trees, Bonner (1985) outlines methods used to preserve germplasm.

Many papers have been written about gene conservation for genera used as exotics. A few examples are Turnbull (1977), for *Eucalyptus*; Keiding and Kemp (1977), for tropical pines and teak; and Koster (1977), for the poplars. So many have been written for individual tree species that it is not suitable to cite them in this chapter.

8.2 WHAT TO CONSERVE IN EXOTIC TREE SPECIES

Most foresters agree that gene conservation of forest trees requires urgent attention (Burley, 1976; Turnbull et al., 1980). The need for conservation exists in all forestry, but there is a real urgency for conservation of species used as exotics. If not done correctly, and soon, many exotic programs will eventually cease to make progress. A number of provenances of desired exotics that are now being used, or that may be of value at a later time, are being severely depleted genetically or even facing extinction. Thus, every exotic forestry program must have as one of its main objectives the preservation and enhancement of the genetic resources that could be of importance now and in the future.

Not all forest conservation efforts emphasize species that are important for wood production for manufacture. There is a very rapid and rising interest in working with trees for energy, soil conservation, or similar uses. For example, 25 such species have been chosen in Central America for collection of seed by the CFI (OFI) (Hughes, 1984); some of these are nearly depleted of desirable trees. This use for exotics was covered in Chapters 1 and 2; the objective here is to point out that frequently it is the dry-zone species used for nonindustrial purposes like firewood that have the greatest need for gene conservation.

Genetic material of species that have adaptations and characteristics for current needs as well as for future unknown problems must be preserved. The forester must be aggressive in conservation because once a gene pool or gene complex has been lost, it is gone forever. We know of numerous valuable provenances where such depletion is taking place. The question often faced is "which ones" should be saved. Money and resources are not available to concentrate on all groups of trees for which action is needed. Decisions must be made about which provenances are most endangered and which are most worthy of attention.

This difficult question of what should be saved was put into perspective by Pryor (1978b) for the eucalpyts when he said:

> The selection of species in *Eucalyptus* is often a perplexing matter because of the very large number in the genus. Experience has shown that a relatively small number of these, perhaps no more than thirty or forty, meet most needs throughout the world.

Despite the objections of the theorists and idealists who think everything should be conserved, practical considerations dictate that some difficult decisions must be made, including *what* group of trees to concentrate conservation efforts upon. Danger of extinction should be a first priority, but this must be supplemented by the potential value of the endangered trees.

Concern was so great for the Central American conifers that the international Central America · and Mexico Coniferous Resources Cooperative, (CAMCORE), was formed (Gallegos et al., 1983; Dvorak, 1981a, 1984) and included companies and governments from eight nations to help conserve the gene resources of the endangered trees (Fig. 8.2). This means that those genes and gene complexes should be saved that have current or possible future economic value or adaptability needed for successful exotic forestry (Zobel, 1971; 1978). The need was expressed by Barnes (1984) as follows: "Genes will be conserved in usable genotypes rather than in trees of no silvicultural use."

Whether one refers to genes or gene complexes, all agree that the preservation of genetic material is critical if maximum long-term gains are to be achieved (Burley and Namkoong, 1980). There are, of course, differences of opinion about just which complexes should be saved and how large the genetic

Figure 8.2. One magnificent but much endangered species is *Pinus tecunumanii* in Guatemala. The stand pictured, and many like it, has been destroyed for firewood within the past five years. Agencies like CAMCORE and CFI (OFI) are attempting to preserve this species.

base needs to be to achieve this. Some foresters consider gene conservation as saving all possible genes or gene complexes within a given species or race, and others look at it as saving those genes or gene complexes that will be most helpful in long-term operational forestry programs. The former group asks, "Who knows when any given gene or gene complex might become desirable?" and thus tries to save all possible genetic material within the population. Because of space, time, and cost limitations, conservation of *all* genes and gene complexes within a species is usually impossible, but the forester must save as many as possible within the limits of finances, personnel, and space.

Gene conservation as applied to an operational exotic forestry program is different from saving genes for some general but undefined future purpose. Often the objective is the prevention of major gene loss from a species or a provenance of a species. An example, listed by Gordon (1968), is *Picea chihuahuana*, a species remarkably tolerant to high concentrations of calcium, and thus of potential future use for special areas as an exotic. Gordon states: "Its present range and pattern of regeneration indicate that *P. chichuahuana* may not long escape extinction." Several other tree species fall into this category, such as the endangered *Abies guatemalensis* (Dvorak, 1984; Donahue et al., 1985), which has future potential for Christmas trees or wood production.

The problem usually faced is not the extinction of an entire species, but rather the severe reduction of the genetic worth of a part thereof (Nikles, 1978; Kleinschmit, 1979b; Dvorak, 1984). Such a danger of loss for *Eucalyptus*, was reported by Turnbull (1977), who stated that none of the approximately 450 species that exist in the genus are in danger of extinction, but a few are definitely faced with extreme genetic impoverishment.

A similar situation occurs in Central America, where only a few pine species are truly endangered but a large number of species have provenances that are being seriously depleted genetically. Darrow and Coetzee (1983) put it this way for Mexico: "The rapid destruction of Mexico's pine forests by uncontrolled cutting and land clearing has already greatly reduced the genetic base of many species. . . . ." Since tree species from this area are a primary source for planting in South America and other tropical and subtropical regions, genetic impoverishment in Mexico and Central America has very great economic and biological importance (Fig. 8.3).

8.2.1 Where Should Action Be Concentrated?

It is axiomatic that gene conservation is needed where stands of desirable species or provenances are endangered because of conversion to agriculture, timber harvesting, fuelwood collection, fires, pest attack, or grazing. But the distribution of the species concerned is also important when making a decision as to what should be saved. For example, the presence of primary and secondary centers for genetic variation have previously been mentioned in Chapter 2 in relation to where to select. They are also of key importance in considerations of gene conservation.

Figure 8.3. Although it is illegal to cut large live trees for firewood in the country where this photograph was taken, the local people need fuelwood and reduce the forest anyhow. The next step is farming and grazing, and then there will be no future pine forest.

Since wild species vary the most genetically near their center of origin (Vavilov, 1930), these areas are of special interest to gene conservation for exotics. According to Moore and Janick (1983), it is important to get representative samples for future use from the center of diversity (Harlan, 1971). The unfortunate situation is that, with few exceptions, the centers of germplasm resources of most plants are threatened with genetic exhaustion or extinction (Frankel and Bennett, 1970). This is not as true for forest trees as it is in agriculture, but the trend in this direction is clear.

The greatest danger of genetic loss in tree species used as exotics occurs in the donor populations for species with restricted ranges or with those having disjunct populations (Fig 8.4). This danger exists especially for unusual ecotypes on unusual sites, and sometimes applies to entire restricted endemic species. If such populations are not conserved, not only will genes or gene complexes be endangered, but entire unique populations and species could be lost. We know of three pine species in Mexico—*P. rzedowski*, *P. maximartinezii*, (Perry, in press) and *P. culminicola* (Passini, 1982)—that are threatened by wood cutting, domestic animals, and attacks of insects and diseases. There are also two in Guatemala—*P. donnel-smithii* and *P. quichensis* (Aguilar, 1961)—where only a few trees are left in the species (Fig. 8.5).

Loss of provenances of both conifers and hardwoods, some of which have nearly disappeared in the last few years (Dvorak and Perry, personal communication), has occurred in the Central American area. The seriousness of the potential losses in Mexico and Central America was inventoried (Anon, 1981b); the major reason listed was rapid human population growth. This region contains species of forest trees used widely as exotics that have tremendous genetic diversity, which are now in danger of being reduced or lost.

Figure 8.4. Some species have very restricted ranges. When farming or logging are followed by fire, as will occur in this stand of *Pinus caribaea* var. *bahamensis*, whole provenances and subspecies can be lost. The location shown is on an island in the Bahamas.

Figure 8.5. *Pinus donell-smithii* is one of the endangered species; it is found at high elevations in Central America. The tree is beautiful and may have value for high-elevation forestry, but only scattered trees remain.

There are many species and sources that are presently not in danger—one example is *Eucalyptus grandis* (Burgess, 1983)—but these must still be watched carefully. Some like *E. grandis* and *Pinus taeda* and some of the tropical pines have been effectively preserved by widespread testing and breeding programs in many countries. One problem mentioned by Burgess is contamination of indigenous provenances through the planting of nonindigenous sources. A good knowledge of a species used as an exotic is necessary to assess the potential dangers of gene losses.

The need for gene conservation for exotic forestry programs is especially critical in the dry tropical areas where the only economically acceptable source of energy is firewood (Wood, 1976; Roche, 1979). Wood gatherers systematically cut the trees closer to their villages, leaving very few trees behind (Fig. 8.6). Because these areas are usually hot and dry, fires are frequent; they are heavily grazed, the soils are poor, and forest regeneration on the exposed sites too often is unsatisfactory.

An attempt is often made to farm the cutover areas, which destroys any remaining seed sources or young trees. Grazing almost always occurs, usually accompanied by fire that destroys any new trees that might have become established. Goats and sheep can be among the worst enemies to trees important as exotics. Thirgood (1983) makes the statement that goats and forests do not mix, and we frequently hear it said and have observed that goats and sheep are the major source of danger to forest regeneration. These animals fre-

Figure 8.6. In much of the tropics, cutting for firewood is a major cause of endangered species. Trees are cut nearest villages whose people are totally dependent on wood as an energy source. Destruction of genetic material can be complete. A large group of people are involved in harvesting firewood, as in Guatemala.

quently prevent reestablishment of trees in cutover areas and thus create a real problem for gene conservation (Zobel, 1967).

Loss of genes and gene complexes by destruction of forest species of value as exotics, caused by shifting agriculture, is becoming more widespread (King, 1979). Especially in the tropical regions, whenever roads are made through the forests, an "army" of colonists usually follows (Fig. 8.7). After the forests are cut, the land is farmed for a short time; it is then often abandoned when the residual nutrients in the soil are gone or after erosion has removed the topsoil. Frequently, the land then grows back to weedy or worthless plants like palms, which do not develop into useful forests. Loss to shifting agriculture is serious indeed as a destroyer of gene complexes in the donor countries.

Fire, insects, diseases, or storms sometimes cause great destruction with resultant gene loss. Even if a new forest should become established after the disaster, there is sometimes gene loss when the original destruction is so widespread that only small islands of parent trees are left or certain trees cannot become reestablished. In Central America, the senior author has seen fires so large (up to 200,000 hectares) and so severe that only very limited natural tree regeneration could possibly occur. In these same areas bark beetles have killed extensive stands of pine that did not become reestablished because of lack of a seed source. Also, frequent burning to create pastures killed any trees that managed to survive or they were eaten by sheep and goats (Thirgood, 1983).

Figure 8.7. Whenever access is made into the jungle, as by a road, colonists follow. They either use shifting cultivation in the forest or, as illustrated by this photograph taken in Colombia, they cut the very young regeneration, which follows logging, for mine props. This leaves a degraded forest, with a resultant loss of genetic material.

It is in areas subjected to the multiple pressures of firewood cutting, fires, insects, and grazing that the emphasis on gene conservation must be concentrated.

Although used only sparingly as an exotic, perhaps the most notable example of widespread loss of genes in a forest species by disease is the American chestnut (*Castanea dentata*) from eastern North America. The chestnut blight, caused by the introduced fungus *Endothia parasitica*, has almost completely eliminated a once widespread and extremely important species. Only occasional sprouts, which are usually killed before reaching maturity, or a very isolated tree, which is often growing outside the species range, are left. The genes and gene complexes of this species have been so reduced that they essentially have been lost. Attempts to replace American chestnut by the exotic Japanese and Chinese chestnuts (*Castanea*) or by hybrid chestnuts have not been very successful.

Another example of a temperate species where some genotypes are becoming lost is *Abies fraseri*. This species is restricted to a few mountaintops in the southern Appalachians in the eastern United States. Although not used for timber production, it has considerable promise as an exotic that will produce high-quality Christmas trees. Natural stands of Fraser fir are being seriously depleted by the balsam woolly aphid (*Adelges piceae*); this introduced pest frequently destroys entire stands. Although reproduction of this fir by seed can be abundant, the younger stands are often attacked and destroyed before reaching reproductive maturity.

Added to the insect depredations is fume damage and acid deposition (as yet undefined), which damages the young trees as well as killing or seriously damaging the reproductively mature trees. If the genetic resources of Fraser fir are destroyed, it would be a severe loss from biological, economic, and aesthetic standpoints; current trends indicate that this could happen unless a vigorous gene conservation effort is instituted.

Logging activities for lumber or fiber can endanger the gene base when frequent fires or grazing, which prevent regeneration, occur after the trees are harvested. Generally, however, natural regeneration will preserve the gene base, although sometimes in a reduced condition.

A serious but too rarely recognized loss of genes results from selective logging of only a few species, but those of the highest value, from the forest. Many conservationists champion selective logging; although the remaining forest may appear to be intact, severe gene loss of certain species can occur. The lack of regeneration of the removed species results partially from a lack of a suitable seed supply and seedbed for regeneration and from competition from less desirable species that prevent the reestablishment of the one that had been selectively logged. There are a few temperate and numerous tropical species for which gene complex loss resulting from selective logging has been, or will soon become, as critical as if the stands had been clear-cut and farmed or grazed. An example is mahogany in Central America.

8.2.2 Cooperative Action—What Is Being Done

The need for international cooperation in gene conservation efforts as well as in exchange and testing of seed of exotics is urgent. This need is emphasized by everyone who works with exotics; examples are Nikles et al. (1978), Burley and Nikles (1973b), Kemp (1971), and Dvorak (1984). Methods of cooperative testing and its relation to gene conservation were described by Nikles and Newton (1984). One section of the 3rd World Consultation on Forest Tree Breeding was given to the need for cooperative action. For example, Dietrichson and Lines (1977) emphasized the need for the temperate region, and Wood and Greaves (1977) covered the tropical pines. Many foresters have emphasized the need in the tropical hardwoods. All persons interested in gene conservation emphasize that it is not a local problem but requires international cooperation if a disaster is to be prevented. The problem is not a lack of recognition of this need, but that too often the needs are fully discussed but not followed through with action.

Many international efforts are coordinated by organizations such as CFI (OFI), CAMCORE, CSIRO, DANIDA, FAO, IPEF, IUFRO,[1] and others like

---

[1] Acronyms are listed in the appendix to this book.

the Southeast Asian Cooperative in Thailand (Granhoff, 1983). Ten countries from Asia, FAO, and Denmark are supporters of the Southeast Asian Cooperative.

Since the endangered species or provenances are in the donor countries, many of which are developing countries, international cooperation is even more essential. Many of the individual donor countries have neither the incentive, the personnel, nor the financial resources to do the necessary job in gene conservation. It is only right that the receptor countries, which use the exotics, participate in gene conservation in the donor countries.

One of the best efforts in gene conservation has been through FAO and its gene conservation committee, the Committee on Exploration, Utilization and Conservation of Plant Gene Resources. This group has been active for many years. FAO publishes a newsletter and annual report, *Plant Genetic Resources*, which contains some excellent information related to gene conservation, danger areas, and endangered species and any conservation actions under way. Of particular value are the Forestry Occasional Papers entitled *Forest Genetic Resources* which carry excellent summaries of work in progress related to forest gene pool conservation.

Because of the crossing of national boundaries, the long-term payout and its social implications, gene conservation must be strongly governmentally supported. Although gene loss within a species may occur in a local area, it usually has broader implications. Since the loss of genetic material may occur in one country but the endangered species may be used in other countries, it is vital that international organizations take the leadership in gene conservation. Recently, the CAMCORE Cooperative, primarily financed by private industry but strongly cooperating with governments and universities, has become a leader in gene preservation activities in Central America, with the material collected being preserved in several of the eight countries in which the cooperative operates (Gallegos et al., 1983). Organizations such as the Queensland Forest Service have started international cooperatives for the exchange of plant material and for conservation (Nikles and Newton, 1983). Similarly, cooperative tree improvement programs have been established in Australia for *Pinus radiata* (Pederick, 1983; Turnbull and Doran, 1983). The program is handled through a Research Working Group, with a special committee for radiata pine. Similar cooperative programs are in South Africa, (Van der Sijde and Denison, 1983), New Zealand, (Wilcox, 1983), Canada, Europe, and elsewhere.

8.3 METHODS OF CONSERVATION

Many publications deal with the methods that can be used in gene conservation; one example is Roche (1975) and another, for gene bank management, is by Konopka and Hanson (1985). In its bulletin on ecological aspects of development in the humid tropics, the National Research Council (1982) states that there are four devices for conserving genetic diversity: viable seed stored at low temperatures and low humidity, *ex situ* clonal repositories, *in situ* populations in natural reserves, and *in vitro* cell lines. Methods in *ex situ* conservation are described by Wood and Burley (1983); Eldridge (1983) covers several field designs used with *Pinus radiata* for conservation of that species. The general concepts of conservation methodology will be briefly summarized in this section; no attempt is made to cover the subject in detail.

No matter what method is used for gene conservation, the objectives are the same. Therefore, different approaches largely revolve around economics and efficiencies. Also, there is nearly always a large component of politics involved.

As mentioned earlier, gene conservation efforts involving plants usually follow one of two general approaches: *in situ*, meaning preservation of trees and stands in natural conditions, or *ex situ*, which refers to saving the genes or gene complexes under artificial conditions, or at least not in their indigenous environment. In an editorial, Chomchalow (1985) proposes that the term *field gene banks* be used where clonal materials are maintained as living collections in a field, orchard, or plantation.

In situ conservation is most discussed by and has the greatest appeal to persons not involved in land management. It means setting aside and preserving the endangered species to prevent further losses within the desired ecosystem (Fig. 8.8). *In situ* conservation is the only method that conserves both the ecosystem and desired species or population. But it is not easy, as pointed

Figure 8.8. *In situ* conservation includes saving endangered species in their natural environment, as shown for this red spruce at high elevations in the southeastern U.S. Care must be taken to specifically save the endangered species, not merely to set aside forests that are of little value for other purposes.

out by Holdridge (1976). Speaking of small developing nations, where frequently the need is greatest, he says:

> There is little reason to expect that governments of these small nations faced with rapidly expanding populations and diminishing resources can establish and maintain forest reserves with the intention of preserving tree species. I recently read a newspaper article by an autonomous agency official stating his belief that the mere declaration of a reserve by the government appeared to constitute an open invitation to exploitation by the public.

This emphasizes the key point that many of the problems with *in situ* conservation are people problems, not biological problems. Often the pressures for *in situ* conservation come from outside sources who have little or no knowledge of the political or social difficulties of establishing preserves.

Many proponents of *in situ* conservation recommend a complete "hands-off" policy regarding the forest to be conserved, although some people advocate control of fires or pests. The hands-off concept has popular appeal but will not maintain the genetic structure of the population of interest because all forests are dynamic and change with time unless man interferes to keep them in a given condition. When a forest stand is left totally untouched and is not managed, the species and gene complex distribution will change as the forest passes through successive stages of development. This is well illustrated by many conifer forest types which have often been established as the result of some past catastrophic change in ecology caused by fires, tornadoes, hurricanes, farming, or insect attacks. A prime example are the pine stands in the southeastern United States. If these subclimax forests are not managed, they usually will be replaced by hardwoods through natural succession and over time the pine component will be greatly reduced. If it is desired to conserve the gene complexes in the pine stands, the *in situ* reserve must be managed to halt the natural succession to a differing species complex.

A special workshop (U.S. For. Ser., 1982) dealt solely with natural diversity in forest ecosystems. Several speakers made the same emphasis as MacCleary (1982), that forest management is required to maintain natural diversity. He states:

> If society wishes that wilderness contain a diversity of plant and animal communities similar to that which existed in pre-settlement forests, active management is needed. Prescribed fire may prove to be a useful tool for this purpose.

Wilcox (1982) and White (1982) both make similar statements: "The strong conclusion is that active and intelligent management will be required in the protection and enhancement of natural diversity. . . . " (Wilcox, 1982).

If genetic resources are to be conserved using *in situ* methods, the need for protection to keep out woodcutters must be recognized. Local governments are not willing to finance guardians year after year to watch over the area, and the genetic diversity of a reserved area can be depleted in a short period of time (Fig. 8.9).

Large forest stands are not needed for *in situ* conservation, despite the common attitude that the larger the area preserved, the better the situation. Although, certainly, large *in situ* conservation stands are not harmful from the genetic standpoint, they impose an excessive economic burden on the organization supporting the conservation effort. Furthermore, society feels the effects since potentially useful forest products may be less available because of the large areas preserved. The desired gene complexes of a species can normally be conserved with a few thousand trees. If these are managed so they can freely pollinate and regenerate, the desired conservation will be accomplished: there is then no need to set aside huge areas for gene conservation. However, small sites can be more easily damaged or destroyed.

It is not possible to set a desired size for *in situ* conservation because this will vary with the genetics of the species and its occurrence in the forest. As an example, Hedegart (1976) suggests for teak that 10 hectares will include 1000–6000 reproductive individuals, which is sufficiently large to preserve the subpopulations of *Tectona*, especially *T. hamiltoniana* and *T. phillipinensis*.

The need for conservation in the Amazon was recently discussed by Davidson (1983b), who emphasized the complexity of preserving the relatively unknown flora and fauna of Amazonica. This includes some of the better known species like Brazil nut (*Bertholletia excelsa*), which is becoming threatened (Fig. 8.10). Often, great urgency in preservation has been expressed to prevent gene

Figure 8.9. Woodcutters often cause heavy losses in Central American reserves. Small countries often do not have the manpower and funds to protect endangered species, many of which are used for exotics.

Figure 8.10. Particularly susceptible to gene loss are scattered high-value trees, such as those in the jungle. Shown is a Brazil nut tree subjected to very extensive harvesting even though it is legally protected. Too little gene conservation is evident in such situations.

loss in the Amazon, but this has been modified by Moeller (1984), who says that reports of widespread forest devastation in the tropical hardwoods are greatly exaggerated. Certainly, devastation occurs in some localized areas and *in situ* preservation must be immediately instituted there. As Cousteau, quoted by Moeller (1984), stated: "Amazonia cannot be preserved indefinitely; this is pure fantasy."

The effort in the tropical hardwoods was also addressed by Davidson (1983b), who discussed the role of protected areas in Amazonia. He feels that maintenance of within-species diversity must be a major objective of conservation of tree genetic resources in the area. The senior author is familiar with two 20,000 ha *in situ* conservation forests in Brazil under the jurisdiction of Companhia Valle de Rio Doce. These areas will conserve species and geographic sources not yet endangered or widely used as exotics, but which may well become more widely used and endangered with time.

There is confusion about saving forests for gene conservation versus saving them for ecological or aesthetic reasons. Although the latter requires large acreages, this is not necessary for gene conservation per se. One prime current example of such confusion is the Amazon region of Brazil. Recently there have been moves to save huge portions of the tropical forests there as a "gene conservation measure." The larger areas may be necessary for ecological conservation, but a few well-chosen forest stands of moderate size will well serve the gene conservation purpose.

Often the wrong forest stands are saved for *in situ* conservation. Stands in unusual environments, such as in high elevations, are often saved rather than the truly needed or endangered populations. Criteria used to determine what should be saved are often steepness of slope or whether the area is too rough or rocky for logging. These are the wrong reasons for preserving an area.

Contamination of desired indigenous stands by pollination from adjacent planted stands is common in some areas, especially in Europe. In parts of Western Europe, it has been stated that there are no truly indigenous Scots pines because of a complete mixture of the indigenous and nonnative sources of this species that have been established in the area. Sometimes it is desired to save thinned stands of exotics to preserve their genetic composition as desirable land races. This is most difficult because other exotics planted nearby may contaminate the stand that is to be saved. In this light, it has been stated that exotic plantations cannot substitute wholly for natural forest as reservoirs of germplasm since they can already be classified as an agricultural crop (O.T.S., 1984).

Numerous examples could be cited of *in situ* conservation. A few will be mentioned here. One, outlined by Letouzey (1985), refers to plans for widespread *in situ* conservation in Cameroon. Many species were mentioned and discussed, legislation planned, and reserves already established. This area is rich in tropical species, some of which have potential as exotics. Another example, by Ng et al. (1985), outlines the situation in Malaysia, listing the species and areas of interest to be saved.

There are many ways to save desired genes or gene complexes using *ex situ* methods, both in temperate or tropical areas (Guldager, 1975). One method is simply to make plantings of the endangered species. This is done by the CAMCORE Cooperative; such a method is also described by Gibson and Barnes (1985) for *ex situ* conservation of endangered Central American pines. They list seed of species and sources available to those desiring to establish *ex situ* stands.

One example of a well-planned gene conservation effort using the method of planting stands is in South Africa. A local gene conservation program was started in 1985. For each of the six major species of interest (*Eucalyptus grandis*, *Pinus patula*, *P. elliottii*, *P. taeda*, *P. radiata*, and *P. pinaster*) approximately 30 mature stands that were not of seed orchard origin and were scheduled to be harvested are identified for gene conservation. The stands are scattered throughout the areas where the species of interest is being grown. Approximately 50 trees are selected from each of these stands; cones are harvested from them and a bulk seed mixture is made for each stand. Seed are then given to the forest manager in the same area for the establishment of a 5-ha gene conservation stand. A register of these stands is kept and the process will then be repeated near the end of each rotation. Stands will be given only the normal silvicultural treatment and management.

Planting as a method of gene conservation is common and relatively easy, but requires good planning and design (Anon., 1977a). The method of using conservation stands is also described by Willan (1984b).

Another common method is through use of vegetative propagation techniques, including grafting, rooted cuttings, and air layering (Longman, 1976). Foresters have a special opportunity since given genotypes and gene complexes can be conserved for many years using vegetative propagules. Rather than having to save large numbers of trees, a few vegetative propagules of the desired genotypes can be established and maintained.

Using a well-designed crossing program, it is possible to preserve in a few individuals the genetic qualities of trees useful for exotics. Not only the endangered limited gene base can be saved, but new gene combinations can be produced. This is especially essential for land races, which can be preserved in clone banks or seed orchards (Zobel, 1971). Such a packaging, crossing and saving of gene complexes will become increasingly important in exotic forestry as indigenous stands come under greater pressures.

Although use of grafts or cuttings is a common and simple way of *ex situ* gene conservation, it poses some difficult operational problems. Considerable area is required and establishment costs can be high. Although the theory is fine, the question always remains of how one is to convince an organization to protect for many years a currently noneconomically important but threatened species. Large costs are involved and immediate returns are not evident.

As the gene banks grow, how should they be managed? Thinning will become necessary for the maintenance of large healthy crowns to enhance seed production for crossing or production of cuttings for grafting. What thinning regime should be followed, that is, should one save all genotypes or remove those genotypes that tests have shown do not contain the desired genetic characteristics? Such difficult operational decisions are too often not considered when gene banks are recommended.

One common *ex situ* method consists simply of saving seed. This has been extensively used and is successful on species whose seed store well. It is not useful on species that have transient viability, where the seeds lose viability after only a few days or weeks. This problem is common in genera like *Populus* and in many of the tropical hardwood species. A major problem with seed storage is that the seed will ultimately lose viability and will need to be replaced, or mutations will occur in the stored seed so the genetic component from the seed will differ from that of the original population. Problems with seed storage methods are covered in Chapter 5. It is sufficient here to cite Longman et al. (1977), who states that lack of regular flowering, heavy predation of fruit, cones, and seed, and difficulties in retaining viability of seed make seed storage as a method of gene conservation ineffective for some species.

Other *ex situ* methods include pollen storage (Franklin, 1983) and *in vitro* techniques such as tissue culture. The former has the disadvantage that some pollens cannot be stored, and even when successful it represents only "half" of the desired plant. Tissue culture is much discussed and will ultimately have great potential for *ex situ* gene conservation. As expressed by Zobel and Talbert (1984), when this method becomes operational, it will be possible to "store" the potential of large numbers of genotypes in a very small area. This is a hope for the future, but as of now the methodology is uncertain (see Chapter 5).

As pointed our earlier, gene conservation not only refers to individual trees but also to populations of trees, such as provenances. These often possess large and important genetic differences; the first major job of gene complex conservation for the forester working with exotics is to save the unique characteristics of geographic races. Differences among provenances usually result from a few differing gene complexes that give the provenance a unique advantage for growth and survival in a special environment. Different gene combinations often are found in the marginal provenances growing in unique environments of wide-ranging species. These fringe populations contain particularly valuable gene complexes since foresters are being forced to grow trees on marginal sites because of the pressures on land for food production. It is of special interest that Davidson (1983) says:

> Some genetic variability within a species may be obtained by selection of geographic races [provenances] and more by selection among individual trees of a geographic race . . . it is the native populations which contain much variation . . . and it is there conservation of genetic resources must occur.

Conserving gene complexes of exotics for adaptability, although the complexes have no particular immediate use raises some unique questions. For example, should seed be collected randomly or only from phenotypes that likely will be of greatest value as exotics? Since there usually is little genetic correlation between adaptability and tree form and utility, saving only the best phenotypes should not result in a loss of adaptability. Thus, many exotic programs select only the best phenotypes to preserve a provenance (Dvorak, 1984); this method is questioned by some. Regardless, enough trees must be chosen to represent a provenance. It's best to start with more than 200 trees, but this often cannot be done. In their calculations, Namkoong et al. (1980) say that at least 50 individuals should be preserved, and potentials for future use will be greatly reduced when 20 or less individuals are represented.

Every forester working with exotics must be concerned about the fate of genes that are currently neutral or gene complexes that have no known economic importance. An example would be genes that would make a tree resistant to an insect or pathogen which is currently unknown in the plantation or which poses no known threat. A prime example of such a new pest in exotics is the pine woolly aphid (*Pineus pini*), which was introduced into Zimbabwe in 1962 and spread rapidly, attacking nearly all hard pines. Great variation among individual trees in resistance to this pest was found (Barnes et al., 1976).

The authors state that "these provenance trials illustrate the principle of adaptation to plantation and local climatic conditions as insurance against possible catastrophe when a new injurious organism is introduced."

It seems evident because of the loss of suitable stands and the difficulties and costs of *in situ* gene conservation that in the future *ex situ* methods—especially those related to packaging of the desired genes that are preserved by vegetative propagation storage—will be the most widely used method of gene conservation in forest trees. For certain species, seed storage will continue to be used. Although normally not viewed in this way, planting of large blocks of trees with a desired background is a form of *ex situ* conservation.

8.4 GENE CONSERVATION IN TROPICAL SPECIES

Much of the recent emphasis on gene conservation has centered in the tropics; Roche (1979) indicates that the most pressing problems are there. To many people, this means hardwoods in the humid tropics. Actually, many of the most endangered species are in the tropical and subtropical low-rainfall areas. This was addressed by Palmberg (1982; 1983a), who emphasized the seriousness of the problem and listed species for use in the arid and semiarid zones suitable for fuelwood and improvement of rural living. Another example is Nicholson (1981), who covered the conservation status of *Acacia mangium*, one of the more valuable species used as an exotic on poor sites. The problems are severe in Central America, where both conifers and hardwoods have heavy pressures, mostly from fuelwood usage and from overgrazing of cut-over forests (Dvorak and Equiluz,1985). Currently, emphasis is greater on multipurpose trees that are valuable for fuel, food, shade, erosion control, and other uses (Burley et al., 1984).

In its report on tropical deforestation, the Committee on Foreign Affairs of the U.S. House of Representatives (Anon., 1980a) states: "The immediate task before us then is to save as much of our genetic heritage as possible by helping countries identify tropical forest areas which contain maximum concentrations of endangered species." The committee makes the assumption that all tropical species should be considered endangered. In our opinion, this expresses an extreme position. Many of the tropical species of concern are rarely used in exotic programs, but they may have great potential in the future and certainly need to be preserved and studied (Anon., 1982c). Some are used for standard products or fibers (Burley and Styles, 1976), and, as recognized by Roche (1979), trees used for other products, such as energy, chemicals, medicine, or erosion control, also need to be emphasized. One group of trees of special concern is the eucalypts, as covered in a publication by Pryor and Briggs (1981). They state that of the 550 known species in Australia, nearly a quarter are at some risk. The 73 most endangered species are described, as well as 52 other species with very limited distributions that are at risk.

A publication of the National Academy of Sciences (Anon., 1982c) lists problems in the humid tropics. This sizable book covers *in situ*, *ex situ*, and *in vitro* lines of gene conservation. It deals especially with storage of viable seed. Emphasis is on the very few species (of the very many usable ones available) that meet human requirements and on the need for a greater utilization of the rich potential available. This applies to forest trees as well as plants for crops.

Despite all the emphasis on tropical species, a knowledge of the basic patterns of variation, flowering, fruiting, and breeding systems is lacking for most species (Kemp, 1978). A number of persons (Myers, 1976; Roche, 1979) feel that the most urgent need in the tropics is for gene conservation in indigenous forests. King (1979) states that the need for food and fuel in the tropics has led to land use resulting in degradation of fragile ecosystems and a resultant depletion of gene pools. Pressures will increase because 35% of the population of the developing countries live in the tropics. All this is aggravated by the limited knowledge about the large number of species that occur per hectare. As pointed out by Lugo and Brown (1981), the issue in the tropics is one of conserving the diversity of forest types rather than individual component species.

Many persons, such as Wood (1976), feel that the pressures on tropical forests can be reduced by growing the easier-to-handle and more productive

Figure 8.11. Compensatory or replacement plantings are made in grasslands such as these on the Meta River in Colombia. Such sites are marginal for tree growth; for example, they are often deficient in boron and phosphorus. But exotic trees can be grown there, thus taking the pressures off the indigenous forests and reducing gene depletion.

exotics on suitable areas and leaving the less operable areas without the pressures which cause loss of genetic material. He called them "compensatory plantations" or, as we referred to them earlier in this book, replacement forests (Fig. 8.11). If this concept is to succeed, the exotics being used now or those of potential use must not become genetically impoverished and gene conservation measures are urgently required (Wetterberg, et al., 1976; Davidson, 1977).

Gene conservation in the tropics appears to be a never-ending, insurmountable task. One realistic approach is to preserve sufficient indigenous jungle to assure the presence of many different species undisturbed in the forest. In its report on tropical deforestation, the Committee on Foreign Affairs of the U.S. House of Representatives states that "as much as 20% of tropical rainforests need to be preserved, in select localities covering distinct ecosystems, in order to ensure preservation of biotic communities with their endemic components" (Anon., 1980a). A concentrated effort should also be made on *ex situ* conservation of those species or sources of special interest. There never will be enough funds or manpower to save everything; a judicious choice of the species and areas on which to concentrate must be made.

8.5 SUMMARY OF GENE CONSERVATION FOR EXOTICS

Gene conservation is related to activities directed at saving genes, gene complexes, and genotypes and, in extreme instances, at preventing extinction of whole taxonomic categories of trees. We prefer the term *gene conservation* to *gene preservation*, but it is of importance to recognize that some persons use the two terms interchangeably.

Gene conservation is vital to all forestry programs; it is especially critical when exotic forestry is being practiced (Brazier et al., 1976; Brune and Melchior, 1976; Kemp et al., 1976). The land race concept, so vital for exotics, must be used. Recognition of the importance of maintaining a proper genetic base and preserving the best for the environments where exotic plantations will be established has been too long delayed.

Concern about gene conservation is urgent for species growing in both tropical and temperate regions. Proposals for gene conservation go back many years; one, by Kanehira (1918), stressed the need for forest conservation in Taiwan of a rare pine (*P. uyematsui*). The basic need is to maintain genetic variation and to assure the continuation of a broad genetic base for both currently useful characteristics and those that may ultimately become of value. Diversity is especially needed in adaptability characteristics to different environments and pests. The packaging of desired characteristics is possible because of the relative genetic independence of adaptive and utility characteristics. The true situation is usually not conservation of single genes but of gene complexes that give a tree its desired qualities. A large literature exists on the conservation of individual species; one example is Donahue (1985), dealing with the endangered *Pinus chiapensis* in Guatemala and Mexico and with *Pinus ayacahuite*.

Gene conservation means different things to different people. To some, it relates to prevention or extinction of a species; to others, it is saving an endangered provenance. Still others view it as the preservation of all the genetic variability present within a taxonomic unit. Most action is needed in donor countries, where the danger is from destruction by fuelwood collectors, harvesting, conversion to agriculture, fires, and grazing.

An important problem concerns where conservation efforts should be concentrated. The "center-of-diversity" versus marginal-population controversy always arises. Certainly, taxonomic entities with restricted ranges and endemic species are often of highest priority. The dry areas near centers of human population are in the most serious condition, usually from firewood-cutters or shifting agriculture. The adverse effects of goat and sheep grazing often is the final action that causes gene loss. Although one tends to think of gene loss as "something that has happened" in the past, current losses are very heavy. In recent years much more attention has been placed on the need for gene conservation in the tropics, both of the indigenous forests and of exotics being used to forest the degraded sites in the area. The need for gene conservation supersedes national boundaries; it is a prime activity where international cooperation is needed.

Conservation efforts can be through either *in situ*, *ex situ*, seed storage, or *in vitro* methods. Although *in situ* methods are more popular and have public support, well-planned *ex situ* methods, such as plantation establishment or vegetative propagation combined with gene packaging, are most efficient. If individual genes or gene complexes are to be saved, the approach would be different than if provenances are to be preserved. If the objective is to save "neutral" genes rather than currently useful genes, the approach will differ still more.

Although the current emphasis is on gene conservation in the humid tropics, care must be taken that forest trees in the temperate and dry tropics are not overlooked; some are in real danger. Pressures on indigenous forests that can result in gene loss can be reduced by planting exotic species as "replacement forests." But to be successful, the gene base of the exotic in the donor country must be carefully protected.

There will never be enough resources to do the gene conservation job in an ideal manner; some hard choices and priorities must be made about where the available funds and manpower will be used. In their discussion of conservation of the genes of the tropical conifers, Dvorak and Laarman (1986) state: "Even if collecting activities intensify, not all conifer populations can be sampled before their demise." An undefined "shotgun" approach, as suggested by many, will result in failure. One objection is the high cost and low financial incentive to do the conservation work. That is the major reason why international cooperation of governments is so strongly recommended. However, in a financial analysis of the CAMCORE Cooperative, which emphasizes gene conservation, Laarman and Dvorak (1985) state that:

> the financial costs of participating in CAMCORE can be justified even when a member's annual level of tree planting is relatively modest. The strictly financial analysis understates true net benefits. For many members, non-financial objectives play a major role in the decision making.

9

WOOD PROPERTIES
OF EXOTIC FOREST TREES

9.1 INTRODUCTION

The tendency in growing exotics has been to use fast-growing species without paying too much attention to the kind of wood produced. This is incorrect and a major concern when exotic forest trees are used. Growing trees for volume yields alone, without consideration for the kind of wood produced, can be disastrous since the wood of exotics often varies in the different environments where they are grown. How much change will occur in wood properties when a tree is grown in an exotic environment depends upon the species and the kind and magnitude of the differences in the environment. The effects of different actions on wood properties of exotics was covered by Ladrach (1986b). He states, " . . . there exists a great opportunity to modify wood properties to suit forest product needs, especially with exotic species." Ladrach outlines silvicultural and parental control methods to achieve this.

The change in wood properties resulting from growing an exotic in the new environment can be massive or of little importance. Time and length of the growth period, growth rate per se, and response to differing moisture patterns, weather sequences, or light qualities can all have an effect (Goggans, 1961; Zobel and Van Buijtenen, 1988). The different qualities of the wood of exotics is causing a change in the quality of the world timber resource; that is described in many papers such as the one by Zobel (1983a).

Although the wood properties of species used as exotics are generally well known and usually thoroughly studied in their indigenous habitat, the information available is sometimes somewhat incorrect or may even be downright misleading relative to wood of the same geographic source when grown in a new environment. This was stated clearly by Zobel (1983b): "It is a major error to think that, because wood of a native species is good, it will be good as an exotic in a different habitat." This concept was illustrated by Wright (1962), who said that the change from the native habitat to the strange habitat affected wood of a number of species, including *Larix decidua*, *Tsuga heterophylla*, *Eucalyptus globulus*, and *E. saligna*. The need to test the wood before establishing seed orchards was mentioned by Thompson and Nelson (1984). Therefore, one of the greatest errors made when growing exotics is to assume that the wood of a species when grown as an exotic will be the same as the wood of the same species in its indigenous habitat or in other exotic habitats.

Anything that alters the growth pattern of a tree can change the wood properties of the tree (Larson, 1973; Zobel and Talbert, 1984). Changes in growth which affect wood can result from different conditions in the exotic environment, from the more intensive management applied to the exotic trees, or from the movement of genotypes and provenances into environments to which they are not well adapted. Wood property alteration can be large with a species like *Pinus caribaea*, which is sensitive to different environments, or small with *Pinus taeda*, whose wood is much less affected by the environment in which the trees grow (Zobel and Van Buijtenen, 1988).

It is generally considered that the wood of hardwoods (angiospersm) is altered less when grown in a different environment than is that of the conifers, but this is not always the case. Generally, the eucalypts tend to maintain quite similar wood characteristics from the indigenous to the exotic environment, while teak (*Tectona grandis*) produces quite different woods in different areas (Keogh, 1980). The effects on wood when moving species or provenances are complex.

Although there are not many absolute rules in forestry, one is that *the wood of an exotic must always be assessed from trees grown in the exotic environment*. It is not yet possible to predict how the wood of a species may differ in the new environment from the indigenous environment. For example, Palmer and Tabb (1971) found that pulping characteristics of *Pinus caribaea* varied so greatly when the same seed source was grown in seven countries that no prediction of pulp quality can be made except from the actual environment on which the trees are planted.

Before the initiation of large-scale plantation programs, managers must decide what kind of wood and products are desired (Dvorak and Zobel, 1985; Ladrach, 1985b). Then they must be assured that the exotic species that is to be used satisfies these requirements. It was stressed by Hughes (1968) that an early evaluation of wood quality in relation to end uses must be made, and the exotic must not only have high yields but it must have desired wood before large-scale tropical plantations are established.

All wood properties may be affected when species are grown as exotics. For example, Darrow and Roeder (1983) reported, in comparative tests of *Eucalyptus urophylla*, *E. saligna*, and *E. grandis* in South Africa, that:

volume production of *E. urophylla* was less than that for *E. grandis* or *E. saligna* of the same age, but because of the higher wood density of *E. urophylla*, the wood mass production of this species was better than that of *E. saligna* and equal to or slightly better than that of ordinary *E. grandis*.

As pointed out in numerous publications (such as those by Einspahr et al., 1969; Barefoot et al., 1970; Zobel and Talbert, 1984), wood density (wood specific gravity)[1] is by far the most important wood property both for pulp and paper and for solid-wood products. As stated for *Pinus radiata* (Anon., 1983d), "Density is the only wood property worth considering because of its significant positive correlation with pulp, paper and timber products." Therefore, many of the examples given in this chapter will concentrate on the differences in wood density that are found when exotic forest trees are grown (Fig. 9.1).

One change in wood almost always related to exotics is the amount (and sometimes quality) of the juvenile wood and especially of the ratio of juvenile to mature wood.

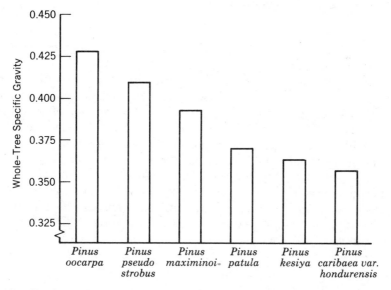

Figure 9.1. Exotics produce wood with greatly differing specific gravities, which must be taken into account when deciding on which species to use. Illustrated are the specific gravities of six different eight-year-old exotic pines grown on similar environments in the lower Andes in Colombia. *P. patula*, *P. kesiya*, and *P. caribaea* had only juvenile wood. (Data from Ladrach, 1986a.)

[1]Wood density and wood specific gravity are commonly used synonymously and express the same thing, although there is a difference in the way they are expressed: density is weight per unit volume while specific gravity is unitless by definition (Ford-Robertson, 1971). When appropriate, we will refer to wood density, but specific gravity will be used frequently because it is commonly found in the literature.

Juvenile wood is that wood formed nearest the pith and has characteristics quite different from the mature wood closer to the bark (juvenile wood has low specific gravity and short tracheids in the pines). There are many publications describing the properties of juvenile wood and its effect on the final product. Much of the information has been summarized in a special chapter by Zobel and Van Buijtenen (1988).

Exotics normally grow at a rapid rate and thus are large enough to harvest when they are young or at short rotations. Furthermore, they frequently are harvested at smaller diameters than indigenous timber, partially because they are primarily used for fiber rather than solid-wood products and partially because they are grown in plantations and economic considerations dictate an early harvest. This was emphasized by Entrican in 1950, who, when referring to exotics, wrote:

> It [wood quality] has been accentuated of course in that we have had to mill immature instead of mature exotics. The product of such trees is so susceptible to decay that to log, saw, season and use in the same careless manner as the indigenous timbers is only to result in tragic building losses with serious prejudice to the future marketing of exotics.

Whatever the cause, harvest early in the life of the tree results in a quite massive change in overall wood properties compared to older trees because of the increase in the percentage of juvenile wood (Zobel, 1981b).

A full presentation of the effect of juvenile wood on forests from tropical exotic plantations was given by Zobel (1985). He summarizes the characteristics of juvenile wood, how and where it is formed, and its effects on wood and product qualities. The important item is that most harvested exotics have considerable juvenile wood, which must be adjusted for during manufacture.

Sometimes normal wood becomes abnormal when a species is grown in an exotic environment. Pines, for example, sometimes develop large radial resinous deposits near the tree center; see Fig. 9.2 for an example from South African grown *Pinus caribaea*. In the eucalypts, unusually high amounts of resinous or phenolic substances occur in fractures in the wood, which sometimes even exudes around knots and cracks in the bark (commonly referred to as kino, which is found in pockets, veins, or rings). This reaction to unusual environments is worse in some species than in others; for example, it is very evident in *Eucalyptus globulus* and *E. viminalis*.

Because of fast growth, poor seed source, and changed environments, many tropical conifers are unusually crooked when grown as exotics (see Fig. 2.1). This results in an abnormal amount of reaction (compression) wood that is very unstable when dried. A similar response, which forms tension wood, does not seem to occur so commonly in the eucalypts, but it is very evident in poorly formed exotic hardwoods such as *Gmelina*, *Leucaena*, and *Robinia*. Although common in the tropics, stem crook in exotics is less evident in the temperate zones and tree form is usually better.

Figure 9.2. Sometimes trees grown in exotic environments produce serious wood defects such as the resin deposits shown in this *Pinus caribaea* grown in South Africa. (Courtesy, S.A. Forestry Research Institute.)

One characteristic of nearly all conifers grown as exotics is that they tend to retain their limbs for a long period of time, so that the logs have an excess of knots and the abnormal wood associated with knots. Frequently, exotics are pruned to produce more clear wood; after a period of healing which covers the branch stub, clear wood is formed. The retention of limbs is one of the greatest causes of wood of exotic conifers being different from the species in its indigenous range. The fast growth of branches and the harvesting of trees at a relatively young age (before limbs are shed) make the problem even more serious. Plantations are usually established at wider spacings than occurs with natural regeneration in the indigenous range from which the exotic was obtained. This also has an effect on limb size and retention. Thus, wood from most exotic conifers has a relatively high proportion of large knots. This tendency to limbiness also occurs in some hardwoods, but there are exceptions to this generality, especially in the eucalypts, most of which shed their limbs when small if grown in competition.

The current trend for greater use of exotic hardwood trees for energy and chemical products is having a profound effect on the kind of wood desired (Goldstein, 1980a). These two uses for wood will become increasingly important in the future. Wood properties needed for other than standard fiber and solid-wood products will have a major effect on the wood desired from exotics. One increasing wood usage is for fuel, where the best wood will have high density, low moisture content, and probably a high extractive content.

The tendency is to emphasize wood qualities of exotic trees as related to fiber properties or for use as energy. Although this is generally correct under tropical conditions, it is not for the temperate and subtropical areas. Here, such as in northern and central Europe, New Zealand, and elsewhere, the majority of the exotics are grown to produce wood for sawtimber, veneer, or other "higher-quality" wood products. The forest economy is dependent on these end products. Pulpwood is normally obtained from the forest as thinnings and tops or as residues from the manufacturing operation.

It is difficult to grow exotics with the desired dimensions, stability, and strength needed for solid-wood products. Growth patterns and tree form are more critical and the provenance used must supply a reasonable percentage of desirable trees per hectare at time of harvest. Rotation ages are longer and mature wood becomes of major importance, so assessment of the value of the exotic for solid wood takes longer than assessment for fiber. If the desired strength and stability are to be obtained, the quality of the wood properties is critical. Particularly frustrating for production of solid-wood products is the larger percentage of juvenile wood, which usually is not desirable for this purpose.

Even when the overall wood properties appear to be desirable, wide growth rings per se create difficulties in both lumber and plywood (Fig. 9.3). Unusual shrinkage and warping will occur, paint is not accepted uniformly, a smooth surface is hard to obtain, and, in plywood, plies primarily of springwood or summerwood are not desirable. The grain of the wood is of considerable importance for some finished products, and wide rings often produce an unattractive pattern.

New manufacturing technologies enabling the use of smaller trees makes the role of juvenile wood and knots even more critical. Therefore, although the importance of solid-wood products from exotic plantations is often not appreciated, it is becoming more significant.

As a result of the need to improve wood of exotics to produce more desirable products, there will be greatly increased genetic manipulation. Most wood properties, and especially wood density, is strongly heritable, so it will be rel-

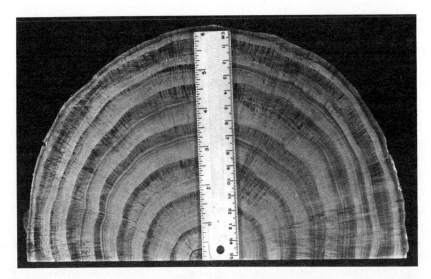

Figure 9.3. With intensive breeding, certain wood properties can be improved, but others may not. Shown is a *Pinus taeda* developed for fast growth and high wood density. Although successful, the wide rings per se make such wood undesirable for certain solid-wood products.

atively easy to produce wood of higher or lower densities (Harris, 1965). In the conifers, with their generally low-density juvenile wood, the improvement needed is primarily to increase wood density. This is not as true for some hardwoods for standard forest products, such as in some of the eucalypts, but is nearly always the case for species to be used for energy production. No matter what kind of wood properties are desired, breeding for better and more uniform wood is going to become increasingly important in exotics and results will be good (Zobel and Van Buijtenen, 1988).

One of the major characteristics of wood of exotics, as well as of indigenous species, is the huge amount of variability from tree to tree. Also for exotics, some variation occurs from provenance to provenance within species. The tree-to-tree differences within provenances are usually very large. This individual variability is a special theme in articles dealing with exotics, such as the one by Taylor (1977). Not only is there variation in wood density and fiber length, but Sesbou (1981) reported variability for shrinkage and wood collapse for *Eucalyptus camaldulensis* trees within provenances. Almost everyone who makes in-depth studies of any wood property of exotics reports large variations. The individual tree differences create difficulties in obtaining clear provenance patterns, but make it ideal for improving wood through breeding since much of the variability is genetic in nature (Smith, 1967).

As should be clearly understood, wood variation among species within genera can be very large, but even this is not always appreciated. In one example of species differences, cited for *Eucalyptus* by Higgins (1985), the mature wood of different species ranged in basic density from 300 to nearly 1000 kg/m³. Extractive amount and nature, and vessel characteristics and abundance, also vary greatly among the eucalypts.

The subject of wood property variation in exotics is suitable for a book in itself. Much has been written and many researchers, such as Palmer and his associates from the Tropical Products Institute, London, England, have specialized in analyses of the wood of exotics for their pulping characteristics (Palmer and Tabb, 1983). Many have published on the wood qualities of exotic species per se, yet surprisingly little is really known about the wood of exotics when grown in different areas. Several chapters of recent books have emphasized the wood properties of exotic forest trees (Zobel and Talbert, 1984; Zobel and Van Buijtenen, 1988); the publication by Burley and Nikles (1973a) has sections dealing with the wood qualities of exotic conifers, mostly of the pines. The theme nearly always revolves around the effects of shorter rotations and thus the large amount of juvenile wood. Since these are covered in detail in other available publications, only a summary will be included in this chapter.

It is important to repeat that wood can be greatly changed by environments that change the growth pattern of trees. This is particularly true of the exotics, where the move is often to extremely different environments and where intensive management is imposed, including the use of fertilizers and lower planting density. The basic rule of testing a species in the new environment before its widespread usage is often overlooked, resulting in the production of large volumes of wood from exotic forest trees for which there is no, or only marginal, use.

The wood of exotics has historically been purchased on a volume basis; this is now changing to weight—that is, tons of wood. The importance of the effect of this, relevant data, and the part played by wood density was described by Ladrach (1986b). The same emphasis was made by Delwaulle (1985) for the eucalypts. All of this points out the necessity of knowing wood properties and not relying solely on volume production when exotic plantations are evaluated.

The wood properties of some conifers and hardwoods when grown as exotics are shown in Tables 9.1 and 9.2.

TABLE 9.1. A Few Selected Publications Related to Wood of Coniferous Forest Trees when Used as Exotics

Species	Ref.	Comments
Pinus elliottii; *P. thunbergii*	Toyama et al., 1959	The tracheids of *P. elliottii* were longer and wider than those of *P. thunbergii;* they increased with age of the wood.
Pinus khasya (kesiya); *P. patula;* *Pseudotsuga menziesii*	Shelbourne, 1963	Timber properties of the best sources of *P. khasya* (*P. kesiya*) grown in N. Rhodesia (Tanzania) were superior to *P. patula* and as good as *Pseudotsuga menziesii* in wood density.

TABLE 9.1. Continued

Species	Ref.	Comments
Picea sitchensis	Brazier, 1967	There is great variation among Sitka spruce trees for all wood properties when grown in Great Britain. Faster-growing trees have lower wood density and increased spiral grain.
Pinus caribaea	Harris, 1970	This species has a remarkably high latewood content and irregular growth rings (false rings) in Kuala Lumpur. Wood density increased from the pith outward. Very little latewood was formed the first 4 growth rings. After that, as many as 10 latewood bands were seen within one year's growth ring. Density did not change from the 7th to 10th ring outward.
Pinus caribaea	Hughes, 1971	There is great variation in wood quality among trees and the potential for developing desired wood is good. Genetic variation is evident and the effect of site on Caribbean pine is great.
Pinus radiata	Shelbourne, 1971	In New Zealand, heritability of wood density was high, contrary to some reports from other areas.
Pinus caribaea	Andrew & Hughes, 1973	In Trinidad, the largest sources of difference in wood density and tracheid length were from pith to bark and from tree to tree. Tracheid length of individual trees varied from 2.7 to 4.5 mm in 12-year-old trees.
Pinus patula	Burley, 1973	The specific gravity values varied from 0.36 to 0.54 in Malawi. The faster-growing trees had lower wood density. There were large tree-to-tree differences in all traits and in tree types and ages.
Pinus elliottii; P. caribaea	De Guth, 1973	*P. elliottii* has a density 24% higher than *P. caribaea,* while the latter has tracheids 10–13% longer than *P. elliottii.* Caribbean pine produces 50% more wood per hectare in Argentina.
Pinus caribaea	Wood et al., 1973	Differences in wood density from 4 climatic zones in Tanzania were huge (22% from one to another). Density was a little higher for slow-growing trees.
Pinus oocarpa	Foelkel et al., 1975	In Brazil, cell length, wall thickness, and wood density all increased with age of the wood.

(*continued*)

TABLE 9.1. Continued

Species	Ref.	Comments
Pinus elliottii	Van der Slooten et al., 1976	In S. Brazil, wood properties were very different among plantations. The authors relate the differences to rainfall and its distribution patterns: higher rainfall produced higher wood density.
Pinus caribaea	Hawkins et al., 1978	In Queensland, Australia, specific gravity is 0.45 for 19-year-old trees; the wood is uniform and easy to work.
Pinus caribaea	Burley & Palmer, 1979	Mean density (12% M.C.) varied from 0.44 to 0.73 g/cm³ for trees in Fiji. Extractives content varied from 3% to 7%.
Pinus caribaea	Falkenhagen, 1979	In South Africa, considerable variability occurs in the wood properties of the varieties of this species, dependent both upon the provenance used and the environment where grown. Pulp yield and wood density were the lowest for var. *hondurensis*.
Pinus elliottii; P. caribaea; P. kesiya; P. oocarpa	Brito et al., 1980	The yields of turpentine when grown in Brazil were high for *P. elliottii* and *P. caribaea*. *P. oocarpa* had the poorest resin qualities and *P. kesiya* and *P. elliottii* had the best.
Pinus caribaea	Aguilar, 1981	In Venezuela, specific gravity of 8-year-old trees varied from 0.31 to 0.49, avg. of 0.37. Tracheid mean length was 3.1 mm, varying from 2.2 to 4.0 mm.
Pinus caribaea	Whyte et al., 1981	Considerable spiral grain was noted in Fiji, but it it seemed not to be correlated with site factors. The effect of spiral grain and of twist with seasoning was related to cull.
Pinus patula	Palmer et al., 1982c	There is a marked increase in wood density with age; least dense 10-year-olds had 325 kg/m³ and most dense 20-year-old samples had 440 kg/m³.
Pinus contorta; Picea abies	Persson, 1982	Wood density and pulp yields per unit volume of wood of the two species is similar. *P. contorta* has more knots. *P. contorta* is suitable for thermomechanical pulp. Quality of sawn timber of the two species is similar but low for export.
Pinus merkusii	Andrew, 1983	This species is a notable source of resinous products, turpentine being of high quality. Wood density is moderate but greatly variable due to resins.

TABLE 9.1. Continued

Species	Ref.	Comments
Pinus caribaea	Brown, 1983	Tree-to-tree and within-tree variation in wood density were very large in Jamaica. Distance from the pith had a marked effect on wood properties.
Sequoia sempervirens	Colbert & McConchie, 1983	Wood density in New Zealand was a low 353 kg/m³ but uniform; characteristics were slightly inferior to the California-grown wood. Wood was stable with no excess shrinkage; heartwood percentage averaged 51% for 40-year-old trees.
Pinus patula; P. elliottii; P. kesiya; P. caribaea	De Villiers, 1983	Differences among species grown in South Africa are considerable and due to radial density gradients in the stem. Spiral grain has an effect on timber defects, especially in *P. patula.*
Pinus caribaea; P. oocarpa; P. merkusii	Harris, 1983	All 3 species have a central core (2 to 4 rings from pith) of low-density wood when grown in Malaya. Outside this, dense wood with many false rings is produced. The steep density gradient ceases about 12 years from the pith.
Pinus contorta; Pinus sylvestris	Martinsson, 1983	The Swedish-grown lodgepole pine has wood properties for pulp and paper as good or better than Scots pine. The wood is useful for sawmill products as well as for pulp and paper.
Pinus caribaea	Mullin et al., 1983a	No differences in wood density of the 3 varieties were found among provenances. There were much higher basic densities in some test areas than in others in Zimbabwe.
Pinus caribaea	Smith, 1983	This species is a good wood producer over a wide range of ecological conditions. Wood quality was relatively similar to other tropical pines in Queensland, Australia.
Pinus caribaea	Woessner, 1983d	In Brazil, var. *caribaea* had the densest wood (specific gravity = 0.40), var. *hondurensis* was intermediate (0.37), and var. *bahamensis* was 0.36.
Pinus patula	Ladrach, 1984f	Great individual tree differences occur in Colombia. Juvenile wood is present; wood in the center and top of trees has less density and shorter tracheids than basal and outerwood.

(continued)

TABLE 9.1. Continued

Species	Ref.	Comments
Pinus kesiya	Mullin et al., 1984	A definite negative correlation was found between wood density and elevation of provenances when grown in Zimbabwe. The authors recommend lower-elevation sources from the Philippines to raise the wood density to an acceptable level.

TABLE 9.2. Some Selected Publications Related to the Wood of Hardwood Exotic Forest Trees

Species	Ref.	Comments
Hybrid poplars	Curró, 1960	Wood density increased from the pith to the bark and from the base of the tree to the top. Moisture content of the wood was higher for trees felled in the winter.
Swietenia macrophylla	Brisco et al., 1963	In plantation-grown trees, specific gravity increased with growth rate. It increased outward from the pith. Whole-tree specific gravity can be accurately estimated from the specific gravity of the corewood and height.
Hybrid poplars	Hamilton & Wendel, 1967	The wood of the highest-density clones in West Virginia was 24% greater than the lightest, but fiber lengths were similar for all clones.
Gmelina arborea	Lamb, 1968	Wood density increases gradually from the pith outward and varies from 25 to 34 lb/ft^3. Wood density decreases very slightly up the tree. Fiber length increases from 0.6 mm at the pith to 1.2 mm the third year and is constant afterwards. Pulping properties are excellent.
Hybrid poplars	Son & Chung, 1972	Ten-year-old trees in Korea showed a very high variation in specific gravity both among trees and among plantation locations.
Eucalyptus camaldulensis; *E. grandis;* *E. tereticornis*	Franklin & Meskimen, 1975	*E. tereticornis* has considerably denser wood (specific gravity of 0.55) than does *E. grandis* or *E. camaldulensis* (0.45). Bark density is the same. Breast height values are closely correlated with whole-tree values.

356

TABLE 9.2. Continued

Species	Ref.	Comments
Cordia alliodora	Stead, 1980	The value of plantation-produced wood for various uses, including pulping, is as yet unknown, although several preliminary studies have been completed. Specific gravity varies from 0.36 in Panama to 0.52 in Venezuela.
Eucalypts	Revell, 1981	Trees should be at least 70 cm in diameter (35–40 years old) in New Zealand in order to reduce growth stresses, to quarter-saw, and to yield high-grade lumber. Wood is good for veneer, furniture, interior finishing, and floors.
Toona ciliata; *Fraxinus uhdei;* *Grevillea robusta*	Buck & Imoto, 1982	Australian toon, tropical ash, and silky-oak produced high-quality sawlogs in 45 years or less in Hawaii.
Acacia mearnsii; *Eucalpytus* spp.	Palmer et al., 1982a	*Acaia mearnsii* grown in Kenya had the most dense wood (590 kg/m^3) compared to the eucalypts, which varied from 470 to 570 kg/m^3. *E. camaldulensis* had a high extractives content.
Eucalyptus nitens; *E. elata;* *E. macarthurii*	Anon., 1983b	The timber density of the five best provenances grown in South Africa did not differ from one another. Wood density of *E. elata* varied from 400 to 600 kg/m^3 and *E. macarthurii* from 450 to 650 kg/m^3.
Eucalyptus deglupta	Davidson, 1983b	Narrow-sense heritability was 0.46 for wood density. The author advises that wood density should be a major property in an improvement program.
Terminalia ivorensis	Durand, 1983	Basic density did not vary much from plot to plot in the Ivory Coast. There was no relationship between basic density and growth rate.
Eucalyptus spp.; *E. saligna*	Ferraz, 1983	There is a close correlation between density increase and soil water deficiency, except in *E. saligna,* which is not sensitive to moisture stress.
Acacia mearnsii; *Tectona grandis*	Gupta & Kukreti, 1983	Acacia wood from India was compared with teak; its properties are inferior to teak. Strength properties are lower than would be expected for a given specific gravity.
Acacia mangium	Keong, 1983	In Malaysia, the wood of this species is good for sawn timber, particle board, and pulp and paper.

(continued)

357

TABLE 9.2. Continued

Species	Ref.	Comments
Eucalyptus nitens	Mullin et al., 1983b	There were significant differences among provenances in basic density, but there were no provenance × site interactions when grown in Zimbabwe.
Gmelina arborea	Woessner, 1983c	Wood density varied among provenances from 0.29 to 0.38 g/cc. Wood density is the most likely characteristic to improve future yields of this species in Brazil.
Gmelina arborea	Akachuku, 1984	In Nigeria, large tree-to-tree differences were found for wood density, fiber length, and fiber proportion among trees of the same age growing in the same environment. Some trees combined good qualities of all three characteristics.

9.2 THE EFFECT OF THE NEW HABITAT ON WOOD

There is always an attempt to match the natural environment of the trees used as exotics to that where they will be grown, but this is rarely possible. Differences may be small and subtle, like a different rainfall pattern or a difference in night temperatures, but even then an effect on the wood can result. An example is when Douglas-fir is grown in the Southern Hemisphere, where the environment is very similar to the indigenous range of the preferred provenance of Douglas-fir. Although the woods are reasonably similar, they differ enough in the growth-ring pattern, amount of resin contained, and proportion of summerwood to springwood to make them less desirable for certain products than wood produced in the indigenous habitat of the species. Some results from growing wood in different environments are listed in Table 9.3.

Frequently, the new environments are greatly different, such as when a species adapted to a continental climate is grown in a Mediterranean climate. If, for example, loblolly pine from the southeastern United States, with its year-round rainfall, is grown in California, with its dry summers, the resultant wood density will be very low. The trees grow normally and the springwood produced early in the year is normal. However, during the time when summerwood formation normally takes place the rains cease, soil moisture becomes very low, and tree growth is greatly reduced. Thus, loblolly pine grown in California is lower in density than in its natural range because of the small amount of high-density summerwood. It is of interest, however, that when grown in California, trees from seed of parents with the highest specific gravity in the East are still higher than those from parents with lower gravities. Thus, the individual inheritance pattern of wood density remains strong even

TABLE 9.3. Change of Wood Properties of Exotics when Grown in Different Environments

Species	Ref.	Comments
Gmelina arborea	Lamb, 1968	Wood density varies little and averages 30 to 31 lb/ft^3 when grown in India, Malaya, Gambia, and Nigeria. Fast growth does not change density.
Pinus caribaea	Harris, 1970	Trees from Kuala Lumpur had excessive false rings and juvenile to mature wood differences. Trees from Jeniang (one site) in N.W. Malaya had normal and definite annual rings, with the wood similar to *P. taeda*. Wood differences between the two sources is dramatic.
Pinus caribaea	Hughes, 1971	There is a remarkable contrast between the wood from Honduras and Fiji; this shows the need to determine the effect of site on wood. *P. caribaea* wood is easily influenced by silvicultural treatments.
Pinus caribaea	Andrew & Hughes, 1973	In Trinidad, there were large differences in wood properties due to differences between sites; one site had tracheids 4.4 mm long and the other, 3.5 mm.
Pinus patula	Burley, 1973	Values for most wood properties varied significantly among sites when the trees were grown in Malawi.
Eucalyptus camaldulensis; E. grandis; E. robusta	Franklin & Meskimen, 1975	There were inconsistencies of wood properties among plantations from the same seed source.
Pinus caribaea	Barnes et al., 1977	Density of wood by sites varied from .31 to .37 g/cm^3 and was highly correlated with soil moisture deficit. Growth rate did not affect basic density. Provenance wood specific gravity ranged from 0.34 to 0.36.
Pinus oocarpa; P. patula; P. kesiya; P. caribaea	Kromhout & Toon, 1978	Wood density varies with species and, where the species is grown in South Africa, also by variety in *P. caribaea*. Lower density is produced in the cooler climates. Variation in tracheid length is smaller. Large individual tree differences are present.
Eucalyptus camaldulensis	Sesbou, 1981	There were great differences among provenances in shrinkage and wood density in Sicily and Calabrica, but much greater uniformity in Morocco.

(continued)

TABLE 9.3. Continued

Species	Ref.	Comments
Pinus radiata	Corson & Foster, 1982	Pulping studies from Australia showed that the influences on wood density resulting from geographical location should have no significant effect on pulp quality even though there are regional specific gravity differences.
Leucaena leucocephala; L. diversifolia	Ladrach, 1984a	Wood density varied among sites from a specific gravity of 0.56 at one test area to 0.46 in another.
Pinus patula	Ladrach, 1984f	In Colombia, plantations at 1750 m elevation have better wood quality than those at higher altitudes.
Eucalyptus saligna; E. grandis	Palmer & Gibbs, 1984	There were significant differences in wood density related to site from three different areas in Uganda.

though the overall average is considerably reduced when loblolly pine is grown as an exotic in a climate with a long dry spell in late spring and summer.

Changes in wood properties caused by differing environments usually cannot be predicted (Zobel and Van Buijtenen, 1988). For example, in some Southern Hemisphere climates where growth conditions are ideal, wood density of *Pinus caribaea* var. *hondurensis* is extremely low (specific gravity = .25–.35), with the trees producing essentially no summerwood. In its indigenous range, or when grown where there are definite wet and dry seasons, the wood of this species is normal (specific gravity = .45–.55) and sometimes is quite dense (0.6–0.7) (Nikles, 1966). Yet when *Pinus elliottii* is grown in the same uniform, good environment, its wood specific gravity can be as high as 0.7–0.8, much higher than the 0.5–0.6 in its natural range. Without actual testing, it would have been impossible to predict that the wood produced by these two species would have responded in diametrically opposite ways to the same exotic environment.

It is known that when a tree is in a state of active height growth, springwood-type cells are formed. Summerwood cells with thick walls are produced only after a "resting" bud has been formed. Therefore, if the tree has constant height growth because of an ideal environment, its wood specific gravity will be very low because of the absence of summerwood formation (Larson, 1973). Often it becomes difficult to distinguish annual rings. Therefore, a species like *P. caribaea* var. *hondurensis*, which responds to the ideal climate by never stopping height growth, is affected differently than *P. elliottii*, which apparently sets a resting bud early, then resumes summerwood growth, which is produced throughout the remainder of the year.

Moisture content of the soil has a major effect on wood properties, and often the reason for changes in wood in exotic environments is the amount and pattern of moisture available to the tree. As an example, in southern Brazil, Van der Slooten et al. (1976) found that the wood density of *Pinus elliottii* was highest in the area of greatest rainfall. Quite frequently, the presence of plentiful moisture during the later part of the growing season, after a resting bud has been formed, results in a continued and high amount of summerwood production. This occurs in climates such as central Florida, where spring growth is good, followed by a late spring drought and formation of a resting bud and start of summerwood formation. After this, plentiful rains occur and continue until winter, resulting in a heavy production of summerwood and thus a high specific gravity.

Many aspects of the environment other than moisture affect wood, but these are less well known and studied. We do know, for example, that in pines an excess of nitrogen produces wood with low specific gravity (Posey, 1964) and a tendency for extension of the production of the period of juvenile wood formation. Conversely, on phosphate-deficient sites the specific gravity of pine is higher than normal; when fertilized with phosphorus, the specific gravity drops, but only to about the normal level. It is obvious that soil fertility plays a role in affecting the wood properties of exotic forest trees.

Numerous other environmental factors can affect wood properties, directly or indirectly; these are summarized by Zobel and Van Buijtenen (1988). Chief among these are elevation and latitude, which are related to day length, and day and night temperatures. Examples of the effect of elevation were given by Mullin et al. (1984) for *Pinus kesiya* in Zimbabwe, where they found a negative correlation between basic density and elevation of the provenance. They recommend more selections from the lower altitudes. Consistent differences in the wood of *Pinus patula* when grown at different altitudes were found by Ladrach (1986b). At age 15, specific gravity decreased for trees grown from 1800 to 3000 m altitude.

As for all tree growth, the law of limiting factors applies. It is often the factors limiting growth in the environment that will affect wood properties. As previously described, the limiting factors can be moisture availability and distribution, nutrients, temperature and its fluctuations, and many others, such as genetic limits of the trees.

Usually, the environmental relationships are not simple but are so complex that interactions among factors make it impossible to pinpoint the effect of a single environment on wood properties. For example, the usual lowered specific gravity related to a high nitrogen content of the soil may not occur if the soils are dry. The tendency towards continuous growth with an ideal environment, which may cause a reduction in the proportion of summerwood, may not occur if some environmental factor, such as a short cold spell or dry spell, causes the formation of a resting bud, however briefly. When this occurs in conifers, the wood may have a large amount of summerwood, as described earlier in the *P. elliottii* example.

Another aspect of the new environment in which exotics are grown is the sometimes intensive forest management applied to the exotic. Quite frequently, site preparation is intensive and planted trees are released from competition by cultivation, by chemicals, or when manual weeding is done. For trees such as the eucalypts, fertilization is commonly practiced. In fact, fertilization is often required to grow forest trees satisfactorily as exotics, especially in the tropical regions where phosphorus, boron, zinc, or other minerals are in short supply. All forest management activities are designed to reduce limiting factors, which will enhance growth. When this is done, growth patterns of the exotic trees are altered and wood properties may be changed (Fig. 9.4).

It is most difficult to pinpoint the effect of increased silvicultural manipulation on wood properties. Some, like the addition of high nitrogen fertilizers on conifers, can often be predicted, but others, like site preparation or cultivation, have not been well assessed as to their effect on wood. Certainly, some effect on wood results since growth patterns are changed, but how much and in what direction generally still remains to be determined. Other changes, such as wide spacing and early harvest, are predictable from the effect of number and size of limbs and the amount of juvenile wood that will be present.

Figure 9.4. Most exotics are managed intensively, usually including fertilization. This often has an effect on wood properties, as can be seen from the compared wood sections from fertilized and nonfertilized pine. Some wood properties are affected positively, some adversely.

9.2.1 The Effect Of Growth Rate

The new environment not only affects the intrinsic wood properties, but it also directly influences the growth rate. Although growth rate per se has little effect on the wood of some species of hard pines in some environments, its effect can be considerable on others (Zobel and Van Buijtenen, 1988). In genera such as *Picea*, some researchers report that low-density wood is related to fast growth, although there is no universal agreement on this. It is true that in some genera and in some species of conifers the faster-growing trees tend to have a lower wood density.

In the hard pines, most reports are that fast growth per se has little effect on wood density, although again there are some reports to the contrary, especially for *Pinus radiata* (Cotterill and Cameron, 1984). These authors discuss methods whereby fast growth and high wood density can be combined. One of the hundreds of studies on the effect of growth rate was made by Palmer and Gibbs (1977) for *Pinus caribaea* grown in Fiji. Slow-grown and fast-grown trees were pulped. There was no significant difference in the density of the wood. In addition, the authors concluded:

> There was no significant difference in the chemical composition of the wood. When cooked by the sulphate process, there was no significant difference in ease of digestion. . . . On the evidence of this trial, it can be concluded that the best course of action for the forester is to grow for volume production.

Although generalizations always have exceptions, it is usually true that fast- and slow-grown hard pines of the same age have similar wood specific gravities. The wood densities of the fast-growing tropical pines are usually low, which results from the trees becoming merchantable at a young age, when they have a high percentage of juvenile wood and thus a low specific gravity (Fig. 9.5).

Almost everyone agrees that fast growth has little effect on the wood of diffuse porous hardwoods but can have a major influence on the ring porous species, which usually have denser wood with fast growth.

The subject of growth rate and its effects on wood properties is greatly studied and hotly debated. It is not suitable to go into further details in this chapter, but it was mentioned here especially to point out the error commonly made with exotics of *confusing fast-growth effects with those of early harvest which result in a high proportion of juvenile wood*. Ring width of fast-growing trees is large near the center of the tree, where juvenile wood with its low gravity is formed. But this is not a cause-and-effect relationship. Trees that initially grow slowly have the usual juvenile wood characteristics regardless of growth rate. The literature is filled with such references as "the wood of exotics is poor or different because of fast growth" where the true situation is that "the wood of exotics is poor or different because of a high proportion of juvenile wood." It was stated by Jacobs (1964) that fast-growing exotics

Figure 9.5. The fast growth of many exotic conifers makes the trees merchantable when most of the wood is still juvenile. This load of small thinnings of tropical pines is from an eight-year-old plantation. Essentially all of it is juvenile wood.

create wood problems because they produce a wide central core of wood with spiral grain and other defects.

If the woods of trees are to be compared, they must be of the same age. Only then can a statement be made, such as that by Taylor (1973), that growth rate does not have a significant effect on specific gravity among trees of *Eucalyptus grandis* in South Africa or, as that by Deleporte (1983) for *Picea sitchensis* in France, that wood density decreases with increasing growth rate. Persons growing exotics must be aware that the wood of exotic pine (for example) has low density and short cells, not because the pine has grown fast per se, but because the fast growth enables harvest at a time when the percentage of juvenile wood is high.

9.3 WOOD PROPERTIES OF EXOTIC CONIFERS

Much of the wood produced in the future by exotic species will be from fast-grown conifer plantations. Although such wood from exotics may be different from that from indigenous forests, it is useful and not necessarily inferior or substandard. The utility of wood from exotic conifers is dependent upon the product to be produced. Special products such as writing paper, tissues, and newsprint can be made efficiently from wood from young conifer plantations that have a high proportion of juvenile wood (Dvorak and Zobel, 1985; Zobel,

1985). A high proportion of juvenile wood is not desirable for solid-wood products or papers that require high tearing strength; for these usages, wood from young softwood plantations is usually inferior.

Tree form of many exotics is poor, resulting in a high proportion of compression wood and large knots (Fig. 9.6). When young exotic conifer plantations are thinned, the combination of juvenile wood, compression wood, and numerous knots may result in poor-quality products. Because of these combined adverse wood properties, paper made from young conifer trees in exotic plantations frequently does not meet the standards for tear strength necessary for the world market (Dadswell and Wardrop, 1959). Despite its somewhat poorer tear, paper made from predominantly juvenile wood is generally useful for consumption within the country where the exotic has been grown. As is commonly done, mills do not pulp juvenile wood alone but use mixtures with mature wood to obtain the required strength properties. In addition to weak paper, the strength, stability, and finishing properties of solid-wood products made from young exotic conifers are poor (Pearson and Gilmore, 1980).

In the conifers, it is suspected but not proven that intensive forest management activities somewhat lengthen the period of juvenile wood formation. Since the intensively managed trees grow rapidly and are harvested at a young age, when juvenile wood makes up a high proportion of the usable wood, the intensive silviculture will affect the kind of wood harvested even though the actual wood properties per se may not be greatly altered. Conifers harvested

Figure 9.6. The initial plantings of unimproved exotics often contain trees with very poor form. Excessively crooked boles, heavy limbs, and foxtails evident in this planting of *Pinus caribaea* var. *hondurensis* produce low-quality wood with much knotwood and compression wood.

at a young age will have shorter tracheids than wood from older trees grown in exactly the same environment.

All species of conifers do not respond the same to exotic environments. As an example, species such as *P. caribaea* and *P. kesiya* may produce wood with essentially no summerwood when grown in environments with ideal growing conditions, while in other exotic environments they develop normal wood. Sometimes unusual wood development occurs with alternating rows of very thick- and thin-walled cells, such as for *P. caribaea* when grown in parts of the Amazon.

9.4 WOOD PROPERTIES OF EXOTIC HARDWOODS

Generally, the wood of exotic hardwoods is more similar to that of the species in its indigenous range than occurs in the conifers. This is because the wood of the hardwoods is usually not changed as much by different environments as is that of the conifers and because the juvenile wood of the hardwoods is more similar to its mature wood than that of the conifers. This statement may not hold as strongly for high-quality finishing woods, since there is only limited experience by which to judge in this area, but it is quite accurate for the wood used for fiber products.

Although the wood of hardwoods is more complex than that of the conifers, and is usually more stable from area to area, there is sometimes enough variation caused by the different environments in which exotics are grown to produce wood that has an effect on the products produced. Therefore, the rule in conifers, to test the wood from the new environment before using exotics on a wide scale, must also be followed for hardwoods. For example, although wood of a given eucalypt species is frequently considered to be reasonably uniform wherever the tree will grow well, the environment in different plantations sometimes produces wood with somewhat differing properties (Hans and Burley, 1972; Taylor, 1973).

The wood properties of hardwoods, just as those of conifers, often vary considerably among individual trees within a provenance. This gives the opportunity to change wood in the desired direction through genetic manipulation (Rudman et al., 1969; Doran, 1974; Plumptre, 1977). Generally, the wood of hardwoods can be quite effectively changed in the desired direction by control of parentage (Fig. 9.7).

The primary hardwoods used for exotics are the poplars, eucalypts, and *Gmelina*, although numerous other species are being used on a lesser scale. (In actuality, one of the most widely planted is the rubber tree [*Hevea* spp.], but it is primarily used for other than wood production.) A lot is known about the wood of these genera and numerous studies (see the following section) have been made on them. Many of the fast-growing exotic hardwoods are not yet planted on a large enough scale to be of major importance on the world mar-

Figure 9.7. The wood of hardwoods can be greatly improved by selection and breeding. An example is the fast-grown *Eucalyptus grandis* used for sawlogs in South Africa. The wood of this species is commonly considered not to be suitable for solid-wood products, but the logs shown produce fine boards. (Courtesy, S.A. Forestry Research Institute.)

ket, although the wood properties of some species grown in the temperate regions as exotics are fairly well known (Barker, 1974; Jett and Zobel, 1974).

The most widely used fast-growing exotics are the eucalypts. Based on the numerous trials already made, the *E. grandis-saligna* complex, *E. globulus*, and *E. camaldulensis* currently are the most important species. In good environments, with good care, and using improved genetic stock, the eucalypts grow very rapidly and produce desirable wood. The many different species and provenances of *Eucalyptus* have greatly diverse wood properties (Foelkel et al., 1975a; Higgins, 1985). Some eucalypt species (*E. deglupta*, for example) have low-density wood while species such as *E. tereticornis, E. citriodora, E. paniculata*, and *E. cloeziana* have higher specific gravity wood particularly suitable for energy production.

Despite this variability of wood properties among species, the group of eucalypts most widely planted has wood in the mid-density range, so that it is suitable for a number of diverse products and has wide utility. The two characteristics most affecting pulp qualities of the different eucalypts are wood density and extractives content (Ferreira, 1968). Older trees frequently have wood with kino deposits or phenolic substances, but young trees are reasonably free of adverse chemicals (Baklein, 1960). Some species have other kinds of deposits that make the wood less usable. For example, we have observed that, in Brazil, some young *E. deglupta* have darkly stained wood near the tree center, often to 30% of its height. The stained wood gives lower yields and limits the possibilities for utilization because of difficulty in bleaching.

Some eucalypts are used for solid-wood products, as reported for *Eucalyptus saligna* by Barr (1983) in New Zealand. He found that the propensity of the logs to end-split or to spring off the saw is probably heritable. Trees with decorative wavy grain produce progeny with the same features. It is possible, particularly with the use of vegetative propagation, to develop sources of relatively straight-grained trees, such as for *E. grandis*, which are suitable for many solid-wood products.

One exotic with great potential in tropical plantations is *Gmelina arborea*; this species grows very rapidly under suitable conditions and is planted in a number of areas such as in the Amazon Basin in Brazil, in Asia, and in coastal Colombia. Its wood and pulping qualities have been extensively studied by many investigators, but little has been published (Palmer, 1973). Many companies have test-pulped it, and reports are that *Gmelina* has a good wood that is easy to work with and suitable for a number of pulp and solid-wood products.

Although the differences in properties between juvenile and mature wood are much smaller in the hardwoods than in most conifers, even these small differences will have an effect when very short rotations are used. In some hardwood genera, such as *Populus* spp., *Fraxinus* spp., and *Platanus* spp. used in short rotations for wood biomass (the "silage" concept; Steinbeck and Brown, 1975), wood properties of the very young trees are quite different from less intensively managed older trees of the same species.

Quite frequently, exotic species are used for biomass production and an assessment of their value for this purpose can only be determined by testing. Related to this are wood qualities of coppice growth. Generally, the wood from coppice stems has been found to be quite similar to seedlings of the same age. This result was reported by Sesbou (1981) for *Eucalyptus camaldulensis*.

9.5 A SUMMARY OF STUDIES ON THE WOOD OF EXOTICS

Several thousand references could be cited listing studies that have been made on the properties, variability, and use of the wood of exotics. Some of these have been selected for mention or discussion in the following section and in Tables 9.1, 9.2, 9.3, and 9.4. Most of the publications refer to studies on specific species. Some especially in-depth studies have been made for certain species, such as that by Sesbou (1981) for the widely planted *Eucalyptus camaldulensis*. He reported upon a number of wood properties such as shrinkage, wood density, and wood collapse from three plantings (two in Italy and one in Morocco) as part of the international study on provenances of the species.

Based upon the literature and our experience, and summarizing the information in Tables 9.1, 9.2, 9.3, and 9.4:

1. Conifers

(a) Wood properties are highly variable from tree to tree, from site to site, by family, and often by provenance source.

(b) Wood density (specific gravity) is the best-known and most important wood property. For many exotic conifers it is marginally low, due to the environment and to the fact that trees are harvested at a young age with a high proportion of juvenile wood.

(c) Despite the somewhat lower wood density and wider annual rings, the wood of exotic conifers is usually useful and sometimes highly desirable for certain products.

(d) Because of the lesser amount of juvenile wood, the wood density of older trees is usually considerably higher than that of young trees (or near the pith or top logs); a similar pattern occurs for cell length (Fig. 9.8).

(e) *Pinus radiata* does not always follow closely the within-tree pattern of other hard pines such as *P. caribaea* and *P. taeda*. The response of *P. radiata* to environmental variations is often more extreme than that of most other hard pines. Some species like *P. caribaea* also are dramatically responsive to extreme environments, sometimes resulting in the production of wood that is marginal for normal usage.

(f) The ability to improve wood properties by genetic manipulation is very good.

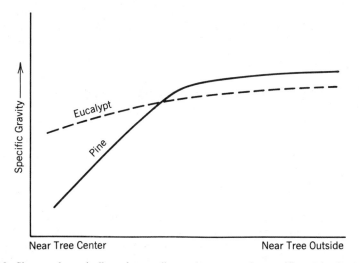

Figure 9.8. Shown schematically and generally are the patterns for specific gravity from the tree center to outside for pine and eucalypts. Note how specific gravity increases more in the pines. The pattern of cell length will be almost similar.

(g) The ability for resin production is good in some species, especially *Pinus caribaea*, *P. eilliottii*, and *P. merkussi*.

(h) Lower- elevation plantings sometimes produce denser wood than high-elevation material.

(i) Silvicultural treatments can have a significant effect on wood of some species.

2. Hardwoods

(a) There is some variation in wood properties within the tree of hardwoods, but not as much as in the conifers. Juvenile wood is present, but has a minimal effect on wood properties. Fiber length varies by location in the tree, but the magnitude is not great. Breast height wood density values are sometimes very close to whole-tree values.

(b) Species differences are huge; this is exemplified by the eucalypts, which vary from having very light to very heavy wood.

(c) Generally, the effect of environment on wood properties is less than that for the conifers. More predictable wood properties will be produced in different environments. However, in some environments, seed source (provenance) differences can be large.

(d) Individual and family differences in wood properties within provenances are very large, often greater than for the conifers. Since much of this is genetically controlled, it is possible to develop strains of hardwoods with desired wood properties by genetic manipulation. This is especially valuable for solid-wood products.

(e) A number of exotic hardwood species can produce high-quality sawlogs. However, growth stresses are often present and trees much have good diameters and straight grain to yield high-quality lumber.

9.6 PRODUCT QUALITY OF WOOD FROM EXOTICS

It is axiomatic that if wood properties vary, product qualities will also vary. This aspect is too often overlooked. As stated by Higgins (1985) following his discussion of the variability in wood among the more than 500 species of eucalypts:

> These and other variable determinants of pulping and paper-making properties make it essential to mention the species when describing eucalypt pulps. The age of the tree has a large influence on the basic density, vessel size and, in particular, extractives content. . . . These requirements are still ignored to a large extent in some important parts of the northern hemisphere.

The concern about the effect of exotic plantations on the wood supply and product quality was covered by Laarman (1980). He discusses the potential competition from exotics but also points out:

> Another limitation for pulp production is that fast-grown pines show reduced fiber quality and yield—they contain a huge proportion of juvenile wood. Solid products have weaknesses related to wide rings and pulp yields are low and have low tear strength.

Laarman concludes: "These factors could lessen Brazil's international competitiveness."

It is not unusual for wood properties of exotics to be such that they make products not acceptable on the world market. This is very true for juvenile pine from some tropical conifers which produce paper with an unacceptably low tear strength (Fig. 9.9). Sometimes no tests have been made of such possible effects, with disastrous results when the paper produced is put on the market. The assumption is frequently made that the paper produced from the exotic will be the same as when produced from its indigenous range; this assumption is dangerous and misleading. Before any large-scale exotic forest program is initiated, the worth of the products made from it must be determined.

A series of studies for this purpose has been made; examples are the results of work on tropical pines by Palmer and associates at the Tropical Products Institute in England; a good example is the paper by Palmer and Tabb (1971) on the pulpwood potential of *Pinus caribaea* from the same lot of seed when grown in seven countries.They rated results as very variable but similar to southern pines of the United States. In the United States, the Institute of Paper

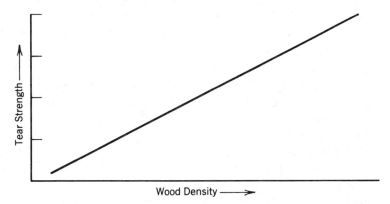

Figure 9.9. Wood properties have a major effect on product qualities. Shown schematically is the relationship between the tear strength of paper and wood density. Low tear strength results from a high proportion of juvenile wood; this is a major problem with exotic pines.

Chemistry in Appleton, Wisconsin, produced an annotated bibliography on silviculture and kraft pulping on *Pinus caribaea* which covered work done to that date. They found that *P. caribaea* had some usuable paper properties while some were inferior. A similar series of studies, by Foelkel et al. (1975), reports that generally the wood of the tropical pines is suitable for sulfate pulping, but yield and tear are somewhat low.

In an attempt to explain the effect of juvenile wood from tropical exotic plantations on the final product, Zobel (1985) states that:

> juvenile wood is here to stay and will make up a large proportion of the wood available from plantations in the tropics. . . . Juvenile wood is not "bad" wood—it is different wood with properties advantageous for some products and not good for others. It is generally inferior for sawn products but produces high quality particle board.

Juvenile wood of conifers is of high quality for papers such as printing papers, newsprint, tissues, and fine papers, but is not the best for papers requiring good tear, such as linerboard.

A few of the major characteristics of products made from fast-growing tropical conifer plantations with a high proportion of juvenile wood is paraphrased below from Zobel (1985) and from Table 9.4:

1. Paper has low tear but high burst strength.
2. Yields of paper per unit volume of wood are low; pulp yields are 5 to 15 % lower than from wood from older trees.
3. Juvenile wood has low cellulose and high hemicellulose yields; chemical requirements and cost of pulping are high.
4. Exotic trees have more compression wood with short cells and greater lignin content, which results in weaker paper that is difficult to bleach (Fig. 9.10).
5. The fibril angle of the wood is flat, resulting in as much as 9% more longitudinal shrinkage than occurs in normal wood. This causes poor quality and unstable solid-wood products.
6. Cells are shorter; the "long-fiber" characteristics that are desired from conifers often are not available in young wood, so mature wood must be included to obtain desired tear strength properties.
7. The moisture content of juvenile wood is usually much higher than that of mature wood, resulting in low yields per unit green weight of wood.
8. Many fast-growing exotics are harvested before much mature wood has formed, so product qualities from exotic plantations are similar to those made from thinnings with a high amount of juvenile wood.
9. Usually the exotic conifers have poor tree form and large limbs. Wood produced has even poorer qualities than result from juvenile wood alone, owing to the knots and compression wood.

TABLE 9.4. Effect of Wood Properties of Exotics on Product Quality: A Few Examples

Species	Ref.	Comments
Pinus caribaea	Hughes, 1971	Little work has been done to establish relationships between wood structural features and product quality. It is badly needed.
Pinus caribaea; P. elliottii; P. patula	Palmer & Tabb, 1971	In South Africa, pulps for *P. caribaea* trees between 9 and 14 years of age were 20% weaker than *P. elliottii* of the same age. The high-density wood yielded superior pulps. *P. oocarpa, P. patula,* and *P. caribaea* had lower-quality pulp than *P. elliottii;* this was true for several countries where the four had been grown.
Pinus caribaea	Boone & Chudnoff, 1972	Compression wood for trees grown in Puerto Rico did not affect specific gravity or modulus of rupture. It reduced modulus of elasticity and increased longitudinal shrinkage. Boards were kiln dried without degrade and were usable and machinable.
Pinus patula	Burley, 1973	The wood is variable from tree to tree and region to region but is acceptable for general utility.
Pinus caribaea	Chong & Palmer, 1973	The pulps had satisfactory alpha-cellulose, adequate but low viscosities, and low brightness for dissolving pulps—useful for some purposes.
Pinus oocarpa	Foelkel et al., 1975	In Brazil, pulp yields, tensile, burst, and tear all increased with age of wood.
Pinus caribaea	Palmer & Gibbs, 1977	When cooked by the sulfate process, there was no difference in the pulps produced in Fiji related to growth rate. The fast-growing trees produced twice the volume; the best is to grow for volume production. Growth rate has little effect on pulp yields and quality.
Pinus caribaea	Worral et al., 1977	Individual 12-year-old trees from Fiji produced markedly different pulps for both quality and yield. Specific gravity variation was high, with tear strength strongly related to it. The pulps were comparable to other pine species.
Pinus caribaea	Hawkins et al., 1978	Recovery of seasoned boards is good from 19-year-old trees (Queensland, Austr.) and only a little lower than from slash pine.

(continued)

TABLE 9.4. Continued

Species	Ref.	Comments
		Sulfate pulps from 11-year-old trees compare with commercial pulps from other species. The timber is useful for both solid wood and pulp and paper.
Eschweilera sagotiana; *Licania venosa;* *Catostemma* spp.	Palmer & Gibbs, 1978	Six hardwood species from Guyana were pulped. Wood density varied from 565 kg/m³ (*Catostemma* spp.) to 879 kg/m³ (*Licania venosa*). *Licania* and *Eschweilera* had lignin contents over 30%, requiring severe pulping for bleached pulp; both also had high silica content, which would cause excess wear in the mill during manufacture.
Pinus caribaea	Burley & Palmer, 1979	Trees pulped from Fiji were within the range of usual kraft pulps. Moderate digestion produced packaging paper; severe digestion produced weak paper suitable for bleaching.
Pinus radiata	Corson & Foster, 1982	New crop trees produce as good-quality refiner mechanical and thermomechanical pulps as did old crop trees. The wood is ideal for high-strength newsprint and printing grades of paper. *P. radiata* wood has good pulp qualities and can be rated with spruce.
Pinus patula; *P. radiata*	Palmer et al., 1982a	In Kenya, the tear strength increased and burst and tensile decreased with age; older trees had higher densities and stronger pulps.
Pinus patula; 5 Eucalypt species	Palmer et al., 1982b	In comparative tests from Kenya, *P. patula* yielded 47% unbleached pulp, the eucalypts over 50%. The older (20-year) *P. patula* made suitable packaging papers. The best eucalypts were better than most commerically used hardwood pulps; brightness was about the same for *P. patula* and the eucalypts.
Albizia; *Gmelina;* *Anthocephalus;* *Schizolobium;* *Terminalia;* *Maesopsis*	Palmer et al., 1983	All genera grown in plantations in Fiji were low density (below 300 kg/m³) except *Terminalia brasii, Gmelina arborea,* and *Maesopsis eminii,* whose density varied from 350 to 415 kg/m³. All pulped well by the sulfate process (except *Terminalia superba*), yielding 47–50% bleachable grade pulp. *T. superba* had high lignin and

TABLE 9.4. Continued

Species	Ref.	Comments
		yielded only 41% pulp using high levels of chemicals for digestion. Bonding strength of all was satisfactory, but only the three high-density ones had tear similar to a hardwood mix from southern U.S.
Pinus kesiya	Hardie & Ingram, 1983	This species has the defects of poor stem form, a large juvenile core, and compression wood when grown in Zambia. Sawn wood showed considerable degrade and instability.
Pinus caribaea; P. radiata	Smith, 1983	Sawn board recovery for 19-year-old trees of *P. caribaea* in Queensland, Austr., was better than *P. elliottii*, although *P. caribaea* had slightly lower wood density. The full range of end uses could be supplied by this species; pulp yields were slightly higher than from *P. radiata*.
Eucalyptus saligna/ grandis	Palmer & Gibbs, 1984	Nine-year-old trees in Uganda had wood density of 431 kg/m^3 and 17-year-old trees had 467 kg/m^3. The 9-year-old trees had the best bonding, the 17-year-old had best tearing strength. Stronger pulp was produced than from mixed hardwoods from the southern U.S.
Pinus caribaea; P. oocarpa	Brito, 1984	Use of thinnings for charcoal gives inferior yield and bulk density from pine compared to hardwood. Briquettes can be made that have good qualities.

In general, the utilization of young, fast-grown hardwoods has only a minor effect on product yields or quality, except for solid-wood products.

The utilization of the wood of exotics is shown by a few selected papers in Table 9.4. These can be generally summarized as follows:

1. The older trees produced the best tear strength, the younger ones the best burst and tensile strength.
2. The exotic conifers produce good refiner mechanical and thermomechanical pulps. This wood is good for newsprint and printing papers.
3. *Pinus caribaea* has had many studies made on it. In some environments and with ages over 10 years, it produces products somewhat similar to the southern pines of the United States, although frequently the pulps are weaker than those from *P. elliottii*.

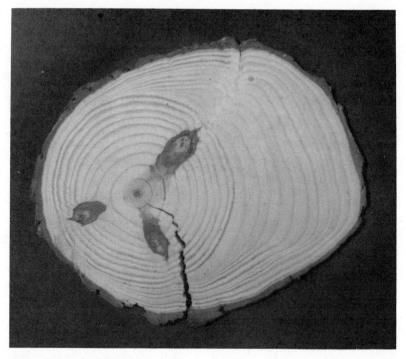

Figure 9.10. Exotic conifers with poor form have much compression wood with high lignin content, which gives weak and unstable lumber and low fiber yields when pulped. Shown is compression wood (the area with wide rings) of a loblolly pine tree that was leaning severely as a result of a storm.

4. High-density wood produces pulps with better tear strength.
5. Wood of young conifers gives inferior yields and bulk density when charcoal is produced.
6. The hardwoods generally give higher yields of fiber products than do the conifers.
7. Eucalypt wood (from average specific gravity trees) usually produces highly desirable pulp. Good pulps are also made from *Gmelina*. Species such as *Terminalia superba* have a high amount of lignin and do not pulp well (Palmer et al., 1983).
8. Although usually considered to be undesirable for solid-wood products, the wood of some eucalypts can be quite valuable if proper seed sources and utilization procedures are followed. As one example of this, Revell (1983) has reported that satisfactory recovery of high-grade timber is possible from several species of *Eucalyptus* when grown in New Zealand. Logs must be large to reduce growth stresses and to quarter-saw boards outside the juvenile core.

9. Because of the effect of the environment on wood, no good prediction of pulping qualities of an exotic can be made unless trees are obtained from the environment in which they will be grown.

Recognizing the effect of harvest at an early age and the effect of different environments on wood properties is essential. In general, the exotics produce products acceptable on the world market, but they are often marginal. Solid-wood products are frequently inferior, although they are quite satisfactory for some species like radiata pine. Sweep in the bole is a common defect in exotics, particularly in the tropics. Often the effect of bole malformations are not measured; however, Cown et al. (1984) reported on the effect of sweep in radiata pine. Straight logs yielded 45% clear grade compared to 34% for moderate sweep and 28% for severe sweep. The caution must be repeated to test the value of the wood from trees of a specific exotic environment before assuming that the product will be usable; this is especially true for the conifers.

9.7 NONCONVENTIONAL USES OF WOOD

Especially in countries where exotics are grown, the forests are used for such things as charcoal, chemicals, or fuelwood, which require wood properties different from those normally considered to be of importance for conventional wood products. For example, low moisture content and high wood density are preferred and often extractives are desired rather than considered a defect. Interest and emphasis on exotics in this area of nonconventional uses of wood is rapidly expanding and, as previously described in this book, are receiving a great deal of support. Work on wood especially suited for these purposes has lagged somewhat, but interest is picking up. For example, in a recent article, Ferreira and dePaula (1983) make an economic assessment of the factors, including wood properties, that affect the costs of producing charcoal.

Fuelwood can be thought of as an unconventional use of wood only in the sense that it is usually not considered when wood properties are discussed. Anywhere from 20% to over half the wood harvested in the world is for fuel-wood, depending upon which author one accepts. Some countries are as much as 90% dependent on wood for energy (Evensen, 1981). Much of the wood used for fuelwood is of low quality or from what is currently considered to be waste. Demand for fuelwood is becoming so great in some areas that high-quality wood must be used, and in a number of countries there is severe competition for wood of any kind for fuelwood. In such areas the need for fuel-wood is starting to be filled by planting exotics. It is so serious in some regions that certain international organizations are trying to develop a greater variety of foods that can be eaten without cooking, so that wood will not be required for cooking. The international organization CARE states in one of its flyers: "By the year 2000, just 17 years away, fuelwood requirements will exceed the available supply by 25%."

The need for fuelwood is steadily increasing. The need to establish energy plantations is becoming more urgent and many of these will use exotic species. As pointed out by Anderson et al. (1983), short-rotation, intensively managed plantations of genetically improved, fast-growing trees will be needed to contribute to energy supplies in the temperate as well as tropical regions. The Swedish Board for Energy (Anon., 1981b) has developed a list of 288 species and 31 genera for use as fuelwood, 27 hardwoods and four conifers.

Although generally little attention has been paid to the quality of wood to be used for energy, the development of slow- but hot- and clean-burning wood is needed. Such wood will have high density, uniformity, and a low moisture content. Some work has been done in this area, and it appears that wood quality more suitable for energy can quickly be developed (Anon., 1978b; Brewbaker and Hutton, 1979; Zobel, 1980a; Smith and Toomey, 1982).

In addition to its use for fuelwood, there is now development in the use of wood more suitable for industrial energy and chemicals. Although this trend is not yet general, the use of wood for energy is quite advanced in some areas of the world (White, 1977; Fege et al., 1979; Smith, 1981).

Much of the wood used for energy and chemicals comes from waste (Zerbe and Baker, 1980), but the forest industry is now growing wood specifically for these unconventional purposes. Special effort has been made to develop forests for energy production in short-rotation energy plantations (Schneider, 1977; Land, 1980). There is major concern in a reduction of land productivity from total tree removal. As pointed out elsewhere, the seriousness of this varies with many conditions. However, it must be considered and, as stated by Castro et al. (1983), "It seems to be not convenient to exploit the crown mainly for short rotations because the increased yield is accompanied by a strong increase in nutrient removal."

The largest use of wood for energy other than for fuelwood is the huge charcoal program to energize the steel industry in Minas Gerais, Brazil. Historically, most charcoal in this region has been obtained from trees from natural forests, but this source of wood is rapidly being withdrawn and the steel companies are growing their own wood needs with exotics (Fig. 9.11). In the states of Minas Gerais and Espirito Santo, approximately 100,000 hectares (250,000 acres) are planted annually with exotics, much of which is converted to charcoal. Most of the faster-growing species of *Eucalyptus* being used do not have ideal wood for charcoal. Some species that have the best wood are slow growers. Since charcoal is best made from high-density, low-moisture-content wood, trees must be developed that both possess such wood and have fast growth. The tree breeder is now being faced with the task of developing trees with the desired wood in the faster-growing species. Good progress has been made that will result in wood quite different from that now preferred for cellulose products.

Another form of energy made from wood in Brazil is alcohol to be mixed with gasoline. Since there is not enough alcohol produced from sugar and

Figure 9.11. Many exotic species are being used for energy plantations. In much of the tropics, charcoal is a major source of industrial energy. The old-fashioned, inefficient charcoal kilns shown in Brazil are currently being improved to become much more efficient.

manioc to supply immediate and future demands, some of the needed alcohol is being obtained from wood.

There has been much progress is using wood for organic chemicals, although operational use has slowed because energy prices have leveled off (Goldstein, 1980b). The interest in using wood for chemicals must be maintained for the time when it will be needed. When the production of chemicals from wood becomes operational, the kind of wood desired will almost certainly differ from that now available. For example, based upon the chemical products being considered, hardwoods are preferred for wood chemical production over conifers.

Wood of exotic species used for energy varies just as it does for those used for wood products. For example, in Colombia, Ladrach (1984a) reported differences in wood density between the provenances of two species of *Leucaena*. He found that the provenances of these species (which are used mostly for fuel) that had high density in one test area also had high wood density in other test areas.

Although only a secondary product from wood, resin produced from exotic conifers is important. Many tests on yield and quality are under way. One example is by Capitani et al. (1983), who found in Brazil that *Pinus caribaea* var. *bahamensis* produced more resin than *P. elliottii*, *P. caribaea* var. *hondurensis*, or *P. oocarpa*. They found no differences in the quality of the resins among the species. Some companies that need resins in their manufacturing process are finding that resin production may be as profitable as wood production. Usually, the trees are tapped for resin just before they are felled. With time, much of the resin supply will come from the "soap" produced in the sulfate pulping process.

A common product from exotic trees is the bark. Of course it is used with fuelwood, but it is also frequently used for fiber products such as particleboard and in pulp. The bark of some eucalypts and *Gmelina* is especially used because the fibers do not differ too much from those in the wood. The amount of bark is particularly important in volume assessment because very frequently plantation yields are reported as overbark rather than as the actual volume of wood under the bark. Some species have relatively small amounts of bark, such as *Eucalyptus* in the Congo, where it makes up 10% or a little more of the total tree volume (Delwaulle, 1985). However, for young tropical pines bark can constitute up to 40% of the total merchantable bole of the tree (Zobel and Van Buijtenen, 1988).

10

POLITICAL AND ASSOCIATED BIOLOGICAL PROBLEMS RELATED TO GROWING EXOTICS

10.1 GENERAL CONSIDERATIONS

Plantation forestry using exotics is increasing at a rapid rate. Its advantages are great; its problems are considerable. It will continue to increase because of need and profitability (Ramirez, 1979; Sedjo, 1983). Although most specific aspects of exotic plantation forestry are covered in other chapters of this book, the one associated with politics and biology is unique and troublesome and will be discussed in this chapter.

Because of the strong environmental interest and concerns of society, the growing of exotics has become somewhat politicized, creating a set of new and unique considerations that must be recognized and dealt with. As with anything that enters the political arena, some problems are real and serious while others are imagined, incorrect, and exaggerated beyond reality. It is the objective of this chapter to cover some biological aspects of exotic forestry that have become politicized and to explain their importance and validity based upon known biological facts and concepts.

Exotics are either "loved" or "hated," depending upon the conditions and persons involved. For example, it is frequently easier to get monetary support for a forestry program that stresses exotics than for one dealing with indigenous species. On the other hand, in some situations the word *exotic* evokes resistance and antagonism and the expression of many fears about their possible disadvantages or the dangers exotics pose to the environment. When political and environmental considerations are added to biological problems related to growing exotics, it sometimes seems that there are no reasonable solutions.

On the surface, the political aspects of growing exotics may appear to be independent of biology, but, in fact, the politicians usually invoke biological, environmental, or conservation factors as reasons for their actions. Therefore, the main objective here is to discuss political aspects as related to biological, environmental, or conservation concepts. This is not easy because it is most difficult to objectively separate facts from hearsay and rumor. Ignorance of the biological principles involved and personal misunderstandings are increased by poor public relations and biased press coverage, sometimes without any scientific explanations, as well as by environmental extremists making unfounded claims. This chapter makes an attempt to discuss scientific explanations of various justifications given by politicians for actions taken in favor of or antagonistic to exotic forestry.

Those who desire information to support claims for or against exotic forestry find that many biological facts are not available and will not be available for a long time—if ever. An example is the predicted change of climate following harvesting of the indigenous forest and the subsequent planting of exotic tree species. One hears such predicted climatic changes cited directly or indirectly, especially in the tropics, but none of them are based upon facts collected over a long enough period of time or on studies large enough or designed well enough to provide sound data. With our current knowledge, any predicted changes in climate are at best suppositions or hypotheses; sometimes they are based upon biologically unsound statements made to further a political objective. The inexactness of available information on environmental changes caused by removal of indigenous forests is emphasized by Whitmore (1981), who states:

> There is rather little knowledge, and therefore less agreement and few generalizations, on the effects of clearing rain forest on the hydrological and mineral cycles or on the recovery of biomass.

There certainly is nothing wrong with the expression of suppositions or hypotheses about the effects of replacing indigenous species with exotics, so long as they do not suddenly become dogma because they appear in print, a situation that is too common, especially if biological objectivity is overlooked by the author in an attempt to further some premise. For example, if a few thousand hectares of jungle are cut and a severe drought occurs in the general area in the next year or two, it is not unusual to hear the claim that the harvesting of the forest was a direct cause of the drought. Frequently, it is overlooked that the drought covered half a continent or that, historically, drought periods have been cyclical in the area whether or not the indigenous forest had been disturbed. Legitimate opinions, ideas, or hypotheses sometimes become "facts" even when the author's statements have been qualified, but the qualifying phrases have been left out of the published quotation. This is frightening, and we have frequently read with dismay quotations credited to us that have left an incorrect impression because the qualifying information had been deleted.

Occasionally, strong dogmas put forth by politicians are based upon biologically incorrect information. One that is frequently promoted in the tropics is that pines use an excess of oxygen and if they are planted on a large scale, people will suffer from an oxygen deficiency and may suffocate. The biological fact is that, whether it be pine, sugarcane, beans or grass, fast-growing young green plants give off oxygen and utilize carbon dioxide. The faster a tree grows, the more oxygen it will produce. Yet it is astounding how many persons express the erroneous concept that pine trees are using oxygen needed for humans or producing too much carbon dioxide (Lugo and Brown, 1981). In addition, more oxygen is generated by oceanic vegetation than by land vegetation and a small change in land vegetation will not have a decisive effect on the oxygen supply.

In addition to pointing out the political aspects of the use of exotics, another objective of this chapter is to indicate what we feel is the true biological situation relative to growing exotics. The problems as well as the benefits from growing exotics will be covered as impartially as possible, using examples or references whenever available. It is especially important to indicate whether specific problems are caused by or are unique to growing exotics or whether indigenous species grown in plantations in the same area have the same effect on the environment and thus on society, the area of concern to the politicians. Too frequently, plantation forestry is equated with growing exotics, and therefore problems which occur in plantations are said to result from exotics and are not simply a result of plantation culture. As stated by Quintana (1981) for the situation in Colombia, "Daily we can hear and read unfavorable comments regarding the possibilities of artificial plantations, which create fear and distrust in the possible potential reforester." We will attempt to separate the general problems of plantation forestry from those that are exclusively caused by the use of exotics.

The political problems associated with exotic forestry really begin before establishment of plantations. The political oversight of not involving the local people results in a lack of understanding of the true biological situation (Ladrach, 1985b). As Ladrach points out, decisions made about growing exotic forests often fail because the biological results of making the plantations are not known by the public. He says of the locals: "Without their cooperation, forestation will usually have a poor chance of success." Many biological problems visualized by the locals could have been avoided if they had been included in the planning phases of the exotic forestry program.

Even though the restrictions to the establishment of exotic forests often are not well understood, support for finding the needed answers is frequently lacking. For example, Johnson (1984) feels that there is purposeful nonsupport for studies in tropical forest areas. He reports that less than 2% of international aid is for forest management and that:

> The international politics of tropical forests have not in recent times encouraged much change in priorities.—Forests, indeed, often act as a carpet under which countries can sweep their "misfit" populations—concessions for their [the forests'] exploitation are often lucrative since they are sources of public revenue or private graft.

The preceding theme was also expressed by Westoby (1984), who feels that it is right for people to be concerned about the destruction of forests, but "they are upset for the wrong reasons—misled by half-truths and irrelevancies given wide circulation by misguided conservationists." He emphasizes that in the tropics the politics of manipulating the army of landless people, and the need for them in the political system which creates localized population pressures, are causing the problems: "the fight to save the tropical forests is a political fight."

The rate at which the tropical forests are being cut and replaced by exotic forests is difficult to measure, and estimates differ widely (Whitmore, 1981; Lugo and Brown, 1981). Having worked in these areas, it is clear to the authors that total land clearing in some regions is proceeding at a rapid rate and that much of the newly created farmland and pastureland soon becomes so marginal, unproductive, and eroded that its only ultimate productive use will be through reforestation. It would often be preferable to plant indigenous tree species, but this is not always possible on these degraded sites (Gallegos et al., 1982), both because the management of the indigenous species is not well known and because the sites have been so altered by mismanagement that they are not suitable for these species (Fig. 10.1). The more hardy exotic species, such as the pines and eucalypts, must then be widely used in planting the degraded sites. Stated briefly, the politics of land use and utilizing forests for agriculture are such that large exotic forestry programs will be required if the lands are to be made even reasonably productive again; this is true both for the tropical and temperate regions.

The reader will ask, "What has this to do with the politics of growing exotics?" Indeed, there is a strong tie. Because of the extensive concern about and study of forests, the following examples will be used to illustrate the relationships between exotic forestry and politics. The need for a better understanding is rapidly expanding. For example, of the 918 million hectares of tropical forests around the world (Leopoldo Brandão, Aracruz Florestal, personal communication), much of the 130 million hectares that are likely to be cut-over before the year 2000 could be used to supply food and fuel for at least 200 million poor people (Johnson, 1984). Most of the wood produced would come from plantations of exotic species, just as much of the food grown there will be of exotic origin.

In their reference to the widely publicized Jari Project on the Amazon River in the state of Para, Brazil, which uses exotics, Fearnside and Rankin (1982) state that "political and bureaucratic decisions affecting the silvicultural operation may have at least as much impact on its [Jari's] ultimate sustainability

Figure 10.1. There are large areas of degraded sites that need to be reclaimed, such as this one in South America. The timber was cut, it was farmed for a short time, then it was grazed and, finally, abandoned. Such land is not suitable for replanting with the indigenous species that were formerly there, but some exotic species can grow remarkably well.

as the many biological and agronomic threats to continued production." In the chapter on Jari in their book *Amazon,* Kelly and London (1983) emphasize that the causes for the sale of the company by Daniel K. Ludwig, the original developer and past owner of the Jari Forestry Project, were primarily political in nature and due to a lack of public relations rather than caused by adverse biological considerations related to the growing of exotics (Fig. 10.2). Similar political problems frequently arise in other operations involving exotics. Unfortunately, however, the ecological problems related to exotic plantations are often given as cause-and-effect reasons for failures of the projects, rather than the true cause, which may be strongly related to political interference.

Compounding the concern for forestry problems with exotics are the frequent "on-again, off-again" forestry programs sponsored within a country by one government and then ignored by the succeeding government. Such political instability results in poorly planned exotic forests and sometimes economically disastrous forestry operations. It disrupts studies necessary for the testing of species and provenances and delays development of the badly needed land races. Lack of continuing support for proper exotic forest development, although often not recognized, is one of the most serious political restrictions to proper use of exotics.

Another political problem when growing exotics relates to the intensity of

Figure 10.2. One of the most publicized uses of exotics is in the Jari operation in Brazil. Here the soils have been graded as most useful for pines (as shown), for *Gmelina,* or for *Eucalyptus.* Much of the total land area is left in the indigenous tropical hardwoods. A large industry is supported by exotic forests.

forest management sometimes required. Because of the nature of the marginal sites on which exotics are often grown and the inherent nature of the exotic species, very intensive site preparation, release from competition, and intensive stand management may be needed. This sometimes includes the use of herbicides or heavy equipment for site preparation, which can be a problem for the politicians and foresters. These management practices are especially noted by the concerned general public and environmentalists, since they may result in excess toxicity or compaction and erosion of the soil. However, some areas such as grasslands require very little management, and thus minimal environmental change results from growing exotic forest trees.

Numerous publications could be cited that deal with the political aspects of growing exotics. It is rare to find a publication that appears to be essentially unbiased. One of the best examples of an apparently fair coverage for the tropics is the book *Amazon* by Kelly and London (1983). Some publications, such as Burch and DeLuca (1983), deal with exotics and the social impact of natural resource policies. One publication by Ladrach (1982) dealt specifically with the questions raised by nonforesters about growing exotics in Colombia and made an effort to relate this to the biological concepts involved.

10.2 THE REPLACEMENT FOREST CONCEPT

Planting exotic forest trees on marginal sites, such as in the grasslands, scrub-brushlands, eroded lands, or abandoned farmlands, has been a long-standing practice. Recently, the term *replacement forests* has been rather universally applied to this practice. It is used to indicate a method of helping to preserve the indigenous forest ecosystems by producing the needed wood without intensively harvesting and managing the remaining indigenous forests (Fig. 10.3). Thus, many of the comments in this chapter regarding exotic forests apply to replacement-type forest operations. This concept was stated similarly for the tropics by Lugo and Brown (1981), who said:

> The faster growth of these species can satisfy the increasing demand for wood and even contribute to reducing deforestation because plantations are more productive than natural forests by a two to ten-fold factor.

There is a lack of knowledge about the true situation regarding the destruction of indigenous forests specifically for the purpose of planting exotics. One often gets the impression that large operations are cutting and often destroying the indigenous timber with the objective of replacing it with exotic species. This idea has become widespread for the tropics, partially from the numerous articles about the Jari operation in the Amazon of Brazil, where, initially, the indigenous timber was replaced by exotics. However, in Jari very little indigenous forest is now being cut, with the bulk of the planting operations replacing exotic plantations that are currently being harvested. But most large exotic operations avoid the indigenous forests and grow the needed timber in the grasslands, scrub-brushlands, or degraded forests where costs are less, markets are closer, and operations are simpler even though growing conditions

Figure 10.3. Much of the wood needs of the world will be supplied by growing exotics on marginal and submarginal agricultural land, such as this area in South America. Wood produced here will relieve the pressures on the indigenous forests. Thus, the concept of replacement forests is becoming widely recognized and hailed by conservationists and used by the forest industry.

usually are not as good as where the indigenous forests are found. In both the tropical and temperate zones, considerable exotic planting is done where indigenous forests were previously cut for agricultural use and have reverted to grass, weeds, or brush, some of which is also of exotic origin, after being abandoned for agriculture.

Most foresters and conservationists agree that, biologically, the best way to manage the tropical and many of the temperate hardwoods is to use natural regeneration systems that avoid high-grading and major species losses, although the economics of such a system is often in doubt. The use of replacement forests enables the forest manager to produce the needed large volumes of wood fiber and energy without intensive management of the natural forests. Replacement forests are widely used where there has been complete destruction of the indigenous forest following cutting by farmers, squatters, or colonists, who remove the trees and then try to farm the land or use it for grazing, often leaving it after a few years in a totally nonproductive state, growing neither crops, pasture, or useful forest trees. Other times, forests will follow the abandonment, but the species and quality may be inferior, suggesting replacement by exotic species. As an example, Burner (1980) states that the average life of a ranch in the Amazon is a mere two to seven years before it is abandoned due to weed or palm growth, erosion, or lack of nutrients.

10.3 BIOLOGICAL, ECOLOGICAL, AND CONSERVATION MISCONCEPTIONS AND POLITICS

Several of the most important biological, ecological, and conservation concepts and relationships that have been used by politicians as a basis for making political decisions about the use of exotics in forestry, both in the tropical and temperate areas, will now be discussed. It is our objective to present the concept and then to point out what we feel to be the true biological and ecological situation relative to its effect on growing exotics.

10.3.1 Conifers Use Excess Oxygen

Perhaps one of the most widely discussed and most incorrect concepts used as a basis for restricting the use of exotics is that *pines use oxygen that should be available to humans* and thus pine planting should be restricted. This often also includes their effect on the carbon cycle.

This concept of excessive use of oxygen by conifers is biologically incorrect. All rapidly growing green plants, be they grass, corn, rice, brush, or trees, use carbon dioxide and free oxygen in the photosynthetic process, that is, in the production of photosynthate necessary for life and growth (Kramer and Kozlowski, 1960). Despite this widely proven physiological reaction in plants, the idea that exotic conifers will deplete the oxygen supply has much popular support in several of the forest areas in the world and has resulted in some major social and economic problems. For example, in one state of a South American country, where the major industry is based upon conversion of the wood from pine plantations into utilizable products, following an environmental and newspaper campaign against pines, the legislature was urged to pass a law prohibiting the planting of pines to "protect the people from a loss of oxygen" (Anon, 1978a). Luckily, pines were not permanently banned and are still being grown and the economy of the region has not been destroyed. Even though the concept of the excessive use of oxygen by pines is biological nonsense, the newspaper had cited a botany professor as the source of its information and many laymen were convinced that this was truly a biological fact which needed to be acted upon.

In a number of forested areas some version of the concept of pines using too much oxygen is cited as a reason for taking restrictive political action. Arguments to the contrary are often ignored (Broeker, 1970). In 1971, Cooper emphasized the huge size of the world oxygen reserves and stated that it is not true that cutting trees might cause an oxygen problem with humans.

Much research has been done on the role of forests in general, and exotics in particular, relative to the global carbon cycle. As an example, Lugo and Brown (1980) and Brown and Lugo (1982) reported on the effect of the carbon cycle related to harvesting in the tropical rain forests. They state that if harvested forests are allowed to regenerate or are planted back to trees, the carbon balance will be easily maintained.

10.3.2 Soil Deterioration from Exotics

It is a common belief that exotic species in some way cause soil deterioration and sometimes soil sterility. Claims of excess nutrient usage by exotics, production of acid soils from accumulation of leaf litter, and even the formation of hardpans are frequently cited as reasons to restrict the planting of exotics. One common concept is that continued cropping over several rotations will result in an overall loss in productivity of the site. This is now being intensively studied. One example was reported by Evans (1983), who stated: "There is no evidence yet of declining productivity with successive rotations in tropical plantations." An example he used was second- and third-rotation pine crops in South Africa. He cautions that data are few and most plantations are in their first rotation. Suitable test areas need to be established and maintained in successive rotations.

The various effects of exotics on soils must be considered and assessed; some are valid and serious while some are minor without basis in fact. It is essential to emphasize that most of the soil changes which result from forest plantations occur whether or not exotic forest trees are used. The soil effects are mostly related to intensive, short-rotation plantation forestry which occurs when either exotic or indigenous species are grown.

The concept that exotics place an especially heavy usage on soil nutrients is quite understandable because there is a heavy nutrient demand from rapidly grown forest plantations that are harvested at short intervals. The bulk of the nutrients present in a tree is in its leaves, small limbs, and bark; little is found in the wood. Nutrient loss from logging is accelerated by "total-tree" harvesting when the bole of the tree is harvested and chipped along with the branches and sometimes with the leaves. This method of total-tree harvesting is especially serious on marginal soils when very short rotations are employed, two conditions commonly encountered when exotics are grown. Renewal of key elements to the soil may then become necessary (Sanchez et al., 1984). Total-tree harvesting is not commonly practiced with most exotics, but it is becoming more widespread and must be considered.

The subject of short-rotation silviculture was covered by Crane and Raison (1983). It was found that *Eucalyptus delegatensis,* grown in Australia, had lesser nutritional requirements (particularly phosphorus) than did *Pinus radiata.* They conclude that this difference holds for short rotations up to seven years, but for longer rotations there is little difference between the eucalypts and other genera.

The exceedingly fast-growing species of *Eucalyptus* and *Gmelina* fill the definition for fast growth and short rotations, and fertilization is often warranted. Especially suspect are the eucalypts. In a study in Spain, Temes (1982) found that "the soils where *Eucalyptus globulus* grows show no signs of degradation or of nutrient reserve loss, no differences in composition—from the oak or pine soils." It is Quintana's (1981) opinion that pines generally are less demanding of nutrients. In fact, he suggests the feasibility of planting badly eroded and degraded areas with pines to help the soil.

Great care must be taken in estimating the economic costs of replacement of actual nutrient loss that occurs when planting exotics. Fearnside and Rankin (1982) calculated a rather substantial loss of nutrients, especially nitrogen, when growing *Gmelina* in the Amazon Basin. They estimated that the total cost to fertilize was U.S. $142.47/ha/yr based upon replacement costs for nutrients lost in the removal of wood and bark and from erosion, or a total cost of $1424.70. Obviously, the cost of fertilizing once a rotation, which would normally be done, was multiplied by each of 10 years in the rotation when these calculations were made. Nutrient loss from harvesting occurs only once a rotation (at time of harvest); in the meantime, there is a recycling of nutrients with litter fall and the natural additions of nutrients from mineral weathering in the soil, biological nitrogen fixation, and nutrient additions from the atmosphere. Costs of using fertilizers must be estimated using realistic values.

There are references in the literature showing that growing trees results in only minor deterioration or sometimes actually in improvement of the physical and nutrient content of the soil; we have observed this as well as greater soil moisture in pine plantations in the llanos (grasslands) of Venezuela. In New Zealand, Cockayne (1914) stated that *P. radiata* did not reduce the fertility of the soil but improved it. Jackson (1973) reported on how tree roots absorb and recycle soil nutrients. We have observed the improvement in soil under exotics in many regions. One example is the increased productivity following establishment of pine in the piedmont soils that had been eroded by farming in the southern United States (Zobel and Davey, 1977).

In a study comparing the effect of the three species *Eucalyptus globulus, Pinus pinaster,* and *Quercus robur* in Spain, Temes et al. (1985) found no differences in soil granulometric composition among the three species. Profile development evaluation, applied to the clay content, did not show evidence of accumulation or losses in any of the profiles studied. The content of exchangeable aluminum, potassium, and magnesium was greatest under the *Eucalyptus.* For this same study, Bard (1984) developed a group of 10 indices and found no difference attributable to different kinds of trees. In Brazil, Haag et al. (1983) found that both pine and eucalypts increased the organic content and nutrient content of the soil. *E. citriodora* improved the magnesium and potassium content of the soil, and leaves of the eucalypts had higher nutrient levels than did *Pinus taeda* needles.

The entire subject of tree plantations as soil builders and site improvement from tree growth in the humid tropics has recently been summarized by Sanchez et al. (1984). They state:

> Little deterioration of soil properties, relative to the virgin forest, were measured during the establishment phase, particularly when a leguminous cover or fertilization was used and the land was cleared by either slash and burn or mechanized land clearing methods that caused little damage to soil properties.

They found little loss in soil chemical properties and were surprised at the dramatic calcium accumulation under plantations of *Gmelina arborea.*

The main deleterious effects of exotic tree crops on soil properties occurs during the plantation establishment phase from site preparation, soil compaction, and erosion. However, trees have an advantage when compared to annual crops because of the longer time they protect the soil surface, the higher biomass, and their ability to recycle nutrients. Yet there is a loss of nutrients, chiefly potassium, from harvesting and leaching prior to canopy closure and a considerable loss of nitrogen, especially when burning is used. This must be replaced by fertilizers if high yields from exotic plantations are to be maintained. If soils have a high native reserve of nutrients, fertilization may not be necessary for several rotations.

There is concern that exotic species, such as the pines, spruces, and eucalypts, poison the soil from an accumulation of leaf litter. (See Section 10.3.5 dealing with poisoning of the soil, or allelopathy.) Sometimes, adverse effects do occur in the cool-temperate climates with species such as spruce, where a strong buildup of leaf litter can occur because of slow deterioration from cool temperatures, which can tie up nutrients, result in an acid surface layer, and cause low biological activity of soil organisms. In the tropics and subtropics, where leaf litter does not accumulate because of rapid decomposition under conditions of high temperatures and plentiful moisture, this problem is less severe. The occasional slight increase of acidity when conifers are grown in the tropics is of no importance to soil productivity and most soils are well enough buffered that significant pH changes will not occur. In some areas, other crops grow well under pine.

The resins and phenols in the leaves of pines and eucalypts do not pose a serious problem, as is sometimes claimed. Actually, contrary to the occasional claims of soil degradation from leaf litter, the soil is usually considerably improved by tree planting because of an enhancement of the water-holding and nutrient-retaining capacities from the increased organic content of the decomposed leaf litter (Zobel and Davey, 1977; Sanchez et al., 1984).

Another claim sometimes made about conifers is that a hardpan is formed by the root pattern of the trees, preventing water percolation and thereby creating a swamp. Most trees have roots that grow to considerable depths unless prevented by a hardpan that existed in the soil prior to planting.

It is thought by some that logging, followed by planting exotics, sometimes creates a "swamp." It is true that when vegetation (such as a forest) is removed from certain "wet-natured" sites, the water table rises because of the reduction in transpirational water loss. When the trees are growing, considerable moisture is removed from the soil by the tree via transpiration of moisture from the foliage to the atmosphere; this keeps the soil reasonably dry. After the vegetation is removed, the transpirational moisture loss no longer occurs and the site sometimes becomes so wet that trees cannot be easily reestablished. The problem of excess moisture following vegetation removal, resulting in a "swamp," is common throughout the world on heavy soils or soils with a hardpan that causes a high water table. But this phenomenon occurs whether replanted with exotic or indigenous species; neither is responsible for creation of a swamp.

Claims are frequently made that pines are harmful to the soil because their roots contain fungi (mycorrhizae) and these fungi may poison the soil. This idea is biologically incorrect. Nearly all plants, including forest tree species, have mycorrhizae of one type or another. The pines, eucalypts, and oaks all have common, "external" ectomycorrhizae that aid in the uptake of nutrients from the soil, while most hardwoods and a few conifers have the "internal" endomycorrhizae. Contrary to being harmful, these fungi are essential for suitable tree growth. Many of the problems related to growing exotics can be traced to a lack of proper mycorrhizal fungi on the roots.

10.3.3 Exotics Use an Excess of Water

One problem commonly associated with growing exotics, particularly *Eucalyptus* (Quintana, 1981), is that *exotics use so much water that they create a desert* (Fig. 10.4). There has been widespread interest in water use by the eucalypts; the literature on the broad subject of the hydrology of eucalypt forests in Australia was covered by Lima (1984). He found that in alpine dry sclerophyll conditions, the soil water regime does not differ among eucalypt forest, grassland, and herbfield. With deeper soils and higher rainfall, some soil water

Figure 10.4. *Eucalyptus* sometimes is said to create deserts by excessive use of moisture. This is not true (see text). In fact, eucalypts can be grown under the most severe of environments, as shown by this *E. camaldulensis* growing north of Santiago, Chile. Nearly one whole year has elapsed with no rain following planting of this stand.

deficit is created by the eucalypts. He found that "comparative studies have shown that the overall soil water regime of eucalypt forests does not differ from that in pine plantations."

A number of studies, such as those by Mello (1961), Karschon and Heth (1967), Ghosh et al. (1978), Golfari (1975a), and Lima and Freire (1976), do not support the contention that the eucalypts or other exotics create deserts from an excessive use of water. For the eucalypts, researchers often find that when the soil is moist, trees of this genera do, in fact, use more moisture than most other trees, but when the soils become dry, they use less with the overall annual moisture usage being about the same for eucalypts as for trees of other genera. Exceptions are species especially adapted for desert conditions, with water-saving morphological or physiological systems, or, to the contrary, genera such as *Salix* and some *Populus* that have poor stomatal closing capacity and thus use excessive amounts of moisture from wet soil during times of hot weather, low humidity, and strong winds (Pryor, 1976). According to Lima (1984), some eucalypt species do not have mechanisms for controlling high rates of transpiration, but the majority of the eucalypts do have control of transpiration rates.

Based upon experience and the literature cited earlier, it can be stated with certainty that growing eucalypts does not cause a desert. In fact, Sampio (1975) found in studies near Campinas, Brazil, that there is more moisture under eucalypt plantations and the soil has better physical features than do adjacent areas without plantations. Osara and Micola (1975) state that 100 years of experience has shown that growth of repeated plantings of exotics in India has been good where rainfall is much less than 1400 mm per year. These authors found that in the fight against deserts, tree plantations are the one viable method and species of *Eucalyptus* have been extensively and successfully used with this objective. In his article, de Camargo (1975) states that there is no justification for the fear of forming a desert by planting *Eucalyptus*.

This does not mean that trees do not use moisture as they grow. It is well understood by all foresters that if trees can be established in overwet sites, the transpiration of water from the trees' foliage will dry the site. This is one of the major reasons for bedding wet sites. The bed enables the tree to become established, and as it grows, the site is dried back to the condition that existed before the original forest was cut. A much-discussed example is the drying of the Pontine Marshes outside Rome where *Eucalyptus camaldulensis* was planted.

Since a number of species of *Eucalyptus,* such as *E. camaldulensis, E. tereticornis,* and *E. cloeziana,* are grown extensively under very low soil moisture conditions, it is easy to see why the idea has developed that the eucalypts cause desert conditions. This belief is heightened by the very vigorous root growth of the eucalypts, which outcompete other crops for the available nutrients and moisture and by the fact that crops adjacent to *Eucalyptus* plantations often wilt early and grow poorly because of the use of the moisture by the eucalypt roots. If the tree roots are cut by subsoiling, the crops adjacent to the *Eucalyptus* trees grow normally. In fact, Pryor (1976) states that:

> [the eucalypts] do not economize on the use of water but have wide ranging root systems and an ability to extract water from soil even though soil moisture tension is higher than that at which more mesophytic plants can extract water. Transpiration rates remain high even though water supply from the soil is dwindling and it is only when severe permanent wilting occurs that there is stomatal closure which inhibits water loss. . . .

He goes on to mention that this pattern varies from species to species.

Sometimes for the eucalypts, but more commonly for conifers grown on deep droughty sands such as the poorer sites in dry portions of the llanos (grasslands) or on shallow soils, the planted trees develop dieback, or even die, after they become pole sized. When the trees are small, transpiration of moisture by the plant is not great enough to deplete the soil moisture, and the water needed by the tree is replenished each year by the rainfall. As the trees become larger, the low and erratic rainfall is not enough to supply the moisture needs. When a droughty period occurs, moisture shortage results in severe top dieback or death. In areas of boron deficiency, dieback also results from lack of boron, which is accentuated under moisture stress. Exotics should not be planted on severely moisture-deficient or shallow soils, except the most hardy species for which drought-hardy land races have been developed.

The measurement of water use by trees and its effect on overall soil moisture is most difficult and sometimes quite imprecise. However, there are useful methods to assess the "droughtiness" of an area, such as Thornthwaite's (1954) concept of evapotranspiration, to determine the soil moisture balance. This has been used in Holdridge's Life Zone System (Holdridge et al., 1971) in which each life zone is represented by the ratio of potential evapotranspiration to precipitation, which is a measure of the water available to the trees.

Although we do not particularly favor legislation, it certainly is the responsibility of government foresters to warn and guide small woodland owners as to which soils are, or are not, suitable for growing different species. We have seen extensive tree-planting operations, sponsored by governments, that were total failures because the landowner was not given the proper technical guidance and planted the incorrect species on soils too droughty for the trees to survive. The political repercussions from such errors are sometimes extensive and too often the conclusion of the public has been that the trees dried out the soil to form a desert when, in fact, it was a "desert" to start with and commercial forest plantations should not have been attempted there.

10.3.4 Forest Plantations Cause Erosion

Unbelievable as it may seem, there are a number of persons who think that *planting trees causes excessive erosion* and it is suggested that exotic planting be stopped because of that adverse effect. In fact, unless poorly done, planting trees helps control erosion. Referring to Colombia, Quintana (1981), states:

> It is commonly said that pine and *Eucalyptus* erode the soil, do not store water and frighten fauna. Really, these statements do not correspond to reality—most of the mountains surrounding the Sabana of Bogota are covered with these two genera, where they are performing a protective task—In several areas of several departments, greater efforts are being made to recover soil using pine.

In another example, in Italy, a very heavy rain caused little soil movement in a 20,000-ha plantation of exotics where extensive erosion occurred before planting the trees (Ghosh et al., 1978). This positive result will only occur, however, when site preparation and planting are well done, preventing excessive water runoff during periods of heavy rains, before the trees have established a canopy and a protective layer of litter and humus. But the authors have even been challenged as to why we plant pines and eucalypts because "their roots make holes in the ground, causing excessive erosion." The biological facts are quite the contrary, and the root channels are points of entry of moisture into the soil, thus limiting erosion. Heavy use of litter under a forest stand for firewood, kindling, or leaf mulch can cause excessive erosion, as will burning, which destroys the litter. It has been stated that the very large leaves of teak matted together to form a "sheet" over the soil over which water ran and which eventually resulted in erosion on the slopes. Sometimes replacement of coniferous forests with certain types of hardwoods result in accelerated erosion because of poorer leaf cover and mulch.

How serious erosion will be in an exotic plantation depends upon the kind of site preparation as well as the kinds of soils and steepness of the slopes planted. In a visit to pine plantations in Colombia, Robert Kornegay, a consultant for the Food and Agriculture Organization of the United Nations, reported that pine plantations strongly improved the hydrological condition of the soil by making for better water holding and infiltration (Ladrach, 1982). Soil loss is critical on steep slopes, such as in the Andes, but even in the Amazon, where rolling topography is common, Fearnside and Rankin (1982) consider loss of soil nutrients from erosion to be important. Soil and nutrient loss from planting exotic forest tree species can mostly be avoided with proper silviculture. There is no question that soil and nutrient loss is much less of a problem in the long term in exotic forestry plantings than in adjacent agricultural lands, where much greater and frequent soil disturbance takes place.

10.3.5 Exotics Are Allelopathic

Exotic tree species are often assumed to be allelopathic; that is, in some manner they poison the soil so that understory vegetation, other trees, and they themselves do not grow well adjacent to one another. Sometimes political decisions are made using soil poisoning (allelopathy) as the reason that exotics should be excluded. Allelopathy occurs in species used as exotics, but it is not unique to them and is certainly well known in many forest tree species (Zobel and Talbert, 1984). In fact, allelopathy appears to be frequent in many of the indigenous tropical hardwoods. It is believed by many foresters that some indigenous species cannot be grown in pure plantations, either because of adverse environmental effects or because of allelopathy.

Although evidence is mostly circumstantial, it is commonly believed that if eucalypts are grown, agricultural crops or other tree crops cannot be successfully planted following harvesting of the trees. One commonly stated reason is that the oils in the eucalypt leaves poison the soil (i.e., they are allelopathic), creating a soil environment unsuitable for growth of other species. This belief that the eucalypts are soil poisoners has been a major argument against using *Eucalyptus* as an exotic species, sometimes leading to legislation against using trees of this genus. In California, the hypothesis was put forth that the oils contained in the leaves of *E. camaldulensis* are harmful to some plants. This concept was covered by Quintana (1981), who explains that no vegetation will grow under *Eucalyptus* plantations because of overdensity and shading out of understory vegetation, but if the plantations are managed to the proper stand density, the ground under the eucalypts will be covered by vegetation.

The exact extent of adverse soil changes from growing *Eucalyptus* that will prevent growing other crops is not definitely known; there is some relationship to soil moisture and allelopathy, as previously mentioned. We have been told— for example, in Brazil—that a crop of coffee trees would not grow well if established on the site of a former eucalypt plantation. However, we have seen some excellent coffee plantings where this assumption has not been borne out (Fig. 10.5). Other examples are the excellent coffee plantations, recently visited by two of the authors, that were growing under a *Eucalyptus* overstory in Colombia (Fig. 10.6). In South Africa, tea and avocado plantations are very successful on land where eucalypt plantations have been harvested. Commonly, we have observed excellent growth of pine, cypress, or other species on the site of former eucalypt plantings. The major difficulty resulting when crops of other species follow eucalypts seems to be the very vigorous *Eucalyptus* sprouts, which create severe competition for light and moisture with the new crop and must be controlled.

Conifers do not appear to be seriously allelopathic (this subject was touched on earlier in the case of needles of pines creating acidic soil conditions). Although most workers concede that pines generally are not a problem relative to soil degradation, statements about pine are often similar to the one made by Fearnside and Rankin (1982) in which they factually state that "pine plantations also have deleterious effects on the soil and undemonstrated long term sustainability." This statement was apparently based on a short visit to the Jari operation in Brazil; it has no basis in fact (Fig. 10.7).

Figure 10.5. Several persons told us that one could not grow agricultural crops following planting of *Eucalyptus*. This is incorrect. Note the excellent growth and vigor of this coffee plantation grown on an area where eucalypts had recently been harvested in São Paulo, Brazil.

Figure 10.6. *Eucalyptus* is sometimes used as a nurse or shade crop, as shown by this excellent coffee growing under an overstory of *E. grandis* in Colombia. We have observed such a relationship on numerous occasions.

Figure 10.7. Sometimes pines also produce a fine nurse crop. Shown here is the fruit lulu (*Solanum quitensis*) growing under *Pinus patula* in the lower Andes of Colombia. The fruit not only grows well under the pine, but it is thought that the pine reduces the nematode population which is so destructive on some fruit varieties such as lulu.

In areas such as in the southeastern United States, pine plantations have been grown over several rotations, with the net result usually being a direct improvement in soil physical and chemical properties, compared to the worn-out agricultural lands on which they were planted (Zobel and Davey, 1977). Despite the constantly repeated (but unsubstantiated) statements in the literature that pines have an adverse effect on soil, the authors know of no instance of scientific proof of this, although formation of podzols has been mentioned. On the contrary, our collective and widespread observations (but not substantiated by data) indicate that in the grasslands, such as the Orinoco Basin of Venezuela and on the eroded slopes of the Andes, even one rotation of pine results in much improved physical and chemical soil properties. Pertinent studies are currently under way.

10.3.6 Cutting Indigenous Forests and Planting Exotic Species Change the Major Weather Patterns

There is no doubt that microclimates are changed by harvesting forests and that humidity and temperature are different in an indigenous forest than in a newly established nearby plantation; this was reported for the tropics, where the humidities are lower and the temperatures higher in the plantations (Johnson, 1984). In the grasslands, mature tree plantations have higher humidity, less wind, and lower temperatures than do the adjacent undisturbed areas.

The major point of contention related to climate is whether major changes in droughts, temperatures, or storm patterns result from planting exotics. Although the literature is filled with statements of changed gross weather patterns following the clearing of indigenous forests, there are no sound data showing that planting exotics change the major weather patterns. In speaking of widespread deforestation in the Amazon, Salate et al., (1978), Fearnside (1979), and Fearnside and Rankin (1982) suggest that deforestation causes decreases in annual rainfall. They go on to state that evapotranspiration (mostly transpiration) accounts for half the water vapor generating rainfall between Belem and Manaus, Brazil (Villa Nova et al., 1976, Salate et al., 1978). We are in no position to question this statement, but we do challenge the statement that planting exotics will lower the amount of evapotranspiration. In fact, well-stocked forest plantations produce a great amount of transpiration. It is obvious that both a reduction in transpiration and an excess of transpiration cannot at the same time be ascribed to planting exotics.

The biological fact is that the transpiration from well-stocked exotic plantations will not be dramatically different from indigenous regrowth forests. If it were possible to clear and keep vegetation off the soil, the suggested changes in transpiration might occur. But those who work in either temperate or tropical forests know how difficult it is to keep regrowth from establishing itself following removal of the forest canopy. The concept that major climatic changes do not occur when exotics are planted is backed by Fearnside and Rankin (1982), who state that at Monte Dourado (Jari) records since 1968 show no trends in rainfall changes or in dry season severity related to clearing and planting exotics. But they add as a final statement: "The time sequence is, however, too short to allow conclusions." Our question is why should there be a change in climate over time since the exotic plantations at Jari are fully stocked, with some now being harvested and replanted and there is no reason why evapotranspiration should be reduced over an extended time period.

There have been a few studies of the effect of plantation forestry on rainfall patterns. One by Pereira (1973) did not find any evidence that the presence or absence of forest trees influenced rainfall. In the Congo, Bernard (1945, 1953) did not report any influence of trees on precipitation in a 1 million km² area. In 1973, Pereira concluded that, although trees affect soil moisture, there is no direct evidence that they affect the quantity of rainfall in a given area.

Overlooked in all the discussion of weather changes is the fact that most of the weather and rainfall patterns are the result of major weather fronts that originate hundreds or even thousands of kilometers away from a given area and whose characteristics are strongly influenced by the patterns in the wind (jet streams) in the upper atmosphere.

10.3.7 Diseases and Insects Are More Severe in Exotics

This broad and important concept was discussed in detail in Chapter 4. To complete this section on politics, some of Chapter 4 will now be summarized, with special emphasis on how pests of exotics relate to political decisions because they may be more severe in exotics.

In 1982, Burdon discussed the validity of the concept that growing exotics is dangerous because "pure, even-aged stands are inherently vulnerable to diseases, insect outbreaks and climatic damage—artificial stands established with exotic species are at much greater risk than natural forests." In New Zealand, where more than two generations of exotic radiata pine have been grown, intensive studies have been made of these claims; Burdon (1982) concludes that evidence does not confirm that pure, even-aged stands are more at risk than mixed stands (the exception being when the stand is monoclonal and lacking in genetic diversity). He states that establishing a tree species outside its natural habitat and domesticating it by intensive silviculture and breeding programs does not necessarily increase susceptibility to pests (Fig. 10.8). Using gall rust on radiata pine as an example, Burdon found that growing a species as an exotic may actually release that species from its natural pests and diseases and thus improve its vigor and performance.

There is no doubt that insects and diseases will appear in exotic plantations (Zobel and Talbert, 1984). Insects and diseases occur in any intensively managed forest areas, whether the trees are exotic or indigenous. The pest problem can be more critical with exotics than with indigenous species because too often exotics are planted offsite (Burdon, 1982; Zobel and Talbert, 1984). Trees growing under stress are more susceptible to a pest than are well-adapted individuals, but experience has shown that pest damage on well-adapted exotics

Figure 10.8. It is commonly thought that plantations of exotics are more susceptible to pests than when indigenous species are used. This is not necessarily so; an example is the severe attack by fusiform rust on the indigenous *Pinus taeda,* where more than half the trees are dead. (Photo courtesy of Wiley & Sons.)

is no worse than on indigenous species. In fact, initially it is often less because of a lack of pests in the exotics, as Burdon (1982) suggests.

Ultimately, indigenous pests will adapt to exotic forest trees. Frequently, a pest from the native range of the species used as an exotic will somehow get to the exotic plantation, where the natural enemies and predators of the pest, which would normally reduce the effect of the pest, may not be present. An often cited example of a pest following an exotic is *Dothistroma* on pine, particularly on *P. radiata.* This disease, which is endemic and not too harmful in the native range of *P. radiata* in California, becomes a massive killer or seriously injures exotic pine plantations in areas such as central Brazil and central East Africa. When the disease was first discovered, political pressures developed in several countries for legislation to stop planting exotic pine, using the destruction of radiata pine as the reason.

In truth, the problems with *Dothistroma* lay partially with the forester. It is now known that *Dothistroma* needle blight is serious where warm, wet climates exist and is less serious where warm and dry or cool and wet conditions are found. For example, in much of Chile *P. radiata* is free from this disease, although it occurs on specific environments and seems to be spreading; the same is true in New Zealand and Australia. The problem arose not because an exotic was planted, but because foresters planted it on the wrong site.

Resistance to damage by animal grazing can be of key importance. For example, some species of eucalypts (*E. globulus*) are not preferred by grazing animals, which give them a distinct advantage. Such unpalatability is important in some species like neem (*Azidiracta indica*), while others, like *Gmelina,* are heavily browsed.

10.3.8 Exotics Fail Because They Are Not Adapted

Perhaps the most common error in growing exotics has been the establishment of *large plantations with a very narrow adaptive genetic base;* this error is rapidly disappearing as testing and development of land races become more widespread. Sometimes the indigenous species used in plantations have narrower gene bases than the exotics because of a lack of a suitable seed source. In both exotic and indigenous plantations, the most common cause for pest attack is the use of a poorly adapted seed source. The resulting plantations are under stress and thus are more easily damaged by pests. The importance of using well-adapted provenances and alternative species and sources to avoid political pressures against exotics because of pest epidemics was emphasized by Ladrach (1982). Nevertheless, restricting the use of exotics because of their supposed great susceptibility to pests, caused by poor adaptability, is a common political argument that has no foundation in fact if the exotics are chosen and grown as they should be. Many of the pest problems result from the poor forestry practices of using poorly adapted sources of seed, regardless of whether exotic or indigenous species are used.

10.3.9 Exotics Destroy Wildlife and Cause Biological Deserts

A frequent claim, widely accepted by the public and used by politicians, is that *exotic plantations become biological deserts* with few birds or other animal life. Another complaint is that there is a major change in the kind of fauna in plantations compared to indigenous forests or grasslands. This latter often occurs because the environment is dramatically altered, such as from dry, windy, hot grassland to cooler, more moist plantations or from tropical hardwoods to exotic conifers.

The authors have observed some remarkable increases in wildlife (birds as well as mammals) in the plantations following the planting of exotics in grasslands. For example, in the llanos of Venezuela, deer essentially did not exist in the grasslands; now they are commonly seen in the large pine plantations in the area. Birds have also increased (Fig. 10.9). In Brazil, both birds and animals are common in the eucalypt plantations, especially at the boundary of the strips of unplanted savanna or indigenous trees along watercourses.

The subject of the relationship between fauna and exotic plantations in Colombia was clearly covered by Ladrach (1982). Other authors, such as Komarek (1971), have emphasized the value of the interface of exotic and indigenous forests for game development. Most industries now leave strips of natural forest along streams and break up their plantations with indigenous forest areas

Figure 10.9. Wildlife, especially deer and birds, often increases when the grasslands are planted to trees. Shown is a deer in a compound in Colombia; these deer are now quite prevalent in some pine plantations. The deer are rarely seen in the grasslands.

between the plantations. Such a combination results in ideal conditions for wildlife.

Eucalyptus plantations have been especially singled out as being adverse for wildlife. In a detailed study by Steyn (1977) in South Africa, the author states:

> The *Eucalyptus* plantations, mainly *E. grandis,* which cover large areas in the north-eastern Transvaal are usually accused of being sterile and unsuitable for birdlife. This supposition is exaggerated and proved to be wrong . . . some less adaptable birds which occur in the area, and which must have inhabited the planted area prior to the establishment of plantations have been driven out.

He goes on to state that the most obvious example is the fruit-eating purple-creasted lourie (*Gallirex porphyreolopus*), which is rarely seen in plantations.

Detailed studies by companies such as Cartón de Colombia (Ladrach, 1982) and Pizano in Colombia have recorded wildlife populations before, during, and after plantation establishment in scrub-brushlands and grasslands. With few exceptions, wildlife has increased when the badly degraded grasslands and scrub-brushland have been replaced by exotic plantations, with strips of un-planted land adjacent to the plantations. In temperate areas, exotic plantations are frequently such a favorite of wildlife that the trees are badly damaged or destroyed by animals from moose to mice.

Sometimes the indigenous fauna damages the exotic plantations. Birds break leaders of trees or eat the buds; antelope, moose, or deer eat off the newly planted trees; porcupines girdle the planted trees; grouse eat spruce buds; and monkeys feed on the cambium of pine. This sometimes prompts foresters to control the pests, which reduces the numbers of certain animals or birds in the plantations.

Using the elimination of wildlife as a political reason to discriminate against planting exotics is not warranted. Changes in kinds of wildlife do occur, but birds and mammals become more prevalent, or are nearly as abundant, in the forest plantations as in the original grasslands and degraded scrub-brushlands or as in the indigenous forest. The requirement should be made that strips of native vegetation be left within plantations and that buffer zones of indigenous vegetation be left along streams. This will result in a much richer fauna than if the exotic plantations had not been established and will enable the continued existence of the wildlife associated with the indigenous vegetation.

10.3.10 Wood Properties of Exotics Are Inferior

It is often felt that *wood of the exotics is inferior* and indigenous species should be used for quality products. This is partially true; the exotics are used primarily to supply energy and pulp from both conifers and hardwoods. A few exotics are grown for timber for furniture or decorative products, but this is a much less common usage than for fiber products.

The major reason that the wood of exotics is desired is that it fills a special need not provided by indigenous species. In fact, it is often political pressure or economic interest resulting from the need for the kinds of wood that can be obtained from exotics that results in the use of exotic species. Wood of known characteristics and utility can be produced very rapidly.

A major error, causing economic chaos and political headaches, is the planting of large acreages of exotic forest trees without a plan for the utilization of the kind of wood that will be produced. When embarrassing surpluses must be left unused or are sold at a low return, some organizations have blamed and banned exotics when in reality it was a lack of planning for use of the wood that caused the trouble in the first place. *Before* exotics are planted, it is necessary *to know the use for which they are destined.* If the kind of wood that exotics produce is needed, exotics should be used, but if that kind of wood is not needed, exotics should not be planted.

As stressed by Zobel and Talbert (1984) and Zobel and Van Buijtenen (1988), the wood of a species may change dramatically when grown in the new, exotic environment. These changes must be known, and an assumption that the wood of the species will be the same in its indigenous range as in its new, exotic habitat is totally unwarranted. One prime example is *Pinus caribaea* var. *hondurensis,* which has very variable wood in different environments, having low-density, light wood in some areas and heavy, high-density wood in others. Such changes were thoroughly documented by Plumptre (1984) and covered in Chapter 9.

A most common problem related to the utilization of exotics is that areas are planted that are too small to efficiently support enough wood for a viable industry. Often, for political reasons, plantings are established as small, separate parcels too distant from one another to combine for a single manufacturing installation. As stated by Entrican in 1950, "of equal importance . . . is the concentration of production in as large plants as practicable." A frequent cause of failure of exotics is their establishment in noneconomic-size units. This political problem of separating plantings is common and continues to be repeated. Loss and disappointment result, not because exotics were planted or their wood was not good, but because of bad planning.

10.4 GOVERNMENT SUPPORT FOR EXOTIC PLANTING

The rapidly growing human population, shifting cultivation, rising beef prices, and the need for pasture have stimulated a widespread elimination of forests in a broad range of climates and on many different soils. It is nearly impossible for small governments in developing countries to restore the degraded lands to productivity by establishing enough forests. However, when planting of the degraded lands is done, exotic species are usually used.

Government agencies vary from enthusiastic to negative in their interest in establishing exotic forest plantations. In many countries, large exotic plantations have been started by one government, then terminated or drastically reduced by the next, and then started again by a third. This produces a timber imbalance, with the result that no industry will make the large investments necessary for manufacturing since there is no assured and continuous timber supply. Political interference and instability of this kind have no special relation to exotic forestry.

Related to the instability in establishing plantations is the follow-up support given to managing them. Frequently, good subsidies are made available to forestry that are used to establish exotic plantations. But sometimes the organization planting the trees is really not interested in forestry, only in getting the planting subsidies. Exotic tree species are frequently used and the wrong species and sources are frequently planted, which in turn are poorly managed and often produce undesirable wood. Massive forestry failures result and then the public often condemns the use of exotic species when the failure is really the fault of the organizations taking the subsidies and the governments giving but not controlling them. Although there are no data on the subject, it is the experience of the authors that nearly half the plantations of exotics established as a result of poorly supervised subsidies have failed through lack of sound follow-up management and care. Despite this, the subsidies have been of great overall benefit to forestry; a prime example is Brazil.

10.5 SUMMARY: POLITICS OF EXOTICS

The authors' summary of the points used to refute some arguments used by some politicians to restrict use of exotics is:

1. In no way will the use of exotics cause a major imbalance in either the oxygen or carbon cycles.
2. Soils are not adversely affected if good silvicultural practices are used.
3. Exotics, including the eucalypts, do not use an excess of water or cause the formation of deserts.
4. Erosion is not caused by exotics if good forestry is practiced.
5. Rarely are exotics allelopathic (i.e., they do not poison the soil).
6. Planting exotics does not alter the major weather patterns.
7. Diseases and insects are not more severe in exotic than in indigenous plantations.
8. When species and sites are properly matched, exotics can produce good yields with minimum failure or dieback.
9. Wildlife is as abundant (but species may vary) in exotic plantations as in degraded sites on which they were established. If strip planting is used, wildlife is more abundant.
10. Wood properties differ from indigenous species but are suitable for the special purposes for which exotics are planted.

Inconsistency in government policies and in the giving and controlling of planting subsidies is a frequent source of problems. But equally poor is the lack of follow-up by those who use the subsidies only as a source of income and not truly for forest production.

A quotation from a speech by Dr. Gustavo Dajer Chadid, minister of agriculture for Colombia, sums up the situation of exotics in general as well as in Colombia (Chadid, 1980):

> We must not be too cautious. Daily it is said that we should not replant with exotic foreign species, which have been shown to be able to grow with a good performance. Do not all races perhaps live together on this earth? Regarding the vegetable kingdom, what kind of valuable arguments can be brought against the cultivation of Australian trees in Colombia? Do not they and the native trees fulfill the same function? Both produce and clean the oxygen that we are breathing; they give a home to the fauna and microfauna, they protect the ground against the direct impact of rain water which is the main cause for erosion. Who can assume under this responsibility a re-forestation plan with native species if we scarcely know the behavior of approximately 10 species and this, only, because they grow in homogeneous forests? We must give up discussions which lead nowhere and only waste time. The country needs to be replanted soon! The exotic species offer us characteristics that nobody can disregard and which are especially advantageous. . . . This, of course, does not imply that the native species do not deserve our attention. . . . Reforestation is a national priority.

The same theme was covered by Quintana (1981), who emphasized that the physiological and ecological effects of all species, whether exotic or indigenous, were similar. He states:

The only difference lies in the fact that some grow quicker than the others and their behavior is known, and that some are foreign and others are Colombian. . . . In my opinion . . . an attack against the exotic species has been established without thinking of the benefits they offer.

Despite the apparent antagonism against exotics in some areas, they are becoming accepted, and even desired, by many. This was shown by Ashcroft (1982), who reported results from a poll of the public in Queensland, Australia, regarding the exotic pine reforestation program. Ninety percent of the respondents expressed a favorable attitude to the plantation program. Results indicated that the public found plantations attractive and interesting rather than monotonous. Ashcroft emphasized the need for combining recreational uses with timber production. Governments are taking a more active part in doing this and must continue to do so.

APPENDIX

A LIST OF SOME OF THE MORE IMPORTANT ACRONYMS RELATED TO EXOTIC FORESTRY

Acronym	Organization	Location
AFOCEL	Association Forêt-Cellulose	Fance
AID	Agency for International Development	United States
ARS	Agricultural Research Service	United States
BANSEFOR	Banco de Semillas Forestales	Guatemala
BLSF	Banco Latinoamericano de Semillas	Costa Rica
BOSTID	Board on Science & Technology for International Development	United States
CAFMA	Companhía Agro Florestal Monte Allegre	Brazil
CAMCORE	Central American and Mexico Coniferous Resources Cooperative	United States
CATIE	Centro Agronómico Tropical de Investigatión Enseñanza	Costa Rica
CFI (OFI)	Commonwealth Forestry Institute (Oxford Forestry Institute)	Great Britain
CIEF	Centro de Investigaciónes y Experiencias Forestales	Argentina
COHDEFOR	Corporación Hondureña de Desarrollo Forestal	Honduras
CSIRO	Commonwealth Scientific & Industrial Research Organization	Australia

(continued)

Acronym	Organization	Location
CTFT	Centre Techníque Forestier Tropical	France
DANIDA	Danish International Development Agency	Denmark
DRNR	El Departamento de Recursos Naturales Renovables	Costa Rica
EMBRAPA	Empresa Brasileira de Pesquisa Agropecuaria	Brazil
ESNACIFOR	Escuela Nacional de Ciencia Forestal	Honduras
FAO	Food and Agriculture Organization (of the United Nations)	Italy
IADS	International Agricultural Development Service	United States
IAWA	International Association of Wood Anatomists	Netherlands
IBPGR	International Board for Plant Genetic Resources	Italy
ICIA	International Crop Improvement Association	—
ICRAF	International Council for Research in Agroforestry	Kenya
IDIA	Instituto Nacional de Tecnología Agropecuaria	Argentina
INIF	Instituto National de Investigations Forestales	Mexico
IPEF	Instituto de Pesquisas e Estudos Florestais	Brazil
ISTA	International Seed Testing Association	—
ISTF	International Society of Tropical Foresters	United States
IUBS	International Union of Biological Sciences	France
IUFRO	International Union of Forest Research Organizations	Italy
NRC	National Research Council	Canada
NTSL	National Tree Seed Laboratory, USDA	United States
OAS	Organization of American States	—

Acronym	Organization	Location
OECD	Organization for Economic Cooperation and Development	Italy
OTS	Organization of Tropical Studies	U.S. and Costa Rica
PRODEPEF	Prójeto de Desenvolvimento e Pesquisa Florestal	Brazil
SAFRI	South African Forest Research Institute	South Africa
SBS	Brazilian Silvicultural Society	Brazil
SEPASAT	Survey of Economic Plants for the Arid and Semi-Arid Tropics	Great Britain
SIF	Sociedade de Investigações Florestais	Brazil
TAPPI	Technical Association Pulp & Paper Industry	United States
TDRI	Tropical Development and Research Institute	Great Britain
UNDP	United Nations Development Program	Italy
UNEP	Untied Nations Environmental Program	Italy
USDA	United States Department of Agriculture	United States
USFS	United States Forest Service	United States

REFERENCES

This list includes a sampling of books, symposia, and bibliographies dealing with aspects of exotics and their development.

Adams, T., and R. K. Campbell (1981). Genetic adaptation and seed source specificity. Seed Cert. Service, Oregon and Washington State Improv. Assoc., Medford, Oregon, pp. 78–85.

Aguilar, J. E. (1961). *Pinos de Guatemala.* Ministério de Agricultura, Guatemala City, 33 pp.

Aguilar, J. E. (1981). Variation in two wood properties of *Pinus caribaea* var. *hondurensis* in 8-year-old plantations in the east of Venezuela with the objective of genetic improvement. Univ. de Los Andes, Facultad de Ciencias Forestales, Mérida, Venezuela, 42 pp.

Ahmad, N., and F. S. Ng (1981). Growth of *Leucaena leucocephala* in relation to soil pH, nutrient levels and *Rhizobium* concentrations. *Malaysian Forester* **44**(4), 516–523.

Akachuku, A. E. (1984). The possibility of tree selection and breeding for genetic improvement of wood properties in *Gmelina arborea*. *For. Sci.* **30**(2), 275–283.

Alazard, L. P., and A. Kadio (1983). Juvenile growth of *Pinus pinaster* cuttings. *AFOCEL,* pp. 119–155.

Almirall, A. L. (1982). Variability of the genus *Pinus* in Cuba. *Acta Botanica Cubana* **12**, 43 pp.

Anderson, H. W., C. S. Papadopol, and L. Zsuffa (1983). Wood energy plantations in temperate climates. *For. Ecol. Mgt.* **6**, 281–306.

Anderson, K. F. (1966). *Economic Evaluation of Results from Provenance Trials.* Seminar, For. Seed and Tree Impr., FAO and Danish Board of Tech. Coop. with Devel. Countries, Rome.

Anderson, R. A., and C. E. Cordell (1979). How to recognize and quantify ectomycorrhizae on conifers. U.S. For. Ser., For. Bull. SA-FB, Atlanta, Georgia, p. 8.

Anderson, R. L., C. H. Young, and J. D. Triplett (1983). Evaluation of five species of pine from Guatemala for resistance to fusiform rust. For. Pest. Mgt. Rept. #RCS-3-83 (mimeo), U.S. For. Ser., Atlanta, Georgia, 15 pp.

Anderson, T. M., G. J. Bacon, and G. M. Shea (1981). Thinning strategies for Honduras Caribbean pine in plantations: An analysis of precommercial and commercial thinnings. Tech. Paper #25, Dept. For., Queensland, Australia, 17 pp.

Anderson, W. C. (1975). Some economics of monoculture. Workshop, South. For. Econ. Workers. Biloxi, Mississippi, 11 pp.

Andersson, E. (1976). *Pinus contorta,* Sågbarhet-impregnerbarhet. Inst. f. virkeslära, Rapport Nr. R 99. Skogshögskolan, Stockholm, 39 pp.

Andrew, I. A. (1983). Wood quality of *Pinus merkusii. Selection and Breeding to Improve Some Tropical Conifers,* Vol. 2. Dept. For., Queensland, Australia, pp. 116–125.

Andrew, I. A., and J. F. Hughes (1973). Variation of wood properties in 12-year-old trees of *P. caribaea* var. *hondurensis* in Trinidad—a summary report. IUFRO Meet. Trop. Prov. & Prog. Res. and Inter. Coop. Nairobi, Kenya, pp. 532–535.

Annila, E., J. Heliövaara, K. Puukko, and M. Rousi (1983). Pests on lodgepole pine (*Pinus contorta*) in Finland. *Commonw. Inst. For. Fenn.* **115**, 1–27.

Anonymous (1959). *Tree Planting Practices in Temperate Asia—Burma—India—Pakistan.* FAO For. Dev. Paper # 14, Rome, 149 pp.

Anonymous (1972). Limiting factors in the growth of plantations of *Cupressus lusitanica* in Antioqia, Colombia. *Jour. Nat. Fac. Agronomy* (Medellin, Colombia) **27**(2), 88 pp.

Anonymous (1977a). *Leucaena. Promising Forage and Tree Crop for the Tropics.* Nat. Acad. Sciences, Washington, D.C., 115 pp.

Anonymous (1977b). Report of the fourth session of the FAO panel of experts on forest gene resources. FAO: FAR/4/Rep. FAO, Rome, 75 pp.

Anonymous (1978a). Reflorestamento na base de *Pinus elliotii* ameaca a fauna e a flora. *LUX Jornal Correio do Povo.* P. Allegre, R. G. S., 1 pp.

Anonymous (1978b). *Leucaena:* The miracle tree. *Africa* **86**, 75.

Anonymous (1980a). *Tropical Deforestation Hearings of Subcommittee on International Organizations of Committee on Foreign Affairs.* Ninety-Sixth Congress, Second Session, Washington, D.C., 446 pp.

Anonymous (1980b). *Pinus Contorta as an Exotic Species.* IUFRO Work. Party, Garpenberg, Sweden, 353 pp.

Anonymous (1980c). *Tropical Woodlands and Forest Ecosystems—A Review.* UNEP Report #1. Nairobi, Kenya.

Anonymous (1981a). Pests and diseases of South African forests and timber. For. & Envir. Conser. Dept. Water Affairs, For. and Envir. Conser. Pamphlet 273 (16 papers). Pretoria, Republic of South Africa.

Anonymous (1981b). Inventory of species and cultivars potentially valuable for forest biomass production. IEA Rept., Nat. Swedish Bd. for Energy Source Dev. NE-17, Stockholm, 43 pp.

Anonymous (1981c). Wood Energy Spec. Edit. 2. *Unasylva* **33**(131), 52 pp.

Anonymous (1981d). Present utilization and potential regeneration of the Pinaceae in the highlands of tropical Mexico and Guatemala. U.S. Man and Biosphere Program, U.S. Dept. State, Washington, D.C., 8 pp.

Anonymous (1982a). Aerial topdressing of forests. What's new in forest research, Bulletin No. 114. New Zealand Forest Service, Rotorua, New Zealand.

Anonymous (1982b). *Leucaena Research in the Asian–Pacific Region.* Workshop, Singapore (1981). Nitrogen Tree Fixing Association, 192 pp.

Anonymous (1982c). *Germplasm and Conservation of Genetic Resources. Ecological Aspects of Development in the Humid Tropics.* National Academy Press, Washington, D.C., 56 pp.

Anonymous (1982d). Annual Report, Prairie Farm Rehabilitation Administration. Indian Head, Saskatchewan, Canada.

Anonymous (1983a). *Mangium and Other Fast-growing Acacias for the Humid Tropics.* Nat. Acad. Sci., Washington, D.C., 41 pp.

Anonymous (1983b). *Innovations in Tropical Reforestation. Calliandra: A Versatile Small Tree for the Humid Tropics.* Nat. Acad. Sci., Washington, D.C., 115 pp.

Anonymous (1983c). Ann. Rept., Wattle Res. Inst. Pietermaritzburg, South Africa.

Anonymous (1983d). Breeding *Pinus radiata.* IUFRO Work. Party, Newsletter No. 5. CSIRO, Canberra, Australia, 40 pp.

Anonymous (1984a). Research Review 1983/84. South Afr. For. Res. Inst. Dir. of For. Dept. of Envir. Affairs, Pretoria, South Africa.

Anonymous (1984b). Comparison between black, green and silver wattle. 37th Rept., Wattle Res. Inst., Pietermaritzburg, South Africa, pp. 20–21.

Anonymous (1984c). *The New Eucalypt Forest.* Proc. Marcus Wallenberg Found. Symp. Falun, Sweden, 29 pp.

Anonymous (1987). Techniques for Producing Fuelwood on Small Farms. CATIE-IUFRO, Turrialba, Costa Rica (in press).

Antonovics, J. (1971). The effects of a heterogeneous environment on the genetics of natural populations. *Amer. Sci.* **59**(5), 593–595.

Armitage, F. B., and P. M. Burrows (1966). Preliminary heritability estimates for *Pinus patula* in Rhodesia. *Rhod. Zamb. Mal. Jour. Agric. Res.* **4**(2), 111–117.

Ashcroft, B. C. (1982). Public attitudes to the exotic pine reforestation programme in southeast Queensland. Tech. Pap. No. 29, Dept. For., Queensland, Australia, 42 pp.

Australian Dev. Assist. Agency (1978). *International Training Course in Forest Tree Breeding: Selected Reference Papers.* Watson Ferguson Co., Brisbane, Australia, 257 pp.

Axelrod, D. I. (1967). Evolution of California closed-cone pine forest. Symp. on Biol. of California Islands, Santa Barbara Botanic Garden, Santa Barbara, California, pp. 93–149.

Badran, O. A., and M. H. El-Lakany (1977). Breeding and improving *Casuarina* for shelterbelt plantations in Egypt. 3rd World Consul. For. Tree Breed. Canberra, Australia, pp. 573–578.

Bain, J. (1979). Forest monocultures—How safe are they? An entomologist's view. *N. Z. Jour. For. Sci.* **9**, 37–42.

Baklein, A. (1960). The effect of extractives on black liquor from eucalypt pulping. *Appita* **14**(1), 5–15.

Ballard, R. (1971). Interrelationship between site factors and productivity of radiata pine at Riverhead Forest, New Zealand. *Plant and Soil* **35**, 371–380.

Ballard, R. (1978). Use of fertilizers at establishment of exotic forest plantations in New Zealand. *N. Z. Jour. For. Sci.* **8**(1), 70–104.

Balneaves, J. M. (1982). Grass control for radiata pine establishment on droughty sites. *N. Z. Jour. For. Sci.* **27**(2), 259–276.

Banks, J. C. (1967). Tree seed certification. Australian For. Res. Work. Grp. #1. Canberra, Australia.

Banks, P. F., and R. L. Barrett (1973). Exotic forest tree seed in Rhodesia. IUFRO Inter. Symp. on Seed Processing, Vol. II. Bergen, Norway, pp. 1–8.

Bannister, M. H. (1962). Some variations in the growth pattern of *Pinus radiata*. *N. Z. Jour. For. Sci.* **5**(3), 342–370.

Bannister, M. H. (1965). The genetics of colonizing species. Asilomar Symp., Pacific Grove, California (Silv. Rept., FRI), 18 pp.

Bannister, M. H. (1969). An early progeny trial in *Pinus radiata*. Juvenile characteristics. *N. Z. Jour. Bot.* **7**(4), 316–335.

Barber, J. C. (1969). Control of genetic identity of forest reproductive materials. 2nd World Consul. For. Tree Breed., Washington, D.C., 7 pp.

Bard, S. (1984). Effectos del *Eucalyptus globulus* sobre la composición de los suelos de Galicia. I. Indice estimativo de la degradación. *Os Usos do Monte en Galicia,* Num. 5, 81 pp.

Barefoot, A. C., R. G. Hitchings, E. L. Ellwood, and E. Wilson (1970). The relationship between loblolly pine fiber morphology and kraft paper properties. Tech. Bull. No. 202, N. C. Agr. Exp. Stat., N. C. State Univ., Raleigh, North Carolina, 88 pp.

Barker, R. G. (1974). Papermaking properties of young hardwoods. *Tappi* **57**(8), 107–111.

Barner, H. (1963). Basic principles of origin certification. 1st World Consul. For. Gen. Tree Impr., Stockholm, Sweden, 8 pp.

Barner, H. (1966). Classification of seed sources. Seminar, For. Seed and Tree Imp., FAO and Danish Board of Tech. Coop. with Devel. Countries, Rome, 19 pp.

Barner, H. (1968). Certification and classification of seed orchards. Scand. Assoc. of Geneticists, Symp. on Seed Orchards, Copenhagen, Denmark, 9 pp.

Barner, H. (1974). Classification of sources for procurement of forest reproductive material. FAO/DANIDA Training Course on For. Tree Impr., Lemura, Kenya, 112 pp.

Barner, H., and H. Keiding (1983). Danish-FAO Forest Tree Seed Center. *Fast Growing Trees. Silvicultura* **32**, 685–695.

Barnes, B. V. (1984). The ecological approach to ecosystem classification. In IUFRO (1984a), Vol. 1, pp. 69–89.

Barnes, R. D. (1973). The Genetic Improvement of *Pinus patula* in Rhodesia. Ph.D. thesis, Univ. of London, 322 pp.

Barnes, R. D. (1977). Variation of growth, stem quality and wood properties in relation to genetic improvement of tropical forest trees. Topic 5: *P. patula*. IUFRO Workshop, Brisbane, Australia, 3 pp.

Barnes, R. D. (1984a). A multiple population breeding strategy for Zimbabwe. In IUFRO (1984b), pp. 619–632.

Barnes, R. D. (1984b). Genotype–environment interaction in the genetic improvement of fast-growing plantation trees. Site Prod. Fast Grow. Plant, Pretoria, South Africa, pp. 197–213.

Barnes, R. D., and G. L. Gibson (1984a). *Conference on Provenance and Genetic Improvement Strategies in Tropical Forest Trees.* IUFRO, Mutare, Zimbabwe, 80 papers.

Barnes, R. D., and G. L. Gibson (1984b). Experimental design, management and selection traits in provenance trials of tropical pines. In IUFRO (1984b), pp. 8–22.

Barnes, R. D., and L. J. Mullin (1984). *Pinus patula* provenance trials in Zimbabwe— Seventh year results. In IUFRO (1984b), pp. 151–152.

Barnes, R. D., and M. A. Schweppenhauser (1978). *Pinus patula* progeny tests in Rhodesia. Genetic control in nursery traits. *Sil. Gen.* **27**(5), 200–204.

Barnes, R. D., and B. T. Styles (1983). The closed-cone pines of Mexico and Central America. *Commonwealth. For. Rev.* **62**(2), 81–84.

Barnes, R. D., R. F. Jarvis, M. A. Schweppenhauser, and L. J. Mullin (1976). Introduction, spread and control of the pine woolly aphid *Pineus pini* in Rhodesia. *South African For. Jour.* **96**, 11 pp.

Barnes, R. D., M. A. Woodend, M. A. Schweppenhauser, and L. J. Mullin (1977). Variation in diameter growth and wood density in six-year-old provenance trials of *Pinus caribaea* on five sites in Rhodesia. *Sil. Gen.* **26**(5/6), 163–167.

Barnes, R. D., J. Burley, G. L. Gibson, and J. P. Garcia de Leon (1982). Genotype–environment interactions in tropical pines and their structure of breeding populations. (Mimeo. Rept.), Oxford, England, 22 pp.

Barnes, R. D., G. L. Gibson, and M. A. Bardey (1983). Variation and genotype–environmental interaction in international provenance trials of *Pinus caribaea* and implications for population improvement strategies. *Fast Growing Trees. Silvicultura* **32**, 761–764.

Barr, N. A. (1983). Sawing qualities of *Eucalyptus saligna* as a guide to selection of trees for breeding and seed collection. *Fast Growing Trees. Silvicultura* **32**, 800–801.

Barrett, R. L. (1978). Forest nursery practice for the wattle regions in the Republic of South Africa. Wattle Research Institute, Pietermaritzburg, South Africa, 56 pp. For. Comm. Res. Bull. No. 2.

Barrett, R. L., and D. T. Carter (1970). *Eucalyptus camaldulensis* provenance trials in Rhodesia (Part 1, early results). Rhodesia For. Comm. Res. Bull. No. 2, Salisbury, N. Rhodesia (Zimbabwe) 50 pp.

Barrett, W. H. (1969). Pine species adaptation to northeastern Argentina: Five years growth. *IDIA* Supplemento Forestal, Buenos Aires, Argentina, pp. 11–26.

Barrett, W. H. (1973). Geographic variation in *P. elliottii* and *P. taeda*. II. Five years of growth in northeastern Argentina. *IDIA* Supplemento Forestal, Buenos Aires, Argentina, pp. 18–39.

Barrett, W. H. (1977). Variation in growth, stem quality and wood properties in relation to genetic improvement of tropical forest trees. Topic 5—*P. patula* IUFRO Workshop, Brisbane, Australia, 3 pp.

Barrett, W. H. (1984). Present status of experimental work on *Pinus caribaea* and *Pinus oocarpa* in the province of Corrientes, Argentina. In IUFRO (1984b), pp. 153–158.

Bassus, W. (1979). Zur epidemiologie forstlicher grosschädlinge in der Tropen. *Beitraege fuer die Forstwirtschaft* **79**(3), 121–124.

Bates, C. G. (1930). The frost hardiness of geographic strains of Norway pine. *Jour. For.* **29**, 327–333.

Bawa, K. S. (1976). Breeding of tropical hardwoods: An evaluation of underlying bases, current status and future prospects. *Tropical Trees—Variation, Breeding and Conservation,* Academic Press, London, 243 pp, pp. 43–59.

Bawa, K. S., and P. A. Opler (1975). Dioecism in tropical forest trees. *Evolution* **29**, 167–179.

Baxter, D. W. (1967). *Disease in Forest Plantations: Thief of Time.* Bull. 51, Cranbrook Inst. of Sci., Cranbrook Press, Ann Arbor, Michigan, 251 pp.

Beek, K. J. (1978). *Land Evaluation for Agricultural Development.* Inter. Inst. for Land Reclamation and Improvement, Pub. #23, Wageningen, Netherlands, 333 pp.

Bell, T. I. (1977). Variation of growth, stem quality and wood properties in relation to genetic improvement of tropical forest trees. Topic 5—*P. caribaea* IUFRO Workshop, Brisbane, Australia, 12 pp.

Bell, T. I. (1979). *Pinus caribaea* seed from Fiji. Fiji Pine Res. Paper No. 4, Lautoka, Fiji. 4 pp.

Benge, M. D. (1982). The miracle tree—Reality or myth? *Leucaena Research in the Asian-Pacific Region.* Workshop, Nitrogen Fixing Tree Assoc. and Inter. Dev. Res. Centre (IDRC-211e), Singapore, pp. 95–98.

Berg, M. A. (1977). Natural enemies of certain acacias in Australia. 2nd National Weeds Conf. South Africa, Stellenbosch, South Africa.

Bernard, A. E. (1945). Le climat écologique de la Cunette Centrale Congolaise. INEAC, Brussels.

Bernard, A. E. (1953). L'évapotranspiration annuelle de la fôret équatoriale congolaise et son influence sur la pluviosité. Comptes Rendus, IUFRO Congress, Rome, pp. 201–204.

Berry, C. R. (1973). The differential sensitivity of eastern white pine to three types of air pollution. *Can. Jour. For. Res.* **3**(4), 543–547.

Bertolani, F., and N. Nicolielo (1979). Behavior and program of genetic improvement of tropical pines in the Agudos Region, São Paulo, Brazil. Paper #18, CAFMA, São Paulo, 19 pp.

Bialobok, S. (1967). Ecotypic variation. *Zarys Fizjologii Sosny Zwyczajnej. (Outline of Scots Pine Physiology)*, Budapest, Hungary, pp. 31–32.

Bialobok, S. (1980). Forest genetics and air pollution stress. *Symp. Effects of Air Pol-*

lutants on Mediterranean and Temperate Forest Ecosystems, Riverside, California, pp. 100–102.

Binet, F. (1963). An instance of interaction of genotype and environment at the population level. *Gen. Today,* Pergamon Press, London, 147 pp.

Bingham, R. T. (1965). Seed movement in the Douglas-fir region. West. For. Gen. Assoc., Boise, Idaho, pp. 30–34.

Bird, N. M. (1984). Variation in volume overbark, stem straightness and longest internode length at 5 years of age between ten provenances of *Pinus caribaea* and two provenances of *P. oocarpa* in Costa Rica. In IUFRO (1984b), pp. 159–167.

Birot, Y., and G. Nepveu (1979). Clonal variability and ortet-ramet correlations in a population of spruce. *Sil. Gen.* **28**(2–3), 37–47.

Björkman, E. (1964). Breeding for resistance to disease in forest trees. *Unasylva* **18**(2–3), 73–81.

Blada, I. (1980). Testing larch clones for *Adelges laricio* resistance. World Conf. Gen. Host–Parasite Inter. in For., Wageningen, Holland, 8 pp.

Boden, R. W. (1958). Differential frost resistance within one *Eucalyptus* species. *Aust. Jour. Sci.* **2**(3), 84–86.

Boland, D. J. (1978). Variation patterns and breeding systems in *Eucalyptus.* Inter. Train. Course in For. Tree. Breed.—Sel. Ref. Topics, Aust. Devel. Assis. Agency, Canberra, Australia, pp. 164–174.

Boland, D. J., and J. W. Turnbull (1981). Selection of Australian trees other than eucalypts for trials as fuelwood species in developing countries. *Aust. For.* **44**(4), 235–246.

Bolstad, P. V., and K. S. Bawa (1982). Self-incompatibility in *Gmelina arborea. Sil. Gen.* **31**(1), 19–21.

Bonkoungou, E. G. (1985). *Acacia albida*—A multipurpose tree for arid and semi-arid zones. FAO, For. Gen. Res. Infor. No. 13, Rome, pp. 30–36.

Bonner, F. T. (1985). Technologies to maintain tree germplasm diversity. Draft copy, Office of Tech. Assess., Congress of U.S., Washington, D.C., 31 pp.

Bonnet-Masimbert, M. (1982). Effect of growth regulators, girdling and mulching on flowering of young European and Japanese larches under field conditions. *Can. Jour. For. Res.* **12**(2), 270–279.

Boone, R. S., and M. Chudnoff (1972). Compression wood formation and other characteristics of plantation-grown *Pinus caribaea.* U.S. For. Ser. Res. Paper ITF-13, Rio Piedras, Puerto Rico, 16 pp.

Booth, J. (1882). *Die Naturalisation ausländischer Waldbäume in Deutschland.* Julius Springer, Berlin, 168 pp.

Borges, R., and A. Brune (1983). Heritability estimates and correlations between characteristics in *Eucalyptus grandis. Fast Growing Trees. Silvicultura* **31**, 525–527.

Boshier, D. H. (1984). The international provenance trial of *Cordia alliodora* in Costa Rica. Prov. and Gen. Impr. Strategies in Trop. For. Trees. In IUFRO (1984b), pp. 168–185.

Bouvarel, P. (1957). Forest genetics and the improvement of forest trees. *Bull. Soc. Bot. France* **104**(7–8), 552–586.

Bowen, M. R., and T. V. Eusebio (1983). *Gmelina arborea.* Flowering and seed studies. For. Gen. Res. Info. No. 12, FAO, Rome, pp. 27–28.

Boyce, J. S. (1954). Forest plantation protection against diseases and pests. FAO For. Dev. Pap. No. 3, Rome, 41 pp.

Brandão, L. G. (1981). Living with nature. Mimeo Rept. (talk given in Rio de Janeiro, Brazil), 11 pp.

Brandão, L. G. (1984). The new eucalypt forest. Symp., Marcus Wallenberg Symposia Proceedings #1, Falun, Sweden, pp. 3–15.

Brazier, J. D. (1967). Timber improvement. I. A study of the variation in wood characteristics in young Sitka spruce. *Forestry* **40**(2), 117–128.

Brazier, J. D., J. F. Hughes, and C. B. Tabb (1976). Exploitation of natural tropical resources and the need for genetic and ecological conservation. *Tropical Trees* **2**, Academic Press, London, 1–10.

Bredenkamp, B. V. (1980). Initial spacing of *Pinus patula* for maximum yield of pulpwood over a 16-year rotation. *S. A. For. Jour.* **115**, 47–49.

Bredenkamp, B. V. (1982). Rectangular espacement does not cause stem ellipticity in *Eucalyptus grandis. S.A. For. Jour.* **120**, 7–10.

Bredenkamp, B. V. (1984). The C.C.T. concept in spacing research—A review. In IUFRO (1984a), Vol. 1, pp. 313–332.

Bredenkamp, B. V., and C. J. Schutz (1984). Precommercial thinning of *Eucalyptus grandis* for mining timber production. *S.A. For. Jour.* **128**, 33–35.

Bredenkamp, B. V., W. E. Malan, and W. E. Conradie (1983a). Some effects of pruning on the growth and timber quality of *Eucalyptus grandis* in Zululand. *Fast Growing Trees. Silvicultura* **31**, 583–588.

Bredenkamp, B. V., J. S. Venter, and H. Haigh (1983b). Early espacement and fewer thinnings can increase profitability of coniferous sawtimber production. *S.A. For. Jour.* **124**, 36–42.

Brewbaker, J. L. (1982). Systematics, self-incompatibility, breeding systems and genetic improvement in *Leucaena* species. *Leucaena* Res. in the Asian-Pacific Region. Workshop IDRC, Ottawa, Canada, pp. 17–22.

Brewbaker, J. L., and E. M. Hutton (1979). *Leucaena*—Versatile tropical tree legume. *New Agricultural Crops,* pp. 207–259.

Bridgwater, F. E., and I. F. Trew (1981). Supplemental mass pollination. *Pollen Management Handbook.* U.S. For. Serv. Agric. Handbook #587, Washington, D.C., pp. 52–57.

Brigatti, R. A., M. Ferreira, A. P. Silva, and M. Freitas (1983). Comparative study of some *Eucalyptus* hybrids behavior. *Fast Growing Trees. Silvicultura* **32**, 761–764.

Brigden, L. G., and E. R. Williams (1984). An assessment of a 5.5-year-old *Pinus caribaea* var. *hondurensis* progeny trial in the Northern Territory of Australia. In IUFRO (1984b), pp. 478–479.

Brigden, L. G., G. C. Cracium, and E. R. Williams (1984). *Pinus oocarpa* provenance testing in the Northern Territory of Australia and a comparison with *P. caribaea.* In IUFRO (1984b), pp. 186–187.

Briscoe, C. B., J. B. Harris, and D. Wyckoff (1963). Variation of specific gravity in plantation-grown trees of bigleaf mahogany. *Carib. For.* **27**(2), 313.

Briscoe, C. B., and R. Ybarra-Coronado (1971). Increasing growth of established teak. U.S. For. Ser. Res. Note ITF 13, Rio Piedras, Puerto Rico, 7 pp.

Brito, J. O. (1984). A technological study of the wood of pine species for the production of charcoal and briquettes. *IPEF* **26**, 25–30.

Brito, J. O., L. E. Barrichelo, and L. E. Gutierrez (1980). Quality of the resins and turpentine of tropical pines. *IPEF* **21**, 55–63.

Brix, H. (1959). Some Aspects of Drought Resistance in Loblolly Pine Seedlings. Ph.D. thesis, Texas A&M College, College Station, Texas, 94 pp.

Brix, H., and R. Van Driessche (1977). Use of rooted cuttings in reforestation. Brit. Col. For. Ser. and Can. For. Ser. Joint Rept. No. 16, Victoria, B. C., Canada, 16 pp.

Broeker, W. R. (1970). Man's oxygen reserves. *Science* **168**, 1537–1538.

Brown, A. G., and J. C. Doran (1985). Variation in growth and branching characteristics of *Pinus attenuata*. *Sil. Gen.* **34**(2–3), 100–104.

Brown, G. A. (1983). A statistical analysis of density variation in *Pinus caribaea* grown in Jamaica. *Selection and Breeding to Improve Some Tropical Conifers,* Vol. 2. Dept. For., Queensland, Australia, Commonwealth For. Inst., Oxford, England, pp. 70–71.

Brown, I. R., and E. M. Sauvé (1975). Effect of exogenous growth substances on cone development in Scots pine (*Pinus sylvestris*). *Can. Jour. For. Res.* **5**(2), 163–170.

Brown, S., and H. E. Lugo (1982). The storage and production of organic matter in tropical forests and their role in the global carbon cycle. *Biotropica* **14**(3), 161–187.

Browne, F. G. (1968). *Pests and Diseases of Forest Plantation Trees.* An annotated list of the principal species occurring in the British Commonwealth. Clarendon Press, Oxford, U.K., 1330 pp.

Brune, A. (1983). Methods of establishing genetic base populations for selection. Designs for long-term ex-situ maintenance of eucalypt gene pools and breeding populations. *Fast Growing Trees. Silvicultura* **31**, 527–528.

Brune, A., and H. N. De Paiva (1983). Induction of coppicing. *Fast Growing Trees. Silvicultura* **32**, 764–765.

Brune, A., and G. H. Melchior (1976). Ecological and genetical factors affecting exploitation and conservation of forests in Brazil and Venezuela. *Tropical Trees* **2**, Academic Press, London, 203–215.

Brune, A., and B. Zobel (1981). Genetic base populations, gene pools and breeding populations for *Eucalyptus* in Brazil. *Sil. Gen.* **30**(4–5), 146–149.

Bryant, P. A. (1984). The impact of fast growth in plantations on wood quality and utilization. In IUFRO (1984a), Vol. 1, pp. 403–416.

Bryndum, K., and T. Hedegart (1969). Pollination of teak (*Tectona grandis*). *Sil. Gen.* **18**(3), 77–80.

Buchert, G. P. (1983). Winter hardiness assessment in seedlings of pure and hybrid pitch pine. 28th Northeastern For. Tree Impr. Conf., Durham, New Hampshire, pp. 94–101.

Buck, M. G., and R. H. Imoto (1982). Growth of 11 introduced tree species on selected forest sites in Hawaii. Res. Paper PSW-169, U.S. For. Ser., Honolulu, 12 pp.

Buol, S. W., and P. A. Sanchez (1978). Rainy tropical climates: Physical, potential, present and improved farming systems. Proc. 11th Int. Soil Ser. Congress, Edmonton, Alberta, Canada, Vol. 2, pp. 292-312.

Buol, S. W., P. A. Sanchez, R. B. Cate, and M. A. Granger (1975). Soil fertility capability classification. *Soil Management in Tropical America,* N.C. State Univ., Raleigh, North Carolina, pp. 126-141.

Burch, W. R., and D. R. DeLuca (1983). *Measuring the Social Impact of Natural Resources Policies.* Univ. of New Mexico Press, Santa Fe, 216 pp.

Burdon, R. D. (1971). Clonal repeatabilities and clone × site interactions in *Pinus radiata. Sil. Gen.* **20**(1-2), 33-39.

Burdon, R. D. (1982). Monocultures—How vulnerable? What's New in Forest Research, No. 115, F.R.I., Rotorua, New Zealand, 4 pp.

Burdon, R. D., and I. J. Thulin (1966). *The Improvement of Pinus radiata.* FRI Symp. No. 6, N.Z. For. Ser., Rotorua, New Zealand, 92 pp.

Burdon, R. D., D. Currie, and C. K. Chou (1982). Response to inoculation with *Diplodia pinea* in progenies of apparently resistant trees of *Pinus radiata. Aust. Plant Path.* **11**(4), 37-39.

Burgess, I. P. (1973). Vegetative propagation of *Eucalyptus grandis. N. Z. Jour. For. Sci.* **4**(2), 181-184.

Burgess, I. P. (1983). The natural appearance of *Eucalyptus grandis,* its distribution patterns in natural forests, its characteristics and conservation. *Fast Growing Trees. Silvicultura* **31**, 397-399.

Burley, J. (1966). Genetic variation in seedling development of sitka spruce, *Picea sitchensis. Forestry* **39**(1), 68-94.

Burley, J. (1973). Variation of wood properties of *P. patula* in Malawi. Proc. Trop. Prov. and Prog. Res. and Inter. IUFRO Coop., Nairobi, Kenya, pp. 574-583.

Burley, J. (1976). Genetic systems and genetic conservation of tropical pines. *Tropical Trees* **2**, Academic Press, London, 85-100.

Burley, J. (1980). Selection of species for fuelwood plantations. *Commonw. For. Rev.* **59**(2), 133-147.

Burley, J., and G. Namkoong (1980). Conservation of forest genetic resources, 11th Commonwealth For. Conf., Trinidad, 25 pp.

Burley, J., and D. G. Nikles (1972). *Selection and Breeding to Improve Some Tropical Conifers,* Vol. I. Commonwealth For. Inst., Oxford, U.K., and Dept. For., Queensland, Australia, 417 pp.

Burley, J., and D. G. Nikles (1973a). *Selection and Breeding to Improve Some Tropical Conifers,* Vol. II. Commonwealth For. Inst., Oxford, U.K., and Dept. For., Queensland, Australia, 466 pp.

Burley, J., and D. G. Nikles (1973b). *Tropical Provenance and Progeny Research and International Cooperation.* Joint Workshop IUFRO in Nairobi, Kenya. Commonwealth For. Inst., Oxford, U.K., 597 pp.

Burley, J., and E. R. Palmer (1979). Pulp and wood densitometric properties of *Pinus caribaea* from Fiji. CFI Occ. Pap. #6, London, 66 pp.

Burley, J., and B. T. Styles (1976). *Tropical Trees—Variation, Breeding and Conservation.* Linnean Soc. Symp. Series No. 2. Commonwealth For. Inst., Academic Press, New York, 243 pp.

Burley, J., and P. Von Carlowitz (1984). Multipurpose tree germplasm. Proc. Planning Work., Washington, D.C., ICRAF, Nairobi, Kenya, 298 pp.

Burley, J., and P. J. Wood (1976). *A Manual on Species and Provenance Research with Particular Reference to the Tropics.* Commonwealth For. Inst., Dept. For. Oxford Univ., Oxford, U.K., 226 pp.

Burley, J., P. A. Huxley, and F. Owino (1984). Design, management and assessment of species, provenances and breeding trials of multipurpose trees. In IUFRO (1984b), pp. 70–80.

Burner, S. G. (1980). Forces of destruction in Amazonia. *Environment* **22**(7), 39.

Butler, C., H. Levack, D. McLean, and J. Sharp (1985). A national exotic forest description system. Work. Pap. No. 3, N.Z. For. Council, Rotorua, New Zealand, 94 pp.

Caballero, M. (1966). Comparative Study of Two Species of Mexican Pine (*Pinus pseudostrobus* and *P. montezumae*) Based on Seed and Seedling Characteristics. M.S. thesis, N.C. State Univ., Raleigh, North Carolina, 140 pp.

Cajander, A. K. (1914). Ulkomaisten puulajien viljelemis—mahdollisuuksista Suomessa. *Metsätaloudellinen Aikakauskirja* **31**(12), 551–558.

Cajander, A. K. (1917). *Mesánhoidon perusteet II. Suomen dendrologian pääpirteet.* Porvoo, Finland, 652 pp.

Callaham, R. Z. (1964). Provenance research: Investigation of genetic diversity associated with geography. *Unasylva* **18**(2–3), 40–50.

Callaham, R. Z. (1966). Tree breeding for pest resistance. Sexto Congresso Forestal Mundial, Madrid, Vol. II, 1291–1297.

Callaham, R. Z., and A. R. Liddicoet (1961). Altitudinal variation at 20 years in ponderosa and jeffrey pines. *Jour. For.* **59**(11), 814–820.

Cameron, J. N., and P. D. Kube (1983). Management of seedling seed orchards of *Eucalyptus regnans.* Selection, strategy and flowering study. *Fast Growing Trees. Silvicultura* **32**, 765–768.

Cameron, J. N., C. Dean, and P. P. Cotterill (1984). Application of multiple trait index selection in *Pinus radiata.* In IUFRO (1984b), pp. 495–496.

Cameron, R. J. (1968). The propagation of *Pinus radiata* by cuttings: Influences affecting the rooting of cuttings. *N.Z. Jour. For.* **13**(1), 78–89.

Campinhos, E. (1980). More wood of better quality through intensive silviculture with rapid growth improved Brazilian *Eucalyptus. Tappi* **63**(11), 145–147.

Campinhos, E., and Y. K. Ikemori (1977). Tree improvement program of *Eucalyptus* spp.: Preliminary results. 3rd World Consul. For. Tree Breed, Canberra, Australia, pp. 717–738.

Campinhos, E., and Y. K. Ikemori (1980). Mass production of *Eucalyptus* spp. by rooting cuttings. In IUFRO (1980), 16 pp.

Cannell, M. G., L. J. Sheppard, E. D. Ford, and R. H. Wilson (1983). Differences in dry matter distribution, wood specific gravity and "foliage efficiency" in *Picea sitchensis* and *Pinus contorta. Sil. Gen.* **32**, 699–702.

Capitani, L. R., G. E. Speltz, and J. O. Brito (1983). Tropical pines potential for resin production in Sacramento, Brazil. *Fast Growing Trees. Silvicultura* **30**, 191–194.

Carmean, W. H. (1984). Site quality evaluation for fuelwood plantations in less developed countries. In IUFRO (1984a), Vol. 1, pp. 111–123.

Carson, M. J. (1977). Breeding for resistance to *Dosthistroma pini*. Breeding *Pinus radiata*. IUFRO Working Party Newsletter No. 1, Canberra, Australia, pp. 2–4.

Carter, C. K., D. Canavera, and P. Caron (1981). Early growth of exotic larches at three locations in Maine. Coop. For. Res. Unit, Res. Note No. 8, Univ. of Maine, Orono, 7 pp.

Castro, D. A., F. Poggiani, and N. Nicolielo (1983). Biomass and nutrient distribution in *Pinus oocarpa* stands at different ages. *Fast Growing Trees. Silvicultura* **30**, 194–198.

Cech, F. C., J. C. Barber, and B. J. Zobel (1962). Comments on "Who wants tree seed certification and why?" *Jour. For.* **60**(3), 208–210.

Chadid, G. D. (1980). Speech by the Minister of Agriculture. II Asamblea General Ordinaria de Ofiliados a ACOFORE (Association Colombiana de Reforestadores). Bogota, Colombia, pp. 14–25.

Chagala, E. M. (1984). *Pinus kesiya* international provenance trial in Kenya at 12 years. In IUFRO (1984b), pp. 188–190.

Chagala, E. M., and G. L. Gibson (1984). *Pinus oocarpa* international provenance trial in Kenya at 8 years. In IUFRO (1984b), pp. 191–203.

Champion, H., and N. V. Brasnett (1958). *Choice of tree species*. FAO For. Develop. Paper No. 13, Rome, 307 pp.

Chanshaima, S. A. (1984). Establishment Techniques for Eucalyptus Species: Effects of Nursery Treatments, Site Preparation and Fertilization on Survival and Growth. Ph.D. thesis, University of Dar es Salam, Tanzania, 171 pp.

Chaperon, H. (1976). Production of hybrid eucalypts in Brazzaville, Congo. 3rd World Consul. For. Tree Breed., Canberra, Australia, 16 pp.

Chaperon, H. (1977). Amelioration genetique de *Pinus caribaea* au Congo, Brazzaville. 3rd World Consul. For. Tree Breed., Canberra, Australia, 12 pp.

Chaperon, H. (1979). New prospects of genetic breeding through vegetative propagation of *Pinus pinaster*. *AFOCEL,* pp. 31–53.

Chaperon, H. (1984). Influence of propagation by cutting on the breeding strategy of forest trees. In IUFRO (1984b), pp. 135–148.

Chaperon, H., J. Y. Fraysse, and D. Leze (1982). Management of the mother trees for the vegetative propagation by cuttings of forest trees: Application to the propagation of *Eucalyptus*. IUFRO Joint Meet. Work. Parties Gen. Breed. Strat. including Multiclonal Varieties. Escherode, West Germany, 63 pp.

Chaperon, H., M. Berger, J. Y. Fraysse, and D. Leze (1983). The quality influence of the mother-plant on vegetative propagation of *Eucalyptus*. *AFOCEL,* pp. 27–53.

Chaves, R., P. Y. Kageyama, and H. T. Do Couto (1983). Estimates of the genetic variation and the heritability for flowering in *Pinus caribaea* var. *hondurensis* and *P. oocarpa*. *IPEF* **25**, 15–23.

Cherrett, J. M., and Peregrine, D. J. (1976). A review of the status of leaf-cutting ants and their control. *Ann. Appl. Biol.* **84**, 124–128.

Chiba, O. (1964). Studies on the variation and susceptibility and the nature of resistance of poplars to the leaf rust caused by *Melampsora laricipopulina*. Bull. Gov't. For. Expt. Stat., Japan, no. 166, Hokkaido, Japan, pp. 85–157.

Chiba, O. (1968). Heterosis in forest tree breeding. 9th Symp. Jap. Soc. of Breed. Tech. Note No. 69, Hokkaido, Japan, 1 p.

Chittenden, A. E., and C. R. Breag (1980). Wood for energy in developing countries. *Commonw. For. Rev.* **59**(2), 193–199.

Chomchalow, N. (1985). Field genebanks in Southeast Asia (editorial). *IBPGR Newsletter* **9**(1), 3.

Chong, W. W., and E. R. Palmer (1973). An exploratory study of the suitability of *Pinus caribaea* for the production of dissolving pulps. Trop. Prod. Inst. L28, London, U.K., 13 pp.

Chou, C. K. (1979). Monoculture, species diversification and disease hazards in forestry. *N. Z. Jour. For. Res.* **9**, 21–35.

Christiansen, M. N., and C. F. Lewis (1982). *Breeding Plants for Less Favorable Environments.* Wiley and Sons New York, 457 pp.

Chudnoff, M. (1973). *Development of the Tropical Wood Resource.* Office Sci. and Tech., AID, Washington, D.C., 72 pp.

Ciancio, O., R. Mercurio, and S. Nocentini (1982). *Le Specie Forestali Esotiche Nella Selvicoltura Italiana.* Ann. dell'Inst. Sperim. per la Selvi, Vols. 12 & 13, Rome, 733 pp.

Cielo, O. J. (1980). Some aspects of fungus in Colombia. Investigaciones Forestales, Bogota, 21 pp.

Claudot, J. (1963). Contribution of Morocco on the genetic improvement of introduced eucalypts in the Mediterranean Basin. First World Consul. on For. Gen. and Tree Impr., Stockholm, Sweden, 15 pp.

Clausen, J., and W. M. Hiesey (1958). *Experimental Studies on the Nature of Species IV. Genetic Structure of Ecological Races.* Carnegie Inst. of Wash. Pub. 615, Washington, D.C.; Summarized in *Madrono* **15**(8), 251.

Clausen, K. E. (1982). Age–age correlations in black walnut and white ash. N. Amer. For. Biol. Workshop, Univ. of Kentucky, Lexington, pp. 113–117.

Clifford, H. T. (1954). Analysis of suspected hybrid swarms in *Eucalyptus. Heredity* **8**(3), 259–269.

Cockayne, A. H. (1914). *Pinus radiata* plantations, effect on soil fertility. *N. Z. Jour. Agr.* **8**, 409–410.

Colbert, C. M., and D. L. McConchie (1983). Some physical properties of New Zealand-grown redwood. FRI Bull. No. 26, New Zealand For. Ser., 11 pp.

Conkle, M. T. (1969). Hybrid population development and statistics. *Sil. Gen.* **18**(5–6), 197.

Conkle, M. T. (1980). Amount and distribution of isozyme variation in various species. 17th Can. Tree Impr. Assoc., Newfoundland, pp. 109–117.

Conkle, M. T., and W. T. Adams (1977). Use of isoenzyme techniques in forest genetics research. 14th South. For. Tree Impr. Conf., Gainesville, Florida, pp. 219–226.

Cooling, E. N. (1968). *Pinus merkusii.* Fast Growing Timber Trees of the Lowland Tropics No. 4, Commonwealth For. Inst., Oxford, U.K., 169 pp.

Cooper, C. G. (1971). Effect of prescribed burning on the ecosystem. Prescribed Burning Symp., Charleston, South Carolina. U.S. For. Ser., pp. 152–160.

Cordell, C. E., and D. H. Marx (1983). The status and practical application of *Pi-*

solithus tinctorius ectomycorrhizae in forest tree nurseries, field forestation and mine land reclamation. U.S. For. Ser. Tech. Rept., Macon, Georgia, 3 pp. (mimeo).

Cordell, C. E., and D. M. Webb (1980). "PT"—A beneficial fungus that gives your trees a better start in life. U.S. For. Ser. Gen. Rept. SA-FRP, Atlanta, Georgia, 16 pp.

Córdoba, A. (1985). Predicting growth and yield for *Pinus patula* plantations: A case study from Colombia. Res. Rept. No. 101, Carton de Colombia, Cali, 16 pp.

Corson, S. R., and R. S. Foster (1982). Refiner pulping of "new crop" *Pinus radiata. Appita* **35**(5), 412–416.

Cotterill, P. P. (1984). A plan for breeding radiata pine. *Sil. Gen.* **33**(2-3), 84–90.

Cotterill, P. P., and J. N. Cameron (1984). Multiple population breeding of radiata pine for growth and wood density. In IUFRO (1984b), p. 499.

Cowling, E. B. (1978). Agricultural and forestry practices that favor epidemics. *Plant Diseases—An Advanced Treatise.* Vol. II: *How Diseases Develop in Populations.* Academic Press, New York, pp. 361–380.

Cowling, E. B. (1979). Effects of acid precipitation and atmospheric deposition on terrestrial vegetation. *Environmental Professional* **1**, 293–301.

Cowling, E. B., and C. B. Davey (1981). Acid precipitation: Basic principles and ecological consequences. *Pulp and Paper,* pp. 182–185.

Cown, D. J., D. L. McConchie, and C. Treloar (1984). Timber recovery from pruned *Pinus radiata* butt logs at Mangatu: Effect of sweep. *N. Z. Jour For. Sci.* **14**(1), 109–123.

Cracium, G. (1977). Variation in growth, stem quality and wood properties in relation to genetic improvement of tropical forest trees. Topic 5: *P. caribaea.* IUFRO Workshop, Brisbane, Australia, 3 pp.

Craib, I. J. (1939). *Thinning, Pruning and Management Studies on the Main Exotic Conifers Grown in South Africa.* Dept. of Agric. and For. Bull. 196. Govt. Printer, Pretoria, South Africa, 179 pp.

Craib, I. J. (1947). *The Silviculture of Exotic Conifers in South Africa.* British Empire For. Conf., London, U.K.

Crane, W. J. (1984). Fertilization of fast-growing conifers. In IUFRO (1984a), Vol. 1, pp. 233–251.

Crane, W. J., and R. J. Raison (1983). The nutritional effect of short rotational silviculture. *Fast Growing Trees. Silvicultura* **32**, 670–672.

Cremer, K. W., C. J. Borough, F. H. McKinnell, and P. R. Carter (1982). Effects on stocking and thinning on wind damage in plantations. *N. Z. Jour. For. Sci.* **12**(2), 244–268.

Critchfield, W. B. (1978). The distribution, genetics and silvics of lodgepole pine. IUFRO, Vancouver, Canada, Vol. I, pp. 65–94.

Critchfield, W. B., and S. L. Krugman (1967). Crossing the western pines at Placerville, California. *Univ. Wash. Arbor. Bull.* **30**(4), 78–81.

Cunningham, R. A., and M. E. Dix (1983). Variation among Siberian elm in their susceptibility to defoliation by the spring cankerworm. 3rd N. Central Tree Impr. Conf., Wooster, Ohio, pp. 190–200.

Curró, P. (1960). Technological investigations on the wood of some Euramerican poplar hybrids. I: Physical and mechanical properties. Pub. Ag. and For. Expt. Center 3, 28 pp.

Dadswell, H. E., and A. B. Wardrop (1959). Growing trees with wood properties desirable for paper manufacture. *Appita* 12(4), 129–136.

Dahlsten, D. L., and D. L. Rowney (1980). Influence of air pollution on population dynamics of forest insects on tree mortality. Symp. Effects of Air Pollutants on Mediterranean and Temperate For. Ecosystems, Riverside, California, pp. 125–130.

Dallimore, W., and A. B. Jackson (1966). *A Handbook of Coniferae and Ginkgoaceae.* Arnold Press London, U.K., 729 pp.

Daniels, F. W., and C. J. Schutz (1975). Rectangular planting patterns in *Pinus patula* stands in the Eastern Transvaal. *For. Inst. S. Africa* 16, 61–62.

Daniels, F. W., and H. A. Van der Sijde (1975). Cold stratification of *Pinus elliottii, Pinus taeda* and *Pinus patula. For. Inst. S. Africa* 16, 63–68.

Darrow, W. K. (1986). Provenance trials of *Eucalyptus saligna* in South Africa: Eight-year results. *S.A. For. Jour* (in press), (Mimeo)26 pp.

Darrow, W. K., and H. Coetzee (1983). Potentially valuable Mexican pines for the summer rainfall region of Southern Africa. *S. A. For. Jour.* 124, 23–36.

Darrow, W. K., and K. R. Roeder (1983). Provenance trials of *Eucalyptus urophylla* and *E. alba* in South Africa: Seven-year results. *S. A. For. Jour.* 125, 20–28.

Darwin, C. (1859). *The Origin of Species.* New American Library, New York, 479 pp.

Das, B. L., and B. R. Stephan (1982). Provenance trials with *Pinus caribaea* and *Pinus pseudostrobus* in Orissa, India. *Sil. Gen.* 31(5–6), 203–208.

Das, B. L., and B. R. Stephan (1984a). Results of a provenance trial with *Pinus caribaea* and comparison with other tropical pines at Koraput, Orissa (India). In IUFRO (1984b), pp. 205–209.

Das, B. L., and B. R. Stephan (1984b). Provenance trial of *Pinus kesiya* in Koraput, Orissa, India. In IUFRO (1984b), pp. 200–203.

Davey, C. B. (1984). Pine nursery establishment and operations in the American Tropics. CAMCORE Bull. No. 1, N.C. State University, Raleigh, North Carolina, 36 pp.

Davidson, J. (1977). Exploration, collection, evaluation, conservation and utilization of the gene resources of tropical *Eucalyptus deglupta.* 3rd World Consul. For. Tree Breed., Canberra, Australia, pp. 75–102.

Davidson, J. (1983a). Progress in breeding *Eucalyptus deglupta. Fast Growing Trees. Silvicultura* 31, 529–533.

Davidson, J. (1983b). Conservation of tree genetic resources: The role of protected areas in Amazonia. *Environmentalist* 3(5), 62–73.

Day, P. R. (1972). The genetics of rust fungi. Biol. of Rust Resis. in For. Trees. NATO-IUFRO Adv. Study Inst. on Gen. Impr. for Dis. and Insect Res. of For. Trees, Moscow, Idaho, pp. 3–17.

de Barros, N. F., and R. M. Brandi (1983). Assessment of growth of provenances of *Pinus kesiya* and *P. merkusii* in Viçosa, M. G., Brazil. *Fast Growing Trees. Silvicultura* 30, 297–300.

Debazac, E. F. (1964). Note on the behavior in France of some Mexican pines. *Rev. For. Franc.* 16(12), 929–935.

DeBell, D. S. (1971). Phytotoxic effects of cherrybark oak. *For. Sci.* **17**(2), 180–185.

de Camargo, A. P. (1975). Estao plantando un deserto? *O Eucalipto e a Ecologia,* Grupo Aracruz, Rio de Janeiro, Brazil, pp. 25–33.

De Graff, H. R. (1978). Analysis of 11 year's growth of Caribbean pine in a replicated Graeco–Latin Square spacing–thinning experiment in Surinam. Dept. Silviculture, Agr. Univ., Wageningen, Netherlands, 58 pp.

De Gryse, J. J. (1955). Forest pathology in New Zealand. N. Z. For. Ser. Bull. No. 1, Rotorua, New Zealand.

De Guth, E. B. (1973). Density and morphology of tracheids in pine species planted in deep red soils in the province of Missiones. *IDIA—Supplemento Forestal,* pp. 1–7.

De las Salas, G. (1980). Salmonwood (*Cordia alliodora*), a promising forest species for the American tropics: Evidence from Colombia and Costa Rica. IUFRO/Mab For. Ser. Symp. Wood Production in the Neotropics via Plantations, Rio Piedras, Puerto Rico, pp. 264–275.

Delaunay, J. (1979). Results of teak provenance studies (*Tectona grandis*) after six years in the Ivory Coast. 3rd World Consul. For. Tree Breed. Canberra, Australia, pp. 273–284.

Deleporte, P. (1983). The variability in inter- and intra-provenance of *Picea sitchensis:* Improvement strategy by vegetative propagation. *AFOCEL,* pp. 283–337.

Delmastro, R. (1983). Cooperative program of genetic tree improvement of *Pinus radiata. Fast Growing Trees. Silvicultura* **32,** 699–702.

Delwaulle, J. C. (1982). Seed production of *Pinus caribaea.* For. Gen. Res., FAO, Info. No. 11, Rome, p. 55.

Delwaulle, J. C. (1985). Paper production from clonal eucalypt stands in Congo. FAO Adv. Comm. Pulp Paper, 26th Session, Rome, 11 pp.

De Muckadell, J. S. (1985). Interim report on the rooting of cuttings from juvenile plant material: *Albizia falcataria, Araucaria cunninghamia* and A. *Hunsteinii,* For. Gen. Res., FAO, Info. No. 14, Rome, pp. 58–59.

Denison, N. P. (1973). Variation in Families of Patula Pine (*P. patula*) Grown at Two Locations in the Republic of South Africa. M.S. thesis, N.C. State University, Raleigh, North Carolina, 133 pp.

Denison, N. P. (1980). Important factors that influence seedling survival with special references to the open-root nursery system. TIMS Seminar on Nursery and Establishment, Sabie, South Africa.

Denison, N. P. (1981). Recent developments in nursery and planting systems in S. A. Forest Investments Limited. *S. A. For. Jour.* **118,** 26–30.

Destremau, D. X., J. N. Marien, and M. Boulay (1980). Selection et multiplication vegetative d'hybride d'eucalyptus resistant au froid. In IUFRO (1980), 13 pp.

De Villiers, A. M. (1983). Observations on the timber properties of certain tropical pines grown in South Africa and their improvement by tree breeding. *Selection and Breeding to Improve Some Tropical Conifers,* Vol. 2. Dept. For., Queensland, Brisbane, pp. 95–113.

Diabate, K. (1977a). Results of tests of provenances of *P. oocarpa* in the Ivory Coast. 3rd World Consul. For. Tree Breed., Canberra, Australia, Vol. 1, pp. 299–306.

Diabate, K. (1977b). Early results from analysis of provenances of *P. caribaea* from the Ivory Coast. 3rd World Consul. For. Tree Breed., Canberra, Australia, Vol. 2, pp. 1–10.

Dietrichson, J. (1968). Provenance and resistance to *Scleroderris lagerbergii (Crumenula abietina)*. The International Scots Pine Prov. Expt. of 1938 at Matrand. Rept. Nor. For. Res. Inst., Vollebekk, Norway, **25**(92), 398–410.

Dietrichson, J. (1970). Geographic variation in *Pinus contorta:* A study aiming at the use of the species for Norway. Nor. For. Res. Inst., Vollebekk, Norway, 140 pp.

Dietrichson, J. (1980). Skal vi ha hvitrussisk gran över hele landet? *Sveriges Skogsv. Förb. Tidskrift* **78**(1–2), 24–34.

Dietrichson, J., and R. Lines (1977). Recent advances from international cooperation in species and provenance selection within the temperate region. 3rd World Consul. For. Tree Breed., Canberra, Australia, pp. 113–126.

Diller, J. D., and R. B. Clapper (1969). Asiatic and hybrid chestnut trees in Eastern United States. *Jour. For.* **67**(5), 328–331.

Dimpflmeier, R. (1959). Hybridization in the Genus *Larix. Forstwiss. Forsch.* **12**, 75 pp.

Din, U. A. (1958). Pines for tropical areas. *Unasylva* **12**(3), 121–133.

Doi, H. (1903). The enactment of the regulations on collection and marketing of *Cryptomeria* and hinoki cypress seeds. *Dai-nippon Saurin Kaihoo [Bull. Jap. For. Assoc.]* **252**, 37–42.

Donahue, J. K. (1985). Conservation efforts for endangered white pines in southern Mexico: *Pinus chiapensis* and *Pinus ayacahuite.* IX World For. Congress, Mexico City, 5 pp.

Donahue, J. K., W. S. Dvorak, E. A. Gutiérrez, and M. B. Kane (1985). *Abies guatemalensis:* A two year status report. CAMCORE Bull. Trop. For. No. 3, Raleigh, North Carolina, 17 pp.

Doran, J. C. (1974). Genetic variation in wood density of *Eucalyptus regnans.* 4th Meet., Res. Working Group, Aust. For. Council, Melbourne, pp. 99–101.

Doran, J. C. (1978). Breeding *Pinus radiata.* Newsletter, No. 2, CSIRO, Div. For. Res., Gippsland, Australia, p. 17.

Doran, J. C. (1983). Recent seed collections of eucalypts in Australia and Indonesia and availability of seed for provenance research. *Fast Growing Trees. Silvicultura* **31**, 443–449.

Dormling, I. (1977). Kritisk nattlängd för knoppsättning hos gran av olika härkomst: Inverkan av ljusintensitet och temperatur. In Experimentell Genekologi. Rapporter och Uppsatser 27. Dep. For. Gen. SLU, Uppsala, Sweden, pp. 18–25.

Dormling, I. (1982). Frost resistance during bud flushing and shoot elongation in *Picea abies. Sil. Fennica* **26**(2), 167–177.

Doull, K. (1973). Bees and their role in pollination. *Australian Plants* **7**, 223–236.

Drew, T. J., and D. E. Cole (1977). Ecological conditions for seed production in *Pinus caribaea* var. *hondurensis* and seed orchard location in Brazil. Tech. Rept. Weyerhaeuser Co., Centralia, Washington, 18 pp.

Ducci, F., and A. Locci (1978). Research on rooting scions from old trees of *Pseudotsuga menziesii. Annali dell'Instituto Sperimentale per la Silvicolture* **9**, 37–70.

Dunberg, A. (1980). Stimulation of flowering in *Picea abies* by gibberellins. *Sil. Gen.* **29**(2), 51–53.

Dunn, M. G. (1965). Radiata pine seed a promising export. New Zealand For. Ser. Reprint No. 171, Wellington, 1 p.

Durand-Cresswell, R., M. Boulay, and A. Franclet (1982). Vegetative propagation in *Eucalyptus. Tissue Culture in Forestry,* Dr. W. Junk Publishers, The Hague, Netherlands, pp. 150–181.

Durand, P. Y. (1983). Variation in the technological quality of the wood of framire in plantations of the Ivory Coast. *Fast Growing Trees. Silvicultura* **32,** 811–815.

Duryea, M. L., and G. N. Brown (1984). *Seedling Physiology and Reforestation Success. For. Sciences,* Oregon State Univ., Corvallis, Oregon, 322 pp.

Dvorak, W. S. (1977). Status of the tree improvement program for *Pinus caribaea* var. *hondurensis* in Fiji. 3rd World Consul. For. Tree Breed., Canberra, Australia, 10 pp.

Dvorak, W. S. (1981a). CAMCORE is the industry's answer to coniferous preservation in Central America and Mexico. *For. Prod. Jour.* **31** (11), 10–11.

Dvorak, W. S. (1981b). *Eucalyptus robusta:* A Case Study of an Advanced Generation Hardwood Breeding Program in Southern Florida. M.S. thesis, School of For. Res., N.C. State University, Raleigh, North Carolina, 85 pp.

Dvorak, W. S. (1982). *Curso Corto Sobre Mejoramiento Genético, Silvicultura Y Manejo Forestal.* CAMCORE and CONARE, Chaguaramas, Venezuela, 192 pp. (N.C. State Univ., Raleigh, North Carolina).

Dvorak, W. S. (1984). Seed collections of coniferous species in Central America and Mexico: A summary of activities of the CAMCORE cooperative since 1980. IUFRO Working Party, Mutare, Zimbabwe, 14 pp.

Dvorak, W. S., and J. Brouard (1986). An evaluation of *Pinus chiapensis* as a commercial plantation species for the tropics and subtropics (in press).

Dvorak, W. S., and T. Eguiluz (1985). Gene conservation of coniferous species in Central America and Mexico. IX World For. Congress, Mexico City, 8 pp.

Dvorak, W. S., and J. G. Laarman (1986). Conserving the genes of tropical conifers. *Jour. For.* **1,** 43–45.

Dvorak, W. S., and B. J. Zobel (1985). Selection of species for industrial pulpwood plantations in developing tropical and subtropical countries. FAO Advis. Comm. Pulp and Paper, Rome, 11 pp.

Dyck, W. J., and J. G. Cooke (1981). Exotic forestry and its effect on water quality *The Waters of the Waikato,* Vol. I. Univ. of Waikato. N. Z. For. Ser. Reprint 1484, Rotorua, New Zealand, 11 pp.

Dyson, W. G., and A. L. Raunio (1977). Revised heritability estimates for *Cupressus lusitanica* in East Africa. *Sil. Gen.* **26**(56), 193–196.

Eberhardt, S. A., and E. Russel (1966). Stability parameters for comparing varieties. *Crop. Sci.* **6,** 36–40.

Eccher, A. (1969). Preliminary observations on trials of some *Pinus radiata* provenances in Italy. 2nd World Consul. For. Tree Breed., Washington, D.C., 1 p.

Eckholm, E. P. (1975). *The Other Energy Crisis: Firewood.* Worldwatch Paper #1, Worldwatch Inst., Washington, D.C., 76 pp.

Eckholm, E. P. (1978). *Disappearing Species: The Social Challenge.* Worldwatch Paper #22, Worldwatch Inst., Washington, D.C., 38 pp.

Edwards, M. W. (1963). The use of exotic trees in increasing production with particular reference to northwestern Europe. 1st World Consul., For. Gen. Tree Impr., Stockholm, Sweden, 8 pp.

Egenti, L. C. (1983a). *Gmelina arborea*—Initial observations on the international provenance trial. *Fast Growing Trees. Silvicultura* **30**, 161-163.

Egenti, L. C. (1983b). *Tectona grandis*—Progress in international provenance trials. *Fast Growing Trees. Silvicultura* **30**, 165-167.

Eidmann, H. (1982). Insekter på contortatall i Sverige. *Sveriges Skogsv. Förb. Tidskrift* **80**(1-2), 59-64.

Eifler, I. (1960). The individual results of crosses between *Betula pendula* and *B. pubescens. Sil. Gen.* **9**(6), 159-165.

Einspahr, D. W., and P. N. Joranson (1960). Late flowering in aspen and its relation to naturally occurring hybrids. *For. Sci.* **6**(3), 221-224.

Einspahr, D. W., J. P. Van Buijtenen, and J. R. Peckham (1969). Pulping characteristics of ten-year loblolly pine selected for extreme wood specific gravity. *Sil. Gen.* **18**(3), 57-61.

Einspahr, D. W., G. W. Wyckoff, and M. Fiscus (1984). Larch—A fast-growing fiber source for the Lake States and Northeast. *Jour. For.* **72**, 104-106.

Eisemann, R. L., and D. G. Nikles (1984). Population–Environmental interactions in Honduras Caribbean pine. In IUFRO (1984b), p. 210.

Eisemann, R. L., D. G. Nikles, and R. S. Newton (1984). The provenance question in Queensland planting of Honduras Caribbean pine. In IUFRO (1984b), pp. 211-213.

Ek, A., and D. H. Dawson (1976). Yields of intensively grown *Populus:* Actual and projected. U.S. For. Ser. Tech. Rept. NC-21, St. Paul, Minnesotta, pp. 5-9.

Ekberg, I., and G. Eriksson (1967). Development and fertility of pollen in three species of Larix. *Hereditas* **57**, 303-311.

El Dafei, A. R. (1983). Eucalypt provenance trials in Sudan. *Fast Growing Trees. Silvicultura* **31**, 430-432.

Eldridge, K. G. (1963). Effect of honeybees on seed production in *Eucalyptus regnans.* For. Tech. Pap. **13**, CSIRO, Canberra, Australia, pp. 6-13.

Eldridge, K. G. (1966). A seed production experiment with *Pinus radiata. Aust. For.* **30**(1), 43-50.

Eldridge, K. G. (1968). Physiological studies of altitudinal variation in *Eucalyptus regnans. Ecol. Soc. Aust.* **3**, 70-76.

Eldridge, K. G. (1974). Progeny testing *Pinus radiata* in Australia. Proc. IUFRO Meet., Stockholm, pp. 385-396.

Eldridge, K. G. (1975). *Annotated Bibliography of Genetic Variation in Eucalyptus camaldulensis.* Trop. For. Papers No. 8., Commonwealth For. Inst., Oxford, U.K., and CSIRO, Canberra, Australia.

Eldridge, K. G. (1976). Breeding systems, variation and genetic improvement of tropical eucalypts. *Tropical Trees—Variation, Breeding and Conservation,* Academic Press, London, pp. 101-108.

Eldridge, K. G. (1978). Provenances and provenance trials. Inter. Train. Course in For. Tree Breed. Sel. Ref. Topics, Aust. Devel. Assis. Agency, Canberra, Australia, pp. 95-100.

Eldridge, K. G. (1983). *Pinus radiata* gene pools for *ex situ* conservation and selection. *Fast Growing Trees. Silvicultura* **32**, 702–704.

Eldridge, K. G., and A. R. Griffin (1983). Selfing effects in *Eucalyptus regnans. Sil. Gen.* **32**, 216–221.

Elgersma, D. M. (1980). Resistance mechanisms of elms to Dutch elm disease. Workshop Gen. Host–Parasite Interactions in For. Wageningen, Holland, 10 pp.

Eliason, E. J. (1963). Tree seed certification and forest genetics. 1st World Consul. For. Gen. Tree Impr., Stockholm, pp. 1–3.

El-Lakany, M. H. (1983). Provenance/site interaction in irrigated plantations of *Eucalyptus camaldulensis. Fast Growing Trees. Silvicultura* **31**, 450–451.

Elliott, D. A. (1976). The influence of disease and insect problems on management practices in the Kaingaroa Forest. *N. Z. Jour. For. Sci.* **6**(2), 188–192.

Enescu, V., G. Popescu, and L. Contescu (1977). Blossoming artificial inducing in a clonal orchard of *Pseudotsuga menziesii.* 3rd World Consul. For. Tree Breed, Canberra, Australia, pp 1071–1077.

Entrican, A. R. (1950). Quality v. quantity in New Zealand forestry and forest products. *N. Z. Jour. For.* **6**(1), 100–111.

Ericsson, T. (1984). Hardiness test of North Swedish pine seed orchard clones. Institutet för skogsförbättring, Årsbok 1983, pp. 48–59.

Eriksson, G., I. Ekberg, I. Dormling, and B. Matern (1978). Inheritance of bud flushing in *Picea abies. Theor. Appl. Gen.* **52**, 3–19.

Eriksson, G., S. Andersson, J. Ifver, and A. Persson (1980). Severity index and transfer effects on survival and volume production of *Pinus sylvestris* in northern Sweden. Studia Forest. Suecica No. 156, Garpenberg, Sweden, 32 pp.

Evans, J. (1978). Long-term productivity in tropical and subtropical plantations. 8th World For. Cong., Jakarta, Indonesia, 8 pp.

Evans, J. (1980). Prospects for eucalypts as forest trees in Great Britain. *Forestry* **53**(2), 129–143.

Evans, J. (1983). Long-term productivity of tropical plantations—An overview. *Fast Growing Trees. Silvicultura* **32**, 678–681.

Evans, J., L. Haydon, and M. Lazzeri (1983). Propagating and planting *Eucalyptus* in Britain. *Arboricultural Jour.* **7**, 137–145.

Evans, J. (1984). *Plantation Forestry in the Tropics.* Clarendon Press, Oxford, U.K., 472 pp.

Evensen, R. E. (1981). Tropical forests in economic development. *Tropical Forests: Utilization and Conservation.* Yale Univ. Press, New Haven, Connecticut, 199 pp.

Fahnestock, G. R. (1983). Possibilities for use of prescribed burning in the management of plantations of *Pinus caribaea* in Venezuela. *Venez. Forestal.* **3**(8), 24–41.

Falkenhagen, E. R. (1978). Thirty five-year results from seven *Pinus elliotti* and *P. taeda* provenance trials in South Africa. *S. A. For. Jour.* **107**, 22–33.

Falkenhagen, E. R. (1979). *Provenance Variation in Growth, Timber and Pulp Properties of Pinus caribaea in South Africa.* Bull. 59, South African For. Res. Ins. Dept. For., Pretoria, 65 pp.

FAO (1966). *World Symposium on Man-Made Forests and Their Industrial Importance.* FAO, Rome, 63 pp.

FAO (1967). Wood: World trends and prospects. FFHC Basic Study No. 16. FAO, Rome, 139 pp.

FAO (1974). *An Annotated Bibliography of Cupressus lusitanica.* FAO, Rome, 64 pp.

FAO (1979). *Eucalypts for Planting.* FAO Forestry Series No. 11. Rome, 677 pp.

FAO (1981a). Map of the fuelwood situation in the developing countries. *Unasylva* **33**(133) (32-page supplement).

FAO (1981b). *Los Recursos Forestales de la America Tropical. Proyecto de Evaluacion de los Recursos forestales Tropicales.* Informe Técnico 1, FAO, Rome, 343 pp.

FAO (1981c). Monthly bulletin of statistics. FAO, Rome, **4**(4), 1–72.

FAO (1981d). Forestry and rural development. FAO Forestry Paper No. 26. FAO, Rome, 35 pp.

FAO (1981e). *Forest Resources of Tropical Africa.* Part I: Regional Synthesis. Tropical Resources Assessment Project, Tech. Rept. 2, FAO, Rome, 108 pp.

FAO (1981f). *Forest Resources of Tropical Asia.* Tropical Forest Resources Assessment Project, Tech. Rept. 3, FAO, Rome, 475 pp.

FAO (1982). *Forest Genetic Resources—Information Number 11.* FAO, Rome, 69 pp.

FAO (1983). *Forest Genetic Resources—Information Number 12.* FAO, Rome, 79 pp.

FAO (1984). Le bois source d'energi. Rapport·sur les problémes forestier No. 1. FAO, Rome, 41 pp.

FAO—DANIDA (1974). *Training Course on Forest Tree Improvement.* FAO/DANIDA 112 (Rome), Limura, Kenya, 344 pp.

FAO—DANIDA (1977). *Savanna Afforestation in Africa.* FAO For. Pap. No. 11 (Rome), Kaduna, Nigeria, 313 pp.

FAO—DANIDA (1980). *Mejora Genética de Arboles Forestales.* [Short Course on Genetics of Forest Trees]. FAO Estudio, Montes No. 20 (Rome), Merida, Venezuela, 340 pp.

FAO—N.C. State University (1969). *Forest Tree Improvement Training Center.* N.C. State Univ., Raleigh, North Carolina, 333 pp.

FAO, IUFRO, and CSIRO (1977). 3rd World Consultation on Forest Tree Breeding, Canberra, Australia, 2 vols.

Farnsworth, D. H., G. E. Gatherum, J. J. Jokela, H. B. Kriebel, D. T. Lester, C. Merritt, S. S. Pauley, R. A. Read, R. L. Sajdak, and J. W. Wright (1972). Geographic variation in Japanese larch in North Central United States Plantations. *Sil. Gen.* **21**(3–4), 65–148.

Fassi, B. (1980). La ruggine vescicilosa del pino Strobo dovuta a *Cronartium ribicola.* Monti e Boschi, Rome, (7–8).

Fearnside, P. M. (1979). O processo de desertificao e os riscos de sua ocurrencia no Brasil. *Acta Amazonica* **9**(2), 393–400.

Fearnside, P. M., and J. M. Rankin (1982). The new Jari: Risks and prospects of a major Amazonian development. *Interciencia* **7**(6), 329–339.

Fege, A. S., R. E. Inman, and D. J. Salo (1979). Energy farms for the future. *Jour. For.* **77**(6), 358–361.

Fenton, R. (1972). Economics of sawlog silviculture which includes production thinning. *N. Z. Jour. For. Sci.* **2**(3), 348–368.

Fenton, R., and J. R. Justin (1972). Profitability of radiata pine afforestation for the export log trade—On site index 95. *N. Z. Jour. For. Sci.* **2**(1), 7–68.

Fenton, R. (1977). Pruning results from 2.44, 4.27 and 5.49m pruned 19 year-old radiata pine. *N. Z. Jour. For. Sci.* **7**(2), 216–239.

Feret, P. P. (1975). Biological significance and problems of pine monoculture. Workshop, Pine Monoculture in the South, Southern Forest Economics Workers, Biloxi, Mississippi, 7 pp.

Ferraz, E. S. (1983). Growth rings and climate in *Eucalyptus*. *Fast Growing Trees. Silvicultura* **32**, 821–822.

Ferreira, F. A., C. S. Hodges, and M. S. Reis (1976). The influence of basal canker caused by *Diaporthe cubensis* on the coppicing of *Eucalyptus* spp. *Brasil Florestal* **7**(25), 13–15.

Ferreira, F. A., M. S. Reis, A. C. Alfenas, and C. S. Hodges (1977). Evaluation of the resistance of *Eucalyptus* spp. to canker due to *Diaporthe cubensis*. *Fitopatologia Brasileia* **2**(3), 225–241.

Ferreira, M. (1968). Studies of the variation of basic density of the wood of *Eucalyptus alba* and *Eucalyptus saligna*. Univ. São Paulo, Piracicaba, Brazil, 71 pp.

Ferreira, M., and P. Y. Kageyama (1977). Program for the genetic improvement of populations of *Pinus oocarpa* in Brazil by the IPEF. Gen. Improve. of Trop. For. Trees. Brisbane, Australia, Vol. 2, pp. 4–7.

Ferreira, M., H. T. Couto, and J. Mascarenhas (1972). Introduction of Mexican pines in the region of Pocos de Caldas, Minas Gerais, Brazil. *IPEF* **4**, 95–103.

Ferrell, W. K., and E. S. Woodard (1966). Effects of seed origin on drought resistance of Douglas-fir (*Pseudotsuga menziesii*). *Ecology* **43**(3), 499–502.

Fielding, J. M. (1970). Trees grown from cuttings compared with trees grown from seed (*P. radiata*). *Sil. Gen.* **19**(2–3), 54–63.

Fielding, J. M., and A. G. Brown (1961). Tree-to-tree variations in the health and some effects of super-phosphate on the growth and development of Monterey pine on a low quality site. Aust. For. and Timber Bur. Leaflet No. 79, Canberra, Australia, 19 pp.

Filer, T. H., and F. I. McCracken (1969). *Clitocybe tabescens* associated with decline and death of Chinese elm and water oak. *Plant. Dis. Reporter* **54**(10), 840.

Filho, E. B., and P. Pacheco (1985). Research task force on leaf-cutting ants. Bull. No. 2, Univ. São Paulo, Piracicaba, Brazil, 13 pp.

Filho, M. T., and T. L. Krugner (1980). Formation of ectomycorrhizae and growth of *Pinus caribaea* var. *hondurensis* seedlings in the nursery artificially innoculated separately with *Thelephora terrestris* and *Pisolithus tinctorius* in the south of Bahia. *IPEF* **21**, 21–37.

Finlay, K. W., and G. N. Wilkinson (1963). The analysis of adaptation in a plant breeding program. *Aust. Jour. Agr. Res.* **14**, 742–754.

Fisher, R. F. (1980). Allelopathy: A potential cause of regeneration failure. *Jour. For.* **78**(6), 346–348.

Fishwick, R. W. (1977). A preliminary assessment of a 9-year-old Southern pine (*P. elliotti* and *P. taeda*) trial with some observations on these species in South Brazil. 3rd World Consul. For. Tree Breed., Canberra, Australia, Vol. 1, pp. 335–339.

Fitzpatrick, E. A. (1980). *Soils: Their Formation, Classification and Distribution.* Longman, London, 353 pp.

Foelkel, C. E., L. E. Barrichelo, and A. F. Milaney (1975a). Study of the *Eucalyptus* spp. wood characteristics and their unbleached sulphate pulps. *IPEF* **10,** 17–37.

Foelkel, C. E., L. E. Barrichelo, A. C. DoAmaral, and C. F. do Valle (1975b). Variation in the wood characteristics and sulphate pulp properties from *Pinus oocarpa* with the aging of forest stands. *IPEF* **10,** 81–87.

Ford-Robertson, F. C. (1971). *Terminology of Forest Science, Technology, Practice and Products* (English ed.). The Multilingual Forestry Terminology Series, No. 1. Soc. Amer. For., Washington, D.C., 349 pp.

Forrest, W. G., and J. D. Ovington (1971). Variation in dry weight and mineral nutrient content of *Pinus radiata* progeny. *Sil. Gen.* **20**(5–6), 174–179.

Fourcade, H. G. (1889). Report on the Natal Forests. W. Watson, Printer to Natal Government, Pietermaritzburg, South Africa.

Fowler, D. P. (1961). Initial studies indicate *Pinus resinosa* little affected by selfing. 9th N.E. For. Tree Impr. Conf., Syracuse, New York, pp. 3–8.

Fowler, D. P. (1964). Effects of inbreeding in red pine, *Pinus resinosa. Sil. Gen.* **13**(6), 170–177.

Fowler, D. P. (1978). Population improvement and hybridization. *Unasylva* **30**(119–120), 21–26.

Fowler, D. P., and R. W. Morris (1977). Genetic diversity in red pine: Evidence for low genetic heterozygosity. *Can. Jour. For. Res.* **7**(2), 343–347.

Fowler, H. G., S. W. Robinson, and J. Diehl (1984). Effect of mature colony density on colonization and initial colony survivorship in *Atta capiguara,* a leafcutting ant. *Biotropica* **16**(1), 51–54.

Franclet, A. (1957). Initial work on genetic improvement of eucalypts. *Annales de la Recherche Forestier au Maroc* **4**(1), 63–86.

Franclet, A. (1979). Micropropagation of forest trees—Rejuvenation of mature trees in vegetative propagation. *AFOCEL* **12,** 3–18.

Franich, R. A., R. E. Gaskin, L. G. Wells, and J. A. Zabkiewicz (1982). Effect of *Pinus radiata* needle monoterpenes on spore germination and mycelial growth of *Dothistroma pini* in vitro in relation to mature tree resistance. *Physiol. Plant Path.* **21,** 55–63.

Frankel, O. H., and E. Bennett (1970). *Genetic Resources in Plants—Their Exploitation and Conservation.* Davis, Philadelphia, Pennsylvania, 176 pp.

Frankie, G. W. (1976). Pollination of widely dispersed trees by animals in Central America, with an emphasis on bee pollination systems. *Tropical Trees—Variation, Breeding and Conservation,* Academic Press, London, pp. 151–159.

Franklin, E. C. (1978). Exotics for hardwood timber production in the Southeastern United States. 2nd Symp. Southeastern Hardwoods, U.S. For. Ser., Atlanta, Georgia, pp. 171–179.

Franklin, E. C. (1979). Model relating level of genetic variance to stand development of four North American conifers. *Sil. Gen.* **28**(5–6), 207–212.

Franklin, E. C. (1983). Strategic uses of pollen in international forest tree improvement. *Fast Growing Trees. Silvicultura* **32,** 705–706.

Franklin, E. C., and R. Z. Callaham (1970). Multinodality, branching and forking in lodgepole pine (*Pinus contorta* var. *murrayana*). *Sil. Gen.* **19**(5-6), 180-184.

Franklin, E. C., and G. Meskimen (1975). Wood properties of some eucalypts for the southern United States. Proc. Soc. Amer. For., Washington, D.C., pp. 454-458.

Friedman, I. (1977). The Amazon Basin, another Sahel? *Science* **197**, 7.

Frochot, H., M. Pitsch, and L. Wharlen (1978). Susceptibility differences of mistletoe (*Viscum album*) to some poplar clones (*Populus* sp.). Congres des Sociétés Savantes, Nancy, France, pp. 371-380.

Froehlich, H. A. (1976). The influence of different thinning systems on damage to soils and trees. Oregon State Univ. Corvallis, pp. 333-342.

Fuentes, J. M. (1972). Interaction between planting site and seed source in loblolly pine. 7th World For. Cong., Buenos Aires, Argentina. 4 pp.

Furukoshi, T., and M. Sasaki (1982). Hybridizations among species belonging to subsect. Sylvestres and their resistance to wood nematodes, including future cross-breeding strategies. Kanto For. Tree Breed. Inst. Ann. Rept. 16, Mito, Japan, pp. 195-225.

Gabriel, W. J. (1975). Allelopathic effects of black walnut on white birches. *Jour. For.* **73**(4), 234-237.

Gallegos, C. M. (1977). Parameters for the Selection of Loblolly Pine *(P. taeda)* Seed Orchard Sites. Ph.D. thesis, N.C. State Univ., Raleigh, North Carolina, 204 pp.

Gallegos, C. M. (1980a). Use of exotics. Trop. Tree Impr., Short Course Session #15, N.C. State Univ., Raleigh, North Carolina, 4 pp.

Gallegos, C. M. (1980b). The pine resources of Guatemala and their association with the coniferous forests of Mexico and Central America. Trop. Tree Impr., Short Course, N.C. State Univ., Raleigh, North Carolina (mimeo rept.), 28 pp.

Gallegos, C. M. (1983). Flowering and seed production of *Pinus caribaea* var. *hondurensis* (results of a worldwide survey). *Fast Growing Trees. Silvicultura* **29**, 84-87.

Gallegos, C. M. (1985). Plantation species for fuelwood in the tropics and subtropics. Plantation Species for the Tropics and Subtropics, Short Course, N.C. State Univ., Raleigh, North Carolina, 18 pp.

Gallegos, C. M., C. B. Davey, R. C. Kellison, P. A. Sanchez, and B. J. Zobel (1982). *Technologies For Reforestation of Degraded Lands in the Tropics.* Cong. of U.S., Office of Tech. Assoc. (Draft for preparation of O.T.A. Report Concerning Sustaining Tropical Forest Resources), Washington, D.C., 131 pp.

Gallegos, C. M., B. J. Zobel, and W. S. Dvorak (1983). The combined industry-university-government efforts to form the Central America and Mexico Coniferous Resources Cooperative. *Fast Growing Trees. Silvicultura* **32**, 707-708.

Gantry, J. Y. (1983). Mother trees and vegetative propagation of Douglas-fir. *AFOCEL,* pp. 191-227.

Garcia, A. S., and E. F. Beronilla (1979). Closed nutrient cycle in tropical rainforests. *Canopy* **5**(7), pp. 3 and 12.

Gathy, P. (1960). International experience on the origin of the seeds of spruce (*Picea abies*) in Belgium. Station de Récherches des Eaux et Forêts Report B, No. 24, Groenendaal-Hoeilaart, Belgium, 32 pp.

Gathy, P. (1961). Preliminary report on the tests on the origins of Douglas-fir (*Pseu-*

dotsuga taxifolia). Station de Récherches des Eaux et Forêts, Report B, No. 26, Groenendaal-Hoeilaart, Belgium, 44 pp.

Geary, T. F. (1984). Flowering limitations on *Eucalyptus* breeding strategies in Zambia. In IUFRO (1984b), pp. 516–517.

Geary, T. F., and C. B. Briscoe (1972). Tree species for plantations in the granitic uplands of Puerto Rico. U.S. For. Ser. Res. Paper ITF, Rio Piedras, Puerto Rico, 14 pp.

Geary, T. F., and J. A. Zambrana (1972). Must Honduras pine be weeded frequently in Puerto Rico? U.S. For. Ser. Res. Pap. ITF 16, Rio Piedras, Puerto Rico, 10 pp.

Geary, T. F., H. Barres, and R. Ybarra-Coronado (1973). Seed source variation in Puerto Rico and Virgin Islands grown mahoganies. U.S. For. Ser. Res. Paper ITF 17, Rio Piedras, Puerto Rico, 24 pp.

Gentle, W. (1970). Incidence of boron and sulfur deficiency in *Pinus radiata* plantations in New South Wales. Australian Plant Nutrition Conf., Mt. Gambier, South Austr., 2 pp.

Genys, J. B., and R. B. Hall (1983). Growth rates of diverse geographic strains of black alder in Maryland's tree nursery. 3rd North Central Tree Impr. Conf., Wooster, Ohio, pp. 44–52.

Gerhold, H. D., E. J. Schreiner, R. E. McDermott, and J. A. Winieski (1966). *Breeding Pest-resistant Trees*. Pergamon Press, Oxford, U.K., 505 pp.

Gerischer, G. F., and A. M. De Villiers (1963). The effect of heavy pruning on timber properties. *For. In. S. A.* **3**, 15–35.

Germishuizen, P. J., and J. P. Marais (1981). Establishment and re-establishment of conifer plantations in the summer rainfall region of Southern Africa. *S. A. For. Jour.* **117**, 55–60.

Gewald, N. J. (1980). Growth data of *Pinus caribaea* var. *hondurensis* in La Yeguada Forest Reserve, Panama. IUFRO—Mab. For. Ser. Symp. Rio Piedras, Puerto Rico, pp. 48–57.

Ghosh, R. C., O. N. Kaul, and B. K. Shubba Rao (1978). Some aspects of water relations and nutrition in *Eucalyptus* plantations. *Indian For.,* pp. 517–524.

Gibson, G. L. (1982). Genotype–environment interactions in *Pinus caribaea*. Commonw. For. Inst., Oxford Univ., U.K., 112 pp.

Gibson, G. L., and R. D. Barnes (1985). Availability of Central American pines for *ex situ* conservation stands, provenance resource stands, breeding populations and provenance testing. For. Gen. Res. Info. No. 13, FAO, Rome, pp. 37–40.

Gibson, G. L., R. D. Barnes, and J. Berrington (1983). Provenance productivity in *Pinus caribaea* and its interaction with environment. *Commonw. For. Rev.* **62**(2), 93–106.

Gibson, I. A. (1979). Diseases of forest trees widely planted as exotics in the tropics and Southern Hemisphere. Part II: The genus *Pinus*. Commonw. Mycological Inst., CFI, Oxford, U.K., 135 pp.

Gibson, I. A. (1980). Two pine needle fungi new to Colombia. *Trop. Pest Mgt.* **26**(1), 38–40.

Gibson, I. A., and T. Jones (1977). Monoculture as the origin of major forest pests and diseases. *Origins of Pest, Parasite, Disease and Weed Problems*. Blackwell, Oxford, U.K., 413 pp.

Giertych, M. (1977). Role of light and temperature in flowering of forest trees. 3rd World Consul. For. Tree Breed, Canberra, Australia, Vol. 2, pp. 1013–1021.

Giertych, M., and H. Fober (1967). Variation among Norway spruce of Polish provenances in seedling growth and nitrogen uptake. 14th Congr. Int. Union, For. Res. Org., Munich, Sect. 22, pp. 536–550.

Gilmour, J. W. (1967). Distribution and significance of the needle blight of pines caused by *Dothistroma pini* in New Zealand. *Plant Dis. Reporter* **51**(9), 4 pp.

Gilmour, J. W., and A. Noorderhaven (1972). Control of *Dothistroma* needle blight by low volume aerial application of copper fungicides. *N. Z. Jour. For. Sci.* **3**(1), 120–136.

Giordano, E. (1960). Observation on some hybrids of *Eucalyptus viminalis* × *E. globulus,* Vol. 4. Center for Agr. and For. Expts., Rome, Italy, pp. 47–52.

Gladstone, W. T. (1980). Silviculture: Growing more wood on less land. TAPPI Ann. Meet., Atlanta, Georgia, pp. 259–265.

Glasgow, L. L. (1975). Public attitudes toward monoculture. Workshop, Pine Monoculture in the South, Southern Forest Economics Workers, Biloxi, Mississippi.

Goddard, R. E. (1969). Slash pine progeny response to di-ammonium phosphate. Coop. For. Gen. Res. Prog., Univ. of Florida, Tree Improvement Tips, No. 16, Gainesville, 2 pp.

Goddard, R. E. (1977). Genotype × environment interaction in slash pine. 3rd World Consul. For. Tree Breed., Canberra, Australia, pp. 761–772.

Goddard, R. E., B. J. Zobel, and C. A. Hollis (1976). Response of *Pinus taeda* and *Pinus elliottii* to varied nutrition. Conf. on Physiological Genetics and Tree Breed., Edinburgh, Scotland, pp. 449–462.

Goggans, J. F. (1961). The interplay of environment and heredity as factors controlling wood properties in conifers with special emphasis on their effects on specific gravity. Tech. Rept. No. 11, School of For., N.C. State Univ., Raleigh, North Carolina, 56 pp.

Goldstein, I. S. (1980a). New technology for new uses of wood. *Tappi* **63**(2), 105–108.

Goldstein, I. S. (1980b). Chemicals from biomass: Present status. *For. Prod. Jour.* **31**(10), 63–68.

Golfari, L. (1963a). Climatic requirements of tropical and subtropical conifers. *Unasylva* **17**(1), 33–42.

Golfari, L. (1963b). Observations about *Cephisus siccifolius* on eucalypts of Misiones. IDIA No. 189, pp. 9–14.

Golfari, L. (1965). Potential regions best for plantations of pine and other conifers in Latin America. IDIA (Suplemento Forestal) **16**, 19–48.

Golfari, L. (1972). Response of some tropical and subtropical conifers to various site conditions in Brazil. *Selection and Breeding to Improve Some Tropical Conifers,* Vol. I, CSIRO, Brisbane, Australia, pp. 264–267.

Golfari, L. (1974). Esquema de zoneamento ecologica florestal para o Brasil. *IBDF,* Rio de Janeiro, Brazil, 127 pp.

Golfari, L. (1975a). Ecological zones in the state of Minas Gerais for reforestation. Serie Tecnica No. 3, PRODEPEF, Brasilia, Brazil, 65 pp.

Golfari, L. (1975b). Fantasias e reallidades sobre plantios de eucalipto e a ecologia. *O Eucalypto e a Ecologia,* Grupo Aracruz, Brazil, pp. Rio de Janeiro, 17–23.

Golfari, L. (1983). Comparison of locations between Australia and Brazil suitable for planting for *Eucalyptus grandis. Fast Growing Trees. Silvicultura* **31**, 406–409.

Golfari, L., and R. L. Caser (1977). Ecological zoning of the northeastern region for experimental forestry. PRODEPEF, Tech. Bull. No. 10, Brasilia, Brazil, 16 pp.

Golfari, L., R. L. Caser, and V. P. Moura (1978). Zoneamento ecológico esquematico para reflorestamento no Brasil. PRODEPEF, Tecnica Serie No. 11, Brasilia, 66 pp.

Gopal, I. F. (1983). Progress of improved seed production of teak in India. *Fast Growing Trees. Silvicultura* **30**, 169–173.

Gordon, A. G. (1968). Ecology of *Picea chihuahuana. Ecology* **49**(5), 880–896.

Granhoff, J. J. (1977). Variation of growth, stem quality and wood properties in relation to genetic improvement of tropical forest trees. Topic 5: *P. caribaea.* IUFRO Workshop, Brisbane, Australia, 5 pp.

Granhoff, J. J. (1983). Report on progress in establishing a Southeast Asian Cooperative Tree Improvement and Seed Procurement Programme. *Fast Growing Trees. Silvicultura* **32**, 709–712.

Granhoff, J. J. (1984). Growth and variation in *Pinus kesiya* at high elevations in Thailand. In IUFRO (1984b), pp. 219–234.

Greaves, A. (1978). *Description of Seed Sources and Collections for Provenances of Pinus caribaea.* Trop. For. Pap. No. 12, Commonwealth For. Inst., Oxford Univ., Oxford, U.K., 98 pp.

Greaves, A. (1979). *Description of Seed Sources and Collections for Provenances of Pinus oocarpa.* Trop. For. Pap. No. 13, Commonwealth For. Inst., Oxford Univ., Oxford, U.K., 144 pp.

Greaves, A. (1982a). *Pinus oocarpa. Annotated Bibliography.* No. F22, Commonwealth Ag. Bur., Oxford, U.K., 70 pp.

Greaves, A. (1982b). A bibliography on *Gmelina arborea* covering the literature from 1920 to 1981. Commonw. For. Inst., Oxford Univ., U.K. (mimeo), 21 pp.

Greaves, A. (1983). A review of the international trials of *Pinus caribaea* and *P. oocarpa. Fast Growing Trees. Silvicultura* **29**, 35–43.

Greaves, A., and R. H. Kemp (1977). Variation in growth, stem quality and wood properties in relation to genetic improvement in tropical forest trees. Prov. Trials and Breed. Programs, IUFRO Workshop, Brisbane, Australia, 9 pp.

Gregor, J. W. (1944). The ecotype. *Biol. Rev.* **19**, 20–30.

Grey, D. C. (1978). A Natural Resource Survey and Afforestation Potential of the Umzimkulu District, Transkei. Unpublished M.Sc. thesis. University of Natal, South Africa, 247 pp.

Grey, D. C. (1983). Forest soils and site requirements of exotic tree species. South African Forestry Handbook. S. A. Institute of Forestry, Pretoria, South Africa, 55–62.

Grey, D. C., A. P. Schönau, and C. J. Schutz (1984). *Symposium on Site and Productivity of Fast Growing Plantations,* 2 vols. IUFRO Pretoria, South Africa, 968 pp.

Griffith, J. A. (1982). Economics and techniques of thinning. *N. Z. Jour. For. Sci.* **12**(2), 38–45.

Grigsby, H. C. (1969). Exotic trees unsatisfactory for forestry in southern Arkansas and northern Louisiana. U.S. For. Ser., Res. Note, SO-92, Southern For. Expt. Sta., New Orleans, Louisiana, 5 pp.

Grijpoma, P. (1976). Resistance of *Meliaceae* against the shoot borer *Hypsipyla* with particular reference to *Toona ciliata* var. *australis*. *Tropical Trees No. 2*, Academic Press, London, pp. 69–77.

Groves, R. H. (1967). Within-species variation in the growth and nutrition of *Eucalyptus cladocalyx*. *Aust. Jour. Bot.* **15**, 161–173.

Grunwald, C., and R. Karschon (1983). Variation of *Eucalyptus camaldulensis* from North Australia grown in Israel. *Sil. Gen.* **32**, 165–173.

Guldager, P. (1975). Ex situ conservation stands in the tropics. *The Methodology of Conservation of Forest Genetic Resources,* FAO, Rome, pp. 85–92.

Guppy, N. (1984). *Tropical Deforestation: A Global View.* Nicholas Guppy, pp. 928–965.

Gupta, V. K., and M. C. Kukreti (1983). A note on physical and mechanical properties of *Acacia mearnsii* from Tamil Nadu. *Indian For.,* pp. 395–400.

Guries, R. P. (1984). Genetic variation and population differentiation in forest trees. 8th N. Amer. For. Biol. Workshop, Logan, Utah, pp. 119–131.

Gutiérrez, G. (1976–82). *Atlas Del Eucalypto.* Min. de Agric., 5 vols., Sevilla, Spain.

Györfey, B. (1960). Hybrid vigor in forest trees and the genetic explanation of heterosis. *Erdesz. Kutatas* (Budapest) **56**(1/3), 327–340.

Haag, H. P., J. V. Filho, G. D. de Oliveira, and J. R. Sarrug (1983). Influence on man-made *Eucalyptus* and *Pinus* forests on soil chemical characteristics. *Fast Growing Trees. Silvicultura* **32**, 643–645.

Hacskaylo, J., R. F. Finn, and J. P. Vimmerstedt (1969). Deficiency symptoms of some forest trees. Ohio Agr. Res. and Dev. Center Bull. 1015, Wooster, Ohio, 68 pp.

Hadders, G. (1977). Experiments with supplemental mass pollination in seed orchards of Scots pine (*Pinus sylvestris*). 3rd World Consul. on For. Tree Breed., Canberra, Australia, 7 pp.

Hägglund, B. (1982). Growth and yield of lodgepole pine in Sweden. *Lodgepole Pine— Our Third Conifer, Sveriges Skogsv. Förb. Tidskrift* **80**(1–2), 31–35.

Hägglund, B., E. Karlsson, J. Remröd, and G. Siren (1979). *Contortatallens produktion i Sverige och Finland.* Projekt Hugin, Rapport nr. 13. SLU, Umeå, Sweden, 133 pp.

Hagner, S. (1979). Optimum productivity—A silviculturist's view. *Forest Plantations— The Shape of the Future.* Weyerhaeuser Sci. Symp., Tacoma, Washington, pp. 49–68.

Hahl, J. (1978). Results from an eight-year-old provenance trial of lodgepole pine (*Pinus contorta*). Infor. No. 4, Found. For. Tree Breed., Helsinki, Finland, 6 pp.

Haigh, H. (1983). Forestry Weed Control. *South African Forestry Handbook,* S. A. Institute of Forestry, Pretoria, South Africa.

Haines, M. W., and S. Tozer (1984). Early performance of *Pinus oocarpa* in within-family provenance trials in the Northern Territory of Australia. In IUFRO (1984b), pp. 240–249.

Hair, D. (1974). Wood requirements and resources. Proc. Fiber Cons. and Util. Seminar, *Pulp and Paper,* pp. 143–162.

Hall, J. P. (1982). Growth and development of exotic tree species in Newfoundland. Information Report N-X-212, Can. For. Serv., St. Johns, Newfoundland, 36 pp.

Hall, J. P. (1984). Field test of exotic larches in western Newfoundland. *Can. For. Serv. Res. Notes* **4**(3), 37.

Hall, R. B., and A. G. Miller (1983). Selection and breeding strategy for an exotic species: *Alnus glutinosa* in North America. 3rd Central States Tree Impr. Conf., Wooster, Ohio, pp. 233–244.

Halos, S. C., and A. H. Abarquez (1984). Response to shoot moth infestation and survival of various tropical pine provenances in Abra, Philippines. In IUFRO (1984b), pp. 258–264.

Hamerick, J. L., J. B. Metton, and Y. B. Linhart (1979). Levels of genetic variation in trees: Influence of life history characteristics. Symp. on Isozymes of N. Amer. For. Trees, Berkeley, California, pp. 35–41.

Hamilton, J. R., and G. W. Wendel (1967). Specific gravity and fiber length of some hybrid poplars growing in West Virginia. Ag. Expt. Stat. Bull. 556T, Univ. of West Virginia, Morgantown, 6 pp.

Han, S. U., S. K. Choi, E. R. Noh, and Y. K. Min (1984). General and specific combining ability for height growth of some plus trees of *Pinus rigida*. Res. Rept. Inst. For. Gen. No. 20, Suwon, Korea, pp. 12–15.

Han, Y. C., and K. Y. Lee (1983). Provenance test of *Pinus strobus* in five plantations at age 15 in Korea. Res. Rept. Inst. For. Gen. No. 19, Suwon, Korea, pp. 73–80.

Han, Y. C., and K. O. Ryu (1984). Height growth of 10 provenances of jack pine (*Pinus banksiana*) at age 10 in the Chunseon area. Res. Rept. Inst. For. Gen. No. 20. Suwon, Korea, pp. 77–81.

Han, Y. C., J. B. Ryu, and G. O. Ryu (1984a). Volume per hectare and per tree of pitch pine and volume increase by provenance and family selection at a provenance test plantation. Res. Rept. Inst. For. Gen. No. 20, Suwon, Korea, pp. 90–94.

Han, Y. C., K. Y. Lee, S. K. Choi, and S. Y. Shim (1984b). Provenance test in Korea of Norway spruce (*Picea abies*) introduced from Romania and West Germany at age of 7 & 8. Res. Rept. Inst. For. Gen. No. 20, Suwon, Korea, pp. 82–89.

Hans, A. S., and J. Burley (1972). Wood quality of eight *Eucalyptus* species in Zambia. *Separatum Experientia* **29**, 1378–1380.

Harahap, R. M., and I. Soerianegara (1977). Heritability of some characteristics in teak. 3rd. World Consul. For. Tree Breed., Canberra, Australia, 8 pp.

Hardie, A. D., and C. L. Ingram (1983). Utilization potentials and problems for exotic conifers in Zambia, with special reference to *Pinus kesiya*. *Selection and Breeding to Improve Some Tropical Conifers,* Vol. 2, Dept. For., Queensland, Australia, pp. 133–147.

Hare, R. C. (1966). Physiology of resistance to fungal diseases in plants. *Bot. Review* **32**(2), 95–137.

Harker, A. P., A. Sandels, and J. Burley (1982). Calorific values for wood and bark and a bibliography for fuelwood. Trop. Prod. Inst. G162, CFI, Oxford, U.K., 20 pp.

Harlan, J. R. (1971). Agricultural Origins: Centers and non-centers. *Science* **174**, 468–474.

Harris, J. M. (1965). The heritability of wood density. IUFRO Sect. 41, Melbourne, Australia, 20 pp.

Harris, J. M. (1970). The wood density of *Pinus caribaea* grown in Malaya as measured with beta rays. N. Z. FRI, For. Prod. Lab. Rept. FP/WG 2, Rotorua, New Zealand, 3 pp.

Harris, J. M. (1983). The use of beta rays to examine wood density of tropical pines grown in Malaya. *Selection and Breeding to Improve Some Tropical Conifers,* Vol. 2, Dept. For., Queensland, Australia, pp. 86–94.

Harris, L. J., J. H. Borden, H. D. Pierce, and A. C. Oehlschlager (1983). Cortical resin monoterpenes in Sitka spruce and resistance to the white pine weevil, *Pissodes strobi. Can. Jour. For. Res.* **13**(2), 350–352.

Hartney, V. J. (1980). Vegetative propagation in the eucalypts. *Aust. For. Res.* **10**(3), 191–211.

Harvey, A. M. (1977). Trials of exotic conifers in the highland region of southeast Queensland. IUFRO Workshop Var. Growth Stem Eval. and Wood Prop. in Rel. to Gen. Impr. of Trop. For. Trees, Brisbane, Australia, 12 pp.

Harvey, A. M. (1983). Growth, volume and value production of patula pine in a free growth spacing trial. Tech. Pap. No. 33, Dept. For., Brisbane, Australia, 40 pp.

Hashizume, H. (1975). Interrelationship of gibberellin and ethrel in the flower bud formation and growth of conifers. *Bull. Tottori Univ. For. No.* **8**, 10 pp.

Hawkes, J. G., J. T. Williams, and R. P. Croston (1983). *A Bibliography of Crop Genetic Resources.* Inter. Board for Plant Gen. Res., Rome, 442 pp.

Hawkins, P. J., D. G. Nikles, and W. J. Smith (1978). Management, wood properties and genetic improvement of Caribbean pine in Queensland. Tech. Paper, Queensland For. Dept. No. 4, Brisbane, Australia, 19 pp.

Hedegart, T. (1976). Breeding systems, variation and genetic improvement in teak (*Tectona grandis*). *Tropical Trees.* Linnean Soc., Academic Press, London, pp. 109–121.

Heimburger, C. C., and C. R. Sullivan (1972). Screening of haploxylon pines for resistance to the white pine weevil. *Sil. Gen.* **21**(3–4), 93–96.

Henson, W. R., L. C. O'Neil, and F. Mergen (1970). Natural variation in susceptibility of *Pinus* to *Neodiprion* sawflies as a basis for the development of a breeding scheme for resistant trees. Yale Bull. No. 78, New Haven, Connecticut, 71 pp.

Hepting, G. H. (1960). Climate change and forest diseases. 5th World For. Cong., Seattle, Washington, Vol. 2, pp. 842–847.

Hepting, G. H. (1963). Climate and forest diseases. *Ann. Rev. Phytopath.* **1**, 31–50.

Herbert, M. A., D. A. Jackson, and R. Verloren van Themaat (1982). Final findings on the response of *Eucalyptus grandis* to fertilizing at De Kaap, Eastern Transvaal. *S. A. For. Jour.* **122**, 53–58.

Herman, B. (1985). The anatomy of some abnormal wood formation in *Pinus taeda.* IUFRO Symp. on Forest Products Research International—Achievements and the Future, Pretoria, South Africa, pp. 6–10.

Hermann, R. K., and D. P. Lavendar (1968). Early growth of Douglas-fir from various altitudes and aspects in Southern Oregon. *Sil. Gen.* **17**(4), 143–151.

Herrera, R., C. F. Jordan, H. Klinge, and E. Medina (1978). Amazon ecosystems:

Their structure and functioning with particular emphasis on nutrients. *Intersciencia* **3**(4), 223–231.

Heybroek, H. M. (1974). Selection pressures on tree populations in different plant formations. IUFRO Meet., Stockholm, Sweden, Session V, pp. 271–282.

Heybroek, H. M. (1980). Monoculture versus mixture: Interactions between susceptible and resistant trees in a mixed stand. Workshop on the Gen. of Host–Parasite Inter. in For., Wageningen, Holland, 20 pp.

Heybroek, H. M. (1982). Monoculture versus mixture: Interactions between susceptible and resistant trees in a mixed stand. *Resist. to Diseases and Pests in Forest Trees* **199**, 236–241.

Higgins, H. G. (1985). Letter from Australia. *Tappi* **66**(2), 24.

Hiley, W. E. (1956). *Economics of Plantations.* Faber and Faber, London, 216 pp.

Hiley, W. E. (1959). *Conifers: South African Methods of Cultivation.* Oxford University Press, Oxford, U.K., 124 pp.

Hillis, W. E., and A. G. Brown (1978). *Eucalyptus for Wood Production.* CSIRO, Australia. Griffin Press, Adelaide, South Australia, 434 pp.

Hinze, W. H. (1984). The Effect of Pruning on Mortality, Volume Increment and Development of Epicormic Shoots in *Pinus radiata.* M.Sc. thesis, University of Stellenbosch, South Africa, 121 pp.

Hirasiro, M. (1918). A proposal to grow seedlings and cuttings of *Cryptomeria* in thorough mixture. *Abstracts of Japanese Literature in Forest Genetics and Related Fields,* **1**(A), 163.

Hodges, C. S. (1976a). Two diseases in plantations of exotic forest tree species in Brazil. For. Devel. and Res., Field Document No. 15, Brasilia, Brazil, 8 pp.

Hodges, C. S. (1976b). A new needle disease of pine in Brazil caused by *Cylindrocladium pteridis.* For. Devel. and Res. Field Document No. 18, Brasilia, Brazil, 4 pp.

Hodges, C. S. (1980). The taxonomy of *Diaporthe cubensis. Mycologia.* **72**(3), 542–548.

Hodges, C. S., J. W. Koenigs, E. G. Kuhlman, and E. W. Ross (1971). *Fomes annosus*—A bibliography with subject index, 1960–1970. U.S. For. Ser. Res. Paper SE-84, Athens, Georgia, 75 pp.

Hodges, C. S., T. F. Geary, and C. E. Cordell (1979). The occurrence of *Diaporthe cubensis* on *Eucalyptus* in Florida, Hawaii and Puerto Rico. *Plant Dis. Reporter* **63**(3), 216–220.

Hodgson, L. M. (1976). Some aspects of flowering and reproductive behavior in *Eucalyptus grandis* at J.D.M. Keet Forest Res. Sta.: Nos. 1, 2, and 3. *S. A. For. Jour.* **97**, 10–18; **98**, 32–43; **99**, 53–58.

Hoffman, D., and J. Kleinschmit (1979). A utilization progam for spruce provenance and species hybrids. IUFRO Norway Spruce Meeting, Bucharest, Romania, pp. 216–236.

Holdridge, L. R. (1976). Ecological and genetical factors affecting exploration and conservation in Central America. *Tropical Trees.* Linnean Soc., London, Academic Press, London, pp. 199–202.

Holdridge, L. R., W. C. Grenke, W. Hatheway, T. Liang, and J. A. Toci (1971). *Forest*

Environments in Tropical Life Zones: A Pilot Study. Pergamon Press, Oxford, U.K., 747 pp.

Holst, M. (1963). Breeding resistance in pines to *Rhyaciona* moths. 1st World Consul. For. Gen. and Tree Impr., Stockholm, Sweden, 17 pp.

Holzer, K. (1965). Standardization of methods for provenance research and testing. IUFRO Kongress, München, West Germany, Vol. III(22), pp. 672–718.

Hood, J. W., and W. J. Libby (1980). A clonal study of intraspecific variability in radiata pine. I. Cold and animal damage. *Australian For. Res.* **10**, 9–20.

Hornbeck, J. W. (1981). Acid rain—Facts and fallacies. *Jour. For.* **79**(7), 438–443.

Horning, W. H. (1961). Society of American Foresters report on a study of seed certification conducted by the Committee on Forest Tree Improvement. *Jour. For.* **59**(9), 656–661.

Horsfall, J. G., and E. B. Cowling (1980). *Plant Disease.* Academic Press, New York, 534 pp.

Hoskins, M. W. (1985). Social forestry. *Bos* **3**(3), 4–13 (AAAS).

Howcroft, N. H. (1974). A racial hybrid of *Pinus merkusii.* Trop. For. Res. Note SR28, Papua, New Guinea, 9 pp.

Howcroft, N. H. (1983). Seed production, genetic variation and conservation of *Araucaria hunsteinii* in Papua, New Guinea. *Fast Growing Trees. Silvicultura* **30**, 266–269.

Hughes, C. E. (1984). Selection of Central American dry zone trees for trials as nonindustrial species. In IUFRO (1984b), pp. 518–520.

Hughes, C. E., and P. S. McCarter (1984). Exploration and seed collection of *Liquidambar styraciflua* in Central America and Mexico. In IUFRO (1984b), pp. 521–524.

Hughes, C. F. (1985). International trial of dry zone species. FAO For. Gen. Res. Info. No. 13, FAO, Rome, pp. 18–20.

Hughes, J. F. (1968). Wood quality in fast growing tropical species: A new approach to species trials. Commonw. For. Inst., Oxford, U.K., 11 pp.

Hughes, J. F. (1971). The wood structure of *Pinus caribaea* in relation to use characteristics, growth conditions and tree improvement. Symp. Sel. and Breed. to Improve Some Trop. Conifers. 15th IUFRO Cong., Gainesville, Florida, 10 pp.

Huhn, M., and H. J. Muhs (1981). Height growth of some interracial hybrids of Norway spruce using selected trees of a north and central European provenance with special regard to between-plot competition. *Sil. Gen.* **30**(1), 25–29.

Hunt, R., and B. J. Zobel (1978). Frost hardy eucalypts grow well in the Southeast. *South. Jour. Appl. For.* **2**(1), 6–10.

Hunt, R. S., and G. A. Van Sickle (1984). Variation in susceptibility to sweet fern rust among *Pinus contorta* and *P. banksiana. Can. Jour. For. Res.* **14**(5), 672–675.

Hunziker, J. H. (1958). Cytogenetic studies of *Salix humboldtiana* and triploid hybrid willows cultivated in Argentina. *Revista de Investigaciones Agrícolas* **12**(2), 155–171.

Hutchins, D. E. (1903). *Transvaal Forest Report.* Pretoria, South Africa.

Huxley, J. S. (1938). Clines: An auxiliary taxonomic principle. *Nature* **143**, 219 pp.

Hyun, S. K. (1967). Physiological differences among trees with respect to rooting. IUFRO Congress (München), Vol. III(22), pp. 168-190.

Hyun, S. K. (1976). Interspecific hybridization in pines with special reference to *P. rigida* × *taeda*. *Sil. Gen.* **25**(5-6), 188-191.

IBPGR (1982). Annual Report. International Board for Plant Genetic Resources, Rome.

IBPGR (1985). *Handbook of Seed Technology for Genebanks.* Vol: I. Principles and Methodology. Vol. II: Compendium of Specific Germination Information and Test Recommendations. Rome.

Ibrahim, S. (1977). Problems of seed production in moist tropical climates. 3rd World Consul. For. Tree Breed., Canberra, Australia, pp. 807-822.

Ilvessalo, L. (1926). Uber die Anbaumöglichkeit ausländicher Holzarten mit spezieller Hinsicht auf die finnische Verhältnisse. *Deutsche Dendr. Gesellschaft* **36**, 96-132.

Ingram, C. L. (1984). Provenance research on *Pinus elliottii* and *P. taeda* in Malawi. In IUFRO (1984b), pp. 265-277.

International Development Research Center (1982). *Leucaena Research in the Asian Pacific Region.* Workshop, Nitrogen Fixing Tree Assoc. (IDRC-211e), Singapore, 192 pp.

ISTF (1984). Brazil needs plantations. (International Society Tropical Foresters) *ISTF News,* p. 7.

IUFRO (1980). *Genetic Improvement and Productivity of Fast Growing Trees.* Symposium and Workshop, São Pedro, São Paulo, Brazil, 716 pp.

IUFRO (1983). *International Symposium on the Breeding of Frost Resistant Eucalyptus. AFOCEL,* Bordeaux, France, 652 pp.

IUFRO (1984a). *Site and Productivity of Fast Growing Plantations,* Symposium, 2 vols., Pretoria and Pietermaritzburg, South Africa, 968 pp.

IUFRO (1984b). *Provenance and Genetic Improvement Strategies in Tropical Forest Trees* (R. D. Barnes and G. L. Gibson, Eds.). Conference, Mutare, Zimbabwe (80 papers).

Ivory, B. J., and D. N. Patterson (1970). Progress in breeding *Pinus radiata* resistant to *Dothistroma* needle blight in East Africa. *Sil. Gen.* **19**, 38-42.

Ivory, M. H. (1972). Pilot plantations of quick-growing industrial tree species in West Malaysia. FAO Tech. Rept. 6, Rome, 46 pp.

Jabil, D. M. (1984). Industrial forest plantations: The future of Asian timber. *Trop. For.* **1**(1), 12-15.

Jackson, B., and W. Dallimore (1926). A new hybrid conifer, *Cupressus Leylandi* (between *Cupressus macrocarpa* and *Chamaecyparis nootkatensis*). *Bull. of Miscel. Info.* **3**, 113-116.

Jackson, D. S. (1973). Soil factors that should influence allocations of land for forestry and agriculture. *N. Z. Jour. For.* **18**(1), 55-62.

Jacobs, M. R. (1964). The use of exotic forest trees. *Jour. Inst. For. Aust.* **28**(3), 150-156.

Jahromi, S. T. (1983). Variation in *Eucalyptus viminalis* with respect to cold resistance and growth. *Fast Growing Trees. Silvicultura* **31**, 502-504.

Jett, J. B., and B. J. Zobel (1974). Wood and pulping properties of young hardwoods. *Tappi* **58**(1), 92–96.

Jiang, I. B. (1982). Growth and Form of Seedlings and Juvenile Rooted Cuttings of *Sequoia sempervirens* and *Sequoiadendron giganteum*. M.S. thesis, School of Forestry, Univ. of Calif., Berkeley, 200 pp.

Jo, D. K., H. M. Kwon, S. K. Choi, and J. H. Kim (1984). Pollen dispersal and effect of pollen density on seed production in *Larix leptolepis* seed orchard. Res. Rep. Inst. For. Gen. No. 20, Suwon, Korea, pp. 58–64.

Johnson, A. G. (1955). Southern pine hybrids, natural and artificial. 3rd. South. Conf. For. Tree Impr., New Orleans, Louisiana, pp. 63–67.

Johnson, B. (1984). The forestry crisis: What must be done. *AMBIO* **13**(1), 48–49.

Johnsson, H. (1957). Some data from tests of North American pines. *Sveriges Skogsv. Förb. Tidskrift* **4**, 23–36.

Johnsson, H., C. L. Kiellander, and E. Stefansson (1953). Production of cones and seed quality in pine grafts. *Sveriges Skogsv. Förb Tidskrift* **4**, 33 pp.

Johnsson, H., A. Persson, and G. Eriksson (1956). Pine types in South Sweden. *Sveriges Skogsv. Förb. Tidskrift* **1**, 47–60.

Jones, N., and J. Burley (1973). Seed certification, provenance nomenclature and genetic history in forestry. *Sil. Gen.* **22**(3), 53–92.

Jonsson, A., G. Eriksson, and I. Dormling (1980). A summary of studies of frost hardiness of *Pinus contorta* seedlings grown in climatic chambers. Pinus contorta as an Exotic Species. Swedish University of Agricultural Sciences, Dep. of Forest Genetics, Research Note No. 30, Garpenberg, Sweden, pp. 75–81.

Kageyama, P. Y., R. Vencovsky, M. Ferreira, and N. Nicolielo (1977a). Genetic variation between provenances of *Pinus oocarpa* in the region of Agudos. *IPEF* **14**, 77–120.

Kageyama, P., R. M. Spelty, A. P. Silva, and M. Ferreira (1977b). Genetic variation within and between the progenies of *Pinus patula* in the region of Telemaco. Instituto de Pesquisas e. Estudos florestais No. 15, Piracicaba, Brazil, pp. 21–39.

Kageyama, P. Y. (1984). Early selection at different ages in programs of *Eucalyptus grandis*. In IUFRO (1984b), p. 525.

Kageyama, P. Y., J. E. Pinto, A. L. Mora, and N. Nicolielo (1983). Half-sib progeny trials of *Pinus caribaea* var. *hondurensis* from selected superior trees of Australian Population. *Fast Growing Trees. Silvicultura* **29**, 97–99.

Kageyama, P. Y., I. E. Pires, and L. E. Herrera (1984). Phenotypic and genotypic variation for foxtailing in *Pinus caribaea* var. *hondurensis*. In IUFRO (1984b), pp. 526–534.

Kalutskii, K. K., G. V. Krylov, and N. A. Bolotov (1981a). Introduction of tree species for the forests of the future: Experience and prospects [in Russian]. *Lesnoi Zhurnal* **5**, 6–14.

Kalutskii, K. K., G. V. Krylov, and N. A. Bolotov (1981b). Prospects for the introduction of tree species when creating the forests of the future [in Russian]. *Lesnoi Khozyaistvo.* **11**, 22–25.

Kanashiro, M., and P. S. Martins (1984). Heteratilia em *Cordia goeldiana* (in press).

Kanehira, R. (1918). *Pinus uyematsui. Jour. Nat. Hist. Taiwan* **7**(33), 164.

Kaplan, L. (1983). Research on irrigation and salt tolerance of *Eucalyptus* in Israel. *Fast Growing Trees. Silvicultura* **32**, 681–682.

Karani, P. K. (1983). Growth potential of *Agathis* in Uganda. *Fast Growing Trees. Silvicultura* **30**, 273–274.

Karani, P. K., and M. A. Chaudhry (1983). Growth and performance of *Araucaria* species in Uganda. *Fast Growing Trees. Silvicultura* **30**, 274–276.

Karlman, M. (1982). Damage to *Pinus contorta* within provenance trials. *Lodgepole Pine—Our Third Conifer. Sveriges Skogsv. Förb. Tidskrift* **80**(102), 49–56.

Karlman, M. (1984). Pathogens and Other Threats to *Pinus contorta* in Northern Sweden. Thesis, Dept. of Ecol. Bot., Univ. of Umea, Sweden, 212 pp.

Karrfalt, R. P. (1985). Procedures for international shipment of seeds and cuttings of forest trees. *Tree Planters' Notes* **36**(3), 26–27.

Karschon, R., and D. Heth (1967). The water balance of a plantation of *Eucalyptus camaldulensis. Conf on Eucalyptus* in Israel, Vol. III, Jerusalem, pp. 35–52.

Kassier, H. W. (1980). An integrated system for forest management and silvicultural planning and control in South African State Forestry. *S. A. For. Jour.* **114**, 1–6.

Kaul, R. N. (1970). Indo-Pakistan. *Afforestation in Arid Zones.* Dr. W. Junk, Publ., The Hague, Netherlands, pp. 155–209.

Kaumi, S. Y. (1977). Variation of growth, stem quality and wood properties in relation to genetic improvement of tropical forest trees. IUFRO Workshop, Brisbane, Australia, Topic 4, 6 pp.

Keays, J. L. (1975). Projection of world demand for wood fibre to the year 2000. 8th Cell. Conf. Wood Chemicals, a Future Challenge. SUNY College Env. Sci. and For., Syracuse, New York, 5 pp.

Keiding, H. (1968). Preliminary investigations of inbreeding and outcrossing in larch *Sil. Gen.* **17**(5–6), 159–164.

Keiding, H. (1970). Evaluation of seed orchards established for the production of hybrid larch (*Larix eurolepis*). For. Tree Imp., Arboretet, Horsholm, Denmark, Vol. 1, pp. 3–24.

Keiding, H. (1985). Teak (*Tectonia grandis*). DANIDA Seed Leaflet No. 4. Humlebaek, Denmark, 21 pp.

Keiding, H., and R. H. Kemp (1977). Exploration, collection and investigation of gene resources: Tropical pines and teak. 3rd World Consul. For. Tree Breed., Canberra, Australia, pp. 13–31.

Keiding, H., and H. C. Olsen (1965). Assessment of stem form in clones and progenies of larch. *Sil. Gen.* **14**(4), 115–122.

Keiding, H., E. B. Lauridsen, and H. Wellendorf (1984). Evaluation of a series of teak and *Gmelina* provenance trials. Tech. Note 15, Danida Forest Seed Centre, Humlebaek, Denmark, 42 pp.

Kelley, W. D., and C. E. Cordell (1984). Disease management in forest tree nurseries. South. Nursery Mgt. Manual. U.S. For. Serv., Atlanta, Georgia, pp. 238–246.

Kellison, R. C. (1967). *A Geographic Variation Study of Yellow Poplar* (Liriodendron tulipifera) *within North Carolina.* Tech. Rept. No. 33, N.C. State Univ., School of For. Res., Raleigh, North Carolina, 41 pp.

Kellogg, W. (1978). Effects of human activities on global climate. World Meteorological Organization, Tech. Note 151, Washington, D.C., 72 pp.

Kelly, B., and M. London (1983). *Amazon.* Harcourt Brace Jovanovich, San Diego, 370 pp.

Kemp, R. H. (1971). Seed sources and procurement of low-altitude tropical pines in Central America. Selection and Breeding to Improve Some Tropical Conifers. 15th IUFRO Congress, Gainesville, Florida, Vol. 1, pp. 9–16.

Kemp, R. H. (1975). Central American pines. *The Methodology of Conservation of Forest Genetic Resources.* FAO, Rome, pp. 57–64.

Kemp, R. H. (1978). Exploration, utilization and conservation of genetic resources. *Unasylva* **30**(119–120), 10–16.

Kemp, R. H., L. Roche, and R. L. Willan (1976). Current activities and problems in the exploration and conservation of tropical forest gene resources. *Tropical Trees* **2**, Academic Press, London, 223–233.

Keogh, R. M. (1980). Teak (*Tectona grandis*) provenances of the Caribbean, Central America, Venezuela and Colombia. Wood Production in the Neotropics via Plantations. IUFRO/Mab. For Serv. Symp., Rio Piedras, Puerto Rico, pp. 343–558.

Keong, T. C. (1983). *Acacia mangium*—A plantation species for *Imperata cylindrica* grassland in Sabah. *Fast Growing Trees. Silvicultura* **30**, 321–326.

Keresztesi, B. (1970). Selection of forest trees and shrubs for improvement of the bee-pastures and in favour of the landscape architecture. 2nd World Consul. For. Tree Breeding, Washington, D.C., Vol. I, pp. 639–652.

Kerr, E. (1972). Trees that resist hurricanes. *The Progressive Farmer* (March), p. 628.

Kershaw, D. J., P. D. Gadgil, G. J. Legget, J. W. Ray, and J. B. Van der Pas (1982). Assessment and control of *Dothistroma* needle blight. FRI Bull. No. 18, Rotorua, New Zealand, 48 pp.

Keys, R. N., F. C. Cech, and W. L. MacDonald (1977). Evaluation of four 25-year-old open-pollinated families of Chinese chestnut. 24th Northeastern For. Tree Impr. Conf., College Park, Maryland, pp. 73–83.

Khalil, A. K. (1984). The potential of poplars in the boreal regions. I. Survival and growth. *Sil. Gen.* **33**(1), 1–7.

Khalil, M. A. (1977). Role of exotic species and provenances in forest improvement in Newfoundland. 3rd World Consul. For. Tree Breed., Canberra, Australia, pp. 191–206.

Kiellander, C. L. (1960). Swedish spruce and continental spruce. *Föreningen Skogsträdsforädling* **3**.

Kiellander, C. L. (1963). Experiences and present situation of foreign tree species and provenances in Sweden. 1st World Consul. For. Gen., For. Tree Impr., Stockholm, Sweden, 17 pp.

King, J. (1965). Seed source × environment interactions in Scotch pines. *Sil. Gen.* **14**, 141–148.

King, J. P. (1980). Variation in specific gravity of 3-year-old coppice clones of *Eucalyptus saligna* growing in Hawaii. *Aust. For. Res.* **10**, 295–299.

King, K. F. (1979). Agroforestry and utilization of fragile ecosystems. *For. Ecol. and Mgt.* **2**(3), 161–168.

King, N. L. (1951). Tree planting in South Africa. *Jour. For. Assoc.* **29**, 19-30.

Kirkpatrick, J. B. (1971). A probable hybrid swarm in *Eucalyptus. Sil. Gen.* **20**(5-6), 157-159.

Klein, J. I. (1971). Performance of Russian Scots pine population in Manitoba and Ontario. North. For. Res. Cen. Infor. Rept. Nor-X-2 Edmonton, Alberta, 12 pp.

Kleinschmit, J. (1977). Problems of vegetative reproduction. 3rd World Consul. For. Tree Breed., Canberra, Australia, pp. 783-798.

Kleinschmit, J. (1979a). Present knowledge in spruce provenance and species hybridization potential. IUFRO Norway Spruce Meeting, Bucharest, Romania, pp. 187-201.

Kleinschmit, J. (1979b). Limitations for restriction of genetic variation. *Sil. Gen.* **28**(2-3), 61-67.

Kleinschmit, J. (1984). Neuere Ergebnisse der Douglasien—Provenienzforschung und Züchtung in der Bundesrepublik Deutschland. *Schweiz. Z. Forstwes.* **135**(8), 655-679.

Kleinschmit, J., and J. Schmidt ((1977). Experience with *Picea abies* cuttings in Germany and connected with large-scale application. Symp., Vegetative Propagation of Forest Trees–Physiology and Practice, Uppsala, Sweden, pp. 65-86.

Kleinschmit, J., J. Racz, H. Weisgerber, W. Dietze, H. Dieterich, and R. Dimpflmeier (1974). Results of the international Douglas-fir provenance test of 1970 in the Federal German Republic. *Sil. Gen.* **23**(6), 167-176.

Komarek, W. V. (1971). Effects of fire in wildlife and range habitats. Pres. Burn. Symp., U.S. For. Ser., Charleston, South Carolina, pp. 46-53.

Konopka, J., and J. Hanson (1985). Documentation of genetic resources: Information handling systems for genebank management. IBPGR, Nordic Gene Bank, Rome, 87 pp.

Koski, V. (1974). On the effect of population size in an areally continuous forest. IUFRO Meet., Stockholm, Sweden, Session V, pp. 253-270.

Koster, R. (1977). Conservation and study of genetic resources of poplars. 3rd World Consul. For. Tree Breed., Canberra, Australia, pp. 45-60.

Kramer, P., and T. T. Kozlowski (1960). *Internal factors affecting growth. Physiology of Trees.* McGraw-Hill, New York, 642 pp.

Kraus, J. F., O. O. Wells, and E. R. Sluder (1984). Review of provenance variation in loblolly pine (*P. taeda*) in the Southern United States. In IUFRO (1984b), pp. 281-317.

Kromhout, C. P., and R. E. Toon (1978). Variation of wood properties of some tropical species grown in plantations in South Africa. *Progress and Problems of Genetic Improvement of Tropical Forest Trees.* IUFRO Symp., Brisbane, Australia, Vol. I, pp. 8-45.

Krutzsch, P. (1974). Provenance trials with lodgepole pine (*Pinus contorta*) in Central Sweden. IUFRO Meet., Röskär, Sweden, 9 pp.

Kung, F. H., and J. W. Wright (1972). Parallel and divergent evolution in Rocky Mountain trees. *Sil. Gen.* **21**(3-4), 77-85.

Kurinobu, S. (1984). A methodological study on the analysis of progeny trial plantations of Japanese larch. Bull. For. Tree Breed. Inst. No. 2, Ibaraki, Japan, 60 pp.

Laarman, J. G. (1980). Exotic plantations and their implications for U.S. forest products trade: A comment. *"Issues in U.S. International Forest Products Trade,"* Resources for the Future—American For. Assn. Workshop, Washington, D.C., 13 pp.

Laarman, J. G., and W. S. Dvorak (1985). Investment in tropical tree breeding and gene conservation: Financial analysis of the CAMCORE Cooperative. 23 pp. (mimeo—N.C. State Univ., Raleigh, North Carolina).

Lacaze, J. F. (1978). Advances in species and provenance selection. *Unasylva* **30**(119–120), 17–20.

Lacaze, M. (1963). The resistance of *Eucalyptus* trees to active limestone in the soil: Report on an early test. 1st World Consul. For. Gen. and Tree Improv., Stockholm, Sweden, 14 pp.

Ladrach, W. (1977). Variation of growth, stem quality and wood properties in relation to genetic improvement of tropical forest trees. IUFRO Workshop, Brisbane, Australia, 2 pp.

Ladrach, W. E. (1978). Tables of volume, green weight, and dry weight of *Pinus patula*. Cartón de Colombia, Res. Rept. No. 38, Cali, Colombia.

Ladrach, W. E. (1980a). *Mejoramiento de bósques a Traves de la Selección Genética.* Quinta Reunión Anual, Investigación Forestal, Cartón de Colombia, Popayan, Colombia, 166 pp.

Ladrach, W. E. (1980b). Thinning of *Pinus patula* by the mechanical and selective method: Results at 10 years. IUFRO/Mab. For. Ser. Symp., Rio Piedras, Puerto Rico, pp. 155–164.

Ladrach, W. E. (1982). *Preguntas y Respuestas—Ecologia Forestal* (booklet). Cartón de Colombia, Cali, Colombia, 72 pp.

Ladrach, W. E. (1983a). Growth and development of the good general combiners of *Pinus taeda* after five years. Res. Rept. No. 88, Cartón de Colombia, Cali, Colombia, 3 pp.

Ladrach, W. E. (1983b). The application of gibberellic acid A-3 to *Cupressus* grafts for increased flower production. *Fast Growing Trees. Silvicultura* **30**, 336–337.

Ladrach, W. E. (1983c). Genetic gains with *Cupressus lusitanica* through six years of tree improvement in Colombia. *Fast Growing Trees. Silvicultura* **30**, 343–346.

Ladrach, W. E. (1984a). Growth of *Leucaena* in the Cauca Valley and the Atlantic Coast after three years. Res. Rept. No. 96, Investigation Forestal, Cartón de Colombia, Cali, Colombia, 6 pp.

Ladrach, W. E. (1984b). San Benito arboretum after 4 years of growth. Res. Rept. No. 93, Investigation Forestal, Cartón de Colombia, Cali, Colombia, 6 pp.

Ladrach, W. E. (1984c). Growth of *Pinus pseudostrobus* and *P. maximinoi* after 5 years. Res. Rept. No. 94, Investigacion Forestal, Cartón de Colombia, Cali, Colombia, 4 pp.

Ladrach, W. E. (1984d). Growth of the arboretum Los Gaviotas after four years. Res. Rept. No. 95, Investigacion Forestal, Cartón de Colombia, Cali, Colombia, 3 pp.

Ladrach, W. E. (1984e). Pests in plantations and their control. Notes from Inter. Short Course on For. Mgt. in the Tropics, N.C. State Univ., Raleigh, North Carolina, 5 pp.

Ladrach, W. E. (1984f). Wood quality of *Pinus patula*. Res. Rept. No. 92, Cartón de Colombia, Cali, Colombia, 17 pp.

Ladrach, W. E. (1985a). Comparisons between provenances and sources of fourteen conifers in the Colombian Andes after five years. Res. Rept. No. 102, Cartón de Colombia, Cali, Colombia, 13 pp.

Ladrach, W. E. (1985b). Guidelines for the development of plantation forestry in the humid tropics for sustained utilization. Winrock International, Washington, D.C., 45 pp.

Ladrach, W. E. (1985c). Stimulation of flowering in the *Pinus patula* seed orchard by the use of fertilization, subsoiling and ringing of the lower branches. Res. Rept. Cartón de Colombia, Cali, Colombia, 7 pp.

Ladrach, W. E. (1986a). Comparisons between provenances of seven conifers in the Andean Region after eight years. Res. Rept. Cartón de Colombia, Cali, Colombia, 14 pp. (mimeo).

Ladrach, W. E. (1986b). Control of wood properties in plantations. IUFRO Congress, Lujbljana, Yugoslavia, 15 pp. (mimeo).

Ladrach, W. E. (1986c). Provenance of *Gmelina arborea:* Results after three and five years. Res. Rept. Cartón de Colombia, Cali, Colombia, 15 pp. (mimeo).

LaFarge, T. (1972). Relationships among third-, fifth-, and fifteenth-year measurements in a study of stand variation of loblolly pine in Georgia. Proc. IUFRO Working Party on Progeny Testing, Macon, Georgia, pp. 7–16.

LaFarge, T. (1974). Genetic differences in stem form of ponderosa pine grown in Michigan. *Sil. Gen.* **23**(6), 211–213.

Lähde, E., M. Werren, K. Etholén, and V. Silander (1984). Ulkomaisten havupuulajien varttuneistä viljelmistä suomessä. [Older forest trials of exotic conifer species in Finland.] Comm. Inst. For. Fenniae 125, Helsinki, Finland, 87 pp.

Lal, R., P. A. Sanchez, and R. W. Cummings (1985). Land clearing and development in the tropics. Inst. Trop. Agric., Ibadan, Nigeria, 450 pp.

Lamb, A. G. (1968). *Fast Growing Timber Trees of the Lowland Tropics No. 1— Gmelina arborea.* Commonw. For Inst., Oxford, U.K., 102 pp.

Lamb, A. G. (1973). *Pinus caribaea. Vol. I: Fast Growing Timber Trees of the Lowland Tropics,* No. 6. Commonwealth For. Inst., Oxford, U.K., 254 pp.

Lambert, M. J. (1984). The use of foliar analysis in fertilizer research. In IUFRO (1984a), Vol. 1, pp. 269–291.

Lambeth, C. C. (1979). Interactions of Douglas-fir Full Sib Families with Field and Phytotron Environments. Ph.D. thesis, N.C. State Univ., Raleigh, North Carolina, 83 pp.

Lambeth, C. C. (1980). Juvenile-mature correlations in Pinaceae and implications for early selection. *For. Sci.* **26**(4), 571–580.

Lambeth, C. C., R. W. Stonecypher, and B. J. Zobel (1982). Early testing on Douglas-fir in phytotron environments—The effect of selection trait and genotype × environment interaction. N. Amer. For. Biol. Workshop, Univ. of Kentucky, Lexington, Kentucky, pp. 137–148.

Lambeth, C. C., R. B. McCullough, and O. O. Wells (1984). Seed source movement and tree improvement in the Western Gulf Region. Symp. Loblolly Pine Ecosystems—West Region, Jackson, Mississippi, pp. 71–86.

Land, Jr., S. B. (1980). Parentage and type of planting stock influence biomass characteristics in sycamore plantations. 27th N.E. For. Tree. Impr. Conf., Univ. of Vermont, Burlington, 10 pp.

Landsberg, H. E., H. Lippman, K. H. Patten, and C. Troll (1963). *Die Jahreszeitenklimate der Erde*. Heidelberg Akademie der Wissenschaften. Springer, Heidelberg.

Langlet, O. (1936). Studien über die physiologische Variabilität der Kiefer und deren Zusammenhang mit dem Klima, Beiträge zur Kenntnis Ökotypen von *Pinus silvestris*. *Meddel. f. Statens Skogsförsöksanstalt* **29**, 219–470.

Langlet, O. (1959a). Polish seed for Sweden. *Särtryck ur Skogen* **5**, 4 pp.

Langlet, O. (1959b). A cline or not a cline—A question of Scots pine. *Sil. Gen.* **8**(1), 13–22.

Langner, W. (1963). Consequences of the development of varieties in forestry. 1st World Consul. For. Gen. Tree Impr., Stockholm, Sweden, 8 pp.

Lanier, L. (1981). La rouille vesiculeuse du pin Weymouth due a *Cronartium ribicola*. Station de Recherches et Expérience Forestier. *Notes Tech. For.* **8**, 11.

Lanly, J. P. (1982). *Tropical Forest Resources*. FAO For. Pap. No. 30, Rome, 106 pp.

Lanly, J. P. (1983). Assessment of the forest resources of the tropics. *For. Abst.* (review article) **44**(6), 287–317.

Lapeyrie, F., and G. Brucket (1982). Protection of *Eucalyptus delegatensis* in regard to limestone by ectomycorrhizae: Preliminary research. *AFOCEL* Annales de Recherches Sylvicoles, pp. 213–232.

Larsen, C. S. (1954). Provenance testing and forest tree breeding. Proc. 11th Cong., IUFRO, Rome, pp. 467–473.

Larsen, E. (1965). A study of the variability of *Eucalyptus maculata* and *E. citriodora*. Leaflet No. 95, For. Timber Bur., Canberra, Australia, 3 pp.

Larsen, E. (1969). Seed procurement for research. 2nd World Consul. For. Tree Breed., Washington, D.C., 6 pp.

Larsen, E., and D. A. Cromer (1970). Exploration, evaluation, utilization and conservation of eucalypt gene resources. IBP Handbook No. 11, *Genetic Resources in Plants*. Blackwell, Oxford, U.K., pp. 381–388.

Larsen, R. T. (1960). The certification of forest tree seed in Britain. 5th World For. Cong., Seattle, Washington, 5 pp.

Larsen, V. B. (1983). Danske skovtraeer, raceförhold, froforsyning og proveniensvalg. *D.S.T.* **68**(1), 1–100.

Larson, P. R. (1973). The physiological basis for wood specific gravity in conifers. IUFRO Div. 4 Meet., Brisbane, Australia, Vol. 2, pp. 672–680.

Laurie, M. V. (1962). Factors in choosing forest species. *SPAN* **5**(1), 22–24.

Laurie, M. V. (1974). Tree planting practices in Africa savannas. FAO Development Paper No. 19, Rome.

Lawrence, T. (1984). *Collection of Crop Germplasm—The First Ten Years, 1974–1984*. IBPGR, Rome, 119 pp.

Leaf, H. L., and H. A. Madgwick (1960). Evaluation of chemical analyses of soils and plants as aids in intensive soils management. 5th World For. Congress., Seattle, Washington, pp. 554–556.

LeCam, J. (1983). Provenance related variability of several criteria in *Pinus contorta*. *AFOCEL,* pp. 229–281.

Ledig, F. T., and M. T. Conkle (1983). Gene diversity and genetic structure in a narrow endemic, Torrey pine (*Pinus torreyana*). *Evol.* **37**, 79–85.

Ledig, F. T., and J. L. Whitmore (1981). Heritability and genetic correlations for volume, foxtails and other characteristics of Caribbean pine in Puerto Rico. *Sil. Gen.* **30**(2–3), 88–92.

Ledoux, P. (1980). Results of a pioneer trial with *Toona ciliata* var *australis* in Belem, Brazil. IUFRO/Mab. For. Ser. Symp. Wood Production in the Neotropics via Plantations, Rio Piedras, Puerto Rico, p. 359.

Lee, K. J. (1979). Factors affecting cone initiation in pines: A review. Res. Rept. Inst. For. Gen. No. 15, Suwon, Korea, pp. 45–85.

Leloup, M. (1956). *Tree planting practices in tropical Africa.* FAO Forestry Development Paper No. 8, Rome, 302 pp.

Letourneaux, C. A. (1957). *Tree planting practices in tropical Asia.* FAO Forestry Development Paper No. 11, Rome, 172 pp.

Letouzey, R. (1985). *In situ* conservation of forest genetic resources in Cameroon. For. Gen. Res. Inf. No. 14, FAO, Rome, pp. 15–31.

Liang, S. B. (1984). The genetic base of *Acacia mangium* in Sabah. In IUFRO (1984b), pp. 597–603.

Libby, W. J. (1973). Domestication strategies for forest trees. *Can. Jour. For. Res.* **3**, 265–277.

Libby, W. J. (1978). The 1978 expedition to collect radiata seed from Cedros and Guadalupe Islands. Newsletter No. 2, CSIRO, *Breeding Pinus Radiata,* Div. For. Res., Gippsland, Australia, pp. 8–12.

Libby, W. J. (1983). What is a safe number of clones per plantation? Tree Improv. Assoc., Toronto, Canada, pp. 221–222.

Libby, W. J., and Hood, J. V. (1976). Juvenility in hedged radiata pine. *Acta Horticulturae* **56**, 91–98.

Libby, W. J., and Rauter, R. M. (1984). Advantages of clonal forestry. *For. Chronicle* **60**(3), 145–149.

Libby, W. J., M. H. Bannister, and Y. B. Linhart (1968). The pines of Cedros and Guadalupe Islands. *Jour. For.* **66**(11), 846–853.

Libby, W. J., A. G. Brown, and J. M. Fielding (1972). Effects of hedging radiata pine on production, rooting and early growth of cuttings. *N. Z. Jour. For. Sci.* **2**(2), 263–283.

Liegel, L. H. (1981a). Preliminary assessment of hurricane wind/rain damage in *Pinus caribaea* and *P. oocarpa* provenance trials in Puerto Rico. South. For. Exp. Stat., Inst. Trop. For., Rio Piedras, Puerto Rico.

Liegel, L. H. (1981b). Seasonal Nutrition of 3 & 4 Year Old *Pinus caribaea* Foxtails and Normal-branched Trees in Puerto Rico. Ph.D. thesis, N.C. State Univ., Raleigh, North Carolina, 76 pp.

Liegel, L. H. (1984a). Ten-year growth results from *Pinus caribaea* and *P. oocarpa* provenance trials in Puerto Rico. In IUFRO (1984b), pp. 326–327.

Liegel, L. H. (1984b). Assessment of hurricane rain/wind damage in *Pinus caribaea* and *Pinus oocarpa* provenance trials in Puerto Rico. *Commonw. For. Rev.* **63**(1), 47–53.

Liegel, L. H. (1984c). Growth and selection traits of Mt. Pine Ridge, Belize, plus-tree progeny in Puerto Rico at 11.6 years. In IUFRO (1984b), pp. 554–555.

Liegel, L. H. (1984d). Results of 5- to 6-year-old provenance trials of *Pinus oocarpa* on eight sites in Puerto Rico. *Sil. Gen.* **33**(6), 223–230.

Liegel, L. H., R. D. Barnes, and G. Gibson (1984). Growth performance and selected assessment of traits of 5.7-year-old *P. caribaea* and *P. oocarpa* in Puerto Rico. *Fast Growing Trees. Silvicultura* **29**, 107–111.

Lima, W. de P., and O. Freire (1976). Evapotranspiração em plantações de eucalipto e de pinheiro e em vegetação herbácea natural. *IPEF* **12**, 103–117.

Lima, W. P. (1984). The hydrology of eucalypt forests in Australia—A review. *IPEF,* **23**, 11–32.

Lindgren, D., P. Krutzsch, J. Twetman, and C. L. Kiellander (1976). *Survival and Early Growth of* Pinus contorta *Provenances in Northern Sweden.* Inst. Skogsgenetik, Dept. For. Gen. No. 20, Stockholm, Sweden, 42 pp.

Lindgren, D., K. Lindgren, and A. Persson (1980). Survival and height increment of *Pinus contorta* IUFRO 70/71 series in Sweden. Pinus contorta *as an Exotic Species.* Dept. For. Gen., Garpenberg, Sweden, pp. 103–133.

Lindgren, L. (1984). Genotype × environment interaction of provenances of *Pinus contorta.* Conf. Geno. × Envir. Inter. *Studia Forestalia Suecia* **166**, 41–44.

Lines, R. (1965). Standardization of methods for provenance research and testing. IUFRO, Sect. 22, Fort-a-Mousson, France, pp. 670–718.

Linnard, W. (1969). Cultivation of eucalypts in the USSR. *For. Abstr.* **230**(2), 199–209.

Linneman, G. (1960). Racial differences in *Pseudotsuga taxifolia* as regards mycorrhiza. *Allg. Forst—u Jagdztg.* **131**(2), 41–47.

Liro, J. I. (1908). *Uredinae Fennicae. Finlands rostsvampar.* Finska litteratursällskapets tryckeri, Helsinki, Finland, 640 pp.

Little, S., and H. A. Somes (1951). No exceptional vigor found in hybrid pines tested. Northeast. For. Expt. Sta. Res. Note No. 10, Philadelphia, Pennsylvania.

Little, S., and I. F. Trew (1976). Breeding and testing pitch × loblolly pine hybrids for the Northeast. 23rd Northeast For. Tree Impr. Conf., State College, Pennsylvania, pp. 71–85.

Loeffler, H. D. (1984). Terrain classification for forestry. In IUFRO (1984a), Vol. 1, pp. 91–110.

Long, A. J., and G. F. Dykstra (1983). Selection and improvement of *Pinus caribaea* in Kalimantan. *Fast Growing Trees. Silvicultura* **29**, 104–106.

Longman, K. A. (1976). Conservation and multiplication of gene resources by vegetative multiplication of tropical trees. *Tropical Trees* **2**, Academic Press, London 19–24.

Longman, K. A., R. R. Leakey, P. Howland, and M. R. Bowen (1977). Physiological approaches for utilizing and conserving the genetic resources of tropical trees. 3rd World Consul. For. Tree Breed., Canberra, Australia, pp. 1043–1054.

Loock, E. M. (1950). *The Pines of Mexico and British Honduras.* So. Afr. Dept. Agr. and For. Bull. 35, Pretoria, South Africa, 224 pp.

Loveday, N. C. (1983). Yield tables for the major timber species grown in South Africa. *Forestry Handbook,* S.A.I.F., Pretoria, South Africa, pp. 134–150.

Lückhoff, H. A. (1949). The effect of live pruning on the growth of *Pinus patula, P. caribaea* and *P. taeda. S. A. For. Jour.* **18**, 24–25.

Lückhoff, H. A. (1956). High pruning in *Pinus patula,* its feasibility, effect on growth and economics. *S. A. For. Jour.* **27**, 55–71.

Lückhoff, H. A. (1964). *The Natural Distribution, Growth and Botanical Variation of Pinus caribaea and its Cultivation in South Africa. Annale Univ. Stellenbosch,* **39**, Serie A, 160 pp.

Lugo, A. E., and S. Brown (1980). Tropical forest ecosystems: Sources or sinks of atmospheric carbon? *Unasylva* **32**(129), 8–13.

Lugo, A. E., and S. Brown (1981). Tropical lands: Popular misconceptions. *Mazingira* **5**(2), 11–19.

Lundgren, B. (1978). Soil conditions and nutrient cycling under natural and plantation forests in Tanzanian highlands. Rpts. For. Ecology and For. Soils, No. 31. Dep. For Soils, Swedish Univ. of Agric. Sciences, Uppsala, 426 pp.

Lundmark, J. E. (1984). Markberedning i allmänhet och inom kyliga klimatlägen i synnerhet. Fjällnära skogsbruk, exkursionsunderlag. Domänverket, Falun, Sweden, pp. 24–27.

Lundmark, J. E., B. Berg, and Å. Nilsson (1982). The influence of *Pinus contorta* on the soil and ground vegetation in comparison with *Pinus sylvestris. Sveriges Skogsv. Förb. Tidskrift* **80**(1–2), 43–48.

Lyr, H., H. Polster, and H. J. Fielder (1967). *Gehölzphysiologie.* VEB Gustav Fischer Verlag, Jena, E. Germany, 444 pp.

MacCleary, D. (1982). Diversity requires active management. Natural Diversity and Forest Ecosystems Symp., Univ. of Georgia, Athens, pp. 87–103.

McCormick, L. H., and K. C. Steiner (1978). Variation in aluminum tolerance among six genera of trees. *For. Sci.* **24**(4), 565–568.

McDonald, C. (1983). Tropical forestry resources—Basis of viability for future projects. PPI 3rd International Pulp Symp., Brussels, Belgium, pp. 19–24.

McDonald, S., and S. L. Krugman (1985). Worldwide planting of southern Pines. Inter. Symp. Nur. Mgt. Proc. South Pines, Montgomery, Alabama, 19 pp.

McNabb, H. S., R. B. Hall, and M. Ostry (1980). Biological and physical modifications of the environment in short rotation tree crops and the resulting effect upon the host-parasite interactions. Workshop Gen. of Host–Parasite Inter. in For., Wageningen, Holland, 13 pp.

Madofe, S., J. A. Mushi, and S. C. Mathias (1984). Performance of five *Pinus merkusii* provenances at Buhindi, Mwanza, Tanzania. In IUFRO (1984b), pp. 335–340.

Male, P. S. (1981). Site index studies of established exotic species for the granite belt region. Res. Pap. No. 11, Dept. For., Queensland, Australia, 36 pp.

Malvos, C. (1983). First result of fertilization trials given to *Eucalyptus* plantations in Madegascar. *Fast Growing Trees. Silvicultura* **32**, 625–626.

Manion, P. D. (1984). *Scleroderis Canker of Conifers.* State Univ. of New York, Syracuse, 250 pp.

Marcos, F. E. (1984). Nothing less than the concerted action of nations. *Tropical Forests* **1**(1), 4–7.

Marien, J. N. (1980). Juvenile selection of frost resistant *Eucalyptus. AFOCEL,* pp. 225-253.

Marien, J. N., and H. Thibout (1978). Natural cross pollination of *Eucalyptus* planted in Southern France. *AFOCEL,* pp. 89-112.

Marquestant, J., H. Thibout, and B. Cauvin (1977). Introduction trial of various eucalypt species in southern France. *AFOCEL,* 294 pp.

Marsh, E. K. (1969). Selecting adapted races of introduced species. 2nd World Consul. For. Tree Breed., Washington, D.C., pp. 1249-1261.

Marsh, E. K. (1978). *The Cultivation and Management of Commercial Pine Plantations in South Africa.* Dept. For., Bull. 56, Pretoria, South Africa, 146 pp.

Martin, B. (1982). Vegetative propagation and breeding: The use of multiclonal variety of hybrid eucalypts in tropical areas. IUFRO Joint Meet. Work. Parties Gen. Breed. Strat. Incl. Multiclonal Varieties, Escherode, West Germany, pp. 64-65.

Martin, B. (1983). International tests with *Eucalyptus. Fast Growing Trees. Silvicultura* **29,** 21-17.

Martin, B., and Cossalter, C. (1976). *The Eucalyptus of the Sunda Isles. Bois et Forêts de Tropiques,* Nos. 163-169 (English trans. by N. Z. For. Ser., Rotorua, New Zealand).

Martinez, H. A., J. Bauer, and J. Jones (1983). *Fuelwood in Central America and the Regional Fuelwood and Alternative Energy Sources Project.* CATIE, Turrialba, Costa Rica, 16 pp.

Martinez, M. (1945). *Las Pinaceas Mexicanas,* Vol. 1. Univ. of Mexico, Mexico City, 345 pp.

Martinez, M. (1948). *Los Pinos Mexicanos.* Ediciónes Botas, Mexico City, 361 pp.

Martinez, M. (1958). The oaks of Mexico XI. *An. Inst. Biol. Univ. Mex.* **29**(1-2), 89-105.

Martinsson, O. (1970). Breeding strategy in relation to disease resistance in introduced forest trees. Sveriges Lantbruksuniversitet Inter. Rept. NR3, Umea, Sweden, 8 pp.

Martinsson, O. (1978). What risks for contorta? *Sveriges Skogs. Förb. Tidskrift.* **5,** 436-440.

Martinsson, O. (1980). Stem rusts in lodgepole pine provenance trials. *Sil. Gen.* **29**(1), 23-26.

Martinsson, O. (1982a). Pathogenic fungi on lodgepole pine. *Lodgepole Pine—Our Third Conifer. Sveriges Skogsv. Förb. Tidskrift* **80**(1-2), 57-58.

Martinsson, O. (1982b). Contortans rotutveckling och stabilitet. *Sveriges Skogsv. Förb. Tidskrift* **80**(1-2), 91-94.

Martinsson, O. (1983). Lodgepole pine in the Swedish reforestation—Problems and prospects. Proc. 4th. Inter. Workshop. Hinton, Alberta, pp. 49-52.

Martinsson, O., and Jan-Erik Lundh (1981). Contortatallens rotstabilitet provenien-sens inflytande. Rotdeformation hos Skogsplantor, Nordiskt Symp. Sveriges Lantbruksuniversitet, Garpenberg, Sweden, 19 pp.

Massavanhane, A. M., and D. Ruden (1984). Early performance in provenance trials with *Eucalyptus* species in Mozambique. In IUFRO (1984b), 1 p. (summary).

Matheson, A. C., and A. G. Brown (1983). Radiata pine breeding manual. For. Res., CSIRO, Canberra, Australia, 11 chapters.

Matheson, A. C., and K. G. Eldridge (1982). Cuttings from young seedlings—A new approach for *Pinus radiata*. Breeding Strategies Including Multiclonal Varieties, Escherode, West Germany, 1 p.

Matheson, A. C., and C. A. Raymond (1984a). Provenance × environment interaction, its detection, practical importance and use in tropical forestry. In IUFRO (1984b), pp. 81–117.

Matheson, A. C., and C. A. Raymond (1984b). Effects of thinning in progeny tests on estimates of genetic parameters in *Pinus radiata*. *Sil. Gen.* **33**(4–5), 125–128.

Mathews, J. (1963). Seed production and seed certification. 1st World Consul. For. Gen. Tree Impr., Stockholm, Sweden, 31 pp.

Matthews, J. D. (1979). Observations on trees and forests in China. The forestry mission to China. Occasional Paper No. 8, For. Comm., Edinburgh, Scotland, pp. 27–58.

Mattos, C. M., and R. Maciel (1984). Competition between natural phosphate and simple superphosphate. In IUFRO (1984a), Vol. 2, pp. 696–689.

Matziris, D. I. (1982). Variation in growth and quality characters in *Pinus pinaster* provenances grown at seven sites in Greece. *Sil. Gen.* **31**(5–6), 168–173.

Mead, D. J., D. Draper, and H. A. Madgwick (1985). Dry matter production of a young stand of *Pinus radiata:* Some effects of nitrogen fertilizer and thinning. *N. Z. Jour. For. Sci.* **14**(1), 97–108.

Meinartowicz, L. E., and A. Schmidt (1978). Investigations into the resistance of Douglas-fir (*Pseudotsuga menziesii*) populations to the Douglas-fir woolly aphid (*Gilletteella cooleyi*). *Sil. Gen.* **27**(2), 59–62.

Melchior, G. H. (1960). The induction of flowering in Japanese larch grafts. *Sil. Gen.* **10**(1), 20–26.

Mello, H. A. (1961). O consumo de agua pelas plantas. Amiario Brasil de Economia Floresta 13, Rio de Janeiro, Brazil.

Mendoza, L. A. (1970). The effects of self-pollination in *Eucalyptus camaldulensis*. *IDIA* (Suplemento Forestal) **6**, 41–45.

Mergen, F. J., and H. Worral (1965). Effect of environment and seed source on mineral content of jack pine seedlings. *For. Sci.* **11**, 393–400.

Mergen, F. J. (1983). Tropical forestry—A challenge to the profession of forestry. Yale School of For. and Env. Studies, New Haven, Connecticut, 23 pp.

Mergen, F. J., J. Burley, and G. M. Furnival (1974). Provenance–temperature interactions in four coniferous species. *Sil. Gen.* **23**(6), 200–210.

Merrifield, L. E., and N. H. Howcroft (1975). *Ceroplastis rubens* damage of *Pinus caribaea* with notes on the scales preference of certain clones of host material. *Sil. Gen.* **24**(4), 110–113.

Meskimen, G., and E. C. Franklin (1984). Hybridity in the *Eucalyptus grandis* breeding population in Florida. U.S. For. Ser. Res. Paper SE-242, Asheville, North Carolina, 15 pp.

Mettler, L. E., and T. G. Gregg (1969). *Population Genetics and Evolution*. Prentice-Hall, Englewood Cliffs, New Jersey, 212 pp.

Mew, G. (1981). Soils information—A basic requirement for exotic forest planning. *N. Z. Jour. For.* **26**(1), 81–95.

Michaud, D. (1978). Growing performances of 184 Douglas provenances in two nurseries. *AFOCEL,* pp. 80–87.

Mikola, J. (1982). Bud-set phenology as an indicator of climatic adaptation of Scots pine in Finland. *Sil. Fennica* **26**(2), 178–184.

Miller, J. T. (1971). Provenance variation in growth rate and other characters in 6-year-old *Pinus contorta* in New Zealand. N. Z. For. Ser. Rept. No. 55, Rotorua, New Zealand, 65 pp.

Miller, J. T., and I. J. Thulin (1967a). The early performance of *Pinus nigra* in New Zealand provenance trials. N. Z. For. Ser. Rept. No. 18, Rotorua, New Zealand, 4 pp.

Miller, J. T., and I. J. Thulin (1967b). Five-year survival and height compared for European, Japanese and hybrid larch in New Zealand. N. Z. For. Ser. Res. Leaflet No. 17, Rotorua, New Zealand, 4 pp.

Mirov, N. T. (1958). Chemistry in the service of silviculture. Proc. Soc. Amer. For., Washington, D.C., pp. 144–145.

Mirov, N. T. (1967). *The Genus Pinus.* Ronald Press, New York, 602 pp.

Mirov, N. T., and J. Hasbrouck (1976). *The Story of Pines.* Indiana Univ. Press, Bloomington, 148 pp.

Mirov, N. T., and E. Larsen (1958). Possibilities of Mexican and Central American pines in the world reforestation projects. *Caribbean Forester* **19**(3), 43–49.

Mitchell, R. G., N. E. Johnson, and K. H. Wright (1974). Susceptibility of 10 spruce species and hybrids to the white pine weevil (= Sitka spruce weevil) in the Pacific Northwest. U.S. For. Ser. Res. Note PNW-225, Portland, Oregon, 8 pp.

Mittak, W. L. (1978). Report concerning classification of the pines of Guatemala and Central America. Mimeo Rept., Tropical Tree Improv. Short Course, Session 15, N.C. State Univ., Raleigh, North Carolina, 27 pp.

Moe, D. (1970). The post-glacial immigration of *Picea abies* into Fennoscandia. *Bot. Notiser* **123**, 61–66.

Moeller, B. B. (1984). Is the Brazilian Amazon being destroyed? *Jour. For.* **82**(8), 472–475.

Moggi, G. (1958). Phenological research on some eucalypt species. *Pubblicazioni del Centro di Sperimentazione Agricola e Forestale* **2**, Rome, Italy, 43–58.

Mohd, W. R., T. K. Chew, and H. L. Wright (1981). A general volume table for *Pinus caribaea* var. *hondurensis. The Malaysian Forester* **44**(4), 425–437.

Molina, A. R. (1964). Coníferas de Honduras. *Ceiba* **10**(1), 5–21.

Mondeil, F. (1984). First results of provenance trials of *Pinus* species in the highlands of Madagascar. In IUFRO (1984b), pp. 348–361.

Monk, R. W., and H. B. Peterson (1962). Tolerance of some trees and shrubs to saline conditions. *Amer. Soc. Hort. Sci.* **81**, 556–561.

Monk, R. W., and H. H. Wiebe (1961). Salt tolerance and protoplasmic salt hardiness of various woody and herbaceous ornamental plants. *Plant Physiol.* **36**(4), 478–482.

Moore, J. N., and J. Janick (1983). *Methods in Fruit Breeding.* Purdue Univ. Press, West Lafayette, Indiana, 464 pp.

Morales, J. (1983). Nursery operations for bare-root *Pinus caribaea* seedling production. *Venez. Forestal* **11**(9), 40–53.

Morandini, R. (1964). Genetics and improvement of exotic trees. *Unasylva* **18**(2-3), 51-59.

Morgenstern, E. K., and A. H. Teich (1969). Phenotypic stability of height growth of jack pine provenances. *Can. Jour. Gen. Cytol.* **11**, 110-117.

Morris, A. R. (1984). International provenance trial of *Pinus kesiya* at age 10 at the Usutu Pulp Company, Swaziland. In IUFRO (1984b), pp. 362-367.

Morris, R. C. (1983). A survey of potential insect pests, their possible impact and natural controls in *Alnus, Salix* and *Populus* energy plantations. For. Energy Agreement, Inter. Energy Agency—Biomass Growth and Production, Maple, Ontario, Canada, 44 pp.

Morris, R. C., T. H. Filer, J. D. Solomon, F. I. McCracken, N. A. Overgaard, and M. J. Weiss (1975). Insects and diseases of cottonwood. U.S. For. Ser. Gen. Tech. Rept. 50-8, New Orleans, Louisiana, 37 pp.

Moura, V. P. (1984). *Eucalyptus camaldulensis* trials in Central Brazil—Third year results. In IUFRO (1984b), pp. 368-370.

Mubita, A. C. (1984). *Pinus merkusii* provenance trial in Zambia. In IUFRO (1984b), pp. 371-379.

Muhs, J. H. (1982). Identifying problems and legal aspects of using multiclonal mixtures. IUFRO Joint Mtg. Work. Par. Gen., Escherode, West Germany, 17 pp.

Muller, H. J. (1959). The prospects of genetic change. *Amer. Sci.* **47**(4), 551-561.

Mullin, L. J. (1969). The potentialities of the pines of Central America and the Caribbean Islands for afforestation in Rhodesia. *Rhodesia Science News* **3**(4), 93-96.

Mullin, L. J. (1984). *Pinus oocarpa* provenance trials in Zimbabwe. In IUFRO (1984b), pp. 380-389.

Mullin, L. J., R. D. Barnes, and R. L. Barrett (1981). The improvement of *Eucalyptus* in Zimbabwe. *S. A. For. Jour.* **118**, 20-25.

Mullin, L. J., and N. P. Denison (1983). The value of importing select genetic resources in exotic tree improvement. *Fast Growing Trees. Silvicultura* **32**, 718-720.

Mullin, L. J., J. Gough, and D. T. Carter (1983a). Provenance trials of *Pinus caribaea* in Zimbabwe. *Fast Growing Trees. Silvicultura* **29**, 116-117.

Mullin, L. J., J. Gough, and D. T. Carter (1983b). Provenance trials of *Eucalyptus nitens* in Zimbabwe. *Fast Growing Trees. Silvicultura* **31**, 480-481.

Mullin, L. J., D. R. Quaile, and W. R. Mills (1984). *Pinus kesiya* provenance trials in Zimbabwe—Twelfth year results. In IUFRO (1984b), pp. 390-403.

Muniswami, K. P. (1977). Population improvement and hybridization—Teak. 3rd World. Consul. For. Tree Breed., Canberra, Australia, pp. 507-544.

Murray, M. (1983). *Lodgepole Pine: Regeneration and Management.* 4th Inter. Work. Can. For. Ser., Hinton, Alberta, pp. 49-52.

Mushi, J. A., and S. Madofe (1984). Performance of two *Pinus taeda* provenance trials at Lushoto and Sao Hill, Tanzania. In IUFRO (1984b), pp. 404-416.

Muttiah, S. (1972). Effect of drought on mycorrhizae of *Pinus caribaea. Selection and Breeding to Improve Some Tropical Conifers,* Vol. I, Commonw. For. Inst., Oxford, U.K. and Dept. For., Queensland, Australia, pp. 133-135.

Myers, N. (1976). An expanded approach to the problem of disappearing species. *Science* **193**, 198-202.

Myers, W., L. Wilson, and J. Bassman (1976). Impact of insects on trees planted for maximum fiber production. Intensive Plantation Culture, U.S. For. Ser. Tech. Rept. N.C.-21, St. Paul, Minnesota, pp. 92–95.

Naccarata, V. A. (1983). Study of *Atta laevigata,* a pest of the pino caribe plantations in southern Monagas state. *Venez. Forestal* **2**(2), 16–39.

Nambiar, E. K., R. O. Squire, R. Sands, and G. M. Will (1984). Manipulation of water and nutrients in plantations of fast growing species. In IUFRO (1984a), pp. 489–504.

Namkoong, G. (1984a). Inbreeding, hybridization and conservation in provenances of tropical forest trees. In IUFRO (1984b), pp. 1–7.

Namkoong, G. (1984b). A control concept of gene conservation. *Sil. Gen.* **33**(4–5), 160–163.

Namkoong, G., and M. T. Conkle (1976). Time trends in genetic control of height growth in ponderosa pine. *For. Sci.* **22**(11), 2–12.

Namkoong, G., R. A. Usanis, and R. R. Silen (1972). Age-related variation in genetic control of height growth in Douglas-fir. *Theor. and Applied Gen.* **42**, 151–159.

Namkoong, G., R. D. Barnes, and J. Burley (1980). *A Philosophy of Breeding Strategy for Tropical Forest Trees.* Trop. For. Pap. No. 16, Commonwealth For. Inst., Oxford, U.K., 67 pp.

Namkoong, G., R. D. Barnes, and J. Burley (1983). Tree breeding strategies and international cooperation. *Fast Growing Trees. Silvicultura* **32**, 721–723.

Napier, I. A., and R. L. Willan (1983). Nursery techniques for tropical and subtropical pines. Tech Note No. 4, DANIDA For. Seed Centre, Humlebaek, Denmark, 22 pp.

Nariyoshi, A. H., B. V. Redko, and S. C. Coutinho (1985). A study of five populations of *Pinus caribaea* var. *hondurensis.* I. Evaluation of wood density in the tree. 18th Cong. Annal. da ABCP-Semana do Papel, São Paulo, Brazil, 18 pp. (mimeo).

National Academy of Sciences (1979). *Tropical Legumes—Resources for the Future.* Washington, D.C., 331 pp.

National Academy of Sciences (1983). *Firewood Crops: Shrub and Tree Species for Energy Production.* Washington, D.C., 237 pp.

National Research Council (1982). *Ecological aspects of development in the humid tropics.* Bull. Nat. Acad. Science, Washington, D.C., 52 pp.

Neil, P. E. (1984). A fast growing tropical hardwood species—*Cordia alliodora* in Vanuatu. In IUFRO (1984b), pp. 423–425.

Nelder, J. A. (1962). New kinds of systematic designs for spacing experiments. *Biometrics* **18**, 283–307.

Nellbeck, R. (1982). Why has Swedish forestry introduced *Pinus contorta* in Sweden? *Lodgepole Pine—Our Third Conifer. Sveriges Skogsv. Förb Tidskrift* **80**(1–2), 17–20.

Nelson, R. R. (1980). Host–parasite interactions and genetics on the individual plant level. Strategy of Breeding for Disease Resistance, Workshop on the Gen. of Host-Par. Inter. in For., Wageningen, Holland, 30 pp.

Ng, F. S. (1983). Flowering of *Pinus caribaea hondurensis.* Forest Genetic Resources, Information No. 12, FAO, Rome, p. 29.

Ng, K. M., S. K. Yap, A. Mohamad, and H. T. Chou (1985). *In situ* conservation of forest genetic resources in peninsular Malaysia. For. Gen. Res. Inf. No. 14, FAO, Rome, pp. 32–47.

Nicholls, T. H. (1979). Dangers of red pine monoculture. 1st N. Central Tree Impr. Conf., Madison, Wisconsin, pp. 104–108.

Nicholson, D. I. (1981). The natural occurrence and conservation status of *Acacia mangium* in Australia. Tech. Note No. 5, Dept. For., Brisbane, Queensland, Australia, 7 pp.

Nicolielo, N. (1984). Behavior of Provenances of *Pinus caribaea* in Agudos Region. M.S. thesis, Univ. São Paulo, Piracicaba, Brazil, 97 pp.

Nicolielo, N., and F. Bertolani (1984). Estudo de Introducáo de Espécíés de Pinus na Regiáo de Agudos—S.P. Silvicultura, Third Brazilian For. Congr., Rio de Janeiro, Brazil, Vol. II, pp. 128–129.

Nienstaedt, H. (1961). Induction of early flowering: A critical review of recent literature. *Recent Advances in Botany* 2(14), 1658–1662.

Nienstaedt, H. (1975). Adaptive variation—Manifestations in tree species and uses in forest management and tree improvement. 15th Can. Tree Impr. Assoc., Toronto, Ontario, Canada, pp. 11–12.

Nikles, D. G. (1966). Comparative Variability and Relationship of Caribbean Pine (*Pinus caribaea*) and Slash Pine (*P. elliottii*). Ph.D. thesis, N.C. State Univ., Raleigh, North Carolina, 201 pp.

Nikles, D. G. (1970). Breeding for growth and yield. *Unasylva* 24(2–3), 9–22.

Nikles, D. G. (1973). Improvement of tropical conifers—Report on a questionnaire. Sel. and Breed. to Improve Some Tropical Conifers, Commonw. For. Inst., Oxford, U.K., Vol. 2, pp. 335–363.

Nikles, D. G. (1977). Variation in growth, stem quality and wood properties in relation to genetic improvement in tropical forest trees. Topic 5: *P. caribaea*. IUFRO Workshop, Brisbane, Australia, 6 pp.

Nikles, D. G. (1978). Establishing and improving the genetic foundations of forest plantations in the tropics. Aust. Nat. Univ., Devel. Studies Center and For. Dept. Canberra, Australia, 12 pp.

Nikles, D. G. (1979). *Genetic Improvement of Tropical Lowland Conifers.* FAO Rept., Rome, 86 pp.

Nikles, D. G. (1981). Some successful hybrid breeds of forest trees and need for further development in Australia. 7th Meet. RWG No. 1—Forest Genetics, Traralgon, Victoria, Australia, 15 pp.

Nikles, D. G. (1984a). Strategies for the incorporation of new provenance material in existing breeding populations of tropical forest trees. In IUFRO (1984b), pp. 118–134.

Nikles, D. G. (1984b). Establishment and progeny testing of clonal seed orchards of *Pinus elliottii* × *P. caribaea* F_1 hybrids in Queensland. In IUFRO (1984b), pp. 567–568.

Nikles, D. G., and J. Burley (1977). International cooperation in breeding tropical pines. 3rd World Consul. For. Tree Breed. Canberra, Australia, pp. 1157–1186.

Nikles, D. G., and R. S. Newton (1983). International cooperative progeny studies of *Pinus caribaea* var. *hondurensis* initiated by Queensland Department of Forestry. *Fast Growing Trees. Silvicultura* 32, 724–729.

Nikles, D. G., and R. S. Newton (1984). Cooperative progeny trials of *Pinus caribaea* var. *hondurensis* initiated by Queensland Department of Forestry: Additional trials, some preliminary results and implications. In IUFRO (1984b), pp. 577–578.

Nikles, D. G., J. Burley, and R. D. Barnes (1978). *Progress and Problems of Genetic Improvement in Tropical Forest Trees*. Proc. Joint Workshop, Brisbane, Australia, Vol. I, 551 pp.

Nikles, D. G., K. P. Haydock, and D. Ratcliff (1977). Population by environment interactions. IUFRO. Var. Growth, Stem Quality and Wood Properties in Relation to Gen. Impr. of Trop. For. Trees, Brisbane, Australia, 11 pp.

Nikles, D. G., T. Spidy, E. J. Rider, R. L. Eisemann, R. S. Newton, and D. Mathews-Frederick (1983). Genetic variation in wind-firmness among provenances of *Pinus caribaea* var. *hondurensis* in Queensland. *Fast Growing Trees. Silvicultura* **29**, 125–130.

Nilsson, B. (1973). Recent results of interprovenance crosses in Sweden and the implications of breeding. 14th Meet. Can. Tree Impr. Assoc., Part 2, Fredericton, New Brunswick, Canada, pp. 3–15.

Nilsson, B. O. (1963). Intraspecific hybridization and heterosis within *Picea abies*. 1st World Consul. For. Gen. and Tree Impr., Stockholm, Sweden, 9 pp.

Nilsson, J. B. (1959). Larch seed and larch hybrids. *Svenska Skogs. Förb. Tidskrift.* **2**, 309–324.

Nixon, K. M. (1974). Early assessment of progeny trials in black wattle (*Acacia mearnsii*). Wattle Res. Inst. Ann. Rept., Pretoria, South Africa, pp. 60–65.

Noh, E. R., S. K. Hyun, J. M. Jo, R. M. Cho, S. K. Lee, J. K. Ahn, and J. J. Kim (1984). Activities related to poplar breeding, cultivation, exploitation and utilization (1980–1984). Res. Rep. Inst. For. Gen. No. 20, Suwon, Korea, pp. 16–45.

Nor, S. M. (1985). Forest problems within the arid parts of the tropics. 17th Exec. Bd. Meet., IUFRO, Malaysia.

Nordic Group of Forest Tree Breeders (1984). Conf. Genotype × Environment Interaction. *Studia Forestalia Suecica,* No. 166, 44 pp.

Nordin, V. J. (1984). *ISTS* (International Society of Tropical Foresters) **5**(4), 1.

North Carolina State University (1980). *Tropical Tree Improvement Short Course,* 2 Vols. Raleigh, North Carolina.

Nwoboshi, L. C. (1984). Growth and nutrient requirements in a teak plantation age series in Nigeria. II: Nutrient accumulation and minimum annual requirements. *For. Sci.* **30**(1), 35–40.

Oda, S., and E. Berti Filho (1978). Growth increment of *Eucalyptus saligna* in areas with different levels of *Thyrinteina arnobia*. *IPEF* **17**, 27–31.

O'Driscoll, M. (1978). Sitka spruce international ten-provenance experiment: Results to end of nursery stage. For. Gen. Res., Info. No. 7, For. Occ. Paper, FAO, Rome, pp. 35–43.

Ohba, K. (1980). Breeding of pines for resistance to wood nematodes (*Bursaphelenchus lignicolus*). Gen. of Host-Par. Inter. in For., Wageningen, Holland, 12 pp.

Ohba, K. (1984). Susceptibility of subtropical pine species and provenances to the pine wood nematode. *Jour. Jap. For. Soc.* **66**(11), 465–468.

Oje, S. A. (1984). Flowering and seed production of *Pinus caribaea* var. *hondurensis* in the pine growing areas of northern Nigeria. In IUFRO (1984b), pp. 584–591.

Okoro, O. O. (1985). Flowering of *Pinus caribaea* var. *hondurensis* in Nigeria. For. Gen. Res., FAO, Info. No. 14, Rome, pp. 7–9.

Olesen, P. O. (1971). Collection of forest tree seed in Mexico. 1968. 15th IUFRO Congress, Working Group on Breed. Trop. and Subtrop. Species, Gainesville, Florida, Vol. 1, pp. 29–37.

Ono, M. (1882). Which grow faster, seedlings or cuttings in the case of *Cryptomeria* or hinoki cypress? *Abstracts of Japanese Literature in Forest Genetics and Related Fields,* Vol. I, Part 1, p. 22.

Oppenheimer, H. R., and A. Halfon-Meiri (1959). Studies on the influence of different soils on growth and chemical composition of Mediterranean forest trees. 9th. Inter. Bot. Cong., Montreal, Canada, IIA, p. 26

Osara, N. Y., and P. Micola (1975). O empacto dos plantações de eucaliptos no equilibrio dos aguas. *O Eucalypto e a Ecologia,* Grupa Aracruz, Brazil, pp. 35–37.

Otarola, T. A., A. L. Ugalde, and M. Reyes (1983). Control of weeds in a plantation of *Eucalyptus camaldulensis* in Nicaragua, study results. CATIE, Turrialba, Costa Rica, 20 pp.

O.T.S. (1984). *Technologies to Sustain Tropical Forest Resources,* U.S. Congress, Washington, D.C., Office of Technology Assessment (F-214), 344 pp.

Owino, F. (1975). Genotypic stability comparisons in loblolly pine. 13th South. For. Tree Impr. Conf., Raleigh, North Carolina, pp. 214–218.

Owino, F. (1977a). Selection of species and provenances for afforestation in East Africa. 3rd World Consul. on For. Tree Breed., Canberra, Australia, Vol. 1, pp. 173–180.

Owino, F. (1977b). Genotype × environment interaction and genotype stability in loblolly pine. II: Genotypic stability comparisons. *Sil. Gen.* **26**(1), 21–26.

Owino, F., and B. Zobel (1977). Genotype × environment interaction and genotypic stability in loblolly pine. I: General introduction and description of the experiment. *Sil. Gen.* **26**(1), 18–21.

Palmberg, C. (1977). Selecting for rust resistance in poplars in Australia. 3rd World Consul. For. Tree Breed., Canberra, Australia, pp. 223–231.

Palmberg, C. (1982). A vital fuelwood gene pool is in danger. *Unasylva* **33**(133), 22–30.

Palmberg, C. (1983a). Conservation of variation in tropical tree species. *Plant Genetic Resources* **55**, 28–31.

Palmberg, C. (1983b). FAO guidelines for seed ordering. For. Gen. Res. Inf. No. 12, FAO, Rome, pp. 30–31.

Palmer, E. R. (1973). *Gmelina arborea* as a potential source of hardwood pulp. *Trop. Sci.* **15**(3), 243–260.

Palmer, E. R., and Gibbs, J. A. (1977). Pulping characteristics of *Pinus caribaea* from Fiji: The effect of rate of growth. Trop. Prod. Inst., London, 15 pp.

Palmer, E. R., and J. A. Gibbs (1978). Pulping characteristics of six hardwoods from Guyana. Trop. Prod. Inst., London, 43 pp.

Palmer, E. R., and J. A. Gibbs (1984). Pulping characteristics of *Eucalyptus saligna/grandis* growing in Uganda. Trop. Prod. Inst., L68, London, 13 pp.

Palmer, E. R., and C. B. Tabb (1971). *Pinus caribaea,* its potential as pulpwood. Trop. Prod. Inst., London, pp. 23–44.

Palmer, E. R., and C. B. Tabb (1983). *Pinus caribaea*—Its potential as pulpwood. *Selection and Breeding to Improve Some Tropical Conifers,* Vol. 2. Dept. For., Queensland, Australia, pp. 23–31.

Palmer, E. R., J. A. Gibbs, and A. P. Dutta (1982a). Pulping trials of wood species growing in plantations in Kenya. Tropical Prod. Inst., L61, London, 57 pp.

Palmer, E. R., J. S. Johnson, S. Ganguli, J. A. Gibbs, and A. P. Dutta (1982b). Pulping trials on *Pinus patula* and *P. radiata* grown in plantations in Kenya, Trop. Prod. Inst. L63, London, 56 pp.

Palmer, E. R., J. A. Gibbs, and A. P. Dutta (1983). Pulping characteristics of hardwood species growing in plantations in Fiji. Trop. Prod. Inst., L64, London, 38 pp.

Panetsos, C. P. (1969). Phenological research on *Eucalyptus camaldulensis* in Greece. For. Res. Inst., Bulletin No. 27, Athens, 16 pp.

Park, H. M., Y. Youn, and K. O. Byun (1984). Specific gravity and moisture content of *Pinus rigida* × *P. taeda*. F_1 cones as maturity indices. Res. Rep. Inst. For. Gen. No. 20, Suwon, Korea, pp. 5–7.

Parry, M. S. (1956). *Tree Planting Practices in Tropical Africa.* FAO For. Devel. Paper No. 8, Rome, 302 pp.

Parsons, P. A. (1983). *The Evolutionary Biology of Colonizing Species.* Cambridge University Press, Cambridge, U.K., 262 pp.

Paschke, J. L. (1979). Age-age Relationships in Loblolly Pine (*Pinus taeda*). M.S. thesis, School of Forestry, N.C. State Univ., Raleigh, North Carolina, 49 pp.

Passini, M. F. (1982). The Mexican stone pines (pinyons) of the Cembroides group. For. Gen. Res. Infor. No. 11. FAO, Rome, pp. 29–33.

Patrick, W. H. (1977). Chemistry of flooded soil and effects on mineral nutrition. U.S. For. Ser., State and Private S.E. Area, Myrtle Beach, South Carolina, pp. 40–48.

Patton, R. L. (1981). Effects of ozone and sulfur dioxide on height and stem specific gravity of *Populus* hybrids. U.S. For. Ser., Res. Pap. NE 471, Broomall, Pennsylvania, 4 pp.

Pauley, S. S. (1956). Natural hybridization of the aspens. *Minnesota For. Notes* **47**, 2 pp.

Pearson, R. G., and R. C. Gilmore (1980). Effect of fast growth rate on the mechanical properties of loblolly pine. *For. Prod. Jour.* **30**(5), 47–54.

Pederick, L. A. (1983). Establishment and progress of cooperative tree improvement programs with *Pinus radiata* in southern Australia. *Fast Growing Trees. Silvicultura* **32**, 736–738.

Pellate, E. De Vecchi (1969). Evolution and importance of land races in breeding. 2nd World Consul. For. Tree Breed., Washington, D.C., pp. 1263–1278.

Penfold, A. R., and J. L. Willis (1961). *The Eucalypts.* Interscience, New York.

Penman, H. L. (1963). *Vegetation and Hydrology.* Common. Bur. Soils Tech. Comm. 53, London.

Pereira, A. R., and G. G. de Paula (1983). Influence of forest productivity on costs of transport of vegetable charcoal in the state of Minas Gerais. *Brasil Florestal* **13**(55), 15–28.

Pereira, A. R., and G. C. Rezende (1983). Influence of cleaning stumps on the vigor of coppice of *Eucalyptus* spp. *Fast Growing Trees. Silvicultura* **31**, 597–599.

Pereira, A. R., A. J. Regazi, J. C. Ribeiro, and L. R. Romalho (1983). Effect of the diameter of the stumps on development of sprouts in *Eucalyptus* spp. *Fast Growing Trees. Silvicultura* **31**, 599-602.

Pereira, A. R., D. C. de Andrade, R. L. Costa, and A. G. de Fonseca (1984). Influence of position of sprouts and height of cut on survival of sprouts in *Eucalyptus grandis. Boletim Técnico* **8**, 59-62.

Pereira, H. C. (1973). *Land Use and Water Resources.* Cambridge Univ. Press, London, 246 pp.

Perry, J. P. (1951). Pine bark beetles of Central Mexico. *Unasylva* **5**(4), 8.

Perry, J. P. (1988). *The Pines of Mexico and Central America.* (In Press)

Persson, A. (1980). *Pinus contorta as an Exotic Species.* Swedish Univ. of Ag. Sciences, Dept. For. Gen. Res. Notes, Garpenberg, Sweden, 353 pp.

Persson, A. (1982). The quality of *Pinus contorta* in comparison to Scots pine and Norway spruce. Pulp, paper and sawn timber. *Lodgepole Pine—Our Third Forest, Sveriges Skogsv. Förb. Tidskrift* **80**(1-2), 37-42.

Persson, A. (1985). Trädslag och kvalitet. *Skogsfakta Konferens* **6**, 52-72.

Petterson, H., and P. Havmöller (1984). Provenance tests and breeding strategies for *Acacia mangium* and *Eucalyptus* spp. in Philippines and India. In IUFRO (1984b), pp. 432-436.

Pharis, R. P. (1976). Manipulation of flowering in conifers through the use of plant hormones. *Modern Methods in Forest Genetics.* Springer-Verlag, Berlin, pp. 265-282.

Pianka, E. R. (1966). Latitudinal gradients in species diversity: A review of concepts. *Amer. Nat.* **100**, 33-46.

Piatnitsky, S. S. (1960). Evolving new forms of oaks by hybridization. 5th World For. Cong., Seattle, Washington, Vol. 2, pp. 815-818.

Piesch, R. F., and R. E. Stevenson (1976). Certification of source-identified Canadian tree seed under the O.E.C.D. scheme. Dept. Fisheries and Environ. Canadian For. Ser. Tech. Rept. No. 19. Ottawa, Canada, 18 pp.

Pisek, A., and W. Larcher (1954). Relationship between drought resistance and frost hardiness in evergreens. *Protoplasma* **44**(1), 30-46.

Plumptre, R. A. (1977). Variation of growth and wood properties in relation to genetic improvement of tropical forest trees. 3rd World Consul. For. Tree. Breed., Canberra, Australia, 28 pp.

Plumptre, R. A. (1984). *Pinus caribaea.* Vol. 2: *Wood Properties.* Trop. For. Paper 17, Commonw. For. Inst., Oxford, U.K., 148 pp.

Pohjonen, V., and M. Nasi (1983). Wet biomass as animal feed—Fodder as a by-product from energy forests. Ministry of Natural Resources, Maple, Ontario, Canada, 22 pp.

Poissonnier, M., M. J. Dumant, and A. Franclet (1983). Acclimatization of *Eucalyptus* clones propagated in vitro. *AFOCEL,* pp. 55-83.

Posey, C. E. (1964). The effects of fertilization upon wood properties of loblolly pine (*Pinus taeda*). 8th South. Conf. For. Tree Impr., Savannah, Georgia, pp. 126-130.

Pousujja, R. (1984). Provenance trials of *Pinus merkusii* in Thailand. In IUFRO (1984b), p. 437.

Poynton, R. J. (1979). *Tree Planting in Southern Africa.* Vol. 1: *The Pines.* Vol. 2: *The Eucalypts.* Dept. For., Pretoria, South Africa, 576 and 882 pp.

Poynton, R. J. (1983). The silvicultural treatment of eucalypt plantations in southern Africa. *Fast Growing Trees. Silvicultura* **31**, 603–605.

Prosser, C. L. (1959). The "origin" after a century: Prospects for the future. *Amer. Sci.* **47**(4), 536–550.

Pryor, L. D. (1950). A hybrid *Eucalyptus. Proc. Lin. Soc. New South Wales* **75**(1–2), 96–101.

Pryor, L. D. (1951). A genetic analysis of some *Eucalyptus* species. *Proc. Lin. Soc. New South Wales* **76**(3–4), 140–147.

Pryor, L. D. (1956). Chlorosis and lack of vigour in seedlings of renantherous species of *Eucalyptus* caused by lack of mycorrhizae. *Proc. Lin. Soc. New South Wales* **81**, 91–96.

Pryor, L. D. (1959). Evaluation in *Eucalyptus. Aust. Jour. Sci.* **22**(1), 45–49.

Pryor, L. D. (1976). *The Biology of Eucalyptus.* Studies in Biology 61. Camelot Press, Southhampton, U.K., 82 pp.

Pryor, L. D. (1978a). Species and species trials. Inter. Train. Course in For. Tree Breed., Sel. Ref. Topics, Australian Devel. Assis. Agency, Canberra, p. 79.

Pryor, L. D. (1978b). Eucalypts as exotics. Inter. Training Course in For. Tree Breed., Sel. Ref. Papers, Australian Devel. Assis. Agency, Canberra, pp. 219–221.

Pryor, L. D., and J. D. Briggs (1981). *Australian Endangered Species: Eucalypts.* Australian Nat. Parks and Wildlife Ser., Spec. Pub. No. 5, Canberra, 139 pp.

Pupo, A. Z., and J. Burley (1973). Progeny test of *P. caribaea* var. *caribaea* at Cajalbana, Cuba. IUFRO, Joint Meet. Trop. Prov. and Prog. Res. and Inter. Coop., Nairobi, Kenya, pp. 510–516.

Quaile, D. R., and L. J. Mullin (1984). Provenance and progeny testing in *Eucalyptus camaldulensis* in Zimbabwe. In IUFRO (1984b), pp. 438–450.

Quintana, H. (1981). III. El bosque artificial como alternativa ecológica y de conservación. Reforestación: La alternativa del futuro. Ministerio de Agricultura, Bogota, Colombia, pp. 17–20.

Radu, S. (1974). *Cultura si valorificarea pinului Strob.* Ceres, Bucharest, Romania, 304 pp.

Radwan, M. A. (1972). Differences between Douglas-fir genotypes in relation to browsing preference by black-tailed deer. *Can. Jour. For. Res.* **2**(3), 250–255.

Ramirez, A. F. (1979). Evaluación económica de la reforestación con fines protectores. Armando Falla y Cia. Ltd., Bogota, Colombia, 7 pp. (mimeo. report).

Ramirez, L. A. (1981). A new disease (*Scirrhia acicola*) associated with the pines of Colombia. Invest. Forestales No. 5, Bogota, Colombia, 8 pp.

Randall, W. K. (1971). Differences among willows in susceptibility to cottonwood leaf beetle. 11th Conf. South. For. Tree Impr., Atlanta, Georgia, 9 pp.

Raunio, A. L. (1973). *Cupressus lusitanica* international (EAAFRO) progeny trial planted in 1966 at Almotonyi, Tanzania. IUFRO Joint Meet. Trop. Prov. and Prog. Res. and Inter. Coop., Nairobi, Kenya, pp. 489–492.

Rauter, M. (1979). Spruce cutting propagation in Canada. Breeding Norway Spruce, Norway Spruce Provenance. IUFRO, Div. 2, Bucharest, Romania, 10 pp.

Rauter, R. M., and J. V. Hood (1980). Uses for rooted cuttings in tree improvement programs. 18th Can. Tree Imp. Conf., Duncan, British Colombia, Canada.

Reed, D. D., R. L. Sajdak, and J. Kotar (1983). Growth comparisons of tamarack and European larch in upper Michigan. 3rd Central States Tree Impr. Conf., Wooster, Ohio, pp. 71-77.

Rehfeldt, G. E. (1979). Ecotypic differentiation in populations of *Pinus monticola* in north Idaho—Myth or reality? *Amer. Natur.* **114**, 627-636.

Rehfeldt, G. E. (1980). Genetic gains from tree improvement of ponderosa pine in southern Idaho. U.S. For. Ser. Res. Pap. INT-263. Ogden, Utah, 9 pp.

Reis, M. S., and C. I. Hodges (1976). Status of forest diseases and insects in Latin America. For. Devel. and Res. Document No. 12, Brasilia, Brazil, 10 pp.

Remröd, J. (1977). Contortatallen. *KSLA Tidsk* **116**(3), 119-149.

Revell, D. H. (1981). Silviculture of eucalypts: New Zealand experience. Proc. Workshop Wood: Future Growth and Conversion, Canberra, Australia, pp. 116-122.

Revell, D. H. (1983). Management of *Eucalyptus* for sawlog production in New Zealand. *Fast Growing Trees. Silvicultura* **31**, 606-607.

Revell, D. H., and J. C. Van Dorsser (1983). Eucalypt plantation establishment in New Zealand using bare-rooted seedlings. *Fast Growing Trees. Silvicultura* **31**, 607-608.

Rhomeder, E. (1961). Problems and suggestions for an international certification of forest seed. *Sonderdruck* **31**(8), 219-221; **30**(9), 253-255.

Rice, E. L. (1984). *Allelopathy.* Academic Press, New York, 422 pp.

Richardson, S. D. (1970). The end of forestry in Great Britain. *Commonw. For. Rev.* **49**, 324-335.

Richardson, S. D. (1973). The availability of supplies from current resources. Symp., The Future Availability of Tropical Hardwoods. Commonw. For. Assoc., London.

Robbins, A. M. (1983). *Pinus caribaea.* Seed Leaflet No. 2, DANIDA Forest Seed Centre, Humlebaek, Denmark, 21 pp.

Robbins, A. M., and C. F. Hughes (1983). *Provenance regions for* Pinus caribaea *and* Pinus oocarpa *within the Republic of Honduras.* Tropical For. Pap. No. 18, CFI, Oxford, U.K., 74 pp.

Roberds, J. H., G. Namkoong, and C. B. Davey (1976). Family variation in growth response of loblolly pine to fertilizing with urea. *For. Sci.* **22**(3), 291-299.

Roberts, R., M. U. Slee, D. G. Nikles, D. Goshnick, and J. Ryan (1983). The times of flowering of clones of *Pinus caribaea* var. *hondurensis* at three locations in Australia. *Fast Growing Trees. Silvicultura* **29**, 133-135.

Rocas, A. N., M. A. Musalem, and T. Eguilez (1977). Establishment of a seed producing area of *Pinus hartwegii. Phytogenetics,* pp. 276-283.

Roche, L. R. (1975). Guidelines for the methodology of conservation of forest genetic resources. *The Methodology of Conservation of Forest Genetic Resources.* FAO, Rome, pp. 107-114.

Roche, L. R. (1979). Forestry and conservation of plants and animals in the tropics. *For. Ecol. and Mgt.* **2**(2), 103-122.

Rockwood, D. L., and T. F. Geary (1982). Genetic variation in biomass productivity and coppicing of intensively grown *Eucalyptus grandis* in southern Florida. N. Amer. For. Biol. Workshop, Univ. of Kentucky, Lexington, pp. 400-405.

Roeder, K. R. (1980a). Early provenance performance of *Eucalyptus citriodora* in South Africa. *S. A. For. Jour.* **113**, 87–89.

Roeder, K. R. (1980b). Variation in growth features of *Eucalyptus saligna* in South Africa. *S. A. For. Jour.* **112**, 36–41.

Rohmeder, E. (1959). Examples of the superiority of foreign provenances over the native races in the species *Pinus silvestris* and *Picea abies*. *Sonderdruck aus Allgemeine Forstzeitschrift* **43**, 1–5.

Roll, R., and J. Pourtet (1949). Catalogue des Espéces Cultiveés dans L'Arboretum des Barres: Angiospermes. Ann. Ed. Eaux For., Nancy, France, 9, pp. 235–664.

Roll, R., and J. Pourtet (1954). Catalogue des Espéces Cultiveés dans L'Arboretum des Barres: Gymnospermes. Ann. Ed. Eaux For., Nancy, France, 9, 254 pp.

Rone, V. (1982). Early tests in clonal breeding of Norway spruce: Experiment results and problems. IUFRO Proc. Joint Meet. Work. Parties on Gen. and Breed. Strat. Including Multiclonal Varieties, Escherode, West Germany, p. 84.

Rosvall, O. (1982). Fröförsörjning och fröplantageprogram för *Pinus contorta* i Sverige. *Sveriges Skogsv. Förb. Tidskrift.* **80**(1–2), 105–108.

Rosvall, O. (1984). Contortatall i nordliga höglägen. In Fjällnära skogsbruk, exkursionsunderlag. Domänverket, Falun, Sweden, pp. 28–29.

Roulund, H. (1978a). Stem form of cuttings related to age and position of scions (*Picea abies*). Forest Tree Improvement No. 13, Arboretet Horsholm. Akademisk Forlag, Horsholm, Denmark, 24 pp.

Roulund, H. (1978b). A comparison of seedlings and clonal cuttings of Sitka spruce (*Picea sitchensis*). *Sil. Gen.* **27**(3–4), 104–108.

Rudloff, W. (1981). *World Climates: With Tables of Climatic Data and Practical Suggestions*. Wissenschaftliche Verlagsgesellschaft, Stuttgart, West Germany, 632 pp.

Rudman, P., M. Higgs, J. Davidson, and N. Malajczuk (1969). Breeding eucalypts for wood properties. 2nd World Consul. on For. Tree Breed., Washington, D.C., 9 pp.

Rudolf, P. O. (1963). Forest tree seed certification in the United States and some proposals for uniformity. 1st World Consul. For. Gen. Tree Impr., Stockholm, Sweden, 9 pp.

Rudolf, P. O. (1966). OECD scheme for control of forest reproductive material. *Jour. For.* **64**(5), 311–313.

Rusk, G. D. (1983). The influence of cost recording on the profitability of growing timber. Proc. SAIF Symp. "Forestry Quo Vadis?," Pretoria, South Africa, pp. 111–120.

Rusk, G. D., J. Kapp, and T. Geraghty (1983). Forestry costs in South Africa. SATGA Doc. 35/1984, Pretoria, South Africa, 39 pp.

Ryu, J. B., D. K. Chang, C. S. Na, and G. S. Jhun (1984a). Selection of early-flowering pitch pine (*P. rigida*) for a hybrid seed orchard. Res. Rep. Inst. For. Gen., No. 20, Suwon, Korea, pp. 12–15.

Ryu, J. B., G. S. Jhun, and H. R. Park (1984b). Comparison of seed production at upper and lower nodes of pitch pine by cone analysis. Res. Rep. Inst. For. Gen., No. 20, Suwon, Korea, pp. 8–11.

Ryynänen, M. (1982). Individual variation in seed maturation in marginal populations of Scots pine. *Sil. Fennica* **26**(2), 185–187.

Salas, F. (1976). Ecological considerations in the Chaguaramas area for *Pinus caribaea*. *Venez. Forestal,* pp. 8–23.

Salate, E., J. Marques, and L. C. Moliou (1978). Origem e distribuicão das chuvas na Amazonia. *Intersciencia* **3**(4), 200–206.

Sampio, A. N. (1975). Os eucaliptos no Brasil. O *Eucalipto e a Ecologia,* Grupo Aracruz, Rio de Janeiro, Brazil, pp. 5–10.

Samuel, C. J., and R. C. Johnstone (1979). A study of population variation in inheritance in Sitka spruce. *Sil. Gen.* **28**(1), 26–32.

Sanchez, P. A. (1976). *Properties and Management of Soils in the Tropics.* Wiley, New York, 618 pp.

Sanchez, P. A., and S. W. Boul (1975). Soils of the tropics and the world food crises. *Science* **188,** 598–603.

Sanchez, P. A., and G. Uehara (1980). Management considerations for acid soils with high phosphorus fixation capacity. *Phosphorus in Agriculture.* Soil Sci. Soc. Amer., Madison, Wisconsin, pp. 471–514.

Sanchez, P. A., C. A. Palm, L. T. Szott, and C. B. Davey (1985). Tree crops as soil improvers in the humid tropics, *Attributes of Trees as Crop Plants.* Inst. Terres. Ecol., Midlothian, Scotland, pp. 331–362.

Sands, R. (1984). Transplanting stress in radiata pine. *Aust. For. Res.,* **14**(2), 67–72.

Sands, R., and E. K. Nambiar (1984). Water relations of *Pinus radiata* in competition with weeds. *Can. Jour. For. Res.* **14**(2), 233–237.

Santamour, F. S. (1965). Rooting of pitch pine stump sprouts. *Tree Planters' Notes* **70,** 32–34.

Santamour, F. S. (1972). Interspecific hybridization in *Liquidambar. For. Sci.* **18**(1), 23–26.

Santos, G., G. M. Gomes, J. C. Zanuncio, and R. M. Brandi (1979). Control of leafcutting ants by the system of thermal spraying, in the region of Timoteo, M.G. *Brazil Florestal* **38,** 18–20.

Sarvas, R. (1962). *Investigations on the flowering and seed crop of Pinus silvestris. Communications Inst. Fores. Fenniae.* 53.4, 198 pp.

Sarvas, R. (1967). Climatological control of flowering in trees. IUFRO Congress, Munich, Vol. 3(22), pp. 15–30.

Sato, S., and A. Brune (1983). Heritabilities and correlation estimations among growth characteristics and for foxtailing growth in *Pinus caribaea* var. *hondurensis. Fast Growing Trees. Silvicultura* **29,** 139–141.

Savage, J. M. (1982). *Ecological Aspects of Development in the Humid Tropics.* Nat. Acad. Press, Washington, D.C., 297 pp.

Scamoni, A. (1950). The further development of artificial pine crosses in Eberswalde. *Der Zuchter* **20**(1–2), 39–42.

Schenk, C. A. (1939). *Fremdlische Wald- und Parkbäume. Die Nadelhölzer.* Paul Parey Verlag, Berlin, 645 pp.

Schlatter, J. E., and V. R. Gerding (1984). Important site factors for *Pinus radiata* growth in Chile. In IUFRO (1984a), Vol. 2, pp. 541–549.

Schmidt, R. A. (1978). Diseases in forest ecosystems: The importance of functional diversity, in *Plant Disease—An Advanced Treatise. Vol. II: How Disease Develops in Populations.* Academic Press, New York, pp. 287–315.

Schmidtling, R. C. (1978). Southern loblolly pine seed orchards produce more cones and seeds than do northern orchards. Flow. and Seed Devel. in Trees. Symp., Mississippi State Univ., Starkville, pp. 177–186.

Schmidt-Vogt, H. (1977). *Die Fichte,* Band 1. Paul Parey, Verlag Berlin, 647 pp.

Schmitt, R. (1972). Intrinsic qualities, acclimatization and growth potential of white pines introduced into Europe with emphasis on *Pinus strobus.* NATO–IUFRO Adv. Inst., Moscow, Idaho. USDA, Washington, D.C., pp. 111–122.

Schneider, M. H. (1977). Energy from forest biomass. *For. Chronicle:* 215–218.

Schober, R. (1963). Experiences with the Douglas-fir in Europe. 1st World Consul., For. Gen. Tree Impr., Stockholm, Sweden, 18 pp.

Schönau, A. P. (1977). Initial responses to fertilizing *Eucalyptus grandis* at planting are sustained until harvesting. *S. A. For. Jour.* **100**, 72–80.

Schönau, A. P. (1982). The planned production period for short rotation *Eucalyptus grandis. S. A. For. Jour.* **122**, 10–13.

Schönau, A. P. (1984). Fertilization of fast-growing broadleaved species. In IUFRO (1984a), Vol. 1, pp. 253–268.

Schönau, A. P., and D. I. Boden (1982). Silvicultural techniques in the establishment of *Eucalyptus grandis.* Symp. on Establishment in Modern Silviculture, Stellenbosch, South Africa, 19 pp.

Schönau, A. P., and R. W. Fitzpatrick (1981). A tentative evaluation of soil types for commercial afforestation in the Transvaal and Natal. *S. A. For. Jour.* **116**, 28–39.

Schönbach, H., and E. Bellman (1968). Frost resistance of progeny from crosses between *viridis* and *glauca* forms of *Pseudotsuga menziesii. Arch. Forstw.* **16**(6–9), 707–711.

Schönbach, H., E. Bellman, and W. Schumann (1966). Early growth and resistance to drought and frost in provenances of Japanese larch. *Sil. Gen.* **15**(5–6), 141–147.

Schopmeyer, C. S. (1974). *Seeds of Woody Plants in the United States.* Agricultural Handbook No. 450, U.S. For. Ser., Washington, D.C., 884 pp.

Schreiner, E. J. (1959). Rating poplars for *Melampsora* leaf rust infection. U.S. For. Ser., N.E. For. Exp. Stat., For. Res. Note. No. 90. Philadelphia, 16 pp.

Schreiner, E. J. (1963). Improvement of disease resistance in *Populus.* 1st World Consul. on For. Gen. and Tree Impr., Stockholm, 21 pp.

Schreiner, E. J. (1965). Maximum genetic improvement of forest trees through synthetic multiclonal hybrid varieties. 13th Northeast. For. Tree Impr. Conf., Albany, New York, pp. 7–13.

Schrum, G. M., and H. D. Gerhold (1970). Heritability estimates for Scotch pine. 2nd Mtg. Work. Grp. Quan. Gen., IUFRO Sect. 22, Raleigh, North Carolina, pp. 87–89.

Schrum, G. M., J. D. Gerhold, R. F. West, and L. S. Hamilton (1975). Genetic variation in Scotch pine. *For. Sci.* **21**(4), 330–339.

Schultz, E. B. (1979). Artificial Cold-hardiness Testing of *Eucalyptus.* M.S. thesis, N.C. State Univ., Raleigh, North Carolina, 61 pp.

Schultz, J. C., and I. T. Baldwin (1982). The significance of physiological and genetic variability in controlling pests of forest trees. 7th. N. Amer. For. Biol. Workshop, Lexington, Kentucky, p. 63.

Schummann, W., and K. Hoffman (1968). Routine testing of frost resistance of 1-year-old spruce seedlings. *Arch. Forstw.* **16**(6–9), 701–705.

Schutz, C. J. (1976). A review of fertilizer research on some of the more important conifers and eucalypts planted in sub-tropical and tropical countries, with special reference to South Africa. Dept. For., Pretoria, South Africa, Bull. 53, 89 pp.

Scott, J. W., P. P. Feret, D. W. Smith, and D. L. Bramlett (1975). Distribution of nitrogen, phosphorus, potassium and calcium in ten families of *Pinus virginiana.* 13th South For. Tree Impr. Conf., Raleigh, North Carolina, pp. 89–92.

Sedjo, R. A. (1983). *The Comparative Economics of Plantation Forestry: A Global Assessment.* Resources of the Future, Washington, D.C., 161 pp.

Sesbou, A. (1981). A Study of the Genetic Variability of the Quality of the Wood and Collapse in *Eucalyptus camaldulensis.* Ph.D. thesis, University of Nancy, France, 145 pp.

Shea, K. R. (1971). Disease and insect activity in relation to intensive culture of forests. 15th IUFRO Congress, Gainesville, Florida, pp. 109–118.

Shelbourne, C. J. (1963). Growth rates, stem form and branching characteristics of five provenances of *P. khasya* grown under plantation conditions in N. Rhodesia. *Commonw. For. Rep.* **42**(4), 334–346.

Shelbourne, C. J. (1971). Wind-pollinated progeny test of radiata pine. N. Z. For. Ser., For. Res. Inst., 1971 Rept., Rotorua, New Zealand, pp. 24–25.

Shelbourne, C. J. (1972). Genotype–environment interaction: Its study and its implications in forest tree improvement. SABRAO Joint Symposia, Tokyo, 27 pp.

Shelbourne, C. J., and I. J. Thulin (1974). Early results from a clonal selection and testing program with radiata pine. *N. Z. Jour. For. Sci.* **4**(2), 387–398.

Shelbourne, C. J., M. H. Banister, and M. D. Wilcox (1982). Early results in provenance studies in *Pinus muricata* in New Zealand. N. Z. For. Ser. Reprint No. 1512, **27**(1), Rotorua, New Zealand, 50–66.

Shepherd, K. R. (1978). General genetics and inheritance. Inter. Train. Course in For. Tree Breed., Selec. Ref. Topics, Aust. Devel. Assis. Agency, Canberra, Australia, pp. 43–60.

Shibata, N., K. Wada, and H. Hara (1970). Investigations on the relationships between environmental factors and the growth of *Pinus densiflora, P. thunbergii* and *P. densithunbergii.* IV: Analysis of nutrient contents in leaves and roots of clones and strains very different in growth. OJI Inst. For. Tree. Impr., OJI Paper Co., Ltd., Tech. Note No. 92, Tokyo, 1 pp.

Shim, P. S. (1974). Growth variation of *Pinus caribaea* var. *hondurensis,* West Coast, Sabah. Malaysian Forest Officers Conf., Sabah, Malaysia.

Shimizu, J. Y., and A. R. Higa (1981). Racial variation of *Pinus taeda* in Southern Brazil up to 6 years of age. *Boletim de Pesquisa Florestal* **2**, 1–26.

Shirley, H. L. (1937). The relation of drought and cold resistance to source of seed stock. *Minnesota Horticulturist,* pp. 1–2.

Shote, E., Z. Hara, S. Ito, and K. Kasaka (1982). Growth of exotic pines. Kanto For. Tree Breed. Inst. Ann. Rept. No. 16, Mito, Japan, pp. 78–86.

Shriner, D. S. (1976). Effects of simulated rain acidified with sulfuric acid on host-parasite interactions. Proc., 1st Symp. on Acid Precipitation and the Forest Ecosystem, U.S. For. Ser. Gen. Tech. Rep. N.E.-23, Philadelphia, Pennsylvania, pp. 919–925.

Silva, R., and R. Arellano (1982). Volume tables by top diameter and commercial length for plantations of *Pinus caribaea* var. *hondurensis* in Cachipo, State of Monagas. *Venez. Forestal* **7**, 1–26.

Silva, R., R. Arellano, J. Tarbes, R. Bellandi, E. Chaves, and E. Moreno (1982). Forest inventory of plantations of *Pinus caribaea* var. *hondurensis* at Chaguaramos, State of Monagas (CONARE Co.). *Venez. Forestal* **7**, 27–30.

Sim, B. L., and N. Jones (1984). Improvement of *Gmelina arborea* in "Sabah Softwoods" plantations. In IUFRO (1984b), pp. 604–609.

Simoes, J. W. (1983). Establishment and management of fast growing forests in Brazil. *Fast Growing Trees. Silvicultura* **29**, 28–34.

Simoes, J. W., R. M. Brandi, and J. R. Malinovsky (1976). Reforestation with fast growth species. *PRODEPEF* No. 6, Brasilia, Brazil, 74 pp.

Skroppa, T., and J. Dietrichson (1978). Survival and early growth of *Pinus contorta* provenances in interior eastern Norway. Rept. Nor. For. Res. Inst. 34, Aas, Norway, 92 pp.

Slee, M. U. (1973). Daylength and temperature performance of *Pinus caribaea,* Brisbane, Australia. *MUS* **9**, 8 pp.

Slee, M. U. (1977a). A model relating needleless shoots and dieback in *Pinus caribaea* to strobilus production and climatic conditions. *Sil. Gen.* **26**(4), 135–141.

Slee, M. U. (1977b). Breeding *Pinus caribaea* for the central lowland tropics. 3rd SABRAD Conf., Canberra, Australia, 7 pp.

Sluder, E. R. (1970). Shortleaf × loblolly pine hybrids do well in Central Georgia. Georgia For. Res. Coun. Res. Paper No. 64, Macon, Georgia, 4 pp.

Smith, D. W., and P. R. Toomey (1982). Specific density and caloric value of trunkwood of white birch, black cherry and sugar maple and their relation to forest succession. *Can. Jour. For. Res.* **12**(2), 186–190.

Smith, H. D. (1975). Potential for foreign production of pine seed for the United States. 13th South. For. Tree Impr. Conf., Raleigh, North Carolina, pp. 27–36.

Smith, N. J. (1981). Fuel forests: A spreading energy resource in developing countries. *Intersciencia* **6**(5), 336–343.

Smith, R. H. (1966). Resin quality as a factor in the resistance of pines to bark beetles. *Breeding Resistant Trees*. NATO and NSF Advanced Study Institute, Pennsylvania State Univ., State College, pp. 189–196.

Smith, W. J. (1967). The heritability of fibre characteristics and its application to wood quality improvement in forest trees. *Sil. Gen.* **16**(2), 41–50.

Smith, W. J. (1983). Wood yield, properties and quality in Queensland-grown *Pinus caribaea. Selection and Breeding to Improve Some Tropical Conifers,* Vol. 2. Dept. For. Queensland, Australia, pp. 45–69.

Smouse, P. E., and L. C. Saylor (1973). Studies of the *Pinus rigida–serotina* Complex. II: Natural hybridization among the *Pinus rigida–serotina complex, P. taeda* and *P. echinata. Annals Missouri Botanical Gardens* **60**(2), 192–203.

Snyder, E. B. (1972). Glossary for forest tree improvement workers. South. For. Expt. Stat., U.S. For. Serv., New Orleans, Louisiana, 22 pp.

Soegaard, B. (1964). Breeding for resistance to insect attack in forest trees. *Unasylva* **18**(2-3), 82-88.

Soegaard, B. (1969). Resistance studies in *Thuja*. Saertryk ur Det forstlige Forsoegsvoesen i Danmark beretning. No. 245(31), 3 pp.

Soerianegara, I. (1980). The alang-alang (*Imperata cyllindrica*) problem in forestry. *Biotrop. Spec.* **5**, 237-242.

Son, D. K., and S. B. Chung (1972). The growth performance and specific gravity of hybrid poplar. Res. Rept. No. 9., Inst. For. Gen., Suwon, Korea, pp. 9-17.

Sorenson, F. C. (1983). Geographic variation in seedling Douglas-fir (*Pseudotsuga menziesii*) from the western Siskiyou mountains of Oregon. *Ecology* **64**(4), 696-702.

Spears, J. S. (1978). Wood as an energy source: The situation in the developing world. 103rd Ann. Meet., Amer. For. Assoc., Hot Springs, Arkansas.

Spidy, T. (1984). Flowering and seeding in *Pinus caribaea* var. *hondurensis* in Queensland. In IUFRO (1984b), p. 610.

Squillace, A. E. (1966). Geographic variation in slash pine. *For. Sci. Mon.* **10**, 56 pp.

Squillace, A. E., and G. R. Gansel (1974). Juvenile-mature correlations in slash pine. *For. Sci.* **20**, 225-229.

Squillace, A. E., and R. R. Silen (1962). Racial variation in ponderosa pine. *For. Sci. Mon.* **2**, 27 pp.

Squillace, A. E., J. G. la Bastide, and C. L. Van Vredenburch (1975). Genetic variation and breeding of Scots pine in the Netherlands. *For. Sci.* **21**(4), 341-352.

Stahl, P. H. (1982). Conditions and problems in reforestation. *Lodgepole Pine—Our Third Conifer. Sveriges Skogsv. Förb. Tidskrift* **80**(1-2), 87-90.

Stahl, W. (1968). *Diplodia pinea:* A preliminary report on some aspects of fungus and host relationship. *Aust. For. Res.* **3**(4), 27-32.

Start, A. N., and A. G. Marshall (1976). Nectarivorous bats as pollinators of trees in West Malaysia. *Tropical Trees—Variation, Breeding and Conservation,* Academic Press, London, pp. 141-150.

Stead, J. W. (1979). Exploration, collection and evaluation of *Cordia alliodora*. For. Gen. Res. Infor. No. 9, For. Occ. Paper 1979/1. FAO, Rome, pp. 24-31.

Stead, J. W. (1980). Commonwealth Forestry Institute International Provenance Trials of *Cordia alliodora*. 11th Commonw. For. Conf., London, 17 pp.

Stebbins, G. L. (1950). *Variation and Evolution in Plants*. Columbia Univ. Press, New York, 643 pp.

Steenberg, B. (1983). Forestry in developing countries. *Kungl. Skogs-och Lantbruksakademiens Tidskrift* **3**, 149-166.

Steinbeck, K. (1966). Site, height and mineral nutrient content relations of Scotch pine provenances. *Sil. Gen.* **15**, 42-50.

Steinbeck, K., and C. L. Brown (1975). Yield and utilization of hardwood fiber grown on short rotations. 8th Cell. Conf., Wood Chemicals—A Future Challenge. SUNY Coll. of Envir. Sci. and For., Syracuse, New York, pp. 63-64.

Steinhoff, R. J. (1974). Juvenile-mature correlations in ponderosa and western white pines. IUFRO Meet. Work. Parties on Population and Ecological Genetics, Breeding Theory, and Progeny Testing, Royal Coll. For., Stockholm, Sweden, pp. 243–250.

Stephan, B. R. (1973). Susceptibility and resistance of Douglas-fir provenances to *Rhabdocline pseudotsugae*. *Sil. Gen.* **22**(5–6), 149–153.

Stern, K. (1960). Concerning a basic difference of forest legislation dealing with seed and plant material in Switzerland and the German Federal Republic. *Schweizerischen Zeitschrift für Forstwesen* **13**, 145–163.

Stern, K. (1972). The theoretical basis of rust resistance testing—Concept of genetic gain in breeding resistant trees. Biol. of Rust Res. in For. Trees, Proc. NATO-IUFRO Adv. Study Ins., Moscow, Idaho, pp. 299–311.

Stern, K., and L. Roche (1974). *Genetics of Forest Ecosystems*. Springer-Verlag, Berlin, 330 pp.

Stern, W. L., and G. E. Voigt (1959). Effect of salt concentration on growth of red mangrove in culture. *Bot. Gazette* **121**(1), 36–39.

Steyn, D. J. (1977). Occupation and use of the *Eucalyptus* plantations in the Tzaneen area by indigenous birds. *S. A. For. Jour.* 100, 56–60.

Stone, E. G. (1982). Observations on forest nutrition research in Australia. *Aust. For.* **45**, 181–192.

Stone, E. L., and G. M. Will (1965). Boron deficiency in *Pinus radiata* and *Pinus pinaster*. *For. Sci.* **11**(4), 425–433.

Stout, A. B., R. H. McKee, and E. J. Schreiner (1927). The breeding of forest trees for pulpwood. *Jour. New York Bot. Gar.* **28**, 49–63.

Streets, R. J. (1962). *Exotic Forest Trees in the British Commonwealth*. Clarendon Press, Oxford, U.K., 765 pp.

Stubbings, J. A., and A. P. Schönau (1980). Management of short rotation coppice crops of *Eucalyptus grandis*. *S. A. For. Jour.* **115**, 38–46.

Styles, T., and C. E. Hughes (1983). Studies of variation in Central American pines. III. Notes on the taxonomy and nomenclature of the pines and related gymnosperms in Honduras and adjacent Latin American republics. *Brenesia* **21**, 269–291.

Styles, B. T., J. W. Stead, and K. J. Rolph (1982). Studies of variation in Central American pines. II: Putative hybridization between *Pinus caribaea* var. *hondurensis* and *P. oocarpa*. *Turrialba* **32**(3), 229–242.

Suassuna, J. (1977). The culture of pine—A perspective and a concern. *Brazil. Flor.* **29**(8), 27–36.

Sucoff, E. I. (1961). Potassium, magnesium and calcium deficiency symptoms of loblolly and Virginia pine seedlings. N.E. For. Expt. Stat. Pap. No. 164, U.S. For. Ser., Philadelphia, Pennsylvania, 18 pp.

Sutton, W. R. (1974). New Zealand experience with radiata pine: Aspects of thinning. *For. Comm. Bul.* **55**, 56–60.

Sutton, W. R. (1984). Economic and strategic implications of fast-growing plantations. In IUFRO Vol. 2, (1984a), pp. 417–431.

Sutton, W. R., and J. B. Crowe (1975). Selective pruning of radiata pine. *N. Z. Jour. For. Sci.* **5**(2), 171–195.

Sweet, G. B. (1963). Significant height differences are shown in seven provenances of

Pinus resinosa, six years after planting in New Zealand. N. Z. For. Ser., Res. Leaflet No. 3, Rotorua, New Zealand, 3 pp.

Sweet, G. B., and R. D. Burdon (1985). The radiata pine monoculture: An examination of the ideologies. *N. Z. Jour. For.* **28**(3), 325–326.

Sweet, G. B., and I. J. Thulin (1963). The performance of six provenances of *Pinus banksiana* in a 7-year-old trial in New Zealand. N. Z. For. Ser., Res. Leaflet No. 2, Rotorua, New Zealand, 3 pp.

Sweet, G. B., and L. G. Wells (1974). Comparison of the growth of vegetative propagules and seedlings of *Pinus radiata. N. Z. Jour. For. Sci.* **4**(2), 399–409.

Szöny, L., and I. Nagy (1968). Frost resistance and growth of Douglas-fir. *Sonderdruck Tagungsberichte* **100**, 65–67.

Taft, K. (1962). The effect of controlled pollination and honeybees on seed quality of yellow poplar (*Liriodendron tulipifera*) as assessed by X-ray photography. N.C. State Univ., School of For. Tech. Rept. 13, Raleigh, North Carolina, 21 pp.

Tanaka, Z. (1883). Be cautious with the introduction of exotic trees. *Ringaky Kyookai Syuusi (Jour. For. Assoc.)* **19**, 205–206. Abstracts of Japanese Lit., Vol. I, Part A, 1970.

Tavitayga, D. (1984). Provenance tiial of *Pinus caribaea* at Koraput (Orissa) India. In IUFRO (1984b), pp. 453–455.

Taylor, C. J. (1982). *Tropical Forestry with Particular Reference to West Africa.* Oxford Univ. Press, London, 163 pp.

Taylor, F. W. (1973). Variations in the anatomical properties of South African grown *Eucalyptus grandis. Appita* **27**(3), 171–178.

Taylor, F. W. (1977). Variation in specific gravity and fiber length of selected hardwoods. *For. Sci.* **23**(2), 190–194.

Taylor, K. L., R. A. Bedding, and R. J. Akhurst (1977). Biological control of *Sirex noctilio.* Australian For. Res. Newsletter No. 4, CSIRO, Canberra, pp. 3–4.

Taylor, R. W. (1983). Timber harvesting techniques in the Republic of South Africa. S. A. Forestry Handbook, S.A.I.F., Pretoria, South Africa, pp. 160–185.

Temes, S. B. (1982). Effect of *Eucalyptus globulus* on Galicia's ecology. 1st Nat. Assembly For. Res., Madrid, Spain, 6 pp.

Temes, S. B., A. R. Rodriguez, D. C. Sotres, P. M. Vasquez, and M. A. Santos (1985). Effectos ecologicos del *Eucalyptus globulus* en Galicia. Estudio comparativo con *Pinus pinaster* y *Quercus robur.* Inst. Nag. de Inves. Agrarias, Madrid, Spain, 381 pp.

Teunissen, P. A., and A. G. Voorhoeve (1973). A preliminary tree improvement programme with *Pinus caribaea* var. *hondurensis* in Surinam. Sel. and Breed. to Improve Some Tropical Conifers, Commonw. For. Inst., Oxford, U.K., Vol. 2, pp. 267–275.

Thielges, B. A., and J. C. Adams (1975). Genetic variation and heritability of *Melampsora* leaf rust resistance in eastern cottonwood. *For. Sci.* **21**(3), 278–282.

Thirgood, J. V. (1983). *Man and The Mediterranean Forest.* Academic Press, New York, 194 pp.

Thompson, D. A., and L. Nelson (1984). Trials with provenances of *P. caribaea, P. oocarpa* and other pines in Jamaica. In IUFRO (1984b), pp. 456–461.

Thornthwaite, C. W. (1948). An approach toward a rational classification of climate. *Geographical Review* **38**, 55–94.

Thornthwaite, C. W. (1954). A reexamination of the concept and measurement of potential evapotranspiration. *Johns Hopkins Univ. Pub. in Climatology* **7**(1), 200–209.

Thornthwaite, C. W., and J. R. Mather (1963). Average climatic water balance data of the continents. Part IV: Australia, New Zealand and Oceana. *Publications in Climatology* **16**(3).

Thulin, I. J., and T. Faulds (1968). The use of cuttings in breeding and afforestation of *Pinus radiata*. *N. Z. Jour. For.* **13**(1), 66–77.

Toda, R. (1970). *Abstracts of Japanese Literature in Forest Genetics and Related Fields,* I-A. Noorin Syuppan Co., Tokyo, 362 pp.

Toda, R. (1972). *Abstracts of Japanese Literature in Forest Genetics and Related Fields,* I-B. Noorin Syuppan Co., Tokyo, pp. 363–918.

Toda, R. (ed.) (1974a). *Forest Tree Breeding in the World.* Govern. For. Expt. Stat. Meguro, Tokyo, 205 pp.

Toda, R. (1974b). Vegetative propagation in relation to Japanese forest tree improvement. *N. Z. Jour. For. Sci.* **4**(2), 410–417.

Toops, C. (1986). The tree that's changing the Everglades. *Amer. For.* **92**(2), 26.

Toyama, S., S. Nishimura, and E. Hoyasbita (1959). On the growth and characteristics of the tracheids of slash pine (*Pinus caribaea,* now *P. elliottii*) in the south of Japan. Breeding of forest trees and its fundamental studies. Fac. Lib. Arts and Educ., Miyaziki Univ., Tokyo, pp. 19–31.

Tozer, S., and R. Robertson (1984). The provenance development of *P. kesiya* in the Northern Territory of Australia. In IUFRO (1984b), pp. 472–477.

Treshow, M. (1980). Interactions of air pollutants and plant disease. Symp. Effects of Air Pollutants on Mediterranean and Temper. For. Ecosystems, Berkeley, California, pp. 103–109.

Troup, R. (1921). *Silviculture of Indian Forest Trees,* 3 vols. Clarendon Press, Oxford, U.K.

Troup, R. S. (1932). *Exotic Forest Trees in the British Empire.* Clarendon Press, Oxford, U.K., 259 pp.

Tucker, R. E. (1975). Monoculture in industrial forestry. Pine Monoculture in the South, South. For. Economics Workers, Biloxi, Mississippi, 32 pp.

Turnbull, J. W. (1977). Exploration and conservation of eucalypt gene resources. 3rd World Consul. For. Tree Breed., Canberra, Australia, Vol. 1, pp. 33–44.

Turnbull, J. W. (1978). Seed collection and certification. Inter. Train. Course in For. Tree Breed., Sel. Ref. Topics, Australian Devel. Assis. Agency, Canberra, pp. 61–78.

Turnbull, J. W., and J. C. Doran (1983). The collection, distribution and improved use of Australian forest gene resources. *Fast Growing Trees. Silvicultura* **32**, 741–743.

Turnbull, J. W., D. G. Nikles, and A. G. Brown (1980). Better use of the gene resources of some Australian forest trees. Eleventh Commonw. For. Conf., Trinidad.

Turner, J. (1984). Site information for plantation establishment and management. In IUFRO (1984a), Vol. 1, pp. 125–138.

Uhlig, S. K. (1979). Epidemien und ihre Bekämpfung bei Pflanzenansucht und Aufforstung. *Beitr. Forstwirtsch.* **79**(3), 118-120.

Ulrich, B., B. Mayer, and P. K. Khanna (1980). Chemical changes due to acid precipitation in a loess derived soil in Central Europe. *Soil Science* **130**, 193-199.

U.S. Congress, Comm. on For. Affairs (1980). *Tropical Deforestation Hearings before the Sub-Committee on International Organizations.* U.S. Gov't. Print. Off., Washington, D.C., 446 pp.

U.S. For. Ser. (1982). *Natural Diversity in Forest Ecosystems.* Proc. of Workshop, Univ. of Georgia, Athens, 290 pp.

Vabre-Durrieu, A. (1954). The hybrid *Tsuga-picea hookeriana* and its parents: Study of seedlings. *Toulouse Soc. d'Hist. Nat. Bul.* **89**, 47-54.

Van Altena, A. C. (1979). Growth comparisons of slash pine and Honduras Caribbean pine at Toolara. Dept. For. Queensland Res. Note No. 28, Brisbane, Australia, 5 pp.

Van Biujtenen, J. P. (1969). Applications of interspecific hybridization in forest tree breeding. *Sil. Gen.* **18**(5-6), 196-200.

Van Buijtenen, J. P., and R. Isbell (1970). Differential response of loblolly pine families to a series of nutrient levels. 1st North Amer. For. Biol. Workshop, Michigan State Univ., East Lansing.

Van Buijtenen, J. P., and K. Stern (1967). Marginal populations and provenance research. IUFRO Congress, Munich, West Germany, Vol. 3(22), pp. 319-331.

Van Buijtenen, J. P., J. Toliver, R. Bower, and M. Wendel (1975). Mass production of loblolly and slash pine cuttings. *Tree Planters' Notes,* 4 pp.

Van Buijtenen, J. P., V. Bilan, and R. H. Zimmerman (1976). Morpho-physiological characteristics related to drought resistance in *Pinus taeda. Tree Physiology and Yield Improvement.* Academic Press, New York, pp. 349-359.

Vanclay, J. K., and T. M. Anderson (1982). Initial spacing effects on thinned stem volumes of slash pine in southeast Queensland. Res. Note No. 34, Dept. For., Brisbane, Queensland, Australia, 9 pp.

Van der Pas, J. B. (1981). Reduced early growth rates of *Pinus radiata* caused by *Dothistroma pini. N. Z. Jour. For. Sci.* **11**(3), 210-220.

Van der Pas, J. B., L. Bulman, and G. P. Horgan (1984). Disease control by aerial spraying of *Dothistroma pini* in tended stands of *Pinus radiata* in New Zealand. *N. Z. Jour. For. Sci.* **14**(1), 23-40.

Van der Sijde, H. A. (1983). Report on the International provenance trials of *Pinus oocarpa* in the Republic of South Africa. *Fast Growing Trees. Silvicultura* **29**, 148-150.

Van der Sijde, H. A., and N. P. Denison (1983). Cooperation in the field of tree improvement in Southern Africa. *Fast Growing Trees. Silvicultura* **32**, 743-745.

Van der Sijde, H. A., M. J. Shaw, and G. Van Wyk (1985). Reaction wood in *Pinus taeda*—A preliminary report. *S. A. For. Jour.* **133**, 27-32.

Van der Sijde, H. A., and J. W. Roelofsen (1986). The potential of pine hybrids in South Africa. *S. A. For. Jour.* **136**, 5-14.

Van der Slooten, J. H., R. W. Fishwick, H. G. Richter, M. Ferreira, and R. G. Motagna (1976). Wood density level of *Pinus elliotti* var. *elliottii* in plantations in southern Brazil. *PRODEPEF* Serie Technica No. 5, Brasilia, Brazil, 47 pp.

Van Laar, A. (1974). Thinning research in South Africa: Aspects of thinning. *For. Comm. Bull.* **55**, 62–71.

Van Rensburg, N. J. (1984). Forest pests and diseases in South Africa. Paper presented at SATGA Congress, Durban, South Africa, 5 pp.

Van Wyk, G. (1976). Early growth results in a diallel progeny test of *Eucalyptus grandis*. I: A field study. *Sil. Gen.* **25**(60), 126–132.

Van Wyk, G. (1977a). Pollen handling, controlled pollination and grafting of *Eucalyptus grandis*. *S. A. For. Jour.* **101**, 47–53.

Van Wyk, G. (1977b). Early growth results in a diallel progeny test of *Eucalyptus grandis*. II: A greenhouse study. *Sil. Gen.* **26**(1), 44–50.

Van Wyk, G. (1981a). Inbreeding effects in *Eucalyptus grandis* in relation to degree of relatedness. *S. A. For. Jour.* **116**, 60–63.

Van Wyk, G. (1981b). Pollen management for eucalypts. Pollen Management Handbook, USDA Forest Service Agric. Handbook No. 587, Washington, D.C., pp. 84–88.

Van Wyk, G. (1983a). Breeding results from two young *Eucalyptus grandis* progeny tests. *Fast Growing Trees. Silvicultura* **31**, 572–575.

Van Wyk, G. (1983b). Clonal seed orchards of *Eucalyptus grandis* in South Africa. *Fast Growing Trees. Silvicultura* **31**, 566–568.

Van Wyk, G. (1983c). Improving forestry yields through genetics. Proc. SAIF Symposium, "Forestry Quo Vadis?" Pietermaritzburg, South Africa, pp. 73–87.

Van Wyk, G. (1985a). Genetic variation in wood preservation of fast grown *Eucalyptus grandis* families. IUFRO Symp. on For. Prod. Research Inter., Achievements and the Future, Pretoria, South Africa, 8 pp.

Van Wyk, G. (1985b). Tree breeding in support of vegetative propagation of *Eucalyptus grandis*. *S. A. For. Jour.*, pp. 33–39.

Van Wyk, G., and E. R. Falkenhagen (1984). Genotype × environment interaction in South African breeding material. Site Prod. Fast Grow. Plant., Pretoria, South Africa, pp. 215–231.

Van Wyk, G., and H. A. Van der Sijde (1983). The economic benefits of forest tree breeding. *S. A. For. Jour.* **126**, 48–54.

Vavilov, N. I. (1926). Studies on the origin of cultivated plants. *Appl. Bot. Plant Breed.* (Leningrad) **16**(2), 1–248.

Vavilov, N. I. (1930). Wild progenitors of the fruit trees of Turkistan and the Caucasus and the problem of the origin of fruit trees. 9th Inter. Hort. Congr., Vienna, Austria, pp. 271–286.

Veblen, T. T. (1978). Guatemalan conifers. *Unasylva* **29**(118), 25–30.

Vélez, E. (1984). Development of 20 families of *Cupressus* from Kenya, Costa Rica, Mexico and Europe after 5 years. Res. Rept. 91, Cartón de Colombia, Cali, Colombia, 5 pp.

Venator, C. R. (1976). Natural selection for drought resistance in *Pinus caribaea*. *Turrialba* **26**(4), 381–387.

Venegas, L. (1981). Ensayos de procedencias de *Pinus caribaea* en los llanos orientales de Colombia, Sur America. Inves. Forestales No. 6, Inst. Nalde los Recursos Naturales Renovables y del Ambiente, Bogota, Colombia, 9 pp.

Venkatesh, C. S., and V. K. Sharma (1976). Heterosis in the flowering precocity of *Eucalyptus* hybrids. *Sil. Gen.* **25**(1), 28–29.

Venkatesh, C. S., and R. K. Vakshasya (1977). Effects of selfing, crossing and inter-specific hybridization in *Eucalyptus camaldulensis*. 3rd World Consul. For. Tree Breed., Canberra, Australia, 1 p.

Venkatesh, C. S., R. S. Arya, and V. K. Sharma (1973). Natural selfing in planted *Eucalyptus* and its estimation. *Jour. Plantation Crops* **1**, 23–25.

Vidakovíc, M. (1962). Establishing seed orchards of forest species outside their area of natural distribution. Tapola, *Beograd* **6**(25–26), 15–19.

Vidakovíc, M., and J. Ashan (1970). The inheritance of crooked bole in shisham (*Dalbergia sissoo*). *Sil. Gen.* **19**(2–3), 94–98.

Vietmeyer, N. (1986a). Another invader: *Melaleuca, Amer. For.* **92**(2), 25.

Vietmeyer, N. (1986b). *Casuarina*: weed or windfall? *Amer. For.* **92**(2), 22–24.

Villa Nova, N. A., E. Salati, and E. Matusi (1976). Estimativa da evapotranspiração na Bacia Amazonica. *Acta Amazonica* **6**(2), 215–228.

Vincent, L. W. (1978). Site-classification for Young Caribbean Pine (*P. caribaea* var. *hondurensis*) in Grasslands in Venezuela. Ph.D. thesis, Univ. of Tennessee, Knoxville, 149 pp.

Von Tubeuf, C. (1927). Das Schicksal der Strobe in Europa. Jahresbericht des deutsches Forstvereins, Munich, West Germany, pp. 348–364.

Vozzo, J. A., and E. Hacskaylo (1971). Inoculation of *Pinus caribaea* with ectomy-corrhizae fungi in Puerto Rico. *For. Sci.* **17**(2), 239–245.

Wadsworth, F. H. (1965). Tropical forest regeneration practices. Proc. Duke Univ. Trop. For. Symp., Bull. No. 18, Duke Univ., Durham, North Carolina, pp. 3–29.

Wakeley, P. C. (1963). How far can seed be moved? 7th South. Conf. For. Tree. Impr., Pub. No. 23, Gulfport, Mississippi, pp. 38–43.

Wakeley, P. C. (1971). Relation of thirtieth year to earlier dimensions of southern pines. *For. Sci.* **17**, 200–209.

Wakeley, P. C., and T. E. Bercaw (1965). Loblolly pine provenance test at age 35. *Jour. For.* **63**(3), 168–174.

Walker, L. C., and R. D. Hatcher (1965). Variation in the ability of slash pine progeny groups to absorb nutrients. *Soil Sci. Soc. Am.* **29**, 616–621.

Wang, C. W. (1971). The early growth of *Larix occidentalis* × *L. leptolepis* hybrids. Station Note No. 17, Univ. of Idaho, Moscow, 4 pp.

Wang, T. T., J. C. Yang, and Z. Z. Chen (1984). Identification of hybridity of *Casuarinas* grown in Taiwan. *Sil. Gen.* **33**(4–5), 128–133.

Wareing, P. F., and K. A. Longman (1960). Studies on the physiology in forest trees. Rep. For. Res. For. Comm., London, pp. 109–110.

Waring, R. H., and G. B. Pitman (1980). A simple model of host resistance to bark beetles. For. Res. Lab. Res. Note 65, Oregon State Univ., School of For., Corvallis, 1 p.

Waters, W. E., and E. B. Cowling (1976). Integrated forest pest management. A silvicultural necessity. *Integ. Pest Mgt.,* pp. 149–177.

Webb, D. B., P. J. Wood, and J. Smith (1980). *A Guide to Species Selection for Trop-*

ical and Sub-tropical Plantations. Tropical Forestry Paper No. 15, CFI, Oxford, U.K., 342 pp.

Webb, L. G., J. G. Tracey, and K. P. Haddock (1967). A factor toxic to seedlings of the same species associated with living roots of the non-gregarious subtropical rain-forest tree *Grevillea robusta. Jour. Appl. Ecol.* **4,** 13-25.

Webb, R. S. (1984). A preliminary investigation of pine rust disease (*Cronartium quercum* f. sp. *fusiforme*) in Guatemala and implications for spread in the Central American region. Inter. Program, Univ. of Florida, Gainesville, 16 pp. (mimeo).

Webster, N., and J. L. McKetchnie (1980). *Websters New Twentieth Century Dictionary,* Unabridged 2nd ed., William Collins, 2129 pp.

Weissenberg, K. von (1982). Erfarenheter av exoter i jord—och skogsbruk. *Sveriges Skogsv. Förb. Tidskrift.* **80**(1-2), 25-30.

Weiying, X., and T. Yongchang (1984). A new hybrid—*Popularis. Scientia Silvae Sinicae* **20**(2), 122-131.

Wells, O. O. (1983). Southwide pine seed source study—Loblolly pine at 25 years. *South. Jour. Appl. For.* **7**(2), 63-71.

Wells, O. O., and P. C. Wakeley (1966). Geographic variation in survival, growth and fusiform-rust infection of planted loblolly pine. *For. Sci. Mono.* **11**, 40 pp.

Wencelius, F. (1977). Plantation comparing provenances of *Pinus caribaea* at Edea (Cameroun). 3rd World Consul. For. Tree Breed., Canberra, Australia, 11 pp.

Wessels, N. O., and H. W. Kassier (1985). A computerized system for forest management and silvicultural planning and control in even-aged plantation forestry. *S. A. For. Jour.* **132,** 62-64.

Wessels, N. O., E. J. Malan, W. H. Hinze, and H. B. Maree (1983). *Silviculture of Pine.* S. A. Forestry Handbook, S.A.I.F., Pretoria, South Africa.

West, G. G. (1984). Establishment requirement of *Pinus radiata* cuttings and seedlings compared. *N. Z. Jour. For.* **14**(1), 41-52.

Westoby, J. (1984). How to save the forests. *Inter. Soc. Trop. For. News* **5**(3), 2.

Weston, G. C. (1957). *Exotic Forest Trees in New Zealand.* Statement prepared for 7th. British Commonwealth Forestry Conference. Australia and N. Z. For. Serv., Wellington, New Zealand.

Weston, G. C. (1971). *The Role of Exotic Genera Other than Pinus in New Zealand Forestry.* FRI Symp. No. 10, N. Z. For. Ser. Rotorua, New Zealand, 258 pp.

Wetterberg, G. B., T. J. Maria, C. S. deCastro, and J. M. de Vasconcellos (1976). *An Analysis of Priorities in Conservation of Nature in the Amazon.* PRODEPEF **8,** 62 pp.

White, E. W. (1977). Wood charcoal as an extender or alternative for coal: An immediately available energy source. *Earth and Mineral Sci.* **46**(4), 25-28.

White, P. (1982). Impacts of cultural and historic resources on natural diversity: Lessons from Great Smoky Mountains National Park, North Carolina and Tennessee. Natural Diversity and Forest Ecosystems Symp., Univ. of Georgia, Athens, pp. 119-132.

Whitesell, C. D. (1974). Planting trials of 10 Mexican pine species in Hawaii. U.S. For. Ser. Res. Paper PSW-103, Honolulu, Hawaii, 8 pp.

Whiteside, I. D., and W. K. Sutton (1983). A silvicultural stand model: Implications for radiata pine management. *N. Z. Jour. For.* **28**(3), 300–313.

Whitmore, J. L. (1980). *Wood Production in the Neotropics via Plantations.* IUFRO Symp., Inst. Trop. For., U.S. For. Ser., Rio Piedras, Puerto Rico, 392 pp.

Whitmore, J. L., and N. F. de Barros (1980). *Pinus kesiya* and *P. merkusii* provenance trial in Puerto Rico. IUFRO/Mab For. Ser. Symp., Rio Piedras, Puerto Rico, pp. 368–378.

Whitmore, J. L., and L. H. Liegel (1980). Spacing trial of *Pinus caribaea* var. *hondurensis.* U.S. For. Ser. Res. Pap. S0-162, Rio Piedras, Puerto Rico, 9 pp.

Whitmore, T. C. (1981). On studying processes and cycles in tropical rain forests. *Commonw. For. Rev.* **60**(2), 113–117.

Whyte, A. G., P. Adams, and S. E. McEwen (1980a). Size and stem characteristics of foxtails compared with *P. caribaea* v. *hondurensis* of normal habit. IUFRO, Div. 5 Conf., Oxford, U.K., p. 59.

Whyte, A. G., P. C. Wiggins, and T. W. Wong (1980b). A survey of spiral grain in *P. caribaea* var. *hondurensis* in Fiji and its effects. IUFRO, Div. 5 Conf., Oxford, U.K., p. 58.

Whyte, A. G., P. Adams, and S. E. McEwen (1981). Foxtailing of *Pinus caribaea* var. *hondurensis* in Fiji: Frequency, distribution of occurrence and wood properties. *For. Ecol. & Mgt.* **3**(3), 237–243.

Wiersma, J. H. (1963). A new method of dealing with results of provenance tests. *Sil. Gen.* **12**(6), 200–205.

Wiersum, K. F., and A. Ramlan (1982). Cultivation of *Acacia auriculiformis* in Java. *Indonesia Commonw. For. Rev.* **61**(2), 135–153.

Wilcox, B. A. (1982). Concepts in conservation biology: Applications to the management of biological diversity. Natural Diversity and Forest Ecosystems Symp., Univ. of Georgia, Athens, pp. 155–172.

Wilcox, M. D. (1980). Genetic improvement in eucalypts in New Zealand. *N. Z. Jour. For. Sci.* **10**, 343–359.

Wilcox, M. D. (1982a). Preliminary selection of suitable provenances of *Eucalyptus regnans* for New Zealand. *N. Z. Jour. For. Sci.* **12**(3), 468–479.

Wilcox, M. D. (1982b). Genetic variation in frost tolerance, early height growth and incidence of forking among and within provenances of *Eucalyptus fastigata. N. Z. Jour. For. Sci.* **12**(3), 510–524.

Wilcox, M. D. (1982c). Genetic variation and inheritance of resistance to *Dothistroma* needle blight in *Pinus radiata. N. Z. Jour. For. Sci.* **12**(1), 14–35.

Wilcox, M. D. (1983). International procurement and exchange of tree breeding material. *Fast Growing Trees. Silvicultura* **32**, 745–749.

Wilcox, M. D., T. Foulds, and T. G. Vincent (1983a). Genetic improvement of *Eucalyptus saligna* in New Zealand. *Fast Growing Trees. Silvicultura* **31**, 578–583.

Wilcox, M. D., D. A. Rook, and D. G. Holden (1983b). Provenance variation in frost resistance of *Eucalyptus fastigata. Fast Growing Trees. Silvicultura* **31**, 521–523.

Wilde, S. A., B. H. Shaw, and A. W. Fedkenheuer (1968). Weeds as a factor depressing forest growth. *Weed Res.* **8**, 196–204.

Wilkinson, R. C. (1973). Inheritance and correlation of growth characteristics in hybrid poplar clones. 20th Northeast. For. Tree Imp. Conf., Durham, New Hampshire, pp. 121–130.

Will, G. M. (1984). Monocultures and site productivity. In IUFRO (1984a), pp. 473–487.

Willan, R. L. (1984a). *A Guide to Forest Seed Handling—With Special Reference to the Tropics.* DANIDA Forest Seed Centre, Humlebaek, Denmark, 36 pp.

Willan, R. L. (1984b). Provenance seed stands and provenance conservation stands. Tech. Note No. 14, DANIDA Forest Seed Centre, Humlebaek, Denmark, 42 pp.

Williams, C., and F. Bridgwater (1981). Screening loblolly pine for adaptability to deep peat sites: A seedling study of two edaphic seed sources from Eastern North Carolina. 16th South. For. Tree Impr. Conf., Blacksburg, Virginia, pp. 143–148.

Wilm, H. W., and C. W. Thornthwaite (1945–46). Report of the Committee on Evaporation and Transpiration. *Transactions of American Geographical Union* **27**, 720–725.

Windsor, G. J., J. Kelly, and W. Gentle (1970). Differences in boron and sulfur nutrition in grafted clones of *Pinus radiata*. Australian Plant Nutrition Conf., Mt. Gambier, South Australia, 2 pp.

Wingfield, M. J., R. A. Blanchetti, T. H. Nicholls, and K. Robbins (1982). The pine wood nematode: A comparison of the situation in the United States and Japan. *Can. Jour. For. Res.* **12**(1), 71–75.

Wittberg, R. A. (1983). Vascular anatomy as a selection criterion for *Verticillium* wilt resistance in Norway maple (*Acer platanoides*). 3rd N. Central Tree Impr. Conf., Wooster, Ohio, pp. 209–220.

Witwer, S. H., and M. J. Buckovac (1969). The uptake of nutrients through leaf surfaces. *Handbuch der Pflanzenernährung und Düngung.* Springer-Verlag, New York, pp. 235–261.

Woessner, R. A. (1980). Plantation forestry and natural forest utilization in the Lower Amazon Basin (Jari). Monte Dourado, Mimeo. rept., 4 pp.

Woessner, R. A. (1983a). Growth of *Eucalyptus deglupta* at Jari on different soils up through age three. *Fast Growing Trees. Silvicultura* **32**, 662–664.

Woessner, R. A. (1983b). *Tectona grandis* provenance trial at Jari—An assessment at 5 years. *Fast Growing Trees. Silvicultura* **30**, 181–183.

Woessner, R. A. (1983c). *Gmelina arborea*—Variation in wood density, height and diameter of the international provenance trial at Jari. *Fast Growing Trees. Silvicultura* **30**, 183–185.

Woessner, R. A. (1983d). Pine genetic improvement program at Jari. *Fast Growing Trees. Silvicultura* **29**, 153–155.

Wood, P. J. (1976). The development of tropical plantations and the need for seed and genetic conservation. *Tropical Trees* **2**, Academic Press, London, 11–18.

Wood, P. J. (1982). Problems of tropical forestry—Some tropical views expanded. *Span* **25**(1), 5–7.

Wood, P. J., and J. Burley (1983). *Ex situ* conservation stands. *Fast Growing Trees. Silvicultura* **29**, 158–160.

Wood, P. J., and A. Greaves (1977). Advances from international cooperation in tropical pines. 3rd World Consul. For. Tree Breed., Canberra, Australia, 12 pp.

Wood, P. J., R. A. Plumptre, and I. D. Gourlay (1973). Wood properties of *P. caribaea* grown in four climatic zones in Tanzania. Meet. Trop. Prov. and Prog. Res. and Inter. Coop., IUFRO, Nairobi, Kenya, pp. 547–551.

Woods, F. W., L. W. Vincent, W. W. Moschler, and H. A. Core (1979). Height, diameter and specific gravity of "foxtail" trees of *Pinus caribaea. For. Prod. Jour.* **29**(5), 43–44.

Woodwell, G. M., J. E. Hobbie, R. A. Houghton, J. M. Melillo, B. Moore, B. J. Peterson, and G. R. Shaver (1983). Global deforestation: Contribution to atmospheric carbon dioxide. *Science* **222**(4628), 1081–1108.

Woollons, R. C., and W. J. Hayward (1984). Growth losses in *Pinus radiata* stands unsprayed for *Dothistroma pini. N. Z. Jour. For. Sci.* **14**(1), 14–22.

World Bank (1980). *Energy in the Developing Countries.* World Bank, Washington, D.C., 92 pp.

Worral, J., J. Burley, E. R. Palmer, and J. F. Hughes (1977). The properties of some Caribbean pine pulps and their relationship to wood specific gravity variables. *Wood and Fiber* **8**(4), 228–234.

Wray, P. H., and L. C. Promnitz (1976). Controlled environment selection of poplar clones. Intensive Plantation Culture, U.S. For. Ser. Tech. Rept. NC-21, Wooster, Ohio, pp. 19–31.

Wright, J. W. (1962). *Genetics of Forest Tree Improvement.* FAO Forestry and For. Prod. Studies No. 16, Rome, 397 pp.

Wright, J. W. (1964). Hybridization between species and races. *Unasylva* **18**(2–3), 73–74.

Wright, J. W. (1970). Ten years of provenance research at Michigan State University and the next steps in tree improvement. 9th Lake States For. Tree Improv. Conf., St. Paul, Minnesota, pp. 8–11.

Wright, J. W. (1976). *Introduction to Forest Genetics.* Academic Press, New York, 463 pp.

Wright, J. W. (1981). The role of provenance testing in tree improvement. *Advances in Forest Genetics.* Ambika Publications, New Delhi, India, pp. 102–114.

Wright, J. W., and H. I. Baldwin (1957). The 1938 International Union Scotch pine provenance test in New Hampshire. *Sil. Gen.* **6**(1), 2–14.

Wright, J. W., and W. I. Bull (1963). Geographic variation in Scotch pine. *Sil. Gen.* **12**(1), 1–40.

Wright, J. W., and L. F. Wilson (1972). Genetic differences in Scotch pine resistance to pine root collar weevil. Nat. Res. Rep. No. 159, Michigan State Univ., Lansing, 5 pp.

Wright, J. W., L. F. Wilson, and W. K. Randall (1967). Differences among Scotch pine varieties in susceptibility to European pine sawfly. *For. Sci.* **13**(2), 175–181.

Wright, J. W., R. A. Read, and W. H. Barrett (1970). Use of geographic variation in the improvement of plantations in Oregon pines in the Republic of Argentina. *IDIA,* Supplemento Forestal, 11 pp.

Wright, J. W., F. H. Kung, R. A. Read, W. A. Lemmien, and J. N. Bright (1971). Genetic variation in Rocky Mountain Douglas-fir. *Sil. Gen.* **20**(3), 53–100.

Yale, R. A., and F. R. Wylie (1983). Subterranean termites in Queensland. Queensland Dept. For. No. 9, Brisbane, 1 p.

Yeatman, C. W. (1976). Seed origin—First, last and always. INFOR Rept. PS-X-64, Petawawa For. Expt. Stat., Chalk River, Ontario, Canada, 12 pp.

Yeh, F. C., A. Brune, W. M. Cheliak, and D. C. Chipman (1983). Mating system of *E. citriodora* in a seed production area. *Can. Jour. For. Res.* **13**(6), 1051-1055.

Yingwanasiri, T. (1980). A review on the genetic improvement of teak. *For. Abst.* **44**(12), 36-41.

Yvory, M. H. (1983). Ectomycorrhizaes of lowland tropical pines. *Fast Growing Trees. Silvicultura* **29**, 95-97.

Zagaja, S. W. (1983). Germplasm resources and exploration. *Methods in Fruit Breeding,* pp. 3-10.

Zaremba, W. (1976). *Logging Reference Manual.* Vol. 1: Timber preparation; skidding by animals and tractors, 377 pp. Vol. 2: Timber skidding by highlead; logging accessories; timber loaders, 421 pp. Vol. 3: Logging roads; timber transportation by suspended cable; supplements, 462 pp. Dept. of For. Bull. 52, Pretoria, South Africa.

Zerbe, J. I., and A. Baker (1980). Forest resources for producing energy. *Bioresources for Development: The Renewable Way of Life.* Pergamon, New York, pp. 278-285.

Zerbe, J. I., J. L. Whitmore, H. E. Wahlgren, J. F. Laundrie, and K. A. Christopherson (1980). *Forestry Activities and Deforestation Problems in Developing Countries.* U.S. For. Ser. Pub. PASA No. AG/TAB-1080-10-78, Washington, D.C., 115 pp.

Zobel, B. J. (1961). Pines in the tropics and subtropics. Proc. IUFRO, 13th Cong., Vienna, Austria, Vol. 1(22/10), pp. 1-9.

Zobel, B. J. (1964). Pines of southeastern U.S., Bahamas and Mexico and their use in Brazil. *Silvicultura em São Paulo* **3**(3), 303-310.

Zobel, B. J. (1967). Mexican pines. FAO Tech. Conf. on Exploration, Utilization and Conservation of Plant Gene Resources, Sect. 6, Rome, Italy.

Zobel, B. J. (1971). Gene preservation by means of a tree improvement program. Proc. 13th Mgt. Comm. on For. Tree Breed. in Canada, Prince George, British Columbia, pp. 13-17.

Zobel, B. J. (1972). Genetic implications of monoculture. 2nd North Amer. For. Biol. Workshop, Oregon State Univ., Corvallis, 10 pp.

Zobel, B. J. (1973). Introduction: Wood of fast growing exotic pines. *Sel. and Breed. to Improve Some Tropical Conifers,* Vol. II. Dept. For., Queensland, Australia, pp. 1-9.

Zobel, B. J. (1978). Gene conservation—As viewed by a forest tree breeder. *For. Ecol. and Mang't.* **1**, 339-344.

Zobel, B. J. (1979). Florestas baseadas em exoticas [Forestry based on exotics]. *Boletim Tecnico* **2**(3), 22-30.

Zobel, B. J. (1980a). Genetic improvement of forest trees for biomass production. *Progress in Biomass Conversion,* Vol. 2. Academic Press, New York, pp. 37-58.

Zobel, B. J. (1980b). The world's need for pest-resistant forest trees. Workshop on Gen. of Host-Parasite Inter. in For., Wageningen, Holland, 14 pp.

Zobel, B. J. (1981a). Vegetative propagation in forest management operations. 16th South For. Tree Impr. Comm. Meet., Blacksburg, Virginia, pp. 149-159.

Zobel, B. J. (1981b). Wood quality from fast-grown plantations. *Tappi* **64**(1), 71–74.

Zobel, B. J. (1983a). The changing quality of the world wood supply. *Wood Sci. & Tech.* **17**, 1–12.

Zobel, B. J. (1983b). Introduction: Wood of fast growing exotic pines. *Selection and Breeding to Improve Some Tropical Conifers,* Vol. 2. Dept. For., Queensland, Australia, pp. 1–3.

Zobel, B. J. (1985). Juvenile wood in tropical forest plantations: Its characteristics and effect on the final product. CAMCORE Bull. on Trop. For. II, Raleigh, North Carolina, 28 pp.

Zobel, B. J., and C. B. Davey (1977). A conservation miracle. *Alabama For. Products* **20**(5), 5–6.

Zobel, B. J., and K. W. Dorman (1973). Loblolly pine as an exotic. For. Gen. Res. Inst. No. 2, Rome, 24 pp.

Zobel, B. J., Y. Ikemori, and E. Campinhos (1983). Vegetative propagation in *Eucalyptus.* 19th Conf. Can. Tree Impr. Assoc., Toronto, Canada, pp. 136–144.

Zobel, B. J., and R. C. Kellison (1984). Wood—Where will it come from, where will it go? Symp., Utilization of the Changing Wood Resource in the Southern United States, N.C. State Univ., Raleigh, North Carolina, 12 pp.

Zobel, B. J., and J. H. Roberds (1970). Differential genetic response to fertilizers within tree species. 1st North Amer. For. Biol. Workshop, Michigan State Univ., East Lansing, 17 pp.

Zobel, B. J., and J. Talbert (1984). *Applied Tree Improvement.* Wiley, New York, 521 pp.

Zobel, B. J., and H. Van Buijtenen (1988). *Wood Variability: Its Causes and Control.* Springer-Verlag, Berlin (in press).

Zobel, B. J., T. E. Campbell, F. C. Cech, and R. E. Goddard (1956). Survival and growth of native and exotic pines, including hybrid pines, in Western Louisiana and East Texas. Res. Note No. 17, Texas For. Ser., College Station, 16 pp.

Zobel, B. J., R. J. Weir, and J. B. Jett (1972). Breeding methods to produce progeny for advanced-generation selection and to evaluate parent trees. *Can. Jour. For. Res.* **2**(3), 339–350.

Zobel, B. J., E. Campinhos, and Y. Ikemori (1982). Selecting and breeding for wood uniformity. *Tappi* **66**(1), 70–74.

Zobel, B. J., R. Umana, W. Dvorak, W. Ladrach, and C. Davey (1985). Political and Associated Biological Problems Related to Growing Exotics in the Tropics and Subtropics of South America Mimeo Rept., N.C. State Univ., Raleigh, North Carolina, 54 pp.

Zsuffa, L. (1975a). Some problems and aspects of breeding for pest resistance. 2nd. World Consul. on For. Dis. and Insects, New Delhi, India, Special Paper, 11 pp.

Zsuffa, L. (1975b). Broad sense heritability values and possible genetic gains in clonal selection of *Pinus griffithii* × *P. strobus. Sil. Gen.* **24**(4), 85–88.

Zucconi, L. (1958). Organogenesis of the flower and embryology in *Eucalyptus camaldulensis. Pubblicazioni del Centro di Sperimentazione Agricola e Forestal* **2**, 59–86.

SPECIES INDEX

Note: The taxonomic names of the many species covered in this book are shown alphabetically in this index, separated into Gymnosperms and Angiosperms. The common names are so varied and different from area to area that often they are of little value. Rather than choose one among many differing common names, we frequently do not show any common name when there is uncertainty. To obtain as much uniformity as possible, pine common names were usually referenced from Mirov and Hasbrouck (1976) and those for *Eucalyptus,* from Hillis and Brown (1978). It was necessary to use other sources for common names not included in these two references.

In the text, the scientific name is listed the first time it occurs although later either the more accepted common name or scientific name may be used. Some species, like *Pinus caribaea, Eucalyptus grandis* or *Pseudotsuga menziesii,* will occur many times while other species may be mentioned just once.

Numbers in *italic* indicate the species is listed in the Reference section of the book rather than in the text.

Gymnosperms

Scientific Name	Common Name	Reference Pages
Abies spp.	fir	5, 13, 210
A. alba	European white fir	298
A. balsamea	balsam fir	302
A. concolor	white fir	302
A. fraseri	Fraser fir	302, 329, 330
A. guatemalensis	Guatemalan fir	324, *429*
A. lasiocarpa	alpine fir	300
A. sibirica	Siberian fir	300, 302
Agathis spp.	kauri pine	*447*
A. macrophylla	—	62
A. robusta	South Queensland kauri	62
Araucaria spp.	—	62, 171, 210, *447*
A. cunninghamia	hoop pine	205, 268, *428*
A. hunsteinii	klinki pine	192, 205, *428, 444*
Chamaecyparis spp.	cedar	*445*
C. nootkatensis	Alaska yellow cedar	121, *445*
Cryptomeria spp.	sugi	206, 220, *429, 443, 463*
C. japonica	Japanese cedar (sugi)	206
Cupressus spp.	cypress	13, 163, 164, 200, 247, 254, 397, *450, 478*
C. leylandi	leyland cypress	121, *445*
C. lusitanica	Mexican cypress	30, 38, 44, 50, 59, 65, 71, 109, 110, 112, 115, 125, 126, 147, 163, 189, 195, 201, 225, *414, 430, 433, 450, 466*
C. macrocarpa	Monterey cypress	121, 225, *445*
Juniperus spp.	juniper	13
J. virginiana	red cedar	287
Larix spp.	larch	5, 106, 107, 117–119, 121, 123, 288, 295, 301, 302, 316, *429, 431, 441, 447, 458, 462*
L. decidua	European larch	55, 119, 121, 122, 303, 346, *419, 467*
L. × eurolepis	hybrid larch	46, 119, 122, 302, 303, *447, 458, 462*
L. laricina	tamarack	46, *467*
L. leptolepis (*L. kaempferi*)	Japanese larch	43, 46, 59, 121, 122, 139, 140, 174, 175, 193, 195, 299, 300, 303, *419, 433, 446, 449, 457, 458, 470, 479*
L. occidentalis	western larch	*479*
L. sibirica	Siberian larch	12, 46, 190, 287, 300–302

(*continued*)

Gymnosperms   Continued

Scientific Name	Common Name	Reference Pages
Picea spp.	spruce	102, 115, 118, 122, 123, 158, 174, 181, 206, 207, 210, 288, 308, 320, 363, 391, 404, *443, 449, 471, 477*
P. abies	Norway spruce	4, 5, 14, 35, 51, 55, 58, 64, 122, 149, 158, 159, 166, 174, 175, 191, 214, 288–290, 299–304, 308, 313, 315, 354, *429, 432, 436, 437, 441, 444, 448, 449, 458, 462, 465, 466, 468*
P. chihuahuana	Mexican spruce	324, *439*
P. glauca	white spruce	287, 300, 308
P. mariana	black spruce	300, 308
P. omorika	Serbian spruce	288
P. pungens	blue spruce	151, 302
P. rubens	red spruce	61
P. sitchensis	Sitka spruce	5, 35, 46, 55, 61, 72, 107, 109, 137, 174, 176, 295, 298, 300–302, 304, 353, 364, *420, 422, 423, 428, 442, 462, 468, 469*
Pinus spp.	pines	2, 5, 6, 8, 13, 25, 101, 115, 120, 122, 123, 125, 141, 153, 164, 166, 168, 171–174, 176, 178, 180, 181, 185, 192, 210, 234, 240, 244, 263, 264, 268, 269, 272, 277, 281, 282, 288, 299, 302, 303, 308, 322, 325, 348, 361–364, 369, 371, 372, 380, 383, 384, 388, 389, 391, 392, 395–397, 399, 401–404, 407, *413–415, 421, 422, 428, 429, 432, 437, 438, 440, 442, 443, 446, 448, 453–456, 458, 459, 461, 462, 465–467, 469, 471, 472, 474, 476, 477, 480, 482, 484, 485*
P. attenuata	knobcone pine	66, 123, 170, 172, 184, *421*
P. × attenuradiata	knobcone × Monterey hybrid	123
P. ayacahuite	Mexican white pine	342, *429*
P. banksiana	jack pine	45, 55, 63, 80, 149, 172, 299, 308, *441, 444, 457, 459, 475*
P. canariensis	Canary Island pine	210, 256
P. caribaea	Caribbean pine	11, 30, 35, 36, 39, 42, 44–48, 50, 53, 55–57, 60–64, 66, 71, 74, 75, 91, 92, 96, 101, 102, 108–110, 119, 122–124, 126–128, 135–137, 144, 148, 154–157, 159, 175–177, 182, 183, 189,

Gymnosperms Continued

Scientific Name	Common Name	Reference Pages
		198, 200, 225, 229, 239, 240, 248, 252, 264, 269, 270, 281–283, 346, 348, 349, 353–355, 359, 363, 366, 369–375, *417–422, 424–428, 432*
var. *bahamensis*	Bahama pine	15, 38, 43, 45, 57, 54, 183, 197, 234, 326, 355, 379
var. *caribaea*	Cuban pine	13, 38, 43, 54, 99, 102, 156, 183, 197, 355, *466*
var. *hondurensis*	Honduran pine	38, 43, 44, 47, 54, 71, 79, 130, 135, 137, 156, 183, 193–199, 225, 232, 234, 282, 347, 354, 355, 360, 365, 379, 404, *413, 414, 420, 424, 429–431, 434, 436, 437, 446, 453, 458, 460, 462, 463, 467, 469, 471–473, 475, 477, 479, 481*
P. chiapensis (*P. strobus* var. *chiapensis*)	Chiapas white pine	46, 48, 50, 62, 342, *429, 430*
P. clausa	sand pine	81
P. contorta	lodgepole pine	4, 5, 12, 30, 35, 38, 46, 49–51, 53, 55, 58, 59, 61, 71, 72, 74, 77, 79, 80, 89, 91, 93, 126, 130, 138, 146, 158, 159, 161, 168, 169, 171, 172, 175, 179, 186, 189, 219, 285, 292, 298–302, 304, 306–318, 354, 355, *414, 423, 426, 429, 440, 444, 446, 447, 449, 453–456, 458–460, 465, 468, 472, 473*
subsp. (or var.) *contorta*	shore pine	39, 54, 307, 309, 310
subsp. (or var.) *latifolia*	lodgepole pine	39, 54, 307, 309, 310
subsp. (or var.) *murrayana*	Murray pine	54, *436*
P. cubensis	—	53
P. culminicola	Potosi pinyon	326
P. densiflora	Japanese red pine	64, 149, 178, 179, *471*
P. donnel-smithii	ocote pine	326, 327
P. douglasiana	Douglas pine	44
P. durangensis	Durango pine	44
P. echinata	shortleaf pine	117, 121, *472*
P. elliottii	slash pine	1, 3, 11, 34, 42–47, 51, 59, 60, 71, 91, 102, 107, 119, 122, 123, 125, 127, 132, 137, 139, 149, 151, 159, 171, 182, 183, 189, 196, 200, 223, 225, 230, 235, 240, 248, 254, 272, 281, 304, 306, 336, 352–355, 360, 361, 370, 373, 375, 379, *414, 418, 427, 432, 434, 438, 445, 461, 467, 473, 476, 477, 479*

(*continued*)

Gymnosperms   Continued

Gymnosperms Continued

Scientific Name	Common Name	Reference Pages
P. peuce	Macedonian white pine	174
P. pinaster	maritime pine	37, 81, 102, 184, 186, 208, 225, 248, 259, 303, 336, 391, *413, 424, 457, 474, 475*
P. ponderosa	ponderosa pine	45, 55, 59, 89, 91, 93, 151, 170, 173, 306, *423, 451, 460, 467, 473*
P. pringlei	Pringle pine	46, 50
P. pseudostrobus	false Weymouth pine	44, 45, 47, 48, 50, 64, 183, 264, 347, *423, 427, 450*
P. quichensis	—	326
P. radiata (P. insignis)	radiata pine (Monterey pine)	1, 14, 31, 39, 42–46, 53, 57, 81, 83, 94, 98, 100–102, 105, 107–111, 123, 126, 139, 148, 149, 154, 158, 161, 162, 165–168, 170–173, 184, 186, 191, 206–208, 215, 220–223, 225, 228, 232–235, 240, 248, 256, 259, 261, 266, 271, 272, 277, 280, 299, 303–306, 331, 332, 336, 347, 353, 360, 363, 369, 374, 375, 377, 390, 400, 401, *415, 416, 422–426, 428–432, 434–436, 443, 445, 453, 456, 457, 464, 469, 471, 474–477, 480–483*
P. resinosa	red pine	80, 96, 136, 158, 171, 184, 216, 217, 221, *418, 435, 461, 475*
P. rigida	pitch pine	45, 111, 117–119, 158, 196, 210, 304, *421, 441, 445, 454, 468, 469, 472*
P. rigida × taeda	pitch-loblolly hybrid	115, 116, 118, 119, 121, 122, 195, 304, 305, *464, 472*
P. rudis	—	44, 45
P. rzedowski	Rzedowski pine	326
P. serotina	pond pine	147, 210
P. strobus	Eastern white pine (Weymouth pine)	97, 122, 174, 184, 287, 293, 294, 304, *418, 433, 441, 452, 466, 470, 479, 485*
P. sylvestris	Scots pine (Scotch pine)	4, 14, 35, 38, 39, 45, 49, 50, 55, 58, 70, 71, 74, 77, 98, 103, 106–108, 122, 126, 137, 138, 146, 149, 158, 159, 161, 166, 168, 170, 171, 174, 176, 186, 287, 289, 292, 300–303, 307–310, 312, 313, 315–318, 355, *418, 421, 429, 432, 440, 448, 449, 458, 465, 468–470, 473, 483*

(continued)

Angiosperms

Scientific Name	Common Name	Reference Pages
Acacia spp.	wattle	8, 22, 52, 152, 185, 201, 226, 229, 235, 238, 248, 262, 280, 304, *418*
A. albida	—	43, *419*
A. arabica (A. nilotica)	—	229
A. auriculiformis	tan wattle	9, 31, 42, *481*
A. dealbata	silver wattle	49, *415*
A. decurrens	green wattle	49, *415*
A. mangium	—	22, 31, 43, 114, 127, 339, 357, *415, 448, 453, 461, 465*
A. mearnsii	black wattle	49, 92, 102, 357, *415, 440, 461*
A. melanoxylon	Australian black-wood	230
A. nilotica (A. arabica)	—	248
A. seyal	shittim	232
A. tortilis	—	229
Acer spp.	maple	*472*
A. plantanoides	Norway maple	172, *482*
Aesculus spp.	buckeye	288
A. hippocastanum	horse chestnut	288
Afzelia spp.	—	241
Ailanthus spp.	—	185
A. altissima	tree of heaven	185
Albizzia spp.	mimosa	248, 274
A. falcataria	batai	205, *428*
Alnus spp.	alder	14, 23, 121, 152, 173, *459*
A. cordata	—	49
A. glutinosa	European black alder	9, 10, 49, 68, 127, 304, *437, 441*
A. incana	—	49
Anthocephalus spp.	—	374
Azadiracta spp.	—	229
A. indica	neem	229, 234, 402
Bertholletia spp.	—	335
B. excelsa	Brazil nut	334
Betula spp.	birch	121, 288, *472*
B. pendula	European white birch	*431*
B. pubescens	white birch	*431*
Bombacopsis spp.	—	51
B. quinata	red ceiba	49, 147, 232, 234
Calliandra spp.	—	152, *415*
C. callothyrsus	—	22, 201
Carya	hickory	287
C. alba (C. tomentosa)	white hickory	287
Cassia spp.	cassia	238, 241
C. siamea	cassia	49, 185, 229

(continued)

Angiosperms Continued

Scientific Name	Common Name	Reference Pages
Castanea spp.	chestnut	329, *429*
C. *dentata*	American chestnut	329
C. *mollissima*	Chinese chestnut	112, *448*
Casuarina spp.	Australian pine	22, 23, 52, 102, 112, 120, 151, *415, 479*
C. *equisetifolia*	she-oak	*479*
C. *glauca*	swamp she-oak	185
Catostemma spp.	—	374
Cedrela spp.	cedar	175
C. *odorata*	cedar	173
Chlorophora spp.	iroko	241
Chukrasia spp.	—	281
C. *tabularis*	—	281
Cordia spp.	laurel	49, 51
C. *alliodora*	salmonwood	8, 43, 52, 67–69, 73, 357, *419, 428, 460, 473*
C. *gerascanthus*	—	49
C. *goeldiana*	—	105, *446*
Dalbergia spp.	sissoo	*479*
D. *sissoo*	shisham	112, *479*
Entandrophragma spp.	sapele	241
Eschweilera spp.	—	374
E. *sagotiana*	—	374
Eucalyptus spp.	eucalypts	1–3, 7, 8, 11, 14, 22, 28, 34–36, 42, 43, 49, 51, 54, 55, 57, 88, 91, 94, 101, 102, 104, 106, 113, 115, 116, 118–123, 127, 130, 141–143, 147, 149, 153–155, 157, 158, 161, 164–166, 168, 171, 174, 178, 180, 181, 187, 190, 193, 196, 197, 200, 205–207, 209, 210, 212, 213, 218, 226, 228, 230, 233, 237, 240, 241, 247, 249, 254, 257, 259, 262–266, 274, 276, 278, 280, 282, 283, 299, 302–306, 319, 322–324, 346, 348, 350, 351, 357, 362, 366–370, 374, 376, 378, 380, 384, 386, 390–398, 402, 403, 406, *415, 416, 419–421, 423–425, 428–438, 440–444, 447, 449, 450, 452, 454, 456, 458, 459, 463–471, 474, 476, 478, 479, 481, 485*
E. *alba*	white gum	39, *427, 434*
E. *camaldulensis*	red river gum	34, 35, 49, 52, 66, 68, 69, 72, 86,

(*continued*)

Angiosperms Continued

Angiosperms Continued

Scientific Name	Common Name	Reference Pages
L. diversifolia	—	360
L. leucocephala	ipil-ipil	8, 22, 52, 66, 69, 72, 113, 360, *413*
Licania spp.	—	374
L. venosa	—	374
Liquidambar spp.	—	*469*
L. formosana	—	122
L. orientalis	—	122
L. styraciflua	sweet-gum	68, 69, 122, 287, *444*
Liriodendron spp.	—	55
L. tulipifera	yellow poplar	55, 193, *447, 475*
Lovoa spp.	—	241
Maesopsis spp.	—	374
M. eminii	—	374
Melaleuca spp.	—	*479*
M. quinquenervia	paperbark	185
Morus spp.	mulberry	185
Platanus spp.	sycamore	368
P. acerifolia	—	287
Populus spp.	poplar	35, 36, 42, 43, 51, 56, 57, 72, 91, 105, 106, 115, 116, 120, 121, 123, 138, 147, 164, 168–171, 173, 175, 206, 208, 220, 230, 302, 304–306, 322, 337, 356, 366, 368, 393, *424, 426, 427, 431, 436, 441, 448, 449, 459, 463, 464, 470, 473, 483*
P. deltoides	Eastern cottonwood	51, 72, 164, 171, 303, *475*
P. nigra	black poplar	171, 303
P. pyramidalis	—	115
P. simonii	—	115
P. tremuloides	trembling aspen	55, 288, *431, 464*
Prosopis spp.	mesquite	22, 229, 238
P. juliflora	mesquite	229
Prunus spp.	cherry	287
P. serotina	black cherry	287, *472*
P. virginiana	—	287
Pterocarpus spp.	—	241
Quercus spp.	oak	42, 54, 105, 147, 153, 168, 187, 301, 302, 392, *456, 465*
Q. pagodafolia (Q. falacata var. *pagodafolia)*	cherrybark oak	180, *428*
Q. robur	English oak	186, 300, 391, *475*
Q. rubra	northern red oak	302

(continued)

Angiosperms Continued

Scientific Name	Common Name	Reference Pages
Rhizophora spp.	mangrove	152
R. *mangle*	red mangrove	152, *474*
Robinia spp.	locust	23, 348
R. *pseudoacacia*	black locust	174, 287, 302
Salix spp.	willow	23, 116, 173, 174, 206, 393, *459, 466*
S. *humboldtiana*	—	*444*
S. *matsudana*	—	115
Schizolobium spp.	Brazilian fire tree	374
Shorea spp.	—	105
S. *robusta*	red meranti	105
Swietenia spp.	mahogany	72, 115, 175, 226, 330, *436*
S. *humilis*	—	48, 66, 174
S. *macrophylla*	mahogany	48, 51, 66, 173, 174, 229, 356, *420*
S. *mahagoni*	—	48, 174
Tabebuia spp.	roble	49, 51
T. *rosea*	roble	49
Tamarix spp.	tamarisk	151, 304
Tectona spp.	teak	51, 72, 101, 113, 115, 138, 152, 241, 248, 278, 322, 334, 396, *421, 439*
T. *grandis*	teak	35, 55, 66–69, 102, 105, 112, 125, 193, 196, 226, 229, 241, 346, 357, *421, 428, 431, 441, 442, 447, 448, 482, 484*
T. *hamiltoniana*	—	334
T. *phillipinensis*	—	334
Terminalia spp.	swamp oak	22, 241, 374
T. *brasii*	—	374
T. *catalpa*	—	52
T. *ivorensis*	framire	357
T. *orientalis*	—	52
T. *superba*	—	374, 376
Toona spp.	—	51
T. *ciliata (Cedrela toona)*	toona	48, 67, 173, 175, 357, *440, 453*
Trema spp.	—	22
Triplochiton spp.	samba	241
Ulmus spp.	elm	171
U. *parvifolia*	Chinese elm	170, *434*
U. *pumila*	Siberian elm	175, *425*

SUBJECT INDEX